CONTEMPORARY ISSUES IN COUNSELING

PAMELA K. S. PATRICK

Capella University

Boston ■ New York ■ San Francisco ■ Mexico City ■ Montreal
Toronto ■ London ■ Madrid ■ Munich ■ Paris ■ Hong Kong
Singapore ■ Tokyo ■ Cape Town ■ Sydney

Executive Editor: *Virginia Lanigan*
Editorial Assistant: *Matthew Bucholtz*
Marketing Manager: *Erica DeLuca*
Production Managing Editor: *Joe Sweeney*
Editorial-Production Service: *SPi*
Composition and Prepress Buyer: *Linda Cox*
Manufacturing Buyer: *Linda Morris*
Cover Administrator: *Kristina Mose-Libon*
Electronic Composition: *SPi*

Graphic illustrations by Evan G. Patrick (www.evangpatrick.com)

For related titles and support materials, visit our online catalog at www.ablongman.com

Between the time Web site information is gathered and published, some cites may have closed. The publisher would appreciate notification where these occur so that they may be corrected in subsequent editions.

ISBN: 0-205-48503-0

Printed in the United States of America
10   9   8   7   6   5   4   3   2   1   RRD-VA   10   09   08   07   06

CONTENTS

CHAPTER FOUR

Research and Counseling Practice: Issues of Application and Integration   **99**
Amanda Costin

CHAPTER SEVEN

Counselors as Advocates for Practice and the Profession   187
Pamela K. S. Patrick

CHAPTER EIGHT

Stress-Induced Challenges to the Counselor Role: Burnout, Compassion Fatigue, and Vicarious Traumatization   210
Pamela K. S. Patrick

CHAPTER ELEVEN

Counseling and Spirituality: Integrating Wellness into Practice   **320**
Ann Hutchinson Meyers

FOREWORD

When I received my master's degree in counseling, Carl Rogers was the most revered professional in the field and William Glasser was an up-and-coming theorist. Mental health centers were relatively new and focused on prevention. School counseling was seen as a way of helping young people consider careers in the sciences and thus serve the good of the nation. It was 1971, and the society of the time was in turmoil with an unpopular war in Vietnam filling the headline news of the day and filtering into the lives of the young in dramatic and often tragic ways.

Needless to say, such is not the scenario of today. While there are still established and novice theorists, the emphasis of almost all practitioners is on short-term treatment. The shine has worn off of mental health, and service for those with disorders is in disarray. Counseling in the schools has broadened but is sometimes compromised by the competing interests and outlook of different disciplines. Fundamentalism, terrorism, and conservatism battle liberalism, progressivism, and radicalism for the minds of youth, midlifers, and the aged. Communism is basically dead, and the cold war is a concept frozen in time. Yet progress in human health and welfare seems to be a stagnant political football that is kicked back and forth by those in legislative positions.

Thus, society has changed, and yet it has not. The needs of the people within it have altered and yet much remains the same but now in different forms and venues. There are multiple values in a culture filled with multitudes from various cultures. Debates on immigration, reparation, and integration fill talk-show airwaves and the pages of general and specialized publications. Amid all of the turmoil, one thing remains constant—there is a need for counseling, prevention, and outreach to individuals, families, and groups. In addition, counselors of all kinds need to know how to impact their clients, their profession, and others most effectively. Furthermore, counselors need to be aware of what trends are emerging and how they are affecting society for better or worse. Therefore, *Contemporary Issues in Counseling* is a vital publication for twenty-first century counseling professionals. Pamela Patrick and her contributors have put together a text that is as timely as any text ever to reach the market.

Within the chapters of this book, you will find facts, figures, and practical suggestions for dealing with current concerns of clients and those who serve them. You will find questions that will make you think and wrestle with ideas and ideologies. *Contemporary Issues in Counseling* covers a plethora of counseling practices within the context, application, and innovation domains of the profession. This book is a stimulating read but a disturbing one as well in that there are no pat answers offered for the complexity of the problems that are addressed. Areas such as politics, research, culture, ethics, advocacy, trauma, and spirituality, all of which impact counseling, are not simply solved. Trends and future directions are not easily teased out of the fabric in which they are tangled.

William Faulkner once purportedly said that "The past is not dead, indeed it is never passed." Patrick and her contributors might say in response, "The present is always with us.

Be prepared." Regardless, *Contemporary Issues in Counseling* is one of those books that should be read and reread because of its significance to our lives as professional helpers. By understanding the issues raised within these pages, we may well come to recognize what we must do to assist our clients, our fellow counselors, and ourselves in getting better instead of bitter. That is worth the investment of time and thought that comes from reading this material. I can think of no better way to spend parts of a day. I greatly value this book and look forward to revisiting it time and time again.

Samuel T. Gladding, Ph.D.
Professor of Counseling
Wake Forest University
President, American Counseling Association (2004–2005)

PREFACE

Counseling is a dynamic and challenging profession. The issues facing the profession and counseling professionals reflect a changing landscape that directly affects how, when, and to whom care can be delivered. At the same time, the problems, life experiences, illnesses, and societal events that impact the mental health and well-being of citizens of all ages are also continually changing. Emotional and psychological problems not imagined one generation ago are now the subject of study, research, and continuing professional education that enables counselor professionals to meet intensified demands for care. As a consequence, professions that are dedicated to offering counseling services are continually challenged to address issues that can impede or facilitate delivery of care.

Whether the counselor is engaged in providing mental health or wellness care to individuals, couples, families, groups, or communities or during times of disaster or extraordinary life events, issues emerge that can directly affect the professional as well as the consumer. In some cases, the issues and debate that drive change in the counseling professions originate in a top-down manner. For example, professional associations serve as forums for identifying issues that have, or should have, an impact on practice, research, or education within counseling. In other cases, the issues that lead to change and growth in counseling practice emerge from the front lines as counselors encounter new and emergent requirements to provide care under circumstances that are stress filled and that require counselors to simultaneously stretch inner resources while relying on well-defined standards of practice.

Contemporary Issues in Counseling originated with the awareness that a dedicated treatment of issues that directly and continually impact counseling practice, research, and education had not been published. Identifying the topics that would form the content of the book involved careful consideration of traditional, current, and anticipated issues that the counseling professions need to address, typically due to social and political forces that are in a constant state of flux. In addition, the book delves into issues that reflect paradigm shifting within and between the counseling professions.

When describing who this book is for, we view *Contemporary Issues in Counseling* as having appeal to traditional counselor education students and faculty as well as counseling professionals who complete training and education in related fields such as counseling psychology or social work. The emphasis in the chapters is on counselors who provide services in a wide variety of settings and in environments that are traditional as well as those that are increasingly complex in a diverse and changing society. In such a contemporary environment, counselors working side by side may have been educated in counselor education programs, schools of social work, or psychology programs. Thus, terms used to refer to counselors are inclusive, recognize that all counselors are members of the larger human services community, and emphasize the emerging goal of collaboration among mental health professionals who are qualified to meet the escalating needs of consumers.

The purpose of this book is to identify and explore core issues that have a direct influence on the counseling professions. For those engaged in preparing to enter the counseling field, as well as practitioners providing direct services to consumers, the book presents contemporary issues that have a direct, lasting, and at times troubling impact on how counseling can be practiced in an ever-changing social context. Although *Contemporary Issues in Counseling* is not designed as an answer or how-to book, it is designed to provoke discussion, debate, and continuing exploration of core issues that counselor professionals must contend with on a daily basis.

Contributors to this text have a depth and breadth of experience as counselors, researchers, and educators in the fields of counseling, psychology, social work, and human services that guide the development of each issue contained in this book. Each chapter describes the nature of the issue, poses challenges, addresses questions, and examines how practice, theory, and research are impacted. Discussion questions are provided for each chapter linked to the material presented. Questions and scenarios are designed to provoke careful analysis of the content and a desire to further explore questions raised.

The book is organized into three sections. In Part I, chapters focus on the context for counseling practice in contemporary society. Current and emergent social, political, and economic forces that directly and indirectly affect how counseling is delivered and how to access needed counseling services are highlighted in Chapters 1 and 2. Issues associated with the evolving multicultural and diverse society in which counseling is practiced is the focus of Chapter 3, and the foundational role of research and its application to practice informs Chapter 4. The bio-psycho-social comprehensive model of counseling practice is presented in Chapter 5.

Part II contains three chapters that address core issues associated with the implementation of the counselor role in therapeutic and professional activity contexts. Chapter 6 explores ethical issues within counseling and emphasizes ethics as a central element of professional identity that must respond to unique as well as familiar ethical challenges, dilemmas, and conflicts. Advocacy as a core aspect of the counselor professional role is the subject of Chapter 7. Using an integrated advocacy model for this essential professional activity, various advocacy activities and roles are identified and defined with the ultimate goal of energizing the reader and providing a stimulating forum to consider a traditional and developing aspect of professionalism. In Chapter 8, stress-induced challenges to practice are identified and linked to burnout, compassion fatigue, and vicarious traumatization. In light of the changing social landscape that now includes the increasing role of counselor professionals in contexts of disaster response, this chapter provides insights of direct relevance to counseling practitioners.

Within the framework of contemporary issues in counseling, a number of innovations in counseling practice are presented in Part III. In Chapter 9, the rapidly evolving field of Internet counseling is examined, with an emphasis on how computer-mediated counseling service delivery can impact consumers and critical ethical issues that arise when counseling becomes a virtual experience. Creative counseling applications discussed in Chapter 10 highlight the challenges as well as the delights of exploring innovative methods to provide counseling services. Counselors as sources for creativity, as well as counselor receptivity to innovation, are a theme throughout this chapter. Within contemporary counseling practice, the role of spirituality as an element of counseling care is explored in an inclusive way. As Chapter 11 unfolds, the reader will find awareness of the needs of consumers for sensitivity about diverse belief systems and the concurrent need for counselor self-awareness

regarding the often pivotal role these aspects of the human experience can have throughout the life span.

Because the counseling professions will continue to be characterized by calls to adjust
to challenges and adapt to changes, the purpose of *Contemporary Issues in Counseling*
will be achieved if the reader engages in debate about the issues presented based on an
enhanced understanding of each topic. It is essential that counselor professionals, both experienced and new to the field, become active participants in the search for solutions to the
problems and challenges identified. As this mission is achieved, counselor professionals
can continue to remain cognizant of the role that dynamic change presents to individual practitioners, students, researchers, educators, and professional associations in contemporary
society.

ACKNOWLEDGMENTS

Collaboration in writing a book creates opportunities to acquire a deeper understanding of
the expertise, enthusiasm, and commitment to professional values of contributors to an
edited volume. The contributors to this book truly embody these qualities, each fully committed to furthering the understanding of the impact of counseling on the lives of those who
seek our help, guidance, and support. As with any writing task that speaks of professional
scholarship, the contributors embraced the challenge, worked diligently to respond to the
editor's feedback and requests for "just one more edit," and remained focused on the end
goal. The depth of counseling experience the contributors brought to each of their topics
reflects the respect and gratitude to the students we teach and the clients who allow us to
share the often arduous journey of counseling and psychotherapy. Each is acknowledged
with appreciation and deep respect.

Thank you also to our reviewers: Seth Brown, University of Northern Iowa; Paige
N. Cummins, East Central University; Sharon Horne, University of Memphis; Brenda Hall,
NCAT State University; Neal Gray, Eastern Kentucky University; Dr. Zaidy MohdZain,
Southeast Missouri State; Marion Schinn, San Jose State University; Dr. Cherryl Galley,
Oakwood College.

PART I

CONTEMPORARY ISSUES: THE CONTEXT FOR COUNSELING PRACTICE

CHAPTER ONE

SOCIAL FORCES AND COUNSELING

Impact on Practice and Preparation

PAMELA K. S. PATRICK

The environment in which counseling professionals practice, teach, conduct research, publish, and advocate is dynamic, changing, and increasingly challenging. Demands to provide counseling during the aftermath of a natural disaster, domestic or rogue terrorism events, or other mass or local crises require counselor professionals to enter environments and provide care to clients, families, and communities at the sites where such events have taken place as well as in home communities. As counselors continue to respond to needs for mental health care alongside other human services providers such as medical, nursing, public health, and law enforcement professionals, the profession itself must continually examine the issues that can impact traditional as well as extraordinary environments for practice.

Amidst these progressive and critically necessary outreach and response efforts, the counseling professional encounters social, economic, and political issues on a daily basis that can directly influence how services are provided. Counseling takes place within the macro- as well as micro-environment and, in turn, has the capacity to influence these systems by positively impacting the lives of individuals, couples, families, and communities. Accordingly, the purpose of this chapter is to provoke debate, discussion, and critique of these issues while recognizing that such engagement with the issues is but one step toward gaining insight into the effects of social, economic, and political forces that form the backdrop to counseling practice, education, research, and advocacy.

Whether the issue is framed as a "challenge," "problem," or "pinch point," the need to respond to current and emerging factors that directly and indirectly determine how counseling is practiced, how counselors are prepared, and who has access to counseling services represents an ongoing source of tension for counseling professionals. According to Horton

(2002), "America's mental health service delivery system is in shambles." The seeming disarray has resulted in a fragmented system that lacks coordination and funding, and is unable to use verified treatments in a consistent manner.

In this chapter, selected social and societal issues become the focus of discussion and examination. Certain issues are only briefly described here since they are the subjects of other chapters in this book (e.g., multiculturalism, spirituality, and counseling). The separation of issues is recognized as an artificial divide. In reality, the day-to-day practice of counseling is inclusive of social, cultural, economic, or spiritual issues of clients as a holistic view of assessment and treatment planning is implemented.

INTERDEPENDENT AND INTERACTIVE SYSTEMS AND FORCES

The practice of counseling, whether in private practice offices, nonprofit agencies, institutional settings, hospitals, or community mental health centers, takes place within a context of social, political, and economic systems (Okun, 2001; McLeod & Machin, 1998; Allen, 1999). Each of these systems interacts with one another to create forces that influence the availability, accessibility, affordability, and accountability of quality mental health and wellness services (see Figure 1.1). At any one time, the impact of changes in one of the social macro-systems can dramatically alter how counselors provide psychotherapy to children and adolescents, adults, families, or entire communities. Although challenges associated with social and societal factors can wreak havoc on mental health service delivery, each also can represent a vital component of a fragile infrastructure that supports the delivery of mental health and wellness services provided by counselors.

FIGURE 1.1   Social Forces Impact Counseling

Counseling cannot and does not take place in a vacuum. The manner in which counseling can be provided is directly affected by social forces; the economic realities that impact consumers, practitioners, and systems of care; contemporary, emergent, and crisis events; and how the counselor integrates social, economic, and political elements into the treatment process based on individual client needs (Clauss, 1998.) It is a complex interplay of factors that continuously interfaces with the counselor's ability to engage in helping as well as at the professional association level that addresses advocacy initiatives. As a contemporary issue in the counseling professions, each of the broad systemic forces to be reviewed in this chapter can individually, as well as collectively, have profound impact on the well-being of consumers and counseling professionals.

The counseling professions have a long history of recognizing and developing services to meet the need for mental health services in schools, communities, and private practice settings (Gladding, 2003; Pistole, 2001). Societal trends, patterns, and changes within families and communities drive the development of mental health counseling programs and methods, as well as the approaches to maintaining mental health and wellness. In the United States, the prevalence, on an annual basis, of diagnosable mental disorders is estimated at 22.1 percent of Americans from the age of 18 and older (NIH, 2004b). Based on the 1998 U.S. Census referencing the residential population, the approximate 1 in 5 individuals affected by mental disorders represent approximately 44 million people. According to the Global Burden of Disease study, unipolar major depression is the leading cause of disability, with reference to the disability adjusted life years (DALYs) measure (NIH, 2004a). According to the President's New Freedom Commission on Mental Health (2004), "The mental health delivery system is fragmented and in disarray . . . lead[ing] to unnecessary and costly disability, homelessness, school failure and incarceration." The impact of mental illness on the economies of businesses, communities, cities, and states is significant. According to research conducted by the Commission, indirect costs are as high as $79 billion per year due to lost productivity, mortality, losses due to incarceration associated with mental illness, and costs to provide care to families and children when wage earners are incarcerated.

While the need for mental health services escalates, and access to the resources to provide services to meet those needs are continually threatened, the value of outcome research directed toward mental health treatment methods has increased. Research findings can dramatically alter how certain therapies are viewed and in some cases result in dramatic changes regarding use of a particular therapeutic approach. Concurrently, the methods used to provide counseling rely on research to support the continuing use of preferred modalities, while at the same time demonstrating efficacy, in order to receive reimbursement from health care and/or insurance providers.

The enormity of the societal factors and forces that interact with social, political, and economic systems must be noted. In this chapter, specific issues are identified, described, and reviewed as each impacts the counseling professions. No attempt is made to provide a comprehensive review since each of these powerful forces, separately, is the focus of bodies of literature in sociology, economics, human services, political science, and public policy. Rather, the emphasis here is to provide a viewpoint that highlights the interrelatedness of socially embedded forces that directly, indirectly, and, at times, reactively affect the counseling professional's ability to serve consumers.

SOCIETAL ISSUES THAT DRIVE COUNSELING PRACTICE

A number of social trends that affect counseling practice have evolved since World War II. Social forces associated with marriage, divorce, child rearing, employment, and gender roles have impacted family functioning and the emergence of complex psychological and emotional problems for children and adults of all ages. Although slight declines in the rate of divorce are noted from year to year, the decreases have not appreciably influenced the stress and strain experienced by individuals, families, and communities affected by this change within family structures. For example, in 2003, there were 4.0 divorces per 1,000 marriages, and in 2004, that rate declined to 3.8 per 1,000 marriages (Centers for Disease Control and Prevention, 2005). Both the positive and negative impact of divorce on adults and children *can* be linked to dissolution of marriage, but can also be linked to a complex array of short- and long-term issues such as predivorce marital conflict, economic impact on parents and children, and preexisting psychological and behavioral problems of parents or children (Parke, 2004; Peres & Emery, 2004). Research data about marriage, divorce, remarriage, and cohabitation suggest that trends that are identified in one decade change the next as more sophisticated research methods are implemented (Bramlett & Mosher, 2002). Thus, counselors must remain cognizant of the impact of marital change on adults and children as well as the accuracy of information about trends and the dramatic media attention paid to each published study on this topic.

Of the major societal issues that directly impinge on the ability of counselors to provide services and consumers to obtain counseling services, five specific issues will be reviewed: demographic trends, information access, health/illness science, disaster/trauma events, and social stigma or bias. Although these issues only "scratch the surface" of a comprehensive list of potential social issues that affect the counseling professions, each highlights the ability of the counseling professions to respond to identified needs for mental health services for individuals, families, groups, communities, and unique populations. Although these issues are contemporary, they represent abiding challenges to all providers of mental health counseling services and programming efforts.

Demographic Trends

By 2010, there will be more than 308 million Americans in the United States, with more than 34 million over the age of 65. Of that number, over 6 million will be 85 years of age or older (U.S. Census Bureau, 2004). According to Table 1.1, the senior elderly (those over 85 years of age) will represent 2 percent of the total population. By 2050, this group is projected to increase to 5 percent of the total population. From 2010 to 2050, the total over-65 age group (including the senior aged) will increase from 11 to 15.7 percent by 2050 (U.S. Census Bureau, 2004). Also depicted in Table 1.1, the population changes anticipated over the next decades will likely generate significant needs for mental health care services in general and specifically will also be linked to needs for increased mental health services that are sensitive to aging issues across all cultural and demographic groups. For example, finding methods to address the mental health needs of an aging population must take into account the imbalance that currently exists regarding

TABLE 1.1   Age Population Projections: 2010–2050

PROJECTION YEAR	AGE 65–84	% OF POPULATION	AGE 85+	% OF POPULATION
2010	39 million	13%	6 million	2%
2030	69 million	20%	9 million	2.5%
2050	66 million	15.7%	18.5 million	5%

Sources: U.S. Census Bureau, *U.S. Interim Projections by Age, Sex, and Hispanic Origin* (2004); Administration on Aging, *Aging into the 20th Century* (1996).

gender, as depicted in Table 1.2. Although estimates vary, U.S. Census Bureau projections clearly indicate that the needs of women, particularly with those in the 85+ age group, will dominate the health care system.

Further changes in the demographic composition of the United States will reflect an increasingly diverse and multicultural population. Based on Census Bureau projections, the ethnic and racial composition of the United States will continue to reflect significant changing demographics. For example, in 2010, Whites will comprise 79 percent of the population, with Hispanics representing 15.5 percent of the total population. By 2050, that proportion will markedly shift: Whites will comprise 50.1 percent of the general population, Blacks 14.6 percent, and individuals of Hispanic origin will increase to an estimated 24.5 percent (U.S. Census Bureau, 2004).

With such dramatic change, how will the counseling professions respond to the development and delivery of mental health services, as well as wellness and self-care strategies, to meet an anticipated increased need for such care? For example, in the United States, there are an estimated 526,000 counselors (Bureau of Labor Statistics, 2004) providing services in mental health settings, schools, rehabilitation facilities, private practice, and substance abuse treatment programs. Population projections indicate that this number must be increased to meet the increasingly complex needs of an aging, diverse, multicultural, and receptive populace. To accomplish this service provider goal and to address the replacement of counselors who retire, leave the

TABLE 1.2   Age and Gender Imbalance: 2010–2050

YEAR OF PROJECTION	MEN (% OF TOTAL)		WOMEN (% OF TOTAL)	
	65–84	*85+*	*65–84*	*85+*
2010	44%	32%	56%	68%
2030	45%	35%	55%	65%
2050	46%	37%	54%	63%

Sources: U.S. Census Bureau, *U.S. Interim Projections by Age, Sex, and Hispanic Origin* (2004); Administration on Aging, *Aging into the 20th Century* (1996).

field, or move to nondirect service positions, 42 percent more mental health counselors will be needed by 2012; the pool of marriage and family therapists needed by that time must increase by 11 percent; and the need for substance abuse and behavioral disorder counselors will grow by 31 percent (Bureau of Labor Statistics, 2004). As experienced clinicians in the "baby boomer" population retire, newly educated and trained counselor professionals will be needed at a rate greater than in previous generations.

Counselors will be faced with a mandate to advocate for the unique needs of a population that is increasingly characterized by (1) longevity, (2) multicultural and ethnic diversity, (3) the use of extraordinary and life-extending medical services, and (4) families who are not able to achieve the middle-class dream of economic stability that supports child rearing and care of the aged in stable environments. To support achieving this mandate, the rate of education and training of counselor professionals must be accelerated to meet these needs. Paralleling these essential components of a mandate to provide counseling care, each of the counseling professions (psychology, social work, human services, and counseling) must continue to incorporate the best of the Information Age technology that exists now, as well as the ever more sophisticated interactive technology formats that can facilitate major aspects of counseling care, education, practice, research, and advocacy.

In addition to the current and anticipated shortage of counselor professionals within psychology, social work, human services, and counseling, the *way* that counseling is practiced and *how* it is delivered also represent an emergent issue that must be addressed. There is a clear and escalating need for more effective, efficient, and consistent clinical practice techniques that are sensitive to changing social demographics, population trends, and the needs for specialized treatment approaches. Moreover, the shortage of well-prepared counselor professionals based on demographics alone is compounded by the increased demands to provide emergency and disaster counseling services that, although essential, can result in relocation of counselor resources away from home communities to sites of disasters for indeterminate time periods.

Information Access and the Internet

At the professional association level, recognition of the value and impact of information on mental health care decision making, self-assessment for the presence of mental health disorders or for self-care, and strategies that promote informed access to mental health care are facilitated through access to knowledge. Consumers can readily access vast amounts of information via the Internet from their personal computers at home, work, public libraries, cyber cafes, and community centers. The barriers to "know" have been effectively removed for millions of consumers of mental health care during the present Information Age.

Recent publications within the counseling professions highlight the role of access to information as a key element in managing mental health care delivery and enhancing the therapeutic process (Goss & Anthony, 2003; Tyler & Sabella, 2003). Easy access to powerful search engines (e.g., www.google.com) provide instantaneous access to information as well as to providers who use websites to promote their services offered in traditional locations as well as via the Internet (Kraus, Zack, & Stricker, 2003).

Each of the major counseling professional associations provides public education information through Internet web portals, in public forums, or in print resource materials. Public education about the benefits of counseling for the treatment of mental disorders as well as for coping with personal life crises, tragedy, disaster, and traumatic events/experiences, and promoting health and well-being is also provided. The American Counseling Association (www.counseling.org), American Psychological Association (www.apa.org), American Mental Health Counseling Association (www.amhca.org), and the National Association of Social Workers (www.naswdc.org), for example, all focus considerable attention on providing information to consumers that clarifies the nature of mental illness and mental health, the use of crisis/trauma resources, and how to maintain high-level wellness and mental health well-being.

Easy access to information related to mental well-being or regarding mental health problems has not been fully realized at this time. Individuals who do not have access to computers or the Internet, for example, are less likely to seek out this form of health education. However, unlimited access to information about health and well-being could be linked to higher rates of early intervention, or to escalated levels of fear and anxiety when information is unfiltered or interpreted by fragile patients, or could both positively or negatively impact treatment outcomes. For the client engaged in counseling, then, the Internet provides access to a volume of information that can be overwhelming and difficult to assimilate in a coherent way. Take the case of Mr. Merrill (fictitious name), who has obviously done some "homework" before his first counseling session.

> Mr. Merrill has been receiving both inpatient and outpatient medical care over the past five months following diagnosis for bladder cancer. After surgery, he has been following the medical treatment regimen prescribed by his urologist and was recently referred to the mental health outpatient clinic, due to concern that he was becoming depressed and anxious. He is being seen for the first time by Dr. Wilson, a licensed professional counselor. After taking a seat in the treatment office, Mr. Merrill produces a set of file folders containing downloaded information about bladder cancer, depression, Prozac, and Wellbutrin. His first questions of Dr. Wilson are guided by the pages he refers to while asking for specific recommendations about which medications he should start on right away.

Professional counselors must recognize how a client's need to have information can be channeled to support a sense of personal control or mastery over a frightening illness, while at the same time providing guidance on effective use of Internet resources. Unguided client self-education through Internet resources may raise anxiety levels, create a demand for immediate results, or lead to confusion that can impede recovery.

Millions of consumers can access the Internet and obtain health-related information, but millions of others cannot due to poor literacy skills. The literacy level of the consumer population can facilitate access to information or impede it. Thus, although it appears that society is awash in information, literally expanding moment to moment, there is a clear and abiding need to ensure that those with nontext-based learning styles also have access to mental health and wellness knowledge. How the counseling professions continue to address this issue of scarcity of information delivery amidst instantaneous access to information for the computer literate remains a challenge.

Evaluating Internet Information.   A concurrent issue relates to the manner in which counseling professionals critically analyze the information that is available on the Internet. As a practice, counseling professionals must understand that information found on the Internet cannot be assumed to be accurate or legitimate by virtue of being in a text format on attractive websites. Rather, the counselor must thoroughly evaluate web-based information before using it to assist clients and provide guidance to consumers who are accessing the Internet for mental health information and services.

Evaluation of website information by counselors as well as lay consumers is a critical ingredient to effective use of this portal to health and well-being resources. Since such information can be used to make health care decisions, it is imperative that both counselor professionals and lay consumers understand the parameters of effective use of the World Wide Web (WWW), as discussed next.

Internet Information Quality Indicators.   Research has verified that the information published on the WWW can be characterized by unevenness (Benigeri & Pluye, 2003; Cline & Haynes, 2001; Peterson, Aslani, & Williams, 2003). Some sites, for example, are sponsored by recognized medical professional associations, such as the American Medical Association, and have established guidelines for content posted on the website used to provide public education (Winker et al, 2000). Other sites are published by private citizens with a knack for computer technology, strong opinions about health issues, or personal experiences they wish to share with other users of the WWW.

Mental health information found on the Internet is equally of inconsistent and uneven quality. Lissman and Boehnlein (2001) found that Internet information about depression frequently failed to align with *DSM-IV-TR* criteria and failed to include accurate information on comprehensive treatment options. Both the risks and benefits to professionals as well as lay consumers of accessing Internet health information is significant. When information obtained is used to make decisions about counseling or other forms of health care, however, accuracy of information is indispensable (Seidman, Steinwachs, & Rubin, 2003). Based on recognition of the crucial role that Internet information can have on health decision making, a new specialization has emerged that holds promise to identify needs for clarity about the nature, format, accuracy, and use of health-related information for both consumers and counseling professionals (Eysenbach & Jadad, 2001). The emergence of this specialization is in concert with the social revolution fostered by wide and easy access to information via the Internet.

Additional features of website quality are needed when the site is designed as a self-help Internet resource for patients with specific health problems. For example, Cummins and colleagues (2003, p. 60) provide clear and thorough guidance on the assessment of health behavior change websites that includes questions designed to critically analyze the focus, purpose, and services provided by a program's website.

1. Does the site *advise* the consumer regarding the need for changes in health behaviors by asking key questions about the site's intended audience and goals?
2. Does the site *assist* the user by providing clear guidance and instructions regarding all facets of the program's options, web-based resources, and interactive elements?

3. Does the site provide *anticipatory guidance* and information about what the consumer can expect as he or she participates in the web-based health behavior change program?
4. Does the site include methods to *arrange follow-up* as an integral element of what the program offers?

For counselor professionals who are considering a website recommendation to clients as part of a comprehensive treatment plan, careful consideration of these elements of the prospective site is necessary. Assessing mental health behavioral health change websites prior to recommending that clients seek information about depression, anxiety, or weight management, for example, can ensure that both counselor and client are comfortable with the addition of a web-based resource to the treatment plan.

Guidelines for Website Quality.   For websites that offer mental health illness or wellness information that is useful to counselors for educational purposes, careful scrutiny of each Internet location, prior to using the information or recommending the sites to clients, can be guided by consideration of key website characteristics. Legitimate, well-supported Internet sites should provide easy access to these key indicators of quality.

1. The purpose of the site should be clearly stated and easily identified by professional and lay viewers. The purpose may include the history, background, and rationale for publishing the site as well as the mission, objectives, and end-user benefits anticipated from accessing the information on the site.
2. The name of the sponsor, originator, and publisher of the site should be prominently displayed on the site. Users benefit from knowing if the sponsor/publisher is well known, trusted, and represents a respected organization, association, or individual.
3. The information contained in the website should be maintained with frequent updates, and the date of the last update should be easily identified. Current information about mental health and illness and wellness topics that reflects up-to-date research and information is of considerable benefit to counselors as a client teaching resource.
4. The perspective, philosophy, and opinions of the sponsors or originators of the site should be easily discerned through clear language, description, and overt position statements. Information that focuses on specific populations, illnesses, or treatment methods is of most benefit to consumers and counselor professionals when the perspective that is communicated is identified.
5. The objectivity of a website should be easily assessed through text and delivery methods. For client/patient information sites that focus on mental health illness or well-being, the most useful sites are typically characterized by a lack of bias in opinion, attitude, or value judgment. Sites that offer a specific opinion regarding mental health issues need to clearly indicate the nature of the nonobjective information published.
6. The well-crafted website useful to the counseling client and professional includes helpful links, resources, and references that are congruent with the purpose of the Internet site. These resources provide related information outlets that can further understanding of the topic being reviewed and lead to information that offers insights into a diagnostic category, for example, that is not contained at the primary site.

7. The accuracy of a website mirrors the value it will have for a counselor or client. Determining the accuracy of information found on the Internet requires the ability to suspend acceptance of the automatic legitimacy of the printed word. Anyone can publish on the Internet or advertise a product that targets a psychological problem or diagnosis and yet have no legitimacy at all. The consumer must therefore retain a degree of skepticism when reading health and medical information found on the Internet. Counselor professionals are able to critique website information and provide clients with insights about the authenticity of mental health information as well as provide guidance to clients regarding Internet sites that are known for accuracy (e.g., American Counseling Association).

8. The appropriateness of Internet information also needs to be assessed by counselors prior to advising clients to seek information about illness or psychological assistance. For example, although there are web-based self-help groups on the WWW, counselors must be cautious in recommending such virtual groups to clients prior to evaluating the services offered. For adolescents, the Internet can be a portal to high-risk behaviors. Counselors working with these populations are well advised to become proficient at evaluating the appropriateness of sites used by clients.

9. The appearance and user-friendly qualities of a website can facilitate use and serve to expand knowledge in highly desirable ways. Websites that are poorly designed, however, can detract from a worthy purpose and increase user frustration. Features of interactivity, including e-mail options, audio messaging, chat rooms, and text that is free of grammatical errors, signal a well-constructed website that could be a valued adjunct to counseling.

10. The ability of disabled clients or counselor professionals to use a website for purposes of information acquisition, communication, or education is linked to the sensitivity of the sponsor to provide disability-friendly access. Websites that also provide language translation options or alternate versions of information in various languages signal a user-friendly, inclusive philosophy that is congruent with the values of counselor professionals in all fields of practice.

The permanence of the WWW is evident and has transformed the social fabric of communities and countries around the globe. The impact of easy access to the Internet for most consumers is a topic for continuing evaluation within the counseling professions. As more consumers enter the mental health care system with more information in hand, professionals must be prepared to respond with guidance on how to effectively use this powerful tool. At the same time, counselors are in a lead position as a profession to address the gaps in access to information for groups and populations who struggle with literacy and access to computer technology.

Science and Mental Health Care

Paralleling the social imperatives linked to availability, accessibility, affordability, and accountability factors within the delivery systems of counseling services are the dramatic increases in understanding the scientific bases of mental health and illness. Research-driven treatment is increasingly recognized as having transformed the understanding of causes and treatments for many major mental health disorders.

Counselors are called on to use information about the biological subsu
and wellness within diverse and complex counseling contexts. For example, applicatio
the biological sciences to counseling practice has demonstrated benefit for issues as wide
ranging as the counselor's own self-care planning (Chandler, Bodenhamer-Davis, Holden,
Evenson, & Bratton, 2001); designing methods of care for children with conduct disorders
(Gerten, 2000); an element of integrated treatment for enuresis in family therapy (Fletcher,
2000); part of a comprehensive family therapy plan for substance abuse (Fals-Stewart &
O'Farrell, 2003); an integrated element of treatment for self-injurious behavior in adolescents (Stone & Sias, 2003); effective counseling with bi-polar diagnosed adolescents
(Wilkinson, Taylor, & Holt, 2002); and treating panic disorder effectively (Beamish, Granello,
& Belcastro, 2003). Discovery of the link between biological heritage and genetic risk
factors is also recognized for aspects of major depression and its treatment (Hazler & Mellin,
2004; Leinbaugh, 2002), for the etiology of schizophrenia (Sawa & Snyder, 2002), and as
it relates to the interaction of genetics and experience in the onset of specific psychiatric
disorders (DeMarco, 2000; Grossman, Churchill, McKinney, Kodish, Otte, & Greenough,
2003; Hyman, 2003).

Scientific contributions to understanding the genesis of major mental health disorders extends to discoveries of the role pharmaceuticals play in facilitating or mediating complex biochemical interactions in the brain and that are used as part of complete treatment
protocols (e.g., selective serotonin reuptake inhibitors [SSRIs] used to treat depression).
Consequently, counselors are called on to understand the scientifically based biological,
cognitive, behavioral, and social research as well as the spiritual dimensions of mental disorders in order to effectively provide counseling and psychotherapy.

Response to Trauma, Violence, Terrorism, and Disaster

Prior to the September 11, 2001, terrorist attack on the United States by a foreign terrorist
group, the counseling professions had developed and implemented a variety of crisis inter-
vention/response methodologies that addressed the role of the counselor following natural disasters (e.g., fire, flood, earthquake), mass killings in schools (e.g., Columbine High School
in 1999), and domestic terrorism (e.g., the Oklahoma City bombing in 1995). To devise crisis intervention and critical incident management protocols, counselors worked within the
frameworks of the American Red Cross, the American Counseling Association, the American
Psychological Association, and counseling specialization, professional, and community-based
programs, such as the United Way. These plans are rapidly mobilized to provide immediate
crisis intervention and counseling outreach during times of mass tragedy and natural disaster as evidenced by the massive outpouring of assistance up to and following national hurricane disasters, such as Hurricane Katrina with its devastating loss of property and lives,
mass population dislocation and relocation, and the first stages of recovery initiated in 2005.

The social context, or landscape, in which counselors provide services has dramatically changed as a consequence of heightened awareness that mass violence, disaster, or
terrorism can occur suddenly and unexpectedly. Mental health profession websites have
incorporated disaster preparedness, crisis response and intervention training, and educational materials specifically directed toward counselor development. For example, the

American Counseling Association provides information and guidance with materials such as "Dealing with Tragedy: Resources" and "Helping Children Cope with School Shootings" (www.counseling.org), and the American Psychological Association offers professional education programs, publications, and consumer information about various aspects of trauma, post-traumatic stress disorder, and disaster preparedness (www.apa.org). In response to the catastrophic aftermath of Hurricane Katrina in 2005, for instance, the American Counseling Association implemented rapid response plans to assist survivors and those displaced by the severity, extent, and duration of the disaster (see www.counseling.org). Similarly, the American Psychological Association published a variety of resources and calls for volunteers to provide assistance as part of partnerships with the American Red Cross and the U.S. Department of Health and Human Services (www.apa.org).

Research verifies the impact of counselor interventions in assisting victims of disaster and terrorism. In school settings, school-counselor–implemented counseling following 9/11 proved effective for children coping with the aftermath (Auger, Seymour, & Roberts, 2004) and for group interventions for child victims of violence (Stein et al., 2003). In traumatic disasters, counseling interventions have proved effective in alleviating severity of symptoms with some groups (Ruzak & Watson, 2001), while not demonstrating significant impact on coping strategies or symptomatology greater than self-help, no intervention, or repeated assessment (Ehlers & Clark, 2003) in others. In addition, there are also reports of mixed results in treatment outcomes when counseling professionals use a psychological debriefing or critical incident stress debriefing model (Litz, 2003; Bisson, McFarlane, & Rose, 2000; Deahl, Srinvasan, Jones, Neblett, & Jolly, 2001). In some cases, there is no measurable impact of the debriefing method; in others, there is some positive impact on well-being and recovery, and in still others, there is a measurable negative impact. The controversy generated by those who do not support the efficacy of the Critical Incident Stress Debriefing (CISD) model suggests the need for controlled, empirical research that clearly identifies the role of this helping method used by counselors.

Schools have become settings in which violence has escalated by students and external perpetrators. School-related violent deaths between 2003 and 2004 alone resulted in stabbings, shootings, and hangings in 25 states for a total of 47 fatalities (Toppo, 2004). Violence and bullying in schools has spawned widespread recognition that counselors, on site, are a first line of intervention as well as prevention of the harm that is inflicted on both the children who are victimized as well as those who are the perpetrators. School-based counselors are serving as trainers to teachers, the community, parents, and students regarding implementation of antibullying and antiviolence programs that involve children who bully and those subjected to this form of violent behavior (Hernandez & Seem, 2004; Hermann & Finn, 2002), for management of crisis and trauma associated with terrorism in school settings (Brock & Cowan, 2004; Schools and Terrorism, 2004), and in devising strategies for assessment, prevention, and early intervention (Daniels, 2002).

Counselors will continue to provide intervention and prevention services for individuals, families, groups, professional cohorts, and communities when natural disasters occur, when violence in schools erupts, following domestic or foreign terrorist acts, and in other contexts in which mass killings take place. Well-constructed research that demonstrates how such services impact the consumer is needed in order to direct the use of the most effective intervention models (e.g., cognitive behavior treatment, psychological debriefing) for affected populations and groups. Questions about the goals for counselor service delivery following natural disaster and mass casualty events can then be more clearly answered. Determining the role of the counselor that is most beneficial as a source of psychological support or "first aid" to surviving victims is essential. Counselor contributions through a staged process in which immediate emotional support is most critical, followed by brief therapeutic intervention, and then by longer-term counseling may be more effective than a single point of intervention. Perhaps a continuum of services is needed while also determining who is best prepared to provide a comprehensive array of mental health services. Whereas intuitively counseling professionals may view this sequencing as logical, the role of empirical research in determining the efficacy of interventions can provide answers that reflect a solid foundation of research.

Mental Illness Stigma, Bias, and Emerging Acceptance

Attitudes toward those with mental illness have historically been characterized by negative stigma and stereotypes. According to Van Dorn, Swanson, Elbogen, and Swartz (2005, p. 153), stigma can be defined

> broadly to include beliefs, attitudes, and behaviors that result in social rejection or isolation of an individual based on any set of characteristics that are perceived by a group to be undesirable or threatening, regardless of whether exposure to the person with these characteristics would actually cause adverse consequences to others.

Social groups can stigmatize those who are perceived to be different due to mental illness or disability, as is often the case with diagnoses such as schizophrenia or other acute psychiatric disorders. Although there are reports of more accepting attitudes toward some psychiatric populations with severe mental illnesses (Angermeyer & Matschinger, 2003a; Newhill & Korr, 2004), the predominant attitude continues to be negative, fear-tinged, and stereotyped (Angermeyer & Matschinger, 2003a; 2003b; McSween, 2002).

Fueling some of the negative stereotypes of mental illness are media depictions that portray acutely mentally ill patients as harmful, posing extreme danger, creating public health problems, or being noncompliant with treatment. These images, repeated nightly on forensic television dramas and comedic programs, intensify the stigma attached to clients receiving community or inpatient mental health treatment from counseling professionals (Byrne, 2000; March, 1999). The consequences of stigma about the mentally ill have an adverse impact on clients as well as children (Wahl, 2003) through images of psychiatric patients as violent or unattractive. Long-term exposure to such negative and fear-inducing depictions can lead to attitudes that are difficult to dislodge. For families of the mentally ill, the phenomenon of "courtesy stigma" (Angermeyer, Schulze, & Dietrich, 2003) includes fear of being contaminated by the mental illness of a parent, sibling, or other family member. The negative attitudes within a community of people about mental illness, for example, can harm the family members who may experience guilt, shame, and a sense of blame for the behaviors of their family member (Corrigan & Miller, 2004).

Counselor Perceptions of Mental Illness.   Counselors are not immune from the pervasive influences of negative attitudes and stigma toward the mentally ill. There is variation in the intensity of mental illness stigma and how it can be influenced by experience with such clients (Van Dorn, Swanson, Elbogen, & Swartz, 2005). Methods that reduce stigma and unwarranted perceptions of dangerousness, for example, can be influenced by contact with the mentally ill in training settings or in community health care settings (Couture & Penn, 2003; Reinke et al, 2004). Witnessing the vulnerability and obvious presence of illness is a powerful counteraction to retention of negative stereotypes. When counselors are in the company of a client who is suffering from schizophrenia, who is frightened, and who is unable to negotiate life effectively, the unusual nature of some of the behaviors becomes understandable as manifestations of illness, not predictors of inevitable dangerousness. When an appropriate medication management and therapy regimen is followed by mentally ill patients, attitudes toward the patient with a depressive mental illness are improved (Sirey et al, 2001). For counselors, efforts to promote adherence to treatment can therefore result in two highly desirable outcomes: (1) the patient's condition can stabilize or improve and (2) attitudes toward the patient held by family, friends, and the community in which he or she lives may become more accepting.

From another perspective, efforts on the part of counselors to advocate for education about the mentally ill, mental illnesses, and the effectiveness of treatment are essential to altering beliefs of consumers and their families. An example of how the social issue of stigma toward the mentally ill can directly impact counseling practice is the NIMBY (not in my back yard) syndrome described by March (1999). When this syndrome appears, it might signal a community rejection of the placement of a half-way house for the chronically mentally ill or residential homes for the homeless mentally ill within a community. Citizens may petition, attend public hearings, and in a variety of ways express fear and anxiety about the placement of such homes within a residential area. These actions often take place as reactions to perceived threats that the mentally ill pose to others in the neighborhood and are a direct reflection of the stigma toward those with mental illnesses that continues to exist.

Implications for Counseling Practice.   The majority of individuals with mental illness do not seek treatment because of their denial of the existence of the illness or seriousness of the symptoms (Kessler et al, 2001). For those who accept that a serious psychological problem does exist, the majority do not seek treatment due to barriers associated with access, financial reasons, or perceptions that treatment is not beneficial (Kessler et al, 2001). The role of the counselor in assisting clients to understand the nature of the psychological problem being experienced, therefore, is a significant one. Clients being seen in a crisis counseling setting, for example, may be overwhelmed by the immediate circumstance and can benefit from the sensitive and knowledgeable care a counselor can provide. Using counseling methods that describe, interpret, and communicate a mental illness diagnosis often is the first step toward guiding a client to seek much needed psychological treatment.

To be effective in reducing clients' nonaccepting attitudes toward mental illness, counselors must have a solid knowledge foundation regarding the complexities of severe mental illness. The social and political factors that are often linked to insufficient levels of service for the mentally ill are the same factors associated with the chronicity of mental illness (e.g., poverty, homelessness, unsafe living environments, and unemployment) (Draine, Salzer, Culhane, & Hadley, 2002). With this understanding, counselors are able to lead advocacy and public education efforts designed to demystify mental illnesses in general, and more specifically, to counteract the negative and stigmatizing portrayals of the mentally ill.

As members of the mental health professional communities in which they reside, counselors can initiate, participate in, and lead in the development and implementation of community-based treatment programs that serve the mentally ill. Programs with a demonstrated effectiveness, such as assertive community treatment (Bond, Drake, Meuser, & Lattimer, 2001), provide intensive multidisciplinary treatment that is associated with reduced inpatient hospitalization, increased quality of life, and, in many cases, stable living environments. With these activities, counselors directly and indirectly begin to alter the mental health literacy (Jorm, 2000) of consumers as well as health care professionals (i.e., the understanding and beliefs held regarding mental disorders and how these beliefs may or may not be associated with help seeking or self-care).

Central to counselors being able to influence the attitudes and stereotyped views of the mentally ill is an understanding of personal biases toward the various populations within what is termed "the mentally ill." Each counselor must ask questions about personal bias that guide recognition of stigma toward the severely mentally ill, the functional mentally ill, and those with undiagnosed mental illnesses. As this self-assessment process continues throughout a career in counseling practice, innumerable opportunities are presented to dispel negative stigma. For example, casual conversation can include negative, judgmental, and ridiculing attitudes toward the mentally ill that take the form of jokes or storytelling about those afflicted with a mental disorder. Counselors can interject corrections or alternative perspectives through their reactions to these encounters while acknowledging how entrenched such stereotypes are within the culture.

Counselors can provide accurate, expert information to those they encounter in practice, through community activities, and in their personal lives that portray those with mental illnesses or disorders in a realistic light. Through participation in lay and professional public education programs, the counselor may provide insights about mental illness that can reduce fear, anxiety, and avoidance of the mentally ill or with reference to initiatives to integrate housing for the chronically mentally ill within community settings. When invited to speak at media events or to provide expert commentary on mental illness to the media, counselors can employ the resources of their professional association to support clear, accurate, and balanced views of the needs of the mentally ill.

Public attitudes toward certain forms of mental illness may be swayed through direct-to-consumer (DTC) advertising on television, radio, and on the Internet that tout the benefits of various psychotropic medications (Gilbody, Wilson, & Watt, 2004; Lenhardt, 2005). A steady barrage of such advertising may, in fact, serve to modify negative views of depression and anxiety as well as certain neurological disorders (e.g., attention deficit hyperactivity disorder) to attitudes of accepting that some psychological disorders are socially acceptable and readily treated through the use of pharmacological agents. Although somewhat biased in perspective (i.e., medicine is the answer to certain mood disturbances), or targeted to specific audiences (e.g., women) using highly persuasive imagery (Peppin & Carty, 2001), overall, the general public may benefit from the limited education that is provided. As a social shift within American culture, the future of DTC advertising may prove to be a beneficial factor in changing some attitudes toward mental illness and health care in general.

The social changes identified in this chapter represent a sampling of factors that impact how counselors deliver services, where helping is provided, and when mental health interventions are used. The backdrop for counseling practice is a society that is influenced by the help it provides to those affected by mental health issues and is, in turn, influenced by social imperatives that direct further change within the professions. One example illustrating this interactive effect has been described (i.e., the evolving role of the counselor as part of trauma response teams in the aftermath of natural disaster, crisis, terrorism, or mass trauma). A second example focuses on the role of stigma toward mental illness and the mentally ill.

It is essential that counselors in practice as well as those in training understand the interactive nature of social factors and societal forces, as these directly and indirectly impact their ability to counsel. At the same time, awareness of these issues and how each continues to change in response to prevailing social trends, patterns, and pressure on vital social institutions ensures that counseling professionals remain sensitized to the lived experience of clients, families, groups, and communities.

DISCUSSION TOPICS AND QUESTIONS

1. The list of social and societal issues that impact counseling clients is potentially limitless. Of the issues discussed in this chapter, select one as the focus for your analysis of how this issue affects counseling practice with children under age 10 and adults over age 65.

2. Select a website that contains information about depression. Discuss the accuracy of the information on the site, verify the sponsor for the site, and evaluate the usefulness of the information to the consumer who is depressed, to the spouse of a depressed individual, and to counselors who care for individuals who are depressed.

3. As you consider the demographic trends discussed in this chapter, as well as updated information that you research, discuss three implications for counseling practice of the data that describe the need for counselors in the United States over the next 10 years.

4. The Internet has generated a revolution in information access for consumers and counseling professionals. Identify three characteristics of the easy access to information that benefit mental health clients and three detractors of access to information on the Internet that pose risks to clients. For the detractor aspect of this topic, focus on adolescents or individuals with addictive or compulsive disorders.

5. Mr. Merrill, described in this chapter, brings copies of downloaded information from the Internet to his fourth session with you, his counselor. The copied information describes a self-help program offered by "Dr. Vone" through her website that offers tapes, books, and herbal remedies that are purported to increase energy for those suffering from depression. What is your response to Mr. Merrill's inquiry about your opinions of this material?

6. Obtain information from your counselor professional association that outlines the requirements for counselors to serve on community-based disaster recovery teams. What are your beliefs about counselors participating on such teams? Under what circumstances would it be appropriate for counselors to decline to do so?

7. The school district in your community will be offering a public education program that will include the topic of grief and bereavement counseling needs for middle school students. You've been asked to prepare a presentation regarding parent responses to the death of a classmate. How does this request reflect social issues that counselors must address in practice?

8. Bullying increasingly is recognized as a significant social issue that counselors in education, community, and practice settings must be prepared to address with parents, children, and education professionals. Discuss the statement and question: Bullying has always existed. Why focus so much attention on it now?

9. Stigma attached to mental illness continues to affect societal responses to the needs of the chronically mentally ill. Discuss the role of the individual counselor in addressing this issue while practicing in an agency or private practice setting.

10. Your client, Ms. Capia, has sought counseling upon referral by her gynecologist with a presenting complaint of sleeplessness. She brings up the topic of direct-to-consumer (DTC) advertising on television as she asks for your views about a newly released sleeping medication. Discuss your stance on DTC in general, and specifically, what would your response be to Ms. Capia's inquiry?

REFERENCES

Allen, J. (1999). Responding to unemployment and inequalities in income and health. *European Journal of Psychotherapy, Counselling & Health, 2*, 143–152.

Angermeyer, M. C., & Matschinger, H. (2003a). Public beliefs about schizophrenia and depression: Similarities and differences. *Social Psychiatry and Psychiatric Epidemiology, 38*, 526–534.

Angermeyer, M. C., & Matschinger, H. (2003b). The stigma of mental illness: Effects of labeling on public attitudes towards people with mental disorder. *Acta Psychiatrica Scandinavica, 108*, 304–309.

Angermeyer, M. C., Schulze, B., & Dietrich, S. (2003). Courtesy stigma: A focus group study of schizophrenic patients. *Social Psychiatry & Psychiatric Epidemiology, 38*, 593–602.

Auger, R. W., Seymour, J. W., & Roberts, W. B. (2004). Responding to terror: The Impact of September 11 on K–12 schools and schools' responses. *Professional School Counseling, 7*, 222–231.

Beamish, P. M., Granello, D. H., & Belcastro, A. L. (2002). Treatment of panic disorder: Practical guidelines. *Journal of Mental Health Counseling, 24*, 224–246.

Benigeri, M., & Pluye, P. (2003). Shortcomings of health information on the Internet. *Health Promotion International, 18*(4), 381–386.

Bisson, J., McFarlane, A. C., & Rose, S. (2000). Psychological debriefing. In E. B. Foa, T. M. Keane, & M. J. Friedman (Eds.), *Effective treatment of PTSD* (pp. 39–59). New York: Guilford Press.

Bond, G. R., Drake, R. E., Mueser, K. T., & Latimer, E. (2001). Assertive community treatment for people with severe mental illness: Critical ingredients and impact on patients. *Disease Management & Health Outcomes, 9*(3), 141–159.

Bramlett, M. D., & Mosher, W. D. (2002). Cohabitation, marriage, divorce, and remarriage in the United States. National Center for Health Statistics. *Vital Health Statistics, 23*(22). Retrieved January 27, 2006, from www.cdc.gov/nchs/data/series/sr_23/sr23_022.pdf.

Brock, S. E., & Cowan, K. (2004). Preparing to help students after a crisis. *Education Digest, 69*, 34–41.

Bureau of Labor Statistics. (2004). Employment by occupation: Counselors. *Occupational Outlook Handbook, 2004–05 Edition*, U.S. Department of Labor. Retrieved May 12, 2004, from www.bls.gov/oco/ocos067.htm.

Byrne, P. (2000). Stigma of mental illness and ways of diminishing it. *Advances in Psychiatric Treatment, 6*, 65–72.

Centers for Disease Control and Prevention. (2005). *Marriage and divorce.* National Center for Health Statistics. Retrieved January 27, 2006, from www.cdc.gov/nchs/fastats/divorce.htm.

Chandler, C., Bodenhamer-Davis, E., Holden, J. M., Evenson, T., & Bratton, S. (2001). Enhancing personal wellness in counselor trainees using biofeedback: An exploratory study. *Applied Psychophysiology & Biofeedback, 26*, 1–8.

Clauss, C. S. (1998). Cultural intersections and systems levels in counseling. *Cultural Diversity & Mental Health, 4*, 127–134.

Cline, R. J. W., & Haynes, K. M. (2001). Consumer health information seeking on the Internet: The state of the art. *Health Education Research, 16*(6), 671–672.

Corrigan, P. W., & Miller, F. E. (2004). Shame, blame, and contamination: A review of the impact of mental illness stigma on family members. *Journal of Mental Health, 13*(6), 537–548.

Couture, S. M., & Penn, D. L. (2003). Interpersonal contact and the stigma of mental illness: A review of the literature. *Journal of Mental Health, 12*(3), 291–305.

Cummins, C. O., Prochaska, J. O., Driskell, M. M., Evers, K. E., Wright, J. A., Prochaska, J. M., et al. (2003). Development of review criteria to evaluate health behavior change websites. *Journal of Health Psychology, 8*(1), 55–62.

Daniels, J. A. (2002). Assessing threats of school violence: Implications for counselors. *Journal of Counseling & Development, 80*(2), 215–219.

Deahl, M. P., Srinvasan, M., Jones, N., Neblett, C., & Jolly, A. (2001). Evaluating psychological debriefing: Are we measuring the right outcomes? *Journal of Traumatic Stress, 14*(3), 527–529.

DeMarco, R. R. (2000). The epidemiology of major depression: Implications of occurrence, recurrence, and stress in a Canadian community sample. *Canadian Journal of Psychiatry, 45*, 67–75.

Draine, J., Salzer, M. S., Culhane, D. P., & Hadley, T. R. (2002). Role of social disadvantage in crime, joblessness, and homelessness among persons with serious mental illness. *Psychiatric Services, 53*, 565–573.

Ehlers, A., & Clark, D. M. (2003). Early psychological interventions for adult survivors of trauma: A review. *Biological Psychiatry, 53*(9), 817–826.

Eysenbach, G., & Jadad, A. R. (2001). Evidence-based patient choice and consumer health informatics. *Journal of Medical Internet Research, 3*(2). Retrieved January 26, 2006, from www.jmir.org/2001/2/e19/.

Fals-Stewart, W., & O'Farrell, T. J. (2003). Behavioral family counseling and Naltrexone for male opioid-dependent patients. *Journal of Consulting & Clinical Psychology, 71*, 432–443.

Fletcher, T. B. (2000). Primary nocturnal enuresis: A structural and strategic family systems approach. *Journal of Mental Health Counseling, 22*, 32–44.

Gerten, A. (2000). Guidelines for intervention with children and adolescents diagnosed with conduct disorder. *Social Work in Education, 22*, 132–145.

Gilbody, S., Wilson, P., & Watt, I. (2004). Direct-to-consumer advertising of psychotropics: An emerging and evolving form of pharmaceutical company influence. *British Journal of Psychiatry, 185*, 1–2.

Gladding, S. T. (2003). *Counseling: A comprehensive profession.* Upper Saddle River, NJ: Prentice–Hall.

Goss, S., & Anthony, K. (Eds.). (2003). *Technology in counseling and psychotherapy: A practitioner's guide.* New York: Macmillan.

Grossman, A. W., Churchill, J. D., McKinney, B. C., Kodish, I. M., Otte, S. L., & Greenough, W. T. (2003). Experience effects on brain development of possible contributions to psychopathology. *Journal of Child Psychology & Psychiatry & Allied Disciplines, 44*, 33–64.

Hazler, R. J., & Mellin, E. A. (2004). The developmental origins and treatment of female adolescents with depression. *Journal of Counseling & Development, 82*, 18–24.

Hermann, M. A., & Finn, A. (2002). An ethical and legal perspective on the role of school counselors in preventing violence in schools. *Professional School Counseling, 6*, 46–55.

Hernandez, T. J., & Seem, S. R. (2004). A safe school climate: A systematic approach and the school counselor. *Professional School Counseling, 7*, 256–263.

Horton, M. F. (2002). *Interim report of the President's new freedom commission on mental health.* Substance Abuse and Mental Health Administration. Retrieved July 5, 2004, from www.mentalhealth.org/publications/allpubs/NMH02–0144/default.asp.

Hyman, S. E. (2003). Diagnosing disorders. *Scientific American, 289*, 96–104.

Jorm, A. F. (2000). Mental health literacy: Public knowledge and beliefs about mental disorders. *British Journal of Psychiatry, 177*, 396–401.

Kessler, R. C., Berglund, P. A., Bruce, M. L., Koch, J. R., Laska, E. M., Leaf, P. J., et al. (2001). The preva-lence and correlates of untreated serious mental illness. *Health Services Research, 36,* 1009–1017.

Kraus, R., Zack, J. S., & Stricker, G. (Eds.). (2003). *Online counseling: A handbook for mental health pro-fessionals.* Oxford, UK: Elsevier Science & Technology Books.

Leinbaugh, T. C. (2001). Electroconvulsive therapy: A primer for mental health counselors. *Journal of Mental Health Counseling, 23,* 36–48.

Lenhardt, E. (2005). Why so glum? Toward a fair balance of competitive interests in direct-to-consumer advertising and the well-being of the mentally ill consumers it targets. *Health Matrix: Journal of Law Medicine, 15*(1), 165–204.

Lissman, T. L., & Boehnlein, J. K. (2001). A critical review of Internet information about depression. *Psychiatric Services, 52,* 1046–1050.

Litz, B. T. (Ed.). (2003). *Early intervention for trauma and traumatic loss.* New York: Guilford Press.

March, P. A. (1999). Ethical responses to media depictions of mental illness: An advocacy approach. *Journal of Humanistic Counseling, Education & Development, 38*(2), 70–79.

McLeod, J., & Machin, L. (1998). The context of counseling: A neglected dimension of training, research and practice. *British Journal of Guidance & Counselling, 26,* Issue 3.

McSween, J. L. (2002). The role of group interest, identity, and stigma in determining mental health policy preferences. *Journal of Health Politics, Policy & Law, 27,* 773–801.

Newhill, C. E., & Korr, W. S. (2004). Practice with people with severe mental illness: Rewards, chal-lenges, burdens. *Health & Social Work, 29*(4), 297–305.

National Institutes of Health (NIH) (2004a). *The impact of mental illness on society.* NIH Publication No. 01-4586. Retrieved February 3, 2004, from www.nimh.nih.gov/publicat/burden.cfm.

NIH (2004b). *The numbers count: Mental illness in America.* NIH Publication No. 01-4584. Retrieved February 3, 2004, from www.nimh.nih.gov/publicat/numbers.cfm.

Okun, B. F. (2001). *Effective helping* (5th ed.). Belmont, CA: Wadsworth.

Parke, R. D. (2004). Development in the family. *Annual Review of Psychology, 55,* 386–399.

Peppin, P., & Carty, E. (2001). Semiotics, stereotypes, and women's health: Signifying inequality in drug advertising. *Canadian Journal of Women & the Law, 13*(2), 326–360.

Peres, T. S., & Emery, R. E. (2004). A prospective study of the consequences of marital disruption for adolescents: Predisruption family dynamics and postdisruption adolescent adjustment. *Journal of Clinical Child and Adolescent Psychology, 33*(4), 694–704.

Peterson, G., Aslani, P., & Williams, K. A. (2003). How do consumers search for and appraise information on medicines on the Internet? A qualitative study using focus groups. *Journal of Medical Internet Research, 5*(4). Retrieved January 24, 2006, from www.jmir.org/2003/4/e33/?&login.

Pistole, M. C. (2001). *Mental health counseling: Identity and distinctiveness.* ERIC-CASS462672. Retrieved January 9, 2004, from www.ericfacility.net/databases/ERIC_Digests/ed462672.html.

President's New Freedom Commission on Mental Health. (2004). *Achieving the promise: Transforming mental health care in America.* Retrieved March 6, 2004, from www.mentalhealthcommission. gov/reports/reports.htm.

Reinke, R. R., Corrigan, P. W., Leonhard, C., Lundin, R. K., & Kubiak, M. A. (2004). Examining two aspects of contact on the stigma of mental illness. *Journal of Social and Clinical Psychology, 23*(3), 377–389.

Ruzak, J. I., & Watson, P. (2001). Early intervention to prevent PTSD and other trauma-related problems. *PTSD Research Quarterly, 12,* 1–7.

Sawa, A., & Snyder, S. H. (2002). Schizophrenia: Diverse approaches to a complex disease. *Science, 296,* 692–695.

Schools and terrorism. (2004, February). *Journal of School Health, 74,* 39–52.

Seidman, J. J., Steinwachs, D., & Rubin, H. R. (2003). Conceptual framework for a new tool for evaluat-ing the quality of diabetes consumer-information web sites. *Journal of Medical Internet Research, 5*(4). Retrieved January 26, 2006, from www.jmir.org/2003/4/e29/?&login.

Sirey, J. A., Bruce, M. L., Alexopoulos, G. S., Perlick, D. A., Friedman, S. J., & Meyers, B. S. (2001). Perceived stigma and patient-rated severity of illness as predictors of antidepressant drug adherence. *Psychiatric Services, 52*(12), 1615–1620.

Stein, B. D., Jaycox, L. H., Kataoka, S. H., Wong, M., Tu, W., Elliott, M. N., et al. (2003). A mental health intervention for school children exposed to violence: A randomized controlled trial. *Journal of the American Medical Association, 290,* 603–611.

Stone, J. A., & Sias, S. M. (2003). Self-injurious behavior: A bi-modal treatment approach to working with adolescent females. *Journal of Mental Health Counseling, 25*, 112–125.

Toppo, G. (2004, June 28). Schools safe, but danger lurks. *USA Today*, pp. 1D, 6D.

Tyler, M. J., & Sabella, R. A. (2003). *Using technology to improve counseling practice: A primer for the 21st century*. Alexandria, VA: American Counseling Association.

U.S. Census Bureau. (2004). *U.S. interim projections by age, sex, race, and Hispanic origin*. Retrieved March 30, 2004, from www.census.gov/ipc/www/usinterimproj.

Van Dorn, R. A., Swanson, J. W., Elbogen, E. B., & Swartz, M. S. (2005). A comparison of stigmatizing attitudes toward persons with schizophrenia in four stakeholder groups: Perceived likelihood of violence and desire for social distance. *Psychiatry, 68*(2), 152–163.

Wahl, O. F. (2003). Depictions of mental illnesses in children's media. *Journal of Mental Health, 12*(3), 249–258.

Wilkinson, G. B., Taylor, P., & Holt, J. R. (2002). Bipolar disorder in adolescence: Diagnosis and treatment. *Journal of Mental Health Counseling, 24*, 348–357.

Winker, M. A., Flanagin, A., Chi-Lum, B., White, J., Andrews, K., & Kennett, R. (2000). Guidelines for medical and health information sites on the Internet: Principles governing AMA web sites. *Journal of the American Medical Association, 283*(12), 1600–1606.

■ ■ ■ ■ ■

CHAPTER TWO

ECONOMIC AND POLITICAL ISSUES

Influence on Counseling Service Delivery

PAMELA K. S. PATRICK

Economics is often viewed as unfamiliar territory to the counseling professional who often enters the profession with minimal academic preparation in the dynamics of economic forces that directly impact the how, where, who, and when of mental health care delivery. In reality, counselors are profoundly influenced by economic and political shifts that can determine whether clients will continue to be employed, or will lose or have to change health care benefit providers, or whether, due to economic factors, the mental health care provider must consider if it is economically viable to remain a mental health service practitioner. Changes in political priorities for legislation as well as the vagaries of the political landscape that can change with each election cycle also influence the environment in which mental health care can or will be delivered. In addition to macro-economic and political variables that affect practice and service delivery, the counseling professions are directly impacted by managed care and politics that result in legislative enactments that alter reimbursements and service access to consumers.

This chapter focuses on understanding how contemporary economic trends and political factors impact access, availability, and affordability of counseling to consumers. These issues often result in decision making that determines health policy making with lasting consequences for individuals, families, and communities. Counselors, therefore, are well advised to consider economic and political issues that are generated far from the sensitive and responsive milieu of client and counselor that is at the heart of the therapeutic relationship.

"IT'S THE ECONOMY"

Counselor professionals are well aware that there are economic factors that support or deter consumers from seeking mental health care. Experience provides ample evidence of this reality in many counseling practices.

> Ms. Thomason had been counseling Alison for three weeks after she left her physically and emotionally abusive boyfriend. Alison had been working with the victim advocate in the state attorney's office and had moved back with her parents while waiting for the trial to begin. Her emotional health was fragile, revealing signs and symptoms of trauma, post-traumatic stress, and healing from the physical injuries she had sustained. Her employee health insurance was adequate, and Alison paid the co-payment for each session. Last week Alison's employer closed one of its restaurants, and she was suddenly unemployed. She called to cancel all remaining appointments.

Economic factors directly impacted Alison. Without a job, she is without health insurance benefits. The macro-economic factors that led her employer to close an unprofitable restaurant directly influenced the micro-viewpoint of the consumer (i.e., without insurance coverage, counseling was an expense that could not currently be managed). Thus, the impact of health insurance availability determined service utilization. These and other factors are the focus of this discussion of issues associated with economic factors and the effectiveness, efficiency, and consistency of mental health care.

Insurance Issues Affecting Mental Health Care

Lack of insurance coverage for mental health care and its cost are cited as the primary delimiters for seeking mental health care (Bossolo, 2004; Sherer, 2004). The majority of consumers in need of mental health care do not seek help due to these factors. According to Sharfstein (as cited by Sherer, 2004, p. 12), 55 to 60 million Americans have no mental health care coverage, placing them in the "so called gray zone, just above the threshold for Medicaid." With over 44 million Americans suffering from mental health disorders, or 1 in 5 in a given year (National Institute of Mental Health, 2005; Satcher, 1999), it is clear that economic issues are of critical importance to the care needs of vast numbers of consumers.

As a core issue impacting the counseling professions, access to mental health care is driven by economics (cost and insurance availability), and each factor is linked to social factors such as employment, employee benefits, lack of health care benefits, and poverty. In addition, when consumers do not have the financial resources to pay for mental health care, personal economic factors are the reason why most do not obtain the care (Bossolo, 2004). Although government-subsidized or government-provided mental health care continues to sustain a level of care to the poor, funding for these services is continually at risk in each community as states struggle to provide continuing funding (McSween, 2002; Satcher, 1999) or cut services. For some, lack of understanding regarding what Medicare covers for mental health services, for example, is a deterrent to seeking services, whereas for other elderly consumers, cost factors over and above what Medicare pays for mental health care is a deterrent (Health Care Economics, 2000). For children and adolescents, it is estimated that three-fourths of the adolescents who need mental health care do not receive it (RAND Health, 2001).

A contemporary example of how economically driven legislative decisions impact consumers of mental health care services is provided by the Medicare Modernization Act (MMA) of 2003. The implementation of this act provides insights into the confusion and disruption to mental health care that is associated with significant legislative changes when interlocking governmental programs such as Medicare and Medicaid for the dually eligible are involved (Elliott, Majundar, Gillick, & Soumerai, 2005; Ryan & Super, 2003). Dually eligible clients who previously received psychotropic medication for mental illness conditions, for example, may experience increased risk for maintaining customary access to prescribed medicines with the implementation of the Part D Medicare drug benefit. Many of these dually eligible patients are least able to self-advocate to seek redress of lost or delayed benefits. Thus, while the MMA legislated by Congress sought to improve access to medicine for those on Medicare, some of the consequences may increase risk to the dually eligible as well as other vulnerable populations.

Economic downturns and recessions result in job loss for millions of consumers and further erode access to the mental health care safety net on which many rely. Additional stresses associated with low-paying jobs, job loss and unemployment, job searching, and financial burdens when family income plummets produce additional sources of acute stress. For individuals with preexisting psychological disorders, these economic factors exacerbate distress while access to mental health services diminishes (Guindon & Smith, 2002; Grove, 1999). In general, men are more significantly impacted by job loss than women (Artazcoz, Benach, Borell, & Cortes, 2004), suggesting that in addition to the inadequacies of the current mental health system for those diagnosed with mental disorders, additional populations, with few resources, are heavily affected by these systemic deficiencies. Amidst this seemingly ever present source of angst, the counselor professional must remain engaged in advocacy efforts at the community and professional organization levels to ensure that the voices of disenfranchised mental health populations are heard and their needs are addressed. At the same time, counselor professionals typically also continue to be engaged in devising other community-based options as stopgap measures for consumers in need of mental health care.

Managed Care: More Questions than Answers?

Managed care is variously described as a systematic approach to rationing health care (Baily, 2003; Sanchez & Turner, 2003), as a method to effectively use available resources (Docherty, 1999), and as a response to the economically driven demand for "technical rationality and efficiency" in health care (Scheid, 2003, p. 142). It is an approach to control the costs of health care as well as the care provided. According to the U.S. Agency for Healthcare Research and Quality (2004), managed care is comprised of

> health insurance plans [that are] intended to reduce unnecessary health care costs through a variety of mechanisms, including: economic incentives for physicians and patients to select

less costly forms of care; programs for reviewing the medical necessity of specific services; increased beneficiary cost sharing; controls on inpatient admissions and lengths of stay; the establishment of cost-sharing incentives for outpatient surgery; selective contracting with health care providers; and the intensive management of high-cost health care cases.

Within the framework of the general label of "managed care organizations" (MCOs) are health maintenance organizations (HMOs), preferred provider organizations (PPOs), individual practice associations (IPAs), and employee assistance programs (EAPs). In general, managed care involves the provision of care to consumers that is provided by counseling practitioners approved by, and included on the approved provider lists of, the managed care organization (i.e., HMO, PPO).

As a "fact of life" for counseling professionals, significant challenges and issues are linked to the revolution in health care rationing that resulted with the spread of MCOs. These issues include the paradigm shift that continues to reverberate throughout the counseling professions; redefinition of treatment goals and how outcomes are measured; access to participation in health care services for consumers and providers; ethical considerations and dilemmas; and quality of care available under the MCO model. Underlying each of these issues is the realization that the transformation wrought by the managed health care movement is primarily driven by economic factors that have led to change in how health care is rationed. Secondary concerns have to do with issues aligned with the rights of all consumers to have access to high-quality health care. As this model continues to refine itself, the fine line between these two often competing motivations will foster intense debate among stakeholders.

Counseling Paradigm Shift.   Managed health care is based on the economics surrounding the explosive costs of providing health care in the United States. According to the Henry J. Kaiser Foundation, national health care expenditures have risen over 88 percent "since 1992 and, at nearly \$1.6 trillion in 2002, are more than six times the \$246 billion spent in 1980" (Lundy, Finder, & Claxton, 2004). This level of expenditure directly impacts the economy, resulting in health care costs that consume 14.9 percent of the country's gross domestic product (GDP) (Lundy, Finder, & Claxton, 2004). Although these figures are dramatic in themselves, projections for national health care expenditures indicate that this percentage of the GDP will escalate to 18.7 percent by 2014 (Center for Medicare & Medicaid Services, 2006). To curb these costs, managed health care systems have been devised and implemented as cost-control measures that propelled a paradigm shift within the counseling professions.

Mental health coverage, both inpatient and outpatient, is covered by virtually all managed health care plans. Co-payments vary, number of sessions per year is typically capped or provided under capitation arrangements, and inpatient care maximums are imposed (Lundy, Finder, & Claxton, 2004). At the same time that expenditures for health care are directly affecting the economy and mental health coverage is provided to the insured, it is estimated that 41.7 to 45.8 percent of Americans do not have health insurance benefits (Cohen & Martinez, 2005; DeNavas-Walt, Proctor, & Lee, 2005; U.S. Census Bureau, 2002). In addition, the projected need for mental health care for the aging population with substance abuse or psychiatric disorders is anticipated to increase by 13 to 50 percent

(Bartels, Blow, Brockman, & Van Citters, 2005). The impact of the health care needs of the uninsured on a public care system under chronic economic strain is immense. For consumers in need of mental health care, these economic forces can directly influence whether care is received, and if it is, whether it is timely and of sufficient length to address care needs.

When "paradigm shift" is defined as a revolutionary way of thinking, or as leading to transformation that is determined by other social, cultural, or political forces, the dramatic changes in how mental health care is provided through managed health care fits the definition. For counselors, the reliance of employers and governmental funding sources on managed health care plans has had a direct impact on practice. The manner in which counselors practice and receive compensation for the services rendered has shifted to meet the demands of a changed marketplace, including the following:

1. How clients are referred to mental health practitioners
2. Who determines when the mental health professional referral will be made
3. How long counseling takes place when managed health care benefits are used as the primary source of compensation
4. Who providers of counseling services will be
5. How outcomes for counseling/psychotherapy will be measured
6. Who receives specialized mental health care and when

From the era when counselors provided services to consumers with no limits imposed by third-party payers to the present time, a reallocation in how services are provided has occurred. The system of care has shifted from a model that relied on counselor professional assessment of client needs for treatment to one in which those parameters are set by external entities. It is now essential that practitioners work collaboratively with external referral sources; seek to become members of PPO, HMO, PPC provider panels; and conform to the requirements defined by such membership.

Impact on Counseling and Psychotherapy Practice.   Many mental health professionals view the establishment of managed health care as an intrusion into the domain of the psychotherapist, resulting in striking changes in the therapeutic process. According to Cowan (2005, p. 27), "There is a very real danger in the current economic climate of mental health care delivery that the field of counseling and psychotherapy could increasingly become a marching ground for an army of therapy 'technicians.'" Others view the presence of managed health care as the new "normal," including its "malignant" intrusiveness into the practice arena (Sperling & Sack, 2002), and have focused on counselor preparation to work collaboratively with HMOs, PPOs, IPOs, and other permutations of managed health care organizations. How to apply psychodynamic psychotherapy in a managed care environment is viewed as virtually impossible or sometimes possible (Sperling & Sack, 2002; Coffey, Olson, & Sessions, 2001). There is recognition, however, that long-term psychotherapy is increasingly becoming an anachronism in contemporary managed care environments as counseling professionals adapt to and adopt brief counseling models as treatments of choice. Debate about the benefits and drawbacks of managed mental health care, therefore, is alive and well.

The impact and influence that various economic forces have on how counseling professionals practice is pervasive. To facilitate the adjustment to the demands and constraints inherent in managed mental health care, training for counselors now must include effective communication with case managers, development of treatment plans in accordance with formats of various managed health care plans, submission of claims forms following managed care organization (MCO) procedures, and methods to address disputes when claims are denied or authorization for continuing care is not forthcoming (Anderson, 2000). In addition, practitioners report an overall negative impact on practice when working with managed health care plans (Scaturo, 2002; Danzinger & Welfel, 2001) while, concurrently, requirements to demonstrate clinical effectiveness have intensified (Christensen, 2001; Whittinghill, Whittinghill, & Loesch, 2000). From the practitioners' perspective, this paradigm change has impacted attitudes of mental health providers toward the managed care systems they interface with that can influence the care that is provided (Jung, Pomerantz, Tuholski, & Sullivan, 2001). There is a perceived and oftentimes real *squeeze* experienced by the counselor, as illustrated by Figure 2.1.

According to the counselor "squeeze" model, pressures to control costs and provide care within a constrained atmosphere press the counselor on one side while requirements to complete treatment within a proscribed number of sessions in order to be in compliance with authorization from the MCO impinges on practice from the other direction. Together, counselors experience demands to provide services using brief models of treatment as the preferred method of intervention rather than the treatment method best suited to the client's mental health needs. In addition, MCO case managers review counselor treatment plans and outcomes as a requirement for membership on MCO provider panels, thereby introducing a third party into a helping relationship that has been traditionally composed of the client and the counselor. This level of intrusion is often viewed by the provider as an unwarranted violation of the treatment environment and contains significant risk to both client and provider.

Impact on Mental Health Care Outcomes.   The impact of managed mental health care on consumer mental health care outcomes varies. Clearly, the need to find ways to manage spiraling health care costs necessitated a radical change in how mental health care is provided to the largest number of consumers while attempting to ensure quality of the care received. Research that measures the efficacy of managed care forms of mental health treatment has

FIGURE 2.1   The Counselor "Squeeze" Model

demonstrated a range of results. When measuring pretreatment and posttreatment outcomes using the Global Assessment of Functioning (GAF), for example, Christensen (2001) found that scores improved significantly following brief marriage and family therapy. Determining how to measure outcomes in a managed mental health care setting, however, is more confounding than this study would suggest.

Measuring treatment outcomes under managed mental health care is extremely complicated due to variance in how (1) "efficacy" is measured and defined across the range of managed care plans; (2) care is accessed and managed over time; (3) imposed limits on length of treatment, diagnosis, and method of treatment is characterized; and (4) data can be compared between MCOs and fee-for-service outcomes. According to Sanchez and Turner (2003), the cost-cutting measures inherent in managed mental health care are not typically linked to types of diagnostic groups, type of provider, level of care needed, or consistent quality index. In addition, to accurately evaluate the impact of managed mental health care, measurement of treatment outcomes and "final conclusions about quality of care must incorporate some aspect of client function or perceived state of well being" (Rohrer & Rohland, 1998).

Access to Managed Care.   In order to participate as a provider of mental health care in the managed care marketplace, counseling professionals must become adept at gaining access to the provider panels or networks that link helper to consumer. According to Danzinger and Welfel's (2001, p. 5) research, 48 percent of the counselors participating in a study investigating the impact of managed care on counseling practitioners indicated that "as counselors they experienced difficulty in getting approved as providers." Although variation and anecdotal evidence exist that access to MCO panels/networks is a straightforward process of application and contractual arrangements with specific managed mental health care organizations, others indicate that gaining access to regional networks can be prevented due to individual plan constraints on who is an acceptable provider (e.g., psychologist, social worker, or mental health counselor).

Advice about how to gain access to provider panels is included in the professional literature and has spawned a cottage industry focused on providing guidance and counselor "how-tos" to gain access to managed care networks (Davis & Meier, 2001; Gibelman, & Whiting, 1999; Browning & Browning, 1996). Performance while an approved provider within an MCO network incorporates another skill set associated with being able to practice successfully in this environment has been accompanied by a second wave of publications that focus specifically on the skill sets necessary for successful practice (Zuckerman & LoPresti, 2003; Fauman, 2002; Clarke, Clarke, & Ross, 2001; Gibelman & Whiting, 1999; Cummings, Cummings, & Pallak, 1996).

Issues to be resolved with reference to gaining access to managed health care provider panels/networks pose specific challenges to counselor professionals.

1. *Ensuring that access to panels/networks is extended to all qualified practitioners in a given geographic area versus limiting membership.* Many panels/networks recruit specific practitioners with master's degrees, referred to as the "lowest competent provider," as a cost-savings measure (Cummings, 1995, 1996). This practice increasingly excludes qualified practitioners, such as psychologists, who represent specializations that are more costly.

At the same time, efforts to ensure that counselors will be included on provider panels has been strengthened by "any willing provider" legal decisions in the courts (Gorin, 2003, p. 4).

2. *Determining the impact of being part of a network on counselor income.* Evidence suggests that being providers on managed health care networks results in less compensation, fewer treatment sessions per client, and significantly increased documentation requirements. Thus, the question is raised: Will counselor professionals continue to seek panel/network provider status or consider building private practices without reliance on managed health care? Publications that address the latter issue provide guidance to mental health professionals in developing managed health care–free practices, touting the benefits of making a fundamental shift back to independent provision of psychotherapy services (Haber, Rodino, & Lipner, 2001; Grodzki, 2000). In addition, there are number of workshops and training seminars offered on the World Wide Web that specifically target practice without managed care (e.g., www.growpublications.com/promote2.htm and www.drelainerodino.com/PractConsult.html).

3. *Accessing managed health care networks/panels, including responsibility to comply with the requirements of every insurance company.* Counselors may find these requirements burdensome, as sources of interference with the quality of services to be provided, as associated with reducing treatment effectiveness, and/or as influencing the quality of the counselor's life as a practitioner. There is additional concern that for some counselors, denial of claims submitted to managed mental health care organizations for a counselor's use of an accurate diagnostic category may lead to use of an acceptable diagnostic category or misdiagnosis in order to receive reimbursement. The conflict for the counselor is well summarized by Braun and Cox (2005, p. 431), who highlight the legal and ethical quagmire that results for counselors "forced to choose between allegiance or compliance–providing needed services to clients or adhering to MCO standards that compromise those services."

Each of these issues holds the potential to directly impact the length of time a counseling professional will remain on a network panel, with some practitioners deciding to alter practice methods, change professional goals in order to retain income levels, and/or experience an increased rate of professional burnout.

As counselors increasingly find it essential to seek provider status on managed care insurance company panels, and based on current trends in the health care industry, significant issues have been raised about the boundaries of practice within the managed health care environment that are of critical concern to counseling professionals.

Ethical Challenges with Managed Mental Health Care

The continuing debate about the impact and efficacy of managed mental health care is frequently paired with discussion of ethical issues. These issues have emerged since the inception of this cost-saving model of health care and show no signs of diminishing. With the introduction of intense case management, referral coordinators, preauthorization requirements, authorization for continuing treatment, records reviews, and a host of other administrative mandates encountered by counseling professionals as network providers, practitioners have raised serious questions about the ethical ramifications of managed health care. It is virtually impossible for the counselor professional to avoid addressing ethical issues when involved in managed care arrangements (Daniels, 2001; Kontosh, 2000; Newman & Dunbar, 2000). The frequency of ethical dilemmas experienced by counselors who provide services through managed care arrangements is extremely high. In Danzinger and Welfel's study (2001), 75 percent of the respondents in the sample reported encountering ethical challenges. Among the most salient issues reflected in the literature are confidentiality of patient records, meeting treatment needs, and competence to practice.

Confidentiality of Patient Records.   In order to obtain authorization to treat a patient, the counselor under a managed care arrangement typically must provide written or verbal information about the client to a managed care staff person. This person, who may or may not hold credentials as a mental health professional, determines, in most cases, whether the provider will receive the necessary reauthorization to continue treatment. Disclosure of confidential patient/client information to a noncredentialed individual raises significant issues for the mental health professional. For example, the American Counseling Association Code of Ethics states in Section B.3, Information Shared with Others, B.3.d. Third Party Payers (American Counseling Association, 2005, p. 8): "Counselors disclose information to third-party payers only when clients have authorized such disclosure."

Prior to joining any managed mental health care organization, it is essential that the counseling professional determine how the organization will honor this ethical guideline. Counselors, in turn, must ensure that the disclosure of information about clients remains protected. The balance between these two competing goals oftentimes produces tension for providers and clients.

The understanding by clients of the limits of confidentiality can directly impact the disclosure of information that is necessary to facilitate treatment. In general, clients make an assumption that confidentiality of treatment information is absolute (Kremer & Gesten, 1998). Further, when informed that confidentiality is not absolute, clients report less willingness to self-disclose (Nowell & Spruill, 1993).

From the client perspective, Kremer and Gesten (2003) found that the most important element of the therapeutic relationship for the mental health client is therapist–client autonomy. Requirements by providers to disclose client information in the context of managed mental health care, when clients are well informed of this requirement, poses the following dilemmas for providers:

1. Disclose information in accordance with MCO demands and fully inform the client according to ethical guidelines and standards of practice. With this compliance comes the risk that clients will then not be as forthcoming about sensitive, confidential information that is needed to fully understand the client's needs.
2. Modify reporting practices to protect client confidentiality as reported by a 1996 study of psychologists. In this study, Murphy, DeBernardo, and Shoemaker (1998) found that 63 percent of the sample "believed that psychologists alter diagnoses or Current Procedural Terminology (CPT) codes in order to protect the patient's confidentiality, future employment, or future medical insurance." This is done by using diagnostic

codes that would be reimbursed while not including Axis II diagnoses that would otherwise be applicable. These practitioners viewed the disclosure of all diagnostic information as potentially compromising to the client's well-being. The legal and ethical implications of incomplete diagnosis information (as discussed by Braun & Cox, 2005) should be addressed by the profession as an anchor point to advocate for systematic change in how managed mental health care is "managed."

3. Along the lines of promoting change regarding how managed care is administered and managed, counselor professionals can advocate for the reinstatement of confidentiality in the client–therapist relationship and reduce the role of utilization review. The cost savings of less utilization review (Sanchez & Turner, 2003) and the lower fees paid to the practitioner could produce additional savings within a system of care that at times seems not to be well managed at all. Confidentiality of client information and the subsequent bolstering of the therapist–client relationship would be immediate beneficiaries of this change.

Meeting Treatment Needs.   Discussion about the impact of managed mental health care on length of treatment and consequently the ability of practitioners to provide appropriate levels of care is an issue that has definite ethical implications.

> Mrs. Phillips has health insurance coverage through her husband's managed care plan. The limit for mental health counseling sessions for each calendar year with this plan is 15 visits. As you begin your counseling work with her in early February, it becomes clear that her mental health issues are complex, are long term, and will require more than a total of 15 sessions. Although this estimation of length of treatment may change, you are becoming increasingly worried about how to plan her care over a limited number of authorized sessions.

Providers of care are often caught between the limits of capitated care, as in Mrs. Phillips's case, and the real-world needs of clients to continue treatment. Treatment plan manuals abound in the literature and emphasize the boundaries of behavioral treatments quite well, but clients do not "fit" neatly into such categories.

In an arrangement in which the counselor has authorization to provide psychotherapy, for example, and the client's presenting and evolving problems clearly indicate a need for long-term treatment, the ethical dilemma becomes evident. Ethical counselors provide the level of care needed by the client, yet when reimbursement for treatment has been exhausted, the therapist is faced with a number of choices that can stretch the practitioner beyond professional and personal comfort zones. For example, therapists who practice in managed care systems must be vocal advocates for client needs, becoming familiar with appeal processes when continued authorization is denied. This time-consuming process requires the counselor to be well versed in the administrative appeals process, adept at crafting documentation that explains the need for continuing care, and consistent in follow-up procedures to ensure that appeals are addressed. Few counselors in training are prepared for this aspect of providing care in the managed mental health care environment, yet it clearly is one of the "tools" in the managed care toolbox for practitioners.

Competence to Practice.   Managed mental health care plans frequently rely on behavioral and/or cognitive outcomes-based interventions and use protocols for treatment of specific psychological disorders. Along with these protocols comes close tracking of results that requires counselors to be competent to practice in such an environment prior to seeking network provider status. Of concern to the profession is the issue of competence to practice when counselor education training programs do not emphasize the preferred treatment methods or procedures associated with managed mental health care practice (Daniels, 2001).

There is variance in the research literature regarding how managed care information is incorporated into graduate counselor training. Almost 60 percent of the reporting program directors (counselor education, social work, and psychology) stated that some content is included in curricula; however, that content is limited to ethical issues, working with diverse clients, using outcomes-based treatments, and/or employing outcome assessment (Daniels, Alva, & Olivares, 2002). In addition, Daniels and colleagues found that the attitudes of respondents to survey questions about managed care were associated with inclusion of content in a particular curriculum. In another survey that specifically focused on counselor education programs (Smith, 1999), 51 percent of the counselor educators who responded to the survey indicated that changes to curriculum had been made to include managed mental health care content and training (i.e., 4 percent making many curricular changes and 47 percent making some changes). These studies highlight the following assumptions that must be used to guide education and training of counselor professionals:

1. Managed mental health care is embedded in contemporary society.
2. Mental health practitioners are increasingly called on to provide care in this cost-conscious monitoring system.
3. Preparation of practitioners must include curricular content and training opportunities.
4. Graduate education training about managed mental health care should incorporate more than "some" preparation—for example, (a) the strengths and weaknesses of managed mental health care; (b) how this system of care directly impacts practice in diverse settings (e.g., agencies, private practice, independent practice groups); (c) needs for specific clinical expertise used by major managed mental health care organizations (e.g., specific treatment modalities and delivery systems); (d) requirements to balance ethical and legal standards of practice with requirements of MCOs for documentation and review of client information; (e) the role of the counseling professional as advocate for managed mental health care clients' access to treatment; and (f) administrative and business competencies needed to function effectively as providers of care.
5. Counselors, when entering professional practice, can then determine the degree of personal involvement with MCOs.

If the counseling professions are to adequately prepare graduates to perform in the real world of managed mental health care, it is logical to assume that inclusion of content and training on this pervasive method of practice must be incorporated into curricula. Although these skill sets should be woven into the educational and training experiences of counseling students (Daniels, 2001), many of these competencies can be acquired postgraduation as well as through continuing education. Reliance on postgraduate voluntary education, however, weakens the imperative to graduate competent, insightful, and adequately prepared practitioners who are both familiar with and able to function in a managed mental health care setting. This stance recognizes that proficiency in operationalizing knowledge after completion of graduate education and training is to be anticipated as well.

On the whole, it is clear that counselor professionals recognize the permanence of managed mental health care while reacting to this paradigm shift with mixed reviews. Some see managed mental health care as a viable experiment designed to ensure that more consumers have access to and receive care, whereas others consider managed care as intrusive and damaging to the therapeutic relationship. A segment of the practicing population choose how much managed care work they will do and devise a satisfactory balance within a practice setting, whereas other counseling professionals reject managed mental health care entirely, preferring to build practices free of any involvement with MCOs. As managed care continues to be modified regarding how care is to be apportioned and given the continuing pressures to control health care costs, counselor professionals will be in the front row of the debate about how best to meet consumer needs for mental health care.

POLITICAL FORCES AND MENTAL HEALTH SERVICES

Social issues that directly and indirectly impact the counseling profession and the process of providing counseling services interact with economic and political issues on a daily basis. The list of potential issues of importance to the counseling professional is long. For the purposes of illustration, the interface of political decision making linked to public safety concerns serves to highlight core issues of importance to the mental health professional.

Nowhere is the interaction of societal problems and politics more starkly brought to the attention of the counseling professional, and the general public as well, as with the interface between mental health and the criminal justice system. Political leaders react to increases in criminal behavior in the general population (a complex set of social problems), in specific groups, and in response to horrendous events such as September 11, 2001. Legislation is passed nationally and at state levels to address criminal behavior, resulting in dramatic increases in incarceration rates, construction of prisons, and in harsh and inconsistent imposition of sentencing guidelines.

Mental Health Services in the Criminal Justice System

Of the over 2,100,000 incarcerated individuals in the United States (Bureau of Justice Statistics, 2005a), it is estimated that 16 percent of state and local inmate populations have a diagnosable mental illness (de Montfort & Oss, 2003). Approximately 1 in 10 state inmates are receiving psychotropic medications (Bureau of Justice Statistics, 2005b). Screening for the presence of mental illness varies from federal to state to community-based incarceration settings (Beck & Maruschak, 2001), with an equal amount of diversity regarding how each jurisdiction provides or does not provide mental health screenings or treatment services. Services typically available to individuals with mental illness in community settings are not consistently or customarily provided to inmate populations. Provision of such services is dependent on practices at community, state, and federal levels with some degree of recognition that providing this care is essential to the rehabilitation and eventual return of the affected inmate to the community (Benson, 2003; Grudzinskas et al, 2005).

There is, however, clear recognition of the role of diagnosable mental illness among a segment of the mentally ill and an increased risk for criminal behavior that leads to incarceration. According to de Montfort and Oss (2003), "Jails essentially have become America's new mental institutions." With the dramatic increase in rates of incarceration for drug offenses, "three strikes, you're out" legislation, and a general "get-tough" attitude pervading national and state legislatures, the needs of inmates convicted of drug offenses, or who have other mental illnesses, have dramatically increased while resources to provide treatment services have declined. At the same time, the incarceration of homeless mentally ill people is viewed all too often as a revolving door that involves repeated periods in prison, relapse of substance abuse disorders, and inconsistent treatment for chronic mental illness (Kushel et al, 2005).

Experts recognize that mental health treatment is essential if the prison population explosion is to be contained. In some jurisdictions, the incarcerated mentally ill population is greater than the population receiving services at community-based centers in the same locations (Faust, 2003). In addition, families unable to access treatment services for mentally ill family members must resort to law enforcement in order to initiate acute intervention. According to Faust (2003), "There is something fundamentally wrong when, for some families, the only way to obtain involuntary treatment for a mentally ill family member is to have that person arrested."

Counselors may encounter unique problems when providing counseling to individuals who are court referred. In many cases, the personal motivation to follow through with sessions is a reflection of the desire of the client to avoid further court sanctions. Counseling in the traditional sense typically relies on the client assuming a degree of personal responsibility for behaviors that led to the sanction of legal authorities. This insight is viewed as a crucial element of change and one that is viewed as supporting lower rates of recidivism. Factors that complicate evaluation of court-ordered counseling, however, include coexisting mental health conditions of the offender, previous history of violating orders of protection, and employment status (Bennett, Call, Flett, & Stoops, 2005). Use of culturally sensitive interventions may or may not have a positive impact on outcomes (Gondolf, 2005), although research that can address client characteristics, medical/psychiatric history, and environmental factors is viewed as essential. Thus, the complexity of the issues that are associated with court-referred counseling, the populations who are subject to such referrals (e.g., batterers, drug abusers), the inconsistent implementation of programs across geographic areas and diverse populations, and a host of other factors necessitate a reformulation of the goals for this form of counseling practice.

Impact on Families.   The impact of incarceration on families can be staggering. Often struggling financially, with substance abuse or domestic violence issues or with special needs children, the impact of jail time extends far beyond the inmate's experience (Raeder,

2001). Mothers who are incarcerated often delegate care for their children to grandmothers, increasing the demands on older women who may have fewer resources with which to provide care (Ruiz, 2002). The impact on children can be profound, with evidence that 1 in 50 children will have to adjust to one or both parents being incarcerated at some time while growing up (Phillips et al, 2002), with an estimated one-half of incarcerated adults being parents (U.S. Department of Justice, 2000). In addition, the incidence of behavioral disorders and other mental health problems of children with parents in jail is significant, ranging from behavior disturbances (e.g., anger, hyper-arousal, attention disorders, and developmental regression) to problems with sleep, self-esteem, and guilt (Wright & Seymour, 2000) to antisocial behavior (Eddy & Reid, 2001). The impact of incarceration on children and families is complex and long lasting. Resources to address the counseling needs of both the inmate mentally ill population, as well as the family residing in communities, range from limited to nonexistent, depending on locale.

Mental health interventions can help ameliorate the impact of separation on children caused by incarceration of parents. Parenting programs held within a prison system can improve relationships between child and parent (Thompson & Harm, 2000) and parenting effectiveness (Eddy & Chamberlain, 2000). Conversely, lack of such therapeutic options can further erode the parent–child bond, often already frayed by divorce, lack of financial support, substance abuse, poverty, and dislocation from a known home to a foster care setting (Eddy & Reid, 2001; Hairston, 2002; Luke, 2002).

Counseling Issues. There are significant implications for counseling professionals of the politically mediated and mandated changes within the criminal justice system, and specifically as these changes affect individuals, families, groups, and communities. Clearly, counselors must be sensitive to the potential impact of incarceration on children and families while interviewing, designing treatment plans, and evaluating outcomes of treatment. Counselor education programs need to incorporate content that describes and evaluates the role of the mental health provider as it relates to the following:

1. Children of incarcerated parents and the impact that this experience has on school performance, social functioning, and peer relationships
2. Developmental impact on children of an incarcerated parent
3. Application of specific interventions for child, adolescent, and adult family members of the incarcerated person
4. Counseling interventions sensitive to the mental health needs of individuals who have been incarcerated and returned to society and their families
5. Impact of the incarceration of parent(s) within the context of the multicultural, ethnic, and diversity characteristics of the family

Political decisions designed to protect the public and promote public safety may indeed succeed in achieving these goals. At the same time, the mental health needs of families and individuals linked to the incarcerated person must be addressed. This seeming invisible population's mental health needs are complex and often interlaced with economic needs created by the absence of the primary wage earner due to confinement in prison. Counselors in community mental health agencies, schools, and institutional health care settings must be aware of the psychological impact of the goals of the criminal justice system and those of the mental health system. Resources to provide mental health services for both the incarcerated population and the left-behind family are limited and seemingly become all too vulnerable to quick-fix cost-cutting measures controlled by political decision makers. As a consequence, these complex and evolving issues will continue to affect individuals, families and communities in varying degrees of severity with short- and long-term psychological and emotional outcomes. The role of the counselor as advocate for these consumers will remain constant as the population of incarcerated individuals continues to increase.

Legislative Mandates

Annually across the United States, in each state legislative body and in the Congress, proposed legislation is considered that impacts how certain mental health and wellness services will be funded by governmental agencies, who will be eligible to receive government-subsidized mental health services, who the providers of such services can be, and how the management of the counseling process must be conducted when governmental funding sources are used. In addition, the legislative groups tasked with protecting the privacy rights of consumers and ensuring that treatments received are appropriate to the presenting problem also engage in establishing law and regulation with these goals in mind. For the counselor professional, legislation can have a significant impact on professional practices in agencies, schools, institutions, community settings, and in private practice. Although many issues can be identified as illustrative of this interactive effect, one example will be the focus of this discussion.

HIPAA: Health Insurance Portability and Accountability Act of 1996.   With passage of the Health Insurance Portability and Accountability Act (HIPAA), providers of health care, including mental health care providers, were required to adhere to a set of requirements designed to limit the amount of client information that can be required by covered entities (e.g., managed care companies, health care clearinghouses, and providers [Cooper, 2005; Jackson, 2004; Holloway, 2003]). This federal legislation seeks to ensure that electronically transmitted information about patients/clients is limited and creates standards regarding how practitioners are to protect and maintain the confidentiality of such information. In addition, the counselor is to provide to the client/patient information about his or her privacy rights and explicitly outline how information about his or her care can be used. Implementation of this legislation includes development of procedures to ensure that all employees understand the regulation, all persons who are involved with the transmittal of information are adequately trained, records and standardized formats are used, and other security safeguard requirements are included in the voluntary compliance with these regulations.

Practitioners exempt from the provisions of this privacy rule include those who never share private health information about clients/patients (with the exception of legal or safety requirements), those who use no administrative staff to process client payment information, and those who do not use electronic or technical devices to transmit client information. In these instances, the practitioner is still required to remain vigilant about HIPAA requirements. The bottom line with HIPAA is this: Any provider who receives third-party payment must be in compliance with HIPAA. In recognition of the complexity of compliance, the

National Institute of Mental Health provides detailed information as guidance to practitioners regarding the requirements for compliance as well as some of the finer nuances of the act (see, for example, www.cms.hhs.gov/HIPAAGenInfo/).

The intent of HIPAA was to protect consumer health care information following the explosive growth of information technologies that accelerated the potential to violate patient rights to confidentiality and security of this information through electronic means of communication. Determining compliance and noncompliance, however, has become a source of frustration for practitioners. For example, it is not definite that the practitioner who does not use electronic claims submission can avoid the HIPAA requirements for notification of clients regarding the privacy rule (Herndon, 2003).

When presented with a consent or HIPAA-compliant information form, clients may tend to sign the forms, according to Freeny (as cited in Jackson, 2004) and not fully understand the ramifications of giving consent. For example, the client may assume that private health information will remain confidential, securely protected, and not available beyond the health care context, only to learn that this is an inaccurate assumption. "Many would be dumbfounded to learn that the government, specifically the U.S. Department of Health and Human Services (HHS), in order to monitor compliance with privacy regulations, has complete access to their medical records, and that law enforcement agencies as well as an array of 'business associates' may claim the right to review records" (Jackson, 2004, p. 11). In addition, although HIPAA provides greater access by patients to their records, HIPAA also requires providers to inform consumers that the provider is not bound to honor such requests and that enforcement of violations to records privacy is not consistent (Morrissey, 2004).

The manner in which the implementation of HIPAA takes place continues to unfold. This requires counselors to continually seek updated information about requirements for the security rule, for example, and this impacts records management as well as decision making about which standards are "required" and which are "addressable" (Cooper, 2005). HIPAA legislation and the HHS rules have created a confusing array of requirements that, when closely examined, do not result in enhanced protection of patient rights to privacy. As practitioners work to be in compliance with HIPAA rules, there is recognition that consumers have lost a degree of their privacy rights, and counseling professionals have had to devise methods to ensure client confidentiality while practicing within the bounds of HIPAA.

Informing clients of HIPAA requirements is now a part of all intake interviews. Materials must be provided to clients to ensure that they are informed of their rights under this act, yet, in spite of measures taken to ensure that clients fully grasp the meaning of the rules, full comprehension is in question. Clearly, HIPAA has generated a cottage industry of trainers and educators to prepare practitioners, as counselor education programs, schools of psychology, and social work programs must now include HIPAA information in their respective curricula.

Licensure and Portability

Counselors licensed to practice in one state cannot easily move to another state and practice without careful analysis of state requirements that may or may not be in alignment with the requirements fulfilled for a current license to practice. Thus, issues of licensure and portability of licensure are of paramount concern to counselors who must relocate from one state to another or who elect to relocate for career advancement or other professional opportunities.

Licensure.   In 1979, Arkansas was the first state to establish a licensure law granting professional counselor licenses for master's-level practitioners (Gale & Austin, 2003). Counselors are now required to fulfill licensure requirements in 50 of the 54 jurisdictions in the United States, with California and Nevada without licensure for counselors (American Counseling Association, 2006). Requirements to obtain licensure are outlined by each state according to state statute and regulated by each state's designated board for the regulation of practice. Licensure establishes a level of consumer protection expectations as well as clearly signifies that the practitioner has met specific educational and training standards expected of the mental health profession.

The American Counseling Association (www.counseling.org) provides extensive information for counseling professionals regarding licensure requirements. Internet links to each state's official website provide detailed information about licensure requirements, examination requirements and schedules, and continuing education expectations. Issues associated with licensure as a counselor professional include the need to support the efforts of state counseling associations and activists to promote licensure laws in the two remaining states lacking this essential consumer protection: California and Nevada.

Portability.   Consider this hypothetical situation:

> Ms. Ramirez is a well-respected licensed mental health counselor in her home state, having worked in a private practice setting for 11 years. She has met all requirements in her state of residence for continuing licensure and has excellent credentials. She recently located a desirable job in Alaska and wishes to accept the position. Upon examining the Alaska's Board of Professional Counselors Professional Counselor Licensure Application, Ms. Ramirez notes that she may well be able to obtain a license to practice under the "Licensure by Credentials" provision that states:

> The board will issue a license to practice professional counseling without examination to an applicant who holds a current license to practice professional counseling in another jurisdiction that has requirements for licensure substantially the same or higher than those of this state (AS 08.29.120(a)). (Board of Professional Counselors, 2004).

> Ms. Ramirez is encouraged and begins the process of locating the documents and obtaining verification forms to submit with her application. She may be successful in securing a license through the licensure by credentials gateway, but she recognizes that there is no portability of her current license in good standing to a different state, and she is having difficulty locating some of the documents required for the application.

States that have counseling practice licensure laws in place typically include an option to obtain licensure through endorsement or review of credentials. States provide guidelines that identify the documentation and verification requirements that must be met before the respective state board reviews the application for endorsement of licensure. Although this process may make it possible for the counselor to obtain a license in a new state of residence eventually, it includes cumbersome requirements that reflect the lack of parity of licensure from state to state within the counseling professions. Thus, a counselor who has obtained a license to practice in one state cannot "carry that credential with them" to another state (Kennedy, 2004).

Two options have been proposed to address the portability or reciprocity issues linked to the ability of licensed counseling professionals to move smoothly from state to state: credentials banks and uniform licensure standards.

Credentials Banks.   One option under consideration, and the subject of concerted implementation effort, is the credentials bank. Within the psychology profession, licensed practitioners who meet specific requirements can register with credentialing organizations such as the National Register or the Association of State and Provincial Psychology Boards (ASPPB). All documents are retained for future retrieval should the psychologist wish to seek licensure in another state and use the documents for that purpose. The submission of credentials ensures that essential materials are "banked" (Hempe, 2004). In addition, the "ASPPB issues a Certificate of Professional Qualification in Psychology (CPQ) to psychologists licensed in the U.S. and Canada who meet standards of educational preparation, supervised experience, and examination performance, and who have practiced a minimum of five years and have no history of disciplinary action" (Hempe, 2004). Licensing boards are encouraged to accept this credential between states as evidence of licensure reciprocity. By 2004, the CPQ was accepted by 27 states. The National Register suggests multiple mechanisms to verify credentials as a more advantageous method to use; that is, individual states could use the CPQ, the NR credential, and/or the American Board of Professional Psychology (ABPP) credential to promote reciprocity goals.

Within the social work profession, the Association of Social Work Boards (ASWB) provides a similar credentials banking service through the Social Work Registry (ASWB, 2004). Described as a credentialing verification service, the registry accepts applications "for social workers' credential information while serving as a verification source for social work licensing boards" (ASWB, 2004). Upon request, social workers currently licensed in one state and wishing to apply for licensure in another state can request that credentialing information be transmitted to a regulatory board.

Through the American Association of State Counseling Boards, the National Credentials Registry has been established to provide credentials banking (AASCB, 2004) similar to that used by the psychology and social work professions. Under this plan, for a fee, licensed counselors can deposit "information about their educational preparation, supervised experience, examination performance, continuing education, and work history" with this service (AASCB, 2004). Counselors who wish to apply for licensure in another state could then request transmission of the information from the AASCB "bank" to the appropriate licensing board.

Establishing Uniform Licensure Standards.   Establishing a uniform licensure standard that would be based on one set of requirements is the focus of efforts by the American Association of State Counseling Boards (Kennedy, 2004). In association with the AASCB-sponsored National Credentials Registry, a two-tiered plan is proposed that would include:

1. Each state board of licensure or professional regulation would agree to use the proposed system to enable licensed counselors to "import" current licensure to another state.

2. Registrants would meet all requirements as outlined by the National Credentials Registry—for example, completion of five years of postlicensure practice, possess a current license in good standing, and have no history of disciplinary actions.

Registrants in the National Credentials Registry would meet all requirements of either Tier I or Tier II criteria matching the requirements of each respective state. For example, a state that requires 48 semester hours for licensure would be designated a Tier I state and a state that requires 60 semester hours would be identified as a Tier II state. Counselors licensed in a Tier I state could move to a state with a Tier I status without having to meet additional requirements, and those from a Tier II state could likewise move to a Tier II state without having to meet additional requirements.

Although this plan is not yet implemented (Williams, 2005), it holds promise to link a "credentials bank" with a structured state-to-state reciprocity system for counselor professionals. If implemented, it additionally would eliminate the need for counselors credentialed in one state within a tier from having to meet additional requirements that many states include in their highly individualized licensure regulations.

Political forces often drive change within the mental health care professions. Whether through national legislation that requires significant change in how the counselor practices, or through state-by-state mechanisms to gain access to the profession, political actions reflect the social and cultural forces that serve as the backdrop for practice. Some of the politically driven changes that the counseling professions have responded to over time are originated by external organizations, groups, or social forces, while others originate from within the profession itself. For example, the California Coalition for Counselor Licensure (CCCL) seeks to "secure and maintain licensure for Professional Counselors in California" (CCCL, 2004). This within-the-profession group seeks to change how counselors are credentialed in California, and this eventual change will have direct impact on how counseling services are provided.

Responding to and initiating change that impacts the counseling professions is a dynamic, challenging, and revitalizing process. It ensures that awareness of the role of political, social, and economic factors that surround the professions is continually used to strengthen the services that mental health consumers receive. At the same time, politically motivated legislation can have a drastic impact on the populations that are in need of mental health services as exemplified by the deinstitutionalization movement that began more than 30 years ago. In contemporary times, deinstitutionalization continues to affect the developmentally disabled, the aged, the homeless chronically mentally ill, and children caught in dysfunctional foster care systems. Responding to political decision-maker changes in resources for mental health care will continue to be a pillar of counselor advocacy.

SUMMARY COMMENT

The topics reviewed in this chapter are vast, complex, and will most likely generate many more questions than satisfying answers. That is one goal of provocative discussion. There are no easy answers to the questions about how economic and political forces impact mental health care and the counselors who provide services to consumers. There is, ideally, a clearer understanding of the complexity of the contemporary and emerging issues that counselor professionals must contend with in the day-to-day world of practice, education, and training. Accordingly, this understanding and vigilance will help the counseling profession deliver more effective, efficient, and consistent services that are desperately needed, given the complexity and interrelatedness of social, political and economic issues. If you, as the reader, complete this chapter with an increased level of understanding of the complexities discussed, one desired outcome has been achieved. If you have many questions about these issues and pursue the debate within your professional community of practice, a second goal has been accomplished. Finally, if your questions motivate you to become more actively involved in your professional association to improve the counseling professions, the third goal has been achieved. Experiencing all three outcomes reflects the vibrancy and dynamism of counseling.

DISCUSSION TOPICS AND QUESTIONS

1. In your community, what has been the impact of state budget allocations on mental health service delivery? For example, in what ways are current levels of service being maintained, reduced, eliminated, or sustained and expanded?

2. As a counselor in a general private practice, you have been asked to speak at a public hearing by the local coalition for the homeless mentally ill. This nonprofit organization is seeking a zoning waiver that would allow it to situate a housing facility for 15 chronically mentally ill patients recently released from prison. The location is a neighborhood with which you're very familiar. What are your reactions to this request? What are the key points that you consider in making your decision to accept or decline the invitation?

3. You are a counselor in a small group practice where Alison (discussed in this chapter) was your client. Now that she has lost her health insurance, how will you address her needs to continue counseling during this stressful period?

4. How does the managed care "squeeze" model affect counselors working in private practice and in community mental health centers? How might the impact vary according to the setting in which counseling is practiced?

5. Mr. Anderson has been a client of yours, having participated in three sessions to date, using his employer-provided PPO benefits. At the beginning of the fourth session, he discloses that he is finally able to talk about his alcoholism for the first time. He then asks you to not include this information in your treatment summaries, since these could be viewed by his PPO care coordinator who might pass this information along to his boss. How will you respond to Mr. Anderson's request?

6. What would you advise the counselor who is providing care for Mrs. Phillips regarding how to plan for her long-term mental health care needs?

7. The issues surrounding HIPAA implementation remain of concern to practitioners. From the consumers' perspective, there are questions about what they understand about HIPAA and the lack of protection that is generated by broad access to their personal medical/health information. How does HIPPA impact the therapeutic relationship and the treatment process?

8. A number of significant economic and political issues have been discussed in this chapter. From your perspective, which would you identify as the top three issues that should be addressed by (1) your counselor professional association (local, state, or national), (2) your state's legislature, and (3) community-based nonprofit agencies?

9. Efforts to review and improve the health care system often involve macro-efforts and micro-efforts. At the macro-level, the Congress may enact legislation that, when viewed from the micro-level of the consumer in need of psychotropic medication, for example, the consequences can be dramatic. What is the role of the counselor in providing guidance to Medicare and Medicaid (dually eligible) clients with regard to the prescription benefit access process? What are the parameters of the role with regard to this topic or others that are associated with access to insurance coverage for mental health care?

10. You have decided that relocation to a different state will be necessary in the next six months. You recently achieved licensure to practice as a mental health counselor in your state. What steps will you take to investigate how to obtain licensure in your anticipated future state of residence? What are the barriers to this process and what are the sources of support you will access?

REFERENCES

American Association of State Counseling Boards. (2004). *AASCB portability policy and procedure.* Retrieved August 6, 2004, from www.aascb.org/pdfs/AASCB%20Portability%20document1-9-04.pdf.

American Counseling Association. (2005). *ACA code of ethics.* Retrieved January 31, 2006, from www.counseling.org.

American Counseling Association. (2006). State licensure chart. Retrieved January 31, 2006, from www.counseling.org/Counselors/StateLicensureChart.aspx.

Anderson, C. E. (2000). Dealing constructively with managed care: Suggestions from an insider. *Journal of Mental Health Counseling, 22*, 343–354.

Artazcoz, L., Benach, J., Borell, C., & Cortes, I. (2004). Unemployment and mental health: Understanding the interaction between gender, family roles, and social class. *American Journal of Public Health, 94*, 82–89.

Association of Social Work Boards. (2004). *Announcements: Social Work Registry.* Retrieved August 6, 2004, from www.aswb.org/.

Baily, M. A. (2003). Managed care and the rationing problem. *Hastings Center Report, 33*, 34–42.

Bartels, S. J., Blow, F. C., Brockman, L. M., & Van Citters, A. D. (2005). *Substance abuse and mental health among older Americans: The state of the knowledge and future directions.* Substance Abuse and Mental Health Services Administration. Retrieved January 31, 2006, from www.samhsa.gov/aging/SA_MH_%20AmongOlderAdultsfinal102105.pdf.

Beck, A. J., & Maruschak, L. M. (2001). *Mental health treatment in state prisons, 2000.* U.S. Department of Justice, NCJ 188215. Retrieved March 12, 2004, from www.ojp.usdoj.gov/bjs/pub/pdf/mhtsp00.pdf.

Bennett, L., Call, C., Flett, H., & Stoops, C. (2005). *Program completion, behavioral change, and re-arrest for the batterer intervention system of Cook County Illinois.* Retrieved September 11, 2005, from www.icjia.state.il.us/public/pdf/ResearchReports/CookCountyDVInt.pdf.

Benson, E. (2003). Rehabilitate or punish? *Monitor on Psychology, 34*, 46–47.

Board of Professional Counselors. (2004). *Professional counselor licensure application.* Retrieved October 1, 2005, from www.dced.state.ak.us/occ/pub/pco4403.pdf.

Bossolo, L. (2004). *Most Americans list lack of insurance coverage and cost as top reasons for not seeking mental health services.* American Psychological Association. Retrieved July 1, 2004, from www.apa.org/releases/insurance.html.

Braun, S. A., & Cox, J. A. (2005). Managed mental health care: Intentional misdiagnosis of mental disorders. *Journal of Counseling & Development, 83*(4), 425–433.

Browning, C. H., & Browning, B. J. (1996). *How to partner with managed care: A "do-it-yourself kit" for building working relationships and getting steady referrals.* New York: John Wiley & Sons.

Bureau of Justice Statistics. (2005a). *Prison statistics: Summary of findings.* U.S. Department of Justice, Office of Justice Programs. Retrieved February 1, 2006, from www.ojp.usdoj.gov/bjs/prisons.htm.

Bureau of Justice Statistics. (2005b). *Mental health treatment in state prisons, 2000.* U.S. Department of Justice, Office of Justice Programs. Retrieved February 1, 2006, from www.ojp.usdoj.gov/bjs/abstract/mhtsp00.htm.

California Coalition for Counselor Licensure. (2004). *Mission statement.* Retrieved August 6, 2004, from www.caccl.org/mission.html.

Center for Medicare & Medicaid Services. (2006). *National health expenditure data: Projected.* Retrieved January 31, 2006, from www.cms.hhs.gov/NationalHealthExpendData/03_NationalHealthAccounts Projected.asp#TopOfPage.

Christensen, L. L. (2001). The practice of marriage and family therapists with managed care clients. *Contemporary Family Therapy, 23,* 169–180.

Clarke, E., Clarke, R., & Ross, E. C. (Eds.). (2001). *Managed behavioral health care handbook.* Boston: Jones & Bartlett Publishers.

Coffey, E. P., Olson, M. E., & Sessions, P. (2001). The heart of the matter: An essay about the effects of managed care on family therapy with children. *Family Process, 40,* 385–399.

Cohen, R. A., & Martinez, M. E. (2005). *Health insurance coverage: Estimates from the National Health Interview Survey, January–March 2005.* National Center for Health, Center for Disease Control and Prevention. Retrieved February 2, 2006, from www.cdc.gov/nchs/data/nhis/earlyrelease/insur200509.pdf.

Cooper, C. L. (2005, March/April). HIPAA reprise: This time it's the security rule. *The National Psychologist, 14,* 7.

Cowan, E. W. (2005). *Ariadne's thread: Case studies in the therapeutic relationship.* Boston: Houghton Mifflin.

Cummings, N. A. (1995). Unconscious fiscal connivance. *Psychotherapy in Private Practice, 14,* 23–28.

Cummings, N. A. (1996). Now we're facing the consequences. *The Scientist Practitioner, 6*(1), 9–13.

Cummings, N. A., Cummings, J. L., & Pallak, M. S. (Eds.). (1996). *Surviving the demise of solo practice: Mental health practitioners prospering in the era of managed care.* Guilford, CT: International Universities Press.

Daniels, J. A. (2001). Managed care, ethics, and counseling. *Journal of Counseling & Development, 79,* 119–123.

Daniels, J. A., Alva, L. A., & Olivares, S. (2002). Graduate training for managed care: A national survey of psychology and social work programs. *Professional Psychology: Research and Practice, 33,* 587–591.

Danzinger, P. R., & Welfel, E. R. (2001). The impact of managed care on mental health counselors: A survey of perceptions, practices, and compliance with ethical standards. *Journal of Mental Health Counseling, 23,* 137–151.

Davis, S. R., & Meier, S. T. (2001). *Elements of managed care: A guide for helping professionals.* Belmont, CA: Wadsworth.

de Montfort, D., & Oss, M. E. (2003). Examining the intersection of the behavioral health and corrections systems. *Behavioral Health Management, 23*(2), 10–14.

DeNavas-Walt, C., Proctor, B. D., & Lee, C. H. (2005). *Current population reports, P60229, Income, poverty, and health insurance coverage in the United States: 2004.* U.S. Government Printing Office. Retrieved February 2, 2006, from www.census.gov/prod/2005pubs/P60229.pdf.

Docherty, J. P. (1999). Cost of treating mental illness from a managed care perspective. *Journal of Clinical Psychiatry, 60* Supplement, 49–52.

Draine, J., Salzer, M. S., Culhane, D. P., & Hadley, T. R. (2002). Role of disadvantage in crime, joblessness, and homelessness among persons with serious mental illness. *Psychiatric Services, 53,* 565–573.

Eddy, J. M., & Chamberlain, P. (2000). Family management and deviant peer association as mediators of the impact of treatment condition on youth antisocial behavior. *Journal of Consulting and Clinical Psychology, 68,* 857–863.

Eddy, J. M., & Reid, J. B. (2001). *The antisocial behavior of the adolescent children of incarcerated parents: A developmental perspective.* Paper presented at the National Policy Conference. From *Prison to home—The effect of incarceration and reentry on children, families, and communities.* Washington, DC. Retrieved March 12, 2004, from http://aspe.hhs.gov/hsp/prison2home02/index.htm.

Elliott, R. A., Majundar, S. R., Gillick, M. R., & Soumerai, S. B. (2005). Benefits and consequences for the poor and the disabled. *The New England Journal of Medicine, 353*, 2739–2741.

Fauman, M. A. (2002). *Negotiating managed care: A manual for clinicians.* Arlington, VA: American Psychiatric Publishing.

Faust, T. N. (2003). Shift the responsibility of untreated mental illness out of the criminal justice system. *Corrections Today, 65*, 2–8.

Gale, A. U., & Austin, B. D. (2003). Professionalism's challenges to professional counselors' collective identity. *Journal of Counseling & Development, 81*, 3–10.

Gibelman, M., & Whiting, L. (1999). Negotiating and contracting in a managed care environment: Considerations for practitioners. *Health & Social Work, 24*, 180–191.

Gondolf, E. W. (2005). *Culturally-focused batterer counseling for African-American men.* U.S. Department of Justice Grant 2001-WT-BX-0003. Retrieved September 11, 2005, from www.ncjrs.org/pdffiles1/nij/grants/210828.pdf.

Gorin, S. H. (2003). The unraveling of managed care: Recent trends and implications. *Health & Social Work, 28*(3), 241–246.

Grodzki, L. (2000). *Building your ideal private practice: A guide for therapists and other healing professionals.* New York: W. W. Norton.

Grove, B. (1999). Mental health and unemployment: Shaping a new agenda. *Journal of Mental Health, 8*, 131–141.

Grudzinskas, A. J., Clayfield, J. C., Roy-Bujnowski, K., Fisher, W. H., & Richardson, M. H. (2005). Integrating the criminal justice system into mental health service delivery: The Worcester diversion experiment. *Behavioral Sciences and the Law, 23*, 277–293.

Guindon, M. H., & Smith, B. (2002). Emotional barriers to successful reemployment: Implications for counselors. *Journal of Employment Counseling, 39*, 73–83.

Haber, S., Rodino, E., & Lipner, I. (2001). *Saying good-bye to managed care: Building your independent psychotherapy practice.* New York: Springer Publishing.

Hairston, C. F. (2002, January). *Prisoners and families: Parenting issues during incarceration.* Paper presented at the National Policy Conference. From *Prison to home—The effect of incarceration and reentry on children, families, and communities.* Washington, DC. Retrieved March 12, 2004, from http://aspe.hhs.gov/hsp/prison2home02/index.htm.

Health Care Economics. (2000, April 7). *Mental health benefits mystery to many Americans.* Retrieved July 1, 2004, from www.psych.org/pnews/00-04-07/mystery.html.

Hempe, S. (2004). *Pack up your license in your ol' kit bag: Professional mobility for psychologists.* American Psychology Association. Retrieved August 6, 2004, from www.apa.org/apags/profdev/mobility.html.

Herndon, P. (2004). The drive for electronic claims. *Monitor on Psychology, 34*, 28–29.

Holloway, J. D. (2003). More protections for patients and psychologists under HIPAA. *Monitor on Psychology, 34*, 22–23.

Jackson, K. (2004). The dark side of HIPPA. *Social Work Today, 4*, 11–13.

Jung, R. M., Pomerantz, A. M., & Tuholski, S. W. (2001). The impact of specific psychotherapist beliefs regarding managed care on prospective psychotherapy clients. *Journal of Contemporary Psychotherapy, 31*, 151–160.

Kennedy, A. (2004, April). ACA, AASCB making licensure portability a reality. *Counseling Today, 46*, 1, 14.

Kessler, R. C., Berglund, P. A., Bruce, M. L., Koch, J.R., Laska, E. M., Leaf, P. J., et al. (2001). The prevalence and correlates of untreated serious mental illness. *Health Services Research, 36*, 1009–1017.

Kontosh, L. G. (2000). Ethical rehabilitation counseling in a managed care environment. *Journal of Rehabilitation, 66*, 9–14.

Kremer, T. G., & Gesten, E. L. (1998). Confidentiality limits of managed care and clients' willingness to self-disclose. *Professional Psychology: Research and Practice, 29*, 553–558.

Kremer, T. G., & Gesten, E. L. (2003). Managed mental health care: The client's perspective. *Professional Psychology: Research and Practice, 34*, 187–197.

Kushel, M. B., Hahn, J.A., Evans, J.L., Bangsberg, D. R., & Moss, A. R. (2005). Revolving doors: Imprisonment among the homeless and marginally housed populations. *American Journal of Public Health, 95*, 1747–1752.

Luke, K. P. (2002). Mitigating the ill effects of maternal incarceration on women in prison and their children. *Child Welfare, 81*(6), 929–948.

Lundy, J., Finder, B., & Claxton, G. (2004). *Trends and indicators in the changing health care marketplace, 2004 update*. The Henry J. Kaiser Family Foundation. Retrieved July 13, 2004, from www.kff.org/insurance/7031/loader.cfm?url=/commonspot/security/getfile.cfm&PageID=36091.

McSween, J. L. (2002). The role of group interest, identity, and stigma in determining mental health policy preferences. *Journal of Health Politics, Policy & Law, 27*, 773–801.

Morrissey, J. (2004). The HIPAA headache. *Modern Healthcare, 34*, 6–8.

Murphy, M. J., DeBernardo, C. R., & Shoemaker, W. E. (1998). Impact of managed care on independent practice and professional ethics: A survey of independent practitioners. *Professional Psychology: Research and Practice, 29*, 43–51.

National Institute of Mental Health. (2005). *Statistics*. Retrieved January 30, 2006, from www.nimh.gov/healthinformation/statisticsmenu.cfm.

Newman, J. F., & Dunbar, D. M. (2000). Managed care and ethical conflicts. *Managed Care Quarterly, 8*, 20–32.

Nowell, D., & Spruill, J. (1993). If it's not absolutely confidential, will information be disclosed? *Professional Psychology: Research and Practice, 24*, 367–369.

Phillips, S. D., Burns, B. J., Wagner, H. R., Kramer, T. L., Robbins, J. M., & Robbins, J. M. (2002). Parental incarceration among adolescents receiving mental health services. *Journal of Child & Family Studies, 11*, 385–390.

Raeder, M. S. (2001). Remember the family: Seven myths about single parenting departures. *Federal Sentencing Reporter, 13*, 251–258.

RAND Health. (2001). Research highlights: Mental health care for youth. Retrieved July 1, 2004, from www.rand.org/publications/RB/RB4541/.

Rohrer, J. E., & Rohland, B. M. (1998). Oversight of managed care for behavioral health services. *Journal of Public Health Management Practice, 4*, 96–100.

Ruiz, D. S. (2002). The increase in incarcerations among women and its impact on the grandmother caregiver: Some racial considerations. *Journal of Sociology & Social Welfare, 79*, 129–148.

Ryan, J., & Super, N. (2003). *Dually eligible for Medicare and Medicaid: Two for one or double jeopardy*. National Health Policy Forum (Issue Brief, No 794). Retrieved January 30, 2006, from http://nhpf.ags.com/pdfs_ib/IB794_Duals_9-30-03.pdf.

Sanchez, L. M., & Turner, S. M. (2003). Practicing psychology in the era of managed care. *American Psychologist, 58*, 116–129.

Satcher, D. (1999). *Mental health: A report of the Surgeon General*. U.S. Public Health Service. Retrieved July 1, 2004, from www.surgeongeneral.gov/library/mentalhealth/home.html.

Scaturo, D. J. (2002). Fundamental dilemmas in contemporary psychotherapy: A transtheoretical concept. *American Journal of Psychotherapy, 56*, 115–134.

Scheid, T. L. (2003). Managed care and the rationalization of mental health services. *Journal of Health and Social Behavior, 44*(2), 142–161.

Sherer, R. A. (2004). Gaps in coverage create health insurance instability. *Psychiatric Times, 21*, 1, 7–8.

Smith, H. B. (1999). Managed care: A survey of counselor educators and counselor practitioners. *Journal of Mental Health Counseling, 21*, 270–284.

Sperling, M. B., & Sack, A. (2002). Psychodynamics of managed care: The art of the impossible? *American Journal of Psychotherapy, 56*, 362–378.

State of Alaska. (2004). *Professional counselor licensure application*. Board of Professional Counselors. Retrieved August 6, 2004, from www.dced.state.ak.us/occ/pub/pco4403.pdf.

Thompson, P. J., & Harm, N. (2000). Parenting from prison: Helping children and mothers. *Issues in Comprehensive Psychiatric Nursing, 23*, 61–82.

U.S. Agency for Healthcare Research and Quality. (2004). *National quality measures clearinghouse (glossary)*. Retrieved July 8, 2004, from www.qualitymeasures.ahrq.gov/.

U.S. Census Bureau (2002). *Health insurance coverage 2002*. Retrieved July 13, 2004, from www.census.gov/hhes/hlthins/hlthin02/hlth02asc.html.

U.S. Department of Justice. (2000). *Special report: Incarcerated parents and their children*. Washington, DC: Bureau of Justice Statistics.

Whittinghill, D., Whittinghill, L. R., & Loesch, L. C. (2000). The benefits of a self-efficacy approach to substance abuse counseling in the era of managed care. *Journal of Addictions & Offender Counseling, 20*, 64–75.

Williams, M. (2005, April). Licensure portability nears enactment. *The Advocate, 29*, 1, 10.

Wright, L. E., & Seymour, C. B. (2000). *Working with children and families separated by incarceration: A handbook for child welfare agencies*. Washington, DC: CWLA Press.

Zuckerman, E. L., & LoPresti, R. L. (2003). *Rewarding specializations for mental health clinicians (clinicians tool box): Developing your practice niche*. New York: Guilford.

CHAPTER THREE

DIVERSITY AND MULTICULTURALISM
Issues in Contemporary Counseling

ALICE YICK FLANAGAN

American society is becoming increasingly multicultural and diverse. Counseling professionals are called upon to understand the import of these societal changes at a deep level in order to meet the mental health and wellness needs of individuals, couples, families, groups, and communities. Pedersen (1991) boldly proclaimed that multiculturalism is a viable fourth force in psychology—a force that has had a profound impact on the counseling professions. This fourth force is now recognized as a required foundational element placed alongside psychoanalysis, behaviorism, and humanism. Similar to these three prominent theoretical orientations, multiculturalism is now recognized as an essential factor in understanding of human behavior. As such, it is infused into the education and training experiences of counselors as a critical element of knowledge that is integrated into practice.

The American Counseling Association (ACA) has woven multiculturalism into the accreditation standards used to evaluate counselor education programs (Council for Accreditation of Counseling and Related Education Programs 2001) as well as throughout its Code of Ethics (ACA, 2005). In addition, the ACA has several divisions that focus on multicultural and/or diversity issues, including the Association for Multicultural Counseling and Development (AMCD) and the Association for Gay, Lesbian and Bisexual Issues in Counseling (AGLBIC).

Fowers and Richardson (1996) noted that multiculturalism is a potent force, with its influence institutionalized in psychology. The American Psychological Association (APA) has included multiculturalism in its accreditation guidelines for psychology programs in academic institutions. The Office of Ethnic Minority Affairs was also established by the APA, with the mission of assisting, coordinating, advocating, and implementing policies on ethnic minority issues (Fowers & Richardson, 1996). In addition, the APA has several divisions established that focus on lesbian, gay, and bisexual issues (Division 44), the study of ethnic minority issues (Division 45), the study of men and masculinity (Division 51), and the study of the psychology of women (Division 35). The Association for Women in

Psychology (www.awpsych.org) provides opportunities for counselors to explore feminist psychological research, activism, and theory.

Within the counseling professions there are both clear and evolving definitions of multiculturalism and diversity. In this chapter, an inclusive approach to the definition of multiculturalism will be utilized, as it considers issues and perspectives that extend beyond ethnic and minority groups. At times, the terms *multicultural* and *diversity* will be used interchangeably, and when the term *multicultural* is used, it is meant to signify beyond the scope of race and ethnicity. An overview of diverse populations that counseling practitioners will encounter in clinical practice is provided. These snapshots of various diverse groups, excluding spirituality and religion covered in Chapter 10, are followed by review of issues associated with counseling practice.

MULTICULTURALISM AND THE FOURTH FORCE IN PSYCHOLOGY AND COUNSELING

Pedersen (1991) explicitly called multiculturalism the "fourth force," to be added to the three dominant perspectives in psychology—psychoanalysis (the first force), behaviorism (the second force), and humanism (the third force). The perspective that multiculturalism is a pervasive force in all aspects of life achieved recognition and acceptance within the counseling professions as a critical element of education, training, and practice. Counseling and therapy are often said to be Western creations that rely on behaviors viewed differently by various cultures. Talking to cure problems, with an emphasis on disclosing private and intimate information to a nonfamily member while focusing on autonomy, is primarily a Euro-American value (Lee & Ramirez, 2000). Recognition that counselors needed to incorporate culture sensitivity into the counseling process led to dramatic change within the counseling field.

During the late 1960s, racial and ethnic minority psychologists began pressuring the APA to endorse their interests. Professional groups representing the interests of racial and ethnic minority psychologists were formed, including the Association of Black Psychologists in 1968, the Association of Psychologists por la Raza in 1970, the Asian American Psychological Association in 1972, and the Society of Indian Psychologists in 1975 (Abreu, Chung, & Atkinson, 2000).

As the field entered the 1970s, there was a surge of research projects and articles discussing how mainstream psychological services were not meeting the needs of racial and ethnic minorities. Pioneers included Paul Pedersen, Derald Wing Sue, and Stanley Sue. Paul Pedersen, in 1973, chaired a panel on multicultural counseling at the APA's annual convention and later published the first book on the subject, titled *Counseling Across Cultures* (Gladding, 2000). Derald Wing Sue contributed the concept of worldviews to multicultural counseling and published his book, *Counseling the Culturally Different*. Racial identity models were developed and challenged mainstream psychological developmental models (e.g., minority identity development [Atkinson, Morten, & Sue, 1993]; black identity development [Cross, 1971]; and black/white racial identity development [Carter, 1995; Helms, 1990]). Stanley Sue discussed the underutilization patterns of mental heath services as well as the poor mental services available for ethnic minorities. This stemmed from the lack of bilingual and bicultural counselors from minority groups who can communicate with clients (Sue, 1988).

By the late 1970s and early 1980s, the term *minority counseling* was replaced with terms such as *cross-cultural counseling* and *multicultural counseling* (Jackson, 1995). Here, "multicultural" did not merely apply to racial and ethnic minorities but extended the umbrella to include other groups with unique characteristics such as gender, age, religion, and sexual orientation (Patterson, 1996). Differences and diversity that existed within oppressed groups were emphasized as well as the call for the development of identity models beyond race and ethnicity identity (Reynolds & Pope, 1991). Feminism, for example, offered alternative perspectives to counseling for women, and similarly, models of identity development and counseling were offered for gays and lesbians (Reynolds & Pope, 1991). Highlighting this period of activism in redefining the essence of counseling was the establishment of professional organizations within the counseling field dedicated to expanding understanding of cultural and diverse populations (e.g., ACA Divisions such as the Association for Multicultural Counseling and Development, and APA Divisions such as the Society for the Psychological Study of Lesbian, Gay and Bisexual Issues). This trend was not limited to psychology and counseling. Other helping professions in the 1970s witnessed an increase of literature in their knowledge bases about multicultural counseling. In social work, terms such as *ethnic sensitive practice, culturally competent practice*, and *culturally diverse practice* were being explored (Fong, 2001). These new expressions indicated a heightening of professional awareness of the necessity to acquire the knowledge and skills sets required by professionals to serve diverse clients.

By the 1980s, the field emphasized the need to focus on specific identifiable competencies with respect to multicultural counseling (Robinson & Morris, 2000). An ethical mandate was pronounced regarding the need to incorporate issues of cultural diversity in education and training. With ethnic minority psychologists continuing to pressure the APA, the Office of Ethnic Minority Affairs was established in 1979, the Board of Ethnic Minority Affairs in 1981, and the Division of Ethnic Minority Affairs in 1986 (Abreu, Chung, & Atkinson, 2000). The APA required cultural competence as part of professional competence. In 1982, the first formal description of multicultural competencies was developed by the Education and Training Committee of APA (Robinson & Morris, 2000). Eleven characteristics were identified as necessary to provide effective counseling services to ethnic minority clients. These characteristics fell into one of three categories: attitudes/beliefs, knowledge, and skills (Robinson & Morris, 2000).

Counseling programs accredited by the Council for Accreditation of Counseling and Related Educational Programs (CACREP) were mandated to include multicultural components in their academic programs. In 1972, the Association for Multicultural Counseling and Development (AMCD) became a part of ACA, dedicated to developing the professional knowledge base in multiculturalism and counseling. From this division, an academic peer-reviewed periodical, *Journal of Multicultural Counseling and Development*, published scholarly articles each quarter on counselor issues in a pluralistic society (Gladding, 2000). By 1991, the AMCD approved a document calling for the need for multicultural counseling, which later led to the 31 multicultural competencies being required in the ACA's accreditation criteria (Sue, Arredondo, & McDavis, 1992; Fong, 2001). Nine criteria revolved around the practitioner's attitudes/beliefs, 11 were knowledge, and the remaining 11 were skills components (Sue et al, 1992).

In 1996, the AMCD published an expanded version of Sue and colleagues' (1992) multicultural competencies, and the AMCD further differentiated between multiculturalism and diversity. According to the AMCD, *multiculturalism* focused on race, culture, and ethnicity, whereas *diversity* referred to other characteristics that may define a person, such as, but not limited to, age, gender, socioeconomic status, religion, sexual orientation, and socioeconomic background (Robinson & Morris, 2000).

Multicultural counseling in the 1990s was a hot topic, and it was proclaimed as the fourth force in psychology. Multiculturalism stood side by side with the traditional schools of thought in counseling and psychology (psychoanalysis, behaviorism, and humanism) (Lee & Ramirez, 2000). The 1990s saw a flourish of empirical research and debates in this area, and the twenty-first century continues to witness a process that has enriched theory, research, and practice within the counseling professions.

MULTICULTURALISM: INCLUSIVE VERSUS EXCLUSIVE DEFINITIONS

In tracing the history of the multicultural movement in counseling, one can see the controversy about the extent to which the definition of multiculturalism should be inclusive to include other minority groups (Pope, 1995). Depending on the camp one is in (i.e., inclusive versus exclusive definition), multiculturalism has expanded from focusing on ethnic minority groups to other groups, such as various subcultures, age groups, gender groups, and the poor. This definition reflects the inclusivity perspective (Patterson, 1996). On the other hand, those who argue for exclusive definitions of multiculturalism believe that the definition should be limited to ethnic minority and racial groups (Locke, 1990).

In taking an inclusive stance, the terms *cross-cultural counseling, multicultural counseling, culturally sensitive counseling, cultural competence*, and *cultural-relevant interventions* all emphasize "differentness." This encompasses age, culture, disability, educational level, religion, sexual orientation, race, gender, and socioeconomic status (Weinrach & Thomas, 1996). Pedersen (1990) also defines culture to encompass ethnographic, demographic, status, and affiliation variables. Ethnographic variables include ethnicity, nationality, religion, and language; demographic variables consist of age, gender, and place of residence; status variables refer to social, economic, and educational factors; and affiliation variables include membership(s) in formal and/or informal networks (Pedersen, 1990).

Williams (2001) argues that people view the world through their own unique set of perceptual filters. These filters have been colored by personal perceptual legacies that reflect an individual's experiences as well as those of his or her family, ancestors, and community. These worldviews are then filtered by multifaceted factors (or lenses), including gender, race, marital status, political affiliation, profession, religion, educational level, family background, and sexual orientation (Williams, 2001). When combined, these factors inevitably shape worldviews. However, these layers are prioritized differently for each individual, and therefore, views of the world are dramatically different from person to person and counselor to counselor.

The proponents of an inclusive definition argue that minority groups share a common identity formation process. The oppression experienced by these groups from the majority culture in terms of the discrimination, prejudice, and bias are similar, all of which ultimately impede the development of minority groups (Pope, 1995). For example, the debate to include gays and lesbians in the definition of multiculturalism is a subject of heated debate. Pope (1995), however, maintains that gays and lesbians are a minority group, as they are a sexual, psychological, and cultural minority. The professional community labeled them "deviant" until in 1973 when the *Diagnostic and Statistical Manual of Mental Disorders (DSM)* no longer categorized homosexuality as a mental disorder. Furthermore, gays and lesbians are frequently set off as outcasts by their families and friends and experience tremendous homophobia within families, communities, and the workplace. Finally, they are cultural minorities because, according to Pope (1995, p. 303), "cultural minority status has been given to groups who are minorities within the majority culture and have their own geographic living areas, economic and social organizations, cultural traditions, and rituals." To take an inclusive stance, counselors would not merely reduce a lived human phenomenon to a single variable (i.e., culture, race, and ethnicity) (Berry, Poortinga, Segall, & Dasen, 1992) but instead, would view culture in a more expansive way.

Diversity-sensitive counseling, therefore, occurs when the counselor wears multiple, unique, and sometimes complex "lenses" while working with clients. Counselors seek to "see" the client's culture in all its facets, as part of the individual's or group's identity. In essence, Weinrach and Thomas (1996) maintain that when speaking of diversity, people should also include in their discourse the diversity of ideas, values, beliefs, interests, personalities, and abilities, and not limit themselves to merely culture, race, and ethnicity. However, Vontress (1988) states that it is the perception of "differentness" that dictates whether an interaction is "cross-cultural." If the counselor and client are culturally different but they *perceive* mutual cultural similarity, even if on the surface, then the interaction is not considered cross-cultural. Conversely, if both the counselor and the client are culturally similar but *perceive* themselves as different from each other, this would be a cross-cultural encounter (Vontress, 1988). Pedersen (1990, p. 94) extends the definition of multicultural counseling even further. He argues, "To some extent, all mental health counseling is multicultural." Every therapeutic encounter is complex and dynamic, since both the client and the practitioner bring with them potential differences in gender, lifestyle, economic status, and/or age in addition to nationality and ethnic differences.

Viewed from another perspective, an exclusive stance posits the importance of focusing only on racial, cultural, and ethnic differences (Locke, 1990). When one overemphasizes the similarities of *all* marginalized groups, one will ultimately reduce the importance of cultural identity, individual characteristics, and unique cultural membership (Locke, 1990). Hence, a more exclusive definition will emphasize these individual characteristics and experiences. Ethnic and racial minorities will often experience culture shock in their new homeland, the stressors associated with cultural and racial discrimination, post-traumatic stress emanating from the war-torn homelands they fled, and learning to cope with new cross-cultural relationships (Nelson-Jones, 2002b). These are unique factors that affect functioning and coping for ethnic minority groups but not necessarily other minority groups. Counselors who use only an inclusive definition of multiculturalism, consequently, will obscure immigrant and ethnic minority groups' unique experiences.

CULTURE DEFINITIONS: CREATING THE CONTEXT FOR COUNSELING

For counselors working with clients who have varied cultural backgrounds and histories, having a definition of culture can guide understanding of client needs, determine how assessment is carried out, support treatment planning, and guide evaluation of outcomes. Definitions of culture, therefore, must be clear and mutually understood by both client and counselor to support the counseling process. Herein lies one of the first culture- and diversity-sensitive aspects of the counselor's therapeutic stance: Focus on learning about each client's cultural and/or diversity background as an integrated element of the initial interview. To accomplish this step, counselors need to consider the many ways that culture can be defined.

Culture as Behaviors

In the 1950s, culture was frequently conceptualized in terms of patterns of behaviors and customs. The emphasis was on a group's habits and behaviors—observable aspects of culture, such as food, dress, music, and art (Jackson & Meadows, 1991). Gordon (1964, p. 32) defined *culture* as

> the ways of acting and the ways of doing things which are passed down from one generation to the next, not through genetic inheritance but by formal and informal methods of teaching and demonstration.

When behaviors are categorized as a dimension of culture, the reference is to objective culture, involving tangible and visible features (Axelson, 1999).

Culture as Shared Knowledge and Values

Culture, of course, includes the observable as well as components that are deep-seated and cannot be easily observed and measured. From this perspective, *culture* is defined as the sum total of knowledge that is disseminated from one generation to the next generation. It includes language; forms of art expression; religion, political, economic, and social structures; norms of behavior, and values (D'Andrade, 1984). In other words, culture structures cognitive reality for a group (Castillo, 1997). In a similar vein, culture has also focused on values, which give meaning to behaviors and subjective culture, and encompass the less tangible and invisible dimensions of shared experience (Axelson, 1999).

Culture as Ethnicity and Nationality

Moving to the 1960s, culture was defined based on ethnographic variables such as nationality, ethnicity, and shared history (Jackson & Meadows, 1991). Influenced by the Civil Rights movement, advocates argued that people of color needed to obtain their legitimate civil rights (Jackson & Meadows, 1991). When culture and ethnicity are intertwined like this, Green (1999, p. 17) observes it is something like a " 'revival,' . . . as something that is 'celebrated' in self-conscious returns to ethnic foods and clothing, traditional religious practices, ethnic festivals, adoption of ethnic personal names, and renewed interest in non-Western (or at least non-American) languages and folklore."

Culture as Worldview

Worldview encompasses assumptions and perceptions about the world and how it works (Sue & Sue, 1999). Ultimately, it influences a group of individuals' behaviors and decision-making processes. Worldviews can help explain why groups of people act as they do and respond to the environment as they do (Jackson & Meadows, 1991). Kluckhohn and Strodtbeck (1961) proposed five different dimensions that comprise a worldview: (1) human nature—how we view human nature; that is, is it good or bad? (2) man and nature—how we view ourselves in relation to nature; that is, do we have control? (3) time—how we view the past, present, and future; (4) activity—how we view "doing" and "being"; and (5) relational—how we view social relations such as family and other social networks.

Culture with Underlying Philosophical Assumptions

Jackson and Meadows (1991, p. 74) argue for the importance of examining the "deep structure of culture as the philosophical assumptions." These structures include ontology, epistemology, cosmology, axiology, logic, and process. Using Asian culture to highlight their points, Jackson and Meadows (1991) note that in many Asian cultures, there is an emphasis on unity. The *ontological* perspective, which focused on the nature of reality, can be characterized as an orientation toward harmony; that is, the world and human beings need to be in harmony (Chung, 1992). The *epistemological* perspective answers the question: What is knowledge? In Asian culture, the philosophy is that there is unity of mind, body, and spirit. In other words, there is no dichotomy between these dimensions (Tseng & Wu, 1985). The *cosmological* question taps into the belief about the order and arrangement of the world. In Asian culture, the view of the world is based on the belief that the parts that make up each person are interrelated and must be in harmony with each other for proper functioning. The *axiological* perspective focuses on the role of values and how they are developed. Asian culture emphasizes values that revolve around family and the collective unit (Uba, 1994). Finally, the Asian *logic* and communication system is circular. Indirect methods of communication are essential to preserve harmony (Okun, Fried, & Okun, 1999). The *process* of bringing about change is founded on relationships and group processes (Chung, 1992).

Culture has been referred to as a way of life. It is a taken-for-granted social concept that is "out there" (Fernando, 2002). Whether one views culture as behaviors, shared knowledge and values, ethnicity, a worldview, or structures with philosophical assumptions about the world, culture is dynamic and not easily defined (Fernando, 2002). It is a flexible system in which people live (Fernando, 2002) and that has potent influence on those lives.

UNIVERSALISM VERSUS CULTURE SPECIFICITY

There is ongoing debate in the field of counseling about the approach practitioners should take when working with multicultural clients. These two orientations have been approached from a universal, or "etic," perspective and from a culture-specific, or "emic," perspective. Each perspective has both benefits as well as drawbacks. A model that bridges the polarization between the "etic" and "emic" perspectives has been conceptualized by scholars in the field and will be considered as it applies to the counseling professions.

The Universalism Perspective ("Etic" Approach)

The term *etic* is derived from the term *phonetic*, which refers to sounds assumed to be universal across all languages. Therefore, etic in psychology and counseling refers to universal behaviors that can be applied to all groups (Lee & Ramirez, 2000). The etic approach asks: Should we assume that human beings are generally alike?

Adopting a universal stance, Fukuyama (1990, p. 7) argues that counseling "recognizes universal processes that transcend cultural variations" and "provides a broad and inclusive perspective for understanding the influences of culture in counseling." She calls this perspective universal or transcultural (i.e., a counseling approach that can be applied to various types of multicultural interactions). In essence, Fukuyama argues for an inclusive definition of multiculturalism since one is not advocating for a particular minority group as justifying for the need for multicultural counseling. Rather, there are universal concepts that exist in any helping relationship, and there are common themes represented among the different minority groups (Fukuyama, 1990). Groups such as women, the elderly, gays and lesbians, and the poor, for example, all experience discrimination, marginalization, and prejudice because they do not fit within the dominant culture power structure.

Similarly, Freeman (1993) argues that one can find the universal in the specific. In other words, there are cultural differences; however, there are those commonalities that exist among all human beings, and the helping relationship builds on this foundation of commonness. For example, when developing or establishing rapport, Sue and Zane (1987) emphasize the importance of two factors—the credibility of the helper and giving the client some form of benefit from the therapeutic interaction. Freeman (1993) maintains that the client-centered approach provides the condition on which to build on the commonalities. An atmosphere where the client defines the problems and solutions, where the counselor listens and "is with" the client, and which promotes honesty are all conditions that assist to build the relationship.

What should be placed at the forefront in counseling are universal human being skills (Nelson-Jones, 2002a). All human beings have the capacity to develop universal mind skills and communication skills, and providing education about these skills can lead to more effective human functioning and pathways to happiness. It is these skills that transcend cultural diversity (Nelson-Jones, 2002a). Proponents of universality do not argue that culture does not play a role in counseling and counseling theories. They do not deny the existence of cultural differences, nor do they argue that there is a cultural bias in Western-style counseling. The emphasis of universality lies in the importance of acknowledging that there are common experiences among minority populations such as discrimination, oppression, worldviews, and need for identity. These dimensions should then be integrated into the counseling process (Lee & Ramirez, 2000).

Some argue that there is risk in using a universal stance. Champagne (1997, p. 28) asserts that an emphasis on multicultural perspectives "undercuts internal cultural/ethnic experiences and differences," and ultimately, classifications contribute and continue to promulgate misunderstandings about internal ethnic political and cultural differences of groups. In a counseling context, when counselors are focused on tailoring interventions and techniques specific to the needs of each multicultural group, they could take on characteristics of the chameleon—constantly changing approaches with clients who are culturally different than themselves (Patterson, 1996).

The Culture-Specific Perspective ("Emic" Approach)

Emic stems from the word *phonemic*, which refers to particular sounds within one language (Lee & Ramirez, 2000). Therefore, in counseling and psychology, emic refers to culture-specific behaviors. The emic approach asks: Should we inquire about the unique cultural characteristics within groups? Locke (1990) advocates for an "emic," "culture-specific," "ideographic," or "provincial" orientation to the study of multiculturalism. This orientation recognizes individual differences within culturally different groups and working with clients within the context of their primary cultural group (Locke, 1990). Therefore, counseling practitioners would intensely study that specific culture and adapt techniques that work with clients from that group (Fukuyama, 1990).

Locke (1990) is concerned that universal perspectives would ultimately encompass so many different groups in the definition of multiculturalism that the sources and interventions for the social problem would become diluted. Worse, a universal view might imply that racism experienced by different cultural groups is no different from racism experienced by White individuals. However, a narrower view of multicultural counseling will take into account individual and institutional racism as factors in perpetuating behaviors against specific culturally different groups (Locke, 1990). Finally, Pedersen (1996) notes that taking a universal approach may trivialize cultural identity.

Some would assert that taking a look at the demographic shifts alone in the United States would argue for a culture-specific orientation. The salience of race is at the forefront in America (McFadden, 1996). In 1990, for example, African Americans constituted 11.7 percent of the population; however, by 2000, African Americans numbered 33.9 million, representing an increase of 12.1 percent of the total U.S. population (U.S. Census Bureau, 2000a). Similarly, the Latino/Hispanic population has grown at a phenomenal rate, increasing from 22 million in 1990 to 35 million in 2000, surpassing the number of African Americans (U.S. Census Bureau, 2000b). Looking at Asians in the United States, the growth of Asian Americans also soared during the 1990s due to high levels of immigration from Asian countries. In 1990, Asian Americans, including Pacific Islanders, numbered

6.9 million in the United States. This increased to 10.5 million by 2000 (U.S. Census Bureau, 2000b). Finally, according to the 2000 U.S. Census, the number of residents in the United States who reported themselves as American Indian or Alaska Native was 2.5 million, which represents 0.9 percent of the U.S. population. This was a 26 percent increase compared to the figures obtained in the 1990 Census. It has been said that by 2050, ethnic minority groups will comprise almost half (47.5 percent) of the total U.S. population. Whites will most likely be a minority group by year 2056 (Lavizzo-Mourey & Mackenzie, 1996).

One of the most prominent arguments for a culture-specific stance is that research shows that traditional mental health service systems do not adequately meet the needs of ethnic minority clients (Sue, 1977). Consequently, counselors must be adequately trained and prepared to communicate and understand values and belief systems of these groups. Cultural competence encompasses respecting cultural diversity and working with clients to enable them to function and cope in both their culture and in the mainstream culture (McFadden, 1996).

Finally, culture-specific proponents maintain that racism, discrimination, language barriers, prejudice, and different cultural value systems color life experiences of ethnic and racial minority groups in ways that make their social realities different from European American groups. Yet, many social science theories—including psychology, counseling, and mental health—are Eurocentric. Thus, scholars have advocated for a distinct epistemology that more accurately depicts the viewpoints of subordinate groups such as ethnic and racial minorities (Padilla, 1990; Stanfield, 1993).

Bridging Perspectives: Not as Polarized as They Appear to Be

The controversy of the "etic/emic" may not be as polarized as it appears to be. Pike (1966), who initially conceptualized the etic/emic dichotomy, himself noted that the two dimensions are merely the same ideas coming from two complementary perspectives. For example, all groups experience happiness (etic); however, the avenues of attaining this emotion may be unique for each group (emic) (Pedersen, 1999). The benefits of both perspectives should be harnessed.

In an attempt to bridge this polarization, Fischer, Jome, and Atkinson (1998) argue for a "common factors" perspective. This perspective maintains that the curative components or attributes of psychotherapy do not necessarily stem from practitioners' theoretical orientation, but rather from attributes underlying all psychotherapies and across all cultures. This common factor perspective was originally articulated by Frank (1961) in *Persuasion and Healing*. Thus, there are common factors to be found in all psychotherapy, and universal elements found in all psychological and spiritual healing across different cultures. However, this needs to be combined with an in-depth knowledge of the cultural context (Fischer et al, 1998).

After reviewing extensive literature about common factors, Fischer and colleagues (1998) summarized these factors into four broad "common factor" categories: (1) the therapeutic relationship, (2) a shared worldview, (3) client expectations, and (4) ritual or intervention. It is important to note that these common factors are not distinct, mutually exclusive entities; rather, there is interplay among all four common factors. The therapeutic relationship consists of a positive and trusting relationship between the client and counseling practitioner. Orlinsky and Howard (1987) characterize the *therapeutic relationship*, where both parties invest emotionally, as empathic and mutually affirming. A *shared worldview* is a common framework, perspective, or "wavelength" in which both the client and the counselor professional operate. It is the ability of the counselor to name the client's distress and explain it, and the willingness of the client to agree with this label that moves the process forward. The third common factor, *client expectations*, refers to the client's hope or faith that there are benefits of the therapeutic process. Finally, the fourth common factor is the *ritual or intervention*. Both the client and the counselor must believe that the intervention is effective in its healing benefits and has the capability of alleviating distress. Thus, one intervention for one client may not necessarily be "effective" for another client unless the client believes in its healing potential.

Using a definition of culture that is compatible with how the counselor provides therapy with culturally diverse clients is a natural outgrowth of reviewing many facets of the topic. Fischer and associates (1998, p. 543) argue that the common factors framework provides a way of unifying the large, and at times, polarized viewpoints about multiculturalism in counseling. Using such an inclusive perspective supports "the process by which they can integrate an understanding of the universal aspects of healing (the skeleton of common factors) with the unique cultural experiences and affiliations of their clients (the flesh of cultural knowledge)." For counselors who seek to infuse multicultural sensitivity and awareness into practice, perhaps the common factors definition of culture does provide the flexibility and focus needed for effective counseling.

COUNSELING THEORIES: CULTURE-FREE OR CULTURE-LADEN

A culture-free theory assumes there are general laws that are capable of explaining all phenomena. Advocates of the existence of culture-free theories adhere to a premise that universal characteristics can be identified in social phenomena, completely independent from specific cultural contexts (Haintrais, 1999). De Anda (1997) defined culture-free theories as theoretical principles about human behavior and dynamics that can be generalized across a range of populations and that can depict these dynamics accurately and in a culturally syntonic manner. She argues that the following five characteristics must exist in order for a theory to be classified as culturally free:

1. *Acontextual*: The concepts can be operationally defined in other cultural contexts. The principle of positive and negative reinforcement can be generalizable to all different populations. The behavior may be culturally bound, and the reinforcers might vary from group to group; however, the principles of learning and reinforcement are maintained. In other words, if a behavior is positively reinforced, the frequency of the behavior will increase in all settings.
2. *Norm-Free*: The theory provides norm-free or value-free guidelines for practice. When theories about human behavior focus on the socialization process, they may be difficult to apply to different groups since socialization is culturally emphasized.

Therefore, stage theories that are developmentally or age-bound may be difficult to apply to other groups.

3. *Self-Corrective*: The variables within the theory need to be operationally defined; that is, one should be able to define the variables in concrete and measurable terms. Consequently, researchers can test the applicability of the theories in other cultural settings and with other populations.

4. *Descriptive*: The theory is descriptive, rather than prescriptive regarding the dynamics of behavior (i.e., identifying what is normal and abnormal). When cultural schemas about what is pathological are embedded in the constructs of the theory, there will be a potential dissonance between the definition of pathology and the group's norms about normality and deviance.

5. *Broadly Heuristic*: Theories that offer general and broad intervention guidelines, as opposed to specific clinical procedures, with rigidly described symptoms will be more generalizable to diverse groups.

The importance of counselors' understanding the implications of culture-free theory is clear. If the theoretical frameworks that a counselor uses to guide treatment assessment, planning, implementation, and evaluation are developed with specific client populations in mind, those theories are not automatically generalizable to populations not included in the initial developmental process. To do so increases risks for incorrect assumptions, misunderstanding the needs of clients, and treatment planning that is based on shaky theoretical ground. Conversely, when a theoretical framework is inclusive and thus able to incorporate culture and diversity issues that clients bring to the therapeutic encounter, the risk for bias is reduced.

UNDERSTANDING DIVERSE POPULATIONS

In the course of counseling practice, some counselors will provide services to clients who have a wide variety of cultural and diverse backgrounds. Others will see fewer clients who have cultural backgrounds different from their own. Understanding major characteristics of culture and diversity, however, has significance for counselors as a general principle. Dr. D realized this recently.

Dr. D practices counseling with five other mental health professionals, including a social worker, a pastoral counselor, a psychiatrist, and two psychologists. The community where she practices is located in a medium-size city with a predominantly homogenous population. She rarely sees clients who have culture or ethnic backgrounds different from her own. Dr. D is well aware of the importance of a multicultural perspective yet has made an assumption for several years about the similarity of her cultural background and that of her clients. When Mrs. E began counseling, Dr. D had to reevaluate her assumptions.

Mrs. E initiated counseling for serious marital discord, and as she described the problems she was experiencing, Dr. D began to sense that what she was hearing did not fit into her understanding of how families of origin function based on her experience personally and with her client population. Fortunately, Dr. D realized that this disconnect in her thinking about family history might reflect a lack of understanding about cultural beliefs that Mrs. E was describing. She then redirected her assessment interview to explore in detail Mrs. E's family background and culture. As it evolved, this became a central issue in the marital counseling that took place with Mr. and Mrs. E.

Culture and diversity form the backdrop to the counseling experience. Counselors risk missing significant information when assumptions are made about a client's cultural background based on superficial physical attributes of client and counselor. This example illustrates the need to consistently acquire and integrate cultural background information into the counseling process.

Understanding the history, qualities, and characteristics of clients' ethnic and cultural backgrounds provides guidance for effective practice. This section of the chapter explores the demographic, social, and psychological issues as well as the cultural values and belief systems of various diverse groups. Since it is beyond the scope of this chapter to cover all ethnic and cultural populations represented in society, four ethnic minority groups (African Americans, Asian Americans, Latino/Hispanic Americans, and Native Americans), and a selection of diversity groups (the elderly, women, gays and lesbians, and the physically disabled) will be the focus of discussion. Because these topics are the subject of extensive publications in the counseling fields, the emphasis here is on identification of *core issues* that counselors are to consider in practice rather than a presentation of counseling methods, techniques, and strategies covered in dedicated texts. Readers are cautioned that cultural values and belief systems are presented as cultural themes and that level of acculturation, immigration status, education, socioeconomic status, religion, and sociopolitical factors color these cultural themes, all of which contribute to their heterogeneity.

African Americans

The experience of slavery in the United States has had the most impact on African Americans' social experiences and realities. The beginning of slavery can be traced to Virginia, when, in 1619, Virginia settlers purchased 20 Africans who arrived in the United States (Kitano, 1997). The institution of slavery worked to eradicate much of African customs, traditions, language, and beliefs; however, despite these efforts, the result, when viewed through contemporary lenses, reveals the emergence of a distinct cultural tradition.

African American family and community life as well as the family institution were disrupted with the start of the slave trade and the slave-based plantation system in the United States. Family life was not encouraged because it would adversely affect slave work productivity on the plantation. Marriage between slaves was not considered legal. Black men were treated like breeders, with the sole purpose of increasing the labor supply, while Black female slaves were sexually exploited by their owners (Hines & Boyd-Franklin, 1996). The system of slavery rendered Africans powerless because a slave's life was contingent on the whims of his or her master. Unfortunately, a slave was a "genealogical isolate" (Kitano, 1997, p. 128), with neither kin nor family security.

Despite the efforts to eradicate the family system, the family has always been the source of tradition for African Americans today and in the past. In Africa, marriage is not considered an individual event; rather, it is a community event that perpetuates family lineage and reinforces a sense of community (Green, 1999). The characteristics described by Hill in 1971 highlighted six characteristics of the African American family of today: (1) strong kinship bonds; (2) strong work orientation in support of family ties; (3) high level of flexibility in family roles; (4) strong achievement orientation, particularly in the area of occupational and educational aspirations; (5) strong commitment to religious values and church participation; and (6) commitment to a language tradition. These qualities and characteristics continue to be integral to understanding African American families while also recognizing that some families struggle in different ways with societal pressures and challenges associated with historical and lived experiences.

Over the years, the family in the African American community has been variously portrayed as disorganized to pathological. In 1965, Daniel Moynihan published a report in which he argued that the Black family was disintegrating, using the high number of divorces, female-headed households, and illegitimate births to substantiate his assertion. Unfortunately, his definition of *family* was based on White-Anglo conceptualizations of family, which is primarily nuclear (i.e., father, mother, and biological children living in one household). On the other hand, African American families are multigenerational and interdependent, with strong roles played by women and men. According to a study by Martin and Martin (1978), a typical extended family network might consist of five or more households centered at a base unit, where the "family leader" resides. Pooling resources is the focal point of such households, demonstrating resourcefulness and flexibility in the face of hardship. It has been said that these strong kinship networks are key in helping African American families cope with the ongoing stressors of racism, oppression, and discrimination.

Issues associated with culture and ethnic experiences of individuals and families impact the health and well-being of African American clients seen by counseling professionals. For example, the self-care strategies used by African Americans who have chronic health problems are associated with the presence or absence of health insurance. Patients with chronic health problems who have insurance engage in biomedically oriented self-care practices to manage these conditions (e.g., diabetes, asthma) more frequently than those who lack access to medical and health resources that would teach the benefits of self-care management of illness (Becker, Gates, & Newsom, 2004). Understanding how self-care is acquired and used by clients is essential to counseling professionals; it is clearly linked to mental health self-care and hence to well-being.

The role of intergenerational support to family members is a significant source of influence within African American families. For young mothers of premature or low–birth-weight infants, for example, grandmothers have assumed a significant role in providing care, support, parenting guidance, and housing for teenage mothers and fathers (Gordon, Chase-Lansdale, & Brooks-Gunn, 2004). In these settings, the young parent has an increased probability of achieving education goals but may not gain parenting competencies that will be needed for independent parenting (Gordon, Chase-Lansdale, & Brooks-Gunn, 2004). For counselors working with adolescents or grandparents in such environments, understanding the benefits as well as the challenges of such coresidence living arrangements guide assessment and intervention.

Saundra, 16 years old, and her grandmother were referred to counseling following a well-baby check-up at the health department. During the visit, the grandmother, Angeline, became angry with Saundra, who arrived late for the appointment, but Angeline would not discuss her reactions with the pediatrician while he was discussing the baby's nutritional needs as a low–birth-weight baby. Both the grandmother and granddaughter agreed to see the counselor who works at the health department following the check-up to discuss the feelings that surfaced during the visit with the physician.

When counseling this family, it will be important to investigate several issues suggested by the scenario: (1) Angeline may be providing the bulk of the infant care while Saundra goes to school, (2) expectations of Saundra may not be clear to her regarding resumption of parenting responsibilities when she returns to her coresidence, (3) Angeline may have expectations of Saundra that do not include a teenage social life that Saundra has reentered, or (4) Angeline may be fatigued and stressed by the caregiving needs she has assumed for her grandchild. These and other issues need to be discussed thoroughly with both Angeline and Saundra before counseling plans can be formulated and implemented. Central to working with this family, as well as with other multigenerational African American families, is recognition of the role that grandparents play in the lives of children and grandchildren and that the extended family is a cultural theme not linked to crisis or deficits. According to Jimenez (2002, pp. 545–546), grandmother care "is a tradition inherited from the strong emphasis on kinship solidarity in Africa, in the slave quarters, and in the lived struggles of African Americans in the United States."

Counselors working with intergenerational African American families must assume variance in how parenting of grandchildren of all ages takes place. Depending on the research evidence, the level of involvement of African American grandparents in providing parenting to grandchildren can range from moderate to high (Lee, Ensminger, & Laveist, 2005). For other multigenerational African American families, the extent of parenting involvement varies over time and can directly impact the health and well-being of the elderly who find themselves in this role. Preexisting health conditions, as well as the demands of child care, can tax the financial, emotional, and physical resources of the aging grandparent (Kropf & Burnette, 2003). Of critical importance are findings suggesting that higher rates of mental health issues such as depression may occur with this population (Minkler & Fuller-Thomson, 1999), rates of coronary heart disease may be exacerbated by the demands of child care (Lee, Colditz, Berkman, & Kawachi, 2003), stress reactions can be intensified (Linsk & Mason, 2004), and less attendance to nutrition, exercise, and smoking cessation may be a negative outcome for caregiving grandmothers (Whitley, Kelley, & Sipe, 2001). In spite of the increased risk for health problems associated with caring for grandchildren by aging grandparents, the rewards of ensuring that children are raised by family and committing to achieve this goal outweigh personal health risks for many who assume this role (Whitley, Kelley, & Sipe, 2001).

In addition to the role of family and kinship bonds within the African American family, issues associated with mental health service utilization reflect various cultural perspectives. For example, there is some indication that African American patients more frequently access mental health care through general medical providers (e.g., general practice physicians) rather than through mental health professionals (Cooper-Patrick et al, 1999). However, access and availability of mental health services for economically marginal African Americans with mental health conditions has been suggested as a variable that directly influences how and when services will be sought and used (Snowden, 2001; Snowden & Thomas, 2000). How, when, and why mental health counseling services are sought may also be influenced by cultural beliefs about mental illness. For example, beliefs about the nature of mental illness or disorders as reflecting spiritual influences, shame, or knowledge of unethical events related to treatment of African Americans in scientific research (e.g., the Tuskegee study) may prevent clients from seeking care for mental health problems (Meinert, Blehar, Peindl, Neal-Barnett, & Wisner, 2003; Waldron, 2003).

Culture influences behavior, thinking, experience, and how individuals, groups, and communities engage with each other in daily living, work settings, and when seeking health care. Counselors who provide care to African American clients must maintain vigilance about the lived experiences of their clients, integrate knowledge about the unique perceptions and belief systems within this ethnic and cultural population, and seek verification of understanding throughout the counseling process. Pursuit of advanced education and training in ethnic and cultural linked behavior, qualities, and characteristics represents an avenue for development of counselor cultural competence throughout a career in counseling.

Asian Americans

Chinese Americans are the largest Asian American group in the United States, and their immigration history dates back to the mid-1800s, occurring in several waves of large migration cohorts (Lee, 1997). The years between 1850 and 1919 marked the first wave, and this influx was triggered by the discovery of gold in California. Filled with dreams of prosperity, many Chinese males, primarily peasant farmers, left their homelands to seek fortune and success in a new land.

The second wave of Chinese immigration was between 1920 and 1942, consisting of Chinese merchants and Chinese wives who were married to U.S. citizens before 1924. The period between 1943 and 1964 marked the third wave of Chinese immigration. In 1945, the War Brides Act was passed, allowing Chinese women to immigrate as brides of men in the U.S. military. From 1965 to 1977, the fourth wave brought Chinese immigrants to the United States under the Immigration Act of 1965. These were working-class families that ended up settling in large urban areas, primarily in cities with Chinatowns. These immigrants worked long hours in factories and restaurants trying to achieve the American dream. Finally, the fifth wave began in 1978, after three decades of the closed-door policy, when immigrants from China were allowed to join their relatives. A large number of students and professionals also immigrated to the United States to pursue their education. A more recent phenomenon consists of Asian immigrants setting up two households, one in the United States for their children to study in the United States and one household in their homelands for the adults to continue working (Lee, 1997).

Filipinos are the second largest Asian American group in the United States, numbering 1.9 million (U.S. Census Bureau, 2002). Most Filipinos in the United States are first generation. Filipino history is very rich, since their culture has been influenced by a series of colonizing and protector countries. The Phillipines were colonized by the Spanish, Americans, and Japanese. In addition, neighboring Chinese, Indonesians, and Asian Indians have contributed to this culture (Sustento-Seneriches, 1997).

In 1763, Spain began its galleon trade from Manila and Cebu, and this sparked the first wave of Filipino immigrants. The second wave of immigrants occurred from 1906 to 1943. These immigrants were male farm workers who were recruited to work the pineapple fields in Hawaii and the farmlands along the West Coast of the United States (Sustento-Seneriches, 1997). Between 1945 and 1965, the United States witnessed another influx of Filipino immigrants. These were Filipino servicemen who fought alongside Americans during the Japanese occupation. Finally, the fourth wave occurred during the 1960s, after the Tydings-McDuffie Act and its lifting of the immigration quota. During this wave, more commonly known as the "brain wave," immigrants consisted of professionals such doctors, nurses, and engineers who came to the United States for more training (Sustento-Seneriches, 1997).

Asian Indians are the most rapidly growing Asian segment of the U.S. population. In 1990, they were the fifth largest Asian group in the country, but by 2000, they represented the third largest Asian group (U.S. Census Bureau, 2002). Immigration by Asian Indians to the United States dates from the middle to late 1800s, with farmers moving into California (Prathikanti, 1997). There, they confronted prejudice and discrimination with widespread anti-miscegenation laws that prevented them from buying or owning real estate or becoming U.S. citizens. Because of the Immigration and Naturalization Act, there was very little immigration from Asia prior to 1965, and consequently minimal numbers of Asian Indians came to the United States. However, after 1965, a second wave of Asian Indians entered the United States because there was a need for physicians, engineers, and technical specialists. These immigrants were young and well educated and spoke English (Prathikanti, 1997). In the 1980s, the United States witnessed the third wave of Asian Indian immigration—family members of professionals from the second wave. These family members were sponsored, and they were generally less educated with less proficiency in English (Prathikanti, 1997).

Although it is essential to stress that there is tremendous diversity within the various Asian subgroups, certain cultural themes can be identified that are reflected within this group of Asian cultures. One predominant theme is clear: Asian cultural values and norms are very different from Western belief systems. In part, these differences stem from the role that Confucianism and Buddhism have played in Asia (Lee, 1996). Western culture emphasizes autonomy and individualism, which are manifested in notions about rugged individualism and democracy. However, traditional Asian culture emphasizes the collective unit, such as the family unit, instead of the individual. Rituals and customs such as ancestor worship, funeral rites, and holiday celebrations all reinforce the fact that individual behavior and actions not only reflect the individual but the entire family system and ancestral lineage (Lee, 1996; Yick & Gupta, 2002).

In general, traditional Asian families are patriarchal; that is, there is a focus on male authority. Roles are clearly defined, with the father having primary authority, and when the father passes away, the eldest son assumes authority (Kitano, 1997). Women are expected to be submissive to their husbands and to be caretakers and nurturers. Counselors working with Asian individuals, families, and groups can incorporate awareness of the cultural values of the traditional family while also exploring changes in beliefs and behaviors as each American-born generation interfaces with the surrounding American culture.

> Jasmine was born in the United States into a large Indian family that adhered to traditional values and expectations for each of the five children. During her second year at college, Jasmine began to experience symptoms of depression and anxiety. Her dorm roommate suggested she see a counselor at the student counseling center on campus. After some consideration, Jasmine scheduled her first appointment and, with intense anxiety, kept the appointment. Steve, the Caucasian male counselor assigned to see Jasmine, is viewed by his peers as a very sensitive and culturally aware counselor. Jasmine, after some coaxing, begins to describe the conflict she is having about her parents' desire that she become engaged to a young man who is immigrating from India to America.

In this situation, a number of issues are linked to how the counselor will assess the presenting problem, develop a counseling treatment plan, and evaluate results. Steve may view this problem as a nonproblem from his personal cultural perspective (i.e., "You're under no obligation to become engaged to anyone you don't wish to be engaged to"). This independent stance is in concert with personal beliefs about romantic relationships. However, even though Jasmine was born in the United States, she may well retain a strong cultural belief that her parents have the right to make such life decisions for her. Steve will need to explore very carefully the many facets of Jasmine's experience and concerns while suspending his personal bias. Recognition that tensions can be generated between traditional and contemporary members of Asian ethnic and cultural populations fosters a collaboration between counselor and client that can reduce the introduction of bias or creating an outcome because it is expected (i.e., the self-fulfilling prophecy) (Patterson, 1996).

Latino/Hispanic Americans

The terms *Latino* and *Hispanic* are labels used to describe people from Cuba, Mexico, Argentina, Colombia, Dominican Republic, Brazil, Guatemala, Costa Rica, Nicaragua, San Salvador, and countries in South America, Central America, and the Carribean (Garcia-Preto, 1996a). Many Spanish-speaking immigrants from Latin America prefer the term *Latino* because it reaffirms their native, pre-Hispanic identity (Falicov, 1998). The terms *Latino* and *Hispanic* are often used interchangeably; however, the term *Hispanic* is generally looked down on because it is associated with politically conservative groups who regard Spanish European ancestry as superior to the indigenous, native groups in the Americas (Falicov, 1998). The U.S. Census Bureau employs the term *Hispanic* in their enumeration of the population, and it generally refers to individuals living in the United States who have descendants from Spanish-speaking Latin American countries or from Spain.

The three largest Latino groups in the United States are Mexicans, Puerto Ricans, and Cubans (Falicov, 1998). According to the U.S. Census Bureau (2000a), Mexicans comprise 60 percent of the Latino/Hispanic group in the United States, and in the last decade, the U.S. Census Bureau (2000a) counted an additional seven million who identified themselves as Mexican. The majority of Mexicans are of mixed Spanish and Indian descent. Mexicans can trace their heritage back to Indian civilizations until the 1500s, when Spanish explorers arrived (Chilman, 1993). From the seventeenth to nineteenth centuries, Spain extended its rule over Mexico, California, and the southwestern United States, where many Mexicans resided. In 1821, Mexico obtained its independence from Spain (Chilman, 1993). From 1846 to 1848, Mexico and the United States were in continual conflict over Texas, which ultimately led to the Mexican-American War. Eventually, the United States acquired Arizona, California, Colorado, Nevada, New Mexico, Utah, and Wyoming, and Mexicans who lived in those states became U.S. citizens (Falicov, 1998).

Family unity, commitment, and obligation are highly regarded values among Latinos/Hispanics (Garcia-Preto, 1996). *Familismo* refers to family interdependence and inclusiveness, and the family goes beyond the nuclear family structures (Falicov, 1998). The family is an extended family system where the boundaries are very permeable, since the family consists of individuals who are not only blood related or related by marriage but also includes *compadres* (Garcia-Preto, 1996a). *Compadres* are godparents, and they provide both economic and emotional assistance. The practice of *hijos de crianza* also adds to the family unit, and this refers to transferring children from one nuclear family to an extended family system in times of crisis. It is characterized by mutual help, protection, and caregiving (Garcia-Preto, 1996a).

In general, Hispanic/Latino culture is organized around patriarchal beliefs. *Machismo* refers to male authority within the family with its responsibility for moral and economic leadership in the household (Green, 1999). Double standards exist: Males have more freedom, particularly in the sexual arena. While premarital sex is forbidden for women, men are encouraged to explore their sexuality. Women are to follow the example of the Virgin Mary (Aragon de Valdez & Gallegos, 1982). They are to demonstrate obedience to their husbands and nurturance to their children. They are the caretakers and nurturers of the home. The authority structure among Latinos/Hispanics can be described as patriarchal; it is also hierarchical. Wives are to submit to and obey their husbands, and children must obey and respect their parents. Children are obligated to demonstrate to their parents *respecto*, which refers to emotional dependence and dutifulness (Falicov, 1998). Child-rearing practices reflect this hierarchy, and punishment, shaming, belittling, and promises are utilized as disciplinary tools (Falicov, 1998) Latino/Hispanic families are also heavily influenced by the Catholic Church. Individuals personalize their relationship with God through special relationships with saints. Offerings, prayers, and lighting of candles are typical rituals followed by the observant Catholic (Garcia-Preto, 1996b). How these complex beliefs relate to counseling practice is partially illustrated by Mrs. Delgado's situation.

> Mrs. Delgado has been referred to you after she was treated in the emergency room for injuries inflicted on her by her husband during a domestic disturbance. He was arrested and is incarcerated until she can arrange bail. She is very anxious when she enters your office and there is visible bruising on her face and arms. Mrs. Delgado speaks English fairly well. She agreed to see you when the ER nurse recommended it because Mrs. Delgado indicated that she is extremely worried about her 10-year-old son, who has been suspended from

school for fighting. According to Mrs. Delgado, this event was the reason that her husband became violent, since they argued about what to do about their son.

The counselor for Mrs. Delgado realizes that the assessment of client needs is complex. Issues of domestic violence, marital discord, potential of future harm to the client by her husband, and parenting are areas to be explored. The counselor in this situation must conduct a careful, sensitive, and thorough assessment. If the counselor is familiar with Hispanic culture, she may find the process of engagement with the client smooth and productive of essential information to guide treatment. Counselors who are not familiar with the beliefs and perceptions linked to Mrs. Delgado's culture, domestic violence within her culture, and parenting challenges in a patriarchal culture must seek knowledge from the literature and through supervision and consultation. Immediate and long-term needs must be integrated into the counselor's plan beginning with the first session.

Native Americans

Native Americans and *American Indians* are terms applied to those who first settled in what is now North America. Early European explorers used the term *Indian* because they believed they had arrived in India following early explorations (Axelson, 1999). However, even the terms employed are highly controversial. Yellow Bird (2001) argues that the terms *American Indians* and *Native Americans* are erroneous because they are not Indian nor did these individuals refer to the United States as "America" until Europeans imposed this name. Instead the terms *First Nations People* or *indigenous peoples* may be more apt to describe the original peoples in America (Yellow Bird, 2001).

Today, Native Americans identify themselves with a particular tribe or clan; however, tremendous diversity exists among clans. Each tribe or clan has different religious practices, customs, and family structures (Sutton & Broken Nose, 1996). There are over 500 different tribes and over 300 reservations (Garrett & Herring, 2001; Sutton & Broken Nose, 1996), but not all Native nations are recognized as federally recognized tribes. Federally recognized tribes are entitled to participate in federally funded services such as the Indian Child Welfare Act (Weaver & White, 1997).

Just as slavery served to oppress and marginalize African Americans, colonialism left an indelible mark on Native Americans. Yellow Bird (2001, p. 63) defines *colonialism* as "the invasion of alien peoples of territories inhabited by peoples of a different race and culture and the establishment of political, social, intellectual, psychological, and economic control over that territory." European American colonizers would control Native Americans by taking children away from their families and placing them in off-reservation boarding schools. Children were taught that they were inferior to Whites and were often subjected to harsh disciplinary tactics when expressing their values (Yellow Bird, 2001).

The family system is the "cornerstone for the social and emotional well-being of individuals and families" (Red Horse, 1981, p. 1). The extended family is common among Native Americans; however, this concept of the extended family is different from what we envision from a Western perspective. For example, the Lakota tribe uses the term *tiospaye*, which constitutes a wide social network, including those who are not biologically related (Weaver & White, 1997). Within Western culture, parents are the primary relationship within the family. However, this is not the case in Native American culture. Grandparents assume a primary role, and, as elders, they are the leaders in the family system, responsible for the day-to-day decisions such as child rearing. Children are taught to treat all elders with respect and to address all elders as grandparents (Weaver & White, 1997).

To demonstrate how boundaries of family members extend, biological parents and aunts and uncles assume a parent role. The term *in-laws* does not exist (e.g., a "daughter-in-law" is instead called "daughter") (Sutton & Broken Nose, 1996). Families are established not only by blood or by marriage. Outsiders such as medicine people and nonblood relatives are also incorporated into the family (Sutton & Broken Nose, 1996). The Lakota have a term *mitakuye oyasin*, which means "all my relations" or "we are all related," to capture the essence of this interconnection between people, linking individuals from past and future generations (Weaver & White, 1997).

Given the value of families, it is not surprising that the collective unit is highly valued. The tribe and family take precedence over the individual. Harmony, cooperation, and according appropriate respect to individuals are emphasized (Brucker & Perry, 1998). Bands reflect this sense of cooperation. *Bands* are mutual assistance societies, whereby members share property (Kitano, 1997). They are characterized by mutual cooperation; in many ways, bands can be viewed as Native Americans' "welfare system." When some are viewed as too wealthy and others left with little sustenance, band organizations ensure that everyone is provided for while promoting a more democratic environment (Kitano, 1997).

Spirituality is a major component in the day-to-day lives of Native Americans who believe in a supreme, omnipotent creator whose name is rarely mentioned because it is so sacred (Pichette & Garrett, 1999). Of the three elements that comprise human beings—the mind, body, and spirit—the spirit is the most important because it is the essence of being (Pichette & Garrett, 1999). The spiritual beliefs and practices of Native Americans have also been a way to overcome despair and cope with the tremendous oppression and European American colonization (Yellow Bird, 2001).

Counseling with Native Americans requires that mental health professionals acquire in-depth knowledge about general as well as specific cultures and tribes. Because Native Americans are significantly underrepresented in counseling research (Delgado-Romero, Galván, Maschino, & Rowland, 2005), this knowledge base is in its early developmental stages. In addition, there is evidence that some Native American populations use traditional healing practices as a first option for care, even when seeking help from primary physicians (Buchwald, Beals, & Manson, 2000). Based on this realization, health care professionals need to consider ways to integrate these practices into counseling care after first learning about the purpose and anticipated outcomes of the practices (Norton & Manson, 1997). For example, in working with Lakota women, counselors need knowledge about how traditional viewpoints have changed in contemporary times, including a deep-seated sense of responsibility to ensure that family traditions and values are upheld while also achieving personal goals as family and community leaders (Roberts, Harper, Caldwell, & Decora, 2003). Finding ways to contribute to society in positive ways can become a therapeutic goal in a counseling setting while continuing to reflect traditional values in the lives of the Lakota women (Roberts et al, 2003, p. 22).

As part of a unique counselor education practicum experience, Anthony is participating as an observer during initial interviews with clients referred to the in-hospital multidisciplinary health psychology clinic. Patients referred for counseling are typically in the hospital due to acute medical problems and are undergoing treatment. Referrals are made by the attending physicians for assessment of psychological or emotional problems that may be interfering with the medical treatment regimen. Anthony has become comfortable with these initial bedside interviews, and now his supervisor, Dr. Phillips, assigns Mrs. Anderson's case to him to allow him to conduct his first solo interview. Mrs. Anderson is a Native American, age 63, with a history of diabetes and chronic lower back pain associated with a severe motor vehicle accident injury seven years ago. The referral notes that Mrs. Anderson is not cooperating with medical treatment designed to teach her how to manage her pain and refuses to speak to the physician or nurses about why she is "being difficult."

For Anthony, or any counselor seeking to establish a therapeutic relationship with a client of Native American heritage, it is essential to prepare for the initial interview by gathering as much information as is available about the individual as well as contextual information about the unique perspectives of the client's tribe. The goals of counseling with Native American clients include careful assessment of (1) level of acculturation (i.e., how the client views himself or herself—traditional, bicultural, assimilated, or marginal); (2) where the person lives (i.e., urban, rural, or reservation); and (3) tribe-specific structure, customs, and beliefs (Garrett & Herring, 2001). This information allows the counselor to gain insight into the lived experience of the client while demonstrating respect and acknowledgment of the importance of this experience in the life of the client. Retaining a nonassuming posture with Mrs. Anderson can assist Anthony in viewing her as the expert about her native culture as he gains insights into her current behavior.

Counseling with culturally diverse clients can be approached through use of the cross-cultural competencies developed by the American Counseling Association that highlight the need to assess personal values, biases, and attitudes regarding multicultural populations; to retain an awareness of the client's worldview; and to use culturally appropriate counseling methods and strategies (ACA, 1992). Using these competencies to guide continuing professional education as well as ongoing practice with culturally diverse clients increases opportunity to provide mental health and wellness services in meaningful ways. In addition, mindfulness about cultural messages that saturate the environment in which counselors and clients live can ensure that contemporary practice can adjust to shifts within and between cultures. The richness and heterogeneity of each of the cultural groups discussed are remarkable, especially in light of the "melting pot" stereotype that has been applied to diversity within the U.S. population.

THE ELDERLY: DEMOGRAPHIC TRENDS AND PSYCHOLOGICAL AND SOCIAL ISSUES

The professional fields of psychology and counseling have long recognized the distinct needs of the elderly. In 1945, the APA's Division on Maturity and Old Age was developed (Heppner, Casas, Carter, & Stone, 2000). The ACA includes the Association for Adult

Development and Aging, founded in 1986, as one of its 17 divisions. Each professional organization addresses counseling, advocacy, and educational issues of specific relevance to adults across the life span.

Demographic Characteristics

The elderly population is defined as 65 years and older and can be placed into three age groups—*young-old* (age 65 to 74 years), *middle-old* (75 to 84 years), and *oldest-old* (85 years and older) (Hutchinson, 1999). The elderly segment within the United States has increased dramatically and is expected to continue to increase at a more rapid pace than the general population (U.S. Census Bureau, 1996). In 2000, there were 35 million elderly in the United States, an increase of 12 percent since 1990 (Administration on Aging, 2001). Today, one in every eight Americans is an elder (Administration on Aging, 2001). By 2020, 14.1 percent of the population will be 65 years of age or older, a 3.1 percent increase from 2010 (U.S. Census Bureau, 2004).

This rapid growth is attributed to the "baby boom" generation and technological and medical advances. The baby boom generation consists of the 75 million Americans born between 1946 and 1964 who will become elders, with 65 years of age defined as elderly, beginning in 2011 through 2029. Second, due to medical advances, life expectancy in the United States has increased by 25 years for men and 30 years for women since 1900 (Ostir, 1999). In a 10-year span of time between 1990 and 2000, average life expectancy increased from 75.4 years to 80 years of age. The increase in the elderly population will concurrently increase the needs for mental health services, social and medical services, and economic support at an unprecedented rate. Life expectancy itself continues to increase for men and women and across major multicultural/ethic groups in the United States (U.S. Census Bureau, 2004), thereby suggesting the need to consider how the mental health needs of a diverse, expanding, and aged population will, and can be, met.

Risks to Health and Well-Being

As life expectancy increases, experts recognize a somewhat disconcerting parallel finding: The morbidity rate (i.e., the incidence of disease) has not decreased (Wolfe, 1993). Specifically, chronic disease and age-related disability are still common and are projected to remain issues of significance to an aging population well into this century. Hypertension, for example, places the elderly at greater risk for strokes and heart disease. More than half of all Americans over the age of 65 have hypertension (Wright, 1995). In addition, nearly a quarter of elders 85 years and older need assistance in order to live independently and 20 percent need help with day-to-day self-care (Atchley, 1997). In 1994, approximately 40 percent of the elderly who were not residing in institutions were limited by chronic illnesses, and of these, about 10 percent were unable to perform some activities of daily living, such as bathing, eating, and shopping (Administration on Aging, 1999).

Most of the issues elders confront revolve around age-related decline and loss (Hill, Thorn, & Packard, 2000). Deterioration in health and cognition occur. Losses may occur on an interpersonal level, such as death of a spouse, friends, and family members; on an occupational level, such as retirement; and on a social level, such as changes in social status, finances, and identity (Bar-Tur & Levy-Shiff, 2000). There is considerable variability in how elders will adapt to each of these changes as well as the challenges inherent in advanced life stages. The extent of an elder's resiliency and resources will play a role in sustaining a sense of well-being during a period of many losses and changes (Bar-Tur & Levy-Shiff, 2000).

With reference to social, physical, and mental changes, the extent to which an elder stabilizes, recovers, or improves following loss experiences is referred to as *resilience* (Ryff, Singer, Love, & Essex, 1998). Resilience is contingent on the amount and quality of the elder's resources in the areas of psychological, biological, social, and sociodemographic domains (Bar-Tur & Levy-Shiff, 2000). Marriage, for example, is a vital social resource that has tremendous impact on an elder's well-being. In fact, studies have demonstrated that losing a spouse is a significant predictor of subsequent illness and earlier death of the surviving spouse (Hutchinson, 1999). The extent of social support also contributes to psychological well-being, which buffers against adverse health effects such as functional impairment, mental health consequences such as depression, and social outcomes such as institutionalization (Bowling & Faquhar, 1991).

In Cummings's (2002) study of 57 elders residing in an assisted living facility, female gender, self-reported health, functional impairment, perceived social support, and participation in activities were significant predictors of psychological well-being. Interestingly, the impact of the variables of gender and health were reduced when social support was introduced into the regression model. In other words, perceived social support plays a large role in psychological well-being. Indeed, it is not necessarily the amount or frequency of involvement of social activities; rather, it is the perception of the quality of relationships that buffers against stress during old age—a time marked by many interpersonal losses.

Some elders will experience economic and financial adjustments that directly impact coping with loss during the elderly years of life. For families headed by a person over 65 years of age, income varies. Approximately 21 percent, for example, have incomes less than $15,000, and 41 percent had incomes of $30,000 and more (Ashford, LeCroy, & Lortie, 2001). Approximately 45 percent of those elders living alone or living with a relative had incomes below $10,000 (Ashford, LeCroy, & Lortie, 2001). Older women are more vulnerable to living in poverty compared to their male counterparts. In 2000, 12.2 percent of elderly women lived in poverty, whereas 7.5 percent of elderly men lived at or below the poverty line (Administration on Aging, 2001). Additionally, without social security benefits, elderly women would experience an increase in poverty as high as 50 percent over current rates. With social security, women account for 70 percent of the elderly poor population (Young, 2004). For widowed women, there is a 400 percent increase in the probability that they will live in poverty after retirement than men who retire. For the single or divorced woman who retires, the risk of living in poverty thereafter is five times more likely than for a married women (Young, 2004).

Elder Abuse

Mr. Jencks had returned to live with his mother, Mrs. Jencks, a widow of 10 years, after his wife kicked him out of the house. During this time, he became depressed and started to drink. Mrs. Jencks's neighbors became concerned recently that Mrs. Jencks had lost weight, looked uncharacteristically sad, and had a disheveled appearance. One day, Mrs. Jencks confided to one of her neighbors that ever since her son returned to live with her, he had been pilfering her social security checks. Initially, she noticed that small amounts of money were missing from her pocketbook, but now, Mr. Jencks threatens her both verbally and physically. Mrs. Jencks told her neighbor that he smashed and threw dishes at her until she handed her over her signed social security check to him. He had found a place that would cash it, no questions asked.

Elder abuse is referred to as an invisible problem, often hidden due to the isolation that many seniors experience in their care or home settings. In addition, societal perceptions about this period in life are still characterized by phrases such as "the golden years," suggesting a time in life when only good things happen, prosperity reigns, and the senior is surrounded by loving and supportive family and social networks. In this idealized world, the elder years are a time when children are grown up and married with families of their own, retirement is planned and anticipated as a positive life transition, and delayed interests can be pursued (i.e., travels and enjoyment of leisure time). Unfortunately, for far too many seniors, this idealized life chapter is not realized. It is estimated that 1.2 million elderly Americans are victims of abuse annually in the United States (Administration on Aging, 1999). In a national study conducted by the National Center on Elder Abuse in 1996, there were a total of 293,000 reports of elder abuse to Adult Protective Services in the United States. This was a 150 percent increase from the 117,000 reports in 1986 (Tatara & Kuzmeskus, 1997). Developing elder abuse incidence data is complex and convoluted. As with other forms of abuse for dependent or health-impaired individuals, abuse of elders is underreported and often perpetrated in the elder's home by a known person or family caretaker as well as in institutional settings (Hawes, 2002).

Pillemer and Finkelhor (1988) conducted one of the most well-known studies on elder abuse. A total of 2,000 noninstitutionalized elders living in the Boston area were surveyed. The researchers found that upon reaching 65 years and over, the overall prevalence rate of abuse was 3.2 percent. Specifically, 2 percent had experienced physical abuse, 1.1 percent experienced verbal abuse, and 0.4 percent experienced neglect. Similar proportions of men and women experienced abuse, and socioeconomic status and age were not related to abuse (Pillemer & Finkelhor, 1988).

Elder abuse also occurs within institutional residential settings where accurate prevalence data are difficult to obtain in spite of legislation mandating the reporting of institutional abuse existing in many states. In one nonprobability study, 36 percent of nursing and aide staff disclosed having witnessed at least one incident of physical abuse by other staff members in the preceding year (Pillemer & Moore, 1990). When asked whether they themselves perpetrated physical abuse against an elderly resident, 10 percent admitted they had (Pillemer & Moore, 1990). A national study of approximately 5,000 nursing homes between 1999 and 2001 found that more than 30 percent of these homes had accumulated over 9,000 abuse violations in this two-year period (Waxman, 2001). Clearly, the incidence of elder abuse, in all of its forms, suggests the need for counselor professionals to maintain awareness of this health issue, to support advocacy efforts on behalf of the elderly who are at risk for abuse, and to incorporate assessment of abuse or neglect when providing mental health services to the elderly.

Based on the challenges, risks, and threats that can impact the aging adult—across all cultural, ethnic, and diversity populations—one could characterize the later chapters of the life span as dangerous, fearsome, and vulnerable. Although there are true risks for many in the aging population, it is also a time in life characterized by resiliency, strength, wisdom, and spirituality. These crucial maturational characteristics have been acquired by the elderly during their journey through life, and thus any stereotypes of the ill, frail, and institutionalized elderly do not do justice to the tremendous vitality that can also be evident during the elderly years of living full and rewarding lives.

Sexuality and the Elderly

One example of elder resiliency and interest in living life to the fullest has to do with sexuality in the latter decades of life. Science has provided methods to ensure that sexual dysfunction associated with aging can be treated for both men and women who retain an interest in physical intimacy (Drench & Losee, 1996). According to Hillman (2000, p. 1), "Despite the potential differences in physical health and living arrangements, elderly adults can and do engage in the same type of sexual behaviors as their younger counterparts." Younger adults may view older adults in their seventies and eighties as nonsexual beings who, according to Butler, Lewis, and Sunderland (1998, p. 183),

1. do not have sexual desires
2. could not make love even if they did want to
3. are too fragile physically and it might hurt them
4. are physically unattractive and therefore sexually undesirable, and
5. would be engaging in behavior that is too shameful and decidedly perverse.

Such assumptions made about limited sexuality in the aging population clearly must be retired and replaced with accurate information about the sexuality and sexual behavior of older adults.

Counselors are likely to find increasing opportunities to provide counseling services to the escalating aged population and must maintain competencies to provide services based on a variety of developmental needs of this diverse population. Assumptions about what is acceptable for elderly adults regarding sexual activity must be carefully verified to ensure that stereotypes of the aged as nonsexual beings do not interfere with the counseling process. Issues of adult sexuality and sexual activity as a continuation of a life-long aspect of intimacy in the lives of clients can be addressed forthrightly and with sensitivity. At the same time, counselors must also be aware of risk factors for aging adults in terms of sexually transmitted diseases such as herpes, HIV/AIDS, or other diseases contracted through high-risk sexual activity (Calvet, 2003). When counseling the aged single client, it is essential that the issue of high-risk sexual behavior be addressed, including the topic of condom use. For counselors, this topic may be an uncomfortable one in general and more specifically with reference to clients who may be similar in age to the counselor's parents or grandparents. Seeking supervision when such issues become apparent is an appropriate strategy to ensure that the client's needs remain at the forefront of the counselor's attention.

WOMEN AS A DIVERSE POPULATION

By the 1970s, the women's movement in the United States had made great strides in raising awareness and implementing advocacy initiatives focused on the social realities impacting women as well as giving women a voice that framed emerging issues. Critically important issues were raised about fundamental assumptions that supported views about women's medical and mental health care needs. Criticisms about how scientific knowledge was formulated and research conducted were raised—for example, *who* defines the problems to be studied? *How* is the research to be conducted that will subsequently be applied to both men and women? *Who* are the research subjects/participants? and finally, *How* do we know that research conducted on male populations has relevance to female populations? Many argued that androcentric bias was introduced at various phases of the research process—from problem and hypothesis formulation, design of the research, data collection, and data interpretation (Harding, 1991). Groups who define what is worthy to be classified as a scientific problem also hold the power to shape perceptions in the world (Harding, 1991). At the beginning of the women's movement, women did not substantially contribute to this scientific process due to the structural obstacles in the scientific and academic community that minimized the opportunity of women to hold prestigious positions in research and scientific institutions.

The majority of early works in the empirical literature have primarily emphasized male and female differences and similarities (Enns, 2000). Minimal work was conducted to portray the unique impact of gender on individual, interpersonal, and structural factors. Out of this gap in the counseling, mental health, and psychology knowledge base, feminist psychotherapy emerged, advocating the view that external sources such as societal ideology and social structures affect behavior (Evans, Kincade, Marbley, & Seem, 2005; Gilligan, 1993). From this perspective, illness or symptoms cannot merely be viewed as internal problems, but as symptoms of oppression (Collins, 2002). Feminist theoretical orientations began to influence traditional psychological perspectives, moving from a limited view of intrapsychic processes to a more encompassing systemic model within larger societal contexts (Collins, 2002). This was in response to the changing social roles and problems encountered by women.

On organization levels, female professionals in psychology and counseling worked to ensure that the study of women's issues was integrated into the knowledge base and that research was promoted and disseminated. The Division of the Psychology of Women (Division 35) of the APA was developed in 1973 and quickly established a peer-reviewed journal, *Psychology of Women Quarterly* (Mednick & Urbanski, 1991). In 1975, APA also organized the Task Force on Sex Bias and Sex-Role Stereotyping in Psychotherapeutic Practice in order to develop training in the area of women's issues and gender bias (Dupuy & Ritchie, 1994). In counseling, similar trends were occurring. The ACA's Code of Ethics (ACA, 2005) addresses nonsexist practice, and the Council for Accreditation of Counseling and Related Educational Programs (CACREP) requires counseling programs to include gender issues in curricula development (CACREP, 2001; ACA, 2005; Dupuy & Ritchie, 1994).

Multiple Role Issues

As women's participation in the workforce has increased, negotiating multiple roles has become inevitable and often times complex. Shaevitz (1984) coined the term *Superwoman Syndrome* to describe women attempting to fulfill roles of wife, mother, employee, housekeeper, nurse, transportation provider, and sometimes student. By 1989, books such as *The Second Shift* by Arlie Hochshield had identified a mega-trend impacting women's lives: working one full-time job outside the home and returning to the homemaker job after the paid work shift is over. Goals to attain perfection in all roles as mother, employee, spouse, friend, daughter, sister, and so on, have been largely influenced by internal pressures. These internal pressures have been developed and reinforced over time by societal standards of what a "good woman" ought to be and how she *should* fulfill multiple obligations (McBride, 1997). Although the "second shift phenomenon" continues to resonate with women, continuous striving to fulfill multiple roles and become expert at multitasking inevitably results in role conflict and increased risk for adverse health consequences. Acceptance of the multiple-role paradigm in the lives of women at current levels of intensity is linked to both individual perception of expectations of women as well as societal and cultural expectations. One way to view this internal role evolution is to consider role centrality.

   Role centrality refers to the degree in which the role that a person develops or accepts serves as a vehicle for defining oneself (Stryker & Serpe, 1994). Therefore, the assumption is that if women are enacting a role that has meaning to them personally, they will be less distressed and experience greater psychological well-being (Thoits, 1992). Martire and Stephens (2000) conducted a study that examined the effects of role centrality for women who are simultaneously wife, mother, employee, and parent care provider and its relationship to depression and life satisfaction. A total of 296 participated in this longitudinal study of middle-generation women who provide care to their parents. The authors found that a greater sense of centrality of mother, wife, and employee roles was associated with higher levels of life satisfaction. A clear sense of employee centrality was associated with less depressive symptoms. These older women did, however, experience more intense effects of stress in relation to the roles of wife and employee. Women indicating centrality of the mother role, however, were protected from the negative effects of stress in this role. These findings suggest that the centrality of the mother role may be stress protective, whereas the role of employee carries higher risk for stress as does the wife role. At the same time, these women reported high rates of satisfaction with the centrality of work, wife, and mother roles. Confusion about how to interpret this study interfaces with the lived experience of women in contemporary society (i.e., many roles are important to women; women fulfill many roles; some of the roles women fulfill generate life satisfaction, whereas others are also linked to stressful outcomes). Maintaining awareness of the meaning of women's roles is an important aspect of counselor assessment.

      Guilt is a common reaction experienced by women who occupy roles of mother and employee. Gilligan (1993) argues that women are socialized with moral principles stemming from the ethics of care, meaning that a woman's identity revolves around relationships and a sense of responsibility for others. Elvin-Nowak's (1999) phenomenological study explored dimensions of guilt with 13 working mothers with at least one child under the age of 12 years. All interviews started off with an open-ended question: "Can you describe a situation in which you experienced feelings of guilt?" Probes were used to help participants elaborate and clarify responses. Findings indicated that the structure of guilt revolves around the relationship and responsibilities linked with the relationship. The responsibility emanates from all directions—responsibility for children, husband, parents, friends, co-workers, and sometimes oneself. Feelings of guilt experienced by these women include everyday guilt, which refers to a feeling that is always present or in the forefront, triggered by certain conditions. It is not necessarily guilt from an individual event; rather, it is feelings of continual responsibility for those around her. Inevitably, these feelings of guilt had to do with their children and what should or should not have been done in caring for and raising them. This study reinforces the notion of Gilligan's (1993) ethic of care and women's struggles with navigating multiple life roles.

Counselor sensitivity to the meaning of multiple roles for women clients goes beyond recognizing the status quo (e.g., the client is mother, wife, caregiver to an aging parent, employee, volunteer, etc.). Counselor assessment can focus more intently on the meaning that these roles have in the life of the client—each role's centrality. Understanding how the client comprehends, incorporates, and values each role can lead to exploration of needs for change in how roles are enacted, to shifting responsibility for certain roles or role components to others, and to a deeper acknowledgment by the client of the meaning that a role has in her life. It is often the process of reframing how the client perceives self in a particular role that can facilitate a healing process, lead to personal growth, and, in many cases, promote decision making that is health-giving rather than health-depleting. At the core of this perspective is acknowledgment that the impact of a vast number of psychological, social, and health issues affect women in ways that are unique, and recognition of this uniqueness can guide effective counseling interventions (Kopala & Keitel, 2003).

Intimate Violence

Domestic violence is a global social problem that extends across social, cultural, ethnic, socioeconomic, and regional boundaries (Fischbach & Herbert, 1997). Domestic violence ranges from physical, verbal, psychological/emotional, financial, and sexual aggression and abuse and is exceedingly complex in how it is researched. In the United States, one of the first national studies was conducted by Straus and Gelles (1990), who found that one-fourth of the couples surveyed reported at least one incident of physical aggression in their relationship. It is estimated that annually, one million women seek medical assistance for injuries resulting from battering (Goodman, Koss, & Russon, 1993). In a more recent national survey conducted among a representative sample of 16,000 men and women, 7 percent of the men and 20.4 percent of the women reported being physically assaulted by a current or former spouse or partner of the opposite sex (Tjaden & Thoennes, 2000). The estimates of intimate partner abuse against women varies, with estimates as high as 1.5 million women being abused by their partners annually (Tjaden & Thoennes, 2000). In 2001, "20 percent of all nonfatal violent crime experienced by women" was associated with intimate partner violence (U.S. Department of Justice, 2003).

Domestic violence does not discriminate according to racial, ethnic, or class boundaries. In a sample of 258 Korean American couples, Kim and Sung (2000) found that 19 percent of Korean Americans experienced at least one incident of minor physical assault by a spouse during the year. In another study with 262 Chinese American men and women in Los Angeles County, Yick (1999) examined the scope of physical and verbal abuse within the last 12 months and during the course of their lifetime. A large percentage (81 percent) reported verbal abuse in the last 12 months and 85 percent reported verbal abuse during their lifetime; 7 percent reported physical spousal abuse in last 12 months and 18 percent for lifetime.

In the southwestern part of the United States, Fairchild, Fairchild, and Stoner (1998) interviewed 341 Navajo Native American women from a health clinic. They found that 52.5 percent reported at least one domestic abuse episode by a male partner during their lifetime, and 16.4 percent reported current domestic violence during the past year. In an American Indian community in Arizona, 31 percent of the respondents reported domestic assaults (Teufel-Shone, Staten, Irwin, Bravo, & Waykayuta, 2005). These figures suggest that domestic violence in ethnic minority families is a distinct social problem, yet it must also be noted that such reports cannot be applied to all members of a particular ethnic or cultural population. For example, Williams and Tubbs (2002) suggest that views of prevalence of intimate partner violence in the African American community can be monolithic, resulting in a "one size fits all" perspective (e.g., occurrence is frequent in African American homes in general). This is an inaccurate assumption for any cultural or ethnic population.

Mental health counselors need to recognize that although gender is an important variable that brings women of all colors together, other elements such as racism, shame, discrimination, language barriers, prejudice, and different cultural value systems color life experiences of ethnic minority women in ways that make their social realities different from Anglo-American women. These differentiating factors can also influence help-seeking behavior when intimate partner violence has occurred. For example, Huisman (1996) found that Asian battered women are less likely to call a hotline for assistance. In addition, Western notions of empowerment may not speak to ethnic minority women whose culture is more collectivistic (Rimonte, 1991); therefore, interventions need to be more culturally sensitive and relevant.

Domestic violence among elderly women is also not atypical. One of the reasons why intimate violence is seldom studied among elderly women is because domestic violence within this population has been investigated primarily in the field of elder abuse rather than domestic violence (Vinton, 1998). Some studies do suggest that intimate violence among older couples can be better understood by the abuser–victim dynamics of the domestic violence model than the elder abuse model, which is based on the concept of caregiver stress (Breckman & Adleman, 1988; Pillemer & Finkelhor, 1988). Reporting of intimate partner violence among older women is limited due to many of the same factors that influence younger women: fear of not being believed, history of growing up at a time when domestic violence was not discussed or disclosed, and misconceptions about the definitions of domestic abuse (Zink, Jacobsen, Regan, & Pabst, 2004).

Studies have generally found that physical abuse among couples declines in old age (Pillemer & Finkelhor, 1988). However, older men, compared to their younger cohorts, are at higher risk for abuse by their wives. In a study conducted by Pillemer and Finkelhor

(1988), older men were twice as likely as women to be abused by their partners. Other studies, however, report that older men are more likely to perpetrate physical violence, whereas older women are more likely to engage in psychological abuse or neglect (Crichton, Bond, Harvey, & Ristock, 1999). Seaver (1996) found that among 132 women, ages 53 to 90, seeking elder abuse services, 58 percent were abused by their husbands. Vinton's study (1992) of 132 older women receiving shelter services reports that the majority were victimized by their spouses.

Dating violence perpetuated against young women has been identified as a significant issue impacting individuals, families, and communities. The following case scenario, unfortunately, is not uncommon:

> Tammy, a 17-year-old junior in high school was recently referred by the school guidance counselor to the nurse when the counselor saw deep bruising on Tammy's arm. The nurse was able to establish rapport with Tammy, and Tammy eventually told the nurse that Dan, her boyfriend, had been waiting for her at her home after school. When she got home late from cheerleading practice, he grabbed her hard and jerked her arm, leaving the bruises. He had accused her of being unfaithful to him, shouting, "You're just a slut!" Apparently, this was not the first incident where she had been physically abused by Dan. Dan was possessive of Tammy, often got into bouts of jealousy, called her constantly on her cell phone, and demanded that she tell him where she was at all times.

According to the U.S. Department of Justice (2003), women ages 16 to 24 are most vulnerable to intimate partner violence. In other words, women are particularly vulnerable and more likely to be victims of dating/domestic violence than men, and most of these women are in their late teens and early twenties (Family Violence Prevention Fund, 2001). Studies on dating violence (specifically, physical aggression) have resulted in prevalence estimates ranging from 14.3 percent to a high of 60 percent (Bernard & Bernard, 1983; Deal & Wampler, 1986; Gray & Foshee, 1997; Riggs, O'Leary, & Breslin, 1990; Neufeld, McNamara, & Ertl, 1999). In addition, stalking is a pattern of violence that is typically linked to prior intimate partner violence (Tjaden & Thoennes, 1998).

The psychological consequences of violence are profound. Victims of intimate partner or marital violence report four times the rate of depression and 5.5 times the suicide attempts compared to their nonvictimized counterparts (Gelles & Straus, 1988). Physical violence is often accompanied by emotional and verbal abuse; consequently, the victim's self-esteem gradually deteriorates, leading to a distortion of reality and an increased vulnerability to anxiety, depression, post-traumatic stress disorder, and a host of somatic symptoms (Coker, Smith, Bethea, King, & McKeown, 2000; Csoboth, Birkás, & Purebl, 2005; Zink, Jacobsen, Regan, & Pabst, 2004).

Based on the pervasiveness of the consequences of intimate partner violence on women of all ages, counselor professionals must ensure that careful assessment of overt symptoms is considered as well as assessment for intimate partner violence when this is not the presenting problem. The issues associated with underreporting and nonreporting of domestic violence provide a clear rationale for such an approach. As with other diversity issues that counselors review with clients and families during the counseling process, awareness of what is not being discussed within a session can lead to a redirected focus on intimate partner violence and abuse when sensitive questions are posed by the counselor.

Counselor knowledge of intimate partner violence and abuse characteristics occurring in all age, cultural, and ethnic populations guides treatment planning. At times this planning and intervention are crisis based when the client is in imminent danger from her intimate partner. Other situations arise during a course of counseling that reveals the ongoing nature of domestic violence that must be addressed in this setting. Recognition that females of all ages continue to be overrepresented in domestic violence statistics does not, however, minimize the rise in domestic violence incidents perpetrated by women (Abel, 2001; Babcock, Miller, & Siard, 2003). Awareness of and sensitivity to the issues associated with intimate partner violence guide treatment planning for both male and female clients. Assumptions about the incidence of domestic violence must be continually tempered with review of current research to ensure that assessment and treatment avoid bias or misunderstanding of the client's reality. Added to this complex mix is an additional layer of sensitivity needed to ensure that ethnic and cultural assumptions about domestic violence are avoided.

SEXUAL ORIENTATION: ISSUES OF COUNSELOR AWARENESS AND SENSITIVITY

The terminology used to identify individuals who are gay, lesbian, bisexual, or transgendered continues to be controversial. There is no universal agreement about terms, and the terms vary across time, geography, and cultures (Hunter, Shannon, Knox, & Martin, 1998). For example, the terminology used for transgendered persons have included "gender bender, gender outlaws, gender trash, gender queer, [and] transsexual lesbian . . . [which] reflects the diversity within this community as well as the ongoing struggle for self-definition" (Carroll, Gilroy, & Ryan, 2002, p. 132). Consequently, it is difficult to conduct prevalence studies to find out how many people in the United States can be designated as members of these diversity groups. One study conducted by Gonsiorek, Sell, and Weinrich (1995) estimated that the prevalence rate for same-gender sexual orientation in the United States ranged between 4 and 17 percent. Ettner (1999) reported that estimates might vary with a range of 3 to 5 percent to a range of 8 to 10 percent for those who fall in the transgender category. Prior to and during the 1950s, homosexuality was illegal in every state (D'Augelli & Garnets, 1995, cited in Hunter et al, 1998). In the 1960s, gays and lesbians were still harassed, and homosexuality was viewed as pathological, or as a condition that had to be socially controlled by treatment or punishment (Hunter et al, 1998).

The gay and lesbian movement emerged with prominence during the 1970s when the Civil Rights movement was at its height. Organizations such as the Gay Liberation Front and Gay Activist Alliance began to promote gay and lesbian rights in the late 1960s, and by the mid-1970s, 5,000 marchers were participating in gay pride parades (Heppner et al, 2000). During this time, in the psychology and mental health fields, the status of homosexuality was still much debated, with the *DSM-III* labeling homosexuality as a psychological disorder (Rubinstein, 1995).

The transgender movement emerged in more contemporary times. In 1992, an international conference on transgender law and employment policy was organized to fight for the rights of transgendered individuals. In 1996, at a meeting of the American Academy of Pediatrics, there was a demonstration on behalf of the rights for infants born with ambiguous genitalia (Carroll et al, 2002). However, the advent of cyberspace technology has helped to disseminate information about transgender issues and has allowed transgendered individuals to provide support to one another through technology (e.g., in chatrooms) (Carroll et al, 2002).

Carroll and Colleagues (2002) note that transgender issues have been pathologized; for example, terms such as *gender dysphoria* and *gender-identity disorder* reflect dysfunction. In the 1950s, individuals who wanted to obtain sex reassignment surgery or hormonal interventions were required to obtain therapy. It was only after therapy had been completed with a positive recommendation from a therapist was the intervention approved. For genital surgery, a second evaluation and recommendation from a mental health professional was required.

The ethical debate revolving around therapy and counseling as tools used to change the sexual orientation of homosexual clients had continued until 1997, when the APA passed a resolution expressing concern about conversion therapy. In 1998, ACA passed a similar resolution (Throckmorton, 1998). In other words, ACA was opposed to conversion or reparative therapies if these therapies depict "gay, lesbian or bisexual youth as mentally ill," or if a counselor spreads inaccurate information or has "unfounded beliefs" about sexual orientation (ACA, 1998, pp. 1–2).

The fields of psychology and counseling have recognized that historically there has been scant scholarly, theoretical, and research materials written to prepare professionals in this area. A series of actions have begun to impact this gap: (1) in 1980, the Committee on Lesbian and Gay Concerns (CLGC) was formed; (2) in 1985, the Society for the Psychological Study of Gay and Lesbian Issues was developed (Division 44) (Heppner et al, 2002); and (3) in 1997, the Association for Gay, Lesbian, and Bisexual Issues in Counseling was formed as a division within the ACA. With the stated mission "to educate mental health service providers about issues confronting gay, lesbian, bisexual and transgender (GLBT) individuals," the ACA recognized the implications for counseling practice of diversity as an inclusive, expanding construct that directly influences quality of services provided (Association for Gay, Lesbian, and Bisexual Issues in Counseling, 1997). As awareness, understanding, and research on the needs of gay, lesbian, bisexual, and transgendered individuals have increased, the ACA Code of Ethics (2005) has recognized the importance of such counselor preparedness by infusing sensitivity to gender issues, for example, in assessment, education, and competence sections of the code.

Heterosexism: Prejudice and Oppression

Much of societal beliefs about gender and sexuality are rooted in *heterosexism*, an orientation that adheres to the notion that individuals' intimate behavior should be directed toward people of the opposite sex (Herek, 2000). Heterosexism can breed prejudice, discrimination, and irrational fears and attitudes toward gays, lesbians, transgendered persons, and other groups who do not conform to societal expectations regarding sexual norms (Lance, 2002).

There are two forms of heterosexism—one operates on a cultural level and one that operates on an individual level (Hunter et al, 1998). *Cultural heterosexism* refers to societal beliefs that heterosexual affection is superior and the only accepted form of sexual expression. This belief is manifested in people's perceptions and the language they employ when discussing or thinking about those with different sexual orientations. For example, in the conservative religious community, gays, lesbians, and transgendered individuals are considered "sinners" and "evil" (Palma & Stanley, 2002). Even in the professional literature, homosexuality was considered a mental illness in the early editions of the *Diagnostic and Statistical Manual of Mental Disorders (DSM)*. Attitudes are then translated into behaviors, and gays, lesbians, and transgendered individuals often face discrimination in their day-to-day lives. Most gays and lesbians are excluded from most civil rights legislation or can be subject to criminal penalties according to sodomy laws (Hunter et al, 1998).

The second form of heterosexism, *individual heterosexism*, is manifested as psychological heterosexism that is expressed in reactions, feelings, and behaviors toward gays, lesbians, and transgendered persons. Open hostility, derogatory jokes and comments, and verbal abuse are common examples of psychological heterosexism (Hunter et al, 1998). Furthermore, not only do nonheterosexually oriented individuals experience these prejudicial attitudes from others but they may also internalize these attitudes, which can ultimately generate intense feelings of low self-esteem and self-loathing. In turn, these dramatic psychological/emotional responses can then lead to a host of mental health issues (Palma & Stanley, 2002). Hence, the counseling professional must be sensitive to the impact of the visible as well as invisible reactions experienced by the gay, lesbian, or transgendered individual client.

Violence and Mental Health

In 1989, the U.S. Department of Health and Human Services estimated that gay adolescents and adults are at greater risk for suicide compared to their heterosexual counterparts. A host of risk factors exist, including lack of social support, ostracism and rejection from family and friends, stress stemming from not conforming to traditional gender roles, and fear of discrimination and prejudice (Sadovsky, 2000). Substance abuse poses another significant risk factor for some nonheterosexual individuals. The prevalence of alcohol abuse is comparable among hetereosexual and homosexual men, but the incidence of alcohol abuse is higher among gay and lesbian women compared to their female heterosexual counterparts (Sadovsky, 2000).

Given the hostile environment that gays, lesbians, and transgendered individuals are exposed to, violence is not uncommon. The following scenario highlights the fact that we live in a homophobic society, where gays and lesbians experience an array of anti-gay victimizations.

> John sensed that he was gay when he started junior high school, but he did not come out until he left home to go to college. Living several thousands of miles from his family, he felt a bit safer in openly stating that he was gay. John's parents were devout Catholics; his father was a public school teacher and football coach. John's two older and younger brothers were all avid athletes. John grew up hearing that "real men" don't cry and never to give up and "tough it out."

John tried his best to fit in with his brothers, but never really managed to do so. It was a relief to go away to college.

In college, John was active in gay and lesbian student organizations and events. He finally told his parents over the holidays during his freshman year. His father was stunned, and the first thing he exclaimed was, "How on earth did I raise a fairy?" His mother cried, asking John to repent because he was going to go to hell. She wanted him to speak to the priest. John was devastated yet he knew that his decision to tell his parents was right for him. Although his visit was shorter than he had planned, he returned to school to a support system that helped him create his identity as a person able to cope with the challenges he faced and would continue to face with his family.

The issue of anti-gay violence and victimization is a severe form of psychological heterosexism (Hunter et al, 1998). Waldo, Hesson-McInnis, and D'Augelli (1998) term this as *heterosexist victimization*, which refers to behaviors ranging from verbal harassment to physical assault and murder (e.g., hate crimes/homicide), stemming from an ideology that stigmatizes nonheterosexual behaviors. According to the Coalition of Anti-Violence Programs, in 1996, there were approximately 2,500 reports of hate-motivated crimes based on sexual orientation, which was a 6 percent increase from 1995 (cited in www.skeptictank.org/agayhate.htm). According to a study conducted by Jay and Young (1977, cited in Herek, 1989), more than a quarter (27 percent) of their 4,400 male respondents experienced at least one incident of physical abuse that was associated with homosexuality, and over three-quarters (77 percent) had experienced verbal abuse. It is likely that these figures are substantially higher, given the reluctance that many victims experience, due to shame, fear, or embarrassment, to discuss similar experiences (Hunter et al, 1998).

There is a developing literature within the counseling professions dedicated to addressing the counseling needs of gay, lesbian, bisexual, and transgendered clients and their families. Although some conflict within the counseling professions exists regarding the focus of counseling (e.g., conversion therapy or addressing presenting psychological or emotional problems using gender-sensitive methods) (Cochran, 2001; Malley, 2002; Milton & Coyle, 1998), the trend is clearly in the direction of developing gender-identity–sensitive methods that guide the counselor's unbiased approach to assessment, treatment planning, and the counseling process.

PHYSICAL DISABILITY: INCLUSIVE CONSIDERATION OF DIVERSITY IN COUNSELING

Although the Civil Rights movement and the passing of the Civil Rights Act of 1964 helped alleviate some of the blatant discrimination toward women and ethnic minorities, particularly in the workplace, individuals with physical disabilities did not see the same gains during this time (Thomas, 2001). In a society that favors fitness, agility, sports, and individualism, individuals with physical disabilities are often shunned or responded to as if they were invisible (Helwig & Holicky, 1994). In 1990, the Americans with Disabilities Act

(ADA) was passed as antidiscrimination legislation with the goal of guaranteeing that Americans with disabilities are treated fairly in the employment, education, health, transportation, and other public service arenas (Colbridge, 2002). *Disability* is defined as either a physical or mental impairment that interferes with at least one major life activity (Colbridge, 2002). Disability can be conceptualized as encompassing three components: (1) a physical and/or mental disorder that interrupts normal processes; (2) impairment, which is defined as the limit or loss of a person's level of functioning due to physical, anatomical, or mental factors; and (3) the inability to perform or the limited ability to function in socially expected roles and tasks (Nagi, 1991).

According to the U.S. Census Bureau (1997), 52.6 million people in the United States had some sort of disability, and 33 million had a severe disability. When examining the adult population (i.e., 21 to 64 years of age), 30.6 million had a disability, and 57 percent of them were employed (U.S. Census Bureau, 2000c). The figures vary by the specific type of disability; for example, it is estimated that annually in the United States, 100,000 people injure their spinal cords, leading to some form of permanent paralysis (Chase, Cornille, & English, 2000). An estimated 14.3 million individuals over 15 years of age have a mental disability—1.9 million with Alzheimer's disorder, senility, or dementia, and 3.5 million with a learning disability (U.S. Census Bureau, 2000d).

Onset of disability also varies. In 2000, the Harris Survey of Americans with Disabilities was conducted with 997 adults with disabilities and 953 adults without disabilities. One-quarter of the sample reported that their disabilities began between birth and adolescence (i.e., 0 to 19 years of age), slightly over one-quarter (27 percent) during early adulthood (20 to 39 years), another 28 percent during middle age (40 to 55 years), and 21 percent after age 55 (National Organization on Disability, 2001).

Significant gender differences exist in the types and prevalence of disabilities experienced. The proportion of men diagnosed with spinal cord injuries and head injuries exceeds that for women by a ratio of four to one (Nosek & Hughes, 2003). Both genders experience back disorders at equivalent rates but this is where the similarities end. Men experience higher rates of cardiovascular diseases (11.4 percent compared to 9.7 percent for women), whereas females are more than nine times more likely to be diagnosed with fibromyalgia, systemic lupus erythematosus (nine times more often), and osteoporosis (four times more frequently) compared to their male counterparts (Nosek & Hughes, 2003).

Psychosocial Adjustment

Research on coping with physical disability has produced divergent views in part because researchers have not come to a consensus about what constitutes "adjustment" or the outcomes that reflect "adjustment" and "coping." For example, does it entail a linear, stage-like progression of reactions or is it individually determined? Or does an individual have to experience a set of psychological reactions such as depression or anxiety (which we typically conceptualize as maladaptive) as part of the adjustment process (Livneh & Wilson, 2003)? The empirical literature, however, is in agreement that personal and contextual variables influence how individuals with disabilities adapt. These variables include sociodemographic variables (i.e., age of onset of disability, marital status, employment, etc.), disability-related variables (i.e., severity of disability, level of functioning), personal-related variables (i.e., self-concept, locus of control), and environmental/social variables (i.e., level of social support, existing environmental barriers) (Livneh & Wilson, 2003; Livneh & Antonak, 1997). There is some evidence that as the interval from the time of injury extends, individuals with disability experience better self-image and less psychological stress (Vappu & Krause, 1998).

The qualitative interviews incorporated into this study indicated that those who were more adjusted were those who had friends and social support who were either physically disabled as well as able bodied and who participated in a range of activities. Those who were not well adjusted were those individuals who looked for a scapegoat among the many doctors and insurance companies involved in their care and those who were continually seeking a new operation or medicine to cure them (Vappu & Krause, 1998). The literature demonstrates that psychosocial outcomes are, in fact, mediated by a host of variables, as illustrated by compliance with prescribed exercise regimens with chronic debilitating physical conditions (Marks & Allegrante, 2005), psychiatric reactions to the vagaries of chronic illness such as multiple sclerosis (Randolph & Arnett, 2005), or coping with the aftermath of cerebrovascular stroke (Murray & Harrison, 2004).

How disabilities are defined and conceptualized also influences client adjustment and achievement of goals for optimal levels of functioning, engagement with daily living, and defining the self. According to Livneh and Parker (2005), psychological adaptation to disability may be viewed through the lenses of four different conceptual models, each having usefulness for counselors working with disabled clients around issues associated with disabling conditions. For example, if the counselor views disability due to a chronic illness as a stepwise, progressive process consisting of accomplishment of successive stages of adjustment (e.g., shock/disbelief, anger, denial, etc.), the counseling interventions reflect this perspective (Livneh & Antonek, 2005). On the other hand, if the counselor views psychological adjustment to disability according to the interactive model, the client's experience includes intraindividual variables such as a physical limitation and the psychological responses, strengths, and limitations of the person. These variables interact with environmental variables that can include social and vocational issues the individual confronts (Livneh & Parker, 2005).

A more contemporary perspective embraces chaos and complexity theory, popularized by Gleick (1987), to suggest that psychosocial adjustment to chronic illness or disability is neither nonlinear (i.e., stage driven) nor limited by interactions between the individual and the environment (Livneh & Parker, 2005). Instead, adaptation can be viewed as dynamic and highly individualized, and therefore counselors need not limit their assessment of client needs to preconceived models of disability coping.

Life Satisfaction

In the 2000 Harris Survey of Americans with Disabilities, only one-third (33 percent) of the sample of disabled respondents stated that they were very satisfied with life compared to two-thirds of their nondisabled counterparts (National Organization on Disability, 2002). However, level of life satisfaction is mediated by a host of factors, such as employment status, level of social support, satisfaction of family closeness, satisfaction with personal assistance, locus of control, and acceptance of disability (Chase et al, 2000). Chase and colleagues (2000) found that individuals with spinal cord injury who took responsibility in directing their personal assistance services reported greater levels of perceived control in their lives and greater life satisfaction. Employment status also predicts life satisfaction, since work can positively affect self-esteem and self-identity. These same researchers found that those who were disabled and employed at least part-time perceived greater control and more satisfaction with life.

In a qualitative study of 18 women with different physical disabilities and varying levels of severity in their disabilities, Nosek, Hughes, Howland, and Young (2004) conducted a focus group and in-depth interviews (for those who were unable to get to the focus group) about how these women defined wellness. One of the prominent themes that emerged was that wellness was integrated with both positive mental health and physical health states. The importance of feeling in control and maintaining hope and optimism, of having supportive friends and family, of engaging in leisure activities, and of experiencing health-promoting behaviors all contributed to positive self-esteem, which ultimately positively impacts life satisfaction and outlook. Alison's situation provides insights that counselors can incorporate into assessment and practice.

> Alison, 23 years old, was born with spina bifida. She underwent multiple surgeries throughout her childhood, and continues to require medical supervision due to the paralysis in her legs that necessitates use of a wheelchair. She is being seen in counseling following a suicide attempt, and has started taking antidepressant medication. As her first session begins, Alison states, "I don't want to talk about my disability at all! I'm here to talk about the break-up with my boyfriend and why he broke up with me. Don't even bring up why I have to use this wheelchair!" The counselor wants to be sensitive to Alison's immediate needs but also thinks that the disability may have been a factor in the break-up.

In Alison's case, she is clearly stating what she wants to focus on during counseling, specifically needing to state the boundaries for the initial session. The counselor is making an assumption that may interfere with "hearing" what Alison has to say in this session, and thus the counselor's sensitivity to the client's disability and its impact may be misdirected. Given the complex myriad of factors that affect the psychosocial well-being of individuals with disabilities, psychologists and counselors must recognize that individuality in adjustment to and coping with disabilities is just that: individualized. Providing relevant and sensitive interventions, then, involves understanding theory and research about various disabilities as well as recognizing that each client presents with a unique perspective.

In addition to sensitivity to client needs in therapy contexts, voices need to continue to advocate on behalf of those with disabilities. In the 1970s, several psychologists with disabilities met at a series of APA conventions (American Psychological Association, 2003). Their efforts led to the formation of a task force that focused on psychology and handicaps. Later, this task force implemented the Committee on Disabilities and Handicaps within APA, which met formally in 1985. This committee continues to ensure that a disability perspective is infused in every aspect of psychology (American Psychological Association, 2003).

The ACA recognized the same need and developed a division identified as the American Rehabilitation Counseling Association (ARCA). This division is charged with educating the public so as to eliminate myths about disabilities and with promoting best practices in clinical practice and expanding the empirical knowledge base (ARCA, 2003). The National Rehabilitation Counseling Association (NRCA) is another organization that represents rehabilitation counselors. The NRCA was founded in 1958 to advance the profession of rehabilitation counseling, and the peer-reviewed journal, *Journal of Applied Rehabilitation Counseling*, seeks to keep rehabilitation counselors abreast of the latest legislation, best practices, and research (National Rehabilitation Counseling Association, no date).

The integration of disability-sensitive practices into research and service delivery represents a significant area in which counselors can implement standards of practice accepted by the counseling professions. For the nondisabled counselor working with disabled clients, it is critically important to acquire knowledge of client needs that spans diversity in disabilities that are inclusive of physical and psychological conditions. He or she must also acquire insight into personal assumptions that are thought to be sensitive to diversity, yet that may also limit the ability of the counselor to fully grasp client needs. As we consider the issues associated with counseling multicultural and diverse clients, ongoing awareness of the unique perspectives of clients serves as a foundational source of expertise that can guide perceptive counseling practices.

MULTICULTURALISM AND DIVERSITY IN COUNSELING: CONSIDERATIONS AND ISSUES

The topics of multiculturalism and diversity are complex and reflect the differences within and between providers and consumers of counseling services. Awareness of these differences supports enhanced practice, curiosity about clients served, and personal growth and expansion as a counseling professional. Issues surrounding the theory, research, and practice linked to multiculturalism and diversity will continue to require concerted attention in counselor education, practice, and advocacy. Although challenges remain in accomplishing the goal of ensuring that all clients receive culture/ethnic/diversity-sensitive counseling services, actions by professional associations as well as counselors in every area of practice have worked toward achieving this goal. With time and continued commitment to this worthy goal, the counseling professions can ensure that caring, sensitive, and highly professional help to clients will become the norm for all clients, regardless of origin, nationality, gender, or ethnicity. This pathway to this goal is clear.

As counselor professionals in counseling, psychology, social work, and human services focus on multicultural and diversity issues as they are presented in practice, it is helpful to conceptualize this process in terms of two central perspectives: (1) foundational knowledge about cultural, ethnic, and diversity populations based on accumulated research; and (2) person-specific knowledge about how culture, ethnicity, and diversity identity are revealed in the lived experience of the client. Each step in the counseling process can be informed by these two levels of awareness, knowledge and sensitivity, as depicted in Table 3.1.

Using the two-perspective approach, counselors will acquire knowledge and information about the client population that includes general themes that characterize the cultural

TABLE 3.1   Culture, Ethnicity, and Diversity: Infusion of Knowledge, Awareness, and Sensitivity into the Counseling Process

COUNSELOR PERSPECTIVE	ASSESSMENT	TREATMENT PLANNING	TREATMENT IMPLEMENTATION	OUTCOME EVALUATION
Population Overview: Acquire multicultural, ethnic, and diversity general knowledge, awareness, and sensitivity information.	Review standards of practice for assessment with multicultural/ diverse populations. Acquire information about client's culture, ethnicity, or diversity population norms.	Review research to identify effective methods and strategies appropriate for client(s) with specific culture, ethnic, or diversity background.	Acquire additional information as treatment progresses; integrate into treatment process through verification with client.	How is outcome evaluated when counseling is provided for population? Do these methods "fit" with current counseling experience? If not, focus on person-specific criteria to determine outcome effectiveness.
⬇	⬇	⬇	⬇	⬇
Individual/Specific: Acquire multicultural, ethnic, and diversity knowledge, awareness, and sensitivity information. What does counselor need to know about this *specific* client?	Develop assessment questions/items or observations focused on lived experience of client linked to culture, ethnicity, or diversity. Does client experience "fit" with general understanding of culture, ethnicity, or diversity?	What will work best for this particular client? Is presenting problem addressed in terms of unique client perspective of lived experience and worldview? Integrate unique perspective of client into treatment plan.	Implement treatment based on person-specific assessment that reflects knowledge of population as well as unique lived experience, nature of presenting problem, and interventions that are culture, ethnicity, and diversity sensitive.	How does client define successful outcome? How does this match counselor's perceptions? Will counselor alter own hypotheses about successful outcomes?
				⬇
				What learnings will counselor identify as result of counseling experience with this client? How will insights be applied to future clients?

or ethnic group. For example, in certain Asian cultures, beliefs about the collective unit or family, as opposed to individual independence, can shape the nature of the psychological or emotional problem that becomes the subject of help-seeking behavior. This general knowledge about a cultural group is quite valuable to the counselor, who then includes it as context to efforts to find out from the client his or her unique perspective. In this way, general information sensitizes the counselor to a cultural difference that must be incorporated into assessment. If the client in this example is a third-generation Asian American, he may not fully subscribe to the dominant belief about individualism, and this understanding then must be taken into account in assessing his needs, receptivity to counseling interventions, or needs to modify initial treatment plans.

It is the counselor's responsibility to ensure that sensitivity to cultural, ethnic, and diversity is communicated to the client in clear and respectful ways that acknowledge what the counselor does and does not yet understand about the population or individual. Participation in multicultural or diversity counseling provides challenging opportunities to rethink assumptions about how people are different from one another in visible ways as well as in ways that we may not often consider. As discussed in this chapter, outward similarities in appearance do not guarantee that the counselor and client are "alike"; rather, the sensitive counselor retains a "no assumptions" posture to ensure that the client's worldview from both the between-culture as well as the within-culture perspectives can be explored.

DISCUSSION TOPICS/QUESTIONS

1. Some people maintain that counseling and therapy are "Western creations." Using an example of a specific ethnic minority group, identify specific cultural value and belief systems associated with the group. Then identify specific values espoused in counseling and therapy. Compare the two lists of values and norms to determine intersections of compatibility or lack of information.

2. You have been asked to form a committee on multiculturalism at your workplace. It has become obvious that two factions within this committee have emerged. One group argues for an inclusive definition whereas the other group firmly believes in an exclusive definition of multiculturalism. In order for you to bring the two groups together, you want to highlight the advantages and disadvantages of each perspective. Summarize the merits and limitations for the inclusive and the exclusive perspectives of multiculturalism and suggest your own solution to this stalemate.

3. Sita has recently attended a group for immigrant women in the community to help them improve their English skills. Sita, her husband, and their two young children recently immigrated from Pakistan. One day, Sita came in with a black eye and some bruises on her neck. The counselor waited until the group was over to ask Sita about her bruises. Sita began to cry. She said that her husband was upset that the long distance telephone bill was so high and that she better obey him and not make so many calls back home to her family. He is the head of the household and she is to obey him. He believes that hitting her every so often is a good disciplining technique to remind her who is the head of the household. Analyze the differences in how a counselor with an "emic" and "etic" perspective would handle this scenario.

4. The purpose of this question is to help increase your self-awareness about the sources of your stereotypes.

   a. Make a list of everything (behaviors, traits, adjectives, images, etc.) you have ever seen, heard, or have been told about Native Americans.
   b. Review your list, and indicate a "P" on any items that are the result of information acquired based on *your personal experiences.*
   c. Review your list, and indicate with an "O" on any items on the list that are the result of information acquired based *on other people in your life* (family, friends, co-workers, etc.).
   d. Review your list, and indicate with an "M" any items that are the result of information acquired by the *media* (television, books, movies, magazines, advertisements, etc.).
   e. Review your list, and indicate other sources where you may have derived your items. Discuss the extent to which these stereotypes are based on reality.

5. Based on your observations, how are cultural and psychological heterosexism manifested in daily life? How do these observations relate to the counselor–client match? Identify four outcomes of a poor counselor–client match. What makes each of these factors detrimental to the success of the counseling experience?

6. In the case of Jasmine, Steve has to find a way to suspend his own judgment about her traditional cultural beliefs while finding common ground to provide counseling assistance. Develop a script for Steve and Jasmine that includes his statements, questions, and comments. Limit this script to a three-minute exchange.

7. As the counselor for Mrs. Delgado, you will need to determine where to focus in terms of the identified problems you'll address in counseling. Discuss how you will determine your treatment goals, the resources you will need to accomplish this task, and any concerns you have about working with this client.

8. You have been seeing Mrs. Graning (72 years old) for two months following the death of her husband after a lengthy illness. Mrs. Graning cared for her husband for three years while he underwent surgery, radiation therapy, and finally chemotherapy. In the session today, Mrs. Graning brings up her dating of a man who attends her grief support group. What are some of the key issues that Mrs. Graning needs to consider before she pursues this relationship further?

9. Carolyn has seen you in outpatient counseling in the past year in association with anxiety management. She has made very solid and sustained progress in counseling and has not been seen for two months. She calls you today because she needs an appointment as soon as she can get one. In this session, Carolyn describes a return of her anxieties since her mother moved in with her. You recall that Carolyn works full-time, has a 14-year-old son in high school, and her husband also works full-time. As Carolyn's counselor, discuss the questions you will ask her as you assess her needs. Describe the rationale for your approach.

10. Review the 2005 ACA Code of Ethics and identify the sections of the code that specifically reference gender diversity. In what ways would these sections apply to assessment and treatment planning when providing counseling for adolescents or midlife adults who are gay or lesbian?

REFERENCES

Abel, E. M. (2001). Comparing the social service utilisation, exposure to violence, and trauma symptomology of domestic violence female victims and female batterers. *Journal of Family Violence, 16*(4), 401–420.

Abreu, J. M., Chung, R. H. G., & Atkinson, D. R. (2000). Multicultural counseling training: Past, present, and future directions. *The Counseling Psychologist, 28*(5), 641–656.

Administration on Aging. (1999). *Older and younger people with disabilities: Improving chronic care throughout the life span.* Retrieved April 23, 2003, from www.aoa.dhhs.gov/factsheets/disabilities.html.

Administration on Aging. (2001). *A profile of older Americans: 2001.* Retrieved April 23, 2003, from www.aoa.dhhs.gov/aoa/STATS/profile/2001/highlights.html.

American Counseling Association (ACA). (1992). *Cross cultural competencies and objectives.* Retrieved October 25, 2005, from www.counseling.org.

ACA. (1998, March). *On appropriate counseling responses to sexual orientation.* Adopted by the American Counseling Association Governing Council, March 27,1998.

ACA. (2005). *Code of ethics.* Retrieved October 19, 2005, from www.counseling.org.

American Psychological Association. (2003). *History of the Committee on Disability Issues in Psychology.* Retrieved June 4, 2004, from www.apa.org/pi/cdip/committeehistory.html.

American Rehabilitation Counseling Association (ARCA). (2003). *Mission.* Retrieved June 4, 2004, from www.nchrtm.okstate.edu/ARCA/.

Aragon de Valdez, T., & Gallegos, J. (1982). The Chicano familia in social work. In James W. Green (Ed.), *Cultural awareness in human services* (pp. 184–208). Englewood Cliffs, NJ: Prentice-Hall.

Ashford, J. B., LeCroy, C. W., & Lortie, K. L. (2001). *Human behavior in the social environment* (2nd ed.). Belmont, CA: Wadsworth.

Association for Gay, Lesbian, and Bisexual Issues in Counseling. (1997). *Mission statement.* Retrieved May 27, 2004, from www.aglbic.org/about/mission.html.

Atchley, R. C. (1997). *Social forces in aging* (8th ed.). Belmont, CA: Wadsworth.

Atkinson, D. R., Morten, G., & Sue, D. W. (1993). *Counseling American minorities: A cross-cultural perspective* (4th ed.). Dubuque, IA: William C. Brown.

Axelson, J. A. (1999). *Counseling and development in a multicultural society* (3rd ed.). Pacific Grove, CA: Brooks/Cole.

Babcock, J. C., Miller, S. A., & Siard, C. (2003). Toward a typology of abusive women: Differences between partner-only and generally violent women in the use of violence. *Psychology of Women Quarterly, 27,* 153–161.

Bar-Tur, L., & Levy-Shiff, R. (2000). Coping with losses and past trauma in old age: The separation-individuation perspective. *Journal of Personal & Interpersonal Loss, 5*(2/3), 263–282.

Becker, G., Gates, R. J., & Newsom, E. (2004). Self-care among chronically ill African-Americans: Culture, health disparities, and health insurance status. *American Journal of Public Health, 94,* 2066–2073.

Bernard, M. L., & Bernard, J. L. (1983). Violent intimacy: The family as a model for love relationships. *Family Relations: Journal of Applied Family & Child Studies, 32,* 283–286.

Berry, J. W., Poortinga, Y. H., Segall, M. H., & Dasen, P. R. (1992). *Cross-cultural psychology: Research and applications.* Cambridge: Cambridge University Press.

Bowling, A., & Faquhar, M. (1991). Associations with social networks, social support, health status, and psychiatric morbidity in three samples of elderly people. *Social Psychiatry and Psychiatric Epidemiology, 216,* 115–126.

Breckman, R. S., & Adleman, R. D. (1988). *Strategies for helping victims of elderly mistreatment.* Newbury Park, CA: Sage.

Brucker, P. S., & Perry, B. J. (1998). American Indians: Presenting concerns and considerations for family therapists. *American Journal of Family Therapy, 26,* 307–319.

Buchwald, D., Beals, J., & Manson, S. M. (2000). Use of traditional health practices among Native Americans in a primary care setting. *Medical Care, 38*(12), 1191–1199.

Butler, R. N., Lewis, M. I., & Sunderland, T. (Eds.). (1998). *Aging and mental health: Positive psychosocial and biomedical approaches* (5th ed.). Boston: Allyn and Bacon.

Calvet, H. M. (2003). Sexually transmitted diseases other than human immunodeficiency virus infection in older adults. *Aging and Infectious Diseases, 36,* 609–614.

Carroll, L., Gilroy, P. J., & Ryan, J. (2002). Counseling transgendered, transsexual, and gender-variant clients. *Journal of Counseling and Development, 80,* 131–140.

Carroll, L. & Gilroy, P. J. (2002). Transgender issues in counselor preparation. *Counselor Education & Supervision, 41*, 233–243.

Carter, R. T. (1995). *The influence of race and racial identity in psychotherapy: Toward a racially inclusive model*. New York: Wiley.

Cashwell, C. S., Young, J. S., Cashwell, T. H., & Belaire, C. (2001). The inclusion of spiritual process in counseling and perceived counselor effectiveness. *Counseling and Values, 45*, 145–153.

Castillo, R. J. (1997). *Culture and mental illness: A client-centered approach*. Pacific Grove, CA: Brooks/Cole.

Champagne, D. (1997). Does the focus on multicultural emphasize differences and foster facial/ethnic stereotypes? Yes. In D. de Anda (Ed.), *Controversial issues in multiculturalism* (pp. 28–33). Boston: Allyn and Bacon.

Chase, B. W., Cornille, T. A., & English, R. W. (2000). Life satisfaction among persons with spinal cord injuries. *Journal of Rehabilitation*. Retrieved January 9, 2004, from www.findarticles.com.

Chilman, C. S. (1993). Hispanic families in the United States: Research perspectives. In H. P. McAdoo (Ed.), *Family ethnicity: Strength in diversity* (pp. 141–163). Newbury Park, CA: Sage.

Chung, D. K. (1992). Asian cultural commonalities: A comparison with mainstream American culture. In S. Furuto, R. Biswas, D. K. Chung, K. Murase, & F. Ross-Sheriff (Eds.), *Social work practice with Asian-Americans* (pp. 27–44). Newbury Park, CA: Sage.

Cochran, S. D. (2001). Emerging issues in research on lesbians' and gay men's mental health: Does sexual orientation really matter? *American Psychologist, 56*, 931–947.

Coker, A. L., Smith, P. H., Bethea, L., King, M. R., & McKeown, R. E. (2000). Physical health consequences of physical and psychological intimate partner violence. *Archives of Family Medicine, 9,* 451–457.

Colbridge, T. D. (2002). The Americans with Disabilities Act: The continuing search for meaning. *FBI Law Enforcement Bulletin*. Retrieved January 9, 2004, from www.findarticles.com.

Collins, K. A. (2002). An examination of feminist psychotherapy in North America during the 1980s. *Guidance & Counseling, 17*, 105–112.

Cooper-Patrick, L., Gallo, J., Powe, N., Steinwachs, D. M., Eaton, W. W., & Ford, D. E. (1999). Mental health service utilization by African Americans and Whites: The Baltimore epidemiologic catchment area follow-up, *Medical Care, 37*(10), 1034–1045.

Council for Accreditation of Counseling and Related Educational Programs (CACREP). (2001). *CACREP accreditation manual: 2001 standards*. Alexandria, VA: American Counseling Association.

Crichton, S., Bond, J., Harvey, C., & Ristock, J. (1999). Elder abuse: Feminist and ageist perspectives. *Journal of Elder Abuse and Neglect, 19*, 115–130.

Cross, W. E. (1971). The Negro-to-Black conversion experience. Toward a psychology of Black liberation. *Black World, 20*, 13–17.

Csoboth, C. T., Birkás, E., & Purebl, G. (2005). Living in fear of experiencing physical and sexual abuse is associated with severe depressive symptomatology among young women. *Journal of Women's Health, 14*(5), 441–448.

Cummings, S. M. (2002). Predictors of psychological well-being among assisted-living residents. *Health & Social Work, 27*, 293–303.

D'Andrade, R. G. (1984). Cultural meaning systems. In R. A. Shweder & R. A. LeVine (Eds.), *Culture theory: Essays on mind, self, and emotions* (pp. 88–119). Cambridge: Cambridge University Press.

de Anda, D. (1997). Are there theories that are sufficiently "culture-free" to be appropriate and useful for practice with multicultural clients? Yes. In D. de Anda (Ed.), *Controversial issues in multiculturalism* (pp. 142–152). Boston: Allyn and Bacon.

Deal, J. E., & Wampler, K. (1986). Dating violence: The primacy of previous experience. *Journal of Social and Personal Relationships, 3*, 457–471.

Delgado-Romero, E. A., Galván, N., Maschino, P., & Rowland, M. (2005). Race and ethnicity in empirical counseling and counseling psychology research. *Counselling Psychologist, 33*(4), 419–448.

Drench, M. E., & Losee, R. H. (1996). Sexuality and sexual capacities of elderly people. *Rehabilitation Nursing, 21*(3), 118–123.

Dupuy, P. J., & Ritchie, M. H. (1994). The inclusion of women's and gender issues in counselor education programs: A survey. *Counselor Education & Supervision, 33*, 238–249.

Elvin-Nowak, Y. (1999). The meaning of guilt: A phenomenological description of employed mothers' experiences of guilt. *Scandinavian Journal of Psych*ology, *40*, 73–83.

Enns, C. Z. (2000). Gender issues in counseling. In S. D. Brown & R. W. Lent (Eds.), *Handbook of counseling psychology* (pp. 601–638). New York: Wiley.

Ettner, R. (1999). *Gender loving care: A guide to counseling gender-variant clients.* New York: Norton.

Evans, K. M., Kincade, E. A., Marbley, A. F., & Seem, S. R. (2005). Feminism and feminist therapy: Lessons from the past and hopes for the future. *Journal of Counseling & Development, 83*(3), 269–277.

Fairchild, D. G., Fairchild, M. W., & Stoner, S. (1998). Prevalence of adult domestic violence among women seeking routine care in a Native American health care facility. *American Journal of Public Health, 88,* 1515–1517.

Falicov, C. (1998). *Latino families in therapy: A guide to multicultural practice.* New York: Guilford.

Family Violence Prevention Fund. (2001, November). Younger women at great risk of intimate partner violence. Retrieved May 5, 2002, from http://endabuse.org/newsflash/index.php3?Search=Article& NewsFlashID=287.

Fernando, S. (2002). *Mental health, race, and culture.* New York: Palgrave.

Fischbach, R., & Herbert, B. (1997). Domestic violence and mental health: Correlates and conundrums within and across cultures. *Social Science and Medicine, 45,* 1161–1176.

Fischer, A. R., Jome, L. M., & Atkinson, D. R. (1998). Reconceptualizing multicultural counseling: Universal healing conditions in a culturally specific context. *The Counseling Psychologist, 26,* 525–588.

Fong, R. (2001). Culturally competent social work practice: Past and present. In R. Fong & S. Furuto (Eds.), *Culturally competent practice: Skills, interventions, and evaluations* (pp. 1–9). Boston: Allyn and Bacon.

Fowers, B., & Richardson, F. C. (1996). Why is multiculturalism good? *American Psychologist, 51,* 609–621.

Frank, J. D. (1961). *Persuasion and healing.* Baltimore, MD: John Hopkins University Press.

Freeman, S. C. (1993). Client-centered therapy with diverse populations: The universal with the specific. *Journal of Multicultural Counseling, 21,* 248–255.

Fukuyama, M. A. (1990). Taking a universal approach to multicultural counseling. *Counselor Education & Supervision, 30,* 6–18.

Fukuyama, M. A. (2000). Integrating spirituality into marriage and family counseling. *The Family Digest, 12,* 7–9.

Garcia-Preto, N. (1996a). Latino families: An overview. In M. McGoldrick, J. Giordano, & J. K. Pearce (Eds.), *Ethnicity and family therapy* (2nd ed.) (pp. 141–154). New York: Guilford.

Garcia-Preto, N. (1996b). Puerto Rican families. In M. McGoldrick, J. Giordano, & J. K. Pearce (Eds.). *Ethnicity and family therapy* (2nd ed.) (pp. 183–199). New York: Guilford.

Garrett, M. T., & Herring, R. D. (2001). Honoring the power of relation: Counseling Native adults. *Journal of Humanistic Counseling, Education & Development, 40,* 139–160.

Gelles, R. J., & Straus, M. A. (1988). *Intimate violence.* New York: Simon & Schuster.

Gilligan, C. (1982,1993). *In a different voice: Psychological theory and women's development.* Cambridge, MA: Harvard University Press.

Gladding, S. T. (2000). *Counseling: A comprehensive profession* (4th ed.). Upper Saddle River, NJ: Prentice-Hall.

Gleick, J.(1987). *Chaos: Making a new science.* New York: Penguin.

Goodman, L. A., Koss, M. P., & Russon, N. F. (1993). Violence against women: Physical and mental health effects. Part I: Research findings. *Applied and Preventive Psychology: Current Scientific Perspectives, 2,* 79–89.

Gonsiorek, J.C., Sell, R. L., & Weinrich, J. D. (1995). Definition and measurement of sexual orientation. *Suicide and Life Threatening Behavior, 25,* 40–51.

Gordon, M. M. (1964). *Assimilation in American life.* New York: Oxford University Press.

Gordon, R. A., Chase-Lansdale, P. L., & Brooks-Gunn, J. (2004). Extended households and the life course of young mothers: Understanding the associations using a sample of mothers with premature, low birth weight babies. *Child Development, 75*(4), 1013–1038.

Gray, H. M., & Foshee, V. (1997). Adolescent dating violence: Differences between one-sided and mutually violent profiles. *Journal of Interpersonal Violence, 12,* 126–141.

Green, J. W. (1999). *Cultural awareness in the human services: A multi-ethnic approach* (3rd ed.). Boston: Allyn and Bacon.

Hantrais, L. (1999). Contextualization in cross-national comparative research. *International Journal of Social Research Methodology, 2*, 93–108.

Harding, S. (1991). *Whose science? Whose knowledge? Thinking from women's lives.* Ithaca, NY: Cornell University Press.

Hawes, C. (2002). Elder abuse in residential long-term care facilities: What is known about prevalence, causes, and prevention. Retrieved May 25, 2004, from http://finance.senate.gov/hearings/testimony/061802chtest.pdf.

Helms, J. E. (1990). *Black and White racial identity: Theory, research, and practice.* Westport, CT: Greenwood.

Helwig, A. A., & Holicky, R. (1994). Substance abuse in persons with disabilities: Treatment considerations. *Journal of Counseling & Development, 72*, 227–234.

Heppner, P. P., Casas, J. M., Carter, J., & Stone, G. L. (2000). The maturation of counseling psychology: Multifaceted perspectives, 1978–1998. In S. D. Brown & R. W. Lent (Eds.), *Handbook of counseling psychology* (pp. 3–49). New York: Wiley and Sons.

Herek, G. M. (1989). Hate crimes against lesbians and gay men: Issues for research and policy. *American Psychologist, 44*, 948–955.

Herek, G. M. (2000). The psychology of sexual prejudice. *Current Directions in Psychological Science, 9*, 19–22.

Hill, R. B. (1971). *The strengths of Black families.* New York: National Urban League.

Hill, R. D., Thorn, B. L., & Packard, T. (2000). Counseling older adults: Theoretical and empirical issues in prevention and intervention. In S. D. Brown & R. W. Lent (Eds.), *Handbook of counseling psychology* (pp. 499–531). New York: John Wiley and Sons.

Hillman, J. L. (2000). *Clinical perspectives on elderly sexuality.* New York: Springer.

Hines, P. M, & Boyd-Franklin, N. (1996). African American families. In M. McGoldrick, J. Giordano, & J. K. Pearce (Eds.), *Ethnicity and family therapy* (2nd ed.) (pp. 66–96). New York: Guilford.

Hochshield, A. R. (1989). The second shift. New York: Penguin Books.

Huisman, K. A. (1996). Wife battering in Asian American communities: Identifying the service needs of an overlooked segment of the U.S. population. *Violence Against Women, 2*, 260–283.

Hunter, S., Shannon, C., Knox, J., & Martin, J. I. (1998). *Lesbian, gay, and bisexual youths and adults: Knowledge for human services practice.* Thousand Oaks, CA: Sage.

Hutchinson, E. D. (1999). *The changing life course.* Thousand Oaks, CA: Pine Forge.

Jackson, A. P., & Meadows, F. B. (1991). Getting to the bottom to understand the top. *Journal of Counseling & Development, 70*, 72–76.

Jackson, M. (1995). Multicultural counseling: Historical perspectives. In J. G. Ponterotto, J. M. Casas, L. A. Suzuki, & C. M. Alexander (Eds.), *Handbook of multicultural counseling* (pp. 3–16). Thousand Oaks, CA: Sage.

Jimenez, J. (2002). The history of grandmothers in the African American community. *Social Service Review, 76*(4), 545–546.

Kim, J. Y., & Sung, K. T. (2000). Conjugal violence in Korean American families: A residue of the cultural tradition. *Journal of Family Violence, 15*, 331–345.

Kitano, H. H. L. (1997). *Race relations* (5th ed.). Upper Saddle River, NJ: Prentice-Hall.

Kluckhohn, F., & Strodtbeck, F. (1961). *Variations in value orientations.* Evanston, IL: Row, Peterson.

Kopala, M., & Keitel, M. (Eds.). (2003). *Handbook of counseling women.* Thousand Oaks, CA: Sage.

Kropf, N. P., & Burnette, D. (2003). Grandparents as family caregivers: Lessons for intergenerational education. *Educational Gerontology, 29*, 361–372.

Lance, L. M. (2002). Acceptance of diversity in human sexuality: Will the strategy reducing homophobia also reduce discomfort of cross-dressing? *College Student Journal, 36*, 598–603.

Lapierre, L. L. (1994). A model for describing spirituality. *Journal of Religion and Health, 33*, 153–161.

Lavizzo-Mourey, R., & Mackenzie, E. R. (1996). Cultural competence: Essential measurements of quality for managed care organizations. *Annals of Internal Medicine, 1124*, 919–921.

Lee, E. (1996). Asian American families: An overview. In M. McGoldrick, J. Giordano, & J. K. Pearce (Eds.), *Ethnicity and family therapy* (2nd ed.) (pp. 227–248). New York: Guilford.

Lee, E. (1997). Chinese American families. In E. Lee (Ed.), *Working with Asian Americans: A guide for clinicians* (pp. 46–78). New York: Guilford.

Lee, R. D., Ensminger, M. E., & Laveist, T. A. (2005). The responsibility continuum: Never primary, coresident and caregiver—Heterogeneity in the African-American grandmother experience. *International Journal of Aging and Human Development, 60*(4), 295–304.

Lee, R. M., & Ramirez, M. (2000). The history, current status, and future of multicultural psychotherapy. In I. Cuellar & F. A. Paniagua (Eds.), *Handbook of multicultural mental health* (pp. 279–309). San Diego, CA: Academic.

Lee, S., Colditz, G., Berkman, L., & Kawachi, I. (2003). Caregiving to children and grandchildren and risk of coronary heart disease in women. *American Journal of Public Health, 93*(11), 1939–1944.

Linsk, N. L., & Mason, S. (2004). Stresses on grandparent and other relatives caring for children affected by HIV/AIDS. *Health & Social Work, 29*(2), 127–136.

Livneh, H., & Antonak, R. F. (1997). *Psychosocial adaptation to chronic illness and disability.* Gaithersburg, MD: Aspen.

Livneh, H., & Antonak, R. F. (2005). Psychosocial adaptation to chronic illness and disability: A primer for counselors. *Journal of Counseling & Development, 83*(1), 12–20.

Livneh, H., & Parker, R. M. (2005). Psychological adaptation to disability: Perspectives from chaos to complexity theory. *Rehabilitation Counseling Bulletin, 49*(1), 17–28.

Livneh, H., & Wilson, L. M. (2003). Coping strategies as predictors and mediators of disability-related variables and psychosocial adaptation: An exploratory investigation. *Rehabilitation Counseling Bulletin, 46*, 194–208.

Locke, D. C. (1990). A not so provincial view of multicultural counseling. *Counselor Education and Supervision, 30*, 18–25.

Malley, M. (2002). Systemic therapy with lesbian and gay clients: A truly social approach to psychological practice. *Journal of Community & Applied Social Psychology, 12*(3), 237–241.

Marks, R., & Allegrante, J. P. (2005). Chronic osteoarthritis and adherence to exercise: A review of the literature. *Journal of Aging and Physical Activity, 13*, 434–460.

Martin, E. P., & Martin, J. M. (1978). *The Black extended family.* Chicago: University of Chicago Press.

Martire, L. M., & Stephens, M. A. P. (2000). Centrality of women's multiple roles: Beneficial and detrimental consequences for psychological well-being. *Psychology and Aging, 15*, 148–156.

McBride, M. C. (1997). Counselling the superwoman: Helping university women cope with multiple roles. *Guidance & Counseling, 12*, 19–23.

McFadden, J. (1996). A transcultural perspective: Reaction to C. H. Patterson's "Multicultural counseling: From diversity to universality." *Journal of Counseling & Development, 74*, 232–236.

Mednick, M. T., & Urbanski, L. (1991). Origins and activities of APA's division of the psychology of women. *Psychology of Women Quarterly, 15*, 651–664.

Mehnert, T., Krauss, H. H., Nadler, R., & Boyd, M. (1990). Correlates of life satisfaction in those with disabling conditions. *Rehabilitation Psychology, 35*, 3–17.

Meinert, J.A., Blehar, M. C., Peindl, K. S., Neal-Barnett, A., & Wisner, K. L. (2003). Recruitment of African American women into mental health research studies. *American Psychiatry, 27*, 21–28.

Milton, M., & Coyle, A. (1998, February). Psychotherapy with lesbian and gay clients. *The Psychologist*, 73–76.

Minkler, M., & Fuller-Thomson, E. (1999). The health of grandparents raising grandchildren: Results of a national study. *American Journal of Public Health, 89*, 1–6.

Moynihan, D. (1965). *The Negro family: The case for national action.* Washington, DC: U.S. Department of Labor.

Murray, C. D., & Harrison, B. (2004). The meaning and experience of being a stroke survivor: An interpretative phenomenological analysis. *Disability and Rehabilitation, 26*(13), 808–816.

Nagi, S. Z. (1991). Disability concepts revisited: Implications for prevention. In A. M. Pope & A. R. Tarlov (Eds.), *Disability in America* (pp. 309–327). Washington, DC: National Academy Press.

National Organization on Disability. (2001). *The nature and severity of disability in America.* Retrieved January 13, 2004, from www.nod.org/content.cfm?id=149.

National Organization on Disability. (2002). *Executive summary: 2000 N.O.D./Harris Survey of Americans with Disabilities.* Retrieved January 13, 2004, from www.nod.org/content.cfm?id=1076#over.

National Rehabilitation Counseling Association. (no date). *History.* Retrieved June 4, 2004, from http://nrca-net.org/history2.html.

Nelson-Jones, R. (2002a). Are there universal human being skills? *Counseling Psychology Quarterly, 15,* 115–120.

Nelson-Jones, R. (2002b). Diverse goals for multicultural counseling and therapy. *Counseling Psychology Quarterly, 15,* 133–144.

Neufeld, J., McNamara, J. R., & Ertl, M. (1999). Incidence and prevalence of dating partner abuse and its relationship to dating practices. *Journal of Interpersonal Violence, 14,* 125–136.

Norton, I. M., & Manson, S. M. (1997). Domestic violence intervention in an urban Indian health center. *Community Mental Health Journal, 33*(4), 331–337.

Nosek, M. A., & Hughes, R. B. (2003). Psychosocial issues of women with physical disabilities: The continuing gender debate. *Rehabilitation Counseling Bulletin, 46,* 224–234.

Nosek, M. A., Hughes, R. B., Howland, C. A., Young, M. E., et al. (2004). The meaning of health for women with physical disabilities: A qualitative analysis. *Family and Community Health, 27,* 6–21.

Okun, B. F., Fried, J., & Okun, M. L. (1999). *Understanding diversity: A learning-as-practice primer.* Pacific Grove, CA: Brooks/Cole.

Orlinsky, D. E., & Howard, K. I. (1987). A generic model of psychotherapy. *Journal of Integrative and Eclectic Psychotherapy, 6,* 6–26.

Ostir, G. V. (1999). Disability in older adults: Prevalence, causes, and consequences. *Behavioral Medicine.* Retrieved September 5, 2002, from www.findarticles.com.

Padilla, Y. C. (1990). Social science theory on the Mexican American experience. *Social Science Review, 64,* 261–275.

Palma, T. V., & Stanley, J. L. (2002). Effective counseling with lesbian, gay, and bisexual clients. *Journal of College Counseling, 5,* 74–89.

Patterson, C. H. (1996). Multicultural counseling: From diversity to universality. *Journal of Counseling & Development, 74,* 227–231.

Pedersen, P. (1990). The multicultural perspective as a fourth force in counseling. *Journal of Mental Health Counseling, 12,* 93–95.

Pedersen, P. (Ed.). (1991). Multiculturalism as a fourth force in counseling (special issue). *Journal of Counseling & Development, 70*(1), 6–12.

Pedersen, P. (1996). The importance of both similarities and differences in multicultural counseling: Reaction to C. H. Patterson. *Journal of Counseling & Development, 74,* 236–238.

Pedersen, P. (1999). Culture-centered interventions as a fourth dimension in psychology. In P. Pedersen (Ed.), *Multiculturalism as a fourth force* (pp. 3–18). Philadelphia, PA: Bunner/Mazel.

Pichette, E. F., & Garrett, M. T. (1999). Cultural identification of American Indians and its impact on rehabilitation services. *Journal of Rehabilitation, 65*(3), 3–10.

Pike, R. (1966). *Language in relation to a united theory of the structure of human behavior.* The Hague, Netherlands: Mouton.

Pillemer, K. A., & Finkelhor, D. (1988). The prevalence of elder abuse: A random sample study. *Gerontologist, 28,* 51–57.

Pillemer, K. A., & Moore, D. W. (1990). Highlights from a study of abuse of patients in nursing homes. *Journal of Elder Abuse and Neglect, 2,* 5–30.

Pope, M. (1995). The "salad bowl" is big enough for us all: An argument for the inclusion of lesbians and gay men in any definition of multiculturalism. *Journal of Counseling & Development, 73,* 301–305.

Prathikanti, S. (1997). East Indian American families. In E. Lee (Ed.), *Working with Asian Americans: A guide for clinicians* (pp. 79–113). New York: Guilford.

Randolph, J. J., & Arnett, P. A. (2005). Depression and fatigue in relapsing-remitting MS: The role of symptomatic variability. *Multiple Sclerosis, 11,* 186–190.

Red Horse, J. (1981). *American Indian families.* Paper presented at the conference on American Indian Family Strengths and Stress, Tempe, AZ.

Reynolds, A. L., & Pope, R. L. (1991). The complexities of diversity: Exploring multiple oppressions. *Journal of Counseling & Development, 70,* 174–180.

Riggs, D. S., O'Leary, K. D., & Breslin, F. C. (1990). Multiple correlates of physical aggression in dating couples. *Journal of Interpersonal Violence, 5,* 61–73.

Rimonte, N. (1991). A question of culture: Cultural approval of violence against women in the Pacific-Asian community and the cultural defense. *Stanford Law Review, 43,* 1311–1326.

Roberts, R. L., Harper, R., Caldwell, R., & Decora, M. (2003). Adlerian lifestyle analysis of Lakota women: Implications for counseling. *Journal of Individual Counseling*, *59*(1), 15–29.

Robinson, D. T., & Morris, J. R. (2000). Multicultural counseling: Historical context and current training considerations. *The Western Journal of Black Studies*, *24*, 239–253.

Rubinstein, G. (1995). The decision to remove homosexuality from the DSM: Twenty years later. *American Journal of Psychotherapy*, *49*, 416–427.

Ryff, C. D., Singer, B., Love, G. D., & Essex, M. J. (1998). Resilience in adulthood and later life. In J. Lomranz (Ed.), *Handbook of aging and mental health: An integrative approach* (pp. 69–96). New York: Plenum.

Sadovsky, R. (2000). Sexual orientation and associated health care risks. *American Family Physician*. Retrieved December 16, 2003, from www.findarticles.com.

Seaver, C. (1996). Muted lives: Old battered women. *Journal of Elder Abuse and Neglect*, *8*, 3–21.

Shaevitz, M. H. (1984). *The superwoman syndrome*. New York: Warner Books.

Snowden, L. R. (2001). Barriers to effective mental health services for African Americans. *Mental Health Services Research*, *3*(4), 181–187.

Snowden, L. R., & Thomas, K. (2000). Medicaid and African American outpatient mental health treatment. *Mental Health Services Research*, *2*(2), 115–120.

Stanfield, J. H. (1993). Epistemological considerations. In J. H. Stanfield & R. M. Dennis (Eds.), *Race and ethnicity in research methods* (pp. 16–36). Newbury Park, CA: Sage.

Straus, M. A., & Gelles, R. J. (1990). *Physical violence in American families: Risk factors and adaptations to violence in 8,145 families*. New Brunswick, NJ: Transaction.

Stryker, S., & Serpe, R. T. (1994). Identity salience and psychological centrality: Equivalent, overlapping, or complementary concepts? *Social Psychology Quarterly*, *57*, 16–35.

Sue, S. (1977). Community mental health services to minority groups: Some optimism, some pessimism. *American Psychologist*, *1*, 616–624.

Sue, D. W. (1981). *Counseling the culturally different. Theory and practice*. New York: Wiley & Sons.

Sue, S. (1988). Psychotherapeutic services for minorities: Two decades of research findings. *American Psychologist*, *43*, 301–308.

Sue, D. W., & Sue, D. (1999). *Counseling the culturally different: Theory and practice*. New York: Wiley & Sons.

Sue, D. W., Arredondo, P., & McDavis, R. J. (1992). Multicultural counseling competencies and standards: A call to the profession. *Journal of Counseling & Development*, *70*, 477–486.

Sue, S., & Zane, N. (1987). The role of culture and cultural techniques in psychotherapy: A critique and reformulation. *American Psychologist*, *42*, 37–45.

Sustento-Seneriches, J. (1997). Filipino American families. In E. Lee (Ed.), *Working with Asian Americans: A guide for clinicians* (pp. 101–113). New York: Guilford.

Sutton, C. T., & Broken Nose, M. A. (1996). American Indian families: An overview. In M. McGoldrick, J. Giordano, & J. K. Pearce (Eds.), *Ethnicity and family therapy* (2nd ed.) (pp. 31–44). New York: Guilford.

Tatara, T., & Kuzmeskus, L. (1997). *Summaries of the statistical data on elder abuse in domestic settings: An exploratory study of staff statistics for FY 95 and 96*. Washington, DC: NCEA.

Teufel-Shone, N. I., Staten, L. K., Irwin, U. R., Bravo, A. B., & Waykayuta, S. (2005). Family cohesion and conflict in an American Indian community. *American Journal of Health Behavior*, *29*(5), 413–422.

Thoits, P. A. (1992). Identity structures and psychological well-being: Gender and marital status comparisons. *Social Psychology Quarterly*, *55*, 236–256.

Thomas, A. (2001). The multidimensional character of biased perceptions of individuals with disabilities. *Journal of Rehabilitation*. Retrieved January 9, 2004, from www.findarticles.com.

Throckmorton, W. (1998). Efforts to modify sexual orientation: A review of outcome literature and ethical issues. *Journal of Mental Health Counseling*, *20*, 283–305.

Tjaden, P., & Thoennes, N. (1998). *Stalking in America: Findings from the National Violence Against Women Survey*. Washington DC: National Institute of Justice and Centers for Disease Control and Prevention.

Tjaden, P., & Thoennes, N. (2000). Prevalence and consequences of male-to-male and female-to-male intimate partner violence as measured by the National Violence Against Women survey. *Violence Against Women*, *6*, 142–161.

Tseng, W. S., & Wu, D. Y. H. (1985). *Chinese culture and mental health*. Orlando, FL: Academic Press.

Uba, L. (1994). *Asian Americans: Personality patterns, identity, and mental health.* New York: Guilford.

U.S. Census Bureau. (1996). *Current population reports, special studies, 65+ in the United States* (pp. 23–190). Washington DC: U.S. Government Printing Office.

U.S. Census Bureau. (1997). *Americans with disabilities.* Retrieved on May 7, 2005, from www.census.gov/prod/2001pubs/p70-73.pdf.

U.S. Census Bureau. (2002a). *The Asian population: 2000.* Retrieved October 25, 2005, from www.census.gov/prod/2002pubs/c2kbr01-16.pdf.

U.S. Census Bureau. (2000b). *The Hispanic population in the United States: March 2000.* Retrieved on May 7, 2005, from www.census.gov/prod/2001pubs/p20-535.pdf.

U.S. Census Bureau. (2000c). *12th Anniversary of Americans with Disabilities Act.* Retrieved June 4, 2004, from www.census.gov/Press-Release/www/2002/cb02ff11.html.

U.S. Census Bureau. (2000d). *Nearly 1 in 5 Americans has some level of disability, U.S. Census Bureau reports.* Retrieved June 4, 2004, from www.census.gov/Press-Release/www/2001/cb0146.html.

U.S. Census Bureau. (2004). *Projected population of the United States, by age and sex: 2000 to 2050.* Retrieved May 25, 2004, from www.census.gov/ipc/www/usinterimproj/natprojtab02a.pdf.

U.S. Department of Justice. (2003). *Intimate partner violence 1993–2001.* Retrieved October 24, 2005, from www.ojp.usdoj.gov/bjs/abstract/ipv01.htm.

Vappu, V., & Krause, C. (1998). Quality of life in individuals with physical disabilities. *Psychotherapy and Psychosomatics, 67,* 317.

Vinton, L. (1992). Battered women's shelters and older women: The Florida experience. *Journal of Family Violence, 71,* 63–72.

Vinton, L. (1998). A nationwide survey of domestic violence shelters' programming for older women. *Violence Against Women, 4,* 559–571.

Vontress, C. E. (1988). An existential approach to cross-cultural counseling. *Journal of Multicultural Counseling and Development, 16,* 78–83.

Waldo, C. R., Hesson-McInnis, M. S., & D'Augelli, A. R. (1998). Antecedents and consequences of victimization of lesbian, gay, and bisexual young people: A structural model comparing rural university and urban samples. *American Journal of Community Psychology, 26,* 307–334.

Waldron, I. R. G. (2003). *Examining beliefs about mental illness among African American Canadian women.* Retrieved October 20, 2005, from https://tspace.library.utoronto.ca/retrieve/889/waldron.pdf.

Waxman, H. A. (2001, July 30). *Abuse of residents is a major problem in United States nursing homes.* Committee on Government Reform, U.S. House of Representatives. Retrieved May 26, 2004, from www.house.gov/reform/min/pdfs/pdf_inves/pdf_nursing_abuse_rep.pdf.

Weaver, H. N., & White, B. J. (1997). The Native American family circle: Roots of resiliency. *Journal of Family Social Work, 2,* 67–79.

Weinrach, S. G., & Thomas, K. R. (1996). The counseling profession's commitment to diversity-sensitive counseling: A critical reassessment. *Journal of Counseling & Development, 73,* 472–477.

Whitley, D. M., Kelley, S. J., & Sipe, T. A. (2001). Grandmothers raising grandchildren: Are they at increased risk of health problems? *Health & Social Work, 26*(2), 105–114.

Williams, M. A. (2001). *The 10 lenses: Your guide to living and working in a multicultural world.* Sterling, VA: Capital Books.

Williams, O. J., & Tubbs, C. Y. (2002). *Community insights on domestic violence among African Americans: Conversations about domestic violence and other issues affecting their communities.* University of Minnesota, Institute on Domestic Violence in the African American Community. Retrieved October 24, 2005, from www.dvinstitute.org.

Wolfe, J. R. (1993). *The coming health crisis: Who will pay for the care of the aged in the twenty-first century?* Chicago: University of Chicago Press.

Wrenn, G. (1962). The culturally encapsulated counselor. *Harvard Educational Review, 32,* 444–449.

Wright, K. (1995). Hypertension. *Gale Encyclopedia of Alternative Medicine.* Retrieved April 23, 2003, from www.findarticles.com.

Yellow Bird, M. (2001). Critical values and First Nations peoples. In R. Fong & S. Furuto (Eds.), *Culturally competent practice: Skills, interventions, and evaluations* (pp. 61–74). Boston: Allyn and Bacon.

Yick, A. (1999). Domestic violence in the Chinese American community: Cultural taboos and barriers. *Family Violence and Sexual Assault Bulletin, 15,* 16–23.

Yick, A., & Gupta, R. (2002). Chinese cultural dimensions of death, dying, and bereavement: Focus group findings. *Journal of Cultural Diversity*, *9*, 32–42.

Young, L. M. (2004). American women in the 21st century: Facts on older women. National Council of Women's Organizations. Retrieved May 25, 2004, from www.womensorganizations.org/pages.cfm?ID=84.

Zink, T., Jacobsen, C. J., Regan, S., & Pabst, S. (2004). Hidden victims: The healthcare needs and experiences of older women in abusive relationships. *Journal of Women's Health*, *13*(8), 898–908.

CHAPTER FOUR

RESEARCH AND COUNSELING PRACTICE

Issues of Application and Integration

AMANDA COSTIN

Effective practice as a counselor requires the application of research-guided knowledge that reflects traditional as well as contemporary theory. Research determines how theory progresses, how practice changes over time, which emerging counseling practices achieve acceptance within the field, and which methods should be "weeded out" when efficacy of outcomes cannot be demonstrated. For any field in the human services to advance, research must consistently be an integrated, a dynamic, and, at times, a debate-provoking ingredient in the helping process.

Research is not a static activity undertaken to complete an advanced academic degree. Rather, it is a process that must be embedded into the way that practitioners *act and think* about the treatment process at each step along the journey taken with clients. Without the element of an evaluation and assessment-based process, counseling practice becomes rudderless and subject to reliance on "shoulds" and "oughts" about the therapist–client relationship. Knowing about the progress of a client's therapy through assessment methods supports ethical and effective practice.

Research, however, can take many forms and is not limited to "one right way" to determine outcomes of counseling. Depending on the context for counseling service delivery, outcomes may be measured in highly structured ways, or via the use of very elegant strategies during individual, family, or group sessions. The purpose of this chapter, therefore, is to explore the underpinnings of outcomes measurement in the counseling field, recognizing that there are many experts in this field who can provide the level of detail and mastery of specific research skills that are beyond the scope of this discussion. The issues surrounding outcome research/measurement and its integration into counseling practice are the focus of this review.

HISTORY OF OUTCOME MEASURES AND EFFECTIVE COUNSELING PRACTICE

Recognition that practice must be guided by research is well understood by counseling professionals from each specialization and field of practice. More than 25 years ago, Wheeler and Loesch (1981, p. 573) wrote, "Significant ideological, theoretical and operation changes—as well as fiscal crises—have necessitated that counselors be concerned about what they do, under the guise of accountability pressures." Knapper (1978, p. 27) emphasized the role of economic factors as a foundational element to research-supported practice by stating, "With increasing competition for the tax dollar, the public demand for counselor accountability may persist." This view reflects a prophetic wisdom in light of the dramatic changes in how economic support for mental health care would change over the ensuing decades. She went on to say that "it may be in the best interest of the profession to seize the initiative by demonstrating collective worth via some accountability strategy thus obviating the need for external monitoring and control. This professional initiative may protect the freedom of counselors to assume their appropriate roles and attend to the individual needs and aspirations of their clients" (p. 27). Noting both the importance of demonstrating accountability in treatment outcomes and the challenges this poses to the profession, Brammer and Whitfield (1972, p. 563) go as far as to say that greater accountability in counseling services has been classified as "everything from the new whipping boy in education to a matter of survival." From these experts came the recognition that not only is research critically important to the counseling field but also the issues that are discussed in contemporary circles are similar to those discussed in the later years of the twentieth century. Although this debate has continued to evolve in the ensuing years, it is clear that the counseling professions now practice within an economic environment that increasingly relies on the capacity to demonstrate treatment outcomes.

THE SCIENTIST PRACTITIONER MODEL AND OUTCOME RESEARCH IN COUNSELING

Despite the history counselors have with recognizing the need for outcome research, many counselors still wonder what outcome research is, why it should be a part of the counseling service delivery process, and what the benefits of research are for the practicing counselor professional. At the most fundamental level of analysis, the rationale for integrating research activities into practice is based on the scientist practitioner model (SPM) of counseling. In this model, theory, research, and practice are linked in such a way that counseling can demonstrate effectiveness, varying levels of effectiveness, or lack of effectiveness of treatments used. Knowledge about the impact of therapeutic methods ensures that treatment is ethically delivered and appropriate to the client's diagnosis. As depicted in Figure 4.1, the SPM relies on knowledge and understanding of theory and prior research to guide the treatment process.

Using a clear, sequential, and scientific process to inform counseling treatment and evaluate the results of treatment ensures that the counseling methods employed are appropriate to the identified problem or diagnosis. With the scientist practitioner model in mind,

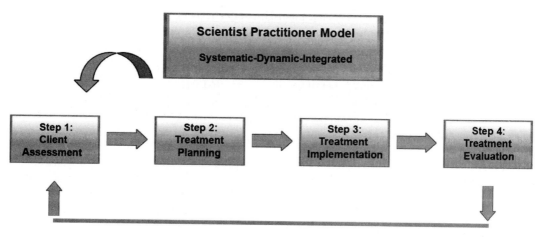

FIGURE 4.1   Application of Research to Practice

outcome research therefore becomes the experimental investigation of the impact of counseling on the client (Lambert, Masters, & Ogles, 1991) and is an essential ingredient of professional practice.

In each step in the scientist practitioner model, counselors engage in a variety of activities designed to evaluate counseling and assess the factors that have the greatest impact on positive outcomes (Walz & Bleuer, 1993). Although Sexton (2001, p. 500) defines outcome research as "focusing on the final result of counseling efforts and . . . the ability to inform what interventions and approaches may work best for which desired outcome," it is clear that the scientific process includes more than identified treatment outcomes. For example, Watkins and Schneider (1991) suggest that outcome research can provide important therapeutic guidelines, test models of clinical practice, and examine whether a counselor's methods of practice are currently supported. In addition, the SPM also provides an outline of the end-to-end process that defines counseling beginning with the first contact between counselor and client through bringing a close to the treatment process.

Outcome research is closely aligned with evidenced-based interventions (Kratochwill & Shernoff, 2004). Both approaches describe the integration of a scientist practitioner approach to the practice of counseling. Thus, the scientist practitioner model is the platform on which outcome research rests. The goals of outcome research are similar to those for evidenced-based interventions and rely on the questioning attitude of the counselor as treatment is planned and implemented (Kratochwill & Shernoff, 2004). For example, Lambert, Masters, and Ogles (1991) suggest retaining an inquisitive demeanor while providing counseling services that incorporate key elements regarding outcomes:

1. Determining if counseling is effective
2. Evaluating the length of effectiveness of treatments
3. Identifying the aspects of counseling that are helpful
4. Analyzing positive outcomes of treatment in terms of therapist technique or client expectations

5. Assessing how to enhance counseling effectiveness
6. Reviewing the match between client need and efficacy of treatment method

With this level of inquiry, the fabric of counseling is strengthened through use of a consistent and systematic set of research-supported steps to guide initial and continuing treatment activities. When viewed in this light, counselors can acquire the mindset to use a scientific approach to support the therapeutic process while simultaneously retaining sensitivity to the art of counseling practice.

IMPETUS FOR OUTCOME RESEARCH IN COUNSELING

Although the scientist practitioner model provides a clear rationale for the ongoing use of approaches to counseling that reflect a systematic research foundation, the discussion of integrating outcome research into counseling practice continues to be discussed in the counseling profession. Although there is a substantial and growing body of research about effective counseling strategies and interventions, many counseling practitioners perceive research as irrelevant, difficult to understand, and impossible to incorporate into daily practice (Ruby, 2005; Sexton, Whiston, Bleuer, & Walz, 1997). In addition, the study of research typically required during the education and training experience is often viewed as a "necessary evil" rather than an essential set of competencies for the counseling professional (Ruby, 2005, p. 60).

From a historical perspective, not long ago counselors were able to treat clients in a manner they personally deemed most therapeutic. Aside from maintaining ethical and legal standards, there was very little accountability for outcomes of counseling practice. Due to a host of factors that have impacted the health care delivery system (e.g., managed mental health care), counselors today are called on more than ever to demonstrate the effectiveness of their counseling interventions. Consequently, counselors are obliged to prove their effectiveness and their ability to make efficient use of limited mental health resources (Burlingame, Lambert, Reisinger, Neff, & Mosier, 1995).

Rather than making clinical decisions based on research findings, some counselors make their clinical decisions based on a hunch or instinct (Sexton, 1996). Some might refer to this as the "art of counseling" (Larner, 2004). Viewed from this perspective, counseling is not a process that is scientific; rather, it relies on a keen sensitivity to the continual flow of information from the client, formation of impressions regarding the client's psychological or emotional needs, and implementation of interventions based on the dynamic interpersonal flow of verbal and nonverbal cues produced by the client. Respecting that varied clinical experiences and acute sensitivity to information produced by clients during the treatment process is certainly relevant and important in therapeutic decision making, such experiences should not, however, be the only factors relied on when making clinical decisions.

Sexton and colleagues (1997, p. 1) reflect on this issue when they state, "We are of the mind that the key factor in therapeutic behavior change is the way in which broad based and systematic knowledge can be skillfully applied by professional clinicians." A key word reflected by this viewpoint is *systematic*: It is the systematic application of a "way of

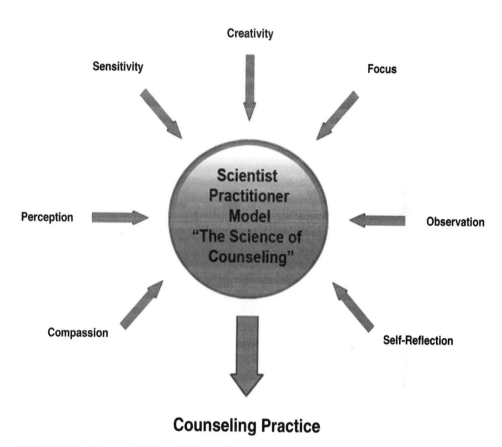

FIGURE 4.2   Integrated View of Counseling Practice

thinking" or being "scientifically minded" (Bieschke, Fouad, Collins, & Halonen, 2004) about research wedded to practice that is at the core of any debate about outcome research in the "real world" of practice. From this combined perspective, both the art and science of counseling can be integrated into practice. As depicted in Figure 4.2, practice reflects the unique characteristics of the counselor who uses the scientist practitioner model. Effective counseling relies on the use of the self of the counselor as well as the systematic approach to assessment, planning, implementation, and evaluation of the counseling process.

If we assume that counseling is both an art and a science, why are many counseling professionals reluctant to use counseling outcome research methods? Larner (2004), Ruby (2005), and Sexton and colleagues (1997) note that this is not a new phenomenon and may be attributed to the following set of myths or beliefs that may explain some of this reluctance:

1. Outcome research does not provide anything relevant to the practitioner in terms of real-world practice.
2. Research results cannot be trusted.
3. Research studies are rigidly designed and examine minute detail, not clinical problems.
4. Outcome research looks only at group differences; practitioners need help with individual clients.
5. Research seeks only statistical significance; practitioners need to know what makes a practical difference.
6. Research focuses on evaluating theory; practitioners need clinical discoveries of new methods.
7. Research requires use of statistical techniques that the counselor views as too complicated or time consuming.
8. There is a lack of collaboration to conduct research in applied settings.

In addition, Sexton (1996, p. 590) systematically reviewed the current status of counseling outcome research with the intent of answering the following questions:

1. Is there a clinically relevant body of outcome research knowledge currently available in the areas in which counselors typically practice?
2. How can the counseling practitioner access this knowledge?
3. To what degree can those findings be confidently applied to clinical practice?

The results of Sexton's (1996, p. 590) study suggested that "there is a large body of outcome research studies investigating numerous client problems and clinical techniques in various areas of practice." This finding supports the reality that counselors have an abundant body of literature to turn to when working with various client problems. However, Sexton points out that although outcome research is in fact available, it is often not accessible. For example, the 365 studies in Sexton's review were published in over 100 professional journals, and of these journals, only 9 were likely to publish more than a single outcome study in a given year (Sexton, 1996). Given the busy lives of counselors, the cost of receiving numerous journals, and the diversity of studies and publications, it is unrealistic to expect counselors to keep up with current studies that are so widely disseminated (Sexton, 1996). Of import in this regard, however, is the dramatic shift in availability of professional literature via Internet search tools, databases, and professional counseling associations. The frequency of practitioner research publications remains a fraction of the potential for this form of research and professional communication, but the number of Internet-delivered counseling journals that are more easily accessed is increasing particularly for members of professional associations in counseling.

To address the issue of practitioner use of research, as well as publishing, Leuger (2002) suggests that the definitions and applications of research methods to clinical practice can be extended beyond the "traditional" model of clinical research. The potential for this perspective is well illustrated by the following case in which Ms. Waterman, a mental health counselor, is currently involved:

Carol initiated counseling following referral by her obstetrical physician two months after the birth of her second child. In the initial session, Ms. Waterman conducted an assessment interview resulting in a preliminary diagnosis of mild post-partum depression. She then developed a counseling treatment plan that focused on the bio-psycho-social aspects of managing post-partum depression. During the fourth session, Carol arrived in an acutely distressed state and spent the session focused on several disturbing dreams she had over the past two weeks. Further exploration of these dreams raised Ms. Waterman's suspicions that Carol might be recalling repressed memories or that the dreams were linked to the heightened stress Carol was experiencing as the mother of an infant, a very active 3-year-old toddler, and the lack of any family support resources. Ms. Waterman revises her treatment plan to include some targeted data gathering around each of these hypotheses and is reconsidering her original diagnosis.

In this case, the therapist is demonstrating flexibility in how she defines the presenting problem, incorporates new information into the diagnostic and treatment planning process, evaluates the continuing flow of information generated by the client's behavior and descriptions, and demonstrates the value of retaining an open mind and scientific perspective while counseling Carol. With this kind of flexible, inquisitive, and curious attitude, Ms. Waterman is viewing her counseling with Carol as a single-case research design that begins with evidence-based treatment goals supported by the literature and research associated with post-partum depression counseling. Ms. Waterman then widens her attention to include other possible issues that Carol is struggling with as more information is revealed. In her treatment notes, she will record her observations, evaluate new information, and link both to her treatment plan as a dynamic source of guidance and evaluation of outcomes. Although technically not a rigorous research study, Ms. Waterman's efforts to use a systematic method to investigate the treatment of her client reflects an understanding of some of the complexities of the scientist practitioner model in the real world of practice.

This brief case serves as an example of evidence-based intervention that could include the use of standardized symptom measurement instruments, self-recordings, and continuing direct observations used during the counseling process. Single-case designs, mental health services research, and case-focused services research, therefore, each hold potential to inform practice beyond the clinical trails model or "gold standard" of randomized control research (Larner, 2004, p. 17). Although Leuger (2002) strongly supports the integration of evidence-based research into psychotherapy practices, he also concurs with Caspar (1997), who found that therapists cognitively move between logical, analytical thinking and intuitive information processing during counseling sessions. Thus, the challenge to counselors is twofold: Retain the focus and intent to understand the client and establish a therapeutic connection to the client as a primary goal of the encounter, and incorporate research-based information and a scientist practitioner focus while practicing.

This balance between the art and science of counseling is based on the therapist's foundation knowledge about psychological disorders, the therapeutic process, and the value of clinical research. In the real world of counseling, both elements of the counseling process become more obvious as well as less overt as the helping process unfolds over time. Highlighting the essential need to ensure that the inner subjective experience (ISE) of the client is incorporated into the counseling process, however, Hansen (2005) admonishes the profession that a "deep appreciation for ISE must animate every element of counseling practice" (p. 414). Hansen's arguments urge individual counselors, counselors in training, and the profession itself to confront trends that place more value on the metrics of practice than on the human therapeutic encounter.

Counseling Effectiveness

From the practitioner's perspective, the value of outcome research lies in its application to day-to-day counseling activities. The counseling professional in private practice, for example, may have daily experiences that reveal effectiveness of interventions. On other days, client progress may be less visible or striking, and this may lead to a process of questioning the efficacy of interventions. For the counselor in an institutional or agency setting, treatment methods prescribed for specific programs may be quite effective for some populations, yet fall short in others. It is at this juncture in reviewing the impact of clinical work that counselors can rely on outcome research knowledge to tease out answers to treatment efficacy questions.

Research in counseling supports an expanding knowledge base on effective treatment practices that spans a century (Whiston & Coker, 2000). To investigate some of the qualities and characteristics of counseling efficacy, Kelly (1996) conducted a literature review study that summarized important advances in clinical knowledge regarding mental health counseling processes and outcomes in a single year, 1994. Although somewhat dated, Kelly's work helps guide understanding of the position that outcome research has in the counseling professions. In his review of the outcome research literature, Kelly limited it to four journals: *Journal of Consulting and Clinical Psychology, Journal of Counseling and Development, Journal of Counseling Psychology*, and *Journal of Mental Health Counseling*.

A number of dominant themes emerged from Kelly's (1996) analysis of clinical mental health counseling outcome research. These themes included recognition that cognitive behavior therapy has demonstrated effectiveness for treating certain psychological disorders (i.e., depression, anxiety, and anger). Further, his findings suggest that "the field has moved beyond questioning whether counseling is effective to considering the most effective counseling techniques for different types of client problems" (p. 12). This study of outcome research clearly indicated that progress has been made in identifying client variables affecting counseling outcome, although most studies continue to compare effectiveness of different techniques. Finally, Kelly noted that although a greater number of counseling process studies have been conducted, the links between counseling process and outcome need further research.

Since Kelly's (1996) work was published, the counseling field has continued to expand the knowledge base that is supported by outcome research, itself based on the scientist practitioner model. As the issue of application of evidence or research-based treatment/counseling methods evolves, questions about counseling effectiveness are now more focused with reference to client populations, counselor characteristics and variables, or other influences that can be present during the treatment process.

An examination of research on the effectiveness of counseling provides additional support for the role of research in practice as a primary outcome of such investigations, as well as a strong source of advocacy within the profession. A core message emerges from this review: Counselors need to retain their research way of thinking or research mindedness "out in the field" as evidence-based practice becomes the expectation throughout the mental health professions and across a landscape that increasingly requires evidence of effectiveness.

Outcome Research Examples.   There have been many studies demonstrating that counseling is effective in helping clients solve problems, reduce symptoms, and improve interpersonal functioning beyond improvements that can be expected to result from naturally existing social supports (Lambert & Cattani-Thompson, 1996). Consideration of "what works in counseling" is explained by Seligman (1995), who reported on a landmark study of psychotherapy conducted by *Consumer Reports*. In this research about psychotherapy, Seligman points out that the recipients of counseling recognized the benefits from treatment, found no significant differences in satisfaction with reference to who provided the counseling, and benefited from long-term counseling more than short-term counseling interventions. These self-reported findings interface well with the Lambert and Cattani-Thompson (1996) research that divided positive counseling outcomes into three categories—the client, common factors, and specific intervention—suggesting that the consumer's opinions of effectiveness must be an integral element of effectiveness. It is important to note, however, that Lambert and Cattani-Thompson do not include the counselor or their techniques as important factors contributing to counseling outcome, and thus, while this categorization of variables is helpful, their perspective is somewhat limited.

According to Lambert and Anderson (1996), the most important variables the client possesses that will impact counseling outcome are severity of disturbance, motivation, capacity to relate, ego strength, psychological mindedness, and ability to identify a focal problem. From another perspective, Lambert and Bergin (1994) reviewed the empirical research of common factors that support positive outcome research. "Common factors across therapies were divided into support factors (i.e., identification with therapist, therapist warmth and acceptance, reassurance), learning factors (i.e., cognitive learning, feedback, insight), and action factors (i.e., modeling, practice, success experiences)" (Lambert & Bergin, 1994, p. 608). Equally important, counselors must understand the role of specific interventions in treatment outcome. The question of whether one technique is substantially different from and more effective than another is still very much debated (Lambert & Cattani-Thompson, 1996). Using a combination of assessment methods, however, counselors can integrate systematic evaluation of practice. For example, Leibert (2006) indicates that counselors can use norm-referenced scales and assessment tools along with ratings of outcomes by clients and counselors. A combined methodology that relies on multiple methods to assess progress can provide insights about progress as well as measurements that, combined, provide evidence of treatment effectiveness.

Conclusions that counselors can use to inform practice are provided by Lambert and Cattani-Thompson (1996, p. 606), who have done an excellent job of reviewing studies on counseling outcome research. The implications for practice described by these researchers were:

1. The effects of counseling are positive at treatment termination.
2. The effects of counseling can be achieved in short periods of time (5–10 sessions) with at least 50% of clients who are seen in routine counseling practice.

3. Twenty to 30% of clients require longer treatment and alternative interventions, but with these efforts, clients will improve significantly. The most likely clients to struggle with brief treatments are poorly motivated, hostile clients who have a history of poor relationships and who expect to be passive recipients of a medical procedure.
4. The effects of treatment seem to be lasting for a majority of clients, with follow-up studies suggesting little decline in 1 to 2 years after termination.
5. Client outcome is largely determined by client variables rather than by the counselor or counseling per se.
6. The best predictors and possibly causes of success outside of client variables are counselor–client relationship factors.
7. Specific techniques seem to be especially helpful with particular symptoms or disorders. Counselors should be aware of the current research regarding these techniques.
8. A portion of clients get worse during counseling. If this is the case, referral and alteration of counseling strategies should be undertaken early in counseling.

The results of this outcome research represent an imperative that counselors must embrace in order to provide the highest quality of care for clients. Furthermore, it has become critical that counselors share this information in a methodical fashion with managed care companies.

Accountability and Managed Care

In addition to providing excellent standards of care to clients, clearly of primary importance to both counselor and client, counseling practitioners cannot overlook the imperative from external sources; that is, the mental health field is being judged on accountability and research evidence of efficacy of practice or evidenced-based treatment (EBT) (Miller, Zweben, & Johnson, 2005; Sexton et al, 1997). Managed care insurance companies control what services are provided to clients and for how long. In fact, outcome research is essential to third-party reimbursement and treatment planning (Granello & Haag, 1998; Miller, Zweben, & Johnson, 2005). Research, not intuition, will justify the need for a particular client's therapeutic plan. Research-based practice guidelines can help clinicians make the case about the effectiveness of a specific counseling plan for a particular client.

Metzl (1998) focused on characteristics of counseling practices that foster reluctance on the part of managed care companies to provide reimbursement, and why managed care companies were at times so reluctant to deal with counseling. Furthermore, issues associated with why insurance plans in every state offered only minimal coverage for mental illness, refused to admit many counselors in their treatment networks, and restricted access to outpatient counseling were also raised. Linked to these factors, many counselors were found to harbor deep-seated reservations about managed care. Describing the relationship between counselors and managed care, Metzl (1998, p. 333) states:

> Managed care companies across the country have treated mental health coverage as if it were a treatment to be avoided at all costs. Claims are frequently denied. Access to care is often heavily restricted. When benefits are provided, they are at a level that many mental health providers find perilously inadequate. Constant and often intrusive assessments regulate the treatment when it begins, and often dictate when it should end. Not enough

support in the face of severe, debilitating, and long-standing afflictions such as major depression, post-traumatic stress disorder, or many personality disorders; and clearly unequal funding compared to that offered for many other treatments available in the health care system.

Managed care has held mental health professionals more accountable for providing evidence of the effectiveness of their techniques than medically based treatments in general. Some managed care insurers refuse to pay for treatments in the absence of proof of their efficacy. In response to this pressure, a database of empirically validated treatments is available (Chambless et al, 1996). Acuff and associates (1999, p. 563) describe the managed care crises in mental health as an "upheaval in the practice community." A well-known mechanism to provide information to counselors regarding accepted mental health treatment protocols is the treatment manual.

The Case for Treatment Manuals

Psychiatrists and psychologists tend to use treatment manuals to guide their practice more than professional counselors. In a managed mental health care environment, the use of treatment manuals conforms to requirements to use only counseling interventions with demonstrated effectiveness. In terms of the scientist practitioner model, it is clear that counselors must take a second look at using treatment manuals when working with clients with specific diagnoses. Use of "canned" treatment protocols clearly poses a risk to the systematic assessment, treatment planning, treatment intervention, and treatment evaluation sequence incorporated into the SPM. As noted previously, despite the growing literature on empirically supported therapies, these evidence-based interventions are rarely used by psychiatrists, psychologists, counselors, and other mental health providers (Connor-Smith & Weisz, 2003). Connor-Smith and Weisz (2003) address the barriers to real-world implementation of research-supported treatments and discuss techniques for making use of current data with the following suggestions:

1. *Flexible Application of Manualized Interventions*: In their study, Connor-Smith and Weisz (2003, p. 5) found that clinicians made the assumption that "every topic and activity outlined were mandatory, to be completed during the scheduled week regardless of session time available, their client's capacity to understand, or crisis in their client's life." As a result, clients often felt misunderstood, rushed, and, at worst, disrespected. Research manuals that outline proven treatments are simply roadmaps for the clinician, outlining core skills and concepts to cover.

2. *Adapting Intervention Structure*: Depending on the client, it may be necessary to add treatment components to the planned intervention outline. For example, depending on the topic area covered, it might be important to devote multiple sessions to a topic that is particularly relevant or to cover content out of order to help meet the client's immediate needs (Connor-Smith & Weisz, 2003).

3. *Adapting Session Content*: "A clinically sophisticated approach does not involve mindless devotion to suggested exercises and assignments, but a skilled plan for presenting the

major intervention components in a way that is meaningful to each client" (Connor-Smith & Weisz, 2003, p. 5). In fact, revising activities, role-plays, and homework assignments are essential to the success of counseling.

4. *Boundaries to Adaptation*: Although adaptation is encouraged, it is important that the key components of the intervention are not lost. "Knowing the difference between an appropriate modification and one that eliminates, or even contradicts a key facet of the program will require a thorough understanding of the underlying principles of the intervention" (Connor-Smith & Weiz, 2003, p. 5).

5. *Maintaining Therapeutic Alliance*: Although client satisfaction may be essential to engage clients, these factors may not lead to change without the inclusion of specific interventions (Connor-Smith & Weisz, 2003). However, showing warmth, empathy, and responsiveness on the part of the therapist continues to be an essential aspect of the counseling relationship.

Although many counselors today value the use of treatment manuals, it is important to outline the various reasons other counselors are opposed to their use.

The Case against Treatment Manuals

According to Erskine (1998), the creation of standardized manuals and guidelines for the practice of counseling is creating a crisis for professional counselors. Manuals are practice guidelines or standardized protocols with empirically validated treatments. Treatment manuals for specific mental health disorders define acceptable counseling and dictate what constitutes appropriate treatment (Erskine, 1998) while reducing counselor–client collaboration in choosing the type, frequency, and duration of counseling. Messer and Wampold (2002) view this disconnect between the science and art of counseling traditionally practiced by most counselors as overlooking the importance of common factors that have been consistently associated with treatment effectiveness. Clearly, the greatest criticism of manuals of standardized techniques is that the counseling relationship cannot be standardized.

According to Erskine (1998), the manuals or standardized protocols are simplistic and rigid remedies for complex human problems and ever-changing relationship difficulties. In addition, manuals focus on a specific form of therapy that is to be applied to a specific list of diagnoses (Beutler, 2000), thereby imposing limits on the counselor's ability to address patient problems flexibly as they arise during psychotherapy. At the same time, a recipe-formatted manualized approach to counseling is simply not compatible with the way that counselors practice in the real world. Beutler (2000, p. 1002) summarizes this intersection between manualized treatment and counselor practices: "It follows, therefore, that adhering to a recipe impedes the operation of clinician judgment and creativity and requires clinicians to constrain the use of their usual interventions." The impact of treatment manuals on practice reflects a continuing source of debate within the counseling professions. Erskine (1998, p. 1) states:

> We psychotherapists endeavor to include our clients in making decisions for their own unique welfare that includes choice of the type of treatment, frequency, duration, objectives, and mutual evaluation of treatment effectiveness. When psychotherapy is governed by statistically

validated techniques or driven by diagnosis-based manuals, the focus on the client's uniqueness is lost and the healing power in the relationship between client and therapist is overlooked. It is essential for the future of psychotherapy that we challenge the manualization of psychotherapy.

Critics state that attempts to standardize counseling practice through the publication of practice manuals ignores the evidence that growth and change occur through the uniqueness of the therapeutic relationship (Erksine, 1998). In addition, Erksine (1998) points out that there exists a potential abuse of manuals by insurance companies that have a profit interest in reducing the number of types of therapies that they will pay for.

The use of treatment manuals by counseling professionals within organizations providing mental health care is difficult to measure. Azocar, Cuffel, Goldman, and McCarter (2003) found that clinicians self-reported high rates of adherence to use of disseminated treatment manuals, yet these self-reports could not be verified by claims data. Requiring the use of a treatment manual, therefore, while lacking a method to ensure that it is being used as intended and that the outcomes of treatment can be associated with the treatment method prescribed in the manual, presents a major drawback to their use.

Another issue of considerable importance has been raised with reference to managed mental health care and the number of sessions provided in such plans. In a study focused on the number of psychotherapy sessions needed to achieve treatment outcomes, length of treatment for a variety of psychological disorders was estimated to be between 13 and 18 sessions (Hansen, Lambert, & Forman, 2002), with 12.7 sessions being identified as linked to improvement for 57.6 to 76.2 percent of the patients. The actual average number of sessions in this study of a national database sample, however, was found to be 5. In viewing these perspectives, questions arise regarding the use of research that verifies the effectiveness of the treatment method as well as managed care authorization for the length of treatment.

Treatment manuals, although introduced as tools to assist counselors in the implementation of empirically validated counseling methods, have generated continued debate and unease within the counseling professions (Beutler, 2000; Messer & Wampold, 2002). The benefits of these tools for practice are well recognized and have led to research to more clearly define the parameters of counseling treatment outcomes. However, the essence of the therapeutic relationship in counseling remains one of the most potent factors in determining how counseling intervention achieves desired outcomes.

Included in therapist variables in a study of master therapists conducted by Sullivan, Skovholt, and Jennings (2005) are qualities and characteristics of the counselor, such as (1) therapist responsiveness and sensitivity to the client, (2) collaboration with the client as an active element of the helping process, (3) formation of an intimate therapeutic relationship as a cornerstone of the therapeutic process, and (4) use of the self of the therapist while engaging with the client and retaining an objectivity about the therapy process. Clearly, these qualities and personal attributes of the competent counselor are not contained in manualized approaches to psychotherapy and further promote a reductionistic view of the counseling process that is not linked to client-centered counseling (Hansen, 2005).

Efficacy versus Effectiveness

Efficacy of counseling can be defined as the results achieved in the setting of a research trial, whereas clinical effectiveness is the outcome of counseling in routine practice (Guthrie, 2000), referred to as evidence-based practice (EBT) (Miller, Zweben, & Johnson, 2005). As researchers have become more concerned with having higher internal validity, the distinction between efficacy and effectiveness becomes greater. As outcome research has grown in sophistication, its relevance to clinical practice has become less clear (Beutler, 2000; Persons & Silberschatz, 1998). Guthrie (2000) suggests that counseling outcome research needs to become more clinically relevant so results can be more easily translated into clinical practice. Although this is an admirable goal, it begs the question that has previously been raised: How will the busy, time-pressured counselor integrate research-based information into practice?

Promoting acceptance of evidence-based research, accumulated in practice settings over time, seems a reasonable proposition to support. Achieving recognition of the potency of this form of research by managed care reviewers in addition to how clinical research is viewed, however, will be challenging. To ensure that consumers of counseling are well served, these two "camps" will need to find a way to devise a middle ground that recognizes the similarities as well as differences in efficacy and effectiveness of research in counseling.

Premise of Outcome Research.   The current premise of outcome research is often focused on the view that something contained in the counseling process results in change beyond that expected by the passing of time, or that the resulting change is in addition to that achieved by a different intervention (Guthrie, 2000). According to Guthrie (2000), most efficacy trials of counseling methods differ from clinical practice in two ways. First, clients are selected according to strict criteria, usually involving diagnostic criteria for one specific mental health condition. Second, counselors who deliver the treatment are highly qualified and experienced and are trained to adhere to a treatment manual (Guthrie, 2000). Furthermore, according to Guthrie, a counseling outcome study is unlikely to receive funding unless the research methodology is robust. However, the higher the internal validity, the less relevance the results may have to clinical practice.

Weisz, Weiss, and Donenberg (1992) suggested that there were six main differences between research counseling and clinical counseling. During *research counseling*, clients (1) are recruited by the researcher, (2) represent homogeneity, and (3) given treatment for one specific problem. Counselors (4) are trained in the specific procedure under study, (5) follow a protocol, and (6) use a treatment manual that includes monitoring of adherence. In *clinical counseling*, clients (1) are referred by others or self-referred, (2) heterogeneous, and (3) may have a range of problems. Counselors have (4) variable training, (5) do not follow a specific protocol, and (6) do not use a treatment manual with monitoring procedures.

Shadish and colleagues (1997) developed three stages by which studies can be judged in terms of clinical representativeness. Stage 1 includes studies that were conducted in nonuniversity clinics, involved clients that were not solicited by the researcher, and involved experienced counselors with typical caseloads. Stage 2 includes all the criteria in Stage 1 plus studies that did not use a treatment manual and did not monitor the implementation of treatment. Finally, Stage 3 includes all of Stages 1 and 2 plus studies that used clients who were heterogeneous in personal characteristics as well as presenting problems, used counselors who were not trained immediately before the study, and used counselors who were free to use a wide variety of procedures. When the researchers reviewed 1,000 counseling outcome studies, they found that only 56 studies passed Stage 1 criteria, 15 passed Stage 2 criteria, and 1 passed Stage 3 criteria.

The question becomes one of balance. If all the studies listed previously have passed Stage 3 criteria, could any inference between cause and effect for the treatment interventions be made? Goldfried and Wolfe (1998) state that counseling outcome research needs to be more clinically relevant without sacrificing all aspects that improve internal validity. Guthrie (2000) makes the following suggestions in order to strike such a balance:

1. The maintenance of treatment integrity using manualized counseling should remain an essential component of any outcome study.
2. Manualized therapies need to be more flexible to individual client requirements.
3. Research counselors need to be more representative of counselors who will be charged with delivering the treatment.
4. Outcome research needs to be targeted toward more clinically relevant and representative client groups.

It would appear that although treatment manuals have drawbacks, when used with caution, they can form a foundation on which to build treatment plans that meet the unique needs of consumers who seek mental health care *and* provide a foundation for practice research. With continued refinement of the content contained in treatment manuals clearly linked to outcome research, the value of this tool can be increased. Essential to such an effort is the need to ensure that interpretation of research results adheres to well-defined principles.

Interpretation of Outcome Research.   Interpreting counseling outcome research results is as critical as the research design. Walz (1993, p. 122) developed 10 principles of counseling outcome research results that apply to both researchers and practitioners alike. These principles are based on Walz's conclusion that "counseling efficacy and advocacy go hand in hand." The principles of counseling outcome research emphasize clarity in identifying the boundaries of the research (i.e., identifying who the research is for, who will benefit, and who the "stakeholders" are in terms of interest in the results). With the advent of technology as a powerful tool for communication, outcome researchers are now encouraged to think beyond the traditional dissemination route (a printed report) and to incorporate electronic or web-based communication channels as well. These extensions of information distribution also can increase the likelihood that audiences who could benefit from exposure to the information can gain access to it in a timely manner (Walz, 1993).

Because counseling research holds the potential for significant impact on how services are delivered, it is essential also to include exploratory efficacy research alongside research that provides confirmation of current methods of treatment outcome. In this manner, the field is strengthened currently while efforts to research newer approaches are undertaken.

As both approaches to efficacy research are implemented, attention to the ethical and legal implications of counseling methods must be integral elements of the research process. Although new forms of counseling may gain notoriety with reference to reported rapid success rates, there can be no substitute for thoughtful, well-constructed research that then verifies dramatic outcomes or not. Counseling research also benefits from research conducted across the spectrum of practitioner settings as well as in traditional institutions of higher education and health care settings. The gap between the "ivory tower" of some research and the world of the practitioner can be a source of the "disconnect" discussed earlier in this chapter (i.e., research knowledge generated in clinical settings not being adapted by practitioners in the field).

Integrating New Knowledge into Practice.   Finally, Walz (1993) has brought up an excellent issue for consideration: the method that practicing counselors can use to integrate new knowledge into practice. How is counselor behavior changed when new research findings are published? An excellent example of this change process is illustrated by the change in practice, training, research, and education within the counseling and psychology professions with reference to multiculturalism and diversity sensitivity. With the advent of research that clearly identified the role of multiculturalism, ethnicity, and diversity variables within the counseling process (see Chapter 2), the methods used to train and educate counselors-to-be changed. Practice changed as the professions of counseling, psychology, and social work, for example, embraced the need to incorporate variables of difference into all areas of the helping process, research, and education. Known as the fourth force in psychology (Pederson, 1991), this change continues to drive research agendas as well as practice applications.

Continuing Professional Research Education.   The counseling professions can promote the usefulness and meaning of research activities as a part of the science and art of counseling through continuing professional education as well as postgraduate life-long learning that could include formal academic coursework, self-study, and collaborations with colleagues who share similar clinical interests. Related to this more expansive view of the potential that research has for practice is the need to demystify the research data analysis process for the practicing counselor. Statistical significance is seen as limited for use in counseling outcome research because it is based on group means and does not provide information on individual variability, nor does it address clinical significance (i.e., the practical importance of client change) that occurs through counseling (Hansen & Lambert, 1996).

Determining the effectiveness of methods used in clinical practice can be made less complex through use of practice-compatible case study methods, for example, that combine a systematic approach to research within the context of the counseling setting. In addition, for those counselors who become more comfortable with the research process as experience is accumulated in practice settings, the option to seek research mentors can be explored. The counselor research mentor can provide guidance, coaching, and mentoring to counselors who see the value of research in practice, yet are not confident in the use of single-subject research designs or statistical analysis options, for example.

ORIGINS OF OUTCOME RESEARCH QUESTIONS

Lambert, Masters, and Ogles (1991) developed major classes of outcome research questions by categorizing them historically. Major Class I (effectiveness) questions ask the basic question: Is counseling effective? Between the 1930s and 1960s, representative questions that were asked about outcome research regarding effectiveness of client-centered therapy were: Do people who participate in counseling change more than people who do not? and Are the effects of therapy are short term or long lasting? (Lambert et al, 1991). Although hundreds of studies have been conducted regarding Major Class I questions, the limitations of these studies were significant. Studies that reported the outcome of treated groups as superior to the outcomes of nontreated groups missed a key element linked to efficacy: The differences reported could not be attributed to the procedures that the researchers believed were effective (Lambert et al, 1991).

The shift in outcome research is classified by Lambert and colleagues (1991) as Class II questions (therapeutic ingredients) that focus on what causes improvement. Representative questions that identify Class II questions include: Are the positive outcomes in counseling due to client expectations or counseling techniques? Are the positive outcomes in counseling due to counselor attitudes, personality, gender, race, or what? Is cognitive therapy more effective than person-centered therapy? and Is group therapy more effective than individual and marriage and family therapy? The between-groups comparison studies produced intriguing results, often subsequently leading to preferences for one form of treatment over another. In contemporary times, the Class II studies continue to weigh heavily on decision makers regarding forms of treatment that will be recognized as having desired efficacy in terms of brevity and cost containment.

Class III questions, as defined by Lambert and colleagues (1991), can be focused on the match between the therapy method and the client in terms of increased efficacy. These research questions also can address questions regarding offering therapy for longer periods of time as a factor to increase outcomes. Another example of a Class III question would seek to answer the question: Does phasing out treatment improve the durability of treatment effects? Enhancement studies hold a critically important position in the pantheon of counseling research formats. It is essential that studies be conducted about variables linked to matching clients to the form of treatment that is known to be most effective for clients experiencing a particular life problem, developmental phase, disorder, or traumatic experience.

Since Lambert and associates (1991, p. 219) suggested this three-part categorization of outcome research questions, other researchers have expanded on this work to devise other terminologies that meet the needs of counselor researchers. Granello and Hill (2005) offer the effectiveness study as a strategy that "can be used by many different types of behavioral treatment facilities to demonstrate treatment success." Using this method, counselors can engage in a systematic research process in practice environments that is uncontrolled for many key variables that would be part of empirical research. Understanding these limitations ensures that conclusions drawn from effectiveness studies are viewed in realistic terms with known limitations.

A research question nomenclature is a valuable tool for the practicing counselor who seeks to integrate research into practice in a more consistent manner. The three classifications present options that clinical as well as practicing counselor researchers can consider and apply with higher levels of sophistication than when these methods were first devised. Research with each of these approaches has been strengthened by each addition to the bodies of literature reporting the studies, and it is this process that, over time, leads to ever-more refined methods to answer research questions in all counseling settings.

COUNSELING OUTCOME RESEARCH MEASUREMENT ISSUES

Counselor effectiveness has historically been evaluated using assessments such as counselor and client self-reports, interviews, simulations, and rating scales. According to Loesch (1995), "Rating scales are the most commonly used method, but no assessment procedure has emerged as the most reliable, valid, and effective." Counselor self-assessments are helpful for a counselor's professional development, and there is certainly value in this. However, according to Loesch (1995), because of their subjectivity, they are rarely generalizable, have not withstood psychometric scrutiny, and are not widely used as an effective means for assessment of counselor performance. As a single data point in a more comprehensive approach to self-evaluation or evaluation of counselor performance, however, the self-report continues to be a valuable tool.

Assessments by clients are widely used because the client is often the individual who can assess how a counselor has performed. Usually, clients assess counselors during postcounseling interviews or by completing rating scales. The use of rating scales completed by clients is one of the most common ways to assess a counselor's performance (Loesch, 1995). The drawback to client self-rating of counselor performance is that these rating scales are often completed immediately after counseling has been terminated; therefore, this immediacy does not take into account change that has been maintained by the client over time.

Steenbarger and Smith (1996) suggest that a continuous quality assessment approach would more accurately provide outcome data, since a high percentage of clients prematurely end treatment before a formal termination process has been initiated. Using this approach, assessment of client progress by the client or therapist is completed periodically throughout the course of treatment, thereby providing opportunity to revise treatment methods and attend to the client's self-assessment information. This method would capture information about the essence of counseling that may include helping methods that clients do not find overtly helpful at the time counseling is delivered, but as time passes, the interventions prove to be powerful and impactful. Evaluations done at the ending of a series of counseling sessions, then, may not reflect the true impact or efficacy of counseling provided. Viewed from a third perspective, evaluations of counseling performance by clients can be restricted in accuracy for another reason: Clients typically are not well versed in what effective counseling methods are, or should be. Thus, when evaluating a counselor, the client can provide personal opinions of the experience, but not an accurate evaluation of how well a counselor delivered a particular method. Objective evaluation of performance is required for this level of evaluation.

Assessment of counselor performance by external objective evaluators is the most frequently used assessment approach, with external evaluators being supervisors, colleagues, or researchers. Rating scales are the most frequently used assessment tools and are developed to assess different aspects of counselor performance and counseling skills (Loesch, 1995). Assessment of noncounseling functions—such as diagnosis, case management, treatment planning, consultation, professional development, and research—is a recent trend in assessment of counselor performance (Loesch, 1995). Loesch points out that assessment of noncounseling functions are often assessed through rating scales by external evaluators, but alternatives such as portfolio reviews are gaining popularity.

Fundamentally, objective evaluation is a powerful mechanism to evaluate counselor performance when the measures used are comprehensive, and the evaluator is skilled in administering the instruments used. Not adequately evaluated consistently is the more interpersonal, "soft," or "art" of counseling that is recognized as essential to effective practice. Thus, although some aspects of the counseling process can be evaluated by the counselor or client through use of structured assessment methods, obtaining information on the more subjective aspects of the art of counseling are not readily subject to the same methods. (How can a counselor be adequately and accurately evaluated on the use of the art of counseling when that is not well defined and difficult to quantify?) It is, however, the art of counseling linked to the science of research-based practice, that, when combined, is readily recognized as excellence, satisfying, and motivating to counselor professionals.

SUMMARY COMMENT

Because research evidence is always incomplete and lacking in comprehensiveness to some degree or another, clinicians are faced with a choice either to use treatments supported by efficacy trials, but relatively untested in clinical practice, or to continue using treatments that have not been tested at all but that "seem" to work (Connor-Smith & Weisz, 2003). Despite limitations in the current outcome research data that are inherent in social science research, using such research is an essential supplement to professional experience (Connor-Smith & Weisz, 2003). Counselors, in fact, have an ethical responsibility to use interventions supported by outcome research before using untested and unproven techniques.

Without credibility and perceived competece, the profession of counseling may struggle for a place among the professions of social work, marriage and family counseling, and psychology (Sexton, 2001). Without scientific support for counseling's effectiveness, there is little justification for regarding counseling as a profession that warrants reimbursement, licensure, and credentialing (Lambert & Cattani-Thompson, 1996).

Watkins and Schneider (1991, pp. 287–296) provide an excellent summation about research in counseling that seems to be the most salient to the conclusion of this chapter. Their postulates about research are as follows:

1. Counseling research can inform counseling practice and be useful to counseling practitioners.
2. Counseling should be guided by professional ethics and standards.
3. There will probably always be some conflict between counseling research and practice.

4. Counseling research has become sophisticated in the research questions asked and in the methodological approaches used.
5. Although research has contributed to establishing the validity of counseling, much more research is needed to develop an empirical base of techniques used in counseling.
6. Counseling research remains committed to seeking out cause–effect relationships.
7. Much more research needs to be done.

The practicing counselor relies on research to guide the care provided in myriad ways. Research forms the scaffolding for counseling interventions that are frequently used, often without overt recognition that the technique or approach originated with research. Other methods are more recent and will continue to require study to ensure that outcomes are consistent and reliable.

In this chapter, although some research from the literature was specific to counseling, there was a great deal of work from our sister profession of psychology. Dr. Howard Smith, the associate executive director for Professional Affairs for the American Counseling Association presented "The Urgency of Outcomes Research for the Counseling Profession" at the 2003 School Counseling Research Summit. Smith (2000, p. 1) states,

> There is a shortage of evidence-based research across the counseling profession. We have borrowed and inferred from the research of our sister professions. We have collected all sorts of anecdotal evidence on effectiveness of counseling, but we have fallen short of doing the heavy lifting of evidence-based research.

Herein lies the path for the future. The counseling profession can take up the banner of evidence-based research across a continuum that is bounded by traditional clinical trials in institutional settings, to agency and organization research in community settings, to single-case research in the offices of private practitioners. Opportunities for collaboration of practitioners in the research process could be facilitated by the professional associations for counseling, social work, and psychology. Cross-discipline collaborations would add an element of richness and relevance to community-based research. The opportunities are limited only by the vision that each counseling professional has to embrace the value and benefits of research/evidence-based methods in the real world of daily practice.

DISCUSSION TOPICS/QUESTIONS

1. Counselors take academic coursework that includes research methods and may conduct forms of research as part of the education and skills training experiences necessary for entry into the profession. Discuss two purposes of research in counseling. Use hypothetical clinical cases to illustrate each purpose.

2. The scientist practitioner model of counseling uses a systematic process to guide the therapeutic encounter between client(s) and counselor. How will you integrate this model into your practice?

3. Evidence-based interventions are supported by research previously conducted with specific populations using specific methods of treatment. Describe how an evidence-based

intervention could be applied in a community mental health agency. Include each step in the SPM as outlined in Figure 4.1.

4. Various terms have been used to describe "research" that could be conducted in practice settings. Evaluate the appeal of two terms (*outcome research* and *evidence-based interventions*) to a mental health counselor in private practice. How could understanding, education, and training in the use of these approaches to research soften the resistance to integrating research into practice?

5. Recognizing that the science and art of counseling can be expressed in practice with individuals, consider how Ms. Waterman could integrate this perspective in a *group counseling* setting with women experiencing post-partum depression. How would she alter her methods for group counseling?

6. Managed mental health care is well situated in the health care industry as a mechanism to control escalating costs while incorporating the need to demonstrate the effectiveness of counseling interventions. Describe how counselors can integrate the art of counseling into practice in the contemporary world of managed mental health care.

7. While at a regional conference attended by counselors and human services professionals, you meet a colleague from your community. As you discuss your practices, you both note similarities in the client populations that you treat and in the methods used. Since one of the sessions that you both attended at the conference discussed research in counseling, discuss how you and your colleague could collaborate on a research project.

8. Research-mindedness represents a consistent way to approach each counseling case beginning from initial interview to termination of treatment. Develop an outline of a continuing education session that could be delivered to a community counseling center staff that highlights two methods to integrate research into the day-to-day practice of the clinicians in this agency.

9. Alison is a 16-year-old high school student referred to you for counseling following a suicide attempt. After an overnight hospitalization during which she was stabilized medically, she was referred to you for outpatient counseling. How will you integrate periodic structured assessment into your treatment plan for Alison? How will the methods you select reflect a continuous quality assessment approach to outcome evaluation of your treatment?

10. Dr. Martinez is a recent addition to the counseling staff at the child advocacy center. She is very interested in providing support to the counseling professionals with whom she works and has excellent empirical research credentials. Prior to approaching Dr. Martinez about mentoring you on a research project, develop a list of discussion questions you could review with her regarding conducting research in this counseling practice setting.

REFERENCES

Acuff, C., Bennett, B. E., Bricklin, P. M., Canter, M. B., Knapp, S. J., Moldawsky, S., & Phelps, R. (1999). Considerations for ethical practice in managed care. *Professional Psychology Research and Practice, 30*, 563–575.

Azocar, F., Cuffel, B., Goldman, W., & McCarter, L. (2003). The impact of evidence-based guideline dissemination for the assessment and treatment of major depression in a managed behavioral health care organization. *Journal of Behavioral Health Services & Reseach, 30*(1), 109–118.

Beutler, L. E. (2000). David & Goliath: When empirical and clinical standards of practice meet. *American Psychologist, 55*(9), 997–1007.

Bieschke, K. J., Fouad, N. A., Collins, F. L., & Halonen, J. S. (2004). The scientifically-minded psychologist: Science as a core competency. *Journal of Clinical Psychology, 60*(7), 713–723.

Brammer, L., & Whitfield, R. P. (1972). A matter of survival. *Impact, 2*(3), 38–45.

Burlingame, G. M., Lambert, M. J., Reisinger, C. W., Neff, W. M., & Mosier, J. (1995). Pragmatics of tracking mental health outcomes in a managed care setting. *Journal of Mental Health Administration, 22,* 226–336.

Caspar, F. (1997). What goes on in a psychotherapist's mind? *Psychotherapy Research, 7,* 105–125.

Chambless, L. D., Sanderson, W. C., Shoham, B., Bennett-Johnson, S., Pope, K. S., Crits-Christoph, P., et al. (1996). An update on empirically validated therapies. *The Clinical Psychologist, 49*(2), 5–18.

Connor-Smith, J. K., & Weisz, J. R. (2003). Applying treatment outcome research in clinical practice: Techniques for adapting interventions to the real world. *Child and Adolescent Mental Health, 8*(1), 3–10.

Erksine, R. G. (1998). Psychotherapy in the U.S.A.: A manual of standardized techniques for a therapeutic relationship. *International Journal of Psychotherapy, 3*(3), 231–235.

Goldfried, M. R., & Wolfe, B. E. (1998). Toward a more clinically valid approach to therapy research. *Journal of Consulting and Clinical Psychology, 66,* 143–150.

Granello, D. H., & Hill, L. (2005). Assessing outcomes in practice settings: A primer and example from an eating disorders program. *Journal of Mental Health Counseling, 25*(3), 218–232.

Granello, P. F., & Haag, D. (1998). Training counseling students to use outcome research. *Counselor Education and Supervision, 37*(4), 224–238.

Guthrie, E. (2000). Enhancing the clinical relevance of psychotherapy outcome research. *Journal of Mental Health, 9*(2), 267–271.

Hansen, J. T. (2005). The devaluation of inner subjective experiences by the counseling profession: A plea to reclaim the essence of the profession. *Journal of Counseling & Development, 83,* 406–415.

Hansen, N. B., & Lambert, M. J. (1996). Clinical significance: An overview of methods. *Journal of Mental Health, 5*(1), 17–25.

Hansen, N. B., Lambert, M. J., & Forman, E. M. (2002). The psychotherapy dose-response effect and its implication for treatment delivery services. *Clinical Psychology: Science and Practice, 9*(3), 329–343.

Howard, K. I., Kopta, S. M., Krause, M. S., & Orlinsky, D. E. (1986). The dose-effect relationship in psychotherapy. *American Psychologist, 41*(2), 159–164.

Kelly, K. R. (1996). Review of clinical mental health counseling process and outcome research. *Journal of Mental Health Counseling, 18*(4), 358–376.

Knapper, E. Q. (1978). Counselor accountability. *Personnel and Guidance Journal, 57,* 27–30.

Kratochwill, T. R., & Shernoff, E. S. (2004). Evidence-based practice: Promoting evidence-based interventions in school psychology. *School Psychology Review, 33*(1), 34–48.

Lambert, M. J., & Anderson, E. M. (1996). Assessment for the time-limited psychotherapies. *Annual Review of Psychiatry, 15,* 23–47.

Lambert, M. J., & Bergin, A. E. (1994). The effectiveness of psychotherapy. In E. Bergin & S. L. Garfield (Eds.), *Handbook of psychotherapy and behavior change* (4th ed.) (pp. 143–189). New York: Wiley.

Lambert, M. J., & Cattani-Thompson, K. (1996). Current findings regarding the effectiveness of counseling: Implications for practice. *Journal of Counseling & Development, 74,* 601–608.

Lambert, M. J., Masters, K. S., & Ogles, B. M. (1991). Outcome research in counseling. In C. E. Watkins & L. J. Schneder (Eds.), *Research in counseling* (pp. 51–83). Hillsdale, NJ: Erlbaum.

Larner, G. (2004). Family therapy and the politics of evidence. *Journal of Family Therapy, 26,* 17–37.

Leibert, T. W. (2006). Making change visible: The possibilities in assessing mental health counseling outcomes. *Journal of Counseling & Development, 84,* 108–113.

Leuger, R. J. (2002). Practice-informed research and research-informed psychotherapy. *Journal of Clinical Psychology, 58,* 1265–1276.

Loesch, L. C. (1995). *Assessment of counselor performance.* Retrieved from the ERIC Document Reproduction Service No. ERIC-RIE0, 19950101.

Messer, S. B., & Wampold, B. E. (2002). Let's face the facts: Common factors are more potent than specific therapy ingredients. *Clinical Psychology: Science and Practice, 9*(1), 21–25.

Metzl, J. M. (1998). Psychotherapy, managed care, and the economy of interaction. *American Journal of Psychotherapy, 52*(3), 332–351.

Miller, W. R., Zweben, J., & Johnson, W. R. (2005). Evidence-based treatment: Why, what, where, when, and how? *Journal of Substance Abuse Treatment, 29*, 267–276.

Nicholson, T. S., & Berman, J. S. (1983). Is follow-up necessary in evaluating psychotherapy? *Psychological Bulletin, 93*(2), 261–278.

Pedersen, P. B. (1991). Multiculturalism as a fourth force in counseling. *Journal of Counseling & Development, 70*(1), 4.

Persons, J. B., & Silberschatz, G. (1998). Are results of randomized controlled trials useful to psychotherapists? *Journal of Consulting and Clinical Psychology, 66*, 126–135.

Ruby, J. R. (2005). Constraints to master's level practitioner research: A literature review. *Counseling: Clinical Psychology Journal, 2*(1), 59–67.

Seligman, M. E. P. (1995). The effectiveness of psychotherapy: The *Consumer Reports* study. *American Psychologist, 50*(12), 965–974.

Sexton, T. L. (1996). The relevance of counseling outcome research: Current trends and practical implications. *Journal of Counseling & Development, 74*, 590–600.

Sexton, T. L. (2001). Evidence-based counseling intervention programs: Practicing "best practices." In D. C. Locke, J. E. Myers, & E. L. Herr (Eds.), *The handbook of counseling* (pp. 499–512). Thousand Oaks, CA: Sage.

Sexton, T. L., Whiston, S. C., Bleuer, J. C., & Walz, G. R. (1997). *Integrating outcome research into counseling practice and training.* Alexandria, VA: American Counseling Association.

Shadish, W. R., Matt, G. E., Navarro, A., Seigle, G., Crits-Christoph, P., Hazelrigg, M., et al. (1997). Evidence that therapy works in clinically representative conditions. *Journal of Consulting and Clinical Psychology, 65*, 355–365.

Smith, H. B. (2000, May). *The urgency of outcomes research for the counseling profession.* Paper presented at the meeting of the School Counseling Research Summit, Amherst, MA.

Steenbarger, B. N., & Smith, H. B. (1996). Assessing the quality of counseling services: Developing accountable helping systems. *Journal of Counseling & Development, 75*, 145–150.

Sullivan, M. F., Skovholt, T. M., & Jennings, L. (2005). Master therapists' construction of the therapeutic relationship. *Journal of Mental Health Counseling, 27*(1), 48–70.

Walz, G. R. (1993). Important consideration in disseminating counseling outcomes research. In G. R. Walz & J.C. Bleuer (Eds.), *Counselor efficacy: Assessing and using counseling outcomes research* (pp. 121–136). Ann Arbor, MI: ERIC.

Walz, G. R., & Bleuer, J. C. (1993). Counselor efficacy. In G. R. Walz & J.C. Bleuer (Eds.), *Counselor efficacy: Assessing and using counseling outcomes research* (pp. 1–4). Ann Arbor, MI: ERIC.

Watkins, C. E., Jr., & Schneider, L. J. (1991). *Research in counseling.* Hillsdale, NJ: Erlbaum.

Weisz, J. R., Weiss, B., & Donenberg, G. R. (1992). The lab versus the clinic: Effects of child and adolescent psychotherapy. *American Psychologist, 47*, 1578–1585.

Wheeler, P. T., & Loesch, L. (1981). Program evaluation and counseling: Yesterday, today, and tomorrow. *Personnel and Guidance Journal*, 573–578.

Whiston, S. C., & Coker, J.K. (2000). Reconstructing clinical training: Implications from research. *Counselor Education and Supervision, 39*(4), 228–254.

CHAPTER FIVE

THE BIO-PSYCHO-SOCIAL MODEL
Integrating Science and Practice

JOANNA OESTMANN

During the seventeenth century, the separation between mind and body was established so that medical science could explore the body and the church could retain the domain of the mind. The latter half of the twentieth century saw the rise in incidence of chronic illnesses (e.g., heart disease, cancer, depression, arthritis, asthma) that appeared to be related to environmental and emotional stresses. Costs to treat these and other emerging chronic illnesses skyrocketed as the scientific movement to explore the mind made dramatic strides in how health care professionals understand the inner workings of the brain.

Concurrent with these advances has been the recognition that humans are part of surrounding cultures and social systems that directly influence how healing takes places. As each frontier was, and continues to be, explored, counseling professionals became intensely interested in the interconnectedness of the mind and body. Thus, at this point in the contemporary practice of counseling, the distinction between mind and body has blurred, and the ancient view of separateness between human behavior and experience has been replaced. Mental health professionals now know that mind–body actions are always mutual and bidirectional, meaning that the body affects the mind and is affected by it in turn. Therefore, the mind–body is best regarded as an overall process that is not easily dissected into separate and distinct parts (Borrell-Carrió, Suchman, & Epstein, 2004; Crick & Koch, 1992).

A large body of scientific evidence supports the effects of an interacting and mutually influential mind-body in contemporary medical science. Research increasingly offers support for this integrated bio-psycho-social model based on the impact of nature (e.g., biological) and nurture (e.g., social) influences on the psychological conditions of patients. For example, counselors now know about the following:

1. The importance of social relationships to health and well-being, and the perceptions of social isolation and aloneness affect many dimensions of human experience. As an

illustration, we know that alterations in cardiovascular and immunological responses during bereavement increase the mortality of the surviving spouse during the first year of bereavement. Other research indicates that social isolation and poor education are linked with increased incidence of disease and death (Dimsdale, 1977; Ott, 2003; Schaefer, Quesenberry, & Wi, 1995). Also, chronic psychological stress and isolation have been associated with heart disease and a weakened immune system.

2. The attitude toward work and work status are related to physical health, mental health, and well-being. As far back as 1973, a task force survey reported that the best predictor for heart attack was the level of job satisfaction, which may related to the observation that heart attacks in the United States cluster on Monday mornings from 8 to 9 a.m. (Kolata, 1986). Factors that offer protection against cardiovascular morbidity and mortality, even in psychologically stressful jobs, include control (personal decision making), challenge (personal growth and wisdom), and commitment to life on and off the job (Kobasa, Maddi, & Kahn, 1982; Parslow, Jorn, & Christensen, 2004).

3. The perceived meaning of an event has direct consequences to health and well-being, including one's mental health. The findings from six studies reached the same conclusion: One's own opinion about his or her state of health is a better predictor of health and well-being than objective factors, such as physical symptoms, extensive exams, and laboratory tests, or behaviors (Idler & Kasal, 1991). Therefore, when negative attitudes and emotions are eliminated or reduced, one's health improves. The "psychological," therefore, can directly influence the "biological," lending further support to the interaction and lack of separateness between mind and body (Gatchel, 2004).

4. The relationship between the physician and patient, and agreement regarding their expectations, brings about a positive placebo response. If this agreement is missing, a favorable response rarely occurs (Hankoff, Englehardt, Freedman, Mann, & Margolis, 1960). Therefore, the relationship and agreement between the therapist and client is extremely important to the outcome of therapy (Shi, Forrest, & von Schrader, 2003).

5. The role of religion/spirituality and health is significant. Research indicates that religion and spirituality are correlated with increased physical and mental health and a lower incidence of a variety of diseases such that infrequent religious attendance should be regarded as a consistent risk factor for morbidity and mortality of various types of illnesses, including heart disease (Levin & Schiller, 1987; Lewis, 2004; Matthews, Larson, & Barry, 1993).

6. The seeming spontaneous remission of cancer and other chronic diseases is a widely documented phenomenon as well as a promising area of research. The relationship between openly facing the disease and its implications are associated with near-equal survival rates, and sometimes a mode of psychological acceptance, not aggressiveness, toward the diagnosis seems to set the stage for remission (Hack, 2004). A caveat to counselors, however, is in order when viewing these exciting findings: The causal factors involved in spontaneous regression of cancer are varied and complex, and therefore these findings must be used with caution. There is no clear and consistent research that verifies the impact of psychological mindset on the biological response rate. However, there is an expanding

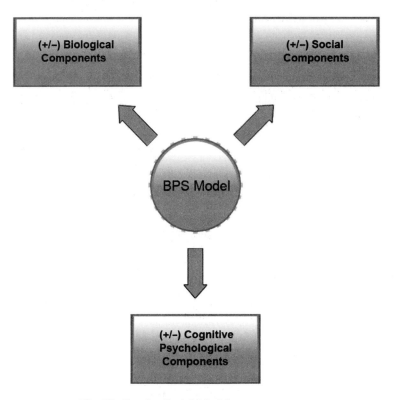

FIGURE 5.1   The Bio-Psycho-Social Model

body of research that emphasizes the qualitative outcomes of a positive mindset with cancer coping.

From these exemplars, the following model of positive and negative biological and social influences can be viewed as having an impact on the subsequent psychological conditions presenting in various patients seen by the psychology and counseling professionals (see Figure 5.1).

Contemporary support for the bio-psycho-social (BPS) model of human behavior was attributed George Engle in 1977. The model was widely embraced and continues to provide insights that guide contemporary counseling practice (Borrell-Carrió, Suchman, & Epstein, 2004). Throughout this chapter, issues associated with this model are explored and evaluated. The implications of each component of the model are reviewed. The biological, psychological, and social aspects of human behavior are considered with an eye on how the knowledge accrued about each element influences counseling professionals. It is recognized that this discussion artificially distinguishes among the biological, psychological, and social components of behavior and external sources of influence on behavior. In reality, these are interrelated and interdependent factors that link to other influences on human behavior (e.g., spirituality and religion, covered in Chapter 11).

CONTEMPORARY VIEWS OF THE BIO-PSYCHO-SOCIAL MODEL

As the twentieth century drew to a close, mental health care experts noted the importance of counseling professionals possessing a basic understanding and familiarity with scientific research, neuroscience, and clinical therapeutics to better meet the needs of their clients (Schwartz, 1982). To ensure that counselors can achieve this knowledge and practice goal, an integrated perspective is needed: the bio-psycho-social model. The BPS encompasses a multilevel, multisystem approach to the assessment of human behavior from individual, family, group, and social system perspectives. As the title suggests, there are three components of this model: the biological, the psychological, and the sociological (Borrell-Carrió, Suchman, & Epstein, 2004; Engle, 1977). When first conceptualized, these components were viewed and treated as individual constructs and as nonintegrative. However, as the counseling professions have developed into more integrative and complex practices, recognition of the interrelatedness of each aspect of this model has increasingly become accepted as holding the potential to favorably impact patient care outcomes (Kerns, Kassirer, & Otis, 2002; Orsulic-Jeras, Shepherd, & Britton, 2003).

In addition, social and political forces such as managed mental health care have forced therapists to use brief intervention models and have stated outcomes that are measurable (Baum, Revenson, & Singer, 2001; Christensen & Miller, 2001; McCann & Lipton, 1998; Prochaska & DiClemente, 1983). Although these, as well as many other challenges to the professions ultimately may produce positive outcomes for consumers and practitioners, other changes have exacerbated problems of access and availability of mental health services.

As a consequence, counseling professionals have increasingly turned to science to define and describe treatment outcomes (Kerns, Kassirer, & Otis, 2002). Counselors have made significant contributions in this regard, adding to the understanding of the role of outcome evaluation and the application of an expanded knowledge base to contemporary practice (Kerns, Kassirer, & Otis, 2002). Some of the factors that have promoted advancement of the BPS model into principles and practice, as related by Borrell-Carrió, Suchman, and Epstein (2004), include the expansion of science and health technology, increased client awareness, emotional and physical curiosity, the ability to research disorders via the Internet prior to treatment, and the desire for clients to seek inclusive treatments, including their subjective experience and biomedical data.

These, and many other issues, can directly impact the counselor's understanding of client behavior, ranging from the presenting complaint that motivated the decision to seek counseling to observed client behavior while providing counseling services. The counselor will need to be more sophisticated in approach to these clients, acknowledge their self-awareness and curiosity, cultivate trust, be empathetic to their individual concerns, provide psychoeducation, and continue to provide information that fosters a therapeutic relationship and further dialoging (Borrell-Carrió, Suchman, & Epstein, 2004). The requirement that counseling professionals provide informed, ethical treatment has increased in complexity and has led to the heightened awareness that multidisciplinary practice requires awareness and use of theoretical and scientific literature.

Defining the knowledge and skills needed by a therapist in the twenty-first century is a challenge, particularly with continuing advances made in the study of the brain, biogenetics, and research on the mind–body connection. At the same time, the American Counseling Association Code of Ethics (2005, p. 9), Standard C.2.a. states, "Therapists practice only within the boundaries of their competence, based on their education, training, supervised experience, state and national professional credentials, and appropriate professional experience." A similar caveat is contained in the ethical code of the American Psychological Association (2002).

In 1982, experts noted the importance of counseling professionals possessing a basic understanding and familiarity of the growing importance of scientific research, neuroscience, and clinical therapeutics to better meet the needs of their clients (Schwartz, 1982). In contemporary times, the explosion of scientific contributions to the understanding of brain functioning and how the brain–body interface operates has led to a restatement of that earlier advisory: Counselors now must ensure that they are abreast of scientific advancements to ensure that treatment provided reflects current knowledge and opportunities to provide up-to-date treatment. Consequently, therapists are responsible for obtaining continuing education and maintaining their knowledge of current professional and scientific information as well as integrating new information into practice to ensure quality outcomes and to monitor effectiveness (Booth, Cushway, & Newnes, 1997).

As part of the professional responsibilities of therapists and counselors in the field of psychology, application of the BPS model for clients has significant implications for assessment, treatment planning and methods, referral decisions, consultation/supervision, practice specializations, and treatment collaboration, as illustrated in Figure 5.2.

> Melinda is a 43-year-old African American female. She presented in counseling stating she was depressed. Among her self-described symptoms were changes in sleep pattern and mood, weight fluctuations, difficulty focusing, and alterations in her social and family relationships for the past six months. Melinda did not have a history of mental illness, significant life stressors, or other personal life changes that coincided with the onset of symptomatology.

In this case, the counselor would do a thorough assessment that focused on evaluating depression, anxiety, and sleep changes in order to arrive at a differential diagnosis. As the assessment

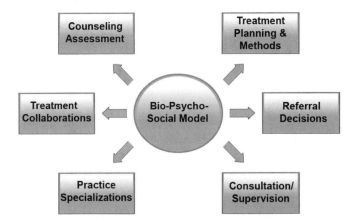

FIGURE 5.2   BPS Model: Implications for Counselors

was conducted, the therapist discovered that the client had not had a medical exam for over 10 years, yet stated that she was in good health. A referral to a physician for a complete physical examination and hormone level assessment, to rule out a biological basis for the reported symptoms, would be necessary based on the BPS model. Collaborating with a physician and other women's health specialists to develop a comprehensive treatment plan, with specific recommendations for the client, represents a methodology that considers mental and physical aspects of health in an atmosphere of trust and collaboration with the client.

As this case illustrates, exciting new developments in the brain–behavior interface, biogenetics, the role of pharmaceuticals in the treatment of neuropsychiatric disorders, and in the interaction between the mind and body await the counselor professional who seeks to incorporate emerging knowledge into practice. In the sections to follow, the three components in the bio-psycho-social model are reviewed as a preamble to examining how each can be applied by today's mental health professional.

THE BIO-PSYCHO-SOCIAL MODEL: BIOLOGICAL COMPONENT

Working within the BPS model, it is important that the counselor have a broad knowledge base regarding each component as well as how each interfaces and interacts. For example, if the counselor is unaware of the variables impacting the development of the brain and associated current research, information might be overlooked that would have a direct impact on treatment planning (e.g., the age at which brain trauma occurs would be an essential item of information to understand onset of behavioral change). In order to understand how knowledge about brain function interfaces with the counseling role, a review of issues associated with this body of knowledge is presented within the framework of the biological component considerations of the BPS model shown in Figure 5.3.

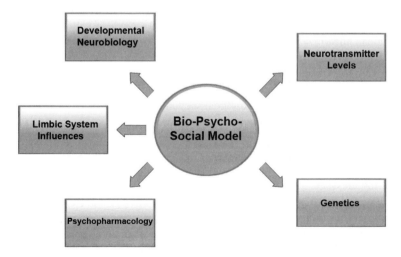

FIGURE 5.3   Biological Component Considerations

As a caveat to the reader, it is important to acknowledge that the counselor's prior knowledge of the brain and its functioning can be at an introductory level. For the counseling practitioner, this foundational knowledge base supports decision making regarding when to refer the client to a neuropsychologist or neurologist, for example, rather than risk practicing outside one's scope of competency. This knowledge foundation serves a second purpose that directly relates to effective practice. Understanding brain function enables the counseling professional to be an astute consumer of medical and psychological reports as well as research findings that can directly link to treatment planning.

The study of the brain provides a basis for the identification and treatment of a variety of physical and mental illnesses. Neuroscience and technological advances such as functional magnetic resonance imaging (MRI) have resulted in a broader understanding of how the brain works by identifying critical chemical and electrical pathways involved in memory, movement, and emotion (Bloom, Nelson, & Lazerson, 2000). Furthermore, the study of the brain is rapidly advancing with the use of magnetic resonance imaging (MRI), positron emission transaxial tomography (PETT), computerized tomography (CT) or computerized axial tomography (CAT) scans, and functional magnetic resonance imaging techniques (fMRI) (Bloom, Nelson, & Lazerson, 2001; Stephen, 2004.) These technological advances have offered new insight into the brain–behavior relationship. For example, researchers have found that many mental and behavioral disorders of childhood once attributed to reinforcement systems or environmental factors actually have a neurodevelopmental or neurochemical basis (Biederman & Farone, 2005; Farrington, 2005). Noteworthy is the benefit this information offers to the conceptualization and treatment of these related biological disorders. Moreover, a review of neurobiology provides the counselor professional with sufficient insight to link biological, psychological, and social factors in the BPS model.

Neurobiology and Neurotransmitters

The development of the neural tissue observed in the embryo early in the first trimester, to the nearly full-size brain and nervous system two years later, follows a relatively predictable pattern of genetically programmed growth (Zhang & Poo, 2001). Brain development seems to be hard-wired, as evidenced by the development/growth of similar physical structures (e.g., human anatomy) and capabilities (e.g., learning, walking, seeing, and hearing) in all human beings. Furthermore, all neurons necessary for the mature development of the sensory, motor, and visual areas in the brain are present at birth (Shonkoff & Phillips, 2000).

The understanding of the neuron's role in sending neurochemical information is important, as it provides insight into how neuropsychiatric (emotional) disorders emerge and progress, and how psychopharmacology interventions may help by targeting specific chemical actions/interactions in the brain. According to Herlenius and Lagercrantz (2004), the neuron consists of four regions: the cell body, dendrites, axon, and terminal buttons. Neurons communicate with each other across a gap located between the neurons, and the dendrites receive the message. The axon is a long tube covered by a myelin sheath that carries a brief electrical/chemical event (action potential) to other cells (Shepherd, 1994). Located at the end of the axon are an axon terminal, a gap or synapse, and another cell's dendrite ready to receive the message (Shepherd, 1994). As the action potential travels down the axon, it reaches the terminal button, and a chemical called a neurotransmitter is released from one neuron to another (Zhang & Poo, 2001). The effect of the neurotransmitter is to either excite or inhibit the message. Other types of synapses are possible as communication takes place throughout the body (Herlenius & Lagercrantz, 2004).

Several neurotransmitters have been identified: acetylcholine, serotonin, dopamine, norepinephrine, epinephrine, and gamma-amino butyric acid (Shepherd, 1994). Neurotransmitters appear to be concentrated in certain brain regions and are part of the electrochemical mechanisms used to communicate the initiation, regulation, and inhibition of simple and complex activities (Verhage et al, 2001). Although research suggests that too much or too little of a neurotransmitter may result in a psychiatric disorder (Matthews, 2001), the complexity of the interactions among billions of neurons is almost unfathomable. Additionally, increases or decreases in one neurotransmitter affects the levels of other chemicals in other brain areas. This effect is also present when medications increase one transmitter to normal levels, thus moving other transmitters in the opposite direction (Matthews, 2001; Shepherd, 1994).

Of these neurotransmitter imbalances, a decrease in dopamine is linked to an increase in hyperactivity and irritability (Matthews, 2001). Norepinephrine is a modulator of other neurotransmitters and is structurally very similar in effects to dopamine (Matthews, 2001). Serotonin plays a central part in impulse control disorders and may result in numerous behavioral disorders such as aggression, impulsivity, inattention, self-mutilation, violent behavior, and violent suicide (Verhage et al, 2001). It is always essential to consider biological factors when conducting patient assessments in order to generate possible diagnoses that can then directly be linked to treatment planning.

> Jennifer was brought to Dr. Wilson's counseling practice when her mother discovered that her daughter was not eating and had fresh scratches and cut marks on her inner forearms. Jennifer has been wearing baggy, long-sleeved shirts, but as the weather became sweltering, Mrs. Stevens became suspicious about her daughter's insistence on wearing this clothing. After much talking and arguing, Jennifer angrily put on a short-sleeved t-shirt that revealed the injuries and admitted that she has not been eating because she is fat.

As the counselor conducts a detailed history and initial interview, knowledge of the role of brain chemistry and neurobiology will guide questions asked of Jennifer and Mrs. Stevens as well as decisions about referrals for medical evaluation, and psychological testing and evaluation by an eating disorders specialist, or involvement of other family members in the treatment process. In addition, understanding of published research will stimulate the counselor to review the role of medication and choice of treatment modality to manage Jennifer's care (Stone & Sias, 2003). With a case as complex as Jennifer's, a variety of physiological issues may come into play when determining underlying causes for her self-injurious behavior. A review of specific elements of neurobiology may provide clues to Jennifer's behavior and guidance for treatment planning.

The Limbic System

The limbic system, an assortment of connected structures located in the central core of the brain, is responsible for various emotions such as rage, fear, aggression, or feelings linked to sexuality (Matthews, 2001). The hypothalamus receives information from the limbic system and can trigger changes/responses (e.g., stress, high blood pressure, rush of adrenaline) in the body associated with the emotion (Millan, 2003; Sala et al, 2004; Shepherd, 1994).

Given the central role of the limbic system in human behavior, ranging from instantaneous responses to threat as well as memory, research has sought to identify how this part of the brain can impact emotional expression, physical health, and emotional health and well-being (Mayne, 2001; Ochsner & Barrett, 2001). Research by Salovey, Rothman, Detweiler, and Steward (2000), for example, indicated that an alarming 50 percent or more of all patients who go to a physician for a physical illness have physical symptoms that are directly caused by emotions. Salovey and colleagues (2000) also contended that there is a physiological reason why emotions can impact health that is directly linked to the brain and hormone levels. Emotional responses are associated with neurological activation and hormonal releases that subsequently can impact health in a positive direction or have harmful outcomes (Mayne, 2001). For example, anger and fear serve to stimulate the amygdala to detect and immediately prepare for responding to threats (real or perceived) (Ochsner & Barrett, 2003). Additionally, a person's inability to express emotions has been found to adversely affect health (Borrell-Carrió, Suchman, & Epstein, 2004).

The impact of the limbic system on behavior and emotional responses is well illustrated for counselors who are working with patients who have chronic pain, are experiencing high levels of stress, or may be struggling with cognitive functioning. Incorporating information about how the brain may be processing stimuli may lead to referrals for medical or psychological evaluation as part of treatment planning.

Pain.   Although pain itself is not an emotion, painful sensations can result in emotions (Borsook & Becerra, 2003; Matthews, 2001). Pain is sensed via pain receptors in the skin, muscles, internal organs, and membranes around the bone. These receptors are more sensitive to firing and easily react to physical stimuli. The pain message is sent along two neural pathways to the brain. The chemical process involved in turning off the pain receptors includes body-produced opiate-like substances and/or endorphins (Shepherd, 1994). Research into the role of endorphins in treating pain is in its infancy yet continues to produce provocative findings that have implications for counseling practice.

The perception of pain is a complex, subjective phenomenon and depends on the meaning that the person assigns to a painful event (Matthews, 2001). Gatchel and Turk (1996) report that pain accounts for more than 80 percent of all primary care visits, affecting more than 50 million Americans and costing more than $70 billion annually in health care costs (as cited in Gatchel & Oordt, 2003). Chronic pain can mask depression or anxiety (Van Houdenhove, Verstraeten, Onghena, and De Cuyper, 1992), and stress and anxiety can significantly influence pain perception (Borsook & Becerra, 2003). The chain reaction of pain perception, emotional response to pain, which leads to the increase in pain perception and experience, forms a circular pattern that if not interrupted can lead to disabling chronic unremitting pain.

The role of the counselor in assessing the role of pain in the life of the client who seeks psychological assistance is clear. Assessment of pain becomes an integral aspect of the comprehensive interview as well as when designing treatment. For example, when initiating counseling with a client who has recently been diagnosed with migraine headaches or who experiences pain associated with life-threatening illness, the counselor may consider incorporating a variety of strategies that address the potential optimization of endorphin secretion. In other instances, the counselor may include patient education about the role of endorphins to block physical pain that should be felt in order to deter harmful behavior such as that associated with self-injurious behaviors. How the client interprets pain, is receptive to a variety of pain control/management methods, or relies on medication to control pain represents vital information that can inform treatment.

Stress.   Emotional reactions related to a stressful event may include intense anxiety (Sala et al, 2004). Stressors and the response to them can jolt the body out of homeostasis. This shift occurs with the secretion of two hormones from the adrenal glands—epinephrine (adrenalin) and glucocorticoids (cortisol or hydrocortisone)—and can be stimulated in relation to an actual event or from anticipation of the event (Millan, 2003). Key factors to the exacerbation of stress responding include lack of (1) an outlet for frustration, (2) a sense of control over events or sources of stress, (3) social support, and (4) confidence that something better will follow (Cheng & Cheung, 2005; Stewart, Davidson, Meade, Hirth, & Makrides, 2000). If these buffers are available, stress may be alleviated; if they are not available, the vigilance to manage or ward off repeated stressful incidents may cause anxiety or become so overwhelming that depression results (Millan, 2003).

For others, the nature of the stressful experiences themselves can foster development of more severe stress-linked physiological and psychological reactions or disorders. Chief among these is post-traumatic stress disorder (PTSD). A detailed study of PTSD is beyond the scope of this chapter, yet central characteristics of this psychological disorder reflect both bio-psycho-social and neurobiological responses that the counselor must incorporate into assessment and therapeutic activities (Soloman & Heide, 2005).

Studies indicate that PTSD connects to a complex interaction between several body and brain chemicals and specific reactions in the brain. Although many of these changes have been documented through study of the brain (e.g., via MRI techniques), as well as through study of body fluids (e.g., blood), the presentation of the changes is not clearly and consistently linked to specific behavioral or psychological responses (Bonne & Charney, 2004). In addition, it must be noted that stress-linked disorders such as PTSD also reflect the stress-diathesis model in which symptoms result from the interaction of inherent dispositions or characteristics (i.e., diathesis) of the individual and the surrounding environment (i.e., stressors) (Mowbray & Holter, 2002). A brief review of selected interactions, however, provides insights into this connection.

The chemical corticotrophin-releasing factor (CRF) is involved in the brain's ability to manage an internal response during a stressful event (Bonne & Charney, 2004; Bremmer et al, 1995). In people with PTSD, CRF is in overdrive, possibly creating increased feelings of fear and anxiety. Support for this theory has been provided through studies comparing healthy individuals with Vietnam veterans suffering from PTSD in which veterans were found to have increased concentrations of CRF (Baker et al, 1999; Bremmer et al, 1995).

Emotions such as fear are likely to produce the emotional and memory symptoms of PTSD. In Vietnam veterans with PTSD, for example, one study found that the amygdala became overexcited, and the veterans had an exaggerated response after hearing combat sounds reminiscent of the traumatic time (Baker et al, 1999). An exaggerated amygdala response is also triggered by viewing pictures of scary faces (Shepherd, 1994), indicating the heightened sensitivity of the brain to a continuum of stress-linked exposures. The range of stimuli that can trigger recall of traumatic experience and reactions include exposure to images, verbal and written recall, or reexposure to a similar stressful event. In addition, it is posited that the hippocampus may be impaired in those with PTSD because it is smaller in size (Bremmer et al, 1995).

The noradrenergic mechanisms explaining the brain's response to stress or perceived stress is the subject of continuing research. The hyperarousal of the noradrenergic system and its interaction with the central nervous system explains much of the reactions that patients experience (Baker et al, 1999). Not all individuals who have experienced traumatic events, however, develop PTSD, and thus the predictability of occurrence requires further research. For the counselor providing mental health or wellness services to patients with PTSD, understanding the underlying neurobiology must be connected to selection of treatment and psychoeducation methods that reflect a comprehensive approach to care (Osuch & Engel, 2004).

Stress may also be related to psychosomatic illness as a category of mental disorders that are often misunderstood. These disorders are not fabricated in a whimsical manner; they are prime examples of the mind's influence over the body. Heszen-Niejodek (1997) reported that individuals have various coping styles and sometimes become sick when an upsetting environmental stress interacts with their individual predisposition toward a certain medical illness. This predisposition may be inherited (genetic), secondary to injury (traumatic), or the result of a dangerous environment or personal habit (environmental) (Heszen-Niejodek, 1997).

Cognition.   Cognition emerges from activity in the brain that can be influenced by bio-psycho-social factors and encompasses the process of knowing (Vander Zenden, Crandell, & Crandell, 2002). The chemical reactions transmitted across synapses in the brain, whether in response to trauma or stress, or simply associated with day-to-day problem solving, are complex and difficult to isolate in a consistent manner. Many neuroscientists agree that what we refer to as cognition involves awareness of our thoughts and behaviors resulting in what is known as meta-cognition (e.g., consciousness, self-awareness) (Ownsworth & Fleming, 2005). Acquisition of language ensures that thinking can be labeled and stored in memory for future access. Therefore, as language develops, so does the capacity for consciousness or self-awareness.

The prefrontal cortex is believed to contribute to a variety of aspects related to thinking (e.g., working memory, planning, foresight, time estimation, strategies, and cognitive flexibility) (Millan, 2003). Injury to these regions can lead to behavioral changes, intense psychological distress, and loss of function. In children who have been exposed to chronic traumatic stress (i.e., child abuse and neglect), as an illustration, right brain development can be impaired (Schore, 2002). With such impairment, chronically abused and neglected children have less capacity to form healthy psychological attachment to caregivers or others.

The brain matures slowly, reaching adult-like functioning during adolescence and continuing into young adulthood (Vander Zanden et al, 2002). After middle age, the number of nerve fibers may decrease, processing of information slows, and changes in the vision, hearing, smell, and movement areas of the brain may result in physical changes in the body (Millan, 2003; Shepherd, 1994; Vander Zanden et al., 2002). Brains do age differently, depending on inherited genes, some lifestyle choices, and life experiences. Because the brain is inextricably dependent on the rest of body, it is difficult to isolate the effects of age on the brain without considering other body organs.

As the brain ages, it may show some mild memory problems, especially regarding proper names and recent events. Interestingly, brain functions used in daily life, such as comprehension and imagination, are as high in older people as in young adults (Millan, 2003; Shepherd, 1994; Vander Zanden et al, 2002). However, when the brain becomes severely impaired and degenerative diseases such as Alzheimer's or Parkinson's disease emerge, depression as a result of disease or as a precursor to these biological changes needs to be considered in the psychological evaluation and treatment plan (Thomsen, Arlt, Mann, Ma, & Ganzer, 2005). Moreover, the importance of family history as it relates to genetic conditions becomes apparent in conditions involving brain functional changes.

Genetics

Genetics or genetic science is concerned largely with examining the relationship between genotypes and phenotypes (Hartwell, Hood, Goldberg, Silver, Veres, & Reynolds, 2003). Many diseases have been successfully identified through isolating disease genes associated with behavioral disorders and mental illness that present unique challenges to our understanding. One problem arises when geneticists try to apply traditional strategies used to identify genes for these complex traits (Hartwell et al, 2003) among an astounding volume of genes in the human genome.

The human genome contains approximately 100,000 to 140,000 genes (Aparicio, 2000; Hartwell et al, 2003). Genes are responsible for providing cells with instructions for producing the specific proteins needed for body functions (e.g., insulin, hormones, enzymes, blood type) as well as regulating the development and functions of the body. An error or mutation in a gene can lead to a genetic disorder (Shepherd, 1994). The "instructions" in the genes are encoded in sequences on a segment of deoxyribonucleic acid, or DNA (Hartwell et al., 2003).

A number of neuropsychiatric conditions have a genetic component that places an individual at a higher risk of developing certain disorders such as autism, Asperger syndrome, anxiety, bipolar disorder, Parkinson's disease, schizophrenia, and Tourette's syndrome, as well as other conditions (Gordon & Hen, 2004; Kendler, 2005; Lyons, & Bar, 2001). Unfortunately, the specific gene(s) involved in these disorders are often unknown, and the interaction with environmental factors in the expression of these illnesses must be considered (i.e., the stress–diathesis view of interaction of inherent factors with the environment). In many cases, therefore, psychiatric disorders are caused by abnormal communication among neurons, some illnesses having a biological basis as well as a behavioral one (Shepherd, 1994), and for others afflicted with mental illness, single life events can trigger the onset of a disorder without a preexisting biological predisposition. In addition, some mental health professionals believe that identification with a genetic disorder creates a stigma that has implications for the client's social status or acceptance, and others think that genetics can help clarify the treatment needed by isolating pharmaceuticals or gene-replacement therapies (Massoud, 2003). Both viewpoints clearly have relevance to how the counseling professional interacts with clients, families, and groups impacted by mental health disorders that have a genetic component.

Many provocative and critically important discoveries through study of the human genome (Cowan, Kopnisky, & Hyman, 2002) have furthered the understanding of mental illness and neurological disorders that counselors are likely to encounter in patient populations in agency or private practice settings. A selection of genetically linked disorders that have particular relevance to counseling practice are considered next with recognition that a comprehensive review is beyond the scope of this chapter. Central to this brief review is the theme of this chapter: Treatment planning by counselors must take into account the bio-psycho-social aspects of human behavior, mental illness, and well-being in order to address patient needs.

Schizophrenia.   Based on family, twin, and adoption studies, researchers know that certain mental disorders are inherited or result from family environment. For example, if one identical twin has schizophrenia, the risk to the other of developing this illness is 45 percent. If one identical twin has autism, the other twin has a 60 percent chance of presenting with the same diagnosis (Massoud, 2003). It is important to note that some twins do not develop these, or other genetically linked disorders, even if they carry the genes (i.e., they carry a predisposition or risk for the disorder without a guarantee that they will develop such a disorder). This finding suggests that environmental factors such as infections, brain injuries early in life, or other factors are involved in determining onset of mental illness.

This interactive effect is illustrated through research findings regarding a general agreement that the genetic risk for developing schizophrenia is dependent on several genes interacting with each other and environmental factors. Analysis of the DNA sequences of people with schizophrenia reveals several genetic variations that increase one's chances for the disorder (Cowan et al, 2002). Similar studies have identified genes associated with depression and bipolar disorder. Although a variant gene HOXA1 related to early brain development may double the chance of developing autism, 99.5 percent of people who have the gene do not develop the disorder (Cowan et al, 2002). Therefore, rather than a single set of genes being involved, the disorders are represented by variations within genes and different combinations of these variant genes. By identifying high-risk clients for acquiring a mental illness, counseling treatment and sensitive treatment planning could begin at the earliest stages of the illness.

Researchers have used neuroimaging to focus on schizophrenia and changes in gray matter of the brain. Using MRI brain scans of the individuals affected, a gradual loss of gray matter in the cerebral cortex (the area responsible for higher thought) was noted as the disease progressed (Van Haren et al, 2003). The changes in the brain reflected the severity of the psychotic symptoms and sensory/motor impairments. This type of information may help when a differential diagnosis is needed, as early detection of schizophrenia helps treatment by delaying the onset of symptoms and/or reducing their severity (Van Haren et al, 2003). In addition, from the counselor's perspective, understanding the dynamics of the neurobiology of the disease can directly guide treatment goals for the client as well as family caregivers.

Attention Deficit Hyperactivity Disorder.   Studies using brain imaging of children with attention deficit hyperactivity disorder (ADHD) have revealed the involvement of several affected cortical pathways (Roth & Saykin, 2004). Due to the complexity of the behavioral expressions of the disorder (e.g., some children present as uninhibited while others exhibit overarousal), it is difficult to isolate specific pathways applicable to the affected population. Furthermore, the symptoms are found mostly in boys, and many specialists believe the disorder involves environmental risk factors and heritable or genetic factors as well (Biederman & Farone, 2005). Neuroscientists are also finding that reading disabilities in some children, but not all, involve phonemic awareness and linguistic-semantic processing changes that may be genetically linked (Roth & Saykin, 2004).

Alcoholism and Substance Abuse.   Substance abuse includes addiction to alcohol and other mood-altering substances. Causes for addictions include genetic factors as well as complex social, environmental, and psychological components. Family alcohol abuse patterns, for example, have been found to increase significantly the risk for onset of alcoholism in children and among siblings (Enoch & Goldman, 1999; Uhl, 1999). Twin studies suggest that genetic contributions to substance abuse onset can be as high as 40 percent (Uhl, 1999). Although this statistic is startling, understanding of the implications must be tempered with the realization that a 40 percent risk to develop substance abuse can also be viewed as a vulnerability, not an inevitability (i.e., destiny) (Hicks, Kreuger, Iacono, McGue, & Patrick, 2004; Tsuang, Barr, Harley, & Lyons, 2001).

The volume of published literature on substance abuse treatment (e.g., books, journals) strongly supports the requirement that substance abuse and alcoholism be considered during the intake process with clients. Awareness of the interplay among biology, genetics, and family history heightens the counselor's sensitivity to issues that will require more than traditional counseling methods to address the potentially life-threatening consequences of substance abuse, misuse, or alcoholism. In addition, the literature provides insights into the addictive process that may be evident in other disorders, such as anorexia and self-injurious behavior (Davis, 2005; Favaro & Santonastaso, 2002).

In any discussion of the role of genetic heritage, mental illness, or neurological disorder, Kendler (2005) cautions mental health professionals to carefully consider the genetic–mental illness link in terms of direct causation. Although evidence strongly suggests genetic links to the emergence of certain mental disorders, other individuals with the same genetic history do not develop these disorders. Thus, the role of the environment, life history, and exposure to life events may trigger onset of symptoms in some of these individuals while not in others. Clearly, more research is needed to refine our understanding of the role of genetics and mental illness as well as mental well-being and resilience.

Psychopharmacology

Psychopharmacology is the study of the effects of any psychoactive drug that acts on the mind by affecting brain chemistry. The use of psychopharmacology in treating mental health clients has increased due to the demands of managed care and to the increased recognition that medication is an important component of a holistic approach to treating mental disorders (Scovel, Christensen, & England, 2002). In addition, more and more counselors and therapists are working with primary care physicians or psychiatrists (Rabasca, 1999). The mental health field recognizes that optimal treatment can be obtained by utilizing therapy and psychopharmacology together (King & Anderson, 2004) in order to optimize both forms of treatment.

Since the 1950s, tranquilizers and antidepressant drugs were marketed to restore mental health or to limit abnormal behavior. Currently, there are five classes of drugs used in the clinical practice of treating mental illness: antipsychotic, anti-Parkinsonian agents, antidepressants, mood stabilizers/anti-manic agents, and anti-anxiety–sedative agents. The action of these drugs on the brain and behavior occurs by affecting the transmission of chemicals at the synapses (Shepherd, 1994). Some drugs copy the action of a neurotransmitter and are called *agonists*, whereas others stop the action of the neurotransmitter and are called *antagonists*. It is hypothesized that drugs interact only with certain receptors (Shepherd, 1994). The role of drugs in the treatment of psychopathology and abnormal behavior, however, does not preclude traditional psychotherapeutic interventions, and, as supported in the literature, both are beneficial to many mental illnesses. Additionally, the treatment of mental illness has improved greatly by reaching millions of people with psychotropic medications to help alleviate their suffering (King & Anderson, 2004).

The limited availability of psychiatrists to prescribe medications has resulted in a movement for prescription privileges for mental health professionals, specifically psychologists (Heiby, DeLeon, & Anderson, 2004; Norfleet, 2002). In addition, Sovel, Christensen, and England (2002) explored the receptivity of mental health counselors regarding prescription privileges and found a high level of interest in this aspect of practice.

Regardless of the potential value to consumers of nonphysicians having prescription privileges, controversy surrounds this issue. Primary concerns include impingement on medical doctors' and psychiatrists' "turf" (i.e., the historic exclusive right to prescribe), the availability of effective training, and the possible reduction in research for psychological causes of mental illness (Scovel, Christensen, & England, 2002). For example, New Mexico enacted legislation granting prescription privileges to psychologists in 2002 (American Psychological Association, 2002; McGrath, Wiggins, Sammons, Levant, Brown, & Stock, 2004), and Canada is considering legislation that would allow prescription privileges for psychologists (Heiby, DeLeon, & Anderson, 2004; Norfleet, 2002). There is considerable discord within this profession regarding such activities. Debate about whether psychologists *want* prescription privileges reveals that a high percentage do not (Hayes, Walser, & Bach, 2002).

Regardless of who prescribes psychotropic medications, it is essential for the counseling professional (mental health counselor, social worker, psychologist, marriage and family therapist) to be aware of the medications clients are taking, the type and impact of medical treatments being used, and who is providing this care. As counseling treatment plans are devised, the role of pharmaceuticals can become a critically important element of care (e.g., the ability to note side effects associated with certain classifications of psychotropic medication). In addition, counselors must be informed about a client's medication practices, since he or she may make a recommendation to a primary care physician that would be in conflict with other medications being prescribed (King & Anderson, 2004). As a member of the treatment team, the counseling professional must be well versed in the role of pharmacology while contributing to the client's overall well-being.

Given the interaction among developmental neurobiology, neurotransmitter levels, limbic system influences, genetics, and psychopharmacology, the counseling professional now has a more comprehensive ability to evaluate the biological component of the BPS model. However, as described earlier, it is not enough simply to treat one system in contemporary counseling practice. Psychological and social systems must also be considered in order to properly evaluate and treat patients.

THE BIO-PSYCHO-SOCIAL MODEL: SOCIAL FACTORS COMPONENT

Just as the behaviors of a person are the direct reflection of perception, values, beliefs, memory, and other biological and cognitive factors, the counselor professional cannot overlook the social components in the bio-psycho-social (BPS) model (Rohrer, Rush, & Blackburn, 2005). Specifically, it is essential that the practitioner consider a multitude of social factors that may include but are not limited to (1) family dynamics; (2) behavioral observations of the client; (3) assessment of values and beliefs that are connected to how the client interprets his or her behavior and presenting problem(s); (4) lifestyle factors and choices; (5) reproductive challenges, (6) chronic and terminal illness conditions, (7) environmental conditions (crisis, acute, long term), and (8) the changes in the mental health field associated with managed care, as illustrated in Figure 5.4. It is important to note that multicultural or diversity qualities and characteristics of clients are also noted within the assessment of each of these factors.

Family Dynamics

As a counseling professional, it is essential to be keenly aware of family dynamics and family issues surrounding the presenting problems being addressed with clients. In the

FIGURE 5.4   Social Component Considerations

case of an adult who has a chronic mental illness or an adolescent being treated for depression, for example, optimal outcomes would be in jeopardy if inquiries and/or involvement of the family or how it functions were to be neglected. Completion of a detailed family history and genogram, including family dynamics and relationships as well as medical/health history, provides insights that guide treatment planning and, ultimately, treatment success.

Using counseling techniques that integrate concerns about health, wellness, and illness also takes into account how family, friendship, and support systems provide a framework for psychotherapy or counseling. The encompassing nature of this approach to the psychosocial aspects of illness can be adapted and expanded by behavioral scientists from different theoretical orientations. (For example, the cognitive behaviorist must explore how troublesome thought patterns are reinforced in the surrounding environment; the family systems therapist working with a multigenerational family must consider how the social experiences of each member may impact the presenting problem.) The family and coinciding social context, therefore, form the backdrop for understanding each element of the client's presenting problem. Whether the client's family is linked with the onset of psychological distress plays only a peripheral role in the client's current life, or has been an abiding resource to the client, inclusion of information about the family supports integration of the BPS perspective into the helping process. Thus, any discussion about behavior is also a discussion about families, since it is in families that each person is exposed to or learns health habits that can impact well-being across the life span.

Behavioral Observations

Counselor professionals may base mental health treatment plans on the behavior presented by the client (i.e., the presenting problem) without assessing the causes of the behavior, such as lifestyle choices, unresolved trauma, or preexisting (often not directly observable) medical conditions. To ensure that all aspects of behavior are incorporated into the awareness and practice of mental health professionals, the American Psychological Association designated 2001 through 2010 as "the Decade of Behavior" (Gatchel & Oordt, 2003, p. xi). The importance of this designation is highlighted by the complexity of the client issues and problems encountered by providers of mental health services. For example, mental health practitioners are now urged not only to see the harmful or distressing emotional, psychological, and social results of client behavior but also to address the mental health and well-being problems that their clients experience that are secondary to lifestyle choices. Such choices can include but are not limited to drinking, substance abuse, domestic violence, and divorce.

In addition, referral sources to mental health professionals provide verification for the impact of behavioral practices on well-being. Primary care physicians see the consequences of patient lifestyle choices and the concomitant increase in illness of smoking, drinking, substance abuse, and inactivity (Gatchel & Oordt, 2003; Mills & Dimsdale, 1991). Counselors working with clients referred by medical professionals, therefore, must incorporate awareness of these lifestyle choices by focusing on all aspects of behavior (i.e., the presenting problem as well as the behavioral choices clients have made).

Assessment of Values and Beliefs

Each client brings to the counseling setting a lifetime of lived experience that is influenced by values and beliefs acquired over the life span. Counselors must acquire an understanding of the unique perspective that the client has about current levels of distress or illness that may reflect beliefs about self, how counselors can help, and why the presenting problem has occurred. Openness to inquire about the client's beliefs, in a nonjudgmental manner, can provide surprising and informative insights into the client's condition.

> Mr. Wyler sought a counselor's assistance following a motor vehicle accident in which he was seriously injured, requiring lengthy rehabilitation over the previous two months and an inability to return to work. The financial hardship on his family was increasing, as he was an independent, long-haul truck driver. His wife returned to work two weeks ago, and since that time, Mr. Wyler has become nervous, dropped out of physical therapy, and was referred to a mental health counselor by his primary physician, noting on the referral summary that Mr. Wyler was no longer cooperating and was jeopardizing his recovery with his noncompliant behavior. As the counselor patiently takes an in-depth history, he inquires about Mr. Wyler's parents and the roles of each in the family. As the story unfolds, it becomes clear that a primary value in Mr. Wyler's life is wage earner, like his father and brother. He feels ashamed about his inability to work and humiliated that his wife has taken a job.

In this brief scenario, the importance of investigating family history as the window to understanding family values becomes clear. If the counselor did not ask Mr. Wyler questions and discuss a wide variety of topics about the meaning of work in his life, he would not have discovered one of the underlying reasons for Mr. Wyler's noncompliant behavior. In addition, the counselor will inquire about Mr. Wyler's cultural beliefs, recognizing that a lifetime of cultural messaging about what his role should be in the family must be taken into consideration as treatment plans are devised. With these insights, the counselor is able to devise a treatment plan that will take into account Mr. Wyler's personal values and cultural perspective while focusing on counseling strategies to assist him to cope more effectively with his current circumstance.

Lifestyle/Environmental Factors

Issues such as smoking, obesity, lack of exercise, and poor dietary habits present health risks to many of the clients seen by counselor professionals (Poston, Hyder, O'Byrne, & Foreyt, 2000; Rohrer, Rush, & Blackburn, 2005). Counselors, as noted previously, must obtain or pursue sufficient medical information from the referral source (the primary care physician, psychiatrist, or other medical professional) to ensure adequate insight into the client's medical status. The stability of the client's medical condition(s) typically assumes priority over any mental health issues being addressed. If the client is not medically stable, counseling or psychological interventions are ill timed and likely to be ineffective. For example, a client's medical referral summary or records might reveal hypertension, diabetes, or lung disease that is complicated by the patient's inability to lose weight or stop smoking. Sometimes a spouse, significant other, or family member might bring up these issues in a therapy session, or the client may present with this issue as a focus of counseling. Addressing health issues as they come up in therapy, while viewing them within the overall BPS context and the meaning each issue has for the client, strengthens the counselor's ability to devise treatment plans that hold promise to positively impact psychological functioning.

Patients being seen by a counselor professional who do not have a presenting problem associated with a medical disorder, or do not have lifestyle risk factors, must also be assessed for physical symptoms. The mental health professional is tasked to remain alert to medical symptoms being expressed during counseling sessions that signal the presence of health problems. For example, patients with untreated hypertension, thyroid dysfunction, sleep disorders, and a host of other medical conditions may present with personality changes, emotional lability, and irritability—all symptoms about which the spouse might be complaining. The therapist must ensure that no underlying physical cause is responsible for some or all of the presenting behavior, and thus makes referrals to the patient's primary care physician or appropriate medical professional for evaluation.

Reproductive Challenges

With today's changing lifestyles and modern medical technology, primary care and other specialist medical providers are able to address increasing numbers of individuals, couples, and families who have psychological or emotional issues associated with reproductive functioning. These problems or challenges can range from unwanted pregnancy, pregnancy loss, infertility, the use of fertility drugs and multiple births, in vitro fertilization, and surrogacy. All of these experiences profoundly impact individuals and families and have significant emotional, psychological, and social correlates.

Pregnancy Loss.   Pregnancy loss affects the whole family. Coping with death is emotionally painful and more profoundly so when the death involves prenatal death. Society's responses to such a loss can lead to various forms of grief and complicated bereavement (Kavanaugh & Trier, 2004). Unfortunately, some people espouse the view that a woman cannot be emotionally attached to a baby who has not lived outside her womb. As a result, women who have experienced pregnancy loss may think that the grief process should be short-lived and temporary. At the same time, spouses or family can hold similar beliefs while the grieving woman experiences emotional devastation. These differences in expectations and experiences of pregnancy loss can be the source of serious discord for couples and can lead to the breakdown of the relationship (Kavanaugh & Trier, 2004). Grieving couples experience an acute sense of loss of control that perinatal death generates. The intensity of the loss is associated with profound distress, and interventions that validate the loss are imperative (Kavanaugh & Trier, 2004; Lang, Goulet, & Amsel, 2004). Counselors must therefore be familiar with the myths and facts surrounding pregnancy loss and acknowledge prenatal loss as a significant event. Such acknowledgment originating from the counselor can create a level of understanding and compassion that allows the grieving couple, woman, or family to embark on the recovery process.

Infertility.   Couples experience many emotional struggles when infertility is being evaluated. These reactions can range from minimal interest in this outcome to major depression, anger, and anxiety, generating concern that the stress associated with infertility may be causing the infertility or the opposite (i.e., infertility itself causes stress) (Wasser, 1994). How the counselor defines the specific issues that each partner is experiencing is a crucial aspect of the treatment process.

Because men and women respond to this challenge differently, the counselor must be sensitive to and consider ethnic and culture issues, language barriers, sex roles, family values and norms, individual feelings, and the couple's options based on their financial situation and the health care system (Wasser, Sewall, & Soules, 1993; Wasser, 1994). Each of these variables can be reflected in how each partner responds to the infertility evaluation, assessment, and intervention process. Whether pregnancy is achieved or not, stress levels typically remain high during the often protracted procedures that must be followed. For example, risk of miscarriage may be high due a number of medically based factors, and thus the couple remains fearful that something will go wrong. For the therapist working with the couple, it is important to maintain awareness of the many issues related to grief and loss, fear and anxiety, depression, differing communications and reactions to treatments, hormonal changes if infertility medications are used, chronic pain, and insomnia that may arise (Wasser et al, 1993; Wasser, 1994).

Many treatments are available to treat infertility. The options available to the couple often depend on their financial resources, motivation, and commitment for exploring all the options. Additionally, counselors may receive referrals to provide counseling for a single woman who wants to explore in vitro fertilization, sperm donation, or surrogacy in order to become a parent. A gay, lesbian, bisexual, or transgender (GLBT) couple may also wish to explore this option to find the most appropriate way to become parents. Because the issues associated with these contemporary reproductive issues may require advanced education and training, counselor professionals receiving referrals for such clients, or who encounter self-referred clients with this presenting problem, must ensure that they are prepared to provide needed care. As with many emerging counseling practice opportunities, it is incumbent on the counselor to ensure that he or she maintains professional ethics of practice by ensuring that knowledge and practice competencies are present and appropriate for the client's needs, or refer the case to a qualified mental health practitioner if it is out of the counselor's scope of practice.

Chronic and Terminal Illness Conditions

When viewing the bio-psycho-social model, counselors are acutely aware that a life span perspective is essential to a clear understanding of client needs. Each stage of life is defined by the developmental changes and challenges that occur. It is during the latter stages of the life span, or when the individual is affected by chronic illness, that many clients can benefit from counseling intervention. Although the inevitability of the end of life is known by all, how each individual or family copes with end-of-life issues varies. For some, the demands of coping with chronic illness are unexpected and can include injuries associated with known and anticipated birth conditions, sudden and unexpected illness, or the consequences of accidental injury.

Coping with chronic illness is one of the most challenging areas in the field of medicine (Meyerstein, 1994; Sharoff, 2004; Stetz & Brown, 2004). As a result of a chronic illness, activities of daily living change, general as well as specific fears emerge, one's sense of control and agency are assaulted, and feelings of helplessness, hopelessness, catastrophizing, and stress impact patients as well as their families (Meyerstein, 1994; Sharoff, 2004; Stetz & Brown, 2004). The experience of chronic or terminal illness affects family life in profound ways, and the way the family handles chronic or terminal illness can strongly influence the course of the illness itself. The family response to chronic illness is influenced by the specific characteristics of the illness, including onset, course, outcome, and degree of incapacitation (Penn, 2001). The fact that many families successfully handle these challenges by developing a new identity and effectively adapting to the illness attests to the rich resources of family strength, flexibility, endurance, and care (Meyerstein, 1994; Sharoff, 2004; Stetz & Brown, 2004).

Counseling methods that foster activation of family resilience resources are part of the counselor's treatment plan when working with the chronically ill. Within this context, the interrelationship between the health of the individual family member and the health of the family unit is connected (Sayger, Bowersox, & Steinberg, 1996). Therefore, when illness occurs (acute, chronic, or life-threatening) with any family member, it is important to assess the needs of all family members who are impacted. As counseling professionals, it is necessary to acquire the knowledge and skills needed to treat the individual within the family constellation. As this is achieved, the counselor is well able to work in a collaborative manner with other involved health professionals and the health care system to achieve positive results (Sayger, Bowersox, & Steinberg, 1996).

Environmental Conditions

The environment in which patients receive counseling services (e.g., mental health care system, community agency, or private practice office) represents a social system that is a central part of the bio-psycho-social model of counseling. While the counselor professional must address the needs of the individual with a psychiatric, psychological, behavioral, or medical diagnosis, the family and the social system(s) in which that care is provided, can directly and indirectly influence how the counselor practices. Consequently, clinicians adopting the BPS model of intervention must also consider the treatment environment and reasons for the referral as factors that impact the outcomes of counseling or psychotherapy interventions (Rohrer, Rush, & Blackburn, 2005).

Managed Mental Health Care.   The enactment of the Health Maintenance Organization (HMO) Act of 1973 is designated as the "birth date" of managed care (Hodgkin, Horgan, & Garnick, 1997). In the modern managed mental health care environment, the very essence of the client–counselor relationship, length of treatment, and designation of outcomes has shifted. What was once viewed as medically necessary and allowable by the treating psychiatrist or psychologist, for example, has evolved into increasingly refined standards of practice characterized by diminished authority to determine the care that is needed. As a consequence, the managed mental care system is a system to be carefully navigated (Hodgkin, Horgan, & Garnick, 1997).

Managed mental health care companies contract with counseling professionals and other health care providers to provide treatment and counseling services for individuals with certain approved diagnoses. Often, there are restrictions on services that can be provided, such as preexisting conditions, financial capitation, and exclusions. Consumers as well as providers are expressing concern about the quality of care and the restrictions to practice and delivery of mental health care based on what is best for the individual client and not what is prescribed by a company to control costs (Hodgkin, Horgan, & Garnick, 1997; Institute for the Future, 2003). Counselor professionals and other health care providers are faced with managed care contracts for provision of services at reduced rates, recertifications, justifications of treatment and recommendations, treatment plan preapproval or preauthorization, and returned claims. Having to consult with the managed care organization for what is deemed medically necessary and waiting for extended periods of time to receive reimbursement for care that has been delivered are problematic issues.

Mental Health Care in a Changing Social Environment.   Current market forces continue to reshape and redefine the delivery of health care. The fee-for-service private sector, employer-sponsored health insurance, and government-sponsored Medicare and Medicaid programs historically paid for an increasingly costly biomedical treatment model that continues to foster alarm and concern among public policy leaders. Spiraling health care costs have increased the nation's appetite for a new recipe to address this escalation in costs (Institute for the Future, 2003). The ingredients of the recipe read like a label for alphabet soup (e.g., HMO, PPO, and PHO) and continue to reflect forms of care designed to address cost and quality factors. The debate rages among consumers wanting adequate, affordable health care coverage; insurance companies needing to decrease costs and increase profits; and mental and physical health care providers compromising their autonomy while halving their incomes.

The Institute for the Future (2003) discussed the transition in the field of mental health care. "The WHO report on the *Global Burden of Disease* stated that mental illness will replace cancer as the number two cause of disability in the next ten years" (as cited in Institute for the Future, 2003, p. 187). A report by the U.S Surgeon General on mental health "confirmed that in any one year, approximately 50 million Americans suffer from mental disorders, and that many do not seek help for their problem because of the stigma associated with these conditions" (p. 187). The climate in which mental health disorders are dealt with, therefore, represents another aspect of the environment component of the BPS model of counseling care.

Counseling Practice in a Changing Environment.   According to Fogel (2003), in the current climate, the practice of psychotherapy is challenged for its very survival. Managed care often dictates the number of sessions one may see a patient. Traditional psychotherapy, as defined by the psychodynamic model, is often discouraged and not reimbursed as readily in today's health care environment. Managed care companies seek quick results with a limited number of sessions, something not traditionally part of psychodynamic therapy, and they do not wish to pay for the long-term relationships that are often necessary for successful treatment. Managed care insurance companies want both scientific efficacy and cost effectiveness before they consider treatments as medically necessary. Even with clinical trials demonstrating evidence for improved benefits with the addition of cognitive-behavioral therapy (CBT) to a treatment regimen, insurers may not necessarily allow for this CBT treatment, as they must first evaluate if this is a "rational" allocation of resources (Fogel, 2003).

Counseling has changed over the last 50 years. In current venues of practice, there are many systems that must interact effectively in order to achieve counseling outcomes. Interfacing relationships between the multiple systems of care must be formed by contemporary counselors in order to ensure that treatment outcomes can be optimized. To be successful in delivering counseling services that takes into account multiple interacting and influential systems such as communities, families, health care clinicians, hospitals and institutions, and insurance or managed care organizations, the counselor may find himself or herself in the explorer role. It is at the intersection of the client's mental and physical health care needs, within a complex environmental context, that the counselor recognizes how inseparable each element is to achievement of desired treatment outcomes.

THE BIO-PSYCHO-SOCIAL MODEL: COGNITIVE PSYCHOLOGY COMPONENT

Cognitive psychology emphasizes the connection between cognitive processes and behavior and has had a preeminent place in psychological research since the 1950s. By the 1960s and 1970s, mental health professionals accepted the theory of sequential cognitive steps, and the developing field of cognitive psychology gained popularity (Eysenck & Keane, 2000; Hunt & Ellis, 1999). This theory concluded that higher cognition abounds in successive, sequential processes, which also influence the BPS model, as shown in Figure 5.5.

Characteristic of this type of cognitive processing is its extension through time and orderly progression from one united representation or idea to another (Hunt & Ellis, 1999). Later steps in the series depend on the contents of the earlier states. In the sequential model, the limbic region is responsible for stimulus-driven information and is referred to as "bottom-up" processing. Bottom-up processing is controlled by features that are essentially taken from the environment rather than by cognitive factors such as learning, memory, spirituality, values, and beliefs (Eysenck & Keane, 2000; Hunt & Ellis, 1999).

Learning and Memories

Memories and how we store them become essential knowledge for the counselor when working with mental health clients. Understanding how memory functions will assist with building rapport and trust and with determining when to moderate or change style of interaction. Sensitivity to client resistance to disclose memories, as an illustration, is supported by an understanding of repressed memory research and consequently can serve as crucial guidance when identifying treatment resources. Counseling professionals not well versed in this literature or confident in psychotherapy competencies with such clients can use this knowledge to make appropriate treatment referrals. For counselors working with clients who are disclosing repressed memories, it is equally important to use understanding of memory during the psychotherapy process. For example, counselors can assist clients to move painful

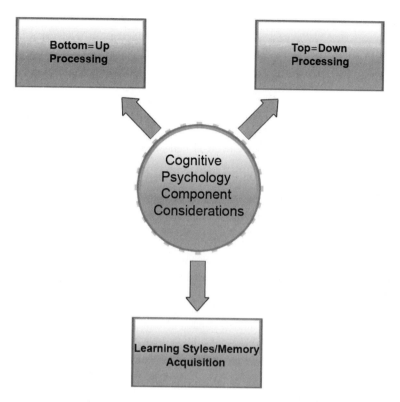

FIGURE 5.5   Cognitive Psychology Component Considerations

memories from short-term memory (STM) by helping them form associations in such a way that the memory is moved to long-term memory (LTM) (Eysenck & Keane, 2000).

In addition to exploring how memory is formed, stored, and retrieved, the discipline of cognitive neuroscience includes the topics of perceptions, thought, concepts, culture, language, problem solving, and mental processes that help control how people acquire, retrieve, and store knowledge (Eysenck & Keane, 2000). The computer, as an exemplar, serves to help counselors conceptualize specific models of the brain, thereby enabling understanding of human thought processes. For example, the conceptualization of a brain model is to view this organ as akin to a computer. Through artificial intelligence, computers organize and solve problems, using heuristics and algorithms to overcome what computers lack in human imagination, ingenuity, and the referential context for situational interpretation (Eysenck & Keane, 2000).

The "top-down" model of cognitive neuroscience (Hunt & Ellis, 1999) describes how information is stored in the brain. Using this method of processing, a person is guided by the information stored in the brain, instead of by information coming in from the environment. Information comes through the upper cortical layers as "top-down" data. This phenomenon can be referred to as the *information-processing paradigm*. Combining Eysenck and Keane's model with Hunt and Ellis's model elicits the study of cognition as a full and complex process that brings great diversity to the study of the how the human brain and mind function (Eysenck & Keane, 2000; Hunt & Ellis, 1999).

How cognition, or the awareness of experience, is put into language is theorized to be stimulus activated. Nathanson (1992) introduced the analogous use of the terms *hardware, software*, and *firmware* to describe the make-up of the human brain (again, using a computer analogy to describe the complexity of brain function). This perspective supports the counseling professional's awareness that humans are genetically programmed to produce their biological systems, and as growth and development progress, additional social programs are learned that affect worldview and interaction within each person's surrounding environment. The hardware (i.e., the human brain) reflects our affinity to all animals, sharing much of the same chemical and biological make-up. What can be termed software (i.e., social conditioning, learning, and experiences) are attributes learned from parents, schools, and communities within an individual's life. The firmware consists of the human genetic code that programs the differences that each person possesses and defines human differences from other animals. Taken together, human hardware, software, and firmware define the diverse and complex humanness that all counselors become familiar with when providing mental health care.

In any field of mental health practice, the counseling professional is interacting with the consequences of cognition. The counselor's behavior, as well, is guided by thought and feeling, mediated by myriad connections in the brain that have been activated by stimuli from environmental or internal sources. As counselors investigate brain function and the expressions of this capacity in thought that directs behavior, it is essential to review continually the implications of this understanding to each area of professional practice. Whether working in social services, counseling, or a health care profession, every counselor professional is continually interacting with the outcomes of cognitive functioning.

THE BIO-PSYCHO-SOCIAL MODEL: APPLICATION TO PRACTICE

Dora is a 79-year-old white female patient who entered a long-term care facility after breaking her hip. Her family abandoned her, sold her home and life possessions, and did not visit her. She was angry, bitter, and resentful; did not participate in activities; did not interact with her peers; was tired all the time; had slow reflexes, muscle weakness, and eczema; and was depressed. The nursing home team referred her for mental health counseling. After an extensive assessment by the counselor, which included depression screening and mental health evaluation, a referral for a medical consultation was initiated, with a specific request to obtain laboratory tests of blood from the patient. Lab reports revealed a potassium deficiency. Once this was corrected through nutrition management and mediation, Dora became active in therapy and all activities, and with her peers, and started working part-time in the thrift shop. Her health has stabilized following a combination of medical, nursing, and counselor intervention.

Because it is recognized that biological, psychological, and social factors directly impact the well-being and illness coping strategies used by clients, the professions of counseling and medicine have increasingly also recognized the need to provide health care academic and training preparation to mental health care providers. With an aging population and a heightened awareness of health issues, individuals and families have become quite assertive in demanding that optimal health care services be available and accessible. Gatchel and Oordt (2003) reported that the vast majority of primary care physicians, nurse managers, and clinic administrators, for example, are highly enthusiastic about integrative bio-psycho-social services. Clients with psychosocial and behavioral needs are prevalent in the medical primary care system. Concurrently, acceptance of the benefits of counseling has also increased. These two converging forces (anticipated increased needs for mental health services and increased consumer awareness of the value of counseling services) make it imperative that mental health professionals continue to become familiar with the role of the counselor professional as a health care team member. At the same time, counselor professionals must also seek knowledge and training that allows them to assume an active role in providing mental health services to families who are struggling with illness, injury, or life-threatening medical conditions. Thus, the following challenges face the counseling professions in this regard:

1. A simmering cauldron of need for health care services exists at the same time that increasing numbers of clients and families lack the resources to obtain care.
2. A need exists to ensure that the quality of mental health and well-being care that is provided meets the same standards for all recipients.
3. There is increasing shortfall of professionals to provide the care.

These practice realities have a direct influence on the counseling professional who seeks to implement a bio-psycho-social model in collaborative practice arrangements. The best features of this holistic approach to mental health care can be implemented into patient assessment, evaluation, and treatment based on the BPS model. Table 5.1 summarizes the core elements of this integrated approach to collaborative counseling care.

Given the considerations for evaluation and treatment of clients in the counseling and psychology professions based on the BPS model, influences in the categories and subcategories highlighted in Table 5.1 can be either positive or negative. In either case, careful consideration of all biological, social and cognitive/psychological categories should be taken into account throughout the evaluation and treatment process beginning with subjective historical reporting by the client.

A successful treatment plan for a client with mental health problems starts with subjective historical reporting by the client. As a member of a client's health care team, the counselor is well positioned to provide crucial insights into the needs of the client and to communicate these findings to referring professionals to ensure that care is coordinated. The counselor does not work in isolation from other health care professionals who also may be providing care to a client. By forming professional working relationships with other members of the health care team, the counselor's perceptions and treatment become integrated into a holistic approach to care.

In the initial stages of counseling, counselor clinicians can use a structured assessment format such as SOAP (Subjective, Objective, Assessment, and Therapeutic and Evaluative Plan). Assessment of psychiatric, behavioral, or lifestyle disorders is typically reflected by symptoms of altered behavior or experience captured in the SOAP history format. While using such a format, or one with comparable detail, it is essential that the counselor ask questions about each component of the bio-psycho-social model, and, if necessary, expand each section of the interview format in order to capture this information. This allows the counselor to attend to related, suspected, or hypothesized impaired biological processes. In some cases, an

TABLE 5.1   BPS Model: Clinical Evaluation and Treatment Considerations

BPS MODEL COMPONENT	SUBCOMPONENT	ASSESSMENT, TREATMENT PLANNING TOPICS, AND EXAMPLES
Biological Influences	Developmental	Premature birth, fetal alcohol syndrome, AIDS
	Neurobiology	Diagnostic results from neuropsychological testing, PET scans
	Biochemical	Biochemical imbalances → mental health symptoms associated with: adrenal dysfunction, blood sugar imbalance, food and chemical allergy, heavy metal toxicity, hormone imbalance, nutritional deficiency
	Neurotransmitter Levels	Serotonin, dopamine, noradrenalin imbalance; stimulant and drug intoxication, or underactive or overactive thyroid that hormone testing (including adrenal stress index, andropause panel, male hormone panel, menopause/PMS panel) could evaluate. Endocrine disorders such as cortisol and adrenaline or underproduction can also contribute to a variety of panic or anxiety symptoms (panic disorder, social phobias, obsessive-compulsive disorder, post-traumatic stress disorder, acute stress disorder, generalized anxiety disorder) Anxiety disorders can cause a variety of symptoms and can be caused by neurotransmitter imbalances. Neurotransmitter levels regulate mood, attention, focus, memory, and concentration. Testing can identify deficient or excessive neurotransmitter levels of serotonin, dopamine, norepinephrine, epinephrine, GABA, PEA, and histamine, and obtain a baseline assessment using a urine or blood sample laboratory analysis. These tests can provide precise information on neurotransmitter deficiencies or overloads, as well as detect hormonal and nutrient co-factor imbalances that influence neurotransmitter production
	Limbic System Influences	Depression, pain, stress, anxiety, changes in drives, such as appetite, thirst, or sexual behavior
	Genetics	Cognition/age, family history; diagnostic test results; related diagnoses
	Psychopharmacology	Chemical imbalances; negative medication effects (e.g., combativeness, tension, sleep changes, delusions, changes in social skills); medication responsiveness

TABLE 5.1   Continued

BPS MODEL COMPONENT	SUBCOMPONENT	ASSESSMENT, TREATMENT PLANNING TOPICS, AND EXAMPLES
Psychological/ Cognitive Influences	Bottom-Up Processing	Processing of data that are driven by features extracted from the environment
	Top-Down Processing	Processing of data that are influenced by what the individual already knows about the information (or past experiences) that is now coming into the system
	Learning Styles	Visual, auditory, kinesthetic
	Memory Acquisition	Long- and short-term memory, including acquisition, consolidation, and retrieval of data; immediate functional issues; long-term issues

underlying disease or injury process is so subtle that it is undetectable (e.g., closed head injury in adolescence). However, with advances in genetics, brain imaging, and basic neuroscience, it is becoming possible to find structural change or a pattern of brain activity that helps to identify disorders. For the counselor professional, referral to primary care physicians or specialists has become part of the decision-making process following initial intake or evaluation.

As science provides ever more sophisticated methods to assess brain function and how the brain interacts with the body to produce symptoms, counselors are called on to use contemporary methods that reflect an expanded view of human behavior. Mind, body, and social environments all deserve special consideration in a comprehensive assessment approach that must be part of the academic and training experiences of counselors across the human services continuum. The ability to provide psychological treatment and counseling services to individuals, families, and groups requires application of such an advanced understanding of the bio-psycho-social model. Failure to do so can result in treating a client for the wrong diagnosis.

Health care and insurance companies are looking for outcome-based mental health treatment. As providers of mental health care, counselors are required to conduct thorough assessments, develop a treatment plan, make recommendations, and follow the recommended guidelines of the health care provider while often working with a primary care physician to provide cost-effective services that validate treatment efficacy. Such *compassionate and competent care*, based on the BPS model, is the responsibility of the counselor professional in contemporary practice.

THE BIO-PSYCHO-SOCIAL MODEL: SUMMARY

The BPS model correlates each element of human behavior and experience within a cohesive whole. When used well, this model of mental health care can determine the quality and effectiveness of the health care delivery system now and well into the future. According to McDaniel, Hepworth, and Doherty (1992), counselors are to act as a vehicle and transcend the changes in the health care system with a focus on the bio-psycho-social model and collaboration with other members of the health care team. In accomplishing this goal, the counseling professional's contributions to the well-being of consumers support change that is sensitive and humane for individuals, families, and health care professionals (Edwards, Patterson, Grauf-Grounds, & Groban, 2001).

The BPS model recognizes that bio-psycho-social crisis can be triggered by medical, psychological, and/or social events that are interrelated. Knowledge of the theoretical bases for understanding the complexities of relationships among clients, their families, health care and managed care providers, the surrounding environment, and personal health issues is a juggling act difficult to master. In such an ever-changing reality, fortunately, there is a growing call to reunite physical medicine and psychotherapy. As Kaplan and Coogan (2005, p. 23) have eloquently stated, "The counseling profession finally has a model sophisticated enough to use across all specialties, modalities, and presenting problems." The bio-psycho-social model focuses on this goal with an understanding that neurobiology, genetics, psychopharmacology, differential diagnostic procedures, environmental/facility factors, family dynamics, overriding managed care, and referring physician preferences all play important and interrelated roles in achieving mental health and well-being.

DISCUSSION TOPICS/QUESTIONS

1. In working with Mrs. Mason, who has recently been discharged from the regional oncology center following treatment of side effects of her radiation treatment (i.e., severe dehydration), you note that she voices a helpless attitude toward her return to her home. What are two issues associated with how she is coping with her illness that could form part of your counseling treatment plan?

2. What social, scientific, and political forces are associated with the development of the bio-psycho-social model? Describe how counseling practice for children with mental health problems has been impacted by one of the forces you have identified.

3. Devise four questions that you would ask a client during an initial interview that focus specifically on the client's health status. How would you modify these items if the client is an 11-year-old girl, a 28-year-old male, or a person of cultural heritage different from your own?

4. Mr. Henderson is a 69-year-old African American widower who began counseling following the recommendation of his family practice physician. His wife died four months ago after eight years of treatment for congestive heart disease. What are likely grief issues and health risks that Mr. Henderson now faces?

5. The neurobiology of the human brain includes complex chemical processes involving neurotransmitters. Using a current popular psychotropic medication as your illustration, describe how this prescribed chemical agent acts on neurotransmission to alleviate depression.

6. Describe the relationship among chronic pain management, stress, and counseling interventions. Identify one counseling strategy that could be part of a treatment plan for patients with fibromyalgia.

7. A genogram completed on the family of one of your clients reveals a significant occurrence of severe mental illness (SMI). Although your client and her parents have not demonstrated

signs or symptoms of SMI, your client becomes increasingly anxious as she discusses the genogram with you. What can you advise her regarding the genetic link to mental illness?

8. What contributions to the health care team can counselors make in a fertility clinic? Identify two counseling strategies that could support the fertility treatment process of couples being seen in this setting.

9. Within the bio-psycho-social model, discuss how the comprehensive assessment process has been influenced by managed mental health care.

10. Two of your clients have recently moved to your area after being relocated following a natural disaster. One of these clients reports that she was sexually assaulted 10 months ago and is just now beginning to feel that recovery is possible. What will you be aware of as you formulate treatment plans for these two individuals that reflects your understanding of the BPS model?

REFERENCES

American Counseling Association. (2005). *Code of ethics*. Retrieved February 6, 2006, from www.counseling.org/Resources/CodeOfEthics/TP/Home/CT2.aspx.

American Psychological Association. (2002). *New Mexico governor signs landmark law on prescription privileges for psychologists*. APA Online. Retrieved September 23, 2005, from www.apa.org/practice/nm_rxp.html.

Aparicio, S. A. (2000). How to count human genes. *Nature Genetics, 25*, 129–130.

Baker, D. G., West, S. A., Nicholson, W. E., Ekhator, N. N., Kasckow, J. W., Hill, K. K., et al. (1999). Serial CSF corticotropin-releasing hormone levels and adrenocortical activity in combat veterans with posttraumatic stress disorder. *American Journal of Psychiatry, 156*, 585–588.

Baum, A., Revenson, T., & Singer, J. E. (2001). *Handbook of health psychology*. Hillsdale, NJ: Erlbaum.

Biederman, J., & Farone, S. V. (2005, July 5). Attention-deficit hyperactivity disorder. *Lancet, 366*, 237–248.

Bloom, F., Nelson, C. A., & Lazerson, A. (2001). *Brain, mind, behavior* (3rd ed.). New York: Worth Publishers.

Bonne, O., & Charney, D. S. (2004). Commentary on "Brain environment interactions: Stress, posttraumatic stress disorder, and the need for a postmortem brain collection." *Psychiatry, 67*(4), 407–411.

Booth, H., Cushway, D., & Newnes, C. (1997). Counseling in general practice: Clients' perceptions of significant events and outcome. *Counseling Psychology Quarterly, 10*, 175–187.

Borrell-Carrió, F., Suchman, A. L., & Epstein, R. M. (2004). The biopsychosocial model 25 years later: Principles, practice, and scientific inquiry. *Annuals of Family Medicine, 2*, 576–582.

Borsook, D., & Becerra, L. (2003). Pain imaging: Future applications to integrative clinical and basic neurobiology. *Advanced Drug Delivery Review, 55*, 967–986.

Bremmer, D. J., Randall, P., Scott, T. M., Bronen, R. A., et al. (1995). MRI-based measurement of hippocampal volume in patients with combat-related posttraumatic stress disorder. *American Journal of Psychiatry, 152*, 973–981.

Cheng, C., & Cheung, M. W. L. (2005). Cognitive processes underlying coping flexibility: Differentiation and integration. *Journal of Personality, 73*(4), 859–897.

Christensen, L. L., & Miller, R. B. (2001). Marriage and family therapists evaluate managed mental health care: A qualitative inquiry. *Journal of Marital and Family Therapy, 27*, 509–514.

Cowan, W. M., Kopnisky, K. L., & Hyman, S. E. (2002). The human genome project and its impact on psychiatry. *Annual Review of Neuroscience, 25*, 1–50.

Crick, F., & Koch, C. (1992). The problem of consciousness. *Scientific American, 267*, 153–159.

Davis, C. (2005). Addiction and the eating disorders. *Psychiatric Times*. Retrieved August 31, 2005, from http://psychiatrictimes.com/p010259.html.

Dimsdale, J. E. (1977). Emotional causes of sudden death. *American Journal of Psychiatry, 134*, 1361–1366.

Edwards, T. M., Patterson, J. E., Grauf-Grounds, C., & Groban, S. (2001). Psychiatry, MFT, & family medicine collaboration: The sharp behavioral health clinic. *Families, Systems, and Health, 19*, 25–35.

Engel, G. (1977). The need for a new medical model: A challenge for biomedicine. *Science, 196*, 129–136.

Enoch, M. A., & Goldman, D. (1999). Genetics of alcoholism and substance abuse. *Psychiatric Clinics of North America, 22*(2), 289–299.

Eysenck, M. W., & Keane, M. T. (2000). *Cognitive psychology*. Hove, East Sussex Psychology Press.

Farrington, D. P. (2005). Childhood origins of antisocial behavior. *Clinical Psychology and Psychotherapy, 12*, 177–190.

Favaro, A., & Santonastaso, P. (2002). The spectrum of self-injurious behavior in eating disorders. *Eating Disorders, 10*, 215–225.

Fogel, J. (2003). Health psychology: A new form of psychotherapy. *Medscape General Medicine, 5*, 1–29.

Frame, M. W. (2003). *Integrating religion and spirituality into counseling: A comprehensive approach*. New York: Thomson, Brooks, & Cole.

Gatchel, R. J. (2004). Comorbidity of chronic pain and mental health disorders: The biopsychosocial perspective. *American Psychologist, 59*, 795–805.

Gatchel, R. J., & Oordt, M. S. (2003). *Clinical health psychology and primary care: Practical advice and clinical guidance for successful collaboration*. Washington, DC: American Psychological Association.

Gordon, J. A., & Hen, R. (2004). Genetic approaches to the study of anxiety. *Annual Review of Neuroscience, 27*, 193–222.

Hack, T. F. (2004). Coping responses following breast cancer diagnosis predict psychological adjustment three years later. *Psycho-Oncology, 13*, 235–247.

Hankoff, L. D., Englehardt, D., Freedman, N., Mann, D., & Margolis, R. (1960). The doctor–patient relationship in a psychopharmacological treatment setting. *Journal of Nervous and Mental Disorders, 131*, 540–546.

Hartwell, L., Hood, L., Goldberg, M. L., Silver, L. M., Veres, R. C., & Reynolds, A. (2003). *Genetics: From genes to genomes* (2nd ed.). Columbus, OH: McGraw-Hill.

Hayes, S. C., Walser, R. D., & Bach, P. (2002). Prescription privileges for psychologists: Constituencies and conflicts. *Journal of Clinical Psychology, 58*, 697–708.

Heiby, E. M., DeLeon, P. H., & Anderson, T. (2004). A debate on prescription privileges for therapists. *Professional Psychology: Research & Practice, 35*, 336–344.

Herlenius, E., & Lagercrantz, H. (2004). Development of neurotransmitter systems during critical periods. *Experimental Neurology, 190*, 8–21.

Heszen-Niejodek, I. (1997). Coping style and its role with stressful encounters. *European Therapist, 2*, 342–351.

Hicks, B. M., Krueger, R. F., Iacono, W. G., McGue, M., & Patrick, C. J. (2004). Family transmission and heritability of externalizing disorders. *Archives of General Psychiatry, 61*, 922–928.

Hunt, R. R., & Ellis, H. C. (1999). *Fundamentals of cognitive psychology* (6th ed.). Columbus, OH: McGraw-Hill.

Hodgkin, D., Horgan, C. M., & Garnick, D. W. (1997). *HMOs' contracting arrangements for mental health care*. New York: Kluwer Academy.

Idler, E. L., & Kasal, S. (1991). Health perceptions and survival: Do global evaluations of health status really predict mortality? *Journal of Gerontology, 4*, 555–565.

Institute for the Future. (2003). *Health & health care 2010: The forecast, the challenge* (2nd ed.). Princeton, NJ: Jossey-Bass.

Kaplan, D. M., & Coogan, S. L. (2005). The next advancement in counseling: The bio-psycho-social model. In G. R. Walz & R. K. Yep (Eds.), *VISTAS: Compelling perspectives on counseling, 2005* (pp. 17–25). Alexandria, VA: American Counseling Association.

Kavanaugh, K., & Trier, D. (2004). Social support following perinatal loss. *Journal of Family Nursing, 10*, 70–92.

Kendler, K. S. (2005). "A gene for" . . . : The nature of gene action in psychiatric disorders. *American Journal of Psychiatry, 162*(7), 243–253.

Kerns, R. D., Kassirer, M., & Otis, J. (2002). Pain in multiple sclerosis: A biopsychosocial perspective. *Journal of Rehabilitation Research and Development, 39*(2), 225–232.

King, J. H., & Anderson, S. M. (2004). Therapeutic implications of pharmacotherapy: Current trends and ethical issues. *Journal of Counseling & Development, 82*, 329–337.

Knishkowy, B., & Herman, J. (1998). Medical family therapy casebook: Ruth's dizziness. *Families, Systems, and Health, 16*, 325–327.

Kobasa, S. C., Maddi, S. R., & Kahn, S. (1982). Hardiness and health: A prospective study. *Journal of Personality and Social Psychology, 42*, 168–177.

Kolata, G. (1986). Heart attacks at 9:00 a.m. *Science, 233*, 417–418.

Lang, A., Goulet, C. C., & Amsel, R. (2004). Explanatory model of health in bereaved parents post-fetal/infant death. *International Journal of Nursing Studies, 41*, 869–880.

Levin, J. S., & Schiller, P. L. (1987). Is there a religious factor in health? *Journal of Religion and Health, 26*, 9–36.

Lewis, S. (2004). Mind, heart, body and soul. *Advances in Mind-Body Medicine, 20*, 3–13.

Lyons, M., & Bar, J. L. (2001). Is there a role for twin studies in the molecular genetics era? *Harvard Review of Psychiatry, 9*, 318–324.

Massoud, S. (2003). Genetic and environmental interactions in psychiatric illnesses. *Journal of Neuropsychiatry & Clinical Neurosciences, 15*, 386–387.

Matthews, D. A., Larson, D. B., & Barry, C. P. (1993). *The faith factor: An annotated bibliography of clinical research on spiritual subjects*. Rockville, MD: National Institutes of Health.

Matthews, G. G. (2001). *Neurobiology: Molecules, cells and systems*. Malden, MA: Blackwell Science.

Mayne, T. J. (2001). Emotions and health. In T. J.Mayne & G. A. Bonanno (Eds.), *Emotions: Current issues and future directions* (pp. 361–397). New York: Guilford.

McCann, S., & Lipton, J. M. (1998). *Annals of the New York Academy of Sciences*. New York: New York Academy of Sciences.

McDaniel, S., Hepworth, J., & Doherty, W. (1992). *Medical family therapy*. New York: Basic Books.

McGrath, R. E., Wiggins, J.G., Sammons, M. T., Levant, R. F., Brown, A., & Stock, W. (2004). Professional issues in pharmacology for psychologists. *Professional Psychology: Research and Practice, 35*, 158–163.

Meyerstein, I. (1994). Reflections on "being there" and "doing" in family therapy: A story of chronic illness. *Family Systems Medicine, 12*, 21–29.

Millan, M. J. (2003). The neurobiology and control of anxious states. *Progress in Neurobiology, 70*, 83–244.

Mills, P. J., & Dimsdale, J. E. (1991). Cardiovascular reactivity to psychosocial stressors: A review of the effects of beta-blockade. *Psychosomatics: Journal of Consultation Liaison Psychiatry, 32*, 209–220.

Mowbray, C. T., & Holter, M. C. (2002). Mental health and mental illness: Out of the closet? *Social Service Review, 76*(1), 135–179.

Nathanson, D. (1992). *Shame and pride*. New York: Norton.

Norfleet, M. A. (2002). Responding to society's needs: Prescription privileges for therapists. *Journal of Clinical Psychology, 58*, 599–610.

Ochsner, K. N., & Barrett, L. F. (2001). A multiprocess perspective on the neuroscience of emotion. In T. J. Mayne & G. A. Bonanno (Eds.), *Emotions: Current issues and future directions* (pp. 38–81). New York: Guilford.

Orsulic-Jeras, S., Shepherd, J. B., & Britton, P. J. (2003). Counseling older adults with HIV/AIDS: A strength-based model of treatment. *Journal of Mental Health Counseling, 25*(3), 233–244.

Osuch, E., & Engle, C. S. (2004). Research on the treatment of trauma spectrum responses: The role of the optimal healing environment and neurobiology. *The Journal of Alternative and Complementary Medicine, 10*(1), S-211–S-221.

Ott, C. H. (2003). The impact of complicated grief on mental and physical health at various points in the bereavement process. *Journal of Death Studies, 27*, 249–272.

Ownsworth, T., & Fleming, J. (2005). The relative importance of metacognitive skills, emotional status, and executive function in psychosocial adjustment following acquired brain injury. *Journal of Head Trauma Rehabilitation, 20*(4), 315–332.

Parslow, R. A., Jorn, A. F., & Christensen, H. (2004). The association between work stress and mental health: A comparison of organizationally employed and self-employed workers. *Work and Stress, 18*, 231–244.

Penn, P. (2001). Chronic illness: Trauma, language, and writing: Breaking the silence. *Family Process, 40*, 33–52.

Pope, K. S., & Vasquez, M. J. (1998). *Ethics in psychotherapy and counseling: A practical guide* (2nd ed.). Princeton, NJ: Jossey-Bass.

Poston, W. S., Hyder, M. L., O'Byrne, K. K., & Foreyt, J. P. (2000). Where do diets, exercise, and behavior modification fit in the treatment of obesity? *Endocrine, 13*, 187–192.

Prochaska, J., & DiClemente, C. (1983). Stages and processes of self-change of smoking: Toward an integrative model of change. *Journal of Consulting and Clinical Psychology, 51*, 390–395.

Rabasca, L. (1999). More therapists are building up their practices by partnering with primary care physicians. *APA Monitor, 30*(4), 1–4.

Rohrer, J. E., Rush, P. J., & Blackburn, C. (2005). Lifestyle and mental health. *Preventive Medicine, 40*, 438–443.

Roth, R. M., & Saykin, A. J. (2004). Executive dysfunction in attention-deficit/hyperactivity disorder: Cognitive and neuroimaging findings. *Psychiatric Clinics of North America, 27*, 83–96.

Sala, M., Perez, J., Soloff, P., Ucelli di Nemi, S., Caverzasi, E., Soares, J. C., & Brambilla, P. (2004). Stress and hippocampal abnormalities in psychiatric disorders. *European Neuropsychopharmacology, 14*, 393–405.

Salovey, P., Rothman, A. J., Detweiler, J. B., & Steward, W. T. (2000). Emotional states and physical health. *American Psychologist, 55*, 110–121.

Sayger, T. V., Bowersox, M. P., & Steinberg, E. B. (1996). Family therapy and the treatment of chronic illness in a multidisciplinary world. *Family Journal: Counseling and Therapy for Couples and Families, 4*, 12–21.

Schaefer, C., Quesenberry, C. P., & Wi, S. (1995). Mortality following conjugal bereavement and the effects of a shared environment. *American Journal of Epidemiology, 141*, 1142–1152.

Schore, A. N. (2002). Disregulation of the right brain: A fundamental mechanism of traumatic attachment and the psychopathogenesis of posttraumatic stress disorder. *Australian and New Zealand Journal of Psychiatry, 36*, 9–30.

Schwartz, G. (1982). Testing the biopsychosocial model: The ultimate challenge facing behavioral medicine? *Journal of Consulting and Clinical Psychology, 50*, 1040–1053.

Scovel, K. A., Christensen, O. J., & England, J. T. (2002). Mental health counselors' perceptions regarding psychopharmacological prescriptive privileges. *Journal of Mental Health Counseling, 24*, 36–50.

Sharoff, K. (2004). *Coping skills therapy for managing chronic and terminal illnesses.* New York: Springer.

Shepherd, G. (1994). *Neurobiology* (3rd ed.). New York: Oxford University Press.

Shi, L., Forrest, C. B., & von Schrader, S. (2003). Vulnerability and the patient–practitioner relationship: The roles of gatekeeping and primary care performance. *Journal of Public Health, 93*, 138–144.

Shonkoff, J. P., & Phillips, D. A. (2000). *From neurons to neighborhoods: The science of early childhood development.* Washington, DC: National Academy Press.

Smith, T. W., Kendall, P. C., & Keefe, F. J. (2002). Behavioral medicine and clinical health psychology: Special issue. *Journal of Clinical and Consulting Psychology, 70*, 459–462.

Solomon, E. P., & Heide, K. M. (2005). The biology of trauma: Implications for treatment. *Journal of Interpersonal Violence, 20*(1), 51–60.

Stephen, K. E. (2004). On the role of general system theory for functional neuroimaging. *Journal of Anatomy, 205*, 443–470.

Stetz, K. M., & Brown, A. M. (2004). Physical and psychosocial health in family caregiving: A comparison of AIDS and cancer caregivers. *Public Health Nursing, 21*(6), 533–540.

Stewart, M., Davidson, F., Meade, D., Hirth, A., & Makrides, L. (2000). Myocardial infarction: Survivors' and spouses' stress, coping and support. *Journal of Advanced Nursing, 31*(6), 1351–1360.

Stone, J. A., & Sias, S. M. (2003). Self-injurious behavior: A bi-modal treatment approach to working with adolescent females. *Journal of Mental Health Counseling, 25*(2), 112–125.

Thomsen, T. M., Arlt, S., Mann, U., Ma, R., & Ganzer, S. (2005). Detecting depression in Alzheimer's disease: Evaluation of four different scales. *Archives of Clinical Neuropsychology, 20*(2), 271–276.

Tsuang, M. T., Barr, J.L., Harley, R. M., & Lyons, M. J. (2001). The Harvard twin study of substance abuse: What we have learned. *Harvard Review of Psychiatry, 9*(6), 267–279.

Uhl, G. R. (1999). Molecular genetics of substance abuse vulnerability: A current approach. *Neuropsychopharmacology, 20*(1), 3–9.

Van Haren, N. E., Cahn, W., Hulshoff, P., Hilleke, E., Schnack, H. G., Caspers, E., et al. (2003). Brain volumes as predictor of outcome in recent-onset schizophrenia: A multi-center MRI study. *Schizophrenia Research, 64*, 41–52.

Van Houdenhove, B., Verstraeten, D., Onghena, P., & De Cuyper, H. (1992). Chronic idiopathic pain, mianserin and "masked" depression. *Psychotherapy and Psychosomatics, 58*(1), 46–53.

Vander Zanden, J. W., Crandell, T. L., & Crandell, C. (2002). *Human development* (7th ed.). New York: McGraw-Hill.

Verhage, M., Maia, A. S., Plomp, J. J., Brussaard, A. B., Heeroma, J. H., Vermeer, H., et al. (2001). Synaptic assembly of the brain in the absence of neurotransmitter secretion. *Science, 287*, 864–869.

Wasser, S. K. (1994). Psychosocial stress and infertility: Cause or effect? *Human Nature, 5*, 293–306.

Wasser, S. K., Sewall, G., & Soules, M. R. (1993). Psychosocial stress as a cause of infertility. *Fertility and Sterility, 59*, 685–689.

Zhang, L. I., & Poo, M. M. (2001). Electrical activity and development of neural circuits. *National Neurosciences, 4*, 1207–1214.

Zuckerman, E. (2000). *Clinician's thesaurus* (5th ed.). New York: Guilford.

PART II

CONTEMPORARY ISSUES: APPLICATIONS TO COUNSELING PRACTICE

CHAPTER SIX

ETHICAL CHALLENGES TO COUNSELING PRACTICE

CHRISTOPHER LUCIES

The counseling professions are characterized by levels of dynamism, demands to respond, and opportunities to address mental health and wellness needs of consumers in ways not conceived of a generation ago. There is an array of theories, therapeutic models, treatment interventions, and research findings from a multitude of disciplines that intersect with the delivery of counseling services to diverse clients, groups, and communities. To prepare for these demands, practicing clinicians as well as graduate counselor education students must be dedicated to expanding theoretical and clinical skills on a continuing basis. One fundamentally important area of practice, however, deserves concentrated attention due to the critical issues raised in each area of practice: ethics.

In recent years, the issues surrounding the role that ethics plays in clinical practice has intensified (Urofsky & Engels, 2003). However, conceptualizing and applying ethical codes is not always an easy process. Modern-day clinicians are confronted with a multitude of challenges that are often complex, philosophical in nature, and linked to changing social and political forces surrounding the practice of counseling (Jennings, Sovereign, Bottoroff, Mussell, & Vye, 2005). These issues are often the result of societal changes; emerging controversial questions generated by research, education, and practice; counselor and client personal and spiritual values; case law; and standards of care.

This chapter provides an overview of the role that ethics play as they relate to the contemporary issues confronted in counseling practice. The purpose of this review is to identify core ethical issues, recognizing that an in-depth treatment of each issue is beyond the scope of this chapter. Several clinical ethical vignettes and discussions are presented to demonstrate the complexity of ethical dilemmas and the ethical decision processes involved in counseling situations. Integrated throughout this chapter are issues associated with the application of American Counseling Association (ACA) Code of Ethics and Standards of Practice (www.counseling.org). Although this code is often referenced as the primary resource for counselors, the Ethical Principles of Psychologists and Code of Conduct will also be referenced (www.apa.org) to reflect the shared values and beliefs about ethical practice held by counseling psychologists.

THE ROLE OF ETHICS

A hallmark of a profession is the construction of ethical codes that guide practice. Professional associations develop codes of ethics and require members to follow them. Failure to follow an ethical code can result in sanctions imposed on the violator by the professional association, yet may not consistently reflect governmental regulation implemented for licensure. Ethical codes are revised periodically or on a scheduled basis according to an association's bylaws to reflect relevant research findings, legal system refinements, and best practices recognized and accepted within the profession. The underlying principles of ethical codes are to prevent client harm, promote client autonomy, and ensure that clinicians do not practice outside of their area of expertise. Ethical and legal complaints filed against counselor professionals are often due to violation of these three underlying principles and result in charges of negligence, incompetence, and noncompliance with standards of care (Corey, Corey, & Callahan, 2003). To ensure that professional codes of ethics and requirements of state licensure boards responsible for monitoring and disciplining licensed practitioners are congruent, licensure boards are increasingly adopting discipline-specific ethical codes (American Psychological Association, 2003).

Counseling ethics serve the following purposes:

1. Ethical standards ensure that client rights and overall welfare are honored.
2. Adherence to an ethical code ensures that counselors practice within the realm of their training and competence.
3. Ethical codes serve as guidelines for professional behavior and as a template when confronting ethical dilemmas.

In recent years, the issues surrounding the *application* of ethics have assumed a magnified role in clinical practice (Bricklin, 2001; Urofsky & Engels, 2003). Clinicians, educators, and professional association leadership recognize that how ethics are conceptualized directly links to how ethics will be applied. Lack of clarity between the desired intent of an ethical code and the real-world needs of practitioners faced with application of ethical codes represents a foundational issue that the counseling professions continually must address. For example, an underlying principle of the ACA Code of Ethics is the *do no harm concept* (Bricklin, 2001). The ACA states its members must promote the "the enhancement of human development throughout the life-span. Association members recognize diversity in our society and embrace a cross-cultural approach in support of the worth, dignity, potential, and uniqueness of each individual" (www.counseling.org). For psychologists, the 2002 Ethical Principles of Psychologists and Code of Conduct "set forth enforceable rules for conduct as psychologists" (p. 2) for members of the American Psychological Association. In practice, questions arise as to how the individual practitioner fulfills this responsibility across a wide array of settings, with increasingly diverse client populations, and in the face of demands for services and dwindling funding or reimbursement resources.

PHILOSOPHICAL CONSIDERATIONS: MANDATORY AND ASPIRATIONAL ETHICS

Preventing client harm and promoting a client's dignity embrace a philosophical orientation. Urofsky and Engels (2003, p. 126) argued for counselor self-awareness and an understanding of how a counselor's interventions influence the overall treatment process as well as its impact on society as a whole:

> Philosophical issues, especially those that are related to moral philosophy, undergird virtually all aspects of counseling [and] require that counselors have an understanding of counseling and ethics that goes beyond the basic knowledge of counseling skills and ethical codes.

Counselors have the choice either to function ethically in a black and white context where each situation is seen through a set of lenses that requires a forced choice between two polar opposite choices (*mandatory ethics*), or implement interventions and honor client welfare that has shades of gray, suggesting a set of lenses through which each situation is viewed individually taking into account a multitude of variables and less emphasis on a forced choice among clear-cut options (*aspirational ethics*). Several researchers (Jordan & Meara, 1990; Kitchener, 1984, 1986; Meara, Schmidt, & Day, 1996) have studied the differences between the mandatory and aspirational frameworks. Mandatory ethics are typically reflected by codes established by professional associations and licensure boards. These codes are considered acceptable ethical and legal standards relative to professional behaviors, clinical procedures, and ethical decision making. Aspirational ethics, on the other hand, embrace the philosophy of client welfare and reflect a transition from viewing ethical challenges from narrow lenses to higher-level ethical thinking and decision making (Bricklin, 2001).

From this perspective, there are several underlying concepts that must be considered, each identifying issues with which the counseling professions must continually struggle (Bersoff, 1995; Corey, Corey, & Callahan, 2003; Kitchener, 1984):

- *Autonomy*: Respecting the client's rights to make decisions
- *Beneficence*: Implementing good counseling work
- *Nonmaleficence*: Avoiding client harm at all costs
- *Justice*: Creating a safe and trusting therapeutic relationship whereby the client's interest comes first

These underlying principles can be viewed as reflecting both a mandatory as well as an aspirational perspective. From the mandatory perspective, all counselor professionals in every context of practice should adhere to these principles. The aspirational perspective adds a different dimension of context to the application of ethics by following each principle yet also considers surrounding influences. For example, a counselor can be charged with a violation of ethical conduct by divulging client information without client permission. From a strict view of the ethical code that addresses confidentiality, this is an accurate assessment. However, on further investigation, the context of the violation may suggest that factors present in the situation mitigate the violation when fully explored. Thus, it is suggested that although the mandatory perspective of applying ethical codes is essential to the safeguarding of the consumer, the aspirational perspective can add a holistic viewpoint to the judgments that will be made.

CORE ETHICAL ISSUE: INFORMED CONSENT

Informed consent is a term that includes ethical and legal implications. The issues associated with ensuring that informed consent is present prior to initiating delivery of counseling services or research activities must be kept at the forefront of treatment planning as well as research design (Corey, Corey, & Callahan, 2003; Leedy & Ormrod, 2005). Counselors and researchers must ensure that all clients and research participants are competent and capable to consent to treatment or to be involved in research and that participation in either activity is voluntarily initiated without coercion. Two issues directly influence informed consent: how informed consent is obtained and how competence to give consent is determined.

Constructing Informed Consent

To ensure that the client or research participant is competent to give consent, the practitioner or researcher must follow clear and consistently used guidelines designed to protect those involved in counseling activities. For example, to "give informed consent," the client must have an understanding of services provided across multiple dimensions. Informed consent forms, therefore, must be precise and detail oriented on the following issues: fees, client/research participant rights, limits of confidentiality, counseling/research interventions, length and frequency of sessions/participation, and the risks and benefits of the activity. Counselors have the added responsibility to disclose the following when in a direct service provider role: fees, educational and clinical training, level of licensure, theoretical approach, client's diagnoses and proposed treatment plan, emergency session(s) options, policies and procedures for client "no shows" or missed appointments, and informing the client of any scheduled vacations and/or prolonged absences by the practitioner. Additionally, all this information must be provided to the client or potential research participant in a manner that is understandable (i.e., language used, grammar, clarity, and so on, must "match" that of the person being informed). Failure to take into account language, culture, or ethnic differences during informed consent procedures can lead to invalidation of the consent given as well as directly impact the effectiveness of treatment or research outcomes.

Competence for Informed Consent

In most contexts, practitioners or researchers can follow well-defined guidelines to obtain informed consent. Certain client populations, however, require additional levels of consideration when devising methods to ensure that informed consent is required and delivered.

For example, determining competency and free will to give consent is challenging with minors, court-ordered clients, and cognitively impaired individuals. One solution to this dilemma is to determine who holds legal guardianship over the client and to obtain parental and/or guardian permission to treat. For minors, adolescents, and court-ordered clients, the clinical challenge is honoring the clients' confidentiality while at the same time providing adequate information to the respective referral sources (e.g., the court, the parents of a teenage child, etc.).

To ensure that informed consent and rights to information are observed, while also sustaining the client–counselor relationship, the counselor or researcher can notify each party to the treatment process about the parameters of confidentiality. When accomplished at the outset of treatment and affirmed as indicated during treatment, required breaks in confidentiality can be recognized as acceptable in a specific context. This form of breaching confidentiality is unique to certain forms of counseling and, although acknowledged by all parties, transforms the nature of the counseling services provided. Issues associated with informed consent are also linked to contemporary changes in third-party payment arrangements (e.g., managed care) as well as governmental statutes that dictate how information about clients is transmitted and protected (e.g., the Health Insurance Portability and Accountability Act [HIPAA]).

CORE ETHICAL ISSUE: ETHICAL DECISION MAKING

As previously stated, ethical codes are guidelines for professional practice and conduct. With that stated, some have argued that codes alone do not always provide a definite solution to ethical dilemmas (Bersoff, 1995; Corey, Corey, & Callahan, 2003; Kitchener, 1984; Urofsky & Engels, 2003). To address this issue, several practitioners and researchers have proposed frameworks within which ethical dilemmas can be addressed. Some of these conceptual frameworks are similar in structure, comprised of specific steps such as identifying the issues, reviewing ethical codes, considering various positive and negative options and consequences, seeking out formal clinical and peer supervision, attaining legal counsel, documenting the results of these meetings, exploring one's conscience and thought processes, and reflecting what was learned. Additional steps include determining and following through on the best choice and evaluating its outcome. Finally, reflecting on the learning experience and avoiding similar situations in the future completes the structured process (Corey, Corey, & Callahan, 2003).

Clearly, a structured decision-making process supports counselors faced with ethical dilemmas. In addition, following a consistent decision-making process also fosters a thought process that can become "second nature." In other words, the counselor faces fewer dilemmas when he or she is confident in how each situation is approached, analyzed, and resolved. Using this, or a similarly structured decision-making process, is compatible with mandatory or aspirational ethical problem resolution as well. It is the process followed in a consistent manner that allows the counselor professional to engage in ethical decision making while reducing uncertainty. Of note is the central placement in the process of seeking professional consultation or supervision when faced with ethical decision-making challenges.

CORE ETHICAL ISSUE: CONFIDENTIALITY
AND PRIVILEGED COMMUNICATION

Confidentiality and privileged communication are concepts comprised of ethical and legal components. Some have proposed that *confidentiality* is the foundation of the counseling relationship and that it builds trust and rapport (Corey, Corey, & Callahan, 2005; Herlihy & Corey, 1996). With trust such a critically important element of the counselor–client relationship, counselors make every effort to maintain confidentiality, and clients assume that information divulged in counseling is protected (Glosoff, Herlihy, & Spence, 2000). Quite frequently, clients will voluntarily sign a release of information for counselors to disclose limited verbal and/or written information. Although such permission is often granted—such as in the case of providing updates to other health care providers, educational systems, attorneys, and significant others—there are occasions when counselors are confronted with a subpoena and/or a court order to disclose confidential material (Corey, Corey, & Callahan, 2005).

Court orders or subpoenas are problematic for the counselor when clients do not wish for their records to be disclosed (Glosoff, Herlihy, & Spence, 2000). A central issue in this situation is the difference between what the client understands as "privileged' or "confidential" and what is considered as such by judicial institutions or legal experts. For example, consider a counselor who receives a court order and/or a subpoena to testify in court and/or a request to surrender counseling records. Unless the counselor privilege is upheld (as determined by a court), the counselor must comply with the court request in order to avoid a contempt of court ruling (Glosoff, Herlihy, & Spence, 2000). When faced with such a request, the counselor is advised to inform the client of the request and then to seek legal counsel before responding to the request. For the counselor, a central issue in such a potentially adversarial situation is protection of client information and the client–therapist relationship that is linked to the treatment process. As with many ethical dilemmas, the counselor's action to inform the client of the request for information by a third party may mitigate harm to the treatment relationship. Consultation with a supervisor or colleague with experience in this area of practice management is advised.

The parameters of *privileged communication* are established by legal statute and/or case law. This specifically implies that clients have the legal right not to authorize any information to be released to the court system and/or to other parties (Corey, Corey, & Callahan, 2003; Glosoff, Herlihy, & Spence, 2000). Unfortunately, privileged communication is not always legally recognized for licensed counselors, marriage and family therapists, and social workers; however, for some professionals, such as licensed psychologists and physicians, both groups legally hold privileged communication (Glosoff, Herlihy, & Spence, 2000). It is important to reiterate that privileged communication is not "owned" by the professional, but rather by the client (Corey, Corey, & Callahan, 2003).

Breaching Confidentiality

In addition to the issues associated with defining privileged communication within different counselor professional licensure categories, there are other circumstances when counselors must break client confidentiality. The ACA Code of Ethics and Standards of Practice (2005) state that when a client is at risk for endangering the self and/or others, confidentiality can be breached. Other examples include the following:

- The client reports involvement in or perpetration of child or elder abuse.
- The client discloses suicidal ideation or intent.
- The clinician assesses a client's suicide risk as meeting established criteria.
- There is evidence of client psychological deterioration to take care of the self.
- There is a risk of homicide posed to others by a client.

The counselor professional is duty bound to breach confidentiality in such situations (Corey, Corey, & Callahan, 2003). These breaks in confidentiality are founded on the ACA Code of Ethics (2005), state laws for mandated reporters and licensure laws, and case law (Corey, Corey, & Callahan, 2003; Golsoff, Herlihy, & Spence, 2000). For psychologists adhering to the APA Ethics Code (2005, p. 8), disclosure of confidential information is acceptable for similar reasons identified in section 4.02 in order to:

1. provide needed professional services;
2. obtain appropriate professional consultations;
3. protect the client/patient, psychologist, or others from harm; or
4. obtain payment for services from a client/patient, in which instance disclosure is limited to the minimum that is necessary to achieve the purpose.

The issues for the practicing counselor include how to sustain an up-to-date knowledge base about reporting requirements and implementing continuing professional development to ensure competence to respond appropriately to situations that may require breaks in confidentiality. As with other ethical dilemmas faced by the counselor professional, seeking peer consultation and supervision when faced with client disclosure of potentially lethal behavior is an imperative (Corey, Corey, & Callahan, 2003).

The Duty to Warn

Specifically breaking confidentiality for suicidal and/or homicidal risk is well established and influenced by case law, legislation, and court rulings and is referred to as the *duty to warn* and as the *duty to protect*. The underlying concept for these warnings centers on the standard of practice that clinicians must protect clients from themselves and/or from others (Melby, 2004). Hence, it is up to the treating clinician to evaluate the client, consult with clinical supervisors, and, within the parameters of reasonable doubt, judge that the client is at risk to harm the self and/or others (Gross & Robinson, 1987).

This standard of practice resulted from the Tarasoff case. In 1969, a student attending the University of California at Berkeley, identified as Prosenjit Poddar, had reported to his psychologist a plan to kill Tatiana Tarasoff, a woman who had refused his advances. The treating psychologist consulted with his supervisor and was directed not to disclose this information to Ms. Tarasoff. The supervisor's rationale was that it would be unprofessional and inappropriate. The treating psychologist followed the supervisor's advice, and several weeks later, Poddar murdered Ms. Tarasoff (Corey, Corey, & Callahan, 1995; Melby, 2004). The Tarasoff decision became a classic ethics case for review, debate, and continuing refinement. In the ensuring years, each mental health profession defined the requirements to breach confidentiality under circumstances involving a client's risk to the well-being or safety of an identifiable other person or persons. In addition, the parameters of the amount of information to be disclosed to fulfill the duty to warn has been narrowed. Thus, counselors implementing a duty to warn action disclose only the information that is essential to implement appropriate actions to protect an identified victim or victims (e.g., see APA Ethics Code 4.05, p. 8). The Tarasoff decision effectively transformed understanding of confidentiality within the mental health treatment context.

The Duty to Warn and HIV

Lately, the duty to warn in some instances has been extended to clients who are afflicted with highly contagious sexually transmitted illnesses. In fact, in recent years, clinicians and researchers (DiMarco & Zoline, 2004; Friedman & Hughes, 1994; Huprich, Fuller, & Schneider, 2003; Keffala & Stone, 1999) have explored the ethical and legal implications with clients who tested positive for the acquired immune deficiency syndrome (AIDS) virus. For example, consider the following clinical vignette:

> Joey is a 37-year-old, White, employed, divorced male who is considered quite a "ladies' man." He is tall, attractive, and very charming. In fact, his marriage resulted in divorce due to his numerous affairs with women, many of whom he met on the Internet. Joey's history indicates that he enjoys the thrill of anonymous and unprotected promiscuous sex. Recently, he met a woman with whom he fell in love. Although he asserts that he loves this woman, he also is seeing other women on the side for "one-night stands." Joey stated to the counselor, "My girlfriend wants me to get an HIV test, and I'll guess I'll do it to get her off my back." Two weeks later, Joey comes into therapy in total disbelief and states to the counselor, "I have it . . . I mean I have HIV. I refuse to tell my girlfriend—she'll leave me. . ."

What is known about HIV is that unprotected sex and exposure to the virus increase the likelihood of contracting AIDS. This disease is life-threatening and afflicts millions. Although there are progressive and promising medications to slow down the progression of the illness, they do not cure the person. From the fictitious case of Joey, there are several ethical issues raised:

1. Does the counselor have the ethical right to break Joey's confidentiality by informing Joey's girlfriend and/or other partners?
2. If the counselor breaks confidentiality, will Joey pursue a malpractice lawsuit?
3. Suppose the girlfriend contracts HIV. Does she have legal recourse against Joey's therapist as a result of a failure to disclose Joey's HIV status?

4. Is it possible that the counselor may be placed on probation and license suspended for breaking confidentiality and/or for not informing Joey's girlfriend and partners?
5. Should the counselor seek out clinical supervision and legal counsel prior to any intervention?

These ethical dilemmas and questions are increasingly becoming universal for contemporary mental health clinicians. Because the issues raised are so complex, there are no simple solutions to resolve the counselor's dilemma. In such cases, there are legal factors, clinical implications, and, for some providers, moral issues that must be addressed (DiMarco & Zoline, 2004). Referencing the landmark Tarasoff decision (Corey, Corey, & Callahan, 2003, p. 334), clinicians who conclude that their client presents a threat to themselves and/or others, counselors have a responsibility to

> use reasonable care to protect the intended victim against such danger; discharge of such duty may require the therapist to take one or more of various steps, depending on the nature of the case, including warning the intended victim or others . . . of the danger, notifying the police, or taking whatever steps are reasonably necessary under the circumstances.

Applying this reasoning to Joey's situation, the Tarasoff case does not conclude that counselors have a legal right to disclose the HIV status to a client's partners in *all cases*. For example, DiMarco and Zoline (2004) claimed there are various states that limit the duty to warn to licensed physicians, whereas some mental health licensure boards allow licensed medical and behavioral health providers to disclose the client's HIV status to unaware partners.

With reference to a client's HIV or AIDS status, the decision to breach confidentiality, regardless of state statutes, generates a plethora of reactions. For example, research has demonstrated that clinicians who are homophobic and who feel socially responsible to protect the public safety are more willing, regardless of their client's HIV exposure to infect others, and those who lack AIDS education, are more apt to break confidentiality (Friedman & Hughes, 1994; Huprich, et al, 2003). For some clinicians, the refusal to breach confidentiality derives from the refusal to compromise the therapeutic relationship at all costs, and thereby, to prevent client harm (Dimarco & Zoline, 2004; Huprich et al., 2003). Thus, two perspectives emerge when considering the duty to inform when the duty is associated with certain potentially lethal diseases.

For direction in resolving ethical issues raised by cases involving fatal and contagious diseases, the ACA Code of Ethics (2005), Section B.2.b., provides clear guidance:

> Counselors may be justified in disclosing information to identifiable third parties, if they are known to be at demonstrable and high risk of contracting the disease. Prior to making a disclosure, counselors confirm that there is such a diagnosis and assess the intent of the clients to inform the third parties about their disease or to engage in any behaviors that may be harmful to an identifiable third party.

Based on these research findings, and the ACA Code of Ethics, is there a middle ground for compromise and/or for ethical decision making? The response is yes. Research has shown that mental health professionals are willing to break confidentiality and follow through on the duty to warn when the client's partner's identity is known, and it has been established that unprotected sex is occurring and is life-threatening (Chenneville, 2000; Huprich et al, 2003).

One strategy proposed with reference to disclosure of HIV status to a client's intimate partner is summed up as a best-case scenario. It involves encouraging the client to disclose and ensuring that the disclosure has taken place. The work of DiMarco and Zoline (2004), Friedman and Hughes (1994), and Keffala and Stone (1999) provides a set of broad guidelines that can form a scaffolding for an approach to the informing process. Each step requires an in-depth exploration of the topic to be addressed, careful delineation of actions to be taken, and methods to verify that the plan has been implemented.

1. Determine if the client is having unprotected sex.
2. Determine if the client has disclosed the HIV status to a partner or partners.
3. Establish the identity of the client's partners.
4. Ascertain if the client is willing to disclose his or her HIV status to the partner.
   a. If yes, it is recommended that a couples session be scheduled to verify that the information has been communicated to the partner.
   b. If yes, have the client sign a release of information prior to the couples session.
   c. If yes or no, explore the option of formulating a contract for safe sex that the client will sign and agree to adhere to with his or her partner(s).
5. Seek clinical supervision and consultation. Carefully document all supervisory and client sessions, contracts, and agreements.

Providing that the client refuses to disclose the HIV status, the following suggestions from the work of Friedman and Hughes (1994) provide insights about how to proceed with reference to the duty to warn ethical guideline.

1. Determine the reasons for the client's refusal to disclose his or her HIV status to his or her partner(s).
2. Evaluate the level of HIV exposure for the partner (i.e., the client refuses to participate in safe sex and has multiple partners in addition to the primary partner).
3. Review the ACA Code of Ethics and state licensure statutes with reference to duty to warn.
4. Review current research that addresses the particular issue that the counselor has encountered as well as prevailing community standards of care.
5. Access clinical supervision and consider seeking legal counsel.
6. Consider the ethical and legal consequences for breaching confidentiality regarding the client's HIV status.
7. Document all client sessions, supervisory and legal consultations, and other considered factors.
8. Arrive at a decision, implement the decision, and document the outcome and rationale for breaching the client's HIV status.

These steps highlight a method that can be used to address a breach of confidentiality based on the counselor's belief that there is a duty to warn, but how the steps to this process unfold will vary. In some cases, the complexity of the client's situation, the counselor's understanding of the facts of the case, and the access to resources essential to support ethical decision making will vary from community to community. Thus, in some cases, steps are repeated as new information is obtained in some settings, whereas in others, the process is clear and the decision to warn another is made with the client's assent and a continuation of a productive therapeutic relationship.

MANAGED CARE AND ETHICAL DILEMMAS

Gone are the days when professional counselors, including the author, could treat a client for weeks, months, or even years at a time without needing to justify to a third party, such as insurance companies, the necessity for treatment. Moreover, these companies neither requested a client's counseling records nor was it necessary to justify one's counseling orientation, theoretical framework, interventions, and treatment plan to external reviewers.

As health care costs increased, health care insurance companies devised a system of care known as *managed care*, designed to control and monitor escalating costs (Dombeck & Olsan, 2002). It was proposed that these companies would ensure that cost-effective treatment would occur by contracting with approved providers to offer time-limited treatment. In general, the emphasis of counseling treatment moved from long-term psychodynamic therapy to brief cognitive-behavioral therapies that addressed clients' concerns in a matter of days, weeks, or a few months (deShazer, 1985; Evans, Valadez, Burns, & Rodriguez, 2002).

Although there is some variation in how each managed care plan implements authorization for treatment, approves treatment plans, or reviews treatment progress, ethical issues associated with these processes have been a source of concern for counseling professionals. For instance, quite frequently treatment plans are submitted to a utilization reviewer (UR), who approves the treatment plan and a specific amount of sessions. These URs are not necessarily licensed master's and/or doctoral clinicians. The focus of the review is to ensure that costs are contained and that treatment is deemed as medically necessary to psychologically stabilize the client.

In managed mental health care, then, the mental health professional–client relationship has been transformed. The client gains access to counseling providers through a provider list, and a third person (UR) is involved in determining whether authorization of treatment will continue or be terminated based on documentation submitted to the plan. To be included on a provider panel, the provider agrees to comply with the requirements the plan demands. From an ethical perspective, the counselor can be faced with an ethical dilemma involving the need to continue to provide treatment beyond the parameters of the provider contract. Should treatment be continued under these circumstances? What are the risks to the client and the counselor? Is this an ethical issue related to premature termination of treatment based on a probability that payment will not be forthcoming? Or should it be resolved only with attention to avoiding malfeasance?

There are both benefits and limitations of being a provider of mental health counseling services for managed care companies (Scaturo, 2002). The benefits are readily apparent, including a reliable source of client referrals, and although the reimbursement rates may be lower than community standards of payment for counseling services, there is a consistent source of managed care income. Some managed care companies provide "bonuses" for counselors who are able to speed up the treatment process and discharge the client (Danzinger & Welfel-Reynolds, 2001; Sanchez & Turner, 2003).

Limitations of participating as a managed care panel provider often emphasize the limits placed on the number of sessions authorized, methods to be used to provide counseling (e.g., time-limited or brief therapy), and using treatment models and interventions that are incongruent to the counselor's theoretical/clinical orientation (Danzinger & Welfel-Reynolds, 2001). Other challenges include disagreement with the UR's judgment relative to the overall treatment process, ranging from the frequency of sessions, to disagreement with the diagnosis, to early termination when the clinician deems it is clinically inappropriate to do so, to the refusal to authorize additional sessions, and to the conflicts between managed care companies' policies and procedures that are in direct conflict with clinicians' ethical codes and values (Sanchez & Turner, 2003).

The ethical issues that the counseling professions are grappling with in relation to managed care have moved through a number of stages since its inception. When first implemented in a widespread manner in the 1990s (Gladding, 2000), the reaction to managed care's intrusion into the therapeutic relationship was strident and characterized by high levels of professional resistance. At the same time, counselor professionals recognized the need to creatively manage health care costs in an atmosphere in which unmanaged spending on treatment approaches of questionable value had exploded.

Reactions to the utilization review process conducted by individuals who may not be licensed mental health professionals was, and continues to be, viewed as ethically compromising to patient confidentiality. Although managed care procedures and practices have in many instances addressed the need to protect client confidentiality, the requirements to document treatment to third parties who may or may not be licensed and qualified to review such material remains a thorny issue in the sides of counseling professionals concerned about the ethical projection of consumers (Danzinger & Welfel-Reynolds, 2001; Sanchez & Turner, 2003).

Legal Issues and Managed Care

A landmark court case, *Wickine v. State of California* (1987), set the precedent that health care professionals must advocate for their clients for additional treatment when it is clinically appropriate to do so, even when managed care companies deem termination must occur. This court case involved a patient who was medically hospitalized for surgery, developed complications, and requested from the managed care company an extension of inpatient days. The UR refused this request, and the patient was discharged, only to develop a blood clot that resulted in her leg being amputated. The patient sued the State of California, and the utilization reviewer was found legally liable for recommending early discharge. Although this case was based on a medical issue, behavioral health care providers and attorneys often refer to this case to ethically and clinically advocate for clients in other areas of practice such as mental health care (Newman & Dunbar, 2000).

A second case, *Wilson v. Blue Cross of Southern California* (1990), determined that a mental health professional does not need to challenge the utilization reviewer's decision.

However, in cases of liability, both the mental health professional and the UR are legally at risk for negligence, which translates into both parties being responsible for premature treatment termination. In addition, recent Supreme Court decisions (Ruger, 2004) found that consumers who are denied managed health care benefits have limited appeal rights. Thus, the counselor professional may well find himself or herself in the position of having to strongly advocate on behalf of clients who need additional mental health care beyond the limits of a particular managed care plan when the utilization reviewer denies such benefits.

> Jerome is a 43-year-old, African American, married male who was referred by his managed care company to see Dr. Francis, a licensed mental health counselor in private practice. Dr. Francis evaluated Jerome and arrived at the diagnosis of post-traumatic stress disorder (PTSD) (American Psychiatric Association, 2000) as a result of reoccurring flashbacks and nightmares of years of childhood sexual and physical abuse. Dr. Francis submitted a treatment plan and requested 12 sessions for cognitive-behavioral therapy with a review by the UR at the sixth session.
>
> As a result of 10 sessions, Jerome learned new skills and was able to manage his PTSD symptoms and even reported feeling better. At the eleventh session, Jerome reported the following to Dr. Francis: "You need to know that although I am feeling better, I've been experiencing these memory lapses, and I see myself floating out of my body. My wife tells me that I am often three different people. Last week I discovered a whole wardrobe that is not my style. I did not buy them and yet my wife insists that she did not purchase them. . . . I don't get it."
>
> Dr. Francis immediately became concerned and suspected that Jerome may have dissociative features or even a dissociative identity disorder (DID) (American Psychiatric Association, 2000). Dr. Francis consulted with his clinical supervisor, who suggested that he call the client's managed care company and request an additional evaluation and counseling sessions. Dr. Francis spoke with a UR and was told, "The patient should have told this to you long ago, and based upon what you are telling me, we do not reimburse for these disorders, and hence you need to terminate therapy immediately and refer the patient to a self-help group. It is impossible to approve any more sessions because he has used his mental health sessions for this year."
>
> Dr. Francis was in a state of disbelief and again called the insurance company and filed a written appeal according to procedures. He was informed he would receive written notification in 30 days of the final decision. Meanwhile, although Dr. Francis is not trained and/or clinically experienced to treat dissociative features and/or DID, he continued to see Jerome on a much reduced sliding-fee scale, which violated his managed care contract, and without contacting his clinical supervisor.

The ethical issues raised by this case are complex and dramatic. Although seemingly reflecting a situation that is of questionable realism, it is likely that practitioners are faced with such complicated ethical decisions more often than can be verified. Based on the hypothetical nature of the case, the following questions and issues are raised:

1. Did Dr. Francis ethically and legally follow the guidelines for best practices and the standards of care of his profession?
2. Is Dr. Francis legally liable for violating the contract and agreeing to continue to treat Jerome on a sliding-fee basis, considering that the managed care company had not yet determined a final decision?
3. Were there other options and/or procedures that Dr. Francis should have followed?
4. Did Dr. Francis violate an ethical code by practicing outside his scope of practice relative to Jerome's additional symptoms?
5. Is it possible that Jerome actually had DID and not PTSD? If this were the case, was Dr. Francis negligent for incorrectly diagnosing the client?

These five issues are a sampling of the questions that can be asked based on the limited information provided. It is the consideration of such cases, however, that brings ethical debate to a new level of analysis. Clearly, significant economic forces that govern much of the mental health care currently provided can further complicate delivery of ethical care.

Linking the Codes of Ethics to the Real World of Counseling

In the fictitious Dr. Francis case, he correctly consulted with his clinical supervisor and followed through on advocating for Jerome by calling the managed care company and pursuing a written appeal for the insurance company to authorize the reevaluation. However, Dr. Francis did not review resource materials that could have more clearly informed his decision making (e.g., as described in both the ACA and APA Codes of Ethics or his state's Counselor Licensure Board relative to expectations of practitioners in such a situation). Additionally, Dr. Francis neglected to consult with the clinical supervisor to report the UR's initial denial decision. Furthermore, Dr. Francis neglected to review his managed care provider contract regarding probable consequences of failing to follow the directive of the UR or of continuing to provide unauthorized care. Finally, to the potential detriment of Dr. Francis's status as a mental health clinician, he did not seek a legal consult to explore the legal implications of his decision options.

It may be viewed as admirable that Dr. Francis was acting in the best interest of the client's welfare by advocating for additional sessions, but the reality is that the original request for treatment authorization was in fact linked to the client's PTSD symptoms, which had significantly decreased over the course of treatment. The client's report of additional symptoms does not indicate that Jerome is in immediate danger to himself and/or to others. At a minimum, then, what is indicated is a risk assessment to determine any potential for danger to self or others, and this request would be viewed by the UR, most likely, in a different light than the request Dr. Francis presented at the original series of authorized treatment sessions. Is it possible that Jerome had two co-occurring diagnoses: PTSD and DID? Alternatively, could it be that Jerome actually had DID and these symptoms were disguised as PTSD?

The issue at hand is that Dr. Francis (a licensed mental health counselor) violated the ACA Code of Ethics (2005, p. 9), Section C.1, Standards of Knowledge, and Section C.2,

Professional Competence. Relative to the standards of knowledge, the Code of Ethics states: "Counselors have a responsibility to read, understand, and follow the *ACA Code of Ethics* and adhere to applicable laws and regulations." Hence, Dr. Francis should have reviewed and considered all ethical concerns. Furthermore, by agreeing to treat Jerome for dissociative and/or DID symptoms, Dr. Francis violated the ethical code that is concerned with professional competence. According to the ACA Code of Ethics (2005, p. 9), Section C.2.a:

> Counselors practice only within the boundaries of their competence, based on their education, training, supervised experience, state and national professional credentials, and appropriate professional experience. Counselors gain knowledge, personal awareness, sensitivity, and skills pertinent to working with a diverse client population.

In view of the issues raised by a single case study, it can be hypothesized that the varieties of ethical issues inherent in contemporary practice environments are also varied, unique, and at times direct and easily resolved, while at other times seemingly with few optimum decision options. Counselor professionals will continue to encounter the demand to follow ethical codes of conduct and standards of practice, and at the same time, respond to client needs for care that can be in conflict with those standards. Review of hypothetical cases promotes careful analysis, reflection, and consideration of how best to use professional resources designed to provide a framework within which to make appropriate decisions.

Preparation for Ethical Practice in a Managed Care Environment

To further explore the issues surrounding ethics and managed care, consider the following self-reflection suggestions. As a practitioner, counselor educator, or researcher, these strategies, when followed consistently, can increase awareness of risks for ethical challenges while introducing a "pause" that supports an informed ethical decision process.

1. Start by self-assessing personal thoughts, attitudes, and beliefs about participation in a managed mental health care environment.
2. Analyze the compatibility of one's preferred therapeutic approach to providing counseling and therapy as compatible or incompatible with managed care. Depending on the nature and outcomes of this review, it may be realistic to reassess how to practice as a counselor in such a system or acquire additional practice competencies.
3. Carefully evaluate personal preferences to provide counseling to specific client populations or in relation to certain psychological disorders. For example, if the provider panel is seeking practitioners with experience and expertise in treating clients with eating disorders, and the counselor does not have the necessary advanced training or competence with such disorders, declining participation on the panel is appropriate.
4. Identify areas for improvement in practice competencies with specific attention to gaps in theoretical foundations, knowledge of diagnostic issues, and unique needs of client populations.

5. Develop a professional plan to review ethical implications of counseling care and management on a regular basis. This can be accomplished with peers or through consultation with a clinical supervisor.

COUNSELING PRACTICE: CHALLENGING ETHICAL ISSUES

A discussion of contemporary ethical issues within the counseling professions could include each ethical standard within a code of ethics and span the professions of counseling, psychology, and social work. For the purposes of this review, however, a number of ethical challenges have been identified as the focus for evaluation. Each ethical challenge is identified, fictitious case illustrations are provided to highlight the context for the issue, and summaries of ethics management are presented.

A significant part of any counselor's overall personal and professional development is self-awareness. It is essential that each counselor determine how cultural background, personal and spiritual values, and biases both positively and negatively impact the therapeutic relationship. Because counselors are not exempt from forming biases, it becomes essential to engage in reflective practices designed to minimize the impact that bias can play while providing counseling services. To minimize and or deny the existence of personal biases or to justify personal values and belief systems, whether subtle or covert, is viewed as unethical (Corey, Corey, & Callahan, 2003). Although such behavior may well be unintentional, it nevertheless demonstrates cultural incompetence and a lack of self-awareness. To assume that theoretical knowledge and clinical interventions will work for all clients demonstrates what Sue and Sue (2003) describe as *cultural encapsulation*. This concept refers to the narrow lenses the counselor can wear relative to how the world is perceived and how others are perceived, and often reflects an unwillingness to step outside of personal safety zones to learn about others who are culturally different.

For the ethical counselor attuned to the importance of a self-reflective stance, the American Counseling Association's position is clear, resolute, and reflected in the Code of Ethics (2005, p. 10):

> Counselors do not condone or engage in discrimination based on age, culture, disability, ethnicity, race, religion/spirituality, gender identity, sexual orientation, marital status/partnership, language preference, socioeconomic status, or any basis proscribed by law.

From the perspective of counselor responsibility to maintain awareness of personal values and beliefs and how these can impact the therapeutic encounter, the ACA Code of Ethics (2005, pp. 4–5) provides explicit guidance: "Counselors are aware of their own values, attitudes, beliefs, and behaviors and avoid imposing values that are inconsistent with counseling goals." Additional guidance is provided by the Association for Multicultural Counseling and Development (AMCD) (1991):

> Culturally skilled counselors seek out educational, consultative, and training experience to improve their understanding and effectiveness in working with culturally different populations.

Being able to recognize the limits of their competencies, they (a) seek consultation, (b) seek further training or education, (c) refer out to more qualified individuals or resources, or (d) engage in a combination of these.

For psychologists, the boundaries of sensitive, self-reflective, and competent practice are specifically delineated in 2.01b in the APA Code of Ethics (p. 5) emphasizing the parameters of professional knowledge in the discipline that must include the following:

> an understanding of factors associated with age, gender, gender identity, race, ethnicity, culture, national origin, religion, sexual orientation, disability, language, or socioeconomic status is essential for effective implementation of their services or research, psychologists have or obtain the training, experience, consultation, or supervision necessary to ensure the competence of their services, or they make appropriate referrals, except as provided in Standard 2.02, Providing Services in Emergencies.

To implement these ethical practices, counseling professionals aspire to model an open and accepting attitude regarding differences among people. This ideal is summed by Rogers's (as cited in Corey, Corey, & Callahan, 2003) unconditional positive regard. Equally important, each counselor professional holds the ideal of having the client's welfare in mind at all times to ensure that client harm is prevented while in the care of the counselor. Within this context, ethical practice with diverse and culturally different clients must safely reside.

It is safe to say that due to equal opportunity laws, societal changes, so-called political correctness, and the emphasis on cultural diversity within the profession, the counselor would avoid overtly biased statements and discriminatory actions toward clients or others encountered in a practice environment, including members of the opposite sex, persons of a different age, or those of a different race or ethnicity. Can it be said the same is true for attitudes toward those who have a different sexual orientation, toward people of differing spiritual/religious values, or in relation to people with disabilities?

ETHICAL ISSUES: DIVERSE BELIEFS AND DO NO HARM

Consider the following fictitious case of Claudia. As the case is reviewed, consider the various ethical issues that potentially could arise in the counselor's thoughts and be revealed in both verbal and nonverbal behavior:

> Claudia is a 68-year-old, African American, lesbian-identified female who practices Spiritualism and is actively dying of breast cancer. Claudia's same-sex partner (Jodie) of 25 years left her for another woman. As a Spiritualist, Claudia has received loving and positive messages from departed loved ones reassuring her of life-after-death and tranquility. Accepting death is not an issue. What is an issue for Claudia are feelings of sadness, anger, and abandonment because Jodie left her.

Out of desperation, Claudia locates a counselor listed in the telephone directory. Her hope is that therapy will enable her to process painful feelings and move through the final stages of her life. During the first session (a clinical evaluation), Claudia shares her story with Dr. Richards, and as she does, she detects discomfort from the counselor, as evidenced by Dr. Richards's body language and facial expressions.

The counselor states the following: "Claudia, you need to know that I am unable to work with you because of my religious beliefs that are against homosexuality and your spiritual beliefs." He continues explaining his views and suggests that if she wishes to address these problems, he is willing to work with her.

The issues raised by the counselor's response to the client's initial description of her reasons for seeking counseling provides ample opportunity to review the ethical issues presented. It is important to note that in using this particular fictitious case example, the intent is to highlight ethical issues, not debate the rights of counselors to hold religious or social beliefs that differ from client beliefs.

Ethical Considerations: Harm to Client Well-Being

A number of ethical violations are illustrated by the case of Claudia. Her experience of entering counseling and encountering a practitioner with beliefs diametrically opposed to hers resulted in a negative outcome for Claudia. In addition, the counselor's behavior clearly was in violation of the ACA Code of Ethics underlying principle to do no harm. When viewing this illustration from the client's perspective, and then from the counselor's, the ethical issues can be identified, recognizing that the counselor's intent to help was not reflected in his actions.

From Claudia's perspective, as the client entering counseling for the first time during a time of distress and medical illness, it is probable that a host of feelings were present (e.g., anger, sadness, disbelief, and feeling devalued and disrespected). For her, the decision to seek counseling assistance was met with highly unsatisfactory results.

From Dr. Richards's perspective, there may have been an intent to find a common ground with Claudia, to "frame" the treatment problem in a way that would be comfortable and familiar to the counselor. However, in offering to address topics that the client did not raise, the goal Claudia had for her counseling was derailed.

According to the ACA Code of Ethics (2005, p. 6), "If counselors determine an inability to be of professional assistance to clients, they avoid entering or continuing counseling relationships. Counselors are knowledgeable about culturally and clinically appropriate referral resources and suggest these alternatives." Dr. Richards, therefore, violated this code by demonstrating disrespect toward the client's beliefs and lifestyle and potentially caused harm to Claudia by not protecting her psychological welfare. Dr. Richards should have provided a referral for Claudia to a counselor who did not have an ideological or religious belief system that would override that of the client.

Ethics Management: Scope of Practice
Self-Reflection

When confronted with diversity issues that reflect client needs that are unfamiliar, contrary to one's own, or that the counselor is not competent to address, it is essential that the practitioner pause, consider all options, and formulate a decision reflecting best ethical practices. The reality of gayness, for some conservative religious groups and clinicians, continues to be an issue linked to beliefs that the client requires a spiritual transformation and reversal therapy to promote heterosexuality (Grant & Epp, 1998; McNeill, 1988; Nicolosi, 1991). It is essential, therefore, that counselors carefully review their respective code of ethics to ensure that compliance to these standards is maintained.

Compliance with the counselor's professional code of ethics is essential yet can be influenced by belief systems that reflect deeply held personal views. There is a well-defined requirement within the counseling professions to ensure that practice throughout a career of helping others with mental health problems is characterized by self-reflection. This practice is woven into each client encounter serving as a compass that guides decision making, supports actions to seek supervision, and corrects a course of action that has been ineffective or caused harm to others.

In Claudia's case, Dr. Richards neither consulted the ACA Code of Ethics prior to informing the client that he would redefine her presenting problem nor sought supervision to address the conflict in beliefs between client and practitioner. The most direct intervention in such a situation, designed to avoid harm to the client and to remain within the counselor's preferred scope of practice, was for Dr. Richards to demonstrate sensitivity to Claudia's presenting problems and requests for counseling while honoring his own beliefs. This can be accomplished by acknowledging a lack of competence to address her presenting problems with a statement such as, "Claudia, you are in a great deal of emotional pain caused by a number of life challenges. Because I am concerned for your well-being, and I lack the skills and knowledge to help you, I am referring you to a qualified counselor with the expertise needed to assist you."

Although there can surely be debate about how to phrase such a referral, the key issues identified include evidence that Dr. Richards has engaged in self-reflection regarding competence to help the client, has determined that he is not prepared to assist her, and has recognized that a referral to another practitioner is required. In this "replay" of the script between Dr. Richards and Claudia, the client is respected, the counselor avoids violation of ethical standards of practice, and the client's needs remain the focus of the encounter.

ETHICS ISSUE: CLIENT ABANDONMENT

Clients who enter counseling typically have an expectation that a course of counseling will be completed with the practitioner according to agreed-upon treatment plans and an understanding of the responsibilities as a client as well as those of the mental health professional providing care. To ensure that this foundation is well constructed during the initial assessment session, informed consent is obtained. As part of the informed consent process, the counselor establishes methods of contact, emergency procedures, and information about unavailability due to illness or time away from the office. Each of these informational items supports ethical practice while establishing initial levels of trust and expectation between client and counselor. Inherent in this process is an expectation that the counselor will be responsive to the client's needs in concert with the guidelines discussed. The therapeutic relationship, therefore, can hinge on the consistent implementation of these mutually understood expectations.

When expectations about access to the counselor are not upheld, clients are placed in potentially risky or life-threatening situations (Doverspike, 1999). Although not viewed as a frequently occurring event, the consequences to clients and counselors alike when such violations of an ethical practice code do occur can be severe. As illustrated by the fictitious case of Amber, untoward outcomes can be unintended.

> Amber is a 37-year-old divorced woman suffering from major depressive disorder (MDD) (American Psychiatric Association, 2000) who has attempted suicide numerous times. She recently began a course of counseling treatment with Dr. Clark. During the second session, Dr. Clark stated, "Remember, I'm here for you." The next day, Amber was feeling suicidal and called Dr. Clark's office on several occasions only to receive a voice-mail message that stated, "Hello. This is Dr. Clark, I'm not in now, please leave a message."
>
> Amber became increasingly distraught, wrote a suicide note, and consumed a bottle of prescription anxiolytic medication. Amber had previously made lunch plans with her roommate Anna. When Anna called Amber to remind her of their lunch plans and received no response, she immediately went to their apartment and discovered the suicide note and Amber, who by then was unconscious. Anna immediately called 911. Amber was admitted through the hospital emergency department to the intensive care unit (ICU) and, after responding to medical intervention, was then transferred to the inpatient psychiatric unit for further treatment.
>
> The hospital medical and psychiatric staff were very concerned about Dr. Clark's nonresponsiveness to Amber's office calls for help as well as to their efforts to contact Dr. Clark. A week after the episode occurred, Dr. Clark returned the hospital's calls and stated, "I'm so sorry. There was an out-of-state family medical emergency with my son. Is Amber okay?" The chief of psychiatry and inpatient treatment team staff were not satisfied with this response and the lack of recognition of the risk Dr. Clark's behavior posed to Amber's well-being. A complaint was filed against Dr. Clark to her state licensure board and to the American Counseling Association Ethics Committee.

In this illustrative case, the central question to be asked is: Did Dr. Clark abandon Amber and her other clients? The answer is yes, according to the ACA Code of Ethics (2005, p. 6) that states, "Counselors do not abandon or neglect clients in counseling. Counselors assist in making appropriate arrangements for the continuation of treatment, when necessary, during interruptions such as vacations, illness, and following termination." A similar caveat is described in the APA Ethics Code (2002, p. 7) that emphasizes the duty of the psychologist to "make reasonable efforts to plan for facilitating services in the event that psychological services are interrupted by factors such as the psychologist's illness, death, unavailability, relocation, or retirement or by the client's/patient's relocation or financial limitations." Regardless of Dr. Clark's reasoning, however, she failed to have a back-up plan or qualified and available coverage for her practice when she was called away on a family emergency. As can be seen in this case, Dr. Clark's absence not only justifies complaints to the state licensure board and to the ACA, but she may also be at risk for facing legal consequences for her behavior.

Ethical Management: Conscientious Coverage

It is not a realistic expectation that counselors will be personally available to all clients 24/7, 365 days a year, but it *is* realistic to expect that arrangements are in place to provide coverage for clients when the counselor professional is away or not available. In this regard, Dr. Clark's well-meaning and apparently caring concern for her client's well-being was not a sufficient rationale to fail to ensure that coverage would be in place while she was away tending to a family emergency. Counselors are obliged to make adequate plans with and for their clients to ensure that care is not unduly disrupted during the counselor's absence (VandeCreek & Knapp, 2001). Furthermore, counselors must specifically inform their clients how to obtain emergency care when emotional crises or mental health emergencies arise. These contingencies should be included in the informed consent process, verified in treatment plans, included in office telephone voice-mail messages, and connected to the availability of another mental health professional designated for such coverage.

ETHICAL ISSUE: DUAL RELATIONSHIPS

Perhaps there is no other topic that holds the potential to cause client harm and to impact client welfare more than the issue of dual relationships. Many dual relationships are considered incompatible and unethical to the counseling process, whereas others do not result in significant harm or exploitation (Glass, 2003; Hill, 2001; Kolbert, Morgan, & Brendel, 2002). For example, a counselor who works and practices in a rural area and frequently interacts with clients at the local parents–teachers association (PTA), at her house of worship, or while shopping. These nonsexual dual relationships must be addressed in an assertive and clear fashion and will remain part of the landscape of the counselor's life (Nigro, 2004). In addition, counselors are very aware of the discomfort generated by being providers of services to people known to them in their home communities and who they will continue to interact with outside the therapeutic environment (Nigro, 2004).

With reference to this issue, the ACA Code of Ethics (2005) provides guidance that addresses the variety of ways that counselors may and should not interact with clients outside the therapeutic context. The code discusses limitations on interaction with clients currently being treated (Section A.5.a), with former clients (Section A.5.b), nonprofessional interactions or relationships (Section A.5.c.), and potentially beneficial interactions with clients outside the counseling relationship (Section A.5.d.). The code also addresses the need for counselors to maintain awareness and engage in appropriate behavior with clients when role changes occur (e.g., from a counselor to a researcher) (Section A.5.e). These guidelines provide clear direction to counselor professionals that are designed to avoid the problems that can arise when dual relationships are anticipated, are formed inadvertently, are unavoidable in certain contexts, or are being considered.

In the APA Ethics Code (2005, p. 6), psychologists are advised to refrain

> from entering into a multiple relationship if the multiple relationship could reasonably be expected to impair the psychologist's objectivity, competence, or effectiveness in performing his or her functions as a psychologist, or otherwise risks exploitation or harm to the person with whom the professional relationship exists. Multiple relationships that would not reasonably be expected to cause impairment or risk exploitation or harm are not unethical.

Counselors clearly are admonished to carefully evaluate the potential risk of engaging in dual relationships in any contexts in which they may arise. It is the counselor's responsibility to ensure that such relationships, when entered into, remain within the narrow bounds of ethical acceptability.

Sexual dual relationships are particularly damaging to clients. These relationships often reflect a counselor's lack of boundaries and personal impairment that impacts therapeutic judgment (Corey, Corey, & Callahan, 2003; Doverspike, 1999). To illustrate the harm that can be perpetrated by a counselor who exploits a client for sexual purposes, the fictitious case of Heather is presented.

> Dr. Milton, a licensed mental health counselor in solo private practice, is counseling Heather about her stated desire to recover from the break-up of her relationship with her boyfriend. Having recently experienced a divorce, Dr. Milton feels lonely and sad that his wife left him for a much younger man. During the sessions with Heather, Dr. Milton perceives Heather's style of dressing as provocative and notes that she frequently touches his arm to emphasize a point she is making. He feels flattered by Heather's behaviors toward him and has gradually extended the length of the sessions with her from 50 minutes to 90. He also has begun to schedule her session as the last appointment for the day and is mindful that he is having sexual fantasies about Heather that include thinking of her as a potential mate.
>
> During one session when Heather was distraught and teary-eyed about her former boyfriend's upcoming marriage, she stated, "I feel so unlovable and alone. Am I that unattractive?" Dr. Milton stated, "You are very upset and you are questioning your self-image. Would you like a hug?" This intimacy initiated a sexual affair with Heather that continued for the remainder of her time in counseling.

Ethical Considerations: Sexual Impropriety

There is a clear-cut, serious violation of ethics illustrated by this case, whether the impropriety was intentional or unintended (Moleski & Kiselica, 2005). Sexual intimacy with clients is explicitly prohibited in ethical codes of conduct and is viewed as one of the most serious violations of professional behavior (Corey, Corey, & Callahan, 2003; Doverspike, 1999). Dr. Milton violated client–counselor boundaries by entering into a sexual relationship with Heather and further violated the ethical codes concerning dual relationships. The ACA Code of Ethics (2005, p. 5) specifically states: "Sexual or romantic counselor–client interactions or relationships with current clients, their romantic partners, or their family members are prohibited." This case exemplifies the mandate that responsibility to maintain professional boundaries resides with the counselor. Compounding the violation of ethical practice standards and harming the client is the abuse of power that also is described. Additionally, it is evident that Dr. Milton either did not access clinical supervision to discuss his sexual fantasies and feelings toward Heather or he ignored the advice from his supervisor to avoid the ethical violation.

Ethical Management: Avoidance of Dual Sexual Relationships

Avoidance of serious ethical violations with clients is based on a consistent practice of self-reflection, use of clinical supervision, and attention to risk factors inherent in practice. Considering Dr. Milton's personal issues relative to his recent divorce, he should have avoided working with clients with similar concerns or made sure that he sought supervision throughout his work with Heather. He could have referred Heather to another provider, recognizing that his personal risk and emotional neediness might interfere with his judgment and competence to treat. When viewed from the perspective of failing to recognize his personal problems of loneliness, desire for emotional comfort, and sexual intimacy needs, he violated another ethical directive: "Counselors are alert to the signs of impairment from their own physical, mental, or emotional problems and refrain from offering or providing professional services when such impairment is likely to harm a client or others" (ACA, 2005, p. 9).

From another perspective, psychologists who have violated APA ethical standards of practice are advised explicitly to "refrain from initiating an activity when they know or should know that there is a substantial likelihood that their personal problems will prevent them from performing their work-related activities in a competent manner" (APA, 2002, p. 5). If Heather's counselor had been a psychologist, Dr. Milton's behavior would reflect his personal problem of loneliness that leads to violation of ethical practice guidelines.

Dual relationships are increasingly being recognized as problematic and linked to the frequency and seriousness of complaints filed against counselor professionals (Corey, Corey, & Callahan, 2003). Nonsexual dual relationships or the potential to form such relationships will continue to confront counselors who strive to remain within the bounds of ethical practice guidelines. Sexual dual relationships, on the other hand, represent serious, career-damaging decisions that harm clients, and thus will remain a contemporary issue for the counseling professions.

RISK MANAGEMENT AND ETHICAL ISSUES

Although it may well be a truism that U.S. society is litigious (i.e., its citizens are prone to file lawsuits in association with real or perceived wrongs at times lacking evidence of harm), it is also a truism that counselor professionals are held to a high standard of professional conduct. Regardless of the societal risk for becoming the subject of a lawsuit filed against a counseling practitioner for unsupported claims, the counselor's best protection against such an event is ethical practice that adheres to ethical codes of conduct and standards of practice. In this chapter, ethical issues that are often the topic of discussion by counselors at conferences, during supervision, or in agency or office settings have been reviewed. Because it is the counselor's responsibility to ensure that professional behavior is evident and that standards of care are always followed, much of risk management is within the counselor's control (Doverspike, 1999). Risk management can be defined in proactive terms to summarize themes presented in this chapter linked to professional risk management strategies. The actions outlined are extracted from a number of sources across counseling professions and reflect a coherent set of actions, ways of thinking, and ethical decision-making practices (Corey, Corey, & Callahan, 2003; Cottone, 2001; Doverspike, 1999; Reamer, 2003).

1. Adhere to and use the professional code of ethics as a living document providing guidance for ethical decision making.
2. Seek consultation and supervision with colleagues, supervisors, and experts with experience and knowledge in ethical practices within the counseling professions.
3. Engage in continuing education and professional development activities with an emphasis on inclusion of risk management, recent research related to practice, legal and regulatory information, and current literature in the field.
4. Maintain accurate documentation in client records, of supervisory sessions, and consultation actions taken in relation to risk management decision making.
5. Practice within the scope of one's area(s) of expertise and avoid accepting or continuing to provide counseling to individuals, families, couples, or groups that are outside these parameters.
6. Follow applicable standards of care.
7. Obtain legal consultation or assistance to verify current practice adherence and/or for the purposes of responding to or initiating actions regarding ethical violations.
8. Ensure that professional malpractice policies are maintained and that benefits and limitations are understood.

CONCLUDING COMMENTS

Practicing ethically begins during the educational process in preparation to enter a professional counseling arena. It continues as a foundation element to effective practice and ongoing development as a professional. This process is a professional journey that is comprised of continual learning, education, clinical supervision, and keeping abreast of the professional literature relative to research, counseling interventions, and current ethical and clinical trends within the field. Knowing thyself is paramount for the prevention of client harm.

As counselors, it is up to each professional to ensure that the counseling care provided is ethical and conforms to established standards of practice. Through the exploration of issues highlighted in this chapter, the reader can reflect on the issues raised by the fictitious cases as well as the review of ethical principles cited. The purpose of this chapter was not to serve as a comprehensive overview of all ethical issues, conflicts, or challenges, but rather to provoke debate and discussion. Although there are continuing social, political, and cultural forces that can influence the counselor professional's daily life as he or she provides counseling services, the rewards of ethical practice are immeasurable.

RESOURCES

Counseling profession ethical standards of practice and codes of ethics include the following professional associations:

American Association of Marriage and Family Therapists (AAMFT)
www.aamft.org/index_nm.asp
Direct path: www.aamft.org/resources/LRMPlan/Ethics/ethicscode2001.asp

American Counseling Association (ACA)
www.counseling.org
Direct path: www.counseling.org/Resources/CodeOfEthics/TP/Home/CT2.aspx

American Mental Health Counselors Association (AMHCA)
www.amhca.org/
Direct path: www.amhca.org/code/

American Psychological Association (APA)
http://apa.org.
Direct path: http://www.apa.org/ethics/

International Association of Marriage and Family Counselors (IAMFC)
www.iamfc.com/
Direct path: www.iamfc.com/ethical_codes.html

National Association of Social Workers
www.socialworkers.org/default.asp
Direct path: www.socialworkers.org/pubs/code/code.asp

National Organization for Human Services (NOHS)
www.nohse.com/
Direct path: www.nohse.com/ethics.html

A compendium of ethical codes of interest to the counseling professions is contained in *Codes of Ethics for the Helping Professions*, 2nd ed., Belmont, CA: Brooks/Cole-Thomson Learning, 2004.

DISCUSSION TOPICS/QUESTIONS

1. In a paragraph, describe in your own words the essence of your professional ethical code. With this in mind, imagine that you live in a small rural community where you know a significant number of the citizens through daily living encounters. You are well respected in the community as a mental health professional and have just received a referral from a family practice physician who has recommended that one of his patients, your son's elementary school teacher, initiate counseling with you. How will you manage this referral?

2. With reference to mandatory and aspirational ethics, describe which of these perspectives most appeals to you. Discuss your rationale.

3. Describe a practice situation that would reflect the intersection of mandatory and aspirational ethics. How will you address ethical dilemmas that are not clear-cut while ensuring that client welfare is not compromised?

4. Informed consent is a foundational ethics tenet. What are the differences in obtaining informed consent from minor children, severely mentally ill clients, and clients mandated to treatment through court referral?

5. Provide a detailed description of the steps you will take to resolve ethical dilemmas. Include the resources you will use, other published resources, individuals, and consultants.

6. Define the differences between confidentiality and privileged communication. Discuss one situation during which confidentiality can be ethically breached, and one situation during which privileged communication can ethically be breached.

7. Ms. Hanson is a licensed marriage and family therapist debating the pros and cons of applying to be a managed care mental health care provider as she plans to enter private practice. She has been a practitioner at an inpatient, residential substance abuse treatment program for six years. What are some of the ethical challenges she may encounter as a private practitioner that she may not have encountered while working in a nonprofit agency setting?

8. Sexual improprieties are arguably the most egregious of ethical violations. Compare the ACA and APA codes of ethics with specific reference to this issue. Identify differences and similarities in how each code addresses sexual improprieties by counselor professionals.

9. In preparing for an extended absence from your practice due to the terminal illness of your father, it is necessary to consider how to provide for the well-being of your clients while you are away. Compose a "notice to patients" that will include the essential information prescribed in your professional code of ethics.

10. Ethical practice is supported by the counselor's ongoing self-reflection activities. Describe your self-reflection practice, identifying current areas of strength as well as areas for continuing growth and development.

REFERENCES

American Counseling Association(ACA). (2005). *ACA Code of Ethics*. Retrieved October 16, 2005, from www.counseling.org.

American Psychiatric Association(APA). (2000). *Diagnostic and statistical manual of mental disorders DSM-IV-TR* (Text Revision) (4th ed.). Arlington, VA: Author.

American Psychological Association. (1998). *Resolution of therapeutic responses to sexual orientation.* Washington, DC: Author.

American Psychological Association. (2002). *Ethical principles of psychologists and code of conduct.* Retrieved October 6, 2005, from www.apa.org.

American Psychological Association. (2003). Legal issues in the professional practice of psychology. Committee on professional practice and standards committee on professional practice. *Professional Psychology: Research and Practice, 34*(6), 595–600.

Association for Multicultural Counseling and Development (AMCD). (1991). Retrieved October 16, 2005, from www.counseling.org.

Bersoff, D. N. (1995). *Ethical conflicts in psychology.* Washington, DC: American Psychological Association.

Bricklin, P. (2001). Being ethical: More than obeying the law and avoiding harm. *Journal of Personality Assessment, 77*(2), 195–202.

Chenneville, T. (2000, December). HIV, confidentiality, and duty to protect: A decision-making model. *Professional Psychology, 31*(6), 661–670.

Corey, G., Corey, M. S., & Callahan, P. (2003, 2005). *Issues and ethics in the helping professionals*. Pacific Grove, CA: Brooks/Cole.

Cottone, R. R. (2001). A social constructivism model of ethical decision making in counseling. *Journal of Counseling & Development, 79*(1), 39–45.

Danzinger, R. P., & Welfel-Reynolds, E. (2001). The impact of managed care on mental health counselors: A survey of perceptions, practices, and compliance with ethical standards. *Journal of Mental Health Counseling, 23*(2), 37–150.

deShazer, S. (1985). *Keys to solution in brief therapy*. New York: Norton.

DiMarco, M., & Zoline, S. S. (2004). Duty to warn in the context of HIV/AIDS: Decision making among psychologists, counseling and clinical psychology *Counseling and Clinical Psychology Journal, 1*(2), 68–85.

Dombeck, M. T., & Olsan, T. H. (2002). Ethics in managed care. *Journal of Interprofessional Care, 16*, 221–234.

Doverspike, W. F. (1999). *Ethical risk management: Guidelines for practice*. Sarasota, FL: Professional Resource Press.

Evans, M. P., Valadez, A. A., Burns, S., & Rodriguez, V. (2002). Brief and nontraditional approaches to mental health counseling: Practitioner's attitudes. *Journal of Mental Health Counseling, 24*, 317–329.

Friedman, A. L., & Hughes, R. B. (1994). AIDS: Legal tools helpful for mental health counseling. *Journal of Mental Health Counseling, 16*(3), 291–314.

Gladding, S. T. (2000). *Counseling: A comprehensive profession* (4th ed.). Upper Saddle River, NJ: Merrill.

Glass, L. L. (2003). The gray areas of boundary crossings & violations. *American Journal of Psychotherapy, 57*(4), 429–444.

Glosoff, H. L., Herlihy, B., & Spence, E. B. (2000). Privileged communication in the counselor-client relationship. *Journal of Counseling & Development, 78*(4), 454–462.

Grant, D., & Epp, L. (1998). The gay orientation: Does God mind? *Counseling & Values, 43*(1), 28–33.

Gross, D. R., & Robinson, S. E. (1987). Hear no evil, see no evil, speak no evil? *Journal of Counseling & Development, 87*(7), 340–344.

Herlihy, B., & Corey, G. (1996). *ACA ethical standards casebook* (5th ed.). Alexandria, VA: American Counseling Association.

Hill, M. R. (2001). Family therapists and religious communities: Negotiating dual relationships. *Family Relations, 50*(3), 199–209.

Huprich, K. S., Fuller, M. K., & Schneider, B. R. (2003). Divergent ethical perspectives on the duty-to-warn principle with HIV patients. *Ethics & Behavior, 13*(3), 263–278.

Jennings, L., Sovereign, A., Bottoroff, N., Mussell, M. P., & Vye, C. (2005). Nine ethical values of master therapists. *Journal of Mental Health Counseling, 27,* 32–47.

Jordan, A. E., & Meara, N. M. (1990). Ethics and the professional practice of psychologists: The role of virtues and principles. *Professional Psychology: Research and Practice, 21*, 107–114.

Keffala, J. V., & Stone, L. G. (1999). Role of HIV serostatus: Relationship status of the patient, homophobia, and social desirability of the psychologist on decisions regarding confidentiality. *Psychology and Health, 14*, 567–584.

Kitchener, K. S. (1984). Intuition, critical evaluation and ethical principles: The foundation for ethical decisions in counseling psychology. *Counseling Psychologist, 12*, 13–55.

Kitchener, K. S. (1986). Teaching applied ethics in counselor education: An integration of psychological processes and philosophical analysis. *Journal of Counseling & Development, 64*, 306–310.

Kolbert, J. B., Morgan, B., & Brendel, J. M. (2002). Faculty and student perceptions of dual relationships within counselor education: A qualitative analysis. *Counselor Education and Supervision, 41*(3), 193–206.

Leedy, P. D., & Ormrod, J. E. (2005). *Practical research: Planning and design* (8th ed.). Upper Saddle River, NJ: Pearson.

McNeill, J. J. (1988). *Taking a chance on God: Liberating theology for gays, lesbians, and their lovers, families, and friends*. Boston: Beacon.

Meara, N. M., Schmidt, L. D., & Day, J. D. (1996). Principles and virtues: A foundation for ethical decisions, policies, and character. *The Counseling Psychologist, 24*, 4–77.

Melby, T. (2004). Duty to warn. *Contemporary Sexuality, 38*(1), 1, 4–6.

Moleski, S. M., & Kiselica, M. S. (2005). Dual relationships: A continuum ranging from the destructive to the therapeutic. *Journal of Counseling & Development, 83*, 3–11.

Newman, J. F., & Dunbar, D. M. (2000). Managed care and ethical conflicts. *Managed Care Quarterly, 8*, 20–32.

Nicolosi, J. (1991). *Healing homosexuality: Case studies of reparative therapy*. Northvale, NJ: J. Aronson.

Nigro, T. (2004). Counselors' experiences with problematic dual relationships. *Ethics & Behavior, 14*(1), 51–64.

Reamer, F. G. (2003). Boundary issues in social work: Managing dual relationships. *Social Work, 48*(1), 121–133.

Ruger, T. W. (2004). The United States Supreme Court and health law: The year in review. *The Journal of Law, Medicine & Ethics, 32*(3), 528–531.

Sanchez, M. L., & Turner, M. S. (2003). Practicing psychology in the era of managed care: Implications for practice and training. *American Psychologist, 58*(2), 116–129.

Scaturo, D. J. (2002). Fundamental dilemmas in contemporary psychotherapy: A transtheoretical concept. *American Journal of Psychotherapy, 56*, 115–124.

Sue, D. W., & Sue, D. (2003). *Counseling the culturally diverse* (4th ed.). Hoboken, NJ: Wiley.

Urofsky, R. I., & Engels, D. W. (2003). Issues and insights: Philosophy, moral philosophy and counseling ethics: Not an abstraction. *Counseling and Values, 47*, 118–129.

VandeCreek, L., & Knapp, S. (2001). *Tarasoff and beyond: Legal and clinical considerations of life-endangering patients* (3rd ed.). Sarasota, FL: Professional Resource Press.

CHAPTER SEVEN

COUNSELORS AS ADVOCATES FOR PRACTICE AND THE PROFESSION

PAMELA K. S. PATRICK

Within the counseling professions, advocacy assumes a variety of forms and consists of activities that can infuse daily practice; occur periodically during professional, community, or consumer outreach events; or be conducted through the counselor's participation in professional associations. In the broadest definition of the term, *advocacy* refers to the process of representing a position, need, or solution to a problem that otherwise would not be heard or addressed by decision makers or those in positions to assist consumer populations. Frequently, advocacy is conducted by human services professionals and counselors who are speaking out about the health or well-being needs of consumers.

Advocacy includes education and promotion of understanding of organizational or governmental decision making regarding consumer needs, while defining *consumer* broadly. A consumer may be a client with a chronic mental illness, a population of consumers with specific health conditions (e.g., chronic mental illness, AIDS, cardiac disease, cancer), or a special needs population that cannot engage in advocacy directly (e.g., developmentally disabled persons). From a profession perspective, advocacy efforts seek to represent the needs and objectives of the profession often through concerted efforts sponsored by the professional association. This may include legislative agenda mapping, advocacy representation during legislative sessions (e.g., state or national), publication and dissemination of position papers, provision of educational resources, and professional development opportunities.

In all its varied formats, advocacy is a dynamic and evolving component of the counseling professional's role. This chapter describes the breadth of advocacy as applied to the counselor role. It then presents an advocacy model applicable to implementing strategic initiatives from the perspective of general organizational activities to client-specific methods. Recognized throughout this presentation is a central tenet of contemporary advocacy in counseling: It is a continuously evolving activity, way of thinking, and central component of counselor identity.

SCOPE OF ADVOCACY FOR THE
COUNSELING PROFESSIONS

The history of counselor advocacy reflects a long and rich involvement in social activism that has directly impacted the lives of mental health patients, promoted changes in social and family conditions within communities, and engaged in "both greatly ambitious and more modest advocacy initiatives" (Kiselica & Robinson, 2001, p. 390). An emphasis on the counselor as advocate was highlighted in 1999 as the Presidential Theme for the American Counseling Association (Kiselica & Robinson, 2001; Toporek, 2000). With this recognition, the methods counselors could use to advocate—as well as the underlying assumptions of advocacy within counseling practice, education, and research—were identified and have continued to evolve since that time. Within the counseling professions, advocacy has assumed a dual role, with both concentrations being viewed as essential to achievement of practice and professional goals (Myers, Sweeney, & White, 2002). As social change agents, counselors engage in activities that are linked to changing the conditions of the lives of clients at the individual, family, group, and community levels.

To accomplish this goal, social activists work to change how client problems are framed, understood, and addressed in order to change perceptions with respect to practice attitudes, social policy, and legislative agendas (Mays, 2000; Wallack, Dorfman, Jernigan, & Themba, 1993). Starkly put, "Advocacy is about power. It means influencing those who have power on behalf of those who do not" (Teasdale, 1998, p. 1). Thus, for the counselor advocating on behalf of clients or populations of clients, it is essential to become familiar with the methods used for effective advocacy in the context of seeking redress, funding support for programs or client needs, or changing social and decision-maker perceptions (Safarian, 2002; Toporek, 2000). A similar awareness and competence is essential when advocating on behalf of the counseling profession.

Advocacy efforts on behalf of the counseling profession have successfully ensured that counselor licensure legislation has been enacted on a state-by-state basis, that counselors have achieved parity in compensation for counseling services in many states, and that counselors have influenced consumer and legislative understanding of the counselor's contributions to mental health care (www.counseling.org; www.apa.org). Whereas efforts must continue in each of these areas to ensure that gains made are retained, the role of advocacy action by counselors has had a demonstrable impact on these outcomes.

As illustrated in Figure 7.1, counselors as advocates can incorporate two broad activity constellations supported by a professional value system and ethical standards. Individual counselors can be involved in both forms of advocacy, focus more exclusively on one area, or move between both. Also noteworthy regarding the role of advocate is the interaction effect that evolves between these parallel advocacy channels. For example, the impact of public policy advocacy can directly change the nature of mental health service availability and access. Conversely, community-based advocacy by counseling practitioners can be used to support legislative advocacy. Through education of legislators and the sponsors of legislation, and by serving as mental health profession experts providing information during public hearings in support of proposed legislation, the counselor advocate can directly influence and inform decision making at local, state, or national levels of government. Similarly,

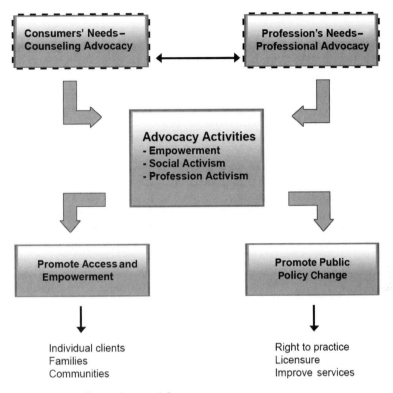

FIGURE 7.1   Counselors as Advocates

the mental health professional can provide perspective by speaking on behalf of consumer groups to further service provision by private foundations or non-profit agencies (e.g., United Way) and funding sources when grant award decisions are being made.

Nature of Advocacy in Counseling

Counseling professionals possess characteristics and qualities that reinforce competence, commitment to the profession, and dedication to achieve goals associated with practice, education, consultation, leadership, and continuing professional growth. These characteristics are incorporated into the practice arena and reflect the ethical values of the individual and profession (Jennings, Sovereign, Bottoroff, Mussell, & Vye, 2005). For the master therapist, the ethical value of beneficence motivates the counselor to "reduce human suffering and to work toward improving the welfare of others" (p. 39). In this context, advocacy work is intermingled with the counseling process as the provider works with individuals, couples, families, or groups. The very characteristics that support effective practice as counselors also support the potential to advocate effectively for others and for the profession (Eriksen, 1997, 1999; Gladding, 2000). Counselors are educated and trained to be sensitive to client needs, to carefully assess presenting problems or needs, to define goals, to implement effective research-based interventions, and to evaluate outcomes (Kiselica & Robinson, 2001; Kurpius & Rozecki, 1992). These same skill sets are directly applicable to the advocacy process.

Using these competencies, advocacy work by counselors on behalf of the counseling professions (e.g., counseling, psychology, and social work) has been responsible for initiating and promoting social change, thereby ensuring that mental health services are made available to consumers (D'Andrea & Daniels, 2000; Goodman & Waters, 2000; Stone, 2003; Weissberg, Kumpfer, & Seligman, 2003). The other form of advocacy that counselors have championed centers on promoting the profession itself, which, over time, results in significant changes in the profession itself (Arredondo & Toporek, 2004; Eriksen, 1997; Lambie & Williamson, 2004). As Myers, Sweeney, and White (2002) have described, these two advocacy channels have at times been viewed as mutually exclusive. The contemporary view, and one that is espoused by professional associations as well as practitioners, is one that recognizes both forms of advocacy as necessary and complementary.

Counseling or Social Activism Advocacy

When used to extend access to consumers of mental health and well-being services, advocacy can consist of empowerment along a continuum that includes teaching, guiding, and supporting clients to seek mental health services; to be assertive with follow through; and to demand action on mental health care needs. Social action forms the other end of the continuum (Toperek, 2000). With social activism, counselor advocates speaking on behalf of clients and their needs can break down barriers that block understanding of differences, thereby promoting a more universalistic view of how, where, and why differences arise (Wallack, Dorfman, Jernigan, & Themba, 1993, p. 11). When viewed from this perspective, problems that counselors seek to address on behalf of their clients "are defined as residing within the social system as opposed to under the skin of the individual." Counselors, therefore, can be intensely involved in advocacy that empowers clients while, at the same time, working to change the social conditions surrounding and supporting the status quo (Kiselica & Robinson, 2001; Lee, 1998; Toperek, 2000).

As outlined by Kiselica and Robinson (2001), advocacy counseling has a long and rich history in seeking to improve the social conditions of mental health clients, families, and communities. Starting in 1905, with Dubois' work to challenge racism, to the 1970s, when counselors increasingly moved into community settings to provide direct services (Kiselica & Robinson, 2001), mental health professionals have pioneered outreach efforts while also focusing attention on promoting change in underlying social conditions and attitudes toward the mentally ill. These efforts have been strengthened through publications that highlight client advocacy that is expanded and inclusive of multiculturalism, gay and lesbian issues, and the impact of age, gender, health, and violence issues on client mental health and well-being (Lewis & Bradley, 2000).

Counselors providing direct mental health or well-being services to individuals, couples, families, groups, or communities encounter the need to advocate on behalf of clients to ensure that care needs can be met, services provided, and education initiated, or to work toward empowerment that leads to achievement of these goals. In this context, the counselor takes action to speak on behalf of a client to a resource (e.g., individual, organization) or decision maker positioned to assist the client. Such intervention can include coaching the client to self-advocate in areas as diverse as cases of sexual harassment (Stone, 2003), to represent family or student needs in a school counseling environment (Field & Baker, 2004; Kurpius & Rozecki, 1992; Musheno & Talbert, 2002), to protect children with reference to suspected child abuse or neglect (Massey-Stokes & Lanning, 2004), to promote understanding of the needs of medically ill patients (Roberts, Kiselica, & Fredrickson, 2002), or to focus on the needs of clients from ethnic or cultural backgrounds that are underserved (Herring, 2000; Arredondo & Vásquez, 2000). Within the advocacy framework, counselors coach clients in empowerment strategies; educate resource sites and organizations regarding the needs of the individual, family, or group; and serve as consultants to further the mental health care agendas of the client.

For many counseling professionals, the role of client advocate is integrated into day-to-day practice activities (Field & Baker, 2004; Leahy, Chan, & Saunders, 2003). Counselors or psychotherapists may telephone a referral source on behalf of a client to obtain information needed for decision making or may coach the client with homework assignments to accomplish this task, providing a report of the outcome at a subsequent session. Would this be termed a form of advocacy? Yes, because it fosters the client's development of self-empowerment or it ensures that a client's needs are met, which are linked to treatment outcomes. The forms that counseling advocacy can take are limited by the ethical standards of practice and the need to ensure that therapeutic boundaries are maintained. Doing for clients what they can do for themselves, or learn to do for themselves, is not viewed as therapeutic, although it may sometimes be an attractive option to save time. Overall, however, the issue for the counselor who assumes an advocacy role with a client is to guide and teach the client to achieve goals without reliance on the counselor.

Another form of counseling advocacy on behalf of clients takes place when the counselor professional becomes a community advocate. This form of advocacy may consist of the counselor's assumption of a leadership role in a community setting, within a nonprofit mental health agency as a board member, or as an initiator of activities that promote mental health care and services to disadvantaged populations. In this capacity, the counselor advocate extends the advocacy for an individual client to a group of clients or population of consumers in need of mental health services. Assuming a leadership role in counteracting the impact of stigma toward those with mental illnesses or psychological disorders also is a critical element of the counselor's contributions to advocacy (Brown & Bradley, 2002). The role of counselor advocate, therefore, is multifaceted and can encompass a range of one-to-one to broader community-based involvements.

Professional Advocacy

In addition to counseling advocacy that focuses on client or consumer needs in a direct manner, another facet of the role is fulfilled by counselors when advocating on behalf of the profession itself: professional advocacy. Table 7.1 summarizes the advocacy activities that are inherent in professional advocacy, illustrating how counselors can engage in advocacy

TABLE 7.1   Professional Advocacy: Opportunities to Promote Counseling Profession Agendas

ADVOCACY ACTIVITY	DESCRIPTION OF ACTIVITY	OUTCOME
Community leadership	Lead, collaborate, network with community-based organizations for legislative agendas; initiate coalition formation; represent mental health professions on coalitions	Represent counseling profession's positions on issues; value added to activity outcomes from mental health perspective
Education (consumer)	Serve as expert to community on mental health issues and topics; engage in media advocacy on behalf of the profession	Accurate dissemination of information to public; representing role of profession to consumer
Education (professional)	Present at local, regional, national professional conferences on advocacy topics; teach counselor education students about advocacy role and purpose	Increase knowledge and understanding of issues facing profession; professional identity as advocate
Legislation promotion	Contact legislative decision makers; FTF legislative advocacy; serve on professional association/ community-based delegation	Inform and influence legislative decision makers
Professional association involvement	Participate in local, regional, state, and/or national professional association advocacy activities seeking "best fit" with personal and professional skill sets; seek education and training for effective advocate competencies	Promote goals of profession and professional association; ensure leadership succession plans
Publishing	Write and seek publication of materials that speak to the role of advocacy; through professional publishing, explain the role of advocate and advocacy opportunities to the counseling professions; inform profession of advocacy research and implications	Increase advocacy interest; update knowledge; refine research agendas
Public policy development	Discern consumer and profession needs; collaborate to write public policy position statements and legislative platforms; disseminate policy information to profession and decision makers	Inform stakeholders; advocacy actions defined; policy reflects contemporary trends and needs
Training	Provide advocacy training at local, regional, national conferences; participate in trainings; seek training opportunities	Increase advocacy competencies and comfort in advocacy role; ensure advocate resources

in diverse ways throughout their careers (e.g., at certain times in a career, one form of advocacy is appealing, whereas at other times, more than one form of advocacy is preferred). Of note regarding the many opportunities available to the counselor advocate is the importance of "best fit" with one's personal characteristics, competencies, and motivation.

Community Leadership

Counseling professionals have the education, training, and experience to serve as mental health care expert resources to their home communities. Through their work in nonprofit agencies, for example, counselors may assume a lead role in advocating for their agency's outreach efforts, coordinate education initiatives designed to teach skills to client populations, or collaborate with other professionals to resolve community problems. In a school setting, the counseling professional may initiate the establishment of advisory boards that advocate for the needs of children in an educational setting (Weist, 2003). While practicing, the counselor conveys the values, actions, and goals of the profession to others. This hands-on form of presenting the counselor role in a community setting is a potent form of advocacy (Eriksen, 1999), albeit an indirect one with reference to overt promotion of the profession.

Another form of indirect advocacy takes place as the counselor engages in outreach efforts on behalf of clients (Kurpius & Rozecki, 1992). In this form of advocacy, the involvement of the counselor in advocating for clients and empowering clients to self-advocate places the counseling professional in the "spotlight" of public opinion, contact with media, and at public forums (March, 1999; Myers & Gill, 2004; Wallack, Dorfman, Jernigan, & Themba, 1993).

Community advocacy requires a willingness on the part of the counselor professional to engage in debate about issues that affect clients or communities, to articulate consumers' and the profession's needs, and to take a visible position within the community. Each of these activities can be experienced as outside the practicing counselor's personal comfort zone. However, when viewed as an element of the professional role, and when activated in accordance with personal comfort levels, mental health professionals add a powerful source of expertise to efforts to ensure that consumer needs are met, can be met, or will be met. In this capacity, the counselor professional "lives the role" that is viewed by the public and those charged with decision making about the level of mental health care services provided.

Education: Consumers

Each counseling profession maintains websites that provide education to consumers about mental health and well-being. On these sites (see counseling: www.counseling.org; psychology: www.apa.org), the public has access to information about these professions and varying amounts of information about mental health and well-being topics. For example, at the American Counseling Association website, the resources pages provide information to consumers on mental health topics and current events that impact health (e.g., crisis intervention, natural and human engineered disaster relief). The American Psychological

Association site includes a consumer-directed "Psychology Topics" section. State counselor professional organizations also provide consumer information on a state-by-state basis.

Public education as an outreach to consumers and providing examples of the value of the counseling professions to consumers represent a tangible form of advocacy, often having an immediate impact of enhancing understanding, providing guidance to access care, or identifying problems having an adverse impact on consumers. Counselors provide educational programming for schools, for mental health agencies, to other counselor professionals, and at community forums. These face-to-face presentations highlight topics that are of direct importance to the attendees. For example, a child abuse prevention coalition might offer educational sessions for parent–teacher organizations, counselors working at domestic violence programs may speak at community awareness events, or counseling professionals may be guests on topical radio programs as the expert providing information about parenting, coping with medical conditions, or adjusting to life-span development challenges. Each of these efforts provides opportunities for the counselor to educate the public in the capacity of the role of mental health professional. Each time these actions are provided, the recipients are exposed to the role of the counselor professional and the value of this role to their well being or potential well-being. Professional advocacy, in this context, provides a direct benefit to the consumer (information, access to resource information) and to the profession (modeling value of counselor role to society).

Education: Professional

Because the overarching goal of advocacy is to improve the mental health care system itself, counselor professional advocates must be prepared to assume an advocate role and acquire the necessary competencies to do so effectively (Eriksen, 1997; Ivey, 1980; Wallack, Dorfman, Jernigan, & Themba, 1993). Through a variety of preparatory channels, counselors learn what advocacy is and how to engage in it, and can receive specialized or advanced training to implement specific aspects of the advocate role. Counselor professionals familiar with the role of advocate and advocacy processes are well positioned to lead the efforts to prepare future advocates as well as provide guidance to currently practicing advocates, for both the profession and as counseling advocates for consumers.

Counselor education programs include advocacy curriculum content according to the Council for Accreditation of Counseling and Related Educational Programs, Standard K.1.g, with reference to professional identity development to ensure that students understand "advocacy processes needed to address institutional and social barriers that impede access, equity, and success to clients" (CACREP, 2001, p. 61). In addition to the requirement to ensure that counselor education students acquire this education and understanding, the American Counseling Association publishes "Advocacy Competencies" (Lewis, Arnold, House, & Toporek, 2005) that provide insights into the role of the advocate, how the role is developed, and how it reflects development of a professional identity. How this aspect of the role is presented to counselor education students varies, with educational content integrated throughout a curriculum (Osborne et al., 1998) or presented in a course dedicated to this purpose (www.capella.edu).

Views of the counseling profession regarding the importance of educating each new generation of counselors about advocacy as an integral element of professional identity are consistent. Within this context, counselors are advised to incorporate learning activities that include interdisciplinary collaborations as a key strategy for advocacy (Bermak, 2000; Myers & Gill, 2004; Myers, Sweeney, & White, 2002), to devise focused and comprehensive measures of student learning outcomes such as portfolios that incorporate the role of advocate (Osbourne et al, 1998), and to ensure that students become familiar with contemporary advocacy methods for both the consumers and counselor professionals (Chi Sigma Iota, 1999).

Although formal advocacy education is a required curriculum element in counselor education programs, research that verifies the application of advocacy knowledge to counseling professional practice is sparse. Field and Baker (2004) report high levels of satisfaction of school counselors who incorporate advocacy of behalf of students into their professional activities. Counseling advocacy is evaluated as "a source of invaluable rewards" (Kiselica & Robinson, 2001) and as advancing the profession itself through efforts to advocate for licensure, to change public policy, and to promote the professional status of the counseling professions (Eriksen, 1997). Continuing professional education is supported by access to materials, information, and resources through professional associations, through regional meetings and conferences, and through listservs to which the counselor subscribes. Rapid communication facilitated by the Internet further increases the counselor's ability to obtain information on issues that directly impact practice as well as events that have affected consumers or the profession. Review of each counselor profession's website is encouraged in order to gain experience in navigating through websites, critically evaluating information contained in websites, and using the information obtained in goal-directed ways.

As the counseling professions continue to capitalize on the capacity for rapid dissemination of information, to provide outreach to counselors and advocacy groups, and to initiate rapid response to emerging issues impacting the professions or consumers, professional advocacy education will be advanced. Taking the step to become an advocate, therefore, is within reach for counselors at all levels of practice.

Legislative Advocacy

The public policy "arm" of professional advocacy focuses on a host of issues that are often linked to specific legislative agendas developed by counselor professional organizations or by advocacy organizations who seek to promote a specific mental health agenda. In psychology, the practice organization has a primary mission "to promote the professional interests of practicing psychologists in all settings through a wide range of advocacy activities, focusing on policy makers, consumers of services, and the healthcare marketplace" (Martin, 2000). For the counseling profession, the American Counseling Association's Public Policy and Legislation webpages include information on annual legislative agendas (www.counseling.org). For example, in 2004, the mission of its Public Policy and Legislative Agenda was to "increase support for professional counselors and their clients in all appropriate Federal and State laws, regulations, and legislation" (ACA, 2005). From this mission statement, specific legislative agenda items were outlined and used as the scaffolding for building an advocacy strategy. This strategy then was used during legislative sessions to advocate for the policies and positions outlined in the strategy.

These two examples illustrate the importance of a clearly constructed advocacy agenda supported by resources—that is, advocacy work that includes a variety of actions that each counselor can implement and resources to engage and guide advocacy efforts. Legislative advocacy may focus on support of legislation that ultimately results in enacting laws that regulate the title and practice of counseling at the state level. Of the 50 states, only Nevada and California lack licensure legislation for the practice of mental health counseling (AMHCA, 2005).

To apprise counseling professionals of advocacy agendas and legislation that can impact practice or access to services, the American Counseling Association publishes *Counseling Today* (www.counseling.org), and the National Board for Certified Counselors (www.nbcc.org) publishes *National Board for Certified Counselors Newsletter*. Each publication contains advocacy guidance as well as timely information relevant to legislative efforts at state and national levels. Calls for support and advocacy for specific pieces of legislation are also disseminated through member listservs during legislative sessions. Other mental health professional organizations publish, either in print format or at websites, advocacy information relative to that association's annual advocacy strategic plan (White, 2002). For psychologists, www.apa.org provides public policy advocacy information. At the state level, counselor associations can provide similar information relative to the legislative session and issues pertinent to the practitioners in that location (FMHCA, 2005).

Advocacy Training

Counselors who engage in professional advocacy often become involved with implementation of the profession's strategic plans or public policy initiatives designed to promote legislation that will impact how counselors practice and whether licensure for mental health professionals will be passed at the state level. The counselors will also serve as spokespersons for specific proposed legislation that holds the potential to increase services to consumers. In this regard, the counselor advocate will benefit from completing training in the use of media advocacy methods, in methods to effectively communicate with legislative delegations or their representatives, and in enhanced competence in crafting communications that are targeted to influence thinking and behavior about specific issues or proposals. Whether the training obtained originates from the counselor's professional association (e.g., see www.counseling.org or www.apa.org) or from community or regionally based advocacy groups, developing advocacy skills strengthens the counselor's ability to influence public policy, to sway decision makers at the legislative level, and to represent the goals of the profession.

Acquiring competence in the use of media (e.g., print, television, radio, Internet) to deliver messages about a cause, issue, or proposal to strengthen the profession increasingly has become an essential tool of the effective advocate (Brawley, 1997; Eriksen, 1997; Kiselica & Robinson, 2001; Myers, Sweeney, & White, 2002; Wallack, Dorman, Jernigan, & Themba, 1993; Wallack, Woodruff, Dorfman, & Diaz, 1999). Counselors may be invited to appear on television or radio programs to speak about the importance of licensure to the profession and to consumers, to host programs that debate issues affecting consumers or practitioners, or to author newspaper articles that provide insights into mental health issues. Each of these activities promotes the image of the counseling profession while also holding promise to promote collaboration with professional groups also interested in advocating for consumers. As summed up by Myers, Sweeney, and White (2002, p. 400), "All counselors have an opportunity, if not a responsibility, to be an advocate for both their clients and themselves." Acquisition of the competencies needed to be an effective advocate supports these goals and can reduce risk for ethical conflicts as well (Lewis & Bradley, 2000).

Professional Association Involvement

Membership and involvement in the counselor's professional association provides diverse opportunities to participate in advocacy. It is through these organizations that major shifts have been initiated in the profession. A contemporary example of this process can be found in the promotion of multicultural and diversity awareness and development of practice guidelines that have emerged within the counseling professions. These activities have been complemented by the integration of multiculturalism in accreditation standards (CACREP, 2001) and in publishing competencies designed to provide guidance to practitioners (Arredondo et al., 1996; Sue, Arredondo, & McDavis, 1992). The professional association therefore serves as the foundation on which change in the profession can take place.

From an advocacy perspective, active involvement in the counselor's professional association can take many forms. Counselors can:

- Participate in regional or state professional association chapter activities (e.g., meetings, special projects, public awareness and education campaigns).
- Assume leadership roles in regional or state associations.
- Start specialized projects within a local or regional area that targets consumer needs (e.g., mental health awareness campaigns sponsored by a local or regional nonprofit agency that is linked to the goals of the professional association's advocacy initiatives).
- Form interest groups linked to a professional association (e.g., women and mental health, adolescent mental health awareness).
- Present at regional, state, or national conferences and conventions sponsored by the professional association.
- Publish in professional association–sponsored publications and magazines.
- Serve on association committees that focus on advocacy initiatives.
- Represent the profession or a cause promoted by the association through media appearances.
- Volunteer to assist at special events.
- Respond to "calls for action" through listservs or action networks.

The possible methods to serve as a professional advocate through involvement in counselor professional associations are continually evolving. As the role of the Internet increases to impact how information can be disseminated, counselors connected to a listserv, e-mail action network, web board, chat room, or real-time debates and seminars, for example, also find expanding opportunities to experience the benefits of the advocacy role.

Publishing

Identifying publication activities as a distinct form of advocacy is critical to the goals of both counseling advocacy and professional advocacy. Counselors who publish professional articles about advocacy further the cause that is espoused, reaching a much larger audience that extends beyond a specific geographic area or a public speaking venue. Within the counseling professions, articles, books, and print matter published by the advocate or profession directly inform the activities of the advocate. Furthermore, publications provide detailed information about the nature of advocacy, importance of advocacy, models of advocacy, and potential impact of advocacy within the counseling professions (Eriksen, 1997; Kiselica & Robinson, 2001; Lee, 1998; Lorion, Iscoe, DeLeon, & VandenBos, 1996; Myers & Gill, 2004; Myers, Sweeney, & White, 2002). Availability of advocacy literature that is expanding and contemporary provides guidance to practitioners, prepares advocates for engagement in advocacy, and serves to highlight areas for improvement.

Publications that address consumer and perceived practice needs raise issues that the counseling professions are charged with addressing. For example, journal articles, books, newsletters, and other print or web-based materials have resulted in a broadened understanding of diversity and multicultural issues within the profession. Within this context, debate about multicultural standards of practice stimulates critical thinking regarding how to implement such guidelines, instigates a review of the value of such standards, or can lead to a reformulation of goals for practice standards (Thomas & Weinrach, 2004; Vontress & Jackson, 2004; Weinrach & Thomas, 2004). Other publications stimulate counselors and other human services professionals to consider core advocacy issues that interface with how professionals confront thorny problems within mental health (Bertelli & Lynn, 2004). Publications also promote consideration of advocacy in practice, furthering a specialization's capacity to advocate for specific populations (e.g., a model of developmental advocacy for school counselors) (Galassi & Akos, 2004).

Another application of advocacy expressed through the professional literature consists of refining the purpose of advocacy as a continuing process and activity that is generative to the profession. These publications include research (Eriksen, 1999; Leahy, Chan, & Saunders, 2003; Myers & Gill, 2004; Tanenbaum, 2005) and manuals to guide advocacy planning and action (Eriksen, 1997; Lewis & Bradley, 2000; Teasdale, 1998; Wallack, Dorfman, Jernigan, & Themba, 1993). Use of the literature both to inform and to drive interest in advocacy is an essential tool for effective advocacy within the counseling professions.

Public Policy Development

Counselor advocates with a keen interest in impacting public policy associated with access to mental health services, licensure legislation, or social issues may find that involvement in constructing position statements is appealing (Abrahamson, Steele, & Abrahamson, 2003; Karlin & Duffy, 2004). Knowledge about consumer needs, previous efforts taken by advocates to address the issues identified, and strong research skills are needed to engage in this form of advocacy. Formulation of policy-focused position statements that will be used by professional associations to advocate must be supported by research that supports the goals of the strategic plan (Biglan, Mrazek, Carnine, & Flay, 2003; Kiselica & Robinson, 2001; Myers, Sweeney, & White, 2002; Wallack, Dorfman, Jernigan, & Themba, 1993).

At a community level, counselor advocates can serve as coalition builders to address local mental health care issues and to promote the mission of the profession. Forming a small core group of counselors and other human services professionals (Eriksen, 1999; Gill, Kewman, & Brannon, 2003) to promote new ways to address complex client issues, such as disabilities, may lead to the development of position statements that are submitted to governmental agencies tasked to address a constituency's needs. Other efforts can result in building long-lasting community-based coalitions that target specific issues such as child abuse prevention, domestic violence, AIDS awareness, and homelessness. Through these ongoing efforts, steady progress can be made to promote prevention and early intervention that directly improve the well-being of constituent populations, while also highlighting the role of the counselor in advocating for legislative change.

The counselor professional as advocate has innumerable opportunities to practice either, or both, forms of advocacy that have been reviewed. At times, the counselor may clearly function as a counseling advocate on behalf of individuals or groups of clients. Working to bring about social change that directly impacts the quality of life of mental health clients is a powerful form of advocacy, bringing both a personal as well as a professional sense of accomplishment and satisfaction. Concurrently, or as the preferred option, counselors can be involved in professional advocacy, working toward improving the profession, thereby also impacting the services that clients ultimately receive. With both core forms of advocacy activity, it is essential that counselor professionals acquire the skills and underlying knowledge that support effective advocacy.

CHARACTERISTICS OF THE EFFECTIVE ADVOCATE

Advocates are optimistic people. They believe it's possible to bring about change for individuals, families, and communities; to influence the decision-making process at the most complex levels of organizations; and to exercise influence at local, state, or national governmental levels in order to promote access to mental health care and well-being services. The literature provides ample evidence of the impact of counseling advocacy on the provision of mental health services to consumers and on behalf of the counseling professions. Counselors are also optimistic when they challenge the profession to change. With an expectation that the dynamics of change are always infused with unknowns, the drive to initiate the change process is pervasive within the counseling professions. Advocacy represents a vehicle for change. As such, the need to ensure that counselors continue to seek out opportunities to advocate for social activism as well as the profession is an imperative. What does it take, then, to be an advocate? What characteristics, qualities, and skill sets are recognized as compatible with effective advocacy? How can the counseling professions build a cadre of advocates that is replenished?

Personal Qualities and Characteristics

The personal qualities and characteristics reviewed here reflect both the literature and the author's extensive experience as an advocate. Although there is minimal research to support the prevalence of these qualities and characteristics with specific reference to how each is applied to advocacy activities, this information is provided as a catalyst to such exploration. Clearly, research that refines understanding of the advocate "profile" would be a valuable contribution when used to recruit, retain, and promote advocay as a counselor role.

Passion and Commitment.   The inner qualities of passion and commitment are foundational to the advocate's role. This commitment is twofold: a clear focus on the topic of advocacy (e.g., preventing child abuse or advocating on behalf of victims of violence) and the capacity to harness these qualities in productive and goal-directed action. Passion for the cause or to speak out on behalf of others is not sufficient for effective advocacy. Combined, however, commitment and passion can be catalytic to the counselor's motivation to acquire the knowledge and expertise for advocacy work.

Drive to Persist.   The advocate's efforts are not always welcomed with open arms. On the contrary, although a cause may be just and the methods used to advocate appropriate, the target of advocacy may be resistant or nonresponsive. For example, when meeting with a legislative delegation to present a nonprofit's legislative platform, the counselor advocate may encounter initial resistance to the proposals that the advocate espouses.

In some cases, the advocate cannot gain access to elected officials to present and discuss a legislative platform. In other contexts, an advocate group can gain access to representatives of the elected official(s), and must persuade this person or group to present the advocate's message in the best light possible to the elected individual. Given that much of what advocates do they do repeatedly on the same topic, it is essential to have an abundance of persistence while moving an advocacy agenda forward. Viewing advocacy from a long-term investment perspective supports persistence.

Toughness and Resilience.   Closely aligned with persistence, the inner quality of toughness or resilience is important for the advocate. Resilience has to do with the capacity to sustain focus amidst contrary feedback, or to bounce back after encountering obstacles. For the counselor advocate, resilience supports a long-range view of the challenges faced with certain advocacy issues and enables the advocate to persist. The adage, "If at first you don't succeed, try, try again" holds true with all forms of advocacy. With a resilient wellspring of resources, the counselor also will find it useful to acknowledge inner resources of toughness. Advocacy, at times, can be heart wrenching. Advocating on behalf of abused and neglected children, for example, places the counselor in contact with the harshest outcomes of harm to a vulnerable population. In some cases, counselors may refer to toughness as "having good boundaries" or "maintaining objectivity." To be sure, these capacities support the toughness and resilience that will be needed when speaking out on behalf of consumers. At the same time, these qualities also come into play when working to enhance consumers' and decision makers' understanding of the contributions of the profession and the needs for consumer protection (i.e., licensure).

Life-Long Learner Attitude.   In the twenty-first century, the language of life-long learning is applied to a process that begins at birth and ends at death. In an information-saturated world, use of information becomes an instrument that supports action, infuses daily living, and provides tools that are used by the advocate. Possession of an "I am always learning" attitude is essential when involved in advocacy and includes an openness to new ideas, strategies, and overcoming personal barriers to success. With reference to "getting the message out," counselor advocates often find it imperative that media channels are used to communicate. These channels are rapid and can support wide dissemination of a key message during a legislative session, for example, that then is linked to a call for action. Comfort in using and accessing media may require that the counselor learn a specific set of skills or extend beyond a current comfort zone of action. Employing a learner attitude facilitates the process with advocacy as well as counseling practice in general. Learning from the process of advocacy strengthens each next action as an advocate.

Self-Confidence.   The inner experience of the self as capable, competent, and committed reflects aspects of the counselor's self-confidence. To speak out on behalf of individuals, groups, or organizations requires self-confidence in a way that is similar to the role of counselors in practice. Effectiveness as a counselor is supported by confidence that the methods used and outcomes achieved reflect the best efforts of the professional. As advocates, this same sense of inner confidence that the actions taken hold the promise of success applies.

Where does the counselor derive this advocacy self-confidence? As part of the entry-level education and training process, self-reflection serves to promote self-awareness of growth and development in the role of counselor. Educators are atuned to the need to elicit this self-reflection quality from the student/learner as the preparation to become a counselor unfolds. As an ongoing process, self-reflection directly links to construction of identity as a practitioner who becomes self-confident and able to practice. When in an advocate role, self-confidence and self-reflection need to form a feedback loop that spurs continued growth and development of the advocate's identity. Reflections about how the advocacy role is fulfilled by each counselor must be reviewed and evaluated as an aspect of this growth process. This information then informs how the counselor views himself or herself as confident, or in need of further training or mentoring, and about how the role is being fulfilled. Further, a self-reflective posture guides the counselor advocate to seek feedback about performance in this role from those impacted by the actions taken as well as peers also engaged in advocacy.

Skill Sets for Effective Advocacy

Personal qualities and characteristics brought to the advocate role are enabled and supported by the development of skill sets, by activating dormant skills, or by applying "tried and true" skills to new situations. A skill is typically considered a competency or action that is taken to successfully produce a specific outcome. Terms such as *tool box*, *set of tools*, and *tool belt* have morphed from a limited application regarding the use of mechanical instruments or devices to get a job done to helping skills used in counseling. These tools become the counselor's skill sets used on behalf of clients or the profession to promote an advocacy agenda.

Communication Competencies.   Counselors are adept at communication. It is the medium through which psychotherapy and counseling are provided, albeit with variation in the amount of verbal exchange between client and helper that is dependent on the theoretical framework of the counselor. When used to promote effective advocacy outcomes, communication competencies shine. It is through targeted, persuasive communication that messages are conveyed, information is transferred, and contact is made with decision makers.

Public Speaking.   The advocate's message is dispersed through public speaking events ranging from presentations at local libraries to national conventions with large numbers in attendance. Framing the message is a critical element of this advocacy activity. Delivery methods are equally vital to the success of the public speaking opportunity. Facility in public speaking can be acquired through training, mentoring, and practice. This form of advocacy is not, however, a one-size-fits-all pursuit. Some counselors are drawn to public speaking, exercising an enjoyable skill set to achieve goals for consumers or the profession. Others find public speaking to be anathema, creating intense anxiety and/or varying levels of discomfort. Recognizing this variance, it is essential that public speaking as an advocacy activity be carefully planned and executed to ensure that counselors who elect to represent a cause or a profession's issue have the skill sets needed for success.

Debate/Position Taking.   Imagine that you have been invited to debate the issue of parity in insurance reimbursement for mental health counselors sponsored by a regional consumer group. This group is keenly aware of the importance of extending access to mental health care in the community and is using the debate forum to explore the issue. As a counselor advocate, your decision to accept this invitation will be dependent on answers to a number of questions: What is the agenda of the sponsor of this event? Who is the intended audience? Who else is being invited as representing an opposing view? Will there be media present? What is the desired outcome? And, most important, Am I comfortable engaging in debates? Because debates may take place face to face, on television, or on radio programs, as the counselor acquires answers for each of these questions, a decision to participate or decline can be made. This form of applying communication skill sets to a debate-advocacy event requires assuming a particular position on an issue and then arguing the various points associated with the issue. Some counselors thrive in such an environment; others easily decline the invitation. Debates can generate considerable interest on topics of timely interest and thus are used strategically to highlight, for example, a professional association's position currently being considered at a state or national legislative level.

Writing.   Clear, thoughtful, and well-crafted writing skills are valuable in advocacy circles. The capacity to communicate an advocacy position serves as the scaffolding of policy statements, strategic plans, and educational materials used in advocacy activities. Counselors with solid writing skills make significant contributions to accomplishment of advocacy goals. Learning how to leverage personal writing competencies, or to acquire them, may involve participation in advocacy trainings that strengthen the application of inherent skills.

Research Skills

Formulating advocacy positions on consumer or the profession's needs relies on research. The personal drive to represent a client's needs, for example, is strengthened when the counseling advocate provides research that supports the need. For issues impacting the counseling professions, data-driven strategies enhance the credibility of the advocacy position and corollary materials (Tanenbaum, 2005). Strategies originally developed in the business world often are used to guide advocacy in the nonprofit sector, recognizing that these methods have a solid backing in research. Thus, counselors often, use "tried and true" methods from other disciplines to lead the development of the human service messages of advocacy.

Time Management and Organizational Skills

It is important to recognize that the counselor advocate often fulfills elements of the role as a volunteer activity. Thus, the application of time management and organizational skills to advocacy activities that are interspersed with a career, a personal life, and family responsibilities is essential. Knowing when to decline requests to volunteer for a special advocacy project is just as important as knowing when to say yes. Retaining balance amidst multiple demands on the counselor's time is mandatory.

Role Balance

Advocate burnout is real. It can result when the complement of advocates is small or dwindling yet strategic plans call for participation from mental health professionals. Counselors who have difficulty declining requests for "one more speaking engagement" or "just one more debate," in the face of obvious need, are at high risk for burnout as advocates. For the counseling professions, therefore, it is imperative that long-range plans be devised that ensure the succession of less experienced advocates to replace those with more experience when a "time-out" is needed or an advocate burns out. In addition, it is essential that counselors understand that although advocacy is part of the professional role, it is typically a voluntary activity. As a result, each counselor must thoughtfully integrate these activities into the overall balance in his or her life.

Coalition- and Partnership-Building Skills

As advocacy continues to contribute to improvements in mental health care, the need to form coalitions and partnerships with the counseling professions and other human services professionals becomes increasingly necessary. Leveraging shared resources and goals of advocacy can significantly extend the impact of outcomes from the consumers' and profession's points of view. Opportunities for coalition building can be fostered at the community level or through professional associations. Central to the success of coalitions are the skill sets previously outlined: communication competencies, research skills, organizational and time management skills, and the constellation of qualities and characteristics unique to counselors. Counselors are adept at working with others, listening, understanding, and devising solutions or achieving resolution. As noted earlier in this chapter, the very skills that make counselors successful as practitioners are the skills that can be instrumental in promoting success in building coalitions, alliances, and partnerships.

CHALLENGES TO ADVOCACY WITHIN THE COUNSELING PROFESSIONS

Advocacy is alive and well in the counseling professions. It serves a vital function to bring forward the agendas that are of keen interest to consumers as well as the profession itself. The effectiveness of counselor advocacy, however, relies on addressing three core challenges: expanding the counselor advocacy corps, providing education and training, and leveraging technology. Investments made now to creatively confront these challenges hold the potential to prepare the counseling professions to meet needs for effective advocacy in a social and professional landscape that is continually required to adjunct and respond to changing demands.

Expanding the Counselor Advocate Population

Although the topic of advocacy is embedded in many counselor education programs, exposure to the application of advocacy while in the student role varies widely from program to program. Variability is desirable when it reflects creative ways to teach the value of advocacy and to provide diverse opportunities to apply what is learned. However, variance that cannot be measured to determine an acceptable baseline of required knowledge and assessment of application skills fosters a view of advocacy that it is "extra" and not an integral element of the practicing counselor's identity. In addition, although a significant percentage of counselor organizations may have mission statements that require involvement in advocacy (Myers & Gill, 2004), an equally significant percentage of such regional, state, and national associations do not. Research that delves into the recruitment and retention of counselor advocates is clearly needed (Myers & Gill, 2004).

When student counselor professionals are completing academic and training requirements, the opportunities to integrate advocacy into the curriculum are innumerable. A concentrated focus on providing learning experiences can result in application of advocacy postgraduation, thus signaling that the number of counselor advocates has been increased (Osbourne et al, 1998). For counselor practitioners, identifying strategies to continue to engage in advocacy becomes more difficult (i.e., competing demands for time in a new career field, needs to ensure that supervision and consultation are used, personal life demands and preferences). These are real-life issues that must be considered when exploring how to expand the counselor advocacy corps now and in the future.

Providing Education and Training

As reviewed in earlier sections of this chapter, education and training form the foundation on which to construct advocacy strategies, to identify activities that are appropriate for each advocacy purpose, and to prepare counselors to implement and evaluate advocacy plans.

How will the counseling professions ensure that advocate education and training promotes a vital renewable resource: counselor advocates who are committed to advocacy? The counseling professional associations provide detailed and updated resource material for this purpose, and counselor education programs include curriculum content in order to meet CACREP accreditation standards. Certified and licensed counselors also are required to complete continuing education programs for renewal of certificates or a license to practice. Therefore, the opportunities to acquire information and knowledge about advocacy abound.

In order to take advantage of resource materials and move the advocate's competence "to the next level," however, it is necessary to ensure that sustained and dynamic advocate training is available. The methods to accomplish this goal could include the following:

- Association-sponsored advocacy trainings as part of continuing education offerings and requirements
- Provision of trainings at conventions, conferences, and seminars that are appealing, dynamic, and enjoyable
- Collaboration with community, regional, or statewide advocate training sessions
- Promotion of advocacy as a practice-building activity with "how-tos" included
- Provision of training opportunities that have immediate impact and outcome

Education about advocacy without the training component risks being "interesting" but not motivational. Together, effective and renewed knowledge about the changing face of advocacy can be connected to updated training opportunities that elicit interest and involvement of each new generation of counselor professionals entering the professions.

Leveraging Technologies

Computer-mediated technologies provide rapid dissemination of information and access to education and training products. Technology can be inspiring in the images and messages that are sent into cyberspace. Expertise in applying effective marketing techniques is increasingly becoming part of the advocate's toolbox. Available applications of technology have much to teach counselors about how to craft messages, present them in appealing and ethical ways, and provide examples that have relevance to accomplishing the mental health professional's goals. Partnering with community-based, grassroots, nonprofit organizations is an excellent strategy to acquire this competence, for these organizations often use the very strategies that the counselor professional could use to further a professional advocacy goal.

Leveraging computer technology to educate about advocacy and to gain experience in applying strategies is increasingly appealing to the innovative educator. Learning modules using interactive simulations, for example, can be designed to provide application experiences for students and be used in continuing education programs as well. Synchronous chat rooms and asynchronous web boards can be used to plan advocacy activities that overcome geographic distance, time zones, and needs to travel for planning meetings. Cybertechnology can be used to research advocacy topics that will further enhance understanding of the barriers and obstacles that must be overcome for advocate success to be realized. The methods that can be devised to take advantage of computer technology to further an advocacy agenda are "virtually" endless. As the technology advances and becomes increasingly more user-friendly, advocates need to be at the forefront of determining how to apply it to advocacy agendas.

Other forms of technology that advocates must continue to become comfortable using include virtual as well as what has now become "traditional" media. Competence to advocate through targeted and effective use of traditional media (television, radio) ensures that the message is disseminated using a different learning portal than the person-to-person mode. A cadre of trained and media-savvy counselor advocates is essential in order to accomplish goals for consumers as well as the profession itself when using media.

SUMMARY COMMENT: ADVOCACY OPENS
A WINDOW TO THE FUTURE

As an issues-oriented chapter, the goal here has been to identify issues, delve into them in some depth, and highlight continuing challenges to the counseling professions relative to the role of counselor advocate. Each issue and challenge requires the concentrated attention of individuals as well as professional associations.

It is fully recognized that much has been accomplished by counselor advocates and that efforts to address the challenges before the professions are in an emergent state. With each new generation of counselor professionals entering the professions, the opportunity to inculcate a deep and abiding belief in the value of advocacy for self, profession, and consumers must be a stated objective of the preparation process. According to Eriksen (1999, P. 33), "Advocacy efforts are critical to the future of the counseling profession." Agreement with this statement may serve to motivate each reader to reflect on a personal advocacy agenda. If this is an outcome from reading this work, one goal has been accomplished. If reading this chapter has instigated a degree of frustration or agitation, another goal has been accomplished. If debate about counselors as advocates has been raised, once again, a successful outcome has been achieved. Given that advocacy is dynamic, each of these responses to considering advocacy from a counselor's perspective is desirable.

DISCUSSION TOPICS/QUESTIONS

1. You have volunteered to assist your state mental health association in developing a public awareness campaign on the topic of adolescent suicide prevention. One of your goals for the campaign is to devise a vignette that will recruit participation in a peer counseling program that will focus on peer-to-peer prevention of suicidal behavior. Write the vignette that you will submit to the planning committee.

2. Involvement in advocacy initiatives can be a reflection of passion for a cause as well as commitment to a professional goal. Describe your rationale for involvement in the public awareness campaign described in item 1.

3. Describe the advocacy training opportunities available to you through your counselor professional association.

4. Identify two computer technology methods of acquiring advocacy skills found on the World Wide Web. How does computer technology support advocacy for your professional association's initiatives?

5. Mrs. Santeras is being seen in outpatient counseling as part of a day treatment program at a community mental health center. During the session today, you noted that she has bruises on her upper arms and is having difficulty concentrating. She has a long-term mental illness and now lives with her daughter, who is raising three adolescent children as a single mother. What are the advocacy implications of your observations of the bruising?

6. After further conversations with Mrs. Santeras, she states, "I have to get out of there. They don't want me anymore." What are the boundaries of the advocate role in this setting? Describe your decision making regarding your next steps in managing Mrs. Santeras's mental health care.

7. You have been asked to write an article for your state counselor professional association with a working title of "Making Advocacy Part of the Counselor's Everyday Life." What are the supports and barriers to your authoring the article?

8. To establish a coalition for child mental health needs in your community, who should be involved in this effort?

9. The legislative session will begin in two months. To advocate for proposed legislation regarding funding for substance abuse treatment, how do the contributions of each of the counselor professionals on the legislative team differ? Focus your analysis on each of these members of the team: counselor education student, consumer of mental health services, private practice counselor, and professional association staff leader for legislative affairs.

10. The regional counselor professional association is facing a leadership gap with the retirement of two key association leaders. You have been identified as a potential co-chair of this organization. What are the factors you will consider before accepting or declining this position?

REFERENCES

Abrahamson, D. J., Steele, A. P., & Abrahamson, L. S. (2003). Practice, policy and parity: The politics of persistence. *Professional Psychology: Research & Practice, 34*, 535–539.

American Counseling Association. (2005). *Public policy & legislation.* Retrieved February 7, 2005, from www.counseling.org/AM/Template.cfm?Section=PUBLIC_POLICY.

American Mental Health Counselors Association (AMHCA). (2005). *Practice resources: State counselor licensure and certification boards.* Retrieved February 1, 2005, from www.amhca.org/practice/.

Arredondo, P., & Toporek, R. (2004). Multicultural counseling competencies = ethical practice. *Journal of Mental Health Counseling, 26*, 44–55.

Arredondo, P., Toporek, R., Brown, S., Jones, J., Locke, D. C., Sanchez, J., et al. (1996). Operationalization of the multicultural counseling competencies. *Journal of Multicultural Counseling and Development, 24*, 42–78.

Arredondo, P., & Vásquez, L. (2000). Empowerment strategies from Latino/Latina perspectives. In J. Lewis & L. J. Bradley (Eds.), *Advocacy in counseling: Counselors, clients, & community* (pp. 45–54). Greensboro, NC: ERIC Clearinghouse on Counseling and Student Services.

Bermak, F. (2000). Transforming the role of the counselor to provide leadership in educational reform through collaboration. *Professional School Counseling, 3*, 323–332.

Bertelli, A., & Lynn, L. E. (2004). Policymaking in the parallelogram of forces: Common agency and human services provision. *Policy Studies Journal, 32*, 167–186.

Biglan, A., Mrazek, P., Carnine, D., & Flay, B. R. (2003). The integration of research and practice in the prevention of youth problem behaviors. *American Psychologist, 58*, 433–440.

Brawley, E. A. (1997). Teaching social work students to use advocacy skills through the mass media, *Journal of Social Work Education, 33*, 445–460.

Brown, K., & Bradley, L. J. (2002). Reducing the stigma of mental illness. *Journal of Mental Health Counseling, 24*(1), 81–87.

Council for Accreditation of Counseling and Related Educational Programs (CACRED). (2001). CACREP accreditation manual. *The CACREP standards*. Alexandria, VA: Council for Accreditation of Counseling and Related Educational Programs.

Chi Sigma Iota. (1999). *Counselor advocacy leadership advocacy report*. Greensboro, NC: Author.

D'Andrea, M., & Daniels, J. (2000). Youth advocacy. In J. Lewis & L. J. Bradley (Eds.), *Advocacy in counseling: Counselors, clients, & community* (pp. 71–78). Greensboro, NC: ERIC Clearinghouse on Counseling and Student Services.

Eriksen, K. (1997). *Making an impact: A handbook on counselor advocacy*. Washington, DC: Taylor & Francis/Accelerated Development.

Eriksen, K. (1999). Counselor advocacy: A qualitative analysis of leaders' perceptions, organizational activities, and advocacy documents. *Journal of Mental Health Counseling, 99*, 17–50.

Field, J. E., & Baker, S. (2004). Defining and examining school counselor advocacy. *Professional School Counseling, 8*, 56–64.

Florida Mental Health Counselors Association (FMHCA). (2005). *Lobbying, legislative updates*. Retrieved February 2, 2005, from www.fmhca.org/lobbying.html.

Galassi, J. P., & Akos, P. (2004). Developmental advocacy: Twenty-first century school counseling. *Journal of Counseling & Development, 82*, 146–157.

Gill, C. J., Kewman, D. G., & Brannon, R. W. (2003). Transforming psychological practice and society: Policies that reflect the new paradigm. *American Psychologist, 58*, 305–312.

Gladding, S. T. (2000). *Counseling: A comprehensive profession* (4th ed.). Upper Saddle River, NJ: Prentice-Hall.

Goodman, J., & Waters, E. (2000). Advocating on behalf of older adults. In J. Lewis & L. J. Bradley (Eds.), *Advocacy in counseling: Counselors, clients, & community* (pp. 79–88). Greensboro, NC: ERIC Clearinghouse on Counseling and Student Services.

Herring, R. (2000). Advocacy for Native American Indian and Alaska native clients and counselees. In J. Lewis & L. J. Bradley (Eds.), *Advocacy in counseling: Counselors, clients, & community* (pp. 37–44). Greensboro, NC: ERIC Clearinghouse on Counseling and Student Services.

Ivey, A. E. (1980). The counselor as psychoeducational consultant: Toward a value-centered advocacy model. *Personnel and Guidance Journal*, 567–568.

Jennings, L., Sovereign, A., Bottorff, N., Mussell, M. P., & Vye, C. (2005). Nine ethical values of master therapists. *Journal of Mental Health Counseling, 27*, 32–47.

Karlin, B. E., & Duffy, M. (2004). Geriatric mental health policy: Impact on service delivery and directions for effecting change. *Professional Psychology: Research & Practice, 35*, 509–519.

Kiselica, M. S., & Robinson, M. (2001). Bringing advocacy counseling to life: The history, issues, and human dramas of social justice work in counseling. *Journal of Counseling & Development, 79*, 387–397.

Kurpius, D. J., & Rozecki, T. (1992). Outreach, advocacy, and consultation: A framework for prevention and intervention. *Elementary School Guidance & Counseling, 26*, 176–190.

Lambie, G. W., & Williamson, L. L. (2004). The challenge to change from guidance counseling to professional school counseling: A historical proposition. *Professional School Counseling, 8*, 124–132.

Leahy, M. J., & Chan, F., & Saunders, J. L. (2003). Job functions and knowledge requirements of certified rehabilitation counselors in the 21st century. *Rehabilitation Counseling Bulletin, 46*, 66–81.

Lee, C. C. (1998). Counselors as agents for social change. In C. C. Lee & G. R. Walz (Eds.), *Social action: A mandate for counselors* (pp. 3–16). Alexandria, VA: American Counseling Association.

Lewis, J., Arnold, M. S., House, R., & Toporek, R. (2005). *Advocacy competencies*. Retrieved February 1, 2005, from www.counseling.org/AM/Template.cfm?Section=RESOURCES.

Lewis, J., & Bradley, L. (Eds.). (2000). *Advocacy in counseling: Counselors, clients, & community*. Greensboro, NC: ERIC Clearinghouse on Counseling and Student Services.

Lorion, R. P., Iscoe, I., DeLeon, P. H., & VandenBos, G. R. (1996). *Psychology and public policy: Balancing public service and professional need*. Washington, DC: American Psychological Association.

March, P. A. (1999). Ethical responses to media depictions of mental illness: An advocacy approach. *Journal of Humanistic Counseling, Education & Development, 38*, 70–80.

Martin, S. (2000, May). Council establishes new organization to enable more advocacy. *APA Monitor on Psychology, 31*. Retrieved February 1, 2005, from www.apa.org/monitor/may00/council.html.

Massey-Stokes, M., & Lanning, B. (2004). The role of CSHPs in preventing child abuse and neglect. *Journal of School Health, 74*, 193–194.

Mays, V. M. (2000). A social justice agenda. *American Psychologist, 55*, 326–327.

Musheno, S., & Talbert, M. (2002). The transformed school counselor in action. *Theory into Practice, 41*, 186–191.

Myers, J. E., & Gill, C. S. (2004). Poor, rural and female: Under-studied, under-counseled, more at-risk. *Journal of Mental Health Counseling, 26*, 225–242.

Myers, J. E., Sweeney, T. J., & White, V. E. (2002). Advocacy for counseling and counselors: A professional imperative. *Journal of Counseling & Development, 80*, 394–402.

Osbourne, J. L., Collison, B. B., House, R. M., Gray, L. A., Firth, J., & Mary, L. (1998). Developing a social advocacy model for counselor education. *Counselor Education and Supervision, 37*, 190–203.

Roberts, S. A., Kiselica, M. S., & Fredrickson, S. A. (2002). Quality of life of persons with medical illnesses: Counseling's holistic contributions. *Journal of Counseling & Development, 80*, 422–432.

Safarian, B. (2002). A primer for advancing psychology in the public sector. *American Psychologist, 57*, 947–955.

Stone, C. B. (2003). Counselors as advocates for gay, lesbian, and bisexual youth: A call for equity and action. *Multicultural Counseling and Development, 31*, 143–155.

Sue, D. W., Arredondo, P., & McDavis, R. J. (1992). Multicultural counseling competencies and standards: A call to the profession. *Journal of Counseling & Development, 70*, 477–483.

Tanenbaum, S. J. (2005). Evidence-based practice as mental health policy: Three controversies and a caveat. *Health Affairs, 24*, 163–173.

Teasdale, K. (1998). *Advocacy in health care*. London: Blackwell Science.

Thomas, K. R., & Weinrach, S. G. (2004). Mental health counseling and the AMCD multicultural counseling competencies: A civil debate. *Journal of Mental Health Counseling, 26*, 41–43.

Toporek, R. L. (2000). Developing a common language and framework for understanding advocacy in counseling. In J. Lewis & L. J. Bradley (Eds.), *Advocacy in counseling: Counselors, clients, & community* (pp. 5–14). Greensboro, NC: ERIC Clearinghouse on Counseling and Student Services.

Vontress, C. E., & Jackson, M. L. (2004). Reactions to the multicultural counseling competencies debate. *Journal of Mental Health Counseling, 26*, 74–80.

Wallack, L., Dorfman, L., Jernigan, D., & Themba, M. (1993). *Media advocacy and public health: Power for prevention*. Thousand Oaks, CA: Sage.

Wallack, L., Woodruff, K., Dorfman, L., & Diaz, I. (1999). *News for a change: An advocate's guide to working with the media*. Thousand Oaks, CA: Sage.

Weinrach, S. G., & Thomas, K. R. (2004). A critical analysis of the multicultural counseling competencies: Implications for the practice of mental health counseling. *Journal of Mental Health Counseling, 26*, 20–35.

Weissberg, R. P., Kumpfer, K. L., & Seligman, M. E. P. (2003). Prevention that works for children and youth. *American Psychologist, 58*, 425–432.

Weist, M. D. (2003). Commentary: Promoting paradigmatic change in child and adolescent mental health and schools. *School Psychology Review, 32*, 336–341.

White, V. E. (2002). Professional advocacy resources for counselors. *ACES Spectrum, 62*, 6.

CHAPTER EIGHT

STRESS-INDUCED CHALLENGES TO THE COUNSELOR ROLE

Burnout, Compassion Fatigue, and Vicarious Traumatization

PAMELA K. S. PATRICK

Counseling professionals are committed to providing psychotherapy, crisis intervention, emergency mental health care, disaster assistance, community-based care, and a diverse and expanding array of services to individuals, families, groups, organizations, and communities. As these services are provided, the counselor expends effort and energy in working with clients to address complex emotional and psychological problems and disorders. The nature of the problems addressed in the counseling process can impact the helper, over time, being linked to a plethora of stress-related experiences with terms such as *compassion fatigue, secondary traumatic stress, vicarious traumatization, vicarious stress*, and *burnout*. In addition, the setting in which care is provided, and the nature of resources available to support the counseling process and the counselor, can increase the risk for onset of these stress-linked phenomena. In some cases, two or more of these responses merge, producing an intense and long-lasting impact on the helper's capacity to provide counseling services. The consequences of long-lasting stress responding in association with the nature of the counselor's work can lead the practitioner to cease practice or leave the profession entirely.

When counselors are not able to ameliorate or avoid the onset of signs and symptoms associated with an experience such as burnout or compassion fatigue, efforts can be initiated to reduce the impact on the individual practitioner. Systemic changes can also be implemented that reduce the impact of stress-related factors in the workplace or organizational context. Understanding the nature of stress-induced responses linked to the counselor role, across settings in which services are provided, is essential for all counselor professionals, whether personally affected, working with others who are at risk, or teaching in counselor education programs preparing future generations of mental health counselor professionals.

Of considerable interest to the counseling professions are contemporary views of how stress-filled experiences inherent in the practice of counseling, and infusing some counseling service contexts, *do not* consistently or inevitably have negative impact on mental health professionals. Resilience, compassion satisfaction, and stamina are three constructs to be investigated in this chapter that suggest alternative mechanisms of adjustment to the stressors encountered by the helping professional. This chapter, therefore, considers the unique as well as shared characteristics of burnout, compassion fatigue, and vicarious traumatization. Methods to prevent onset of each stress-linked phenomenon and strategies to intervene when one or more are present are considered. Woven into this discussion is a keen awareness of the toll that stress takes on the counselor professional and how this toll can lead to significant outcomes for the profession as a whole as well as for the individual counselor and the clients who are served.

A MULTIPLICITY OF TERMS

Various, often overlapping, terms are used to describe the experiences of counselors who are suffering psychologically or emotionally as a direct result of the work they do. Certain formulations of these stress-induced experiences have been labeled as *compassion fatigue, secondary traumatic stress, vicarious traumatization*, and *burnout*. Within the professional literature, there is similarity and shared characteristics within the definitions of some of these terms, although several are used consistently to describe experiences with which counselors readily identify. An attempt is made here to describe the signs and symptoms of stress-induced counselor trauma while recognizing that a disclaimer is required. Each of the human experiences to be reviewed is "soft around the edges"; that is, what impacts one individual may not impact another working in the same setting, with the same client population, or under the same circumstances. The self of the counselor varies, as does each counselor's responses and reactions to stressors. Thus, this discussion takes into account the individualized nature of the persona of the counselor who is at risk and/or resistant or resilient to the impact of burnout, compassion fatigue, or vicarious traumatization. In an effort to focus this review while analyzing the issues associated with each construct, discussion of secondary traumatic stress (STS) and secondary traumatic stress disorder (STSD) is subsumed within the description of vicarious traumatization.

In addition to these three conceptualizations of intense stress-induced responses to counseling work, the phenomenon of countertransference is reviewed. Mentioned in the literature alongside compassion fatigue, vicarious traumatization, and burnout, countertransference is a familiar aspect of counseling practice that students and practitioners must continually remain attuned to when providing counseling services. Within the framework of stress-induced responses that counselors may encounter, however, countertransference takes on a more defined and specific meaning.

STRESS-INDUCED RESPONSES AND
COUNSELOR IMPAIRMENT

The psychological, physical, emotional, and spiritual toll that burnout, compassion fatigue, and vicarious traumatization can have on individuals and their families and friends can be short-lived or long-lasting. In addition to the individualized impact of stress-induced reactions on counselors are the potential adverse consequences of these stress-induced reactions on clients and the work settings in which they provide counseling. For some counselors who suffer from burnout, compassion fatigue, or vicarious traumatization, changes in the quality of counseling practice emerge that pose risk to clients.

> Miranda is an experienced professional counselor in private practice. She has been accepting more referrals of new clients at a greater rate than usual because one of her office partners is on maternity leave. After completing her seventh session of the day, preceded by three days of similarly high rates of seeing clients in individual and couples therapy, she has one more session to conduct before wrapping up case notes and reviewing the next day's schedule. As she begins the last session of the day, she becomes anxious, preoccupied, and fidgety. She is not attending to the client's description of the problems he's having with his teenage son. Miranda excuses herself from the session. While leaving the treatment room, she realizes that she missed following up on a crucial piece of information disclosed by her previous client that could suggest risk for suicide. She also realizes she was just as distracted in that last session as she is in the current one.

Miranda's excessive counseling workload may well be linked to changes in her level of attentiveness, suggesting that significant risk to her clients is emerging and must be addressed. The American Counseling Association (ACA) Code of Ethics (2005, pp. 9–10) identifies impairment of counselor professionals as inextricably linked to competence to practice: "Counselors are alert to the signs of impairment from their own physical, mental, or emotional problems and refrain from offering or providing professional services when such impairment is likely to harm a client or others." Awareness of the potential to harm is essential, as illustrated by Miranda's insight gained in a nonstop work schedule in the midst of a therapy session.

The ACA Taskforce on Counselor Wellness and Impairment links the construct of professional impairment with stress-induced reactions in its definition and description of risk factors associated with counselor impairment:

> Therapeutic impairment occurs when there is a significant negative impact on a counselor's professional functioning which compromises client care or poses the potential for harm to the client. Impairment may be due to:
>
> - Substance abuse or chemical dependency
> - Mental illness
> - Personal crisis (traumatic events or vicarious trauma, burnout, life crisis)
> - Physical illness or debilitation
>
> Impairment in and of itself does not imply unethical behavior. Such behavior may occur as a symptom of impairment, or may occur in counselors who are not impaired. (www.counseling.org/taskforce/tf_definitions.htm)

Not all counselors who suffer from burnout, compassion fatigue, or vicarious traumatization will become impaired according to this definition, but some will meet the criteria and therefore be at risk for violation of ethical standards of practice.

For psychologists, the American Psychological Association Code of Ethics (2002, p. 5) has language similar to that of the ACA Code of Ethics (2005) with reference to the responsibilities of the counseling professional who is experiencing personal problems or conflicts that could be linked to stress-induced responses to the counseling role:

> (a) Psychologists refrain from initiating an activity when they know or should know that there is a substantial likelihood that their personal problems will prevent them from performing their work-related activities in a competent manner.
>
> (b) When psychologists become aware of personal problems that may interfere with their performing work-related duties adequately, they take appropriate measures, such as obtaining professional consultation or assistance, and determine whether they should limit, suspend, or terminate their work-related duties.

Implicit in this language is recognition that any factors that result in the inability of the psychologist to perform his or her counseling responsibilities in an ethical manner may suggest the presence of impairment. In addition, colleagues working with a counselor who is presenting signs and symptoms of impairment, regardless of the sources of causation, are ethically responsible to (1) provide assistance to the colleague that helps him or her recognize the signs and symptoms of impaired professional behavior, (2) provide supervision and consultation to colleagues who are impaired, and (3) intervene in the counseling practice of an impaired colleague to ensure that clients are not at risk or harmed by the counselor's behavior (ACA, 2005).

BURNOUT

In 1974, Herbert Freudenberger brought attention to the phenomenon of burnout in the social and human services professions (Freudenberger, 1974). This early work helped professionals from all helping disciplines begin to recognize and label a set of experiences that had been mysterious, troublesome, yet often thought of as "part of the job." Freudenberger identified the signs and symptoms of burnout (Freudenberger, 1974, 1975; Freudenberger & Richelson, 1980), spurring research and practice application across the human services (Farber, 1983), counseling (Savicki & Cooley, 1982), and health care professions (Patrick, 1981a, 1981b, 1984a, 1984b, 1984c, 1987a, 1987b). As originally conceptualized, burnout included emotional, psychological, physical, social, and spiritual characteristics experienced by helping professionals in varying levels of intensity.

Presentation of Burnout

Burnout consists of a gradual onset of signs and symptoms linked to the work experience. The linkage to the work site—whether private practice, agency, institutional, or community based—is central to the burnout construct. These experiences or reactions to stress can be identified through research using such instruments as the Maslach Burnout Inventory (MBI) or Maslach Burnout Inventory-General Form (Maslach, Jackson, & Leiter, 1996). The MBI represents the most used survey tool to measure the burnout construct within the human services, within organizational contexts, and in international studies of burnout.

Based on results from research using the MBI and MBI-GF, the following three factors have consistently been found to be correlated with the burnout experience (Bakker, Demerouti, & Schaufeli, 2002; Schaufeli & Greenglass, 2001; Schaufeli, Salanova, Gonzalez-Roma, & Bakker, 2002):

> *Emotional exhaustion*: The feeling of being emotionally overextended, drained, and exhausted by the helping experience
>
> *Depersonalization*: The feeling of detachment or distancing from those being cared for; a pulling away from closeness to recipients of care
>
> *Decline in sense of personal accomplishment*: The sense of competence and success achievement in the work being done to care for others

When burnout is present, the counselor professional feels emotionally drained and exhausted, feels detached and distant from clients, and may describe a diminished sense of personal accomplishment or efficacy about the counseling services being provided. As a process (Figley, 1995), or an outcome of a stress-saturated work environment, burnout can include a range of signs and symptoms reported in the literature.

The presentation of burnout is unique to each counselor or human services professional's experience. The manifestations of burnout have included behavioral and interpersonal responses such as shifting in attitudes toward recipients of care, reduced tolerance to frustrations associated with helping, conveying disapproval to clients for noncooperation, interpersonal distancing from clients, and a general change in attitude from positive to negative about the nature of the work experience. Increased use of psychological defense mechanisms such as rationalization, displacement, projection, and denial has also been reported.

Descriptions of declines in self-image, decreases in flexibility and tolerance for frustration, and changes in expression of emotions and experience of moods (Balevre, 2001; Kahill, 1988; Patrick, 1984b, 1987b) are also associated with the experience of burnout. Emotional exhaustion is also similar to the concept of vital exhaustion described by Appels, Falger, and Schouten (1993), in which the affected person feels mentally and physically exhausted, demoralized, and less competent.

The counselor or client experiencing burnout may describe depressive symptomatology specifically with reference to emotional exhaustion (McKnight & Glass, 1995). Burnout can be present without any evidence of depression as well. Although the role of burnout in *onset* of depression has not been confirmed, depressive symptomatology can be distinguished from the three MBI burnout factors (Bakker, Schaufeli, Demerouti, Janssen, & Van Der Hulst, 2000; Iacovides, Foudulakis, Moysidou, & Ierodikonou, 1997)—that is, when there is evidence of burnout (as measured by the MBI) and depression (as measured by the Beck Depression Inventory, Zung scale, or General Health Questionnaire), each "stands alone" as a distinct experience. There is no consistent evidence that burnout causes depression and no evidence that individuals who burn out will become depressed. What does seem to be clear is that stress-filled employment settings are associated with higher rates of burnout and, in some, higher rates of depression (Tennant, 2001). For many who experience burnout, it is the emotional exhaustion that reverberates with psychological distress and associated reactions to the long-term impact that this distress can have on mental health and well-being (Maslach, 2001).

Physical signs and symptoms linked to the experience of burnout have been reported that reflect job stress-related health problems (e.g., headaches, gastrointestinal disturbances, sleep disturbances, activity and energy level changes, and lowered resistance to illness) (Patrick, 1981a; Steptoe, 1991). However, a firm link between burnout, per se, and health problems has not been consistently verified in the literature (Maslach, 2001). Age or years of experience, however, may have some bearing on the onset of burnout. The preponderance of evidence suggests that there is a negative correlation between age and experience and onset of burnout (Brewer & Shapard, 2004). Although the-new-to-the-profession, or younger, practitioner may be more at risk for burnout, as experience is acquired and the counselor ages, this correlation evens out. Thus, experience and/or use of effective coping strategies reduces risk for burnout. This finding has implications for the counseling professions' preparation of counselors in training and those first entering practice (i.e., if a portion of the risk for burnout is associated with age or experience, it is logical to include this characteristic in burnout prevention and skills coping training).

Assessment and Measurement of Burnout

The capacity of the Maslach Burnout Inventory to measure the burnout construct has been found to be stable and valid. Extensive factor analysis has demonstrated its validity for a host of occupational and health settings as well as for international populations (Schutte, Toppinen, Kalimo, & Schaufeli, 2000). With reference to longitudinal research, the instrument (in its general form) has been used to determine that role conflict has a statistically significant relationship to depersonalization (an MBI factor) but not with personal accomplishment (an MBI factor) (Peiro, Gonzalez-Roma, Tordera, & Manas, 2001). Noteworthy in this study, as well as in others, is that the presence of a sense of depersonalization and emotional exhaustion does not positively correlate with sense of accomplishment (Lee & Ashworth, 1996). However, over time, when role ambiguity is present, sense of accomplishment is diminished. This research suggests that the helping professional who experiences burnout can continue to retain a sense of accomplishment in the work that is done, while feelings of burnout evolve and develop. In addition, such findings allude to the possibility that each factor in the MBI is influenced differently depending on workload and role stressors.

Other measures of burnout have focused attention on the multidimensionality of the MBI suggesting that a unidimensional approach may more accurately reflect the emphasis on emotional exhaustion as a core construct that is consistently present for those experiencing burnout. The dimension most often noted as consistently present, intensely experienced, and as having the most negative impact when burnout occurs is emotional exhaustion (Schaufeli & Enzmann, 1998; Van Dierendonck, Schaufeli, & Buunk, 2001). Although this approach to weighting the burnout factors is appealing, there is insufficient research to justify collapsing the factors into one. It is more realistic to view the burnout experience as multifaceted, each factor interacting with another, and taking place within an individual who brings to the experience personal characteristics, history, and social support resources that interface with workplace stressors (Boyle, Grap, Younger, & Thornby, 1991; Piedmont, 1993).

The Stress Profile is a multifaceted instrument used to measure stress in private life, at work, and at leisure. Included in this measure are 18 items that focus on burnout and that have been validated with well-known burnout scales (Pines' Burnout Measure, Hallsten's Burnout Scale, Shirom's Burnout Scale, and the MBI) (Hallman, Thomsson, Burell, Lisspers, & Setterlind, 2003; Setterlind & Larsson, 1995). Using this instrument, researchers have been able to embed responses to burnout items within a profile that includes 15 other main fields of inquiry. The instrument has effectively been used to measure burnout as part of a constellation of stress factors that impact coronary heart health of women in a rehabilitation program (Hallman et al, 2003), law enforcement officers (Grossi, Theorell, Jurisoo, & Setterlind, 1999), and bullying in work settings (Mikkelsen & Einarsen, 2001). Because the instrument has been used extensively in diverse health- and nonhealth-related occupational settings (Brewer & Shapard, 2004), the MBI continues to be the instrument of choice for researchers investigating burnout in the human services professions.

Within the health care professions, the Staff Burnout Scale for Health Professionals (SBS-HP), a variation of the MBI (Boyle et al, 1991; Jones, 1985; Rich & Rich, 1987), has been used with health professions populations (e.g., nurses). Although specifically emphasizing work-related stress responses and presence or absence of burnout, the scale does not align with the MBI three-factor model. Instead, it measures dimensions of burnout descriptive of the experience along behavioral, cognitive, and psychophysiological dimensions (Boyle et al, 1991). This instrument is useful for screening of stress-linked burnout reactions, and when used with the MBI, collectively can produce a more comprehensive description of the burnout phenomenon across a wide variety of professions and occupations.

Burnout and Counselor Professionals

Within the human services, health care, and mental health professions, evidence of the prevalence and intensity of burnout has been linked to mental health work in general (Ross, Altmaier, & Russell, 1988; Walsh & Walsh, 2001), clergy (Golden, Piedmont, Clarroucchi, & Rodgerson, 2004; Grosch & Olsen, 2000), rehabilitation counselors (Layne, Hohenshil, & Singh, 2004), mental health counselors (Kee, Johnson, & Hunt, 2002), psychotherapists (Raquepaw & Miller, 1989), nurses (Burke & Greenglass, 2001; Edwards, Coyle, & Hannigan, 2000; Balevre, 2001), social workers (Lewandowski, 2003), and psychologists (Ackerley, Burnell, Holder, & Kurdek, 1988; Mills & Huebner, 1998). The human services professions that are most involved with providing counseling services to individuals, families, and groups are most at risk for a gradual, insidious onset of burnout as well as a heightened sensitivity to the risk factors inherent within these counseling professions for burnout. It could be hypothesized that the mental health professional would be able to avoid burnout, due to well-honed skills of self-assessment and self-awareness, but far too many counselors succumb to the daily stress that surrounds them. Counselors are not immune to the emotional exhaustion, irritability, frustration, and sense of futility that can gradually surface in high-stress work environments. For this reason, it is essential that counselor professionals in *any* area of practice retain not only an awareness of risk factors but also a willingness to use tried and tested strategies to prevent, avoid, or reduce the impact of work-related stressors.

Burnout Self-Awareness and Self-Assessment

It is evident that counselors, psychologists, social workers, clergy, and other human services providers all have a degree of risk for burnout associated with the nature of the services provided to individuals, couples, families, groups, and community agencies. Since burnout is linked specifically to the stress-induced responses generated by the job, a segment of the intervention strategies described as applicable to burnout treatment or prevention focus on the job setting. Other strategies emphasize personal self-care, vigilance for warning signs of onset or risk, and analysis of personal characteristics that suggest risk for burnout.

In determining how best to resist burnout, or cope with it effectively when it develops, researchers have identified specific variables that interact with the environmental stressors found in the workplace. A central factor that has been found to correlate with burnout, or risk for burnout, is the personality of the professional. Lawrence (1984) suggested that reactions to job stress are a function of three factors: personality factors (e.g., aggressiveness, defensiveness), stressors (e.g., danger, problems with supervisors), and behavioral responses (e.g., coping mechanisms, denial). Personality characteristics have been linked to higher rates of burnout (Downey, Rappoport, & Hemenover, 2002; Layman & Guyden, 1997; Piedmont, 1993) and with the three factors of the BMI (emotional exhaustion, depersonalization, and personal accomplishment) assessment instrument. Other research has identified risk for burnout or the burnout experience to be equally correlated with personality disposition and work experience (Burisch, 2002). Determining "the" causes of burnout is consistently confounded by the internal qualities and characteristics of the counselor professional—the self of the therapist. Why some counselors avoid burnout or reduce its impact and others progress to a burned-out state in the same environment is a persistent question for researchers in this area of human services.

Reports of emotional exhaustion are linked to the nature of the counselor's practice in agency, private office settings, community mental health, health care organizations, and home-based care. Responses to the work of counseling others who are emotionally wounded, psychologically suffering, acutely or chronically mentally or physically ill, affected by substance abuse, or struggling with intense family or relationship issues can be directly impacted by the nature of the environment in which the counseling work is performed. In settings that are characterized by consistent and high levels of social support, for example, the risk for burnout is reduced. The personal characteristics of each counseling professional interface with the workplace burnout risk factors as well. To effectively address burnout in the counseling professions, therefore, it is essential that burnout be viewed as

- Linked to the stressors embedded in the locale in which the work is done
- Developing over time as the counselor practices
- Being influenced by other unique factors brought to the work site by the individual counselor

Burnout has unique characteristics when compared to other stress-induced phenomena (to be discussed). It can also include characteristics of the work experience that are identified as predictive or descriptive of compassion fatigue or vicarious traumatization. This overlap in characteristics of the workplace supports a view of stressor-induced responses to counseling practice as interrelated, complex, and evolving. When viewed from an overarching perspective, the stress experienced by the counseling professional at a work setting may include stressors that lead to burnout and stressors that are specifically related to client populations and subsequently lead to trauma-associated reactions. Counselors who specialize in working with clients who have experienced sudden, unexpected traumatic events or who have histories of traumatic experiences may therefore encounter an accelerated risk for more intense reactions, such as compassion fatigue or vicarious traumatization.

It can be hypothesized, based on the fact that the counselor's exposure to stressors, trauma associated or otherwise, originates at the work site. Although it is essential that the counselor's stress-induced reactions are understood, it is also important to explore the interrelationships of burnout as trauma-linked counselor experiences as well. Thus, the counselor who experiences compassion fatigue may well also be feeling burned out. A counselor who suffers from the effects of vicarious trauma also may feel depleted of emotional and compassion resources as well as the emotional exhaustion described by "burnout."

IMPACT ON COUNSELING PROFESSIONALS OF EXPOSURE TO CLIENT TRAUMA

Counseling environments that serve individuals, families, couples, or communities that have been impacted by traumatic experiences and events include a potential, and some would say, an inevitability that trauma-related reactions within the caregiver will emerge. Within the context of providing mental health care to victims of traumatic events, counselors are exposed to the extraordinary levels of stress responding and post-traumatic stress reactions, within the clients served, that can directly impact the counselor's capacity to function effectively and/or sustain self-care practices and well-being. Such counselor work environments can foster emergence of compassion fatigue and/or vicarious traumatization within counselors.

Terms found in the literature that refer to what appears to be similar experiences of counselor responses to the stresses and strains of providing mental health services, not referred to or linked with burnout, include *compassion fatigue* (Joinson, 1992), *empathy fatigue* (Stebnicki, 2000), *vicarious trauma* (Trippany, Kress, & Wilcoxon, 2004), *traumatic countertransference* (Collins & Long, 2003a), and *secondary traumatic stress* (Stamm, 1999). Noteworthy in a review of the many terms used to describe an array of psychological and emotional consequences of caring is a clustering of the experiences into two categories: compassion fatigue and vicarious traumatization. The framework that guides this discussion is a variant of countertransference known as *traumatic countertransference*.

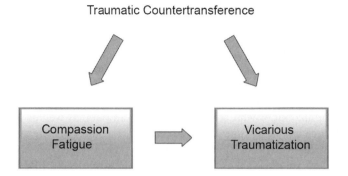

FIGURE 8.1   Trauma Therapy Risk Model

The model that describes the relationship of traumatic countertransference to compassion fatigue and vicarious traumatization is depicted in Figure 8.1.

Traumatic Countertransference

Attempts to conceptualize the impact of exposure to the traumatic experiences of clients have included review of the role of countertransference in the life of the counseling professional. When this aspect of the psychotherapeutic process is applied to the counselor–client relationship in the context of trauma therapy, the term has been described as *traumatic countertransference* (Collins & Long, 2003b; Figley, 1995; Salston & Figley, 2003) or defensive countertransference (Wilson & Lindy, 1994). In this examination of the impact of caring for survivors of trauma across diverse contexts, traumatic countertransference is the foundation on which compassion fatigue and vicarious traumatization rests. Certain elements of the countertransference process seem particularly salient when applied to working with trauma survivors. The therapist's own unresolved conflicts or issues may become manifest in the counseling process when a trauma survivor's experience is similar to that of the counselor. In addition to these responses, or distinct from them, are responses of the therapist to client descriptions of experiences, emotional expressions, and behaviors associated with traumatic events (Salston & Figley, 2003).

When mental health professionals counsel clients who have immediate, recent, or previous trauma experiences, the boundaries between therapist and client can be impacted. The extent of the client's pain and suffering, presence of PTSD, the scale of the traumatic experiences encountered by the client, and/or the nature of the traumatic event that caused a post-traumatic stress response becomes intermingled with the empathic counseling process. As the empathic connection with the client is formed, the counselor moves emotionally and psychologically closer to the client's inner world of trauma. Therapeutic boundaries that enable the counselor to provide caring, yet objective, therapy can become porous or permeable under these conditions (Valent, 1999). As this porosity weakens the therapeutic boundary between therapist and client, risk for development of compassion fatigue and vicarious traumatization emerges.

Research exploring the parameters of countertransference indicates that this dynamic feature of counseling can "take the form of distorted perceptions of clients, inaccurate recall of client material; reactive, defensive mental activity; blocked understanding; uncertainty; and changes in treatment planning" (Rosenberger & Hayes, 2002, p. 269). Within the context of counseling PTSD in women with substance abuse diagnoses, for example, Cramer (2002, p. 199) describes the push and pull of countertransference forces within the therapist–client relationship. The demands of providing counseling to clients who are addicted to drugs or alcohol or who are poly-substance abusers, as well as survivors of trauma, can result in heightened vulnerability to traumatic countertransference that is expressed as vicarious trauma. For therapists working with child sexual abuse survivors, the distortions in empathy and the desires to protect the client can override the boundaries necessary for effectiveness (Harper & Steadman, 2003; Kinzie & Boehnlein, 1993). The blurring of the therapeutic boundary can result in a lessening of client autonomy, high therapist anxiety, or a therapist who takes "control of the therapeutic agenda."

The manner in which traumatic countertransference is manifested in the counseling session reflects more than an anticipated need to address this issue in any therapeutic relationship. In the context of working with traumatized clients, the therapist is exposed in three ways:

1. To the content of the client's experience that may range from child sexual abuse to traumatic mass casualty or disaster situations
2. To personal reactions that directly impact the helping relationship
3. To real-life exposure to disaster events and traumatic events taking place in the therapist's home community

It is analogous to an emotional or cognitive override mechanism that "kicks in" when the counselor is flooded with the enormity of the client's experience, his or her own reactions to these descriptions, or the actual scene of devastation where the counselor is providing emergency services. Therefore, when engaged in counseling victims of trauma, the therapist's own reactions can impede treatment progress while leaving the counselor to cope with the outcomes of traumatic countertransference: compassion fatigue or vicarious traumatization.

Compassion Fatigue

Identified in the early 1990s (Joinson, 1992), *compassion fatigue* refers to the experience of diminished or exhausted compassion (as an inner resource) that helpers can experience as they provide care to others. In certain contexts, compassion fatigue is reported as a reaction to social problems, such as hunger and famine that are unremitting and devastating, that lead to a kind of numbness within helpers and observers of the suffering of others (deWaal, 1995; Schubert, 1988). Within the health care professions, including mental health care, compassion fatigue has been viewed as part of or synonymous with secondary traumatic stress (STS) (Figley, 2002a; Jenkins & Baird, 2002), as a related variable to burnout and countertransference by others (Salston & Figley, 2003), and as a form of caregiver burnout (Figley, 2002b). Others clearly state that "compassion fatigue is NOT 'burnout'" (ACE Network, www.acenetwork.com/index.html), referring to compassion fatigue as "absorbing the trauma through the eyes and ears of your clients." The nuances that separate these terms suggest that the experiences are overlapping, or that use of certain terms is more user-friendly (e.g., *compassion fatigue* vs. *secondary traumatic stress*), or that the nature of these complex phenomena is simply not yet fully defined or agreed on.

Differentiating compassion fatigue from the emotional exhaustion factor identified by Freudenberger (1974) and Maslach, Jackson, and Leiter (1996) results in the description of an experience that is qualitatively more intense and potentially debilitating than what is reported as associated with burnout. Whereas burnout is linked to the stressors within a particular work environment, compassion fatigue is specifically related to the nature of the counseling work with clients (i.e., the very nature of the content or material that is the subject of counseling sessions). The counselor extends empathy, compassion, and caring to the client as the psychotherapeutic process unfolds. When repeatedly faced with the intense, disturbing, and devastating information shared through the client's narratives, the therapist's capacity to sustain compassion and empathy can erode when witnessing the suffering of others. Counselor professionals who listen to the stories of fear, pain, and anguish of others may feel similar fear, pain, and anguish because they care (i.e., are empathic). Clearly, a counselor who is suffering from compassion fatigue can also then experience burnout, especially as the cumulative effect of the workplace stressors combine with the distress originating from the nature of the client experience. Conversely, counselors who are suffering compassion fatigue may be at high risk for burnout (Collins & Long, 2003a).

Characteristic of compassion fatigue is a rapid onset (Figley, 1995). Symptoms of compassion fatigue can be physical (e.g., susceptibility to illness) or psychological (depression, grief, sadness, anxiety, rage, dread, horror) (Valent, 2002). Additional symptoms can include intrusive images, nightmares, and numbing or distancing from clients (Valent, 2002). Counselors listening to and engaging with client who have histories or recent experiences that are traumatic may find, in a seemingly sudden manner, they no longer feel compassion for these clients.

To be effective in helping others in the counselor role, the capacity to be empathetic to the client's emotional distress, while retaining a degree of objectivity and boundaries, is what is often referred to as the *art* of counseling. This ability to care and express empathy (empathic concern) (Figley, 2002a) is at the center of the therapeutic alliance. When the client's suffering—and the impact of that suffering on current functioning, quality of life, contagion to personal life, and psychological symptoms—exhausts the counselor, compassion fatigue has developed.

Measuring Compassion Fatigue.   Since Freudenberger's initial definition of burnout in 1974 to contemporary efforts to refine compassion fatigue, research has been conducted to verify the frequency, pattern, parameters, and intensity of each construct. Research that attempts to measure compassion fatigue has focused on the work of Figley (1995) through use of the Compassion Satisfaction/Fatigue Self-Test for Helpers (Figley, 1999). This 66-item instrument is divided into two sections: Items About You, and Items About Being a Helper and Your Helping Environment. Using a five-point rating scale, respondents use a self-assessment approach to rating the presence of thoughts, feelings, experiences, and impressions about each of these two broad parameters. Included in the scoring guide are directions about the interpretation of the scores obtained. Outcomes are a "Potential for Compassion Satisfaction," "Risk for Burnout," and "Risk for Compassion Fatigue." The Compassion Fatigue Self-Test (CFST) for Psychotherapists includes the same sections, although there is scant published research on its use within the mental health professions (Jenkins & Baird, 2002). A third variation of the original Compassion Fatigue Scale (Figley, 1995) contains 30 items using a 10-point Likert-type rating scale titled the Compassion Fatigue Self-Test-Revised for Care Providers (Gentry, Baranowsky, & Dunning, 2002).

With each instrument, counselors can acquire valuable information about personal levels of compassion fatigue. There is, however, a need for in-depth research that distinguishes among each of these constructs, within different populations of counselor professionals, under varying circumstances in which care is provided, and across geographic locations (Gentry, Baranowsky, & Dunning, 2002).

The most recent CFST instrument's items seem to be designed to bridge the gap in our understanding of how burnout, compassion fatigue, and vicarious traumatization each impacts the mental health professional or other human services caregiver. In addition, research that identifies interactive effects between the three components of the instrument could help clarify the occurrence of each within different human service provider populations.

When considering the limited research based on this self-test, results indicate that compassion fatigue is only one side of a two-sided coin. Although compassion is a foundational characteristic of the effective mental health professional, there is a need to view it also as a source of satisfaction within the counselor role. The flip side of the coin, therefore, is compassion satisfaction—the joy, appreciation, and professional satisfaction that is derived from having guided another along the path toward a degree of healing from the pain, isolation, and fear that can color a life impacted by traumatic events or experiences. For example, using the CSCF instrument, Collins and Long (2003b) suggest that for a sample of health care providers who work with seriously traumatized clients, level of compassion satisfaction appears to be a protective factor with reference to compassion fatigue and burnout. Seeing client improvement was viewed as a positive source of gratification for these professionals. These results support additional programs of research that focus on the role of protective factors that appear to be associated with resilience or hardiness, two topics to be reviewed in this chapter.

Overlapping Constructs.   The literature that defines compassion fatigue is intertwined with that of secondary trauma and secondary traumatic stress (STS) (Figley, 1995, 1999). Literature that focuses on STS often overlaps with that of vicarious traumatization. One distinguishing feature between the indistinct boundaries between these constructs, however, is the methods used to measure each. Compassion fatigue and STS seem to be rather consistently measured using the CFCS self-test, whereas vicarious traumatization has an evolving literature using a more targeted instrumentation, the Secondary Traumatic Stress Scale (STSS) (Bride et al, 2004). In addition, compassion fatigue has a "softer" connotation than secondary traumatic stress and is viewed as a normative response that helpers have to the nature of the helping process (Figley, 1995).

Replenishing the Compassion Reservoir.   The impact of compassion fatigue on helping professionals is extensive, pervasive, and often not identified in a timely manner. Counselors on the front lines of trauma care are at risk for compassion fatigue by virtue of the work performed (i.e., it is "normal" in the context in which the counselor works) (Arvay & Uhlemann, 1996; Figley, 1995; Inbar & Ganor, 2003; Schwam, 1998). Is it possible that it is inevitable that the counselor serving traumatized clients will experience compassion fatigue at one time or another? The very nature of compassion is a giving of an aspect of oneself to another. If the counselor continually practices within a context of high emotional intensity that requires this giving process, can she or he maintain sufficient levels of compassion to continue in the giving role? What are the qualities and characteristics of the individual counselor that reduce this risk, mitigate the severity of compassion fatigue when it does occur, or prevent onset entirely? These are critical issues for the counseling professions.

In the contemporary climate in which natural disaster, terrorist attacks, and other forms of mass casualties may occur, counselors will continue to be providers of emergency mental health, crisis intervention, and continuing counseling services to victims. As a consequence, the need to ensure that counseling professionals are well prepared for the impact of providing help to trauma survivors becomes imperative.

Vicarious Traumatization

Counselors who provide services to clients who suffer from posttraumatic distress disorder (PTSD), or clients who have experienced trauma without being diagnosed with PTSD, can experience vicarious traumatization (McCann & Pearlman, 1990; Pearlman & Saakvitne, 1995). *Vicarious traumatization* (VT) consists of a "transformation of the inner experience of the therapist that comes about as a result of empathic engagement with clients' trauma material" (McCann and Pearlman, 1990, p. 145). It is hypothesized that the counselor engaged in the intense treatment process with victims of trauma become traumatized themselves as they are exposed to listening to the narratives of clients. Counselors providing crisis counseling or supportive mental health services during incidents of mass casualties, natural or human-caused disaster, or in circumstances in which the injuries or deaths are extraordinary in potential impact also can experience vicarious trauma. Terms used interchangeably with VT include *secondary trauma, contagious trauma*, and *victims by proxy* (Winget & Umbenhauer, 1982).

Although there is some disagreement about the strength and consistency of evidence in support of the construct of vicarious traumatization (Sabin-Farrell & Turpin, 2003), the consensus in the literature supports its existence and its potentially debilitating impact on mental health care workers.

Symptoms of Vicarious Traumatization.   The impact of client traumatic narratives, themes, depictions, and responses to treatment that can activate powerful feelings and reactions within clients can mimic PTSD-like symptoms within the therapist. The origin of the traumatic event and its scope of devastation influence the degree of VT within counselors (Batten & Orsillo, 2001; Wee & Myers, 2002). Following the Alfred P. Murrah Federal

Building bombing in Oklahoma City in 1995, research conducted with disaster mental health workers found that the severity of the stress symptoms within this group of providers was higher than other emergency and disaster relief workers (Wee & Myers, 2002). For counselors assisting those impacted by the New York World Trade Center terrorist attack in 2001, reports of shock, emotional exhaustion, overwhelm, and fear were found among counselors who provided counseling assistance yet resided outside the New York area (Batten & Orsillo, 2001). More intensive personal reactions were noted by therapists who lived closer to the disaster area and who then encountered repeated exposure to client reports of trauma impact as counseling sessions progressed (Palm, Smith, & Follette, 2001). With the exposure to the narratives, and the behavioral, emotional, and psychological reactions that clients experience during the course of counseling, the counseling professional may develop mental images of the client's depiction of events. It is suggested that when this occurs, the counselor can experience some of the intensity of the client's experience, including PTSD-like feelings associated with the traumatic event (Schauben & Frazier, 1995; Steed & Downing, 1998).

In addition to direct exposure to the client's traumatic experience and its consequences, the signs and symptoms of vicarious traumatization that resemble those of PTSD (American Psychiatric Association, 2000) include reexperiencing traumatic feelings and reactions, increased arousal, intrusion, impairment, and persistent avoidance (Bride et al, 2004; Kassam-Adams, 1999; Lerias & Byrne, 2003). According to Lerias and Byrne (2003), the reexperience of trauma can include dissociation to the trauma that represents a significant diagnostic criterion for this counselor response to trauma counseling. Persistent avoidance of reexperiencing the feelings associated with the exposure to the client's trauma can include emotional distancing from review of the client's descriptions during the counseling session and redirecting counseling sessions away from trauma content (i.e., the silencing response) (Baranowsky, 2002).

An intensified emotional and cognitive arousal can also occur when the counselor is exposed to a one-time traumatic event or description from a client, through repeated exposure to the event narratives, or through the community-based heightened level of arousal when the disaster occurs in the counselor's home community (Myers & Wee, 1999). The impact on the counselor's personal life can also be similar to that of the client who experiences post-traumatic stress (e.g., anxiety about safety, amplified sense of vulnerability, decreased social interaction, and emotional pulling away from family and friends). Symptoms experienced by the counselor, additionally, can include sleep disturbances, heightened emotional sensitivity, difficulty concentrating, intrusive thoughts, and changes in how the counselor views the world.

Impairment of performance may develop when the counselor is experiencing symptoms of VT. Although decrements in counselor performance may not be severe (Brady, Guy, Poelstra, & Fletcher, 1999; Lerias & Byrne, 2003), the impact on practice capabilities can result in performance changes that hold the potential for negative impact on client well-being (Valent, 1999). Over time, with repeated exposure to the VT experience and gradual intensification of the counselor's reactions to the content described by the client, the effectiveness of the counselor's practice may be reduced. Counselor education and training emphasize the integral nature of self-reflection and the use of personal self-awareness to prevent negative impact on clients of the counselor's personal experiences or reactions, but when VT is present, the counselor's self-reflection "radar" may not identify this impact.

Trauma Exposure Risk Factors

For counselors providing services to victims of trauma associated with natural disaster, terrorism events, or other incidents that result in traumatic impact (i.e., war, torture), the risk of impact with single or ongoing exposure to the client experience can be high. Whether the outcome for the therapist or counselor is labeled secondary traumatic stress disorder or vicarious traumatization, the common thread in these experiences is *exposure to traumatic client experience*. With this exposure, the counselor, through listening and seeing the impact of the traumatic experience on the client, family, group, or community, begins to experience similar feelings. Thus, the depiction of this experience as "secondary" trauma aptly describes how the reaction is acquired and reflects agreement among experts in the field of traumatology (Figley, 1999).

Nature of Trauma Event.   The nature of the traumatic experience that the client has gone through also directly impacts the counseling professionals who are at the site to provide mental health assistance during a disaster, mass casualty, or terrorism attack. Mass casualty situations, for example, due to their size and scope, can overload and overwhelm the psychological capacity of the counselor to remain in the setting for an extended period of time. Intensity and duration of exposure, alone, then, can be a core factor in the development of vicarious traumatization signs and symptoms. The sudden demand to appear on site to provide critical mental health care to victims or disaster relief workers adds a dimension of stress to the counselor's experience.

> Dr. B is a member of the disaster response team in her home community. When the hurricanes of 2005 occurred, she provided mental health care at an evacuation center for children who had been evacuated from New Orleans and transported to Texas following Hurricane Katrina. Following a day of working with the children, who were still disheveled, disoriented, and frightened, she returned home. In her words, "I cried and cried. It was just horrible what these children have gone through. I can't get them out of my mind. It never even entered my mind to prepare emotionally and psychologically for the day. I thought as a counselor I had good boundaries and was fairly impervious to the trauma that would surround me in the evacuation center. It truly did take me by surprise, and that really is the problem with vicarious trauma, isn't it? Particularly for counselors who feel they have the tools to fend it off" (Anonymous, personal communication, October 17, 2005.)

In this illustration, Dr. B spent a day with the child survivors of trauma and was intensely impacted. She had a vicarious experience of trauma impacting her emotional well-being that can be short-lived or long-lasting. For other counseling professionals, time on site and extent of need for crisis counseling can intensify the counselor's exposure to the trauma victim's experience (Chrestman, 1995; Palm, Polusny, & Follette, 2004; Robinson, Clements, & Land, 2003; Wee & Myers, 2002). In these settings, the counselor is subject to direct, often sudden, exposure to the impact of the trauma. He or she has entered the event after the first impact of the trauma-inducing event (i.e., natural or mass casualty disaster), and this stage of disaster aftermath then becomes the counselor's initial exposure to the traumatic event. Thus, the counselor who is expected to provide care to victims of the event can become victimized by the overwhelming nature and scope of the event itself as well as witnessing the harm to victims.

A number of elements have been considered as risk factors to the development of vicarious traumatization. In addition to sudden exposure to emergent disaster events, characteristics of the counselor who provides services to trauma victims have been considered. In isolation, each of these risk factors is reviewed, recognizing that a predictive model must take into account how factors interact, combine, or facilitate one another to describe the counselor's risk for VT.

Previous Personal Trauma Experience.   When considering the degree of vulnerability that counselors have for developing VT, a personal history that includes experience of traumatic events is viewed as increasing risk or as having minimal correlation with risk to develop VT. In reviewing the relationship of personal history of trauma with onset of VT symptoms, it is essential to be mindful of the complexity involved in defining "history of trauma." Few studies have focused on type of personal trauma history as this relates to the counselor's current caseload, to variance in how personal life trauma does or does not interface with the trauma experiences of clients, or how personal trauma experience that is tempered by time, therapy, or personal or spiritual life views interacts with vulnerability to VT.

Social work clinicians who have a personal history of sexual trauma or abuse are more likely to develop symptoms of vicarious traumatization when working with sexual assault victims (Cunningham, 2003). In a study of psychotherapists and symptoms of PTSD, Kassam-Adams (1999) reported an increased risk for development of symptoms in association with counseling trauma victims, with an emphasis on the clinician's personal history of childhood trauma. A prior history of having experienced trauma may be associated with desire to work with trauma survivors in the counselor role. For example, Pearlman and Saakvitne (1995) suggest that counselors with a history of sexual trauma may prefer working with clients who have suffered traumatic life experiences. For these mental health professionals, it is hypothesized that there is a sensitized ability to use the insights gained through personal healing from trauma to guide current counseling interventions.

Viewed from another perspective, Follette, Polusny, and Milbeck (1994) found that mental health professionals experienced less intense VT symptoms when compared to the symptoms experienced by law enforcement officers. Although each professional group experienced significant levels of distress, the symptoms reported by the counseling professionals were overall less intense. This finding is consistent with that of Schauben and Frazier (1995, p. 61), who suggest that "counselors who have been victimized themselves are not more distressed by doing trauma work than are counselors without a victimization history." It is important to note that the therapists in this study also found that the impact of working with trauma survivors does include elements of emotional drain and frustration with some of the organizational barriers to ensuring that clients receive care.

Research suggests that there is a varying relationship between the counselor's personal history of trauma and how he or she may respond to the experience of counseling victims of trauma. Limited research indicates that the type of trauma experienced by the counselor and that the use of counseling to resolve the psychological wounds of being traumatized may mediate the risk for VT (Bell, Kulkarni, & Dalton, 2003).

Experience in the Counselor Role.   Length of time in the counselor role was found to ameliorate the risk for vicarious traumatization (Cunningham, 2003) or, conversely, to be associated with intensification of the VT experience (Pearlman & MacIan, 1995). The type of trauma experienced by the client also is viewed as a factor associated with risk to develop VT symptoms. Counselors working with cancer patients did not experience increased risk for VT, whereas caseloads that included sexual assault survivors did increase the risk to develop VT (Cunningham, 2003). In Nelson-Gardell and Harris's (2003) study of child welfare workers, the age of the provider was found to correlate with onset of VT symptoms more than years of experience in the field (i.e., the younger the practitioner, the higher the incidence of symptoms).

Origin of Trauma Experienced by the Client.   The origin of the trauma experienced by the client also affects the risk for VT. Traumatic experiences that are of human origin (i.e., physical or sexual abuse, acts of terrorism) are associated with more intense reactions within the helping professional (Danieli, 1994; Pearlman & Saakvitne, 1995). The pain and suffering of the victim can be directly linked to the human actions and motivations that led to harming others (e.g., the Holocaust, school shootings). Natural disaster and mass casualty accidents, however, are often viewed as chance occurrences over which victims and survivors have no control. The aftermath must be faced by survivors and those who care for them, yet there is no willful human causation involved. For acts of domestic or international terrorism, the scope of human violence and malevolence intensifies the reactions of both survivors and caregivers. Thus, the counseling professional who is exposed to trauma may have a different reaction to trauma exposure that is influenced by the source of trauma causation.

Assessment and Measurement
of Vicarious Traumatization

Recognition that the VT construct is complex and that it shares some of the features of burnout and compassion fatigue suggests that the assessment and measurement of its presence is also complex. In view of the challenges inherent in devising instruments that can be useful to the practicing clinician and researcher, a number of strategies have been pursued that have resulted in development of measurement tools. These tools have been employed in research emphasizing compassion fatigue as well as VT.

A number of instruments have been developed to measure the presence of vicarious trauma signs and symptoms, and to differentiate VT from burnout, compassion fatigue, and secondary traumatic stress. These tests and scales have been devised to identify the presence

TABLE 8.1   Self-Assessment: Vicarious Trauma and Stress-Induced Correlates

SCALE IDENTIFICATION	FORMAT AND FOCUS
Compassion Satisfaction/Fatigue Self-Test for Helpers	66 items; Likert scale; three risk domains identified (compassion satisfaction; burnout; compassion fatigue) (Figley, 1999, pp. 18–19)
Impact of Event Scale (IES-R)	22 trauma-related items; Likert scale; three subscales (avoidance, intrusion, hyperarousal) (Weiss & Marmar, 1997)
Secondary Traumatic Stress Scale	17-item self-report measure; Likert scale; three factors identified (intrusion, arousal, and avoidance) (Bride et al, 2004)
Trauma and Attachment Belief Scale (TABS)	84 items across five areas of psychological need sensitive to trauma (intimacy, esteem, control, safety, trust); Likert scale; 10 subscales (Pearlman, 2003) Note: Replaces the Traumatic Stress Belief Scale (Revision L) (Pearlman, 2003)
Trauma Symptom Inventory (TSI)	100-item self-report format; measures 10 clinical scales, with five closely aligned with *DSM-IV-TR* for post-traumatic stress disorder symptomatology (Briere, 1995)

and outcome of trauma-induced experience with clients as well as with counseling professionals. Table 8.1 provides a summary of these tests, scales, and questionnaires, along with descriptive information, that may be of assistance to counseling professionals who wish to further explore this aspect of vicarious traumatization.

The roles that mental health professionals fill have expanded dramatically over the past decade and at a startling pace since 9/11. The involvement of counseling professionals in helping trauma survivors in diverse, intense, highly stressful, and demanding contexts is rapidly evolving. Thus, the potential for adverse impact on the helper must be carefully evaluated to ensure that proactive strategies can be devised to mediate negative effects of providing trauma mental health care. It is clear that the effort to develop assessment and measurement methods to identify symptoms of VT in mental health professional populations or clients is a dynamic area of investigation. The impact of VT on the professional can be severe and lasting, and therefore continued effort to refine instrumentation, ensure that it is used within the mental health professions, and introduced in counselor education programs is essential.

Sensitivity to the impact on counseling professionals of trauma exposure, acquired through the counseling process with individuals, groups, communities and at disaster events, includes an emphasis on the need for prevention and intervention planning. The very nature of the counseling work that is performed with trauma victims or during traumatic events suggests that the experience of vicarious trauma symptoms is a normal reaction to the extraordinary narratives, symptoms, and suffering of those receiving care (O'Halloran & Linton,

2000; Palm, Polusny, & Follette, 2004; Schauben & Frazier, 1995). As the most desirable option, use of prevention, early intervention, and coping strategies hold the promise of ameliorating the potentially severe consequences of absorbing the suffering of clients while providing mental health care (Schauben & Frazier, 1995; Stamm, Varna, Pearlman, & Giller, 2002). When counseling victims of trauma, the professional is called on to use empathic skills and caring, recognizing that the very actions and capacities to connect emotionally with clients can lead to vicarious traumatization (Nelson-Gardell & Harris, 2003). While respecting that VT, as well as burnout and compassion fatigue, can have devastating consequences, these stress-induced experiences also can be viewed from a different perspective.

RESILIENCE: IMPACT ON BURNOUT, COMPASSION FATIGUE, AND VICARIOUS TRAUMATIZATION

Review of counselor stress responding, in all of its work-related manifestations, reveals a provocative finding that gives one pause to consider the flip side of the coin. Why do some counselors *not* succumb to the effects of work-related stress and instead resist burnout, compassion fatigue's negative influence, or the loss of perspective that can occur with vicarious traumatization? Some counselors working with trauma victims can avoid the effects of compassion fatigue or vicarious trauma or appear to be able to manage such symptoms well. These counseling professionals seem to resist the negative impact of stressors encountered while providing psychotherapeutic services to clients. Instead of assuming that burnout, compassion fatigue, and vicarious traumatization are inevitable in the life of the practicing mental health professional, it may well be that there are qualities or characteristics of the counselor, settings in which counseling takes place, or an interactive effect of these two variables, that mitigate risk for development of these phenomena.

Resilience is defined as the individual's capacity to bounce back or recover after being exposed or reacting to stressors. More specifically, this complex construct is described as the capacity for "positive adaptation within the context of significant adversity" (Luther, Cicchetti, & Becker, 2000, p. 543). Over time, the resilience process "does not function uniformly and automatically, but waxes and wanes in response to contextual variables," (Tusaie & Dyer, 2004, p. 4). Arrington and Wilson (2000) discuss these contextual variables as including culture and diversity background of the individual linked to resistance or vulnerability to developmental risk factors.

The aftermath of a resilient response is return to a steady state of functioning, or homeostasis, with an awareness of the importance of the events experienced. In a highly stressful counseling context, the counselor who is resilient is not immune from the intensity of stressors, but rather implements coping strategies that reduce the negative impact of the events or experiences. It is hypothesized that there may be constitutional factors within caregivers that appear to be associated with less reactivity to stressors (Bonanno, 2004).

Counselors with built-in psychological protective qualities may experience the exposure to sources of burnout or vicarious trauma, for example, in ways that are qualitatively different when compared to the response styles of helpers who do not have similar qualities or who work in settings that lack social supports (Bonanno, 2004; Collins & Long, 2003b). The protective factors for resilient counselors include personal hardiness, defined as the manner in which the professional approaches the helping process (Stamm, 1999). Included in hardiness are qualities of perceived control and commitment, and viewing the work performed as challenging and holding potential for personal growth (Bonanno, 2004; King, King, Fairbank, Keane, & Adams, 1998). Within this context, the "hardy" counselor who encounters highly stressful work with clients has a lower risk for compassion fatigue or vicarious traumatization, or is resilient when impacted by these counseling experiences. This effect, however, requires research attention to determine the impact of personal qualities of hardiness across treatment settings and in relation to supports that may be in place known to enhance coping capacities.

Satisfaction with the work performed may be protective to counselors providing mental health services in highly stressful work contexts. When considering compassion fatigue, for example, therapists exposed to the traumatic experiences of clients do not always become emotionally depleted (Kessler, Sonnega, Bromet, Hughes, & Nelson, 1995; Stamm, 1999). Counselors working with survivors of trauma, including the emergency work performed during mass casualty events, report high levels of personal satisfaction in being able to positively impact the lives of clients (Bell, 2003; Collins & Long, 2003b). This sense of personal satisfaction represents a form of psychological protection or buffer against onset of compassion fatigue and vicarious trauma. The capacity to avoid the pitfalls of compassion fatigue, secondary traumatic stress responding, or burnout has also been referred to as *stamina* (Osborn, 2004, p. 319) and includes the capacity to "keep one's outlook positive and one's work fresh, relevant, and rewarding." The approach described by Osborn emphasizes ways of thinking and behaving that counselors can adopt to sustain well-being in the face of multiple sources of stress found in contemporary practice.

Given that personal characteristics and qualities do exist that provide a steady internal guidance system useful while working in highly stressful environments, counselors can take measures to capitalize on this knowledge. Skovholt (2001, p. 147) describes the "danger of one-way caring" being balanced with "constant investment in a personal renewal process." When counselors place the caring for others higher than self-preservation, for example, the risk for burnout escalates. Focusing on self-care guides ongoing renewal that supports sensitive and compassionate counseling. Thus, there are actions counselors can take to avoid or reduce the impact of burnout, compassion fatigue, or vicarious trauma, and ways to maintain a healthy internal guidance system that fosters resilience, a sense of hardiness, and life balance.

A COUNSELOR SELF-CARE MODEL

The nature of counseling practice, regardless of the setting in which it takes place, includes stressors. Although similar to any work setting that can include stress-filled elements, the stressors inherent in the workplace for counselors reflect the pain, suffering, and trials faced by clients who seek mental health and wellness assistance. To maintain counselor sensitivity, compassion, astute judgment, and one's own inner balance, it is essential that a self-care standard of practice be maintained. In addition, with attention to self-care as an

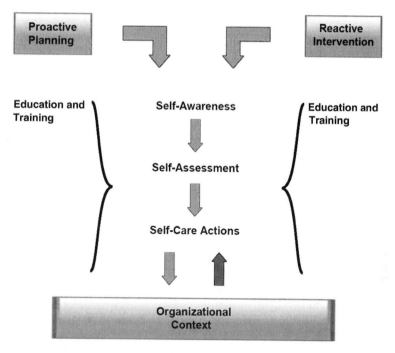

FIGURE 8.2   Counselor Self-Care Model

integrated element in the counselor's life balance philosophy, issues of counselor impairment can be addressed in a proactive manner. Within the standard of practice presented here are two key elements: self-awareness and self-assessment. With the personal information and insight gained from self-awareness and self-assessment, self-care actions can be planned and implemented.

In dissecting this counselor self-care model (see Figure 8.2), each element is considered, while recognizing that how each counselor approaches the issues associated with burnout, countertransference, compassion fatigue, and vicarious traumatization will vary. Resources to address each phenomenon also vary within the organizational, private practice, or community context in which counseling is provided. Taking this variation into account, let's review how the proactive planning and reactive intervention might be evident to counseling practitioners.

Proactive planning and reactive intervention are represented along a time continuum spanning the initial education and training experiences counselors complete prior to entering practice. Because education and training are continuing elements of the counselor's professional role, further education and training are often needed to address reactions to the experience of being in practice. During the counselor education and training experience, programs include curricular elements that specifically focus on professional identity development and self-care/wellness planning. Within this context, the counselor acquires self-awareness skills linked to continuing self-assessment, both competencies essential for effective counseling practice. Using these skills and insights, the counselor devises proactive self-care plans.

When symptoms of burnout, compassion fatigue, or vicarious traumatization are evident, the counselor is tasked with devising reactive interventions using these same competencies—self-awareness, self-assessment, self-care actions. Devising or revising self-care plans once symptoms have evolved are supported by education, training, and supervision. The model is connected to the organizational or systemic context in which the counselor practices, providing an interaction of elements that can support the counselor or detract from effective stressor coping.

Education and Training

While providing services in diverse settings, a counselor's practice typically will include clients who have experienced highly stressful life events or traumatic experiences (Kitzrow, 2002; Marotta, 2000). From schools to mental health agencies to private practice, individuals, couples, families, and groups seek counseling assistance to cope with the aftermath of traumatic experiences brought on by natural or human-engineered disaster, life-threatening accidents, loss and grief, and the consequences of injury or illness. Recognizing that counselors can anticipate encountering clients with such presenting problems, educational preparation that includes skills development specifically directed toward counseling those impacted by trauma is essential.

Initial Education and Training.   Students who have coursework that includes information about burnout, compassion fatigue, and vicarious trauma have opportunities to explore how stress impacts both personal and professional life. Some counselor education programs report offering some coursework that includes information and treatment guidance applicable to working with survivors of sexual abuse (Kitzrow, 2002). The offerings, however, range from an elective or required course, to additional training incorporated into other courses. Experts in traumatology strongly advocate for the inclusion of educational preparation in the treatment of survivors of trauma as a mechanism to strengthen practice competencies (Follette, Polusny, & Milbeck, 1994; Pearlman & Saakvitne, 1995).

Education that targets the unique skills needed to provide ethical treatment to trauma survivors, while retaining professional boundaries, is essential prior to entering practice and then periodically throughout the counselor's career. Just as there are guidelines for practice associated with treating clients with PTSD (Marotta, 2000), there also is a need to have standards of practice focused on counselor needs to address burnout, compassion fatigue, and vicarious traumatization risk factors. Such standards could be formalized in terms of practice competencies, or could consist of practices that each counselor implements as part of self-care planning.

In recognition of the increased risk for negative impact of exposure to client traumatic experience for the novice counseling practitioner (Cunningham, 2003; O'Halloran & Linton, 2000), anticipatory preparation through formal education channels is essential. Suggestions include taking a course on stress management offered through a college or university, completing continuing professional development short courses, or participating in professional conference presentations on coping with burnout, compassion fatigue, or vicarious traumatization. As education and training take place, it is essential that participants retain awareness that exposure to traumatic material can result in unfavorable reactions. For example, in a review of child abuse and neglect training, Jones (2002) noted the adverse impact that exposure to graphic visual images of abuse had on trainees. Considering this potential impact when planning presentations ensures that sufficient support resources and time to review adverse reactions is incorporated into education and training offerings. In addition, the novice counselor must be advised to ensure that adequate supervision and consultation resources are available prior to working with survivors of trauma and to remain cognizant of the requirements to only practice within areas of competence.

Specialized Professional Training.   Counselors in practice benefit from continuation of therapeutic and self-care skills training as this professional development activity relates to provision of services to victims of trauma and high-stress work environments (Bell, Kulkarni, & Dalton, 2003; Pearlman & Saakvitne, 1995; Schauben & Frazier, 1995). Self-study goals can be accomplished through readings, attendance at professional conferences, and intensive training programs accessed through Internet resources (e.g., the International Society for Traumatic Stress Studies, www.istss.org/students/training.cfm). Although not linked to licensure requirements as a mental health professional, certification in specialized subspecialty fields of practice (Remley, 1995), such as trauma counseling, is a viable option to strengthen competencies as a trauma counselor who is mindful of the need to also attend to self-care while serving others.

In addition to the methods found in a structured intervention, training, and education program, related strategies as well as more intensive interventions may be required when vicarious traumatization has developed. The risk to clients with reference to ethical practice and ability to focus on client therapeutic needs when experiencing VT are significant (Collins & Long, 2003b; Munroe, 1999); thus, attention to personal risk factors is imperative. Practitioners who fail to attend to intensity and rapid onset of symptoms of personal distress, may find themselves engaged in self-protective behaviors that harm client well-being. Issues that should be addressed during counseling sessions with traumatized clients can be avoided, or, if expressed, the counselor can over- or under-respond to the therapeutic need. These potential problems can be reduced or directly addressed by a thoughtful, planned, and balanced approach to VT prevention and intervention.

The goals of education and training programs consist of both preparation (proactive) strategies in anticipation of working in high-stress counseling environments and responsive strategies (reactive) to address the consequences of high-stress counseling work. Within formal academic settings, or within the workplace or environment in which mental health services are provided, these methods focus specifically on the rigors of fulfilling the role of counselor.

Programmatic and Organizational Support

Professional training that addresses the unique treatment issues of trauma survivors, as well as the impact of providing counseling to those who have been traumatized, is a central concern from the organizational perspective. Work settings with missions to provide mental health services to trauma survivors—whether children, adults, families, groups, or communities—can provide fundamental support to staff who directly interface with the client population.

Specialized training and institutional support resources can reduce or mediate the negative impact of exposure to client traumatic experiences (Bell, Kulkarni, & Dalton, 2003; Chrestman, 1999; Nelson-Gardell & Harris, 2003). Included in organizational support resources are training opportunities targeting the types of trauma found in the client population (Myers & Wee, 1999; Schauben & Frazier, 1995) and developing social support resources among peers (Boyle, Grap, Younger, & Thornby, 1991; Etherington, 2000; Inbar & Ganor, 2003).

The organization in which the counselor works can provide support to counselors in high-stress environments through workload management strategies. Counselors should practice only within their particular areas of expertise rather than be asked or required to extend beyond those parameters (Osborn, 2004). Total number of clients requiring acute trauma services should be monitored to ensure that counselors are not overloaded with trauma cases (Etherington, 2000; Trippany, Wilcoxon, & Satcher, 2003; Trippany, Kress, & Wilcoxon, 2004) and thereby destined for burnout or compassion fatigue. Additionally, caseload volume is related to degree of exposure to the traumatic material presented by clients. From this perspective, monitoring workload takes on an added urgency in terms of the overall number of traumatized clients seen and the nature of the trauma exposure for counselors (Figley, 2002b). Balancing the counselor's caseload, therefore, is a shared responsibility to be reviewed by the counselor, the organization, and the supervisor or practice consultant.

Rudolph and Stamm (1999) advocate for organizational policy and administrative leadership that would highlight specific areas of organizational support for the mental health professional at risk for vicarious trauma. These strategies hold promise to reduce risk for VT and to address it effectively when developed:

1. When a high percentage of clients are trauma survivors in a particular setting (e.g., rape crisis center), the counselor's caseload must be reduced.
2. Increase the time dedicated to discussing cases, addressing helper reactions to providing care, and debriefing.
3. Ensure that counselors use personal leave time to replenish inner resources and well-being.
4. Consider accessing mental health care resources not associated with the workplace as sources of support, guidance, and treatment.
5. Ensure that supervision resources are available and used.

These and other strategies originate from within the organization and can facilitate effective coping with the high-stress demands of working with trauma survivors while ensuring that adequate support services are in place for providers.

Other organizational efforts to provide support to counselor professionals include content and experiential learning opportunities across a broad array of stress-induced responses while attending to the more intensive elements common to the trauma exposure aspect of the individual counselor's experience. An excellent example of an intervention program designed specifically for the effects of compassion fatigue is the Accelerated Recovery Program (ARP) model (Gentry, Baranowsky, & Dunning, 2002) that uses a standardized five-session format to cover seven distinct treatment components. The program addresses prevention as well as intervention by addressing the therapeutic alliance, quantitative and qualitative assessment, anxiety management, narrative, exposure/resolution of secondary traumatic stress, cognitive restructuring, and an aftercare plan (Gentry, Baranowsky, & Dunning, 2000, pp. 129–130). The comprehensive nature of the treatment program suggests an optimal approach to providing both education and practical self-care information to the counselor professional. Empirical research is essential to verify the efficacy of this approach across diverse populations of mental health care providers who are at risk for compassion fatigue. The issues associated with counselor well-being and effectiveness when practicing in high-stress settings are also addressed by the counselor's individual actions (internal origin) associated with self-awareness and self-care.

Self-Awareness

During the counselor education and training experience, an emphasis is placed on acquiring self-awareness as a fundamental competency directly connected to the role of counselor professional. Self-awareness includes the capacity to self-monitor reactions and responses to the client, the environment in which counseling is taking place, and personal reactions and feelings while maintaining a degree of objectivity. Each of these variables can influence the therapeutic process and the capacity of the counselor to effectively practice.

When burnout, compassion fatigue, or vicarious traumatization begin to develop, each can directly impact the counselor's ability to retain an ongoing process of self-awareness and self-reflection due to the presence of symptoms associated with any one of these three phenomena. Some symptoms are so intense in impact that self-assessment practices that would ordinarily take place are neglected. For example, in times of mass casualty disasters during which counselors are providing care to survivors, the ability of the helping professional to step back, self-assess, and take appropriate action based on that self-reflection can be significantly reduced. The nature of the experience blocks effective self-assessment. In such instances, assessment must come from other sources such as supervisors, peers, family, or friends that alert the counseling professional to the presence of symptoms.

Self-awareness consists of elegantly simple as well as singularly complex elements. To be self-aware, the counselor sustains a continuous innerdialogue that asks questions about the self while in the role of therapist to others, such as.

- How am I feeling as I provide counseling services today (lately, these days)?
- What am I feeling and thinking during the day that reflects my inner experience, sense of well-being, and level of stress responding?
- Am I in touch with my physical self while attending to my own emotional, psychological, social, and spiritual well-being?
- Am I feeling disconnected from my inner experience of being in the therapist role, or am I ensuring that I attend to this core issue about myself daily (weekly, every now and then)?

By asking these questions, self-awareness is activated and connected to self-assessment. Along a continuum of professional self-care planning, therefore, self-awareness leads to the process of self-assessment that targets in a more concerted manner personal risk factors for burnout, compassion fatigue, and vicarious trauma, and that identifies evidence of harmful stress-responding patterns.

Self-Assessment

Awareness of the disease or "ill health" (Maslach, 2001) associated with stress-induced phenomena can alert the counselor to the need to attend to the emergence of signs and symptoms (i.e., to self-assess). Self-awareness also enhances the counselor's capacity to self-assess well *before onset* of signs and symptoms of harmful stress responding. Colleagues or supervisors may provide feedback on observable changes in behavior and performance that suggest symptoms are present or evolving rapidly. With integration of this self-awareness information into one's ongoing self-reflection practices, the counselor can determine how burnout, compassion fatigue, or vicarious traumatization is impacting practice, job satisfaction, one's personal life, and overall well-being. Self-assessment allows the counselor to determine the parameters of the stress-induced experience from both a personal and professional perspective.

Use of self-assessment surveys, scales, and tests is quite helpful in this regard. Instruments are available on the Internet that emphasize key components of the workplace experience and that provide insights, for example, into the burnout experience or potential for burning out. Each of these instruments is generic; that is, each reflects the areas of the work experience that impact human services professionals, including counselors, as well as the nondirect human service sector. Well-constructed, self-assessment Internet accessible measures include the Burnout Self-Test (www.mindtools.com/stress/Brn/BurnoutSelf Test. htm), the Burnout Potential Inventory (www.deeroaks.com/images/burnout_question-naire.pdf), and the Job Burnout Inventory (www.secretan.com/burn.html). When viewing these self-assessment instruments and comparing them with previously published self-assessment surveys (Patrick, 1981a, 1982), application to the unique characteristics of the counselor role can be made.

Instruments focusing on compassion fatigue can be found in published sources as well as on the Internet (Figley, 1999; Stamm, Larsen, & Griffel, 2003) at www.isu.edu/~bhstamm/tests/satfat_english.htm and www.isu.edu/~bhstamm/tests/ProQOL.pdf. Used to self-screen for symptoms of compassion fatigue, however, scores obtained on validated instruments can be used to consider the next steps in addressing the impact of burnout, compassion fatigue, or vicarious trauma on the personal and professional life of the counselor. For vicarious trauma (secondary traumatic stress), the Secondary Traumatic Stress Scale is in the preliminary stages of development (Bride et al, 2004), and may not yet be in a format for wide use as a self-assessment instrument.

Nonstandardized Self-Assessment.   Through use of self-assessment instruments or self-reflection methods (e.g., journaling, supervision), counselors can become more informed about personal stress reactions and responses to on-the-job experiences. In Table 8.2, a burnout self-assessment checklist is presented that encompasses the major categories of the burnout experience. Since this self-assessment is not a standardized instrument, it is designed to be used as an individualized self-check that alerts the counselor to the need to attend to specific areas of self-care. Counselors can complete the checklist, noting items that are present as well as whether those items that are bothersome to them. Using this self-reflective information then guides planning for self-care, seeking assistance from others, and communicating about these feelings. The process of focusing on self-assessment raises

TABLE 8.2   Self-Assessment of Counselor Burnout

BURNOUT COMPONENT	SELF-ASSESSMENT TOPIC	PRESENT? YES	NO
Emotional (General)	I feel energized at the end of my work day. I feel emotionally drained at the end of the day at work. This emotional tiredness occurs two or more days per week. When I think about it, I'm aware that there are certain clients that drain me more than others. This has increased over the past year. When I self-reflect about how I relate to my colleagues, I must admit that I am more irritable than I used to be. My colleagues, friends, or family have advised me that I am more irritable these days. My colleagues, friends, or family tell me that my irritability seems to be more associated with my job than our relationship(s). I focus more attention on meeting the needs of my clients than on my own needs.		
Physical	I have more difficulty recovering from minor ailments than I used to have. My slower recovery from minor ailments seems to be more related to my fatigue and attitude than to other factors in my life. Demands of my work make it difficult to for me to maintain regular medical check-ups. I cancel my own health care appointments if clients want to schedule during those time periods. I haven't kept up with my annual health care check-ups this past year. I tend to ignore my own advice when it comes to exercise. I tend to ignore my own advice when it comes to nutritional health. I tend to ignore my own advice when it comes to regular practices of rest and relaxation.		
Quality of Work	As a counselor, I feel that my work is inconsistent in terms of quality. I do not have a supervisory relationship that supports my counseling work. The quality of my counseling work is satisfactory. I used to set goals for my professional development, but lately find that is too time consuming. I am a solo practitioner and do not have weekly contact with colleagues in my field. The paperwork that I complete has become routine, boring, and mechanical in how I complete it. I could do a better job of follow-up with my clients but am too tired to do so. My counseling work is safe and ethical yet uninspiring according to my standards.		

(Continued)

TABLE 8.2   Continued

BURNOUT COMPONENT	SELF-ASSESSMENT TOPIC	PRESENT? YES	NO
Attitudes toward Clients	I've noticed changes in how I view my clients over the past year. My attitude toward my clients is not as positive as I would like it to be. I attribute my change in attitudes toward my clients as a reflection of fatigue. I attribute my change in attitudes to the clients I work with. I have days when I struggle to retain an open attitude toward my clients' problems. I find myself mentally wandering during sessions with my clients. I used to use tardiness to an appointment with me as a therapeutic issue but now feel resentful when a client is late. I have a harder time addressing very intense issues with clients because I've become more impatient.		
Job Satisfaction	I sometimes feel that being a counselor is not the right profession for me. My enthusiasm for my counseling work has declined. If I had it to do over again, I would not become a counselor. I don't want to have to keep up with the paperwork demands of counseling. I find myself looking at the clock during sessions more than I used to. The nature of my counseling practice has become dissatisfying to me over the past year. If I could change some aspects of my practice, I would enjoy it more. I plan to stay in counseling for the financial benefits, not the inherent nature of the work		
Support Systems	I don't see my friends or people in my support system as often as I did six months ago. I haven't attended a professional conference, seminar, or workshop in the past year. I complete my CEU requirements online or through home study courses, not attending professional meetings. My family tells me I'm "no fun anymore." When I'm with friends or family, I feel preoccupied with problems associated with my job. I find it hard to ask friends or family to listen to my job-related frustrations. I feel like I'm a "broken record" when it comes to complaining about my job. If asked directly, I don't think I could identify who is really in my "support system."		

the level of self-awareness and therefore results in learning more about the self. It is this insight that can foster increased self-knowledge that directly links to development of self-care plans. Self-care plans are applicable to prevention of stress-linked exacerbation of gradual and acute stress reactions as well as intervention to reduce symptoms or to manage them effectively. In order to retain professional competencies and effectiveness in the counselor role while working with those who have been traumatizey, it is essential that the counselor proactively engage in the use of self-awareness, self-assessment, and self-care strategies.

Self-Care Actions

Many of the self-care actions presented in Table 8.3 are "tried and true," having extensive backing in the stress management, burnout, compassion fatigue, and vicarious traumatization literature. The work of Skovholt (2001) provides detailed insights into "the caring cycle" that includes (1) the professional development continuum, (2) patterns of responding to stress across this developmental continuum, (3) methods to sustain the professional self, (4) strategies to incorporate focus on the personal self of the counselor, and (5) suggestions on how counselors can maintain stress self-awareness throughout a career in counseling. Because there is overlap in strategies espoused by various experts with reference to preparing for effective management of stress responding regardless of source of causation, however, no attempt is made here to provide a comprehensive cataloging of potential methods and activities. Such resources are available in the literature, offered at professional conferences and workshops, and are the subject of specialized training.

Inherent in this discussion is an emphasis on what the counselor can do individually to prepare for and react effectively to stressors while working in a variety of counseling settings. Complex issues associated with organizational stress prevention and management interventions are addressed in a limited manner in this chapter. The literature provides a diverse and rich source of guidance when considering how to impact workplace factors that are associated with onset of burnout, compassion fatigue, and vicarious traumatization (e.g., Leiter & Maslach, 2005). It is recognized that many of the strategies reviewed take place within organizational settings; thus, the interaction between what the individual counselor can do and how the organization responds is considered. Each strategy represents a commitment of *attention* and *intention* to implement, over time, a consistent self-care plan designed to support and nurture the mental health professional's well-being, competence, and functioning.

Personal Self-Care.   Prevention of the adverse consequences of providing counseling services is based on implementation of personal self-care. Actions that promote a healthy lifestyle, nutrition, and rest are central to personal self-care (Inbar & Ganor, 2001; O'Halloran & Linton, 2000; Palm, Smith, & Follette, 2001, 2002; Strumpfer, 2003). Regular practices of exercise, play, recreation, and spiritual/religious involvement interact with physical self-care to promote optimal well-being. Within a framework of devising personal self-care as conscious and planned, the counselor recognizes that use of self-care measures is within the realm of personal control. For counseling professionals working in settings that often impose demands for quick action, immediate response, and preparedness for the unexpected, having a foundational self-care plan provides ongoing backup that

TABLE 8.3 Self-Care Plan Template

The assumptions I make about my self-care:

- I am committed to ensuring that I can practice my profession as a counselor in an ethical and professional manner.
- Because the stressors inherent in counseling practice can lead to burnout, compassion fatigue, or vicarious traumatization, I am committed to my self-care plan.
- My plan is based on my unique needs and resources.
- I make this agreement with myself, knowing that self-reflection, self-assessment, and self-awareness are activities that I engage in as a professional in the helping professions.

Actions that I will take to ensure that my self-care plan is balanced and meets my needs to prevent stress-induced reactions or to address my reactions as they arise follow:

Type of Care Activities, Plans, Goals

Physical Self-Care

Exercise plan and activities:	For example: Type, frequency, location
Healthy nutrition goals and needs:	For example: Daily dietary needs; food choices; goals
Sleep plan:	For example: Bedtime, naps, presleep routine
Rest and relaxation:	For example: Methods, use of music, baths, aromatherapy

Recreational Self-Care

Play activities:	For example: Daily, weekly, or other frequencies
Laughter program:	For example: View funny films; find humor around me
Vacation and time off:	For example: how much personal time off (PTO) remains; how was it used this year?
Hobbies and relaxing interests:	For example: life-long learning activities; crafts; sailing
Athletic activities:	For example: With family; member of team

Social Support Self-Care

Interaction with friends:	For example: Frequency of contact; with whom?
Interaction with family:	For example: How often? Where? Occasions?
Social gatherings:	For example: attend parties; host parties
Outreach to friends/family:	For example: initiate contact; travel to visit

Spiritual/Religious Self-Care

Prayer/meditation practice:	For example: How often? When? Where?
Attend services:	For example: How often? When? Where?
Seek guidance:	For example: From pastor, spiritual mentor

Other Self-Care Activities:

	Unique to you; your lifestyle; your interests

can sustain resolve, commitment, and passion to remain in the field of practice. It is while consciously using self-care activities to relieve stress, reduce tension, and disconnect from the intensity of counseling work that psychological, physical, spiritual, and emotional batteries can be recharged.

One method that counselors can use to be mindful of the importance of self-care when in high-stress work environments is the self-care plan. The self-care plan template provided here reflects the self-care topics discussed in this chapter and is designed to serve as a working guide that changes over time. Central to effective use of such a template is regular review of personal progress, modifying the plan as change takes place, use of the tool in supervision, and, finally, dedication to a mindful approach to managing stress. Completing each section of the template requires attention to the topics in each component of the plan as each relates to self of the counselor. In itself, attending to the items may strengthen awareness of the importance of issues raised while working on the template.

> Karen attended a workshop on burnout prevention sponsored by her regional counselor professional association. She sensed that the workshop would "speak to her," but did not anticipate the insights she would gain. Part of the workshop was to fill out the Self-Care Template and then discuss the plan with two other people in a small group of other participants. When Karen began to discuss her template, she became tearful and quiet. She had been able to hold the tears back while she wrote on the template, but now she accepted a tissue from one of the small-group members who leaned in gently toward Karen and said, "Karen, what is it about your template that brings these tears?" Karen began to talk about how she realized that she just does not laugh much anymore, hasn't been to a movie or concert in the past three years—all since she started working at the acute inpatient unit at the medical center. As she discussed her awareness of the blank spaces on her template, Karen gained important insights into how she is struggling with burnout on her job.

When counselors are experiencing symptoms of burnout, compassion fatigue, or vicarious trauma, they very often find that self-care activities have been sporadic or ceased entirely. The consequences of stress responding signal the need to reinvigorate self-care actions, once again, at a conscious and mindful level, often gaining understanding about the value of enjoyment and support found in these activities. Over time and with a renewed commitment to self-care, the benefits of these practices will become apparent in reduced negative impact of stressors on well-being. It is important to note here that implementation of self-care is not a "cure-all" to work-related stress. The sources of stress may well remain unremitting. However, when used with regularity, self-care strategies alter the response patterns of the counselor to those sources of stress and distress.

Social Support Systems.   Research highlights the role of social support systems as antidotes to the potential ravages of burnout, compassion fatigue, and vicarious traumatization (Collins & Long, 2003a; Inbar & Ganor, 2001; Kee, Johnson, & Hunt, 2002; Skovholt, 2001). Social support consists of the relationships the counselor has with others at work, within one's personal life, and within the community. These supportive relationships are found in social networks that provide psychological, emotional, spiritual, and health benefits (Anthony & O'Brien, 1999) and can serve as early warning systems to the counselor who is experiencing symptoms of burnout, compassion fatigue, or vicarious trauma.

Social support system maintenance is an essential element of counselor self-care. Connections with friends, family, and community contacts serve as prevention measures for stress-linked reactions to the counselor's work. In some cases, however, time or work pressures experienced by the counselor can lead to neglect of the support system's mainte- nance and use. Ideally, members of the counselor's support system will bring this neglect to the attention of the helper. The professional, then, will ideally "hear" this feedback as helpful and supportive and as motivation to redirect attention to self-care maintenance.

Supervision and Consultation.   Of the many strategies reported as effective in resisting as well as coping effectively with burnout, compassion fatigue, or vicarious trauma, ongoing supervision and use of consultation resources are repeatedly cited (Azar, 2000; Collins & Long, 2003b; Cramer, 2002; Etherington, 2000; Pearlman, 1999; Salston & Figley, 2003). In addi- tion, ongoing supervision and consultation is an essential component of professional growth and development as a practitioner and is inextricably linked with working through counter- transference reactions emerging while providing mental health care (Harper & Steadman, 2003).

Supervision for counseling professionals can be provided by a designated co- professional with specific expertise in providing guidance and coaching to the counselor, or by peers who assume this role upon request. As a regular element of the counseling prac- tice experience, supervision provides the opportunity to explore personal reactions to clients, symptoms associated with secondary exposure to trauma, issues raised in therapy, and to identify overall well-being and satisfaction. Skillful supervision can be process-oriented, designed to "examine the state of the treatment relationship" (Cramer, 2002, p. 206). In this context, issues can be raised about symptoms of burnout, compassion fatigue, or vicarious traumatization in a "safe harbor" (Etherington, 2000, p. 379), which also includes confrontation of nonproductive or potentially harmful professional and personal behavior.

Supervision as well as consultation with colleagues about particularly challenging treatment experiences is a "must have" for the counselor professional working with sur- vivors of trauma. Supervision sessions represent an essential stress-release mechanism that allows the counselor to explore the treatment issues encountered, to take part in per- sonal stress management activities, to evaluate one's effectiveness as a counselor, and to receive supervisory support. Working in isolation is a professional "no-no" in the practice of trauma therapy, since the risk for compassion fatigue and vicarious trauma are significant, pervasive, and potentially devastating to the counselor and to client welfare.

Sense of Humor.   Within this framework, use of humor to alleviate stress and insert emotional distance from counseling work can produce healthy outcomes (Inbar & Ganor, 2003; Pearlman, 1999; Skovholt, 2001). Laughter and a sense of humor allow for tension reduction and are used within parameters that are understood by peers and supervisors, while ensuring that clients are not privy to these moments of expressing anger, frustration, or a sense of futility. Within the context of a social support system, humor and laughter (including "gallows humor") can be an important element of an overall self-care plan and retaining balance among work, family, social activities, and one's inner spiritual life.

Mentoring and Being Mentored.   There is surprisingly little mention of the role of mentoring as part of the self-care planning process for counselors at risk for burnout, compassion fatigue, or vicarious traumatization. It is within a mentor–mentee relationship, however, that counselors who are experienced in managing personal stress responding can provide guidance and coaching to novice practitioners as well as those new to the specialized role of trauma therapist. *Mentoring* is defined as the provision of guidance, support, advising, and coaching that promotes successful practice. Within this framework, the mentor can prepare the counselor with realistic expectations about practice in highly stressful work environments or with specific client populations by focusing on development and growth of counselor competencies.

The benefits of mentoring relationships to counselors include access to role models in the work setting, assistance in assimilating into the work setting, and historical information and successful practice guidance. Although the role of mentor may include features of supervision, it also stands alone as a valuable source of coaching, development, and growth as a counseling professional that extends beyond direct service provision. In contexts characterized by high stress and exposure to traumatic client experiences, the mentor–mentee professional relationship adds significant strength to the overall self-care plan resources available to the counselor professional.

The potential number and variety of potential strategies appropriate for incorporation into a prevention or intervention self-care plan are limited only by the creativity, focus, and intention of the counselor professional. Workshops, seminars, and conference presentations are dedicated to this topic within each of the counseling professions, as are continuing education programs and Internet-delivered learning modules. As outlined in the Counselor Self-Care Model, training, education, and supervision are continuing threads woven throughout an individualized self-care plan. Counselors are expected to ensure that continuing professional development activities meet goals for support of practice competencies. This outcome carries added import for counselors providing services to survivors of trauma. Although it is not possible to avoid burnout, compassion fatigue, or vicarious trauma entirely, it is reasonable to set expectations that can be met to identify the best fit of counselor-to-client population, and to remain vigilant regarding self-care.

ISSUES IN CONTEMPORARY COUNSELING PRACTICE

When considering stress, exposure to client trauma, and the counselor's personal experience with traumatic events, the interactive effect of the work setting and client population is recognized as holding the potential to adversely impact the counseling professional. Within the counseling professions, there is a clear need to address these issues in order to ensure that current practitioners can continue to function effectively as mental health professionals within contexts of high demand and high stress. In reality, counselors will find it difficult to avoid burnout or the harmful impact of compassion fatigue or vicarious trauma if the environment in which the counselor practices is nonsupportive. Work settings that are infused with stressors and demands to serve clients regardless of the cost to the practitioner's well-being can counteract the self-care efforts of the helper. The interactive effect of individual self-care and organizational supports must be addressed in counseling work settings if the high cost of helping others is to be reduced, attenuated, and managed well.

The issues faced by the counseling professions are complex and multifaceted. Each advance in counselor role development is accompanied by needs for adjustment that include education, training, and creation of support resources. Because the mental health professions have assumed a lead position in providing care to victims of trauma in any setting that such physical, emotional, and psychological injury can occur, a concomitant need has emerged to ensure that the provider's needs for care are not neglected. Trauma, disaster, and crisis counseling call on the counselor to perform effectively, even when the setting is fraught with anxiety, fear for one's personal safety, and potential for physical or psychological harm. The world truly has changed. The counseling professions, in turn, have been responsive to the need to care for the well-being of survivors of trauma. In recognition of this change in the role of the counselor, it is incumbent on counselors themselves, employers of counselors, and the organizations in which counselors work to proactively address the risk for counselor burnout, compassion fatigue, and vicarious traumatization.

DISCUSSION TOPICS/QUESTIONS

1. Each of the stress-induced reactions discussed can impact counselors in unique as well as similar ways. Discuss two compelling reasons why counselors must attend to signs and symptoms of burnout and compassion fatigue.

2. In the case of Miranda, what are the actions that she should take to address the immediate needs to ensure that her potentially suicidal client is protected? What advice would you give her if she consulted with you about this experience?

3. Consider the statement: "Counselor burnout is inevitable." Develop two arguments that support this statement and two arguments that counter this statement.

4. Phil is a well-respected counselor in your community. He has presented a number of times at statewide conferences on topics linked to survivors of child physical and sexual abuse. He is widely admired as a professional who is focused and compassionate. What are the risks to Phil for burnout, compassion fatigue, or vicarious traumatization?

5. Victor and Carol are in practice in a small community. Both are doctorate-prepared counselors, licensed, and involved in the local coalition for the homeless. Carol has been increasing her volunteer hours at the coalition to provide guidance to homeless families. She also has a full-time practice that is very demanding. Victor is noticing that her physical fatigue level is increasing, and decides he has to discuss his observations with her. As they begin to talk, Carol states, "Victor, I'm thinking that since I have room in my house, with the kids married and gone, that I could offer a temporary home to one or two of my homeless families. What do you think?" How should Victor respond? What are the issues raised by Carol's statement and behavior with reference to stress-induced reactions?

6. As the occurrence of major natural disasters seems to increase, you're aware that the acute and long-term mental health needs of victims of such events are significant and complex. You decide to explore involvement with the local disaster response coalition. Identify and

discuss the pros and cons of involvement based on insights you have about your own sensitivities and stress-response style.

7. In the case of the counselor who provided mental care to children evacuated from New Orleans to Texas following Hurricane Katrina, the reactions to the traumatic experiences of the children had great impact on the professional. What could Dr. B have done to better prepare for this work? What can Dr. B do in the aftermath of this experience to heal?

8. Self-care is generally accepted as a basic element of burnout prevention. What are three strategies that you can use at you attempt to convince your colleague, Gerry (who is skeptical about burnout being "real"), that focusing on self-care makes sense as he begins a career as a counselor in an acute inpatient psychiatric hospital?

9. Complete the Self-Care Plan Template. Discuss what you've learned about yourself, how you integrate balance into your personal and professional lives, and specific steps you can take to strengthen this plan.

10. You and three of your counselor colleagues have decided that it's time to tackle how clients are scheduled for appointments at the mental health clinic where you all work. Currently, each of you receives new referrals in a random manner (i.e., clients make appointments, and the scheduler sets up appointments for anyone who has an opening). This method does not take into account the acuity level or type of counseling problem that the client has. What are the burnout and vicarious traumatization risks associated with this kind of scheduling? What are some alternative scheduling options?

REFERENCES

Ackerley, G. K., Burnell, J., Holder, D. C., & Kurdek, L. A. (1988). Burnout among licensed psychologists. *Professional Psychology: Research and Practice, 19*(6), 624–631.

American Continuing Education Network (ACE). (2004). *Compassion fatigue: The stress of caring too much*. Retrieved September 24, 2004, from www.ace-network.com/index.html.

American Counseling Association. (2005). *ACA Code of Ethics*. Retrieved October 16, 2005, from www.counseling.org.

American Counseling Association. (2003). *Task Force on Counselor Wellness and Impairment: Risk factors*. Retrieved October 19, 2005, from www.counseling.org/taskforce/tf_riskfactors.htm.

American Psychiatric Association. (2000). *Diagnostic and statistical manual of mental disorders, fourth edition (DSM-IV-TR)*. Washington, DC: Author.

American Psychological Association. (2002). *Ethical principles of psychologists and code of conduct*. Retrieved October 19, 2005, from www.apa.org/ethics/code2002.pdf.

Anthony, J. L., & O'Brien, W. H. (1999). An evaluation of the impact of social support manipulations on cardiovascular reactivity to lab stressors. *Behavioral Medicine, 25*, 78–87.

Appels, A., Falger, P. R., & Schouten, E. G. (1993). Vital exhaustion as risk indicator for myocardial infarction in women. *Journal of Psychosomatic Research, 37*, 881–890.

Arrington, E. G., & Wilson, M. N. (2000). A re-examination of risk and resilience during adolescence incorporating culture and diversity. *Journal of Child and Family Studies, 9*(2), 221–230.

Arvay, M., & Uhlemann, M. (1996). Counselor stress in the field of trauma: A preliminary study. *Canadian Journal of Counseling, 30*, 193–210.

Azar, S. T. (2000). Preventing burnout in professionals and paraprofessionals who work with child abuse and neglect cases: A cognitive behavioral approach to supervision. *Journal of Clinical Psychology, 56*, 643–663.

Bakker, A. B., Demerouti, E., & Schaufeli, W. B. (2002). Validation of the Maslach Burnout Inventory—General Survey: An Internet study. *Anxiety, Stress & Coping, 15*, 245–260.

Bakker, A. B., Schaufeli, W. B., Demerouti, E., Janssen, P., & Van Der Hulst, R. (2000). Using equity theory to examine the difference between burnout and depression. *Anxiety, Stress & Coping, 13,* 247–268.

Balevre, P. (2001). Professional nursing burnout and irrational thinking. *Journal of Nurses in Staff Development, 17,* 264–271.

Baranowsky, A. B. (1999). The silencing response in clinical practice: On the road to diaglogue. In C. R. Figley (Ed.), *Treating compassion fatigue* (pp. 155–170). New York: Brunner-Routledge.

Batten, S. V., & Orsillo, S. M. (2001). *Therapist reactions in the context of collective trauma. AABT: Articles on trauma.* Retrieved November 4, 2004, from www.aabt.org/.

Bell, H. (2003). Strengths and secondary trauma in family violence work. *Social Work, 48,* 513–522.

Bell, H., Kulkarni, S., & Dalton, L. (2003). Organizational prevention of vicarious trauma. *Journal of Contemporary Human Services, 84,* 463–470.

Bonanno, G. A. (2004). Loss, trauma, and human resilience: Have we underestimated the human capacity to thrive after extremely aversive events? *American Psychologist, 59,* 20–28.

Boyle, A., Grap, M. J., Younger, J., & Thornby, D. (1991). Personality hardiness, ways of coping, social support and burnout in critical care nurses. *Journal of Advanced Nursing, 16,* 850–857.

Brady, J. L., Guy, J. D., Poelstra, P. L., & Fletcher, B. (1999). Vicarious traumatization, spirituality, and the treatment of sexual abuse survivors: A national survey of women psychotherapists. *Professional Psychology: Research and Practice, 30,* 386–393.

Brewer, E. W., & Shapard, L. (2004). Employee burnout: A meta-analysis of the relationship between age or years of experience. *Human Resource Development Review, 3,* 102–123.

Bride, B. E., Robinson, M. M., Yegidis, B., & Figley, C. R. (2004). Development and validation of the secondary traumatic stress scale. *Research on Social Work Practice, 14,* 27–35.

Briere, J. (1995). *The Trauma Symptom Inventory professional manual.* Odessa, FL: Psychological Assessment Resources.

Burisch, M. (2002). A longitudinal study of burnout: The relative importance of dispositions and experiences. *Work & Stress, 16,* 1–17.

Burke, R. J., & Greenglass, E. R. (2001). Hospital restructuring, work–family conflict, and psychological burnout among nursing staff. *Psychology and Health, 16,* 583–594.

Chrestman, K. R. (1999). Secondary exposure to trauma and self-reported distress among therapists. In B. H. Stamm (Ed.), *Secondary traumatic stress: Self-care issues for clinicians, researchers, and educators* (pp. 29–36). Lutherville, MD: Sidran.

Collins, S., & Long, A. (2003a). Too tired to care? The psychological effects of working with trauma. *Journal of Psychiatric & Mental Health Nursing, 10,* 17–28.

Collins, S., & Long, A. (2003b). Working with the psychological effects of trauma: Consequences for mental health-care workers—A literature review. *Journal of Psychiatric & Mental Health Nursing, 10,* 417–424.

Cramer, M. A. (2002). Under the influence of unconscious process: Countertransference in the treatment of PTSD and substance abuse in women. *American Journal of Psychotherapy, 46,* 194–210.

Cunningham, M. (2003). Impact of trauma work on social work clinicians: Empirical findings. *Social Work, 48,* 451–460.

Danieli, Y. (1994). Countertransference, trauma and training. In J. P. Wilson & J. D. Lindy (Eds.), *Countertransference in the treatment of PTSD* (pp. 368–388). New York: Guilford.

deWaal, A. (1995). Compassion fatigue. *New Statesman & Society, 8,* 13–16.

Downey, R. G., Rappoport, L., & Hemenover, S. (2002). Personality and job burnout: Can coping skills reduce job burnout? *Behavioral Sciences: Psychology,* Report No. A573604. Retrieved October 5, 2004, from www.stormingmedia.us/57/5736/A573604.html.

Edwards, D., Coyle, D., & Hannigan, B. (2000). Stress and burnout in community mental health nursing: A review of the literature. *Journal of Psychiatric and Mental Health Nursing, 7,* 7–14.

Etherington, K. (2000). Supervising counselors who work with survivors of childhood sexual abuse. *Counselling Psychology Quarterly, 13,* 377–389.

Farber, B. A. (Ed.). (1983). *Stress and burnout in the human service professions.* New York: Pergamon.

Figley, C. R. (1995). *Compassion fatigue: Coping with secondary traumatic stress disorder in those who treat the traumatized.* New York: Brunner/Mazel.

Figley, C. R. (1999). Compassion fatigue: Toward a new understanding of the costs of caring. In B. H. Stamm (Ed.)., *Secondary traumatic stress* (2nd ed.) (pp. 3–28). Baltimore, MD: Sidran.

Figley, C. R. (2002a). Compassion fatigue: Psychotherapists' chronic lack of self-care. *Journal of Clinical Psychology, 58*, 1433–1442.

Figley, C. R. (Ed.). (2002b). *Treating compassion fatigue.* New York: Brunner-Routledge.

Follette, V., Polusny, M., & Milbeck, K. (1994). Mental health and law enforcement professionals: Trauma history, psychological symptoms, and impact of providing services to child sexual abuse survivors. *Professional Psychology: Research and Practice, 25*, 275–282.

Freudenberger, H. J. (1974). Staff burnout. *Journal of Social Issues, 30*, 159–165.

Freudenberger, H. J. (1975). The staff burnout syndrome in alternative institutions. *Psychotherapy Research & Practice, 12*, 72–83.

Freudenberger, H. J., & Richelson, G. (1980). *Burnout: The high cost of high achievement.* New York: Doubleday.

Gentry, J. E., Baranowsky, A. B., & Dunning, K. (2002). The Accelerated Recovery Program (ARP) for compassion fatigue. In C. R. Figley (Ed.), *Treating compassion fatigue* (pp. 123–137). New York: Brunner-Routledge.

Golden, J., Piedmont, R. L., Clarrocchi, J. W., & Rodgerson, T. (2004). Spirituality and burnout: An incremental validity study. *Journal of Psychology and Theology, 32*, 115–125.

Grosch, W. N., & Olsen, D. C. (2000). Clergy burnout: An integrative approach. *Journal of Clinical Psychology Session, 56*, 619–632.

Grossi, G., Theorell, T., Jurisoo, M., & Setterlind, S. (1999). Psychophysiological correlates of organizational change and threat of unemployment among police inspectors. *Integrative Physiological and Behavioral Science, 34*, 39–42.

Hallman, T., Thomsson, H., Burell, G., Lisspers, J., & Setterlind, S. (2003). Stress, burnout and coping: Differences between women with coronary heart disease and healthy matched women. *Journal of Health Psychology, 8*, 433–445.

Harper, K., & Steadman, J. (2003). Therapeutic boundary issues in working with childhood sexual-abuse survivors. *American Journal of Psychotherapy, 57*, 64–79.

Iacovides, A., Foudulakis, K. N., Moysidou, C., & Ierodikonou, C. (1997). Burnout in nursing staff. Is there a relationship between depression and burnout? *International Journal of Psychiatry in Medicine, 29*, 421–433.

Inbar, J., & Ganor, M. (2001). Trauma and compassion fatigue: Helping the helpers. *Journal of Jewish Community Service*, Winter-Spring, 109–111.

Jenkins, S. R., & Baird, S. (2002). Secondary traumatic stress and vicarious trauma: A validational study. *Journal of Traumatic Stress, 15*, 423–432.

Joinson, C. (1992). Coping with compassion fatigue. *Nursing 92, 22*, 16, 116, 118–119, 121.

Jones, J. W. (1985). Staff burnout scale for health professionals. In J. V. Mitchell, Jr. (Ed.). (1985). *The ninth mental measurement yearbook.* New York: McGraw-Hill.

Jones, K. D. (2002). The impact of learning about child abuse trauma. *Journal of Humanistic Counseling, Education and Development, 41*, 45–51.

Kadami, M. A., & Truscott, D. (2003). Vicarious traumatization and burnout among therapists working with sex offenders. *Traumatology, 9*, 216–230.

Kahill, S. (1988). Interventions for burnout in the helping professional: A review of the empirical evidence. *Canadian Journal of Counselling Review, 22*, 310–342.

Kassam-Adams, N. (1999). The risks of treating sexual trauma: Stress and secondary trauma in psychotherapists. In B. H. Stamm (Ed.), *Secondary traumatic stress* (pp. 37–48). Baltimore, MD: Sidran.

Kee, J. A., Johnson, D., & Hunt, P. (2002). Burnout and social support in rural mental health counselors. Retrieved October 2, 2004, from www.marshall.edu/jrcp/sp2002/Kee.htm.

Kessler, R. C., Sonnega, A., Bromet, E., Hughes, M., & Nelson, C. (1995). Post-traumatic stress disorder in the National Comorbidity Survey. *Archives of General Psychiatry, 52*, 1048–1059.

King, L., King, D., Fairbank, J., Keane, T., & Adams, G. (1998). Resilience-recovery factors in post-traumatic stress disorder among female and male veterans: Hardiness, post war social support and additional stressful life events. *Journal of Personality and Social Psychology, 74*, 420–434.

Kinzie, J. D., & Boehnlein, J. K. (1993). Psychotherapy of the victims of massive violence: Countertransference and ethical issues. *American Journal of Psychotherapy, 47*, 90–103.

Kitzrow, M. A. (2002). Survey of CACREP-accredited programs: Training counselors to provide treatment for sexual abuse. *Counselor Education & Supervision, 42*, 107–118.

Lawrence, R. A. (1984). Police stress and personality factors: A conceptual model. *Journal of Criminal Justice, 12*, 247–263.

Layman, E., & Guyden, J. A. (1997). Reducing your risk for burnout. *Health Care Supervisor, 15*, 57–69.

Layne, C. M., Hohenshil, T. H., & Singh, K. (2004). The relationship of occupational stress, psychological strain, and coping resources to the turnover intentions of rehabilitation counselors. *Rehabilitation Counseling Bulletin, 48*, 19–30.

Lee, R. T., & Ashworth, B. E. (1996). A meta-analytic examination of the correlates of the three dimensions of job burnout. *Journal of Applied Psychology, 81*, 123–133.

Leiter, M. P., & Maslach, C. (2005). *Banishing burnout: Six strategies for improving your relationship with work*. New York: John Wiley & Sons.

Lerias, D., & Byrne, M. K. (2003). Vicarious traumatization: Symptoms and predictors. *Stress and Health, 19*, 129–138.

Lewandowski, C. A. (2003). Organizational factors contributing to worker frustration: The precursor to burnout. *Journal of Sociological and Social Welfare, 30*(4), 175–185.

Luther, S. S., Cicchetti, D., & Becker, B. (2000). The construct of resilience: A critical evaluation and guidelines for future work. *Child Development, 71*, 543–562.

Marotta, S. A. (2000). Best practices for counselors who treat posttraumatic stress disorder. *Journal of Counseling & Development, 78*, 492–495.

Maslach, C. (2001). What have we learned about burnout and health? *Psychology & Health, 16*, 607–611.

Maslach, C., Jackson, S. E., & Leiter, M. P. (1996). *Maslach Burnout Inventory manual* (3rd ed.). Palo Alto, CA: Consulting Psychologists Press.

McCann, I. L., & Pearlman, L. A. (1990). Vicarious traumatization: A framework for understanding the psychological effects of working with trauma. *Journal of Traumatic Stress, 3*, 131–149.

McNight, J. D., & Glass, D. C. (1995). Perceptions of control, burnout, and repressive sympotomatology: A replication and extension. *Journal of Consulting and Clinical Psychology, 63*, 490–495.

Mikkelsen, E. G., & Einarsen, S. (2001). Bullying in Danish work-life: Prevalence and health correlates. *European Journal of Work and Organizational Psychology, 10*, 393–413.

Mills, L., & Huebner, E. (1998). A prospective study of personality characteristics, occupational stressors, and burnout among school psychology practitioners. *Journal of School Psychology, 36*, 103–120.

Munroe, J. F. (1999). Ethical issues associated with secondary trauma in therapists. In B. H. Stamm (Ed.), *Scondary traumatic stress: Self-care issues for clinicians, researchers, and educators* (pp. 211–229). Baltimore, MD: Sidran.

Myers, D., & Wee, D. F. (1999). Strategies for managing disaster mental health worker stress. In C. R. Figley (Ed.), *Treating compassion fatigue* (pp. 181–211). New York: Brunner-Routledge.

Nelson-Gardell, D., & Harris, D. (2003). Childhood abuse history, secondary traumatic stress, and child welfare workers. *Child Welfare, 82*, 5–27.

O'Halloran, T. M., & Linton, J. M. (2000). Stress on the job: Self-care resources for counselors. *Journal of Mental Health Counseling, 22*, 354–364.

Osborn, C. J. (2004). Seven salutary suggestions for counselor stamina. *Journal of Counseling & Development, 82*, 319–328.

Palm, K. M., Polusny, M. A., & Follette, V. M. (2004). Vicarious traumatization: Potential hazards and interventions for disaster and trauma workers. *Prehospital and Disaster Medicine, 19*, 73–78.

Palm, K. M., Smith, A. A., & Follette, V. M. (2001). *Trauma therapy and therapist self care. AABT: Articles on trauma*. Retrieved November 4, 2004, from www.aabt.org/.

Patrick, P. K. S. (1981a). Burnout: Antecedents, manifestations and self-care strategies for the nurse. In L. B. Marino (Ed.), *Cancer nursing* (pp. 113–135). St. Louis, MO: C. V. Mosby.

Patrick, P. K. S. (1981b). *Health care worker burnout: What it is, what to do about it*. Chicago: Inquiry Books.

Patrick, P. K. S. (1982). Burnout: Understanding its causes. *Free Association, 9*, 1–4.

Patrick, P. K. S. (1984a). Professional roles at risk for burnout. *Family & Community Health, 6*(4), 25–31.

Patrick, P. K. S. (1984b). Preventing burnout: Coordinating the employee health function. *Family & Community Health, 6*(4), 76–92.

Patrick, P. K. S. (1984c). Organizational burnout programs: Nursing administration as the trend setter. *Journal of Nursing Administration, 14*(6), 16–21.

Patrick, P. K. S. (1987a). Hospice caregiving: Strategies to avoid burnout and maintain self-preservation. *The Hospice Journal, 3,* 223–253.

Patrick, P. K. S. (1987b). Hospice caregiving: Strategies to avoid burnout and maintain self-preservation. In L. F. Paradis (Ed.), *Stress and burnout among providers caring for the terminally ill and their families* (pp. 223–253). New York: Haworth.

Pearlman, L. A. (1999). Self-care for trauma therapists: Ameliorating vicarious traumatization. In B. H. Stamm (Ed.), *Secondary traumatic stress: Self-care issues for clinicians, researchers, and educators* (pp. 51–64). Baltimore, MD: Sidran.

Pearlman, L. A. (2003). *Trauma and Attachment Belief Scale: Manual.* Los Angeles, CA: Western Psychological Services, Inc.

Pearlman, L. A., & MacIan, P. S. (1995). Vicarious traumatization: An empirical study of the effects of trauma work on trauma therapists. *Professional Psychology: Research and Practice, 26,* 558–565.

Pearlman, L. A., & Saakvitne, K. W. (1995). The therapeutic relationship as the context for countertransference and vicarious traumatization. In L. A. Pearlman & K. W. Saakvitne (Eds.), *Trauma and the therapist: Countertransference and vicarious traumatization in psychotherapy work with incest survivors* (pp. 15–32). New York: W. W. Norton.

Peiro, J. M., Gonzalez-Roma, V., Tordera, N., & Manas, M. A. (2001). Does role stress predict burnout over time among health care professionals? *Psychology & Health, 16,* 511–525.

Piedmont, R. L. (1993). A longitudinal analysis of burnout in the health care setting: The role of personal dispositions. *Journal of Personality Assessment, 61,* 457–473.

Raquepaw, J. W., & Miller, R. S. (1989). Psycho-therapist burnout: A componential analysis. *Professional Psychology: Research and Practice, 20,* 32–36.

Remley, T. P., Jr. (1995). A proposed alternative to the licensing of specialties in counseling. *Journal of Counseling & Development, 74,* 126–129.

Rich, V. L., & Rich, A. R. (1987). Personality hardiness and burnout in female staff nurses. *Image: Journal of Nursing Scholarship, 19,* 63–66.

Robinson, J. R., Clements, K., & Land, C. (2003). Workplace stress among psychiatric nurses: Prevalence, distribution, correlates & predictors. *Journal of Psychosocial Nursing and Mental Health Services, 41,* 32–41.

Rosenberger, E. W., & Hayes, J. A. (2002). Therapist as subject: A review of the empirical countertransference literature. *Journal of Counseling & Development, 80,* 264–270.

Ross, R. R., Altmaier, E. M., & Russell, D. W. (1989). Job stress, social support, and burnout among counseling center staff. *Journal of Counseling Psychology, 36*(4), 464–470.

Rudolph, J. M., & Stamm, B. H. (1999). Maximizing human capital: Moderating secondary traumatic stress through administrative and policy action. In B. H. Stamm (Ed.), *Secondary traumatic stress: Self-care issues for clinicians, researchers, and educators* (pp. 277–290). Baltimore, MD: Sidran.

Sabin-Farrell, R., & Turpin, G. (2003). Vicarious traumatization: Implications for the mental health of health workers? *Clinical Psychology Review, 23,* 448–481.

Salston, M., & Figley, C. R. (2003). Secondary traumatic stress effects of working with survivors of criminal victimization. *Journal of Traumatic Stress, 16,* 167–174.

Savicki, V., & Cooley, E. J. (1982). Implications of burnout research and theory for counselor educators. *Personnel and Guidance Journal, 60,* 415–419.

Schauben, L. J., & Frazier, P. A. (1995). Vicarious trauma: The effects on female counselors of working with sexual violence survivors. *Psychology of Women Quarterly, 19,* 49–64.

Schaufeli, W. B., & Enzmann, D. (1998). *The burnout companion to study and practice: A critical analysis.* London: Taylor & Francis.

Schaufeli, W. B., & Greenglass, E. R. (2001). Special issue: Job burnout and health. *Psychology & Health, 16,* 4.

Schaufeli, W. B., Salanova, M., Gonzalez-Roma, V., & Bakker, A. B. (2002). The measurement of engagement and burnout: A two sample confirmatory factor analytic approach. *Journal of Happiness Studies, 3,* 71–92.

Schubert, R. F. (1988). Africa, famine and compassion fatigue. *Vital Speeches of the Day, 54,* 501–504.

Schutte, N., Toppinen, S., Kalimo, R., & Shaufeli, W. (2000). The factor validity of the Maslach Burnout Inventory-General Survey (MBI-GS) across occupational groups and nations. *Journal of Occupational & Organizational Psychology, 73,* 53–46.

Schwam, K. (1998). The phenomenon of compassion fatigue in perioperative nursing. *AORN Journal, 68*, 642–648.

Setterlind, S., & Larsson, G. (1995). The stress profile: A psychosocial approach to measuring stress. *Stress Medicine, 11*, 85–92.

Skovholt, T. M. (2001). *The resilient practitioner*. Boston: Allyn and Bacon.

Stamm, B. H. (1999). Measuring compassion satisfaction as well as fatigue: Developmental history of the compassion satisfaction and fatigue test. In C. R. Figley (Ed.), *Treating compassion fatigue* (pp. 107–119.). New York: Brunner-Routledge.

Stamm, B. H., Larsen, D., & Griffel, K. (2003). *Measures of traumatic stress and secondary traumatic stress*. Retrieved November 10, 2004, from www.isu.edu/~bhstamm/ tests.htm#TEST%20NAME.

Stamm, B. H., Varna, E. M., Pearlman, L. A., & Giller, E. (2002). The helper's power to heal and to be hurt-or helped—by trying. *DC Register Report: A Publication of the National Register of Health Service Providers in Psychology*. Retrieved November 11, 2004, from www.isu.edu/~bhstamm/tests/S_VT%20One%20Page%20Handout.pdf

Stebnicki, M. A. (2000). Stress and grief reactions among rehabilitation professionals: Dealing effectively with empathy fatigue. *Journal of Rehabilitation*, Jan–March, 23–29.

Steed, L., & Downing, R. (1998). A phenomenological study of vicarious traumatisation amongst psychologists and professional counselors working in the field of sexual abuse/assault. *Australasian Journal of Disaster and Trauma Studies, 2*, 1–8.

Steptoe, A. (1991). Invited review: The links between stress and illness. *Journal of Psychosomatic Research, 35*, 633–644.

Strümpfer, D. J. W. (2003). Resilience and burnout: A stitch that could save time. *South African Journal of Psychology, 33*, 69–80.

Tennant, C. (2001). Work related stress and depressive disorders. *Journal of Psychosomatic Research, 51*, 697–704.

Trippany, R. L., Kress, V. E. W., & Wilcoxon, S. A. (2004). Preventing vicarious trauma: What counselors should know when working with trauma survivors. *Journal of Counseling & Development, 82*, 31–37.

Trippany, R. L., Wilcoxon, S. A., & Satcher, J. F. (2003). Factors influencing vicarious trauma for therapists of survivors of sexual victimization. *Journal of Trauma Practice, 19*, 47–60.

Tusaie, K., & Dyer, J.(2004). Resilience: A historical review of the construct. *Holistic Nursing Practice, 18*(1), 3–8.

Valent, P. (1999). Diagnosis and treatment of helper stresses, traumas, and illnesses. In C. R. Figley (Ed.), *Treating compassion fatigue* (pp. 17–37). New York: Brunner-Routledge.

Van Dierendonck, D., Schaufeli, W. B., & Buunk, B. P. (2001). Towards a process model of burnout: Results from a secondary analysis. *European Journal of Work and Organizational Psychology, 10*, 41–52.

Walsh, B., & Walsh, S. (2001). Is mental health work psychologically hazardous for staff? A critical review of the literature. *Journal of Mental Health, 10*, 121–129.

Wee, D., & Myers, D. (2002). Response of mental health workers following disaster. The Oklahoma City bombing. In C. R. Figley (Ed.), *Treating compassion fatigue* (pp. 57–83). New York: Brunner/Rutledge.

Weiss, D. Y., & Marmar, C. (1997). The impact of event scale-revised. In J. Wilson and T. Keane (Eds.), *Assessing psychological trauma and PTSD: A practitioner's handbook* (pp. 399–411). New York: Guilford.

Wilson, J. P., & Lindy, J .D. (1994). Empathic strain and countertransference. In J. P. Wilson & J. D. Lindy (Eds.), *Countertransference in the treatment of PTSD* (pp. 5–30). New York: Guilford.

Winget, C. N., & Umbenhauer, S. L. (1982). Disaster planning: The mental health workers as "victim-by-proxy." *Journal of Health and Human Resources Administration, 4*, 363–373.

PART III

CONTEMPORARY ISSUES: INNOVATIONS IN COUNSELING PRACTICE

CHAPTER NINE

INTERNET COUNSELING
Trends, Applications, and Ethical Issues

PAMELA K. S. PATRICK

Imagine a national conference attended by counselors, human services professionals, and a variety of counseling practitioners where the topic of one breakout session is Internet counseling. Following the presentation, the speaker opens up the question and answer period with, "What are your reactions to the presentation and to Internet counseling in general?" The responses are immediate, energetic, and challenging. From one participant comes, "I think this is just so exciting! To think that some forms of counseling can be offered using technology just makes sense," while another states, "This is opening counseling to quackery! Anyone can set up a website, put out their cyber-shingle, and end up hurting the public." As the discussion continues, others voice concerns for how to uphold ethical standards, how to manage payment and reimbursement, how to avoid the pitfalls of misrepresentation by clients, and how to handle malpractice and negligence risks. As the session comes to a close, the speaker is impressed with the complexity of the concerns voiced as well as the overall feel of the discussion as positive, hopeful, and thoughtful.

As the hypothetical conference session discussion reveals, the very notion of Internet counseling sets teeth on edge for some, whereas others see it as an exciting and innovative method to extend mental health and wellness care that capitalizes on technology. The counseling professions are continually changing in order to respond effectively to emerging needs of consumers and the professionals who deliver counseling services. Over the past few decades, familiar tried-and-true counseling service delivery methods have changed, others have been updated yet continue to be delivered within familiar formats, and in some cases, "traditional" counseling practice models have stopped offering services altogether. While the counseling professions have been undergoing these changes, often driven by social and political factors, computer technology has become both more sophisticated and accessible. Generations of children are now growing up with a high level of comfort and proficiency in computer use. Homes, schools, businesses, and public institutions now commonly use computers to conduct business, maintain records, communicate, educate, conduct business, and achieve parity of data access in a rapidly changing global community.

The extension of computer technology to the counseling professions, therefore, reflects a continuing *theme of change* within the helping professions and society as a whole. As a consequence, the counseling professions have begun the process of considering how to integrate computer technology in appropriate ways while adhering to the values and standards that guide practice, research, and education in an increasingly computer-saturated society.

With the advent of computer technology, and the increasingly user-friendly enhancements of this communication and data management device, counseling practitioners, educators, and researchers now have more options to provide mental health and wellness assistance than at any previous time in modern history. At the same time, consumers of counseling services now can access educational and psychological help in ways that have generated intense debate within the counseling professions (Childress, 1998; Fenichel, 2001; Holmes, 1997; Lee, 1998; Sussman, 1998) that continues to the present time.

New developments, however, bring both desired enhancements to the counseling profession as well as risks and cautions to the practitioner and consumer. In this chapter, issues associated with Internet counseling are addressed, with full recognition that as this material is written, the implications of Internet/online counseling are in a dynamic state of change, refinement, and ongoing debate.

DEFINING INTERNET COUNSELING

Simply stated, *Internet counseling* can be defined as the delivery of counseling or psychotherapy services through computer-mediated formats. Terms used to describe counseling conducted over the Internet include *Internet therapy* or *psychotherapy* (Pergament, 1998; Stofle, 1999); *cybertherapy, e-therapy,* or *e-mail therapy* (Jerome, 1999; Manhas-Baugus, 2001); *computer-mediated counseling* or *psychotherapy* (Cohen & Kerr, 1998; Lebow, 1998; Walther, 1996); and *online counseling* (Alleman, 2002; Wright, 2002). Varying combinations of the key terms *cyber*, *online* or *Internet* and *counseling* or *psychotherapy* appear to be interchangeable when describing counseling services delivered over the World Wide Web. For the purposes of this discussion, we will use the term *Internet counseling* to refer to the online delivery of mental health and wellness services by counselors.

The prime vehicle used to deliver counseling services is the Internet, or the World Wide Web. The Internet consists of a global network of connections among computers (hosts) whose purpose is the exchange of information or data. It is a "virtual" space "in which users send and receive e-mail, log in to remote computers, and browse databases of information" (Levine, Baroudi, & Young, 2000; Internet Glossary, www.mantex.co.uk/samples/glo.htm). The extensions of Internet-mediated communication methods change at an astounding rate. It is not unusual to note the announcement of a new form of Internet communication technology that appears in December, for example, to be considered "outdated" within months of the time of its first introduction.

Within this virtual communication space, counselors and consumers of counseling services are able to engage in varying forms of interaction through the touch of a keyboard or portable wireless miniature keypad. Participants using Internet communication become familiar with words and terms that are rapidly being woven into everyday conversation.

Professional interaction at the interpersonal, professional presentation, and publication levels of discourse are incorporating Internet jargon with more frequency.

Professionals and mental health service consumers are increasingly familiar with terms and phrases, for example, such as *e-mail, www, URL, chat room, website, blog, text message, spam, LOL* and *emoticons, link, attach the file to an e-mail*, and *search engine*. Each term or phrase represents a readily understandable element of Internet use that counselors can employ when engaged in Internet counseling activities. When working with children and adolescents, in fact, counselors are well advised to ensure that they are familiar with current terminology used by these increasingly technology-sophisticated clients. Counselors as well as counseling clients who use the Internet to access counseling services or information about counseling do not have to possess a high level of technological sophistication. Understanding the fundamental meaning of commonly used terms, however, is necessary in order to access a targeted website and to use the site effectively.

INTERNET COUNSELING: CONTEXTUAL ISSUES AND CHARACTERISTICS

The Internet is an intriguing concept, an evolving reality, and a lightning rod for debate regarding the nature of counseling. Through a series of key strokes, one can obtain in-depth information on all manner of health and wellness topics, access treatment information, identify potential providers of health care services (including mental health assistance), and interact with others who have a similar medical/health problem, overcoming geographical distance, time zones, and diversity of culture. The Internet makes this possible for millions of consumers on a daily basis as they participate in web discussion groups or blogs, post messages to message boards, or subscribe to listservs that provide desired information or resources. For others, however, access to Internet technology poses challenges due to issues associated with poverty, disability, and other factors associated with the "digital divide" (Warschauer, 2004).

Demographics of PC and Internet Use

For the consumer or potential consumer of Internet counseling, the reasons to select this new option rather than the face-to-face traditional format for counseling reflect a variety of personal needs, barriers to access or use of the face-to-face option, and preferences for the Internet method of engaging in the counseling process. With ownership of personal computers and broadband connectivity estimated at 80 percent by 2010 (Fitchard, 2003), the population of individuals who may consider Internet counseling holds the potential to increase at a stunning rate. This is especially impressive, given the estimation in 2002 that 165.75 million were "online," representing 59.1 percent of the population in the United States (NUA, 2003). The presence of personal computers at this level of penetration into the population suggests a general comfort with technology, recognition of its usefulness as a communication enhancer, and/or integration of the personal computer as an essential household management labor-saving device. Presence of computers in the home, at work, in public institutions, at cyber-cafes, in community centers, and so on, also coincides with public comfort and familiarity with online access, perceived importance of easy access, and desire to have user-friendly Internet connections.

Variance in Internet access between rural and urban households narrowed to 2 percent by 2000, increased in lower-income to upper-income households, within multicultural groups, and across educational levels, and includes all age groups (NTIA, 2002). Discrepancies in Internet access via personal computers among ethnic populations pose challenges to access to online services of all kinds, inclusive of Internet counseling. For example, cost is a factor for some Blacks and Latinos who are less likely to have access to in-home computers than non-Latinos (Fairlie, 2003). For the elderly who have limited financial resources, personal computer ownership may be addressed through public channels of access (e.g., public libraries or through free television access programs) (Keil, Meader, & Kvasny, 2003). Although limitations in ownership of home personal computer technology exist, the most pervasive pattern for this electronic information and communication medium can be characterized as increased ownership of personal computers, greater variation in methods to access the Internet (e.g., text messaging with cell phones), and extension of broadband or fast access to diverse geographical areas throughout the country.

The potential population of individuals, couples, families, and groups who may consider the Internet counseling option therefore expands with high rates of personal computer ownership or access (including laptop computers and handheld devices such as the Blackberry (Fels, Samers, & Robertson, 2003)) that are increasingly being recognized as "equalizers" that reduce barriers to communication, information, and opportunity. Clearly, many do not have access to the technical proficiencies or resources associated with computer/Internet use, but far more are able and receptive to learning how this pervasive device can be used in everyday and unique ways to enhance health and well-being.

Computers, the Internet, and Counseling Professionals

Users of computer technology include counseling professionals. The demographic statistics cited include counselors as part of the population of owners of PCs and users of the Internet. Counselors use computers to engage in communication with colleagues, in their personal lives, to obtain treatment information, to prepare and process business data and compensation claims, to engage in assessment activities, and to prepare and store records. Aside from the application of the technology to the counseling process itself, counselors are already a key group of professional users of computers and the Internet.

Counseling has traditionally relied on the establishment of an intimate, caring relationship between client and therapist that takes place in a face-to-face atmosphere of trust, security, and safety. Within the therapy setting, most often an office-like environment that is configured to be physically comfortable and aesthetically pleasing, the therapeutic process unfolds over the course of treatment sessions. In couple, family, or group settings, a similar format is used to work with clients to achieve identified treatment goals.

The face-to-face encounter incorporates visual observation of expression, body posture, and a host of nonverbal cues that are incorporated into the counselor's assessment and evaluation of the treatment process. Volumes have been written about the critical importance of the dynamic exchange that occurs between client and therapist during counseling sessions, all of which has enriched the field of counseling and guided counselors in training to develop both a theoretical framework and skill sets that support the therapeutic process. These qualitative elements of the counseling process continue to be salient to the profession, and there is no indication that these core qualities of the art and science of counseling will diminish in importance. However, with the advent of Internet counseling, the debate about how the "traditional" qualities of the counseling process can be expressed in a virtual environment has been intense.

On the one hand, some counselor professionals subscribe to the belief that counseling cannot be effective when the core elements of the human encounter are not *physically* or *visually* present. Thus, *Internet counseling* is an oxymoron: two words that when put together have a contradictory or sharply incongruous meaning. From this perspective, there is doubt that *Internet*, a virtual space that exists in an invisible location, can be linked with *counseling*, a term that is used to describe an intimate, intense face-to-face human interaction. The juxtaposition of these two terms is often the source for reactions ranging from confusion to varying degrees of indignation.

On the other hand, counselor professionals who have begun to pioneer use of the Internet to deliver *selected* counseling services to consumers find that the two seemingly contradictory terms can be blended effectively. These professionals have carefully begun to map the possibilities of Internet counseling in specific ways by establishing parameters of practice that serve as guideposts to those who wish to consider providing services via the Internet (American Counseling Association, 1999). While the profession will continue to debate the efficacy of Internet counseling, and must do so to ensure that standards of practice and ethical issues are addressed, the characteristics of Internet counseling, the user of Internet counseling, and issues associated with the providers of Internet counseling can be examined.

Issues surrounding the "rightness" of offering certain counseling services over the Internet perhaps reflect a core paradigm shift within the profession. There are those who will remain skeptical of Internet counseling based on strongly held beliefs about the philosophical and theoretical underpinnings of the therapeutic process. Within the debate about new and evolving methods to provide mental health services, the traditionalist view, as well as the contemporary view of the potential value of Internet counseling, must coexist. The needs of consumers for multiple pathways to access mental health and wellness counseling services dictates that multiple pathways be available. The Internet is one such pathway for consumers and providers.

The Appeal of Internet Counseling

The reasons that a potential consumer of mental health services would select the Internet counseling option can be categorized as combinations of internal and external factors. Descriptions of these factors reflect contemporary and emerging personal motivations and many of the social demands that directly influence use of mental health services. Some of these same factors may influence counselors to consider offering Internet counseling and will be the subject of discussion in later sections of this chapter.

Access. With availability of personal computers connected to the Internet, a world of information, services, entertainment, work-related resources, and opportunity to explore one's interests is possible for each user. The implication of uncomplicated entrée to information, by anyone, at any time, from any location, can be summed up as *easy access*. Individuals and families can be involved in counseling via the Internet who would not be able to participate in the therapeutic process otherwise (Lee, 2000; Boer, 2001; Dunaway, 2000; King, Engi, & Poulos, 1998; Sussman, 1998).

Easy access represents the most logical of rationales for seeking counseling from an Internet counselor (Robson & Robson 2000; Sussman, 1998). Far too many individuals live in remote, rural areas where a minimal level of mental health services is available. For these individuals, there is no access to mental health services other than through the Internet or, in some cases, through telephone counseling. From the privacy of their homes, a client can engage in Internet counseling with a professional who may be located many hundreds of miles away from the home of the consumer. Thus, barriers of long-distance travel, and the time necessary to travel, are eliminated with Internet counseling.

Individuals who are handicapped or disabled, and who often are not able to access counseling services offered in locations that require travel, verbal communication, or face-to-face encounter, can have increased access to counseling services delivered online (Griffiths, 2001; Dunaway, 2000). For individuals who can use voice-activated software or other assistive devices to activate and use computers, participation in Internet counseling sessions offers an option to address personal issues or problems that is reflective of the technological marvels of the computer age. Removal of barriers to access is perhaps one of the most persuasive arguments in support of Internet counseling, and for the disabled, availability of counseling services by qualified professionals offers mental health treatment that previous generations were denied.

Internet counseling offers groups of consumers access who are often "invisible" to the dominant society. For example, family caregivers are often isolated socially, unable to leave dependent loved ones unsupervised, and, at the same time, can experience intense emotional distress linked to the demands of caring for others on a 24/7 basis. The psychological distress associated with the caregiving role is intense, often generating mental health conditions such as depression and anxiety (Li & Sprague, 2002; Marks, Lambert, & Choi, 2002; Townsend, 2002; Chambers, Ryan, & Connor, 2001; Cummins, 2001; Laditka & Pappas-Rogich, 2001). In addition, preexisting caregiver mental health disorders can be exacerbated by the demands of caring for chronically medically or mentally ill family members, aged spouses or relatives, or relatives with long-term, life-threatening illnesses or conditions. For these individuals, counseling services that could assist with psychological coping, stress management, and development of strategies to manage the care-giving responsibilities they have assumed are often out of reach. They are not able to leave loved ones unattended, travel to a counselor's office or clinic, or afford the services of practitioners qualified to assist them. For those familiar with home personal computers, Internet counseling offers access to counseling and perhaps a window of hope that they would otherwise not have.

Because computers offer the possibility of communication in ways that were unimagined in previous generations, language barriers can now be overcome via computer technology and software that allow two or more people to converse in different languages (Babel Fish Translation, 2003; Smartlink, 2003; Systran, 2003). Translation from one language to another can occur via the computer, thus facilitating verbal text-based communication. Applied to the counselor–client relationship, this capability now offers access to clients with limited or minimal proficiency in a therapist's native language, or vice versa, to communicate in text-based exchanges within the parameters of the counseling relationship.

Efficiency.   Closely linked with easy access is the inherent efficiency found with Internet counseling. *Efficiency* refers to the optimal use of a client's time and resources to connect to mental health services. With Internet counseling, the client does not wait in a waiting room and does not have to contend with natural elements that can impede access to a counselor's office, and it can take place in an asynchronous manner. For the client, access, then, is optimized by the anytime/anywhere qualities of Internet access. When traveling, for example, a client can continue with counseling sessions so long as Internet access can be accomplished using a personal computer or laptop.

Efficiency is also facilitated by the medium itself. The process of preparing and typing responses inserts a "pause" in the response-reply format of the typical counseling session. With Internet counseling, the client and therapist reply to one another, asynchronously (not in real time), thus allowing time to think, reflect, and review previous session material. For many clients, this becomes an appealing aspect of the interaction.

> Carlin is struggling with a major life decision and has been participating in Internet counseling sessions with Dr. B. In the last session, Dr. B made three observations of factors that might be hindering Carlin's capacity to make the decision she stated repeatedly that she had to make. The time between her last contact and the next one is used by Carlin to formulate two scenarios of decision making. She types these out, reviews them, and reconsiders her previous replies to Dr. B's observations of her struggle. In this process, she begins to see the path to a solution. She forwards her two scenarios, her thoughts and reactions while she worked on the issue, and her solution to Dr. B. For this client, the process of working through the problem she faced took place while traveling, using her laptop computer, and storing each segment of her analysis over a two-day period. She had made an agreement with Dr. B to send a reply by a specific date in spite of a busy work-related travel schedule.

Employment Compatibility.   For some potential mental health counseling clients, the requirements to fulfill employment duties prevent involvement in counseling at a level of frequency that is desired, or that would be indicated to achieve treatment goals. Time away from the job may simply not be reasonable from the client's point of view. In such cases, Internet counseling represents a viable option for clients to continue with mental health treatment during off-work hours, on a regularly scheduled basis, and with consistency.

The location of an individual's place of employment may also present a significant barrier to counseling services. Although data are lacking on the demographics of users of Internet counseling services, it is recognized that with the extensions of wireless Internet access, geographical areas that previously had limited and unreliable access to the Internet will increasingly not face this barrier. The rapidity with which past technological advances have been made suggests that access to the Internet, and Internet counseling services, will be unlimited in the near future.

Privacy.   For both clients and counselors, the Internet environment is characterized by a form of invisibility. Unless each party to a communication uses a miniature camera linked to a PC (e.g., videochat format with live voice and video such as "cuseeme"—www.cuseeme.com), the therapeutic relationship is typically formed without a visual image of each person, or audio transmission of voice tone or inflection. Thus, a high degree of personal privacy is characteristic of Internet counseling (Wright, 2002; Boer, 2001; Sussman, 1998). For many, this is an attractive characteristic of the Internet counseling method and a quality that increases the likelihood that counseling assistance will be sought.

This sense of personal privacy, combined with convenience, can therefore be an inducement to access counseling services for those who might not otherwise consider seeking counseling that required loss of this level of privacy. An additional feature of the privacy afforded Internet counseling participants is the hypothesized reduction in concern about being stereotyped as "mentally ill" when using mental health services in traditional formats. It is not unusual for some clients to have experienced intense levels of anxiety when initiating counseling services that might include being observed entering or leaving the practitioner's office. For some, this anxiety can be so intense that the client will avoid the assistance that counseling provides in order to avoid any perceived stigma attached to the process.

Privacy also becomes a crucial factor in the decision to access counseling when issues such as shame or abuse have been experienced by the potential client. Beginning to explore these issues in the privacy that is created by the online environment may provide an additional inducement to explore Internet counseling. For one who may never have voiced feelings or memories about previous painful experiences, for example, beginning the description in written format in the privacy of one's home can be perceived to be less threatening than in a face-to-face encounter. The material can be examined and reviewed before submitting it to the therapist, similar to the manner in which many counselors use journaling or other expressive activities to access psychological healing processes. Privacy, therefore, can be a factor that leads some clients to consider Internet counseling, and as such, it is an *option* that can increase the probability that certain clients who need psychological assistance will do so.

For others who select Internet counseling as a preferred first step (or only step) to seek counseling, issues associated with physical appearance and characteristics are diminished or eliminated in the online context. The focus for the client or the therapist is directed to the material presented in the text that is exchanged and not influenced by outward appearance (i.e., visual anonymity) that includes ethnic or racial characteristics, body type, evidence of injury or malformation, or other physical traits (Joinson, 2001; Robson & Robson, 2000). For the client, the comfort of presenting the self without concern for how these characteristics would be viewed or evaluated by the therapist, as an unknown helping professional, could be a powerful driver toward Internet counseling services.

Text-Reliance Attraction.   Related to the privacy that is afforded to the Internet counseling client is the method used to communicate between therapist and client: the written word.

Whether in a chat format, e-mail, or asynchronous counseling interactions, the client and the counselor are communicating through writing (Wright, 2002; Wright & Chung, 2001; Murphy & Mitchell, 1998). The advantages of this format include the measured pacing of interaction. The client and the counselor have time to compose replies, feedback, and analysis, or compose questions, or present arguments or state positions, or to use the interval between postings to consider what has been written. This kind of "pause" can be therapeutically valuable in the counseling process (Wright, 2002; Miller & Gergen, 1998) for both client and therapist.

With Internet counseling, a record of interaction is created and is retained by both client and therapist for future review or reference. Whether in real or asynchronous time, each person has access to the conversation that has taken place. This material can then be used for review purposes later, to refer to when questions arise between sessions, or to serve as the record of treatment progress or research. Drawbacks to the transcript as archive of sessions also exist (e.g., protecting confidentiality according to professional standards of practice and exercising caution and care in writing responses to clients in recognition of the limitations of the non–face-to-face context). For example, casual comments about progress or lack of progress in counseling made by the counselor can be hurtful or interpreted as criticism.

For many clients, the activity of writing enhances awareness of feelings, thoughts, and memories. As part of the therapeutic process, accessing emotions coincides with addressing problems that led to help-seeking behavior. Writing about one's feelings and thoughts in a journal or narrative format, with the guidance of the therapist, becomes a powerful mechanism to make progress in achieving treatment goals. When viewed from this perspective, Internet counseling is another option that uses writing for therapeutic purposes in addition to using the written word to engage in interpersonal interaction. The downside of this characteristic of Internet counseling is associated with the client's facility as a writer and typist. Although not a factor that can prevent effective use of Internet counseling services, the capacity to type and write at a proficient level certainly enhances the ability to engage in this process.

Another perceived benefit of text-based counseling communication is personal freedom. When writing about one's feelings, thoughts, experiences, history, memories, or current life circumstances, use of the writing medium to compose and conceptualize the material is facilitated when the client determines when to write, where to write, and how much of the written material will be shared. Although other clients share this ability when writing is used as part of face-to-face (FTF) counseling, in the online environment, the social pressure or expectations to produce writing for the therapist to review may be reduced in the virtual environment. In this way, the client exercises an additional layer of control over how much personal information or expression is shared with the counselor and how it will be phrased and presented.

For many, verbal exchange is comfortable and may actually limit identification of psychological issues that are linked to emotional distress. Facility with the spoken words can "mask" feelings and conflicts and extend the time in counseling while the client skirts issues or struggles with personal comfort in the therapeutic encounter. In the Internet counseling environment, the person who is facile with spoken words in the FTF context may find it a challenge to express him- or herself when required to do so as part of Internet counseling. These potential clients may avoid Internet counseling for this reason. Or, due to circumstances that preclude FTF counseling, these clients may find that although online counseling becomes the most viable option, it requires reliance on text-based communication that removes the use of FTF interaction patterns from the exchange. From this perspective, the requirement to write to another person (the therapist), or to write about one's inner experiences, worries, fears, memories, or problems calls on skills and commitment that otherwise would be avoided or delayed. For clients who are motivated to seek counseling, and cannot access the traditional FTF format, learning to write-through-the-therapy is a unique challenge.

The skill set of writing is not required in traditional talk therapy. The therapist and the client may elect to incorporate written materials into the therapy process or use it as the starting point for exploration of difficult, sensitive, or painful issues. In Internet counseling, however, writing and the written word become the vehicle that makes counseling possible. Nonverbal cues are missing in this format, whereas use of expressive techniques within the confines of the text-based format are highlighted.

A personal preference for a text-based counseling venue may be evident for some who engage in Internet counseling. Current generations of young adults have been raised with computer technology as "normal" tools that enhance entertainment, education, and learning, and that serve as information resource devices. Consumers of mental health services will be derived from this increasingly sophisticated population of computer users (Alleman, 2002; Robson & Robson, 2000; Guterman & Kirk, 1999). For these technology users, as well as an expanding cohort of older, mature adult computer technology users, personal comfort with computer communication may serve to "normalize" help-seeking behavior in the form of Internet counseling. One might hypothesize, in fact, that computer technology users with high levels of personal comfort in text-based communication would be more likely to access counseling services, when in need, via the Internet than in a traditional format. Although research evidence for this hypothesized relationship is lacking, anecdotal and preliminary research suggests that high levels of affective expression do occur in the Internet counseling format (Alleman, 2002; Collie, Mitchell, & Murphy, 2001; Freeny, 2001; Anthony, 2000). For these individuals, skill in expressing oneself in text-based interactions is preferred, less anxiety provoking, and more appealing as a primary method to address personal issues or problems. Thus, Internet counseling represents an extension of options to access counseling that otherwise might not occur.

Internet counseling also offers the hesitant client an opportunity to "try on" the counseling experience with less investment of time, financial resources, or personal inconvenience than with the traditional counseling option. It is possible that anxiety associated with the FTF encounter may delay or block some clients' help-seeking behavior. In the virtual environment, however, some of these barriers may be lifted due to the structure of the text-based method of communicating. Clients retain control over when a session is addressed by when he or she logs on to the computer; the therapist also has this degree of freedom to manage time and to plan replies.

Nature of Psychological Disorder.   Certain psychological disorders pose barriers to the client considering counseling. Individuals who suffer from phobic disorders—such as agoraphobia, acute bereavement, and psychological disorders associated with debilitating medical conditions—can participate in Internet counseling as the initial step that leads to a FTF encounter for more intensive therapy, as the sole format for receiving counseling services, or as part of the follow-up and aftercare process associated with inpatient or out-patient counseling (Klein & Richards, 2001; Carlbring, Westling, Ljungstrand, Ekselius, & Andersson, 2001; Freeny, 2001; Graham, Frances, Kenwright, & Marks, 2000; King & Poulos, 1998). As an adjunct to FTF counseling, Internet counseling offers a source of support and continued connection to the therapeutic process that can enhance recovery and serve as the "bridge" from no therapeutic assistance to a time when the client can access FTF counseling. In addition, for those clients residing in rural areas that lack mental health counseling services who have psychological diagnoses that can be addressed via Internet counseling, the Internet-based modality offers hope and help.

Cost Factors.   Dependent on the Internet counseling services accessed, there is some evidence that Internet counseling services are less costly than many fee-for-service rates in the FTF environment (Dunaway, 2000; Heinlen, Welfel, Richmond, & Rak, 2003). Key to evaluating cost factors is recognition that Internet counseling "sessions" are typically asynchronous and are not based on the same standard of therapist–client time found in the FTF office setting and typically do not conform to traditional office hours. For example, clients can write to the therapist in an asynchronous manner and read replies from the counselor at any time of the day or night. The costs associated with delayed communication that can occur when a client must contact a counselor, set up an appointment, travel to the office, and arrange work or personal life schedules to attend counseling sessions is not present in the asynchronous Internet counseling process. Cost-benefit analyses of Internet counseling compared to FTF counseling remains to be conducted across multiple venues in which these services are made available (e.g., comparable diagnoses of clients receiving counseling in each format, evaluation of Internet counseling practitioners' variance in fee schedules, services provided, formats for payment for services, and evaluation of insurance reimbursement policies regarding mental health service payment schedules).

Internet counseling "sessions" may be billed to the consumer for specific time increments of the counselor's time (e.g., in 15-minute increments), for a series of sessions that are agreed on at the onset of the counseling process, be "free of charge" for the first session, or require credit card information on a "secure" site before counseling begins. Variation in payment for Internet counseling services currently is the norm in this form of counseling. A search on the Web, in 2003, using terms such as *online psychotherapy* and *cost*, produced approximately 200 "hits" that provided information about the cost of Internet counseling services. By 2005, the total "hits" had risen to over 550 references. Many provider sites highlight the issue of cost effectiveness of Internet counseling services, either as individual practitioners or as a group of counselors offering web-based counseling.

Clearly, the issue of cost is of concern to consumers in an era of managed care curtailment of coverage for mental health diagnoses (i.e., limitations on the annual number of sessions covered or need to seek preauthorization prior to accessing mental health services). Charges for Internet therapy will vary with website provider information on rates, credentials, time increments and charges, and use of credit cards or other forms of payment (Ainsworth, 2004). Review of websites indicates that payment is expected from the client directly, and if the client then wishes to pursue reimbursement of a health insurance provider, the client assumes that responsibility. Thus, Internet counseling is a private pay service that in some cases may be less costly than similar services rendered in a FTF setting.

Risk Takers.   Although difficult to measure in terms of research, and only hypothesized here, it is possible that some clients who prefer Internet counseling over the FTF format do so because they are drawn to the most contemporary, "leading edge" option supported by technology. Comfort with computer technology, which is linked to the characteristics of convenience and efficiency in the privacy of one's home, draws this consumer to the Internet when seeking help with personal problems, searching for information to solve a problem, coaching to learn skills to solve problems or to enhance well-being, or to begin a process of gaining insight into thoughts and feelings. For these individuals, the quality of being "first," or "first adopters," may be what attracts them to Internet counseling. The question arises, then, as to the benefit these clients receive from Internet counseling when the motivation to establish a counseling relationship is based on the "adventure" of the encounter versus the personal commitment to address personal problems. As with many of the reasons to access Internet counseling that have been reviewed, the "risk-taker hypothesis" requires research to verify its accuracy.

Reasons to access Internet counseling range from intense need based on the lack of any other mental health counseling services to personal preference to use a hi-tech device to address personal problems in a text-based format. As illustrated in Table 9.1, the appeal of Internet

TABLE 9.1   Appeal of Internet Counseling

APPEAL FACTOR	CHARACTERISTICS OF THE APPEAL
Access	Overcomes barriers of time, distance, geographical location, disability, confinement or travel limitations, language differences
Efficiency	Uses consumer and provider time on anytime, anyplace basis
Employment compatibility	Employment schedule/demands can be overcome associated with shift work, travel requirements, work location changes
Nature of psychological disorder	Psychological problems with FTF meetings avoided; allows those confined with complex medical conditions to seek counseling; offers continuing connection with counselor that transcends appointment schedules
Cost factors	May be less costly when compared to traditional counseling; fee for service basis attractive to providers; eliminates travel and transportation costs; reduces scheduling time; changing work schedules to attend sessions avoided; fee schedules vary; third-party reimbursement not available
Privacy	Non-FTF counseling viewed by some as a positive feature; clients avoid visual stereotyping based on physical characteristics; reduced anxiety associated with FTF interaction or disclosure of highly sensitive personal information
Text reliance	Measured pace of writing preferred; provides transcript of interactions; can use narratives as therapeutic tool and key treatment strategy; freedom to express self in privacy without interruption; can promote deeper levels of self-reflection; strong facility with writing an asset; can "try on" counseling at a distance
Risk taker	Appeals to innovators and first adopters of new counseling delivery system; high level of comfort with computer technology facilitates engagement

counseling encompasses a variety factors, characteristics, and motivations that may lead consumers, or counseling professionals, to explore this technology-based delivery system. As one contemporary method to become involved in counseling, Internet counseling will continue to attract some while lacking in appeal for others. This reality applies to both consumers and practitioners. Clearly, research attention that seeks to answer the question "Why do people choose Internet counseling?" is needed before the counseling professions can fully address the complex issues that it generates.

Drawbacks of Internet Counseling

The traditional method in engaging in psychotherapy consists of the face-to-face meetings in which the therapist and client are in close physical proximity, speaking and interacting in real time, and are surrounded by the complex, diverse, and finely nuanced behavioral cues that are visible and expressed in that context. For both therapist and client, this environment is rich in nonverbal communication, surrounding stimuli, and physical elements that are absent in the online counseling format. The absence of the nonverbal informative qualities found in the FTF encounter suggests to some counseling professionals that Internet counseling is "a poor substitute for face-to-face communication" (Day & Schneider, 2000, p. 203) or "cannot be compared to face-to-face counseling" (Anthony, 2000, p. 626).

It is clear that Internet counseling is *not the same* as counseling that occurs in an FTF context, and thus, from a logical point of view, it cannot be measured against a single psychotherapy delivery system as either good, bad, or neutral. Recognition that Internet counseling is *different*, not better than traditional counseling, suggests that a review of its limits and problems, as summarized in Table 9.2, will further enlighten our understanding of its role in mental health counseling service delivery.

Confidentiality Not Guaranteed.   Much concern has been voiced about issues of confidentiality in the Internet counseling environment. Counselors who offer Internet counseling services should provide specific information and guidelines that promote confidentiality of information exchanged over the Internet, yet there is inconsistency in compliance (Heinlen, Welfel, Richmond, & Rak, 2003). Sophisticated encryption programs can be used to "scramble" messages to and from client and therapist, yet risks to confidentiality of the text-based communication record remain. For example, a client using a home personal computer may have counseling session transcripts viewed by family members who also have access to the device (Paris, 2001). If a computer is used at one's workplace for this activity, employers have access to that material as well.

Media reports describe dramatic "hacking" events that typically consist of ingenious attacks on specific computer security systems of governmental agencies or high-profile businesses. As social protest, these incidents reflect the risk that is inherent in a virtual communication environment when an individual or group wishes to gain access to a specific system as a prank or to attempt to damage the system. For the mental health client using Internet counseling services, risk of having a home computer system hacked most likely is low. However, as a symbol of the vulnerability of the Internet to unauthorized access to private records and data, it must be viewed as part of the risk to confidentiality of counseling information (Segall, 2000).

TABLE 9.2   Drawbacks of Internet Counseling

DRAWBACK	CHARACTERISTICS OF INTERNET COUNSELING
Confidentiality not guaranteed	Specific encryption and confidentiality safeguards essential; protection from computer hackers required
Encounters viewed as shallow	Method is impersonal; relies on an electronic device to discuss intimate problems—an oxymoron; no visual or behavioral cues to assist with assessment or counseling
Disinhibition effect	Over–self-disclosure can occur; civility in communication can be ignored due to visual anonymity; intensity of interaction can be superficial or inauthentic
Not applicable to complicated mental disorders	Exclusion of clients who are at risk for suicide or homicide or who have complex psychiatric disorders (e.g., self-mutilation, eating disorders, dissociative disorders); not useful with clients who engage in subterfuge or deception or for clients who can best be cared for when direct observation of behavioral and psychological cues is essential to treatment effectiveness
Counseling psychotherapy	Not possible to conduct psychotherapy over the Internet; the nature of Internet counseling may be a form of psycho-education, information sharing, or conversation only; research is needed to determine the parameters of Internet counseling and the existence of Internet psychotherapy
Consumer protection issues	No regulation of Internet counseling or websites that offer services; potential for deception is high; unlicensed practitioners can offer services; ethical violation risk may be significant; authenticity information varies from site to site

Shallow Encounters?   There are mixed opinions on the level of interpersonal intimacy that is established in Internet counseling. Reports of high levels of expressed feeling and self-disclosure are remarked on as a positive, but perhaps not anticipated, finding (Freeny, 2001; Grohol, 2000; Anthony, 2000). The *impersonal nature* of communication that uses an electronic mechanical device and an invisible cybernetwork to discuss *personal problems*, feelings, and life struggles would seem to be an oxymoron—two incongruent activities existing simultaneously in the same space. In the FTF encounter in counseling, visual cues associated with body posture, movements, gestures, facial expressions, and the overt as well as nuanced qualities of speech and discussion are present and are included in the assessment process.

In a virtual session, taking place at different times and across time zones without access to this observational information, the therapist must rely on typed text, skillful questioning delivered in writing, and use of expressive icons or shorthand. For example, emoticons and acronyms help to enliven a text-based exchange. Proficient computer communicators integrate phrases such as *laughing out loud* with LOL, *by the way* with BTW, and *in my humble opinion* with IMHO. Being expressive is not limited by the online format; observation (without webcams technology) of the client's behavior is. Thus, overall, the online counseling process provides a method to learn about the client's affective and cognitive state in a limited manner that is applicable to specific client populations. These encounters are not the same as those in a traditional setting, yet they are able to reveal issues that the client wishes to address in a setting that allows for highly expressive written exchange.

Disinhibition Effect.   A somewhat surprising phenomenon has been observed with reference to Internet counseling and online communication. It is called the "disinhibition effect" (Alleman, 2002; Joinson, 1998; Walther, 1996; Suler, 1996) or the "intimate stranger phenomenon" (Snow, 2001). *Disinhibition* refers to the level of disclosure that occurs in an online context. Online therapists report high levels of disclosure (Alleman, 2002; Freeny, 2001; Joinson, 2001) often at a rate that is much more rapid and intense in comparison to how this process evolves in traditional counseling sessions. It is hypothesized that the capacity to retain a degree of anonymity facilitates the ease with which online clients immerse themselves in the disclosure of personal information and explore sensitive personal issues. In other online contexts (e.g., chat rooms), establishment of intimate relationships has been reported with reference to romantic affairs and high levels of self-disclosure as well as giving emotional support to others (Donn & Sherman, 2002; Whitty, 2002; Levine, 2000; Nice & Katzev, 1998).

Whether self-disclosure and expressions of emotional intimacy are of the same quality or intensity as those expressed in traditional therapy is a research question worthy of investigation. However, the argument can be made that the level of self-disclosure and expression of emotion in each context are to be evaluated based on the context in which they occur, and as such should not be compared to a single standard of "validity" derived from the traditional FTF model of providing counseling.

Not Applicable to Complicated Mental Disorders.   Psychotherapy methods are developed, researched, and applied to client populations that will most benefit from each treatment approach. Similarly, Internet counseling methods are applicable to specific client populations and not appropriate for others. Experts in this area of practice suggest that a number of client populations are not suitable for online counseling due to the severity of the disorder.

Individuals who are at risk for self-injurious behavior or who pose a threat to the safety of others are not suitable for Internet counseling (Robson & Robson, 2000; Alleman, 2002; Stofle, 2001). Websites produced by licensed mental health counselors or psychologists who adhere to professional codes of ethics and standards of practice include specific limitations to accepting clients who are suicidal or homicidal. For example, at thetherapistonthenet.com, the following disclaimer is prominently posted:

> This service is not intended for individuals who are contemplating suicide or are suffering from a severe mental or emotional disorder. If this describes you, please contact a mental health professional or contact a suicide prevention hotline in your area. (www.thetherapistonthenet.com)

A review of current websites of licensed counseling professions provides insights into the consistency of these advisories.

The ethical and competent Internet counselor will take measures to ensure that he or she adheres to the standards of practice that coincides with licensure and certification requirements and thus prepares them to assess suicide risk. In addition, the licensed practitioner has access to published standards of practice and must ensure that these Internet counseling specific guidelines are followed (e.g., ACA Code of Ethics, 2005). It is reasonable to assume, however, that some online clients will enter a state of suicide risk that was not present or anticipated at the outset of Internet counseling. For this reason, the online counselor must obtain necessary identifying information about the client in a manner quite like that of the therapist in a traditional setting to establish a baseline of understanding of the individual's behavior. With this information, the therapist is better equipped to evaluate the responses of the client and determine if a substantial change has occurred that suggests risk for suicide or self-injurious behavior. Therefore, the online counselor who is compliant with professional ethical standards takes measures to avoid establishing a counseling relationship with at-risk clients, and takes measures to ensure client safety when a change in status signals movement to an at-risk state.

Because Internet counseling is not for everyone, certain clients with complex psychiatric diagnoses should not use Internet counseling (Suler, 2001). Instead, they need to seek the professional counseling assistance of qualified mental health professionals near their geographical location. For example, Stofle (2001) states that individuals with a borderline personality disorder or a psychotic mental state should not be treated online. Completion of a detailed intake form prepared by the online therapist and available at the therapist's website would include this information as part of the initial data collection procedures. The impersonal nature of the online environment, and the need of these clients for the personal interaction and observation that can take place only in the FTF setting, directs the Internet counselor to refer these potential clients to professionals close to their location.

Complex psychiatric conditions such as self-mutilation, dissociation, or other severe psychiatric behaviors that can be missed or overlooked in text-based counseling are unsuitable for online counseling. Clients struggling with such severe mental disorders must be seen by mental health professionals in FTF settings in which visual contact and observation can more effectively be used to assess needs and provide treatment. When text is the primary form of communication, it can be used to deceive self and others as to current status or change in condition, and/or to assume a false identity that reflects a dissociative state. Certainly the argument can be made that clients in the FTF setting also can deceive the therapist. Deception can occur in both settings, and the astute, qualified mental health professional is able to identify such behavior in both settings. As another area of research in Internet counseling, determining the best "fit" for client/diagnosis and the best counseling method is essential as this growing practice area expands.

Certain medical conditions have significant psychological/psychiatric features that reduce the appropriateness of Internet counseling as the sole method of engaging in the psychotherapy process. When the client's physical appearance must be observed by the therapist during counseling sessions, the online method of providing counseling is not appropriate. Clients with eating disorders, such as anorexia, benefit from observations made by the therapist of physical appearance and status of well-being. Individuals with neurological disorders involving balance, coordination, or cognitive processing changes cannot be observed in the virtual environment. Direct observation during FTF counseling sessions can identify important signs of distress, exacerbation of condition, or presence of previously unidentified symptoms. In an asynchronous environment, for example, a client who is suffering from cognitive impairment could "mask" symptoms. For instance, the communication between counselor and client does not take place in real time; thus, the client unknowingly may select "good" times to engage in writing that effectively prevents identification of emerging deficits. In such a hypothetical situation, the client could continue in Internet counseling for some time without being evaluated or diagnosed.

Psychotherapy versus Counseling.   Depending on who is defining terms, psychotherapy, e-therapy, and Internet counseling are considered to be different activities (Maheu & Gordon,

2000; Metanoia, 2001a). Practitioners may or may not make similar distinctions. For some, *counseling* is an inclusive term that represents a wide, often complex array of services provided by the mental health professional. Others use the term *psychotherapy* to signify the same set of activities, but with an emphasis on the level of intensity of the interactions and length of treatment. Concern arises within the counseling professions regarding how or if Internet counseling can accommodate psychotherapy. From another perspective, counselors question what actually takes place in Internet counseling when compared to psychoeducation, conversation, or forming a cyberfriendship. Determining the parameters of Internet counseling, Internet psychotherapy, helpful conversation with an expert, and other descriptions of what takes place between counselor professional and client requires in-depth research and exploration.

Consumer Protection Issues.   Protection of the users of counseling services is a cornerstone of the profession. In an Internet counseling environment, however, ensuring that consumers are protected must be viewed from a different perspective. The safeguards that must be in place are different from those in a traditional setting regarding how they are implemented in cyberspace. The consumer protection issues that must be addressed by Internet counselors are highlighted by the reality that the Internet is an open, unregulated environment. For example, anyone can construct a website advertising counseling services. In a recent study by Heinlen, Welfel, Richmond, and Rak (2003), a survey of websites offering Internet counseling found that eight months after the initial review of available sites, 37 percent were no longer "up" or operational. Additionally, of the 136 sites sampled by these researchers, none was found to be compliant with the National Board of Certified Counselors (2005). Consumers seeking Internet counseling services, if not advised to carefully check the licensure/certification status of the provider, can assume that a well-constructed website reflects the authenticity of the counselor's background and skill. Since licensure or certification is designed to ensure that consumers can expect competency and preparation of the provider according to standards that are verified by the state, the nonlicensed practitioner poses a threat to the well-being of consumers.

In traditional counseling settings (e.g., private practice or a mental health clinic), a counselor is permitted to offer mental health services within the state of licensure or certification and within the defined parameters of the licensure or certification scope of practice. If practice is to occur in a different state, the counselor must seek licensure in that state. With the Internet, state borders can easily be breached to provide services across state lines. Consumer safety can be directly impacted by such breaches of licensure. For example, individuals who are unqualified to provide counseling services in one state can provide counseling in another state via a website that can be accessed from any point on the globe. Issues of legal liability and risk to consumers are substantial when this occurs. For injured or harmed consumers, questions arise about where to file a claim—in the state of client residence or in the state of provider residence. Presently, the client's state statute(s) that govern liability are considered in determining how a claim would be processed (Metanoia, 2001b; Hughes, 2000; Sussman, 1998). Until such time that claims against cybertherapists are brought into the judicial system and decisions are made about the geographical locus of liability, this issue will remain hazy and poses potential harm to consumers.

In spite of state licensure/certification rules/statutes that specifically prohibit online counseling by providers (e.g., Texas) (White, 2002), there is evidence that counseling services by licensed providers are being offered in states (e.g., Texas) where they do not have licensure. This appears to be taking place without consequences to these providers (Grohol, 2000). The National Board of Certified Counselors' Principle 13 regarding Internet counseling addresses this issue:

> Local, state, provincial, and national statutes as well as codes of professional membership organizations, professional certifying bodies, and state or provincial licensing boards need to be reviewed. Also, as varying state rules and opinions exist on questions pertaining to whether Internet counseling takes place in the Internet counselor's location or the Internet client's location, it is important to review codes in the counselor's home jurisdiction as well as the client's. Internet counselors also consider carefully local customs regarding age of consent and child abuse reporting, and liability insurance policies need to be reviewed to determine if the practice of Internet counseling is a covered activity. (www.nbcc.org/webethics2)

Questions arise regarding the *actual* impact of state regulation of counselor practice in this evolving area of specialization. It appears that the value of licensure and/or certification could become muted or devalued when it is not a requirement to practice from state to state—so long as it is Internet counseling or so long as the provider avoids prohibitions to do so across state lines.

Another illustration clearly outlines the limits of Internet counseling for licensed counselor professionals. California law mandates that online mental health services be provided only by a licensed clinical psychologist or physician (Sussman, 1998) to California residents. How this proscription is reinforced to ensure that California psychologists do not offer services to non-California residents is unclear. In addition, questions also arise regarding the extent or existence of malpractice insurance coverage when services are provided over the Internet.

The American Counseling Association Code of Ethics states that "counselors . . . do not provide on-line counseling services to clients located in states in which counselors are not licensed" (ACA, 1999, p. 4). The question then becomes, with reference to Dr. Wilson, a fictitious licensed counselor in this state: If the ethical standard is to avoid practicing across state lines, why would a counselor who otherwise abides by and supports the ethics of the profession engage in prohibited practice? The impact of Dr. Wilson's behavior on consumers is troubling, since it suggests that there may be cause for concern that other violations of ethical standards could occur. Consumers may not be aware of the significance of such behavior by a counselor professional who he views as an expert.

Websites offering online counseling vary in depth of information provided, clarity of stated limitations, comprehensiveness of intake information gathered, disclaimers, crisis referral information, and description of provider credentials (Heinlen et al, 2003). Consumers who are in psychological or emotional distress and are seeking help may not be skilled in determining a qualified provider from an unqualified one when the website "looks" good and is visually appealing. For the consumer, the existence of a website devoted to Internet counseling does not automatically indicate authenticity or ethical practice.

The issues associated with Internet counseling are obviously complex, and many are yet to be resolved by the counseling professions. Risk to consumers exists with this form of counseling, as with all forms of counseling. With the Internet, however, the virtual environment has the aura of a "new frontier" with some of the challenge, allure, and perhaps a false sense of security that is unlike any other form of counseling activity. Comfort with the use of a home or office PC, however, does not equate with competence to begin to offer Internet counseling services. How this unique form of counseling service delivery can be effectively and ethically practiced must be analyzed cautiously and carefully.

PRACTICE IMPLICATIONS OF INTERNET COUNSELING

Thinking about setting up an Internet counseling practice would include varying combinations of excitement, anxiety, curiosity, and recognition that much needs to be done to ensure that the outcomes could be managed. For the purposes of discussion, Ms. Carter will be the subject of an exploration of the issues associated with the decision to initiate an Internet counseling practice.

When first considering this option, Ms. Carter considers that she has been in practice with a small group of four licensed counselor professionals, including a clinical social worker, a psychologist, a mental health counselor, and a marriage and family therapist, for 15 months while she has been completing postgraduate supervision. She recently completed this requirement and successfully achieved licensure status. She has been intrigued with the possibilities that the Internet offers for delivery of counseling services, and is now ready to investigate how it could be initiated.

Ms. Carter will need to address a host of issues before making the decision to initiate an Internet counseling practice, and another set of issues must be addressed regarding the structure of such a practice should she decide to pursue the proposal further. Making the decision to start up an Internet counseling practice will require the development of a feasibility study that includes each of the topics summarized in Table 9.3. These topics, as well as others that can be identified when focusing on a specific form of Internet counseling (e.g., links to websites for self-help support groups when the counselor specializes in substance abuse Internet counseling), are considered essential during the decision-making process (Alleman, 2002; Gross, 2000; Suler, 2001; Baltimore, 2000).

Self-Assessment and Self-Reflection

Some forms of counseling may be intriguing due to the innovation involved, the uniqueness of the proposed treatment method, or, in some cases, how it is applied in unusual situations. For the counselor professional who is intrigued by the possibilities that Internet counseling suggests, it is essential that a period of self-assessment and self-reflection take place prior to embarking on a new venture. Self-assessment often is composed of a series of questions that the individual asks himself or herself in an effort to understand personal motivations for making a change. Among the questions that could be asked are the following:

Why am I intrigued by Internet counseling?

What are my goals for this form of practice?

What do I have to gain or lose if I start up such a practice?

TABLE 9.3 Internet Counseling Practice Feasibility Study

FEASIBILITY FACTOR	TOPICS TO CONSIDER PREDECISION
Engage in self-assessment/self-reflection	Personal motivation to investigate Internet counseling Compatible qualities and characteristics Potential gains or losses Personal and professional readiness Experience in Internet counseling
Develop knowledge base	Understand research regarding efficacy of Internet counseling Identify counseling methods suitable to Internet delivery Explore Internet options as adjuncts to traditional counseling
Study ethics and principles of practice	Review and understand codes of ethics and Internet practice principles Evaluate how confidentiality can be maintained Incorporate specific, detailed informed consent procedures
Assess technical skill competencies	Competency to use the Internet and computer technology Writing proficiency assessment Cost analysis for start-up budget and sustaining financial support
Perform risk assessment	Regulatory limitations and consequences Take ACA online continuing education course on cybercounseling

> Am I ready professionally and personally for the demands of this form of counseling?
>
> What is my inventory of personal qualities and characteristics that would well interface with Internet counseling?

Obtaining answers these questions, as well as others, could include discussion with family and friends. In Ms. Carter's case, she has four professional colleagues with whom to talk. She also might seek consultation from her supervisor, a mentor from graduate school, or professionals who are currently engaged in Internet counseling practice. The goal of this first phase of the feasibility study is to ensure that her goal is reasonable for her and that she is clear about the reasons she wishes to pursue this option.

Evaluate Current Knowledge Base

Internet counseling consists of applying counseling principles through an invisible communication channel with clients who may never be seen. To establish that this can be accomplished in a professional manner, Ms. Carter must acquire a knowledge base about the nature of Internet counseling. A central issue in this exploratory phase is developing an understanding of the efficacy of Internet counseling. Consideration of efficacy assumes that Internet counseling is a contemporary option to deliver certain counseling services (i.e., it is not going to "go away"). To date, the evidence for efficacy of counseling delivered online is anecdotal as well as research based, although the body of published research is limited.

Efficacy of Internet Counseling. Efficacy of a counseling treatment rests on methods based on theory that define the nature of psychological disorders. From this understanding, systematic research either verifies efficacy of the method or fails to demonstrate effectiveness. Methods that are not supported by outcome research are then not recognized as effective for continued use. With Internet counseling, the emphasis is on both the methods used to counsel and the method used to deliver the counseling services. Ms. Carter needs to understand the outcome of research that supports the efficacy of Internet counseling as well as the paucity of research that has been published.

Internet counseling has been applied to the treatment of the fear of public speaking (Bottela, Banos, Guillen, Perpina, Alcaniz, & Pons, 2000); career counseling and guidance (Boer, 2001; Clark, Horan, Kovalsky, & Hackett, 2000; Tait, 1999); providing education and counseling to HIV/AIDS patients (DeGuzman & Ross, 1999); rehabilitation counseling (Hampton & Houser, 2000); marriage and family therapy (Jencius & Sager, 2001); avoidant personality disorder and social phobia (King & Poulos, 1998); panic disorder (Klein & Richards, 2001); couples group therapy (Sander, 1999); and recurrent headache (Stroem, Patterson, & Andersson, 2000). As can be seen, research reports on the application of Internet counseling to diverse mental health problems and needs present an interesting picture of the current status of research activities.

While the reported research describes specific diagnoses within subject populations studied, when reviewing a sampling of websites devoted to provision of online counseling services, some providers list a wide range of problems/topics/disorders that can be addressed, from the counseling perspective, by these Internet providers (DMOZ, 2002) (e.g., anxiety, anxiety attacks, anger management, alcohol and drug abuse, addictions, ADHD, ADD, brief online therapy, chronic pain, chronic illness, depression, divorce recovery, domestic violence, eating disorders, employment issues, entertainment industry pressures, false memory syndrome, family troubles/problems, grief and bereavement, insomnia, marital problems, obsessive-compulsive disorder, phobias, panic disorder, parenting, PTSD, recovery from trauma, relationship problems, self-esteem, sexual issues, stress, and women's issues). Other sites offer more focused and limited services by individual practitioners, or within a group practice, an expanded array of problems, issues, or diagnostic categories are considered during the pretreatment assessment before determining suitability for Internet counseling (e.g., www.asktheinternettherapist.com/). Detailed information about fees structured for licensed counselors who provide Internet counseling can also be found in the National Directory of Online Counselors (ISMHO, 2003).

Internet Counseling Methods.   In reviewing efficacy research, Ms. Carter will also begin to understand which counseling methods for providing counseling and psychotherapy are appropriate over the Internet. Research dedicated to determining treatment outcome when counseling services were solely delivered through the Internet is limited. Cognitive behavior therapy programs delivered online report varying results, with statistically significant improvement in distress, depression, and anxiety with reference to tinnitus (Kaldo-Sandröm, Larsen, & Andersson, 2004), improvement in depression coping skills for mild to moderate levels of depression (Clarke et al, 2002), and significant reductions in depression and anxiety over the course of web-based treatment (Christensen, Griffiths, & Korten, 2002).

In each of these treatment programs, the treatment modules based on cognitive behavioral principles were web-based, accessed by the clients through Internet connection, and included e-mail communication. For patients with more severe levels of depression, improvement was minimal and not statistically significant (Clarke et al, 2002), suggesting that one explanation for this finding may lie in the subject selection for the study that included individuals with serious levels of depression. It is possible that such clients are unsuitable for this form of treatment if Internet counseling is the only method of treatment used.

For mental health disorders related to eating behavior problems, Internet counseling combined with Internet education was associated with greater achievement of weight loss goals than Internet education alone (Tate, Wing, & Winett, 2001). Reducing risk factors for eating disorders involving an Internet-based educational and counseling program resulted in significant reductions in weight concerns and disordered eating behavior and attitudes (Winzelberg et al, 2000). Each of these studies provides preliminary evidence that very challenging mental disorders can be favorably impacted by use of Internet treatment methods, or Internet-based education and counseling combined. In a different study, researchers found no differences in the ratings of online or FTF counselors when receiving treatment for anxiety. Both sets of counselors were viewed as similar in expertness, trustworthiness, and attractiveness (Cohen & Kerr, 1998), with the latter variable being of particular interest when considering the "virtual" characteristic that did not include visual cues of the counselor.

Personal Experience of Internet Counseling.   Before Ms. Carter initiates a business plan to offer Internet counseling, it is strongly recommended that she explore this experience herself. Although it is not an expectation that all counselor professionals have personal experiences similar to their clients, when deciding whether to use a new practice delivery system, acquiring personal experience of the new delivery system can inform decision making in ways that studying the delivery system cannot.

For Ms. Carter, it will be essential that she clearly evaluate her personal and preferred practice method to determine if it is compatible with the strengths and limitations of an Internet delivery system. Discussion with peers and her supervisor should prove invaluable during this stage of the feasibility study.

Blended Internet Counseling Options.   One of the more appealing forms of Internet counseling, and one that is seemingly more readily accepted by traditional counselor professionals, is to use it as an adjunct to traditional practice. When used in an adjunctive manner, the counselor can use a personal website to provide information or assignments that are to be completed by the client or participants in an Internet therapy group that is linked to the counselor's FTF office practice.

Adjunctive Internet counseling has been reported as effective in promotion inclusion of distantly located family members while family therapy is in progress. In this context, the involvement of family who lives at a distance increases the communication that then supports the therapeutic process (King, Engi, & Poulos, 1998). In a study of Internet counselor practitioners, Maheu and Gordon (2000) report that 46 percent of survey respondents use real-time chat rooms for clients who are currently being treated, and 82 percent use e-mail to provide counseling communication. These results are similar to those seen by Lazlo, Esterman, and Zabko (1999), who found the use of chat rooms by surveyed providers was at 54 percent, with 75 percent of the sample using e-mail as the primary form of interaction with clients.

Ms. Carter's understanding of the use of e-mail and chat rooms as supplements to traditional counseling practice expands the possibilities for integrating Internet communication with clients into her practice. Internet counseling clients report higher scores on a measure of working alliance formation in comparison to FTF clients in a study reported by Cook and Doyle (2002), suggesting that treatment for anxiety and depression can be effective in a virtual environment that includes individual text-based and chat room communication. In addition to the adjunctive nature of chat rooms, Internet counselors can refer to online support groups to add important elements of assistance to clients.

Another adjunctive option Ms. Carter can consider as she becomes familiar with the parameters of Internet counseling is the online support group. Such virtual groups can be accessed independently by consumers without referral from a counseling professional, or can be a highly valued resource used in the counseling process. Virtual support groups mimic their use of traditional counseling (i.e., in a support group, members communicate with others who have similar problems and therapists facilitate this form of support, networking, and interaction). In the virtual world of the Internet, a support group has few boundaries and thus has both strengths and cautions that counselor professionals must carefully evaluate.

In the Internet support group, limited research indicates that high levels of support, mutual acceptance, positive feelings, and acceptance occur in a manner similar to that occurring in the FTF group meeting (Gary, 2001; Gary & Remolino, 2000; Miller & Gergen, 1998; Salem, Bogat, & Reid, 1997). Women seeking services in Internet support groups or chat rooms are cautioned to carefully monitor involvement in recognition of the risk for victimization in online chat rooms and other Internet points of contact with individuals who pose risk to their safety, such as stalking or identity deception (Finn & Banach, 2000). With a lack of standards and methods to enforce standards of behavior on the Internet, whether in a chat room or in support group format, counselors who consider referral of clients to support groups must carefully evaluate the sites before making a referral—as would any counselor practicing in a FTF environment. Clients also need to be advised about the risks inherent in unmonitored support groups, listservs, or chat rooms (e.g., how to review a website to identify sponsorship, "netiquette" expectations, legitimacy of the group facilitator if one is identified, and protection of personal information).

Combining Multiple Options. In addition to text-based online communication, Internet counselors may elect to incorporate real-time chat on the provider's website, or make a referral to web-based support groups where the option for real-time chat is provided. When viewed from this perspective, Internet counseling begins to mirror the FTF method of delivering counseling services. For example, the provider conducts a FTF counseling session and decides to add a group discussion (chat room or asynchronous web-board) to the client's treatment plan. She or he then provides a referral to specific support groups for additional assistance between sessions (web support groups, listservs).

Study Ethical Guidelines and Principles

As Ms. Carter reads about Internet counseling and uses the Internet to investigate the many topics that will inform her decision making about starting a virtual practice, she will note that the most often cited issue discussed in the Internet counseling literature is ethics.

It is assumed in this discussion that online counseling practitioners are obliged to adhere to the same ethical standards as counselors in traditional settings. Adhering to the traditional standards of practice in a nontraditional setting is essential for this form of counseling to remain viable. The method of delivering counseling services does not mitigate this professional responsibility. With this in mind, it is equally important to note that observance of ethics and standards of practice are implemented in ways that are different from in FTF encounters.

Codes of Ethics and Internet Counseling. In recognition of the differences and challenges inherent in the delivery of counseling services over the Internet, counselor professional associations have devised codes of ethics that specifically emphasize factors that counselors should be aware of, examine, and integrate into online practice. The first codes were formulated by the American Counseling Association (ACA) as "Ethical Standards for Internet Online Counseling" (ACA, 1999), and the National Board of Certified Counselors (NBCC) with a statement of principles (NBCC, 2005). Each of these codes or principles signals recognition that, within the professional association representing counselor practitioners or certification bodies, Internet counseling practice can be included within the associations' missions. Central to these ethical statements is the recognition that ethical standards of conduct and practice must be followed when providing services in any practice environment—virtual or traditional. Such progressive action indicates recognition of an emerging trend in delivery of counseling services and awareness that incorporating technology-based delivery systems is not contrary to competent, ethical practice standards.

Specialized codes of ethics should be used in conjunction with a profession's general code of ethics and standards of practice. Unfortunately, research suggests that compliance with the NBCC standards for Internet counseling are not consistently followed. In a study by Heinlen and (2003), a survey of Internet counseling services and websites found low levels of compliance with the NBCC Standards. The majority of the providers described as credentialed mental health practitioners and para-professional practitioners failed to follow the profession's standards of ethical practice. More dramatically, a return to the websites eight months after data collection found that more than one-third of the sites were inactive. In a study by Shaw and Shaw (2006), similar low levels of compliance with professional codes of ethics was found in a survey of 88 online counseling websites that provided services offered by licensed counselors, psychologists, social workers, and marriage and family therapists. Using a 16-item checklist based on the American Counseling Association ethical standards for Internet online counseling, Shaw and Shaw (2006) found an alarming lack of compliance with the clearly stated ethical requirements on key ethical standards (e.g., client abandonment, informed consent, and confidentiality waivers). The implications for consumers of these findings include potential harm associated with "disappearing" therapists, misrepresentation of professional credentials, potential fraud with reference to payment for services that are no longer offered, misrepresentation of services offered, and a host of other ethical and legal outcomes. Future research is needed to delve more deeply into the methods of practice used by licensed or certified counselors to determine how practice actually takes place, how providers are interpreting the ethical standards of practice within the context of e-therapy, and why providers ceased delivering e-therapy services. This finding strongly suggests that Ms. Carter's feasibility study must take into account the projected longevity of her Internet practice.

In addition to the counseling profession, other human services professions have addressed Internet counseling as well. Since Ms. Carter works with a multidisciplinary team of counselor professionals, it is incumbent on her to understand what her officemates must be familiar with if their participation becomes part of her feasibility study. The National Association of Social Workers (1996) (NASW News, 2001) addresses Internet counseling through its Ethical Standards by emphasizing informed consent in Standard 1.03, (e), Informed Consent, as follows: "Social workers who provide services via electronic media (such as computer, telephone, radio, and television) should inform recipients of the limitations and risks associated with such services." Implied competencies to provide online counseling by social workers is inferred in Standard 1.04, Competence, that emphasizes practice within the professional's "boundaries of [his or her] education, training, licensure, certification, consultation received, supervised experience, or other relevant professional experience." In addition, according to the ethical standards for social workers, practice areas that are new or unfamiliar to the professional are initiated only after receiving appropriate "study, training, consultation, and supervision from people who are competent in those interventions or techniques" (Standard 1.04, (b)). These practice standards can be interpreted to clarify how social workers who wish to provide counseling services online are to proceed (i.e., preparation beforehand in recognition of a new practice application).

The American Psychological Association has defined a similar path to establishing how psychologists are to approach online delivery of psychological services. In a recent Code of Ethics revision, specific ethical principles have been incorporated into the 2002 revision of the Ethical Principles of Psychologists and Code of Conduct (APA, 2002). Rather than devise a specific subset of counselor ethics tailored to Internet counseling, this revision of the APA Code incorporates recognition of the unique characteristics of the Internet delivery system in the Ethical Standards (i.e., 2. Competence, 2.01 Boundaries of Competence, c and e) (p. 1064). In Standard 2.01, c, psychologists "planning to provide services, teach, or conduct research involving populations, areas, techniques, or technologies new to them undertake relevant education, training, supervised experience, consultation, or study." This standard speaks clearly to the requirement that psychologists seek preparation for internet counseling ventures *prior* to offering such services. As a professionwide expectation, this would be a reasonable standard to establish throughout the counseling professions.

For the psychiatry profession, Hsiung (2001), and others, have been involved in the development of principles of ethics for online mental health services in conjunction with the International Society for Mental Health Online (ISMHO and the Psychiatric Society for Infomatics (PSI) (PSI, 2000). These standards have been developed as a joint effort by these two professional organizations, but do not reflect the formal position on Internet delivery of mental health services of the American Psychiatric Association. Rather, these suggested voluntary standards represent a collaborative attempt to define ethical standards that extends beyond the bounds of a specific profession.

Confidentiality and Informed Consent Issues.   The unique features of a text-based system of communication generates issues associated with privacy and confidentiality based on transmission of information over the Internet. At several points in the information exchange sequence, risks to confidentiality exist (i.e., point of origin security of messages, storage of messages in secure computer files, encryption, and the extent of information that is stored, since communication in counseling takes place in written format (ISMHO, 2000; Manhal-Baugus, 2001). The Internet counselor must take all "typical" measures to protect client confidentiality as well as applying these standards to a virtual environment of interaction.

Internet counseling clients must be informed of the limits to guaranteeing confidentiality that are unique to the Internet. At the same time, clients must understand that some risk to confidentiality exists in general with any counseling environment. Methods used by the counselor must be explained to the client regarding the website's security options and information storage. For example, clients can be provided options regarding encryption, required to obtain such software or downloads, or be referred to free downloads. If more desirable, the communication between counselor and client can take place through engaging in e-mail without additional layers of security (Alleman, 2002; Sussman, 1998). The NBCC Standards (2005) require that Internet counselors "inform web clients of the encryption methods being used to help insure the security of client/counselor/supervisor communications." Additional standards address issues of security and storage of client information (i.e., text-based communications such as e-mail, test results, or session notes) and practices that protect clients, promote efficacy of methods used, safety of clients, and off-line communication agreements.

For many counselors, the text-based format ensures that counselor–client communication is documented, available for review by the client or counselor, and allows verification of messages sent and received. As one element of the process of assuring that clients are informed at the beginning of the counseling process, as well as during the interaction, the text archive of sessions provides clear documentation of this activity.

Boundaries of Practice.   Counselors are obliged to practice within their bounds of professional competence. In the online environment, however, there is concern that counselors without specific preparation for Internet counseling practice are, in fact, embarking on such practice in an unregulated, largely free-wheeling environment (New Therapist, 2000). In addition, questions of protecting the public from imposter clients (Suler, 1996, 2000; Lee, 1998), victimization (Finn & Banach, 2000), and practitioners who violate legal proscriptions on practice beyond one's state of licensure must be considered (Alleman, 2002; Hughes, 2000). How the counseling professions devise standards and promote public policy that protects both client and practitioner rights to practice are quickly emerging as complex issues that demand measured, research-based attention. The need to address these issues takes on a higher level of urgency in an environment that is characterized by split-second transmission of information.

At this point, Ms. Carter has learned a great deal about the nature of Internet counseling. She has studied current Internet counseling websites to learn about the layout and content that should be included to ensure that the site she markets includes all essential features according to American Counseling Association (www.counseling.org) and International Society for Mental Health Online (www.ISMHO.org) principles. As she continues her feasibility study, she recognizes that the intrigue associated with Internet counseling will need to be bolstered by intense preparation prior to entering the world of Internet counseling. She has some doubts about how realistic it will be for her to start up such a practice, but decides to continue to explore key issues.

Assess Technology Competencies

As with any area of practice that is new to a counselor, the need for skill sets and competencies appropriate to that area of practice must be acquired *before* provision of services begins. While computers are ubiquitous in office management, professional documentation, report preparation, professional presentations, educational experiences, and in e-mail communication both professionally and in one's personal life, these competencies may not represent sufficient preparation to embark on the provision of Internet counseling.

Skill assessment should include the current level of proficiency in use of computer technology and the Internet (Collie, Mitchell, & Murphy, 2000). Because Internet counselors are using the Internet as a delivery system, they also use it to evaluate websites that offer support services to clients and that might be appropriate for their clients. Skills in discerning who produces and sponsors a website are essential, since some are commercially focused and may not be helpful to clients. Comfort in accessing the Internet, using search engines, finding research articles and information, and linking with other Internet counselors is essential. Technical resources are essential for design, setup, and maintenance of Internet counseling websites. Although the counselor may well have many of these competencies, backup resources will ease anxiety and ensure that once put on the internet, the site will be functional. Review of Internet resource checklists that describe the skills needed will facilitate this skills assessment process.

Because writing skills are so critical to the success of Internet counseling, Ms. Carter will need to carefully evaluate her writing competencies. Consultation with colleagues as well as mentors who have knowledge of her communication proficiencies can provide helpful insights. If this competency is not well developed, success as an Internet counselor is jeopardized.

Finally, the basics of technology ownership must be addressed. Ms. Carter needs to budget for the necessary computer technology, web design, encryption software, digital camera, web hosting, and associated equipment and high-speed or broadband Internet access costs. Included in this budget are mechanisms to process payment for services (e.g., "PayPal®" or debit/credit card) and other costs that will emerge as the Internet counseling business is established.

Risk Assessment

Feasibility studies that precede decision making about a new venture include a risk assessment. In such an assessment, the pros and cons of the proposed business are identified and considered. The risk assessment that Ms. Carter decides to include in her study of Internet counseling includes issues associated with many of the topics covered in this chapter. In addition, because Ms. Carter has progressed to this point in her study of the Internet counseling practice option, she decided to take an online course offered by the American Counseling Association (Bloom, Walz, & Ford, 2005) that focuses on the key factors that she has been studying. With this additional preparation, she anticipates being able to make her decision with higher levels of clarity.

Regulatory Limitations and Resources.   Legislation defines the scope of practice for most counselor professionals who deliver direct counseling services. If a counselor's state of residence has a legal mandate to restrict practice to the confines of the state's geographical boundaries, such as California (Manhal-Baugus, 2001; Sussman, 1998) and Texas (White, 2002), counselors must honor that restriction. Clearly, if Ms. Carter resides in one of these two states, she will have to carefully monitor where potential clients live and exclude those who live outside her state.

Knowing what the requirements are in her state is critical, because there is some evidence that licensed counselors may not be aware of the prohibitions to practice Internet counseling. According to Maheu and Gordon (2000), in a study of online practitioners, 78 percent of licensed or certified respondents provided services to individuals not living in the provider's state of residence. In addition, 74 percent were uncertain about the telehealth laws in their states. Ignorance of legal statutes designed to govern practice parameters is not an acceptable rationale to engage in unethical professional behavior.

In continuing her risk assessment, Ms. Carter realizes that she needs to learn about the regulatory jurisdiction in her state that monitors and reviews professional practice, in addition to her voluntary adherence to ethical codes of conduct and standards of practice. She learns that this responsibility is assumed by the Board of Professional Regulation where she lives, but she is confused about the role of the board in the states in which her potential clients reside. At this point, she recognizes a very thorny issue that could hold the potential for serious legal repercussions if claims of malpractice arise while she was practicing as an Internet counselor. State regulation for Internet counseling can range from very specific to vague and is subject to interpretation in each state (Hughes, 2000; Love, 2000).

Licensure, Malpractice Coverage, and Backup.   As previously noted, it will be very important for Ms. Carter to ensure that her scope of practice boundaries are defined and enforced. She is a licensed mental health professional and has malpractice insurance. She now understands the limits for her Internet counseling practice, and decides to accept only clients who can produce residency proof applicable to her geographical location. She now turns to ensuring that she has adequate professional backup and coverage for client emergency, crisis, and other situations that would involve her not being able or present to respond to Internet client needs. As she identifies who could provide this coverage for her practice, she realizes that this person or group would have to have similar preparation and awareness that she now has regarding the parameters of Internet practice.

Scope of Practice.   Startup of an Internet counseling practice requires marketing activities typically accomplished through setup of the website that will be the entrance to the practice for Internet clients. Included in the self-marketing process is awareness of risk factors that must be explicitly addressed prior to activation of the site. Self-marketing of competencies that a counselor may well possess in the traditional person-to-person setting is not automatically transferable to the text-based online venue. From the consumer perspective, Ms. Carter will consider how to communicate her competencies within her scope of practice in such a way that this information is clear, balanced, and accurate. Having colleagues review her website materials can serve as a kind of field test to ensure that she has achieved this goal.

Related to this issue is a study by Barthelmeus (2000) indicating that the amount of detailed information on a website of a mental health counseling provider was *inversely* related to the desirability to use such a provider; that is, the more detailed the informed consent information, the less likely the subject would select that online provider. Overall, this sample preferred the face-to-face encounter over the online delivery system, yet clearly indicated that depth of information influenced decision making in a hypothetical situation. With a heavy emphasis in the Internet counseling literature to establish standards that clearly and fully provide informed consent, this finding is somewhat puzzling, yet it serves to illustrate the need for programs of research that investigate how clients select an Internet provider and how the provider offers self-market services.

Supervision and Consultation.   Ethical practice as a provider of counseling services includes the judicious use of supervision and consultation. Supervision provides backup to counselors when difficult situations arise in counseling sessions, when unusual problems are presented, and when the counselor needs to review progress of treatment. The value of advice from Ms. Carter's colleagues will be an integral part of her Internet practice. It also will help her continue to develop her proficiencies, promote continued professional growth and development, and provide guidance on ethical quandaries and treatment issues. If Ms. Carter did not have a nearby practice group to seek this support from, she would need to develop a supervision and consultation relationship with counselor professionals in her community of practice. In addition, given the virtual nature of Internet practice, she may find it instructive and helpful to seek supervision and consultation from experienced Internet providers. Central to her successful use of supervision and consultation will be the awareness, knowledge, and sensitivity that these resource professionals possess regarding Internet counseling's unique features.

As Ms. Carter completes her feasibility study, she is aware that her effort has met a key criterion for setting up a new practice: She has explored the skill sets and competencies appropriate to her work as an Internet counselor *before* provision of services begins. She also realizes that although computers are ever-present in office management, professional documentation, report preparation, professional presentations, and e-mail communication both professionally and in one's personal life, these competencies may not be sufficient preparation to engage in a business venture involving Internet counseling. With the detailed information contained in her feasibility study, Ms. Carter now must decide whether to proceed to develop a business plan.

THE FUTURE OF INTERNET COUNSELING

How the counseling professions address the issues associated with the practice, regulation, and monitoring of Internet counseling has begun within professional associations as well as in related specialization organizations. Credentialing, practice within the scope of licensure, ethical practice on the Internet, and outcome research are topics to be addressed.

Internet Counselor Competencies

Competencies for Internet counselors are designed as principles that support standards for successful and effective practice and that have been provided by the American Counseling

Association (1999) as well as specialization organizations such as the International Society for Mental Health Online (ISMHO, 2000). These preliminary principles provide guidance for the online practitioner regarding ethics and standards of practice and conform to other ethical codes of conduct in stating, "The counselor should remain within his or her boundaries of competence and not attempt to address a problem online if he or she would not attempt to address the same problem in person" (ISMHO, 2000). In addition, in an ISMHO position paper by Fenichel (2001), a strongly worded statement further supports the rationale for specific preparation of online counselors: "Online mental health professionals should not only be every bit as qualified as offline practitioners, but have additional training, competencies, and skills which facilitate ethical, professional practice."

A precursor to any effort to certify counselors as possessing the skill sets and competencies to deliver online counseling services is the identification and verification of the competencies that a counselor should possess and demonstrate in order to achieve certified status. Collie, Mitchell, and Murphy (2000) describe e-mail, text-based skill sets identified as effective in conducting Internet therapy sessions. Included in their descriptive research is the need for the therapist to employ a therapy method that "fits" with text-based communication. For these practitioners, solution-focused brief therapy methods (e.g., emotional bracketing, use of stories and metaphors, and descriptive immediacy) are employed. Regardless of the psychotherapy method used, however, an overarching set of competencies were identified as essential to the successful practice of online counseling that mimic those previously identified: competence with the use of computer technology; competence to construct a website that conforms to ethical standards of practice of one's profession; competence to limit online counseling practice to clients with psychological disorders that can realistically benefit from non-FTF therapy; competence to express relationship-building activities in typed text messaging; competence to apply therapeutic treatment/counseling methods that best "fit" the text-based format; and competence to evaluate the efficacy and application of Internet resources as adjuncts to online counseling.

While credentialing of counselors who practice online could remain a voluntary option exercised by practitioners who seek to reassure consumers and establish credibility of mental health services delivered, a limited number of formal mechanisms to certify Internet counselors are currently offered. Certification could be required by the counselor professional associations as a way to provide authentication that the practice is sanctioned by the profession and that special competencies are required. It is possible that certification of a service delivered in a worldwide context may prove to be too daunting a task for some or all of the professional associations. Newly offered credentialing may fill part of this void by serving as a model for other counselor professional organizations to follow. Clearly, the issue of credentialing will demand attention as the Internet counseling alternative continues to provide access and services to an expanding population of consumers.

Consumer Protection in the Virtual World

The lure of the Internet, the increasingly user-friendly nature of software applications, and the ease of access to the Internet may falsely assure counselors that it is safe to assume that proficiency with a home PC is sufficient preparation to enter the world of Internet counseling practice. Without a method to credential Internet counselors that recognizes the unique features and competencies associated with providing services in this environment, as well as mechanisms to prepare counselors with necessary skill sets and proficiencies, the potential for unintended harm to clients remains a risk. A strong position should be taken by the counseling professions (e.g., APA, ACA) on this issue. Such a position would not imply that current Internet counselors lack ethics or fail to take measures to protect consumers; it would, however, indicate that in this rapidly evolving area of practice, attention to counselor preparation within counselor education programs and credentialing is emerging as a fundamental issue that must be addressed. There clearly is a need to fully define the skill sets that are most applicable to delivery of high-quality, ethically sound counseling services via the Internet delivery system.

Certification Models

Certification of Internet counselors is not yet a prerequisite to enter this field of practice. It is assumed that licensure or certification of the provider that conforms to state requirements is sufficient to ensure consumer protection. This is debatable, since the lack of regulation of the Internet and who promotes themselves as Internet counselors increases the risk that nonlicensed practitioners could harm consumers. In addition, without a mechanism to certify this form of practice, given that it is such an innovation within the professions, lends further support to "outside-the-box" thinking with reference to certification and regulation of access to practice. This issue is a sticky one because it pushes both state regulatory boards and the professional associations to promote a layer of certification in addition to that already required.

The Center for Credentialing and Education (CCE) (2004) has developed a credential for distance counseling comprised of training that culminates in the designation of Distance Credentialed Counselor (DCC) (www.cce-global.org). In addition and prior to the CCE effort, a web-based organization devised an interim solution. Metanoia (www.metanoia.com) compiled a listing of Internet psychotherapy/counseling providers. This organization checks the credentials of its listed practitioners with their appropriate licensing bodies. In addition, the Mental Health Net (www.cmhc.com) has rated each of the sites listed on Metanoia. An additional service provided by Mental Health Net is a "Credentials Check" website that lists the credentials of Internet counseling providers. Included in the information is the degree of the provider, professional license number, and a link from the practitioner's website to Credentials Check. This helpful service is provided at no cost to the consumer and can provide valuable information that verifies minimal professional practice requirements identified by this organization.

Reciprocity and Regulatory Issues

The thorny issue of Internet counselors practicing in states in which they are not licensed elevates reciprocity of licensure to new heights within the counseling professions due to the "reach" of the Internet to cross all state and international borders. Currently, most states require a formal process of application, review of credentials, and possibly retaking a licensure examination in order to secure the right to practice in a new state of residence. This process is essentially suspended when counselors can practice anywhere due to access through the World Wide Web.

Linked to this issue are questions that put the spotlight on determining where counseling services are actually being delivered during the Internet counseling process. For example, the counselor's messages to clients originate in the geographical location of the computer that records it (the counselor's office location where the keyboard resides). The message then is transmitted over the Internet to a client who could reside in the counselor's same state or in another state. Where, then, is the counseling taking place? As an illustration, consider this situation: An Internet counselor travels to attend an annual conference, or flies to Canada to provide consultation to a hospital conglomerate. While traveling, she wishes to maintain her Internet practice with clients but is aware that questions may arise about this continuation that suggest risk for violating licensure statutes, create problems with malpractice coverage, or result in ethical lapses. Guidance on how to manage these realities of the global context in which counseling can now take place must be developed by the counseling professions.

Internet Counseling Research

Research is central to the success of Internet counseling and how it is refined. Although the list of potential research topics is lengthy, most of the publications that address Internet counseling are descriptive in nature, with a relatively limited number of research reports to date. Research has provided some recognition that certain psychological disorders are unsuitable for Internet counseling. These include severely depressed individuals at risk for suicidal behavior (Freeny, 2001; Stofle, 1999, 2001), persons with severe psychopathology (Suler, 2001), and individuals in crisis situations (Childress, 1998). Descriptions of the use of e-mail to facilitate psychological treatment for anorexia nervosa (Yager, 2000), various anxiety disorders (Cohen & Kerr, 1998; Carlbring et al, 2001; Klein & Richards, 2001), post-traumatic stress and grief (Lange, van de Ven, & Schrieken, 2001), tinnitus (Andersson, Stromgren, Strom, & Lyttkens, 2002), personality disorder (King & Poulos, 1998), group therapy (Barak & Wander-Schwartz, 2000), panic disorder (Carlbring et al, 2001), and family therapy issues (Jencius & Sager, 2001; King, Engi, & Poulos, 1998) have been reported with positive results.

To further investigate treatment efficacy, however, it will be necessary to determine from clients how the online delivery method impacted the treatment experience. Cook and Doyle (2002) provided initial insight along these lines with reference to the therapeutic working alliance. The results from this study indicate that there are no significant differences between online and face-to-face methods of providing counseling services. Replication of this research with other client populations is indicated. In addition, research that identifies more definitively the optimal client populations or disorders most amenable to Internet counseling, with empirical research demonstrating treatment outcomes, is needed.

The results of limited research conducted to date suggest several issues that must be addressed regarding the use of Internet counseling. Topics that require research investigation include the frequency of patient management problems encountered by licensed/certified Internet providers of mental health services; effective methods to screen online clients prior to initiating counseling; evaluating screening protocols used and which screening

TABLE 9.4   ISMHO Case Study Group Discussion Topics: Internet Counseling

Methods of Internet Counseling

- Identification of the communication methods that are either adequate or preferable for client assessment
- Examination of the relationship between previous and concurrent counseling with online therapy
- Description of ethnic and multicultural issues that impact Internet counseling
- Evaluation of online resources appropriate to inclusion in the Internet counseling process

Internet Client Factors

- Determination of how client knowledge, computer skills, access to the Internet, and familiarity with the Web platform impacts the counseling experience
- Investigation of client knowledge and experience in using online communication and engaging in online relationships
- Clarification of client competency and "best fit" with reading and writing associated with text-based communication
- Exploration of relationship between diagnosis, personality type, and reason to seek counseling with suitability for online counseling
- Explanation of the impact of medical or physical factors on the Internet counseling process

---

methods can be verified in a consistent manner; and identification of methods to terminate Internet counseling and criteria for this decision. Research that begins to provide answers to these questions is essential.

Methodologies that access Internet counseling providers for such study must be inclusive of practitioners who subscribe to professional standards of practice, such as those published by the National Board of Certified Counselors (NBCC, 2005), the American Counseling Association (ACA, 1999), and the International Society for Mental Health Online (2000), as well as providers with service-offering websites who do not identify themselves as subscribing to these professional association standards. Web-based data collection methods are obvious strategies to use for these investigations.

Research that identifies the suitability for Internet counseling/therapy has been the focus of the ISMHO clinical case study group (Suler, 2001, p. 675). The group is "devoted to the discussion of psychotherapy cases and professional clinical encounters that involve the Internet." When viewed through the lenses of the researcher, the questions identified by the clinical case study group reflects research topics of major import to the counseling professions (see Table 9.4). As these and other issues are researched, practitioners can anticipate publication of study results that will enhance knowledge, guide practice, and lead to further refinement of the parameters of Internet counseling service delivery.

Internet Counseling and Consumer Education

Internet counselors using the World Wide Web to deliver mental health and wellness services typically incorporate various kinds of consumer health education as part of the healing and/or change process. Counselors frequently recommend readings and community resources to clients as adjuncts to treatment. The Internet is used by consumers to research issues related to personal life problems, psychological disorders, and medical illnesses or conditions. Counselors will increasingly be called on to know about computer-mediated information and resources as part of counseling and to make informed referral to clients about such resources.

In counselor-produced and counselor-maintained websites, information about mental health issues, listing of links to websites that contain related information or assistance, and links to listservs, chat rooms, support groups, or web boards can be provided as educational resources to the public. Additionally, websites can be used to promote understanding of mental health issues and the counseling professions, and to demystify the counseling process. Many such sites now exist on the Web, and many more will be opened in the coming years as counselors who have been "raised with computers" realize the outreach and patient education potential of the Internet. From the professional association perspective, ensuring the quality of mental health and wellness information could be enhanced by development of materials that Internet counselors could place on their websites. As a professional association branding activity, the professional association could then offer this material only to licensed and/or certified professionals.

Collaboration of Counseling Professions

Collaboration among the counseling professions (e.g., APA, ACA, NASW, APA-psychiatry) in the development of accepted standards of practice for delivery of Internet counseling and psychotherapy would significantly clarify treatment parameters and provider competencies, and support consumer protection. As Internet counseling continues to define itself, it will be imperative that Internet practitioners continue to take the lead in defining practice parameters while working with professional associations along these same lines. This partnership suggests the potential for collaboration across the counseling disciplines (i.e., mental health counseling, marriage and family therapy, social work, psychology, and psychiatry). Such a collaborative, across-discipline approach would more accurately reflect key characteristics of the Internet delivery system itself (e.g., far-reaching, global access, and synchronous or asynchronous time frames).

Clearly, such a collaborative effort would be groundbreaking in uniqueness and impact. Typically, the boundaries between the counseling professions emphasize the differences in how services are provided, variance in preparation requirements, diversity of counseling strategies, and distinctiveness of FTF service delivery location. In the online environment, these differences are less obvious or visible to the client, and as a consequence, perhaps these differences could be reduced in import with reference to the traditional barriers to collaboration among the counseling professions. Optimizing the potential for Internet counseling, while promoting professional collaboration that recognizes the promise of the Internet, can increase access to mental health services for those who might not otherwise receive assistance.

The Future Is Now

The practice and potential of Internet counseling creates varying degrees of discomfort and enthusiasm among providers (Alleman, 2002; Anthony, 2000), theoreticians (Kuntze et al, 2002; Burnett-Stuart, 2001; Dryden, Mearns, & Thorne, 2000), counselor educators (Patrick, 2005; Lewis, Coursol, & Herting-Wahl, 2000; Walz, 2000), and professional associations (Menon, 2001; NASW News, 2001). It signifies that a dramatic change in how counseling services will continue to be delivered has begun, and it is unlikely that such services will diminish or cease to exist given the continuing expansion of the Internet and its applications. Grohol estimated that by 2005, there would be over 5,000 Internet counselors/practitioners (New Therapist, 2003). Given this potential, combined with research that supports the efficacy of Internet counseling as effective within the bounds of appropriate client populations, Internet text-based therapy can expand alongside traditional methods of service delivery. The potential efficacy of Internet-based counseling service delivery, as well as enhancement of counseling activities with use of web-based resources, is recognized within the counseling professions with increasing frequency (Goss & Anthony, 2003; Kraus, Zack, & Stricker, 2003; Tyler & Sabella, 2003).

The operative word when discussing Internet counseling is *different*. This counseling method and delivery system creates access to therapy in a manner that is *different* from the traditional FTF method. Clients who use Internet therapy are receptive to a *different* method to seek counseling. Treatment outcomes associated with Internet counseling, may also *differ* in ways yet to be defined. The promise of the Internet to extend access to mental health counseling services is undeniable. With the concerted commitment of the counseling professions to address ethical, practice, and research issues, this promise to consumers can be fulfilled.

What conclusions can be drawn about the future of Internet counseling? Limited research suggests that it is effective for specific psychological problems (e.g., certain anxiety disorders, personal growth issues), helpful to clients when counseling methods blend well with the Internet delivery system (e.g., brief models of therapy that can rely on text-based communication), and appropriate for clients who require anytime-anywhere-asynchronous access to mental health services. Internet counseling, then, is fast becoming a recognized form of counseling and, at the same time, is generating ongoing debate about practitioner issues, profession-related response to this phenomenon, and the need to address risks as well as benefits to consumers.

DISCUSSION TOPICS QUESTIONS

1. Consider how technology has become a topic of discussion within the counseling professions. What are your personal opinions regarding this method to deliver counseling services? Would you consider using it yourself?

2. Compare the ethical standards of practice for the American Counseling Association and the 1999 standards for Internet online counseling (both are found at www.counseling.org). How are these standards different? How are they similar? What are the unique issues addressed by the Internet online counseling standards that are not emphasized in the ACA Ethics Code?

3. Based on one counseling theory of your choice, debate the merits of considering Internet counseling as a form of counseling or psychotherapy. Identify the pros and cons of your position.

4. In the unregulated environment (cyberspace) in which Internet counseling takes place, consumer protection issues are significant. Discuss how Internet counseling could be regulated and who should provide the regulation or oversight.

5. Describe the essential information that a counselor should include in his or her new website that will be the acess portal for consumers seeking Internet counseling.

6. Devise a checklist for your colleague who is considering the startup of Internet counseling as an adjunct to his current practice as a licensed mental health counselor. Discuss why these items are on the checklist.

7. Which theoretical frameworks are best suited to Internet counseling? Describe why one theoretical framework "fits" well with Internet counseling and why another does not.

8. In talking with an experienced counselor who has been in private practice for over 10 years, you learn that this well-respected professional is offering Internet counseling to clients in Ohio. She lives in Texas. What are the implications of this disclosure?

9. When using supervision in the Internet counseling environment, how would it differ from supervision obtained in a FTF setting? What are the strengths and barriers of Internet counseling supervision?

10. Ms. Carter has completed her feasibility study, and now moves toward making a decision to proceed with developing a business plan or to not proceed further with this initiative. What factors do you think will sway her one way or the other?

REFERENCES

Association for Counselor Education and Supervision (ACES) Technology Interest Network. (1999). *ACES guidelines for online instruction in counseling education*. Retrieved January 6, 2003, from www.acesonline.net/onlineguidelines.htm.

Ainsworth, M. (2004). *ABC's of Internet therapy: Talk to a therapist online*. Retrieved September 18, 2005, from www.metanoia.org/imhs/.

Alleman, J. R. (2002). Online counseling: The Internet and mental health treatment. *Psychotherapy: Theory, Research, Practice, Training, 39*, 199–209.

American Counseling Association. (1999). *Ethical standards for Internet online counseling*. Retrieved November 27, 2002, from www.counseling.org/resources/internet.htm.

American Psychological Association. (2002). Ethical principles of psychologists and code of conduct. *American Psychologist, 57*, 1060–1073.

Andersson, G., Stromgren, A. G., Strom, L., & Lyttkens, L. (2002). Randomized controlled trial of Internet-based cognitive behavior therapy for distress associated with tinnitus. *Psychosomatic Medicine, 64*, 810–816.

Anthony, K. (2000). Counselling in cyberspace. *Counselling Journal, 11*, 625–627.

Babel Fish Translation. (2003). AltaVista's Babel Fish Translation Service. Retrieved January 19, 2003, from http://world.altavista.com.

Baltimore, M. L. (2000). Ethical considerations in the use of technology for marriage and family counselors. *Family Journal, 8*, 390–393.

Barak, A., & Wander-Schwartz, M. (2000). Empirical evaluation of brief group therapy conducted in an Internet chat room. *Journal of Virtual Environment, 5*. Retrieved January 26, 2003 from www.bradeis.edu/pubs/jove/html/v5/cherapy3.htm.

Barthelmeus, S. J. (2000). Disclosure of limitations, risks, and benefits of online counseling services: An investigation of the effects of differing amounts of information on perceived desirability. *Dissertation Abstracts International, 60*, 3556B (University Microfilms No. AEH9938258).

Bloom, J., Walz, G., & Ford, D. (2005). *Cybercounseling: Going the distance for your clients.* American Counseling Association online courses. Retrieved September 21, 2005, from www.counseling.org.

Boer, P. M. (2001). *Career counseling over the Internet.* Mahwah, NJ: Erlbaum.

Bottela, C., Banos, R., Guillen, V., Perpina, C., Alcaniz, M., & Pons, A. (2000). Telepsychology: Public speaking fear treatment on the Internet. *CyberPsychology & Behavior, 3,* 959–968.

Burnett-Stuart, J. (2001). The technological psyche: A challenge to psychodynamic counseling? *Psychodynamic Counselling, 7,* 431–445.

Carlbring, P., Westling, B. E., Ljungstrand, P., Ekselius, L., & Andersson, G. (2001). Treatment of panic disorder via the Internet: A randomized trial of a self-help program. *Behavior Therapy, 32,* 751–764.

Center for Credentialing and Education. (2004). *Distance credential counselor (DCC).* Retrieved December 16, 2004, from www.cce-global.org/dcc.htm.

Chambers, M., Ryan, A. A., & Connor, S. L. (2001). Exploring the emotional support needs and coping strategies of family carers. *Journal of Psychiatric & Mental Health Nursing, 8,* 99–106.

Childress, C. (1998). *Potential risks and benefits of online psychotherapeutic interventions.* Retrieved November 27, 2002, from www.ismho.org/issues/9801.htm.

Christensen, H., Griffiths, K. M., & Korten, A. (2002). Web-based cognitive behavior therapy: Analysis of site usage and changes in depression and anxiety scores. *Journal of Medical Internet Research, 4.* Retrieved January 26, 2003, from www.jmir.org/2002/1/e3/.

Clark, G., Horan, J. J., Kovalsky, T., & Hackett, G. (2000). Interactive career counseling on the Internet. *Journal of Career Assessment, 8,* 85–93.

Clarke, G., Reid, E., Eubanks, D., O'Connor, E., DeBar, L. L., Kelleher, C., Lynch, F., & Nunley, S. (2002). Overcoming depression on the Internet (ODIN): A randomized controlled trial of an Internet depression skills intervention program. *Journal of Medical Internet Research, 4.* Retrieved January 26, 2003, from www.jmir.org/2002/3/e14/index.html.

Cohen, G. E., & Kerr, B. A. (1998). Computer mediated counseling: An empirical study of a new mental health treatment. *Computers in Human Services, 15,* 13–24.

Collie, K. R., Mitchell, D., & Murphy, L. (2000). Skills for on-line counseling: Maximum impact at minimum bandwidth. In J. W. Bloom & G. R. Walz (Eds.), *Cybercounseling and cyberlearning: Strategies and resources for the millennium* (pp. 219–236). Alexandria, VA: American Counseling Association and CAPS, Inc.

Collie, K., Mitchell, D., & Murphy, L. (2001). E-mail counseling: Skills for maximum impact. *ERIC/CASS Digest, EDO-CG-01-03.* Retrieved March 23, 2003, from http://ericcass.uncg.edu/digest/2001-01.html.

Cook, J. E., & Doyle, C. (2002). Working alliance in online therapy as compared to face-to-face therapy: Preliminary results. *CyberPsychology & Behavior, 5,* 95–105.

Cummins, R. A. (2001). The subjective well-being of people caring for a family member with severe disability at home: A review. *Journal of Intellectual & Developmental Disability, 26,* 83–100.

Day, S. X., & Schneider, P. (2000). The subjective experiences of therapists in face-to-face, video, and audio sessions. In J. W. Bloom & G. R. Walz (Eds.), *Cybercounseling and cyberlearning: Strategies and resources for the millennium* (pp. 203–218). Alexandria, VA: American Counseling Association and ERIC Counseling and Student Services Clearinghouse.

DeGuzman, M., & Ross, W. M. (1999). Assessing the application of HIV and AIDS related education and counseling on the Internet. *Patient Education and Counseling, 36,* 209–228.

DMOZ Open Director Project. (2002). *Mental health counseling services online: individual practitioners.* Retrieved January 26, 2003, from http://dmoz.org/health/mental_health/counseling_services/online/.

Donn, J. E., & Sherman, N.C. (2002). Attitudes and practices regarding the formation of romantic relationships on the Internet. *CyberPsychology & Behavior, 5,* 107–123.

Dryden, W., Mearns, D., & Thorne, B. (2000). Counselling in the United Kingdom: Past, present and future. *British Journal of Guidance & Counselling, 28,* 467–483.

Dunaway, M. O. (2000). Assessing the potential of online psychotherapy. *Psychiatric Times, 18.* Retrieved November 17, 2002, from www.psychiatrictimes.com/p001058.html.

Fairlie, R. W. (2003). *Is there a digital divide? Ethnic and racial differences in access to technology and possible explanations.* Retrieved September 18, 2005, from www.ctcnet.org/ctc/ucsc/digitaldivide_ethnic_racial.pdf.

Fels, D., Samers, P., & Robertson, M. (2003). *Use of asynchronous Blackberry technology in a large children's hospital to connect sick kids to school*. Paper presented at the International Conference on Computers in Education, Hong Kong. Retrieved September 18, 2005, from www.wch.org.au/emplibrary/edinst/Blackberry_Paper.pdf.

Fenichel, M. (2001). *A response to the Clinical Social Work Federation position paper on Internet text-based therapy*. Retrieved November 27, 2002, from http://ismho.org/issues/cswf.htm.

Finn, J., & Banach, M. (2000). Victimization online: The down side of seeking human services for women on the Internet. *CyberPsychology & Behavior, 3*, 243–254.

Fitchard, K. (2003). *Metrics: Catching up to the PC*. Retrieved September 18, 2005, from www.telephonyonline.com.

Freeny, M. (2001). Better than being there. *Psychotherapy Networker, 25*(2), 31–39, 70.

Gary, J. M. (2001). Impact of cultural and global issues on online support groups. *ERIC/CASS Digest*. Retrieved November 27, 2002, from http://ericcass.uncg.edu/digest/2001-01.html.

Gary, J. M., & Remolino, L. (2000). Online support groups: Nuts and bolts, benefits, limitations and future directions. *ERIC/CASS Digest*. Retrieved November 27, 2002, from www.ericfacility.net/ ericdigests/ed446330.html.

Goss, S., & Anthony, K. (Eds.). (2003). *Technology in counseling and psychotherapy: A practitioner's guide*. Hampshire, UK: Palgrave Macmillan.

Graham, C., Frances, A., Kenwright, M., & Marks, I. (2000). Psychotherapy by computer. *Psychiatric Bulletin, 24*, 331–332.

Griffiths, M. (2001). Online therapy: A cause for concern? *The Psychologist, 14*, 245–248.

Grohol, J. (2000). Online therapy: A minefield of treasures. *New Therapist,* May/June. Retrieved November 17, 2002, from www.newtherapist.com/groho117.html.

Gross, S. J. (2000). Updating the prospects for online counseling and psychotherapy. Retrieved September 21, 2005, from www.helphorizons.com/vo/library/article.asp?id=185.

Guterman, J. T., & Kirk, M. A. (1999). *Mental health counselors and the Internet*. Retrieved November 21, 2002, from www.counselingzone.com/internet/.

Hampton, N. Z., & Houser, R. (2000). Applications of computer-mediated communications via the Internet in rehabilitation counseling. *Journal of Applied Rehabilitation Counseling, 31*, 3–9.

Heinlen, K. T., Welfel, E. R., Richmond, E. N., & Rak, C. F. (2003). The scope of webcounseling: A survey of services and compliance with NBCC standards for the ethical practice of webcounseling. *Journal of Counseling & Development, 81*, 61–69.

Holmes, L. (1997). *You can't do psychotherapy on the net, yet*. Paper presented at the American Psychological Association Annual Convention, August, 1997. Retrieved November 29, 2002, from http://mentalhealth.about.com/library/weekly/aa010499.htm.

Hsiung, R. C. (2001). Suggested principles of professional ethics for the online provision of mental health services. *Medinfo*. Amsterdam: IOS Press. Retrieved November 29, 2002, from http://cmbi.bjmu.edu.cn/news/report/2001/medinfo_2001/papers/Ch15/590_Hsiung.pdf.

Hughes, R. S. (2000). Cybercounseling and regulations: Quagmire or quest? In J. W. Bloom & G. R. Walz (Eds.), *Cybercounseling and cyberlearning: Strategies and resources for the millennium* (pp. 321–338). Alexandria, VA: American Counseling Association and CAPS, Inc.

International Society for Mental Health Online (ISMHO). (2000). *Suggested principles for the provision of mental health services*. Retrieved November 27, 2002, from www.ismho.org.

International Society for Mental Health Online (ISMHO). 2003. National directory of online counselors. Retrieved June 28, 2006, from www.etherapyweb.com.

Jencius, M., & Sager, D. E. (2001). The practice of marriage and family counseling in cyberspace. *The Family Journal: Counseling and Therapy for Couples and Families, 9*, 295–301.

Jerome, L. W. (1999). Telehealth: Clinical tool for psychology. *National Psychologist, 9*(5), 7–8.

Joinson, A. N. (1998). Causes and effects of disinhibition on the internet. In J. Gackenbach (Ed.), *The psychology of the Internet* (pp. 43–60). New York: Academic Press. Retrieved December 17, 2002, from http://iet.open.ac.uk/pp/a.n.joinson/papers/disinhibition.PDF.

Joinson, A. N. (2001). Self-disclosure in computer-mediated communication: The role of self-awareness and visual anonymity. *European Journal of Social Psychology, 31*, 177–192. Retrieved December 17, 2002, from http://iet.open.ac.uk/pp/a.n.joinson/papers/self-disclosure.pdf.

Kaldo-Sandröm, V., Larsen, H. C., & Andersson, G. (2004). Internet-based cognitive-behavioral self-help treatment of tinnitus: Clinical effectiveness and predictors of outcomes. *American Journal of Audiology, 13*, 185–192.

Keil, M., Meader, G. W., & Kvasny, L. (2003). *Bridging the digital divide: The story of the free internet initiative in LaGrange, Georgia.* Proceedings of the 36th Hawaii International Conference on System Sciences—2003. Retrieved September 18, 2005, from http://www.hicss.hawaii.edu/HICSS36/HICSSpapers/ETEPO05.pdf.

King, S. A., Engi, S., & Poulos, S. T. (1998). Using the Internet to assist family therapy. *British Journal of Guidance and Counselling, 26*, 43–52.

King, S. A., & Poulos, S. T. (1998). Using the Internet to treat generalized social phobia and avoidant personality disorder. *CyberPsychology & Behavior, 1*, 29–36.

Klein, B., & Richards, J. C. (2001). A brief internet-based treatment for panic disorder. *Behavioural & Cognitive Psychotherapy, 29*, 113–117.

Kraus, R., Zack, J. S., & Stricker, G. (Eds.). (2003). *Online counseling: A handbook for mental health professionals.* Oxford, UK: Elsevier Science & Technology Books.

Kuntze, M. F., Stoermer, R., Mueller-Spahn, F., & Bullinger, A. H. (2002). Ethical codes and values in a virtual world. *CyberPsychology & Behavior, 5*, 203–206.

Laditka, S. B., & Pappas-Rogich, M. (2001). Anticipatory caregiving anxiety among older women and men. *Journal of Women and Aging, 13*, 3–18.

Lange, A., Van de Ven, J.-P., & Schrieken, B. (2001). INTERAPY. A treatment of posttraumatic stress through the internet: A controlled trial. *Behavioral Therapy and Experimental Psychiatry, 32*, 73–90.

Laszlo, V., Esterman, G., & Zabko, S. (1999). Therapy over the Internet? Theory, research & finances. *CyberPsychology & Behavior, 2*, 293–307.

Lebow, J. (1998). Not just talk, maybe some risk: The therapeutic potentials and pitfalls of computer mediated conversation. *Journal of Marital and Family Therapy, 24*, 203–206.

Lee, C. C. (1998). Counseling and the challenges of cyberspace. *Counseling Today*, April, 5.

Lee, C. C. (2000). Cybercounseling and empowerment: Bridging the digital divide. In J. W. Bloom & G. R. Walz (Eds.), *Cybercounseling and cyberlearning: Strategies and resources for the millennium* (pp. 85–93). Alexandria, VA: American Counseling Association and ERIC Counseling and Student Services Clearinghouse.

Levine, D. (2000). Virtual attraction: What rocks your boat? *CyberPsychology & Behavior, 3*, 565–573.

Levine, J. R., Baroudi, D., & Young, M. L. (1997). *The Internet for dummies* (4th ed.). Foster City, CA: IDG Books.

Levine, J. R., Baroudie, D., & Young, M. L. (2000). The Internet for dummies: Starter kit. New York: John Wiley and Sons.

Lewis, J., Coursol, D., & Herting-Wahl, K. (2000). Electronic portfolios in counselor education. In J. W. Bloom & G. R. Walz, (Eds.), *Cybercounseling and cyberlearning: Strategies and resources for the millennium* (pp. 171–184). Alexandria, VA: American Counseling Association and CAPS, Inc.

Li, Y., & Sprague, D. (2002). Study on home caregiving for elders with Alzheimer's and memory impairment. *Illness, Crisis & Loss, 10*, 318–334.

Love, J. S. (2000). Cybercounselors v. cyberpolice. In J. W. Bloom & G. R. Walz (Eds.), *Cybercounseling and cyberlearning: Strategies and resources for the millennium* (pp. 339–360). Alexandria, VA: American Counseling Association and CAPS, Inc.

Maheu, M. M., & Gordon, B. L. (2000). Counseling and therapy on the Internet. *Professional Psychology: Research and Practice, 31*, 484–489.

Manhal-Baugus, M. (2001). E-therapy: Practical, ethical, and legal issues. *CyberPsychology & Behavior, 4*, 551–563.

Marks, N. F., Lambert, J. D., & Choi, H. (2002). Transitions to caregiving, gender, and psychological well-being: A prospective U.S. national study. *Journal of Marriage & Family 64*, 657–667.

Menon, G. (2001, July). Caution urged before web counseling. *NASW News*. Retrieved November 29, 2002, from www.socialworkers.orfg/pubs/news/2001/-1/web.htm.

Metanoia. (2001a). *ABC's of Internet therapy.* Retrieved December 17, 2002, from www.metanoia.org/imhs/index.html.

Metanoia. (2001b). *E-therapy history and survey*. Retrieved December 17, 2002, from www.metanoia.org/imhs/history.html.

Miller, J. K., & Gergen, K. J. (1998). Life on the line: The therapeutic potentials of computer-mediated conversation. *Journal of Marital and Family Therapy, 24*, 198–202.

Murphy, L. J., & Mitchell, D. A. (1998). When writing helps to heal: E-mail as therapy. *British Journal of Guidance and Counseling, 26*, 21–32.

National Association of Social Workers. (1996). *Code of ethics*. Retrieved November 29, 2002, from www.socialworkers.org/pubs.code/code.asp.

NASW News (2001). *Licensing group looking toward standards*. Retrieved November 29, 2002, from www.socialworkers.org/pubs/news/2001/07/standards.htm.

National Board for Certified Counselors. (2005). *The practice of Internet counseling*. Retrieved September 21, 2005, from www.nbcc.org/webethics2.

National Telecommunications and Communication Administration (NTIA). (2002). *A nation online: How Americans are expanding their use of the Internet*. Retrieved December 17, 2002, from www.ntia.doc.gov/ntiahome/dn/index.html.

New Therapist (2000). *The ethics and law of online therapy*. Retrieved November 27, 2002, from www.newtherapist.com/ethicsonline.html.

New Therapist (2003). *Online therapy: A minefield of treasures*. Retrieved January 9, 2003, from www.newtherapist. com/grohol7.html.

Newburger, E. C. (2000). *Home computers and Internet use in the United States: August 2000*. Retrieved December 17, 2002, from www.census.gov/prod/2001pubs/p23-207.pdf.

Nice, M. L., & Katzev, R. (1998). Internet romances: The frequency and nature of romantic on-line relationships. *CyberPsychology & Behavior, 1*, 217–223.

NUA Internet Surveys. (2003). *How many are online?* Retrieved January 15, 2003, from www.nua.ie/surveys/how_many_online/n_America.html.

Paris, J. J. (2001). Ethical issues in cybermedicine: Patent-medicine salesmen did not go out of style with the Conestoga wagon. *America, 184*, 15–24.

Patrick, P. K. S. (2005). Online counseling education: Pedagogy controversies and delivery issues. In G. R. Walz & R. K. Yep (Eds.), *VISTAS: Compelling perspectives on counseling 2005* (pp. 239–242). Alexandria, VA: American Counseling Association.

Pergament, D. (1998). Internet psychotherapy: Current status and future regulations. *Journal of Law Medicine, 8*, 233–280.

Psychiatric Society for Infomatics (PSI). (2000). *ISMHO/PSI suggested principles of professional ethics for the online provision of mental health services*. Retrieved November 27, 2002, from www.dr-bob.org/psi/suggestions.approved.html.

Robson, D., & Robson, M. (2000). Ethical issues in Internet counseling. *Counselling Psychology Quarterly, 13*(3), 249–257.

Salem, A. D., Bogat, G. A., & Reid, C. (1997). Mutual help goes on-line. *Journal of Community Psychology, 25,* 189–207.

Sander, F. M. (1999). Couples group therapy conducted via computer-mediated communication. A preliminary case study. *Computers in Human Behavior, 12*, 301–312.

Segall, R. (2000). Online shrinks. *Psychology Today, 33*, 38–43.

Shaw, H. E., & Shaw, S. F. (2006). Critical ethical issues in online counseling: Assessing current practices with an ethical intent checklist. *Journal of Counseling & Development, 84*, 41–53.

Smartlink Corporation. (2003). Smartlink translation software. Retrieved January 19, 2003, from www.smartlinkcorp.com.

Snow, S. (2001). *Is online counseling ethical?* Retrieved November 11, 2002, from http://commcure.com/ethicsonline.html.

Stofle, G. S. (1999). *Thoughts about online psychotherapy: Ethical and practical considerations*. Retrieved November 11, 2002, from http://members.aol.com/stofle/onlinepsych.htm.

Stofle, G. S. (2001). *Choosing an online therapist: A step-by-step guide to finding professional help on the web*. Harrisburg, PA: White Hat Communications.

Stroem, L., Patterson, R., & Andersson, G. (2000). A controlled trial of recurrent headache conducted via the internet. *Journal of Consulting & Clinical Psychology, 68*, 722–727.

Suler, J. (1996). *The psychology of cyberspace.* Retrieved November 11, 2002, from www.rider.edu/users/suler/psycyber/psycyber.html.

Suler, J. (2000). *The disinhibition effect.* Retrieved November 11, 2002, from http://enotalone.com/article/2458.html.

Suler, J. (2001). Assessing a person's suitability for online therapy: The ISMHO clinical case study group. *CyberPsychology & Behavior, 4,* 675–679.

Sussman, R. J. (1998, June). Counseling over the Internet: Benefits and challenges in the use of new technologies. *Counseling Today, 8,* 28.

Syntran Corporation. (2003). Systran Information and Translation Technologies. Retrieved December 19, 2003, from www. systran.com.

Tait, A. (1999). Face-to-face and at distance: The mediation of guidance and counseling through the new technologies. *British Journal of Guidance and Counselling, 27,* 113–122.

Tate, D. F., Wing, R. R., & Winett, R. A. (2001). Using Internet technology to deliver a behavioral weight loss program. *Journal of the American Medical Association, 285,* 1172–1177.

Townsend, A. (2002). Employed family caregivers of cognitively impaired elderly: An examination of role strain and depressive symptoms. *Aging & Mental Health, 6,* 55–62.

Tyler, J. M., & Sabella, R. A. (2003). *Using technology to improve counseling practice.* Alexandria, VA: American Counseling Association.

Walther, J. B. (1996). Computer-mediated communication: Impersonal, interpersonal and hyperpersonal interaction. *Communication Research, 23,* 4–43.

Walz, G. R. (2000). Summing up. In J. W. Bloom & G. R. Walz (Eds.), *Cybercounseling and cyberlearning: Strategies and resources for the millennium* (pp. 417–420). Alexandria, VA: American Counseling Association and CAPS, Inc.

Warschauer, M. (2004). *Technology and social inclusion: Rethinking the digital divide.* Cambridge, MA: MIT Press.

White, R. (2002). *LPCs and Internet counseling: Ethical considerations.* Retrieved November 15, 2002, from www.tmhca.org/ethics.htm.

Whitty, M. T. (2002). Liar! Liar! An examination of how open, supportive and honest people are in chat rooms. *Computers in Human Behavior, 18,* 343–352.

Winzelberg, A. J., Eppstein, D., Eldredge, K. L., Wilfley, D., Dasmahapatra, R., Dev, P., & Taylor, C. B. (2000). Effectiveness of an Internet-based program for reducing risk factors for eating disorders. *Journal of Consulting & Clinical Psychology, 68,* 346–350.

Wright, J. (2002). Online counselling: Learning from writing therapy. *British Journal of Guidance & Counselling, 30,* 285–298.

Wright, J., & Chung, C. (2001). Mastery or mystery? Therapeutic writing: A review of the literature. *British Journal of Guidance and Counselling, 29*(3), 277–291.

Yager, J. (2000). E-mail as a therapeutic adjunct in the outpatient treatment of anorexia nervosa: Illustrative case material and discussion of the issues. *International Journal of Eating Disorders, 29,* 125–138.

Young, K. S. (2005). An empirical examination of client attitudes toward online counseling. *Cyberpsychology & Behavior, 8*(2), 172–177.

CHAPTER TEN

INNOVATIVE COUNSELING METHODS

Evolving Applications to Practice

BENJAMIN V. NOAH

Counseling has continually evolved since its inception as theory, research, and contemporary sociopolitical forces have influenced and been integrated into practice. Along one continuum, counseling as a profession evolved from the guidance movement to client-centered to brief therapy treatment methods (Gladding, 2003). By the 1970s, the movement to require state licensure for counselor practice was initiated and currently includes 50 of 54 jurisdictions (ACA, 2005a; Gladding, 2003). Another developmental continuum bridges the traditional educational setting for counselor preparation to the electronic age (i.e., from "ivy-covered" walls to online degree programs and Internet counseling) (Attridge, 2004; Page et al, 2003). Delivery of counseling can be mapped along another continuum that originated with Freud's couch to an acceptance of Internet counseling (Kraus, Zack, & Stricker, 2003).

New applications of theory and research may lead to innovative methods to provide counseling interventions, or counseling interventions may be offered without the foundations of theory and research and be viewed as examples of innovation. In some cases, new applications are "grafted" onto well-established methods of counseling, and in other instances, critical issues of ethics, credentialing, and research emerge. This chapter presents an overview of innovative methods of counseling. Some are reflective of familiar counseling methods, whereas others are defined as unique methods to provide mental health care. As specific methods of delivering counseling are identified, it is recognized that all possible forms of innovative applications of counseling theory and research are beyond the scope of this chapter.

COACHING

When discussing or researching the topic of coaching, one immediately encounters problems of definition and standards of practice. In counseling, *coaching* is "a technique for helping individuals, couples, or families make appropriate responses by giving them verbal instructions"

(Gladding, 2001, p. 25). "*Career coaching* is the term used in business and industry to signify the efforts engaged in by managers to facilitate the career development of employees" (Hall & Associates, 1986, as cited in Isaacson & Brown, 2000, p. 13). Executive coaching has existed for at least 25 years and is based on an organizational leadership protocol (Stern, 2004). An entirely different definition is provided by the International Coach Federation (ICF, 2005a, ¶ 1 and 2):

> Professional coaches provide an ongoing partnership designed to help clients produce fulfilling results in their personal and professional lives. Coaches help people improve their performances and enhance the quality of their lives.
>
> Coaches are trained to listen, to observe and to customize their approach to individual client needs. They seek to elicit solutions and strategies from the client; they believe the client is naturally creative and resourceful. The coach's job is to provide support to enhance the skills, resources, and creativity that the client already has.

A "hot topic" for the counseling profession is *life coaching* (S. T. Gladding, personal communication, January 27, 2005). Life coaches help people with relationship issues, career change, debt, and family problems to "liberate" and "set them on a new course" (Life Coaching Institute, n.d.). These last two definitions are noticeably similar to counseling practice, and some in this industry acknowledge the need to distinguish coaching as "people development" that is different from counseling, therapy, consulting, and the practice of psychology (Grant, 2003; Walker, 2004). Use of the life coaching terminology to describe the activities of these practitioners skirts the boundary between practice that requires licensure or regulation that is designed to protect consumers. The life coach engages in human services activities that have been created and defined by an emerging industry that is populated by both non–mental health professionals as well as counseling professionals.

A three-level certification process does exist for those who practice as coaches and is available through the International Coach Federation. Increasing numbers of ICF-approved training hours and client coaching experience hours are required to progress from the Associate Certified Coach to the Master Certified Coach level (ICF, 2005b). Self-study training courses are available for a fee (LCI, n.d.). The self-study required hours of training for the entry-level Associate Certified Coach credential (ICF, 2005b) consists of a minimum of 60 hours of training and 250 hours of client experience.

A different form of coaching consists of career coaching and is reflected in the activities carried out by career counselors who have academic and training experience according to established standards. Career coaching methods differ from more traditional career counseling by incorporating a more directive approach to problem solving, by providing coaching in nonoffice settings (e.g., the client's home or place of employment), and by the period of time necessary to achieve client outcomes (three to six months or longer) (Chung & Gfroerer, 2003). In addition, career coaches may or may not have a career counseling background.

Coaching is included as part of the competencies of the career development facilitator (CDF) as described by the National Career Development Association (NCDA, 2005). In addition, coaching activities within the realm of career counselor preparation is supported by education program accreditation through the Council for Accreditation of Counseling and Related Educational Programs (CACREP) (2001, pp. 102–103). With this assurance and background, certain career development specialists provide consumers with assurance that ethical practices are addressed by counselors practicing this form of coaching. However, for counselors *without* such training and educational preparation (often not at the master's degree level), there is significant risk that "without training in counseling, assessment, and psychology, career coaches are essentially practicing counseling without a license in a totally unregulated, 'unprofessional' environment." Thus, the risk to consumers is twofold: Persons performing career coaching or other forms of coaching may be practicing outside of their areas of expertise, and without sufficient basic education and training in this field of practice, these providers may be offering services outside appropriate and ethical practice boundaries.

Issues to Consider: Coaching

As the counseling professions consider how "coaching" is impacting practice as well as consumers, a number of issues are raised that directly influence how this activity is viewed and practiced. With the increase in coaching marketing efforts on the Internet, for example, there is some urgency for the counseling professions to address the implications of coaching on the safety and well-being of consumers. Among the considerations that will require attention are the following topics.

Research.   There is a need for more research regarding what makes "good coaching" (Stern, 2004) as well as its effectiveness (Grant & Zackon, 2004). For anyone interested in converting a private practice into a coaching practice, for example, there are "how-to" resources available that will guide one through the transition (Williams & Davis, 2002). Other publications abound and are marketed through the Internet, media outlets, and book venders. One can find a number of books at the various coaching websites; however, there is no indication that these publications are research based. The ICF does have a Code of Ethics, but it has a scant three sentences concerned with research (2005c).

Although the boundaries between counseling and coaching require further delineation, several issues must be addressed to provide a research- and outcomes-based foundation for this practice. Determining how coaching "works" according to the standards that other counseling and human services providers adhere to presents challenges in a number of ways. Coaching seems to include concepts and methods strikingly similar to counseling and psychology, yet research to support such claims is lacking (Grant, 2000, 2003). According to Grant (2003, p. 254), the life coaching definition used in a study of impact on a group of consumers consists of "a collaborative solution focused, result-orientated and systematic process in which the coach facilitates the enhancement of life experience and goal attainment in the personal and/or professional life of normal, non-clinical clients." In this study, participants in a program of life coaching reported improvements in mental health, goal attainment and quality of life, suggesting a positive outcome for this sample of 20 clients.

Because research guides evidence-based practice in counseling, the paucity of research in the life coaching field clearly suggests a need to engage in focused short- and long-term study of the impact on consumers.

Theory.   The theoretical foundations of life coaching are portrayed as cross-disciplinary practice implemented by managers, teachers, consultants, psychologists, sales people, executives, and counselors primarily through telephone communication (Bluckert, 2004; Grant & Zackon, 2004). Life coaching interventions can be based on theories well validated by psychology and the counseling professions, such as solution-focused theories and cognitive-behavioral theory.

The borrowing from counseling and psychology theoretical foundations does, in fact, provide a form of research-based support for life coaching. However, this observation may support life coaching as more within the scope of practice of the academically prepared and trained counseling practitioner rather than a person who completes a self-study program. Future research and theory building is needed to determine if the cross-disciplinary approach is sufficient to support life coaching, or executive coaching in general, thus leading to the development of research and practice that demonstrates distinctions between counseling and coaching.

Practice.   Addressing behavioral, psychological, emotional, and spiritual/religious issues that may be associated with life transitions traditionally has been within the realm of counseling professionals or spiritual/religious professionals who have training, education, and experience in addressing such complex issues. Without mechanisms to regulate practice and to monitor adherence to ethical standards of the life coach, ensuring that practitioners remain within the scope of noncounseling activities is unclear. Qualifications to seek a life coaching credential appear to be expensive in terms of financial investment, and currently there is no third-party reimbursement for the services delivered by the coach as there is for licensed counseling professionals. The absence of regulation of life transition coaching suggests that individuals may enter this arena of practice lacking a depth of understanding of the interpersonal experiences that can emerge during the course of intense interaction. Limiting the scope of the role is a step in the right direction, yet the impact of life transition coaching on consumers is not well researched or verified.

Consumer Protection.   The amount and format of training to become a life transition coach could result in competence to assist a person facing certain life changes. However, of significance is the fact that there is no consumer protection regulation in place to verify the qualifications of coaches or to prohibit practice to those who are qualified or certified at the minimal level currently available. In addition, with the use of the Internet as a key marketing mechanism for coaches, regulation of claims for effectiveness are neither verified nor regulated. Thus, the unsuspecting consumer is potentially at risk when using the services of a coach who may or may not have achieved a minimal proficiency in this form of helping interaction. Among many questions and concerns that can be raised about life transition coaching, issues of competence and professional practice must be considered by the counseling professions in light of the potential risk to consumers.

Use of a premier Internet search engine, Google, results in identifying numerous individuals and companies advertising services as "coaches" (i.e., life coaches, personal coaches, life transition coaches). In considering the emergence of the coach role, questions arise regarding the impact of this new form of human service on the income and prestige of the counseling profession. Further, perhaps the Council for Accreditation of Counseling and Related Educational Programs (CACREP) could consider including coaching-related training in graduate counseling programs (S. T. Gladding, personal communication, January 27, 2005).

Linked to the emergence of the coach role, other roles could be viewed as versions of nonprofessional coaching. For example, should media therapists, such as Dr. Phil and Dr. Laura, be considered within the broad category of coaching for their five-minute "advice" sessions that are televised or broadcast as entertainment or as forms of counseling? With the evolution of coaching and coaching-like roles that depend on interaction and offering help to individuals who seek guidance, it is essential that the counseling professions maintain vigilance about the impression clients may develop of therapy from their encounters with coaches.

Although coaching may indeed be of benefit to certain groups of consumers, the issues surrounding the lack of regulation of training and education of coaches, as well as the lack of research that verifies efficacy of outcomes, are central themes that must be addressed. The boundaries between counseling and coaching may be very permeable from the perspective of the consumer who is not sophisticated about methods of helping that are well grounded in research and those that are entering the marketplace without a similar foundation. As a significant contemporary issue in the counseling profession, life transition coaching is a topic that will continue to provoke debate.

CRITICAL INCIDENT STRESS DEBRIEFING

On August 20, 1986, Patrick Sherill walked into the Edmond, Oklahoma, post office where he worked. He was armed. His rage with his co-workers would leave 15 dead (including his suicide) and 6 wounded. The National Organization for Victim Assistance (NOVA) was requested to assist with the trauma. This was NOVA's first community response, and the lessons learned became the genesis of the National Crisis Response Team initiative (NCRT, 2004). Previously, this service was not available to emergency responders, although in retrospect it was clearly needed. Individual counseling was offered to crisis team responders, but was not used due to the stigma associated with seeking what was perceived as "mental health" care. For the crisis responders in that 1986 event, anger, nightmares, and anxiety were experienced at the time and during subsequent calls to go to other crisis scenes. This carry-over lasted for months, and there is still some holdover on each anniversary of this event (J. R. Griffith, personal communication, January 17, 2005). Since then, crisis response teams have been deployed to the Gulf Coast and Florida following hurricanes, to California after earthquakes, to Oklahoma City in 1995, to Colorado following the Columbine shooting, to New York City in 2001 (Comer, 2004; Reid, et al, 2005), and to other natural and human-generated disaster sites each year.

Based on this experience and events that have transpired since the 1980s, mental health professionals have developed methods to address crisis-related responses among crisis responders. Counselor intervention for those who provide emergency care in complex, intense, and often potentially life-threatening contexts is considered an innovative application of counseling to a contemporary and emerging area of practice.

Stress was recognized as a psychological concept by the ancient Greeks. "People are disturbed not by things but by the views they take of them" (Epictetus, as cited in Pulley, 2004, ¶ 11). Physiological explanations of stress predominated in the nineteenth and twentieth centuries, culminating in the work of Hans Selye (1956), who defined the general adaptation syndrome. Since the time of Selye's pioneering work, stress and its aftermath have come full circle, and is again viewed as psychological phenomena of crucial importance to the well-being of first responders (Pulley, 2004).

Viewed more as a community issue rather than as an individual mental state (Comer, 2004), a diagnosis of critical incident stress (CIS) is not found in the *Diagnostic and Statistical Manual of Mental Disorders (DSM-IV-TR)*. "Historically, CIS was called other names, including traumatic stress, combat fatigue, and rapid-onset burnout. Simply put, CIS results from any situation that causes emergency personnel to experience unusually strong emotional reactions that could interfere with the ability to function" (Pulley, 2004, ¶ 21). These reactions may emerge in association with a diverse array of workplace or work-related activities.

As a sociocultural model of therapy, the critical incident stress debriefing (CISD) model evolved to guide intervention for first responders (Comer, 2004). In this context, "CISD is a generic label applied to a variety of group process protocols used in a variety of settings, with a variety of groups, and is . . . a facilitator-led group process conducted soon after a traumatic event with individuals considered to be under stress from trauma exposure" (Hiley-Young & Gerrity, 1994, ¶ 2).

Hiley-Young and Gerrity (1994) believed there were important differences between critical incidents and community disasters that were not being recognized by practitioners, perhaps raising expectations that could not be met by the procedures and protocols currently in place. Since then, others have expressed concern about the effectiveness of CISD (Gist & Woodall, 1999, as cited in Comer, 2004; van Emmerik, Kamphuls, Hulsbosch, & Emmelkamp, 2002), whereas others suggest a different approach that is community based and focuses on a continuum of care to address acute posttraumatic stress reactions (Macy et al, 2004). Pulley (2004) points to a federal study of responders to the 1995 Murrah Federal Building bombing that found higher incidents of divorce and continuing need for mental health services five years after the explosion. He also cautions that flawed studies should not detract from the benefits of CISD.

Of the models used in psychological debriefing, CISD is the most popular (McNally, 2004). Other models include, but are not limited to, traumatic event debriefing (TED) (Bell, 1995); process debriefing (PD), based on research in Europe (Dyregrov, 1997); and brief eclectic psychotherapy (BEP) (Gersons, Carlier, Lamberts, van der Kolk, 2000). Although there is debate in the literature about the efficacy of CISD (Devilly & Cotton, 2003; Robinson, 2004) when applied to diverse and often highly unique events and locations, it remains a model of crisis intervention that counselors must become competent to use prior to engaging in disaster relief activities.

Critical incident stress debriefing is a group process with group members being selected to complement each other (i.e., firefighters, law enforcement, trauma first responders). Typically, this is accomplished through identification of the individuals associated with a particular job or the role of the person in the incident (e.g., police with police, medic with medics, etc.). This allows group members to share feelings with others who have had a similar experience doing similar work. The debriefing moves through seven phases, beginning with an introduction to the process, moving through progressively intense debriefing sessions, and concluding with a summary of the event and the opportunity for participants to clear up any misunderstandings (MacDonald, 2003; Pulley, 2004; McNally, 2004). The CISD team conducts a team debriefing process after an incident has occurred and debriefings are completed. This is as much for psychological reasons as for operational and logistical processing (Pulley, 2004).

Training for professionals wishing to be on a CISD or CISM (critical incident stress management) team may be found through contact with a number of provider or professional organizations. The National Organization for Victim Assistance (NOVA) was founded in 1975 to provide research and training for individuals and agencies that give aid to victims and witnesses to traumatic events (NOVA, 2005). The International Critical Incident Stress Foundation (ICISF) offers training in conjunction with other organizations, including the United Nations, the American Red Cross, and the Salvation Army (ICISF, 2004). Members of the American Counseling Association (ACA) may receive training through the American Red Cross Disaster Mental Health Training offering at the association's annual conference. Attendance at the ACA conference training varies depending on the presence or absence of critical/disaster events in the news that are at the forefront of each participant's attention prior to conference registration (H. Clubb, personal communication, January 19, 2005). Clearly, predisaster training and preparation not linked to the recency of traumatic events would be more desirable and, in many communities, has taken place as a form of preparing mental health professionals to provide "psychological first aid" (Reid et al, 2005; Wilson, Raphael, Meldrum, Bedosky, & Sigman, 2000, p. 184).

Issues to Consider

Issues to consider affect more than just the first responders. I attended a number of town meetings with a U.S. Congressman in the weeks following 9/11. A number of attendees at these meetings reported similar symptoms to critical incident stress (CIS) in themselves and/or their children. When asked what to do, my (not facetious) answer was simply to turn off the television. This raises an issue that counselors and the counseling professions need to consider: Is it beneficial to citizens to consume unlimited, graphic, and intense "information" about traumatizing events during the 24-hour news cycle? One could make the case for such exposure as heightening the risk of viewers of all ages for vicarious CIS reactions. It would seem logical that advisories to citizens be issued regarding the potential impact of unlimited and extended viewing and hearing about disasters, domestic or international terrorism, war news, or other traumatic events. This has special import with reference to the television viewing habits of children. Counseling associations, as well as counselors, need to be ready to address the possible impact of media saturation following critical incidents.

Critical incident stress debriefing is designed to provide support, information, and assistance to those who are impacted by performing job duties under often extraordinary circumstances. It is not designed as a psychotherapeutic intervention, but as a short-term, time-limited form of early intervention. There clearly may be a need for follow-up counseling with the victims of trauma, but this often does not follow CIS intervention/debriefing (S.T. Gladding, personal communication, January 27, 2005). The current research has results ranging from mixed to highly effective concerning the efficacy of CISD and similar models in preventing of the later development of PTSD (Deahl et al, 2001; McNally, 2004; MacDonald, 2003; Richards, 2001; Robinson, 2004). In the wake of 9/11 and a host of natural disasters within the United States as well as in foreign countries, it is necessary that the counseling professions initiate research on the long-term effectiveness of CIS interventions. With such a longitudinal approach to research, it may be possible to construct a view of the critical stress response process along a continuum that includes CIS debriefing as well as other forms of acute and long-term counseling interventions.

According to some, the history of the inclusion of PTSD in the *Diagnostic and Statistical Manual of Mental Disorders* resulted from a confluence of politics, faulty research, and federal funding (Burkett & Whitley, 1998; Sommers & Satel, 2005). It will be essential that the counseling professions avoid a repeat of such a confluence of factors in any efforts to include CIS in the next edition of the *DSM*. With the hypothetical inclusion of CIS in such a revision of the diagnostic nomenclature, it will be important to ensure that this variant of PTSD will result in increased help for those affected while also spurring additions to counselor education and training agendas. The continuing occurrence of catastrophes, both natural and human made, will ensure a need to have well-prepared counselors available to help victims. Additional research on the effectiveness of CISD and follow-up activities, for victims and helpers, is therefore clearly needed.

INNOVATIVE USES OF GROUP THERAPY

Group counseling and psychotherapy have existed since the mid-1880s. The *moral therapy* movement in England used a structured, sheltered, and humane approach to successfully help mental patients. In the twentieth century, group work evolved through Alcoholics Anonymous and the group dynamics of Kurt Lewin to support cooperative learning groups (Gladding, 1995). Fads in group therapy have come and gone (e.g., the encounter and marathon groups), yet the group model of therapy has changed little in recent years (S. T. Gladding, personal communication, January 27, 2005). More contemporary applications of group counseling/therapy methods reflect the ongoing evolution within the field of counseling practice while recognizing that the longevity of such innovative applications relies on outcome research. Three examples are described as illustrations of innovative applications of group therapy methods: sandtray, marathons, and adventure-based counseling.

Sandplay: An Innovative Group Approach

Sandplay, and the less structured sandtray therapy, was introduced by Dr. Margaret Lowenfeld in the 1920s and was further developed by Dora Kalff in the 1930s (Homeyer & Sweeney, 1998, as cited in McCown, 2004; Kennedy, 2005; Sweeney, Minnix, & Homeyer, 2003). Developed for one-on-one counseling, sand therapy is finding applications in a number of settings such as group therapy with parents of adolescents in substance abuse treatment (James & Martin, 2002).

The tray of sand, with or without miniatures, allows unconscious thought and imagination to become visible—it becomes a metaphor for aspects of a person's present life or themes that are thought to be associated with the psychological issues that led to help seeking. "When practiced in a group setting, sandtrays recognize and honor the varying developmental levels within the group, thereby enabling children, regardless of cognitive functioning levels, to participate and express their feelings" (McCown, 2004, p. 5). The healing process occurs without need for interpretation, verbalization, or conscious awareness (Hunter, 1998, as cited in McCown, 2004, p. 6; Sweeney, Minnix, & Homeyer, 2003).

The Sandplay Therapists of America (2004) maintain their own research journal and training workshops. With its reliance on symbolism and creative interaction, counseling based on the sandtray may be viewed as a bridge to creative arts and play therapies. The training and preparation essential to effective use of this method of helping is extensive. As with other forms of play therapy, there is an emphasis on the empirical base for the methods used, while recognizing that some of the underlying constructs to the method may not be easily measured.

Group Therapy with Targeted Populations: Marathons and Adventure-Based Counseling

Group therapy methods have a long and well-defined history within the counseling professions, but how methods are used with unique, diverse, and newly defined populations reflect extension of these methods in innovative ways. For example, Stranger and Harris (2005) describe the application of the marathon group therapy session in a university counseling center. Many in the counseling professions recall the use of the marathon group approach to intense psychotherapeutic or personal growth seminars starting in the 1960s. While use of intense and extended sessions in a mini-marathon (four to six hours) or a full marathon (typically over a weekend) is less common in the age of managed mental health care, this option presents opportunity for counselors who seek to work with populations who would respond favorably to such an opportunity.

A variation of what could be taking place over a long weekend or for consecutive weeks consists of adventure-based counseling (ABC) (Fletcher & Hinkle, 2002; Schoel & Maizell, 2002). This form of counseling combines counseling processes delivered during outdoor, or adventure, environments. Used in one-to-one family or group formats, ABC holds promise as a primary treatment or as adjunctive to more traditional counseling that occurs in an office or clinic setting. The intensity of ABC, as depicted in certain reality television programming, can focus on issues of particular importance to youth at risk, with organizational teams, or with families struggling with relationship dynamics (Gass, 1995; Fletcher & Hinkle, 2002). When applied to group therapy with families, the delivery of adventure family therapy may focus on goals for enhanced family recreation, enrichment, or therapy (Burg, 2001). Using similar methods to adventure-based counseling, adventure family therapy seeks to blend elements of family therapy with adventure counseling strategies and methods. As an adjunct to family therapy or as a free-standing method to provide counseling, both ABC and adventure family therapy hold promise as methods that can promote optimal outcomes in these unique group settings.

Issues to Consider

The counseling professions have a number of terms used to describe working in groups: group counseling, group dynamics, group intervention, group process, and group therapy, to name a few. With a multiplicity of terms to describe the inner workings of the group therapy experience, or use of group formats to provide a variety of counseling interventions, there is a need to clarify terminology. Clarification may emerge as innovative group treatment methods are developed and the need for definitive terminology to distinguish innovative applications from traditional group therapy methods emerges. What is clear, regardless of the volume of terms used to describe the group counseling process, is recognition that there is a renewed focus on the potential that group methods hold for counseling that focuses on psychological disorders as well as health and wellness.

To practice in environments or with methods new to the counselor, it is essential that sufficient education, training, supervision, and consultation be part of the exploration of innovative methods in counseling. Continuing professional education and advanced practice certifications are required. With adventure-based counseling, the two pillars of the method must be in place before embarking on work with individuals or groups (e.g., counseling competencies in intense group work and the physical and athletic competencies associated with outdoor adventure activities used in this approach) (Fletcher & Hinkle, 2002). Research that provides evidence of efficacy of adventure-based counseling methods is essential (Newes, 2001) and should address diverse populations who may benefit from this group approach.

As the sandplay and adventure-based counseling examples illustrate, applications of creative counseling methods to help clients achieve well-being can reflect nontraditional methods that are not yet widely in use. Attention to the ethical issues and risk factors to both client and counselor associated with new areas of practice must be addressed. Finally, research is needed that verifies the effectiveness of innovative application of group methods to the treatment of clients with mental disorders, as well as promotes a high level of wellness. Although the counseling fields have much to offer to consumers with traditional methods of mental health and wellness care, they also have significant opportunity to expand the scope of ethical practice with integration of innovative adjunctive or primary forms of group counseling into a variety of practice venues.

CREATIVE ARTS IN THERAPY

Creative art is a broad term that is inclusive of art, music, dance, imagery, literature, drama, and humor in counseling (Gladding, 2005). The Association for Creativity in Counseling (ACC) is the American Counseling Association's newest division, recognizing the growth of the arts as adjunct forms of therapy. The ACC's "primary goal in forming this association was to create an inclusive forum for counselors, counselor educators, creative arts therapists and counselors in training to explore unique and diverse approaches to counseling" (ACC, 2004, ¶ 1). The division has its own journal, newsletter, and professional training and development opportunities.

Historically, the use of the arts in counseling (for healing) was both universal and ancient: Healing mandalas among Buddhists and the Navajo, and guidance through storytelling, dance, and visual symbols have been in use for centuries (Ziff & Beamish, 2004). Contemporary music (e.g., rap music) has been used to focus on such issues as self-esteem, social skills development, anger management, and other factors associated with urban adolescent behavior (DeCarlo, 2000–2001). Music therapy has also been used to favorably impact teacher burnout in conjunction with cognitive-behavior therapy (Cheek, Bradley, Parr, & Lan, 2004). Use of writings and drawings with children who have been traumatized following a dramatic escape from a home country and subsequent arrival in a new country as refugees facilitates communication about the experiences and expression of often powerful, overwhelming affect (del Valle, McEachem, & Sabina, 1999). Caron (2005) describes the benefits of using movies as part of the counseling process. Clients completing homework assignments to view a specific film can gain insights in ways that might not emerge in the face-to-face encounter (Higgins & Dermer, 2001; Koch & Dollarhide, 2000). When client and counselor view a movie together, the ability to stop-start the film allows discussion of insights and feelings that can accelerate progress made in counseling.

Both music and art therapy have their genesis in the 1930s, with significant growth following World War II. The American Art Therapy Association (AATA) and the American Music Therapy Association (AMTA) maintain research and certification programs (AMTA, 2004; AATA, 2003). Recognition that counselors may not seek advanced certification or graduate education in these specializations raises important issues for the counselor with creative capabilities in the arts. One of the conundrums of integrating art into counseling is illustrated by the following personal example:

> I have never been trained in art therapy (ergo, no certification). However, I have been an artist for as long as I can remember. A few years back I stopped counseling adults and college students and started working with at-risk students in kindergarten through grade 8 (possible candidates for CISD). When I started doing group therapy with six- to eight-year-olds (in the small town where I was born), I found myself feeling a bit out of place. The children's primary need was self-esteem. My art has long been a source of self-efficacy. Why not use art to build self-esteem in the children?
>
> Two girls in one group illustrate the concept. Both are 8 years old and the middle of three girls in their respective families. Both are living in families headed by single mothers, with a history of abuse by the men in their lives, and are poor. The way I teach drawing is by giving the children choices: What animal will we draw? Is it happy or sad? Do we want to draw the body? If so, what is the position—asleep, walking, or sitting? The girls have not had the option of choices, so they are excited to suddenly have choices. Teaching the girls to draw cartoon animals gave them a start on self-esteem—something to hold up to the world and say, "I did this." This small start in self-esteem has resulted in the girls showing improved grades in school, better relations with siblings and mothers, and feelings of success. Question: Does my use of art in therapy in counseling constitute a breach of ethics, since I'm not certified in art therapy?

The question raised by this personal example is often at the heart of creativity in counseling practice. If the counselor is competent as a counselor, and also as a musician, artist, dancer, or sculptor, for example, finding appropriate and ethical ways to use this capacity within the counseling context can enrich the counseling experience for client and counselor.

Integration of counselor-unique qualities and expertise in the arts into counseling practice may well require that supervision is sought as an objective review of the work being performed. From one perspective, the supervisor or consultant would then also need some degree of competence in the use of creative methods in counseling, or from a different perspective, perhaps this form of professional interaction could take place with experts in the processes of counseling who would be open to learning about a creative counselor's practice. In this way, the supervision and consultation experience becomes enriching for both participants.

Issues to Consider

Counselor education programs focus primarily on preparing students for licensure through fulfilling accreditation requirements for academic coursework and skills training in preparation for entry to the profession. Often there are few elective course options that could lead to exploration of creative enhancements to counseling skill sets and competencies. Given these limitations, it may well be time to include at least one class on the use of the arts as a vehicle to accomplish counseling treatment goals such as that proposed by Ziff and Beamish (2004). These authors developed a workshop-style class for their students to provide an experiential introduction to using the arts in therapy, as well as ethical considerations peculiar to the arts in therapy. Students in this class gained experience in engaging in arts activities as well as exploring how a variety of arts can be integrated into practice.

Creative art activities can be integrated into counseling practice as adjunctive to the therapeutic methods used without the counselor having achieved a specialized certification (e.g., play therapy certification). For example, when counseling with young children, the medium of expression that they are most familiar with is drawing, coloring, and working puzzles. The counselor who is building rapport with a four-year-old, for example, may ask her to "draw a picture" as a general invitation or to "draw a picture of your family doing something." In this situation, the counselor observes how the child approaches and completes the task as well as talking about the drawing produced. As with many creative methods, counselors can use music, film, and self-produced art as a bridge to discuss painful experiences with clients of any age.

Integration of metaphors and storytelling enriches the counseling interaction between therapist and client. Use of storytelling, drawing, or writing allows clients to express themes and feelings, and to address counseling issues that otherwise might not be identified. In the context of developing a story or narrative, the client accesses the art of expression to see, experience, and work with the therapist to resolve often complex and painful personal experiences (Cowan, 2005; Snow, Ouzts, Martin, & Helm, 2005). Use of storytelling or personal myth-building exercises in counseling is an innovative method that is revitalized through use with diverse clients, groups, and families, often resulting in dramatic strengthening of understanding and resolution of long-standing emotional issues. Central to the use of the arts and creativity, therefore, is recognition of the counselor's comfort level in doing so, clear understanding of the potential outcomes, and ready access to the support and guidance that supervision provides.

THE LATEST FAD OR THE FUTURE OF COUNSELING?

Numerous therapy approaches have been developed that seemingly were greeted as the "next big movement" in the counseling profession. These approaches found adherents, initiated a flurry of research, in some cases garnered media attention, and originators or adherents offered training workshops and certifications to prepare counselors to offer the treatment method. Practitioners then marketed their certifications as an added value to clients with specific psychological, social, or personal life problems. Once the initial flurry of activity passed, reference to the new methods typically faded from the professional literature (similar to the previously mentioned encounter group movement of the 1960s). In considering innovations in counseling practice, two contemporary counseling approaches are described that continue to attract interest within the counseling professions. As each is discussed, consider the question: Will time consider each as a passing fad or as an abiding form of counseling that will continue to be viable well into the future?

Eye Movement Desensitization and Reprocessing

Eye movement desensitization and reprocessing (EMDR) began as an idea formulated by Francine Shapiro while she was walking in a park in 1987 (Carroll, 2003; EMDR Institute, 2004). The method is premised on the belief that eye movements (i.e., rapid saccadic eye movement) have a "desensitizing effect" on negative emotions and distressing memories. A counselor using this method believes that the focused eye movements interact with cognitive components of brain function that helps to reduce symptoms of clients who have a diagnosis of PTSD. Initial studies conducted by Shapiro supported the efficacy of this method (EMDR Institute, 2004; Shapiro & Maxfield, 2002). Controversy in the literature, however, raises the issue of counselors using an intense form of intervention that may or may not have a solid physiological foundation with clients who have a serious and complex psychological disorder. Post-traumatic stress disorder is one such disorder with a complicated neurobiology and a diverse array of symptoms, sources of causation, and risks to the client's overall well-being (Osuch & Engel, 2004). In addition, reviews of the literature on the efficacy of EMDR research suggest that more rigorous designs are needed as well as careful analysis of research outcomes (Hertlein & Ricci, 2004).

Although EMDR has been referred to as "science or wizardry, with little middle ground" (McCabe, 2004), it has been applied with success to the treatment of various forms of traumatic memory and intrusive thoughts about traumatic experiences as part of sex therapy (Koehler, 2002; Zangwill, 2004), to specific forms of severe trauma experience (Lamprecht, et al, 2004), to treat dental phobia (DeJongh, van den Oord, & ten Broeke, 2002), to address childhood sexual abuse (Snyder, 1996), to work with couples addressing trauma effects (Capps, 2006), and to treat chronic pain (Grant & Threlfo, 2002). Other studies indicate that EMDR is no more effective than nondirective treatment (Lytle, Hazlett-Stevens, & Borkovec, 2002), and that outcomes of EMDR research can be influenced by significant issues of design that impact determinations of EMDR treatment effects (Capps, Andrade, & Cade, 2005; Maxfield & Hyer, 2002; Shapiro, 2002).

At this point, one can quickly become involved in a "war of research" with the disciples of EMDR presenting efficacy studies to support the approach and the detractors presenting research that questions the entire concept. A review of these opposing viewpoints presents a "rematch" of a historically intriguing period in the annals of psychology regarding research involving Freud's theory with the "true believers" biased toward their view and the behaviorists having their own contradictory biases on the meaning of reality (Torrey, 1992). Perhaps it is the passion generated by such debate, when new theories and treatments are implemented, that continues to invigorate the counseling field. One could hypothesize that without new theoretical and practice developments, the field would cease to grow or sustain its viability and vitality.

Eye movement desensitization and reprocessing belongs with the power therapy approaches—for example, visio/kinesthetic dissociation (V/KD), traumatic incident reduction (TIR), emotional freedom technique (EFT), and thought field therapy (TFT) (Commons, 2000). Each of these approaches is also involved in the war of research with opponents and skeptics who view these methods as pseudoscience. For adherents on both sides, these approaches become paradigms or shared assumptions that support the method's legitimacy. Kuhn (1970, p. 94) cautioned, "When paradigms enter, as they must, into a debate about paradigm choice, their role is necessarily circular. Each group uses its own paradigm to argue in that paradigm's defense." Thus, when innovative methods of counseling are introduced, they can collectively or individually begin a shift in the construction of how counseling is conceptualized. Counseling techniques that integrate neurobiology into the treatment process add dimensions of challenge to our understanding of the boundaries of therapy. As such, the debates about each new form of treatment should remain robust and multidimensional in order to sift the fad from the enduring therapeutic tool.

Narrative Methods

Innovative counseling methods consist of unique forms of counseling, such as EMDR, that blend several elements of theory into a new form of helping. Other forms of counseling that reflect innovation are derived from a desire to generate insight through activation of the client's inner world of thought, feeling, and experience. One such contemporary therapeutic method is narrative therapy.

Narrative therapy originated in Australia with the work of David Epston and Michael White in 1990 (Gladding, 2001; Seligman, 2001). Narrative therapy is "a post modern and social construction approach to change based on narrative reasoning, which is characterized by stories, meaningfulness, and liveliness" (Gladding, 2001, p. 80). The therapeutic process begins much like the existential counselor asking the client, "What does it mean to be you?" This begins the search for meaning and value in the client's life (Deurzen-Smith, 1988). The narrative counselor collaborates with the client in developing a new "story" of himself or herself. The old story is deconstructed and externalized. Changing the story encourages externalizing the problems in order to solve them (Gladding, 2001; Seligman, 2001).

Narrative approaches have been successfully used in a number of settings, such as family counseling (Gladding, 2001; Muntigl, 2004), where the values of constructing stories can focus on the desired outcomes of change and growth in ways that are appealing to family members, respectful of divergent viewpoints, and rich in detail that might not otherwise emerge. The narrative approach can be used in career counseling for adults to change the "work story" (Goodman, 2003) in recognition that the more standard use of instruments (e.g., career inventories) typically are less effective with adults who are struggling with career issues. The approach has been successfully used to prevent PTSD as part of cancer recovery (Petersen, Bull, Propst, Dettinger, & Detwiler, 2005) and to cope with trauma associated with terrorism (Tuval-Mashiach, Freedman, Bargai, Boker, Hodar, & Shalev, 2004). In Australia, narrative therapy has been used with girls hospitalized for anorexia nervosa (Bardick et al, 2004; Segal, 2002). The potential of restorying one's life, problems, and psychological issues through narrative approaches is impressive. Within an eclectic approach to counseling, for example, narrative therapy provides a bridge between the multiple contexts of a client's life (e.g., culture, medical diagnoses) and alternative ways to explain and address identified problems (Gutterman & Rudes, 2005).

Issues to Consider

How well does the latest "fad" or "future counseling theory" hold up when evaluated according to Popper's (1963) principle of falsifiability, risky predictions, and postdiction? Is EMDR sufficiently research based at this time to be considered a legitimate, albeit out of the usual realm of the counselor's practice, form of helping those experiencing intense distress associated with PTSD? Is the risk of avoiding harm to clients adequately addressed by the procedures that guide the treatment to allay anxiety about client well-being? Individual practitioners as well as the profession itself will continue to be watchful about these issues as part of the mandate to ensure that consumers of mental health services are protected and well served.

Central to dissecting this issue is recognition that determining effectiveness is influenced by how the end result of counseling is defined. For example, if the interpretation of effectiveness is the client's reports of improvement and decrease in symptoms following a course of EMDR treatment, a desirable outcome has been achieved. If the interpretation of effectiveness is the capacity to use scientific measurements of brain blood flow or biochemical blood analysis as a correlate of reports of treatment effectiveness, EMDR may not produce such outcomes. If the therapist's evaluation of treatment outcomes does or does not coincide with self-ratings by clients, questions can arise about how to interpret treatment effectiveness.

As with many counseling methods, each practitioner settles on a particular theoretical framework that guides intervention. This first-level framework is usually acquired during the initial counselor education experience yet may well evolve as the world of practice, client needs, and the field itself transforms the counselor either slowly or dramatically into a seasoned practitioner. Professionals are inherently suspicious of the "next best thing" when it comes to the lives and well-being of consumers. This protective stance is part and parcel of the professional's sense of ethical responsibility and integrity. Thus, when a new therapeutic modality is touted as producing dramatic results requiring minimal investment of time with clients to apply, or in other ways seems "too good to be true," professional wariness is justifiably aroused.

According to Kuhn (1970, p. 15), "History suggests that the road to a firm research consensus is extraordinarily arduous." Has the research for EMDR been "extraordinarily arduous," and are there sufficient conclusions drawn to reduce the level of skepticism that remains within the profession regarding this method of treatment? Or, perhaps a different question needs to be asked: How does the counseling profession incorporate an acceptance of different treatment methods without dramatically altering the foundation of the profession? Ideally, counselors who wish to incorporate a new method do so with a clear understanding of the theoretical and research scaffolding of the approach and thereby avoid the "latest fad."

Narrative methods of counseling have not garnered a similar amount of skepticism as EMDR. Perhaps this is due in part to the symbiosis that narrative therapies have with traditional talk therapies, psychotherapy that relies on understanding of intrapsychic processes, and in the familiar vocabulary used. Counselors are accustomed to listening to the stories of clients, yet narrative therapies take this to a new level of activity, suggesting that building the narrative by the client takes on a deeper meaning and has a greater impact during the healing process.

IN SEARCH OF "WHY?"

Counselors are trained to avoid "why" questions, as the client may view such inquiry as negative or accusatory (Seligman, 2001). For many, the question is unanswerable and creates frustration. However, it is the unstated reason individuals seek counseling—trying to answer the "why's" of life. "Why" questions are contemplated, and sometimes answered, in the realms of religion and philosophy.

Immanuel Kant placed freedom, immortality, and God beyond either proof or disproof (Copleston, 1961). Ergo, the existence of a deity is beyond the limits of reason—to be contemplated but never known (Kant, 1781/1952). For counselors, the struggle to develop concepts of spirituality and religion within the context of counseling has become increasingly recognized as viable and rich areas of exploration (see Chapter 11 for an in-depth review of this topic). Within the counseling profession, professional associations such as the Association for Spiritual, Ethical, and Religious Values in Counseling (ASERVIC) are engaged in conducting research on the role, impact, and outcomes of integrating concepts of religion and faith within counseling. As these efforts develop and make substantial contributions to the practice of counseling, there is a parallel increase in the growing number of certifications being developed for "spiritual" and Christian counseling.

Typically, state counselor licensure laws include exemption language for counselors working in religious settings that eliminate the need for a license to practice. Questions arise in this regard with reference to assurances of consumer protection by unlicensed counselors, adherence to ethical standards of practice, and peer review of performance. As these concerns are addressed by practitioners who base counseling treatment on religious principles or tenets, additional questions arise regarding the need for standards of practice and accountabilities that are similar to those required of licensed mental health practitioners.

Christian Counseling Certification

The American Association of Pastoral Counselors (AAPC) was founded in 1963 to certify individuals, training programs, and counseling centers (AAPC, 2005a). The AAPC maintains a three-tiered certification process (Certified Pastoral Counselor, Fellow, and Diplomate).

The entry-level credential requires a graduate degree in theology or pastoral counseling, church endorsement, three years of ministry experience, and supervised pastoral counseling experience. The fellow and diplomate designations build on the initial certification in both training and experience (AAPC, 2005b). These requirements incorporate verification of the credentials of pastoral counselors that can provide assurance to consumers regarding ethical standards of practice. However, not all certifications are created equal within this specialized area of practice.

The National Christian Counselors Association (NCCA), established in 1983, offers training programs, certification, and licensure for Christian counselors. The NCCA is very emphatic that its license is in ministry and not a state license to practice outside of a church setting. Licensure and certification is available only to those who have completed an NCCA training program, and the curriculum is available at 12 participating colleges. Malpractice insurance is available through Lloyds of London (NCCA, 2005). When considering the potential impact to ethical practice and consumer protection, several concerns arise with reference to the efficacy of this form of nonregulated "recognition": (1) the web-based materials associated with this organization emphasize the marketing of a nonstandardized assessment instrument (Temperament Analysis Profile) developed by the organization; (2) there is no indication on the site of an accreditation agency for the training offered (NCCA, 2005); and (3) assurances or information about how the practice of certified counselors will be monitored to ensure adherence to ethical standards of practice is lacking.

The Association of Christian Counselors (AACC) was initially founded as a forum for the exchange of ideas and information. Since 1989, it has grown into a multifaceted organization that supports a number of training programs, maintains its own research journals, and supports outreach programs. This author (a founding member of the association) participated in a "community meeting" several years ago where the topic of discussion was whether AACC should develop a certification for Christian counselors. The organization does not have specific educational requirements for membership and many members do not having formal training or graduate degrees in the helping professions. Consequently, a professional certification was not created by this organization. Individuals receive completion certificates for training programs, but these are not intended to signify more than the completion of training.

Issues of Concern

The three organizations described each provide a set of lenses through which to view "Christian" or "spiritual/religious" counseling. For consumers, knowledge of the underlying premises of certification as a Christian counselor can be confusing in itself. That is, when three different models are presented, consumers are faced with questions about identifying a counselor who is credentialed and prepared to address mental health issues from a spiritual/religious or Christian religious perspective. In addition, Christian counselors who are not licensed mental health providers are obligated to clearly distinguish the nature of the services they provide from those offered by licensed counselors. Counseling professional organizations can provide accurate information to consumers about the counselor selection process that recognizes the potential benefits of religion-based counseling while also providing guidance on qualifications that are appropriate to the client's need.

As an innovative method of providing counseling, religion-based or Christian counseling has acquired recognition as a viable method to counsel in specific settings and contexts. It is essential, however, to recognize that counselors who elect to integrate personal religious or spiritual beliefs into the counseling process must do so with a clear understanding of the potential impact on clients. Seeking supervision on a regular basis, as with all innovative methods that do not yet have a solid foundation of outcome research, is an essential ingredient along the time line of integration or deemphasis of innovations in counseling practice.

Philosophical Counseling

Does philosophy hold the answer to the eternal "why" question? Seneca's answer is instructive: "Shall I tell you what philosophy holds out to humanity? Counsel. . . . You are called in to help the unhappy" (Seneca, as cited in Raabe, 2002, p. 1). Proponents suggest that there is a growing movement to build philosophical counseling into a recognized counselor specialty, whereas others debate the viability of the movement (Knapp & Tjeltveit, 2005). Raabe believes that philosophical counseling is the answer to the underemployment of philosophy graduates that fosters career options outside of academia. Although this rationale to expand a discipline's scope of influence has practical implications for employment or economic success, it raises serious issues about the motivation of unlicensed academically prepared professionals who enter a field of human services practice.

The application of philosophical treatment methods with nonmental health clients is referred to as *narrow-scope philosophical counseling* (e.g., addressing professional ethical dilemmas from a philosophical perspective) (Knapp & Tjeltveit, 2005). Use of the method, for some proponents, focuses solely on providing philosophically based talk therapy for the nonmentally ill consumer (Paden, 1998). Marinoff (1999) is emphatic that this is "therapy for the sane," while being an alternative to "disease-ifying" psychology and psychiatry. Aside from the antipsychology/psychiatry posture that this view suggests, philosophical perspectives on certain life issues or concerns often have a role to play in promoting well-being for consumers who seek this form of intervention or traditional counseling.

Broad-scope philosophical counselors provide services to clients who have identified mental health diagnoses or who would otherwise be counseled by mental health counselors as psychotherapy clients (Knapp & Tjeltveit, 2005). According to Marinoff (2003), changing the view of mental "illness" from a "disease" model to a "dis-ease" model provides a rationale to use philosophy to regain a sense of well-being. When used as part of a treatment plan by qualified mental health practitioners, philosophical counseling becomes a viable alternative to traditional therapy. It is the application of the philosophical perspective as the sole method of counseling delivered by individuals without appropriate credentials or licensure that represents a significant unresolved issue for the proponents of this approach. An effort to address one element of this issue is represented by the credentialing offered by the American Philosophical Practitioners Association.

Certification as an associate or fellow in philosophical counseling is gained through the American Philosophical Practitioners Association (APPA). The mission of the APPA "encourages philosophical awareness and advocates leading the examined life. Philosophy can be practiced through client counseling, group facilitation, organizational consulting or educational programs. APPA members apply philosophical systems, insights and methods to the management of human problems and the amelioration of human estates" (APPA, 2005). For licensed counselors, this additional level of training and education can position the counselor professional to integrate philosophical perspectives into counseling in a concerted manner. Additionally, when narrow- or broad-scope philosophical counseling is used by licensed counselors, standards of practice and ethical guidelines provide essential practice boundaries and consumer safeguards (e.g., practicing within the counselor's areas of competence).

Issues to Consider

As with other forms of nontraditional counseling, core issues of ethical practice by counselors who self-identify as philosophical counselors must be addressed. For example, initiation of the philosophical counseling client–counselor relationship must include review of client expectations. Consumers may see the "counselor" designation of the philosophical counselor without understanding what this means in comparison to, for example, how a mental health counselor approaches therapy. Counselors interested in the philosophical perspective seek advanced education and training to ensure that differences between traditional forms of psychotherapy and philosophical counseling can be clearly explained, questions can be answered, and expectations can be fully understood before initiating a course of treatment.

Additional questions regarding the acceptability of philosophical counseling as a primary treatment method arise with reference to insurance reimbursement. With the emphasis on brief therapies in the contemporary managed mental health care environment that currently exist, clients would rightly have valid questions about insurance coverage for this form of counseling. Counselors, in such situations, would be required to disclose this information to the client. Failure to do so would be a breach of ethical standards of practice for licensed counselors.

The counseling professions would benefit from discussion of the rationale for the movement of philosophers away from academia and into counseling practice. In addition, consideration of how to integrate the best of what the philosophical counseling perspective brings to traditional practice methods could result in added benefits to both practitioners and clients. It would seem appropriate to explore how counseling theory, research, and treatment methods can be brought into the preparation of philosophers who wish to become counselors, and to carefully define what the parameters of such a role would be. The need to ensure consumer protection and ethical standards of practice for a unregulated form of counseling is essential. Research that identifies the efficacy of philosophical counseling will foster increased understanding of outcomes as well as provide broader support within the counseling professions of the purpose and intent of this innovative method.

CONCLUSIONS AND PERSPECTIVE

Nontraditional counseling approaches that seek to blend spiritual, religious, or philosophical perspectives with the helping process are often viewed as adjunctive; that is, *in addition* to use of methods that are based on theory and research, counselors add techniques or perspectives that expand the repertoire of the counseling professional. Alternative methods enrich practice as well as provide opportunity to meet unique needs of clients. However, alternative methods that are not based on well-developed theory and research can increase consumer risk with reference to protection of well-being when innovative or alternative methods lack the stringent ethical standards of traditional counseling practice. Consideration of these issues leads to thoughtful analysis by the counseling profession, as well as individual counselor professionals, regarding governmental regulation of practice for religion-based or philosophical counselors. The pros and cons of consumer protection legislative actions, for example, could be viewed as a violation of church–state separation, yet without thoughtful debate, consumer protection and ethical practice issues remain unresolved.

In reviewing the history of innovation in the counseling profession over the last few decades, seemingly new approaches to therapy are often found to lack "legs"; in other words, they are not viable over time to continue as legitimate methods to help consumers travel the often arduous path toward healing. Pseudoscientific approaches and questionable therapies arise, become popular and intriguing, then often subside or disappear entirely when unable to withstand the scrutiny of research, debate, and evaluation of outcomes. The traditional standards for counseling professional practice still set accepted and recognized expectations for consumers. The counseling professions *do* rely on research to provide direction to "what works." The professionals who provide counseling that impacts lives, address issues ranging from life-threatening illness, to trauma recovery, to marital and family issues, and the host of troubling mental health issues encountered in practice must have a foundation that is solid, reliable, and lasting.

While innovative methods are brought forth, the contemporary climate of managed care and cost containment leads to questions that must be at the forefront of debate about any new therapy. In addition, legal and ethical issues also influence how new methods are introduced, used, and evaluated with a constant need for vigilance regarding liability issues. Another challenge to the counseling professions is to attend to how each professional's creativity and drive for innovation will be influenced by societal and political issues such as tort reform, changes in consumer protection legislation, economic issues associated with fees charged and reimbursement schemes for innovative methods, and public education to establish realistic expectations of the counseling experience.

Certification to practice is a time-honored and recognized mechanism to signal that a provider of mental health care is qualified to practice. However, the number of certifications for specialized practice continue to increase, suggesting a conundrum: Certification provides a degree of evidence to consumers that the counselor has acquired expertise, yet the certification itself may lack a backbone of legitimacy, thereby voiding the patina of legitimacy. It is important to realize that there is variance regarding the meaning of certifications that are not regulated and offered by self-proclaimed counselor professional organizations. Completing a set of academic courses, for example, does not ensure that the certificate recipient is adequately prepared to provide counseling services using innovative methods.

Although there are caveats to consider regarding innovative counseling methods, simultaneously innovation and creativity reflect the promise for the future of the counseling professions. It is through the careful review of innovative methods that those with solid foundations can be integrated into the counselor's repertoire of helping methods. Over time, diffusion of innovation takes place (Rogers, 2003, p. 5) "in which an innovation is communicated through certain channels over time among the members of a social system. It is a special type of communication, in that the messages are concerned with new ideas." For the counseling professions, the diffusion of new ideas has continually led to significant development of theory, research, and applications to practice that has fostered the well-being of clients served. It is this dynamic nature of counseling that spurs renewal of the counseling professions.

DISCUSSION TOPICS/QUESTIONS

1. One of your colleagues at the mental health center is considering a change of career. You've discussed it with him a number of times. After reading about coaching, you're considering suggesting that your colleague explore talking with a life transitions coach. As preparation for your talk with your colleague, describe the potential benefits of life transition coaching as well as the limitations.

2. In preparation to discuss life transition coaching with your colleague, you've surfed the Web for information. Provide a critique of one of the websites you located. Include in your critique the objectives of the site, the services or education offered, and the sponsor of the site. Summarize your opinion of this website in terms of it meeting professional standards you're familiar with for licensed counselors.

3. Many innovative methods used by counselors as adjuncts to therapy are very contemporary and recently introduced. How will you determine the effectiveness of an innovative counseling method that you're interested in exploring?

4. Counseling that focuses on mental health care for clients who have experienced trauma can be implemented along a continuum of time from the onset of the traumatic event to years later in the client's life. What educational and training experience would you need to provide trauma counseling services to children or adolescents?

5. Group counseling methods are familiar to the practicing counseling professional as a strategy to address many complex mental health problems in a collective environment. Identify two ways that music could be used in a group setting. Include in your description the type of music that would be used, the goals for using it, and expected outcomes.

6. Robert is a counselor in training. He readily admits that he has no artistic talent whatsoever, yet he has recently read an article about how to use drawing in working with adolescents who are in a substance abuse outpatient treatment program. What advice would you give Robert regarding use of drawing with these clients? What are the advantages of using drawing with adolescents? What are the drawbacks?

7. There are many certifications available to the counselor professional, with many offered by professional associations or educational institutions. In what ways is the proliferation of certifications helping the counseling professions? Next, discuss the message that consumers receive when they see certification certificates on the walls of a counselor's office. Identify three reasons why certifications are helpful and necessary, and three reasons why they may hinder the counseling profession's status.

8. Governmental regulation of counseling practice is well established. Is government regulation of practice always the best option to ensure adequate qualification of counselors? Defend your answer.

9. An entry-level EMDR training session is being offered in your area. What factors will you evaluate about EMDR before making a decision about beginning or "passing" on this opportunity to begin EMDR training?

10. Counselor professionals may learn of innovative counseling methods through professional publications, the media, or serendipitously while surfing the World Wide Web. What are the positive and negative consequences of a counselor getting quickly "on board" with a new therapy approach?

REFERENCES

American Association of Pastoral Counselors (AAPC). (2005a). *About pastoral counseling*. Retrieved January 30, 2005, from www.aapc.org/about.htm.

American Association of Pastoral Counselors. (2005b). *Categories of membership*. Retrieved January 30, 2005, from www.aapc.org/membership.htm#associate.

American Art Therapy Association (AATA). (2003). *Frequently asked questions*. Retrieved January 29, 2005, from www.arttherapy.org/aboutarttherapy/faqs.htm.

American Counseling Association (ACA). (2005a). *State licensure*. Retrieved February 7, 2006, from www.counseling.org/Counselors/StateLicensureChart.aspx.

American Counseling Association (ACA). (2005b). *Code of ethics*. Retrieved October 9, 2005, from www.counseling.org/PDFs/ACA_2005_Ethical_Code10405.pdf.

American Music Therapy Association (AMTA). (2005). *Frequently asked questions about music therapy*. Retrieved January 29, 2005, from www.musictherapy.org/faqs.html.

American Philosophical Practitioners Association (APPA). (2005). *Mission statement*. Retrieved January 20, 2005, from www.appa.edu/.

Association for Creativity in Counseling (ACC). (2004). *Goal statement from Thelma Duffey, Ph.D.* Retrieved January 29, 2005, from www.aca-acc.org/about_acc.htm.

Attridge, W. C. (2004). *Current practices & future implications for Internet counseling*. U.S. Department of Education, Office of Educational Research and Improvement, National Library of Education (ERIC Document Reproduction Service No. ED478222).

Bardick, A. D., Berries, K. B., McCulloch, A. R. M., Witko, K. D., Spriddle, J. W., & Roest, A. R. (2004). Eating disorder intervention, prevention, and treatment: Recommendations for school counselors. *Professional School Counseling, 8*, 2.

Bell, J. L. (1995). Traumatic event debriefing: Service delivery designs and the role of social work. *Social Work, 40*(1), 36–43.

Bluckert, P. (2004). The state of play in corporate coaching: Current and future trends. *Industrial and Commercial Training, 2*, 53–56.

Burg, J. E. (2001). Emerging issues in therapeutic adventure with families. *Journal of Experiential Education, 24*, 118–122.

Burkett, B. G., & Whitley, G. (1998). *Stolen valor*. Dallas, TX: Verity.

CACREP. (2001). Standards for career counseling programs. *CACREP Accreditation Manual 2001 Standards*. Alexandria, VA: Council for Accreditation of Counseling and Related Educational Programs.

Capps, F. (2006). Combining eye movement desensitization and reprocessing with gestalt techniques in couples counseling. *The Family Journal, 14*, 49–58.

Capps, F., Andrade, H., & Cade, R. (2005). EMDR: An approach to healing betrayal wounds in couples counseling. In G. R. Walz & R. K. Yep (Eds.), *VISTAS: Compelling perspectives on counseling 2005* (pp. 107–110). Alexandria, VA: American Counseling Association.

Caron, J. C. (2005). DSM at the movies: Use of media in clinical or educational settings. In G. R. Walz & R. K. Yep (Eds.), *VISTAS: Compelling perspectives on counseling 2005* (pp. 179–182). Alexandria, VA: American Counseling Association.

Carroll, R. T. (2003). Eye movement desensitization and reprocessing (EMDR). *The skeptics dictionary.* Retrieved February 27, 2005, from http://skepdic.com/emdr.html.

Cheek, J. R., Bradley, L. J., Parr, G., & Lan, W. (2004). Using music therapy techniques to treat teacher burnout. *Journal of Mental Health, 25*(3), 204–217.

Chung, Y. B., & Gfroerer, M. C. A. (2003). Career coaching: Practice, training, professional and ethical issues. *The Career Development Quarterly, 52,* 98–157.

Comer, R. J. (2004). *Abnormal psychology* (5th ed.). New York: Worth.

Commons, M. L. (2000). The power therapies: A proposed mechanism for their action and suggestions for future empirical validation. *Traumatology, VI, 2,* Article 5. Retrieved May 6, 2005, from www.fsu.edu/~trauma/v6i2/v6i2a5.htm.

Cook, R. T. (2004). Myers-Briggs type indicator. *The skeptic's dictionary.* Retrieved January 22, 2005, from http://skepdic.com/myersb.html.

Copleston, F. (1961). *A history of philosophy* (vol. VI). Westminster, MD: Newman.

Cowan, E. W. (2005). *Ariadne's thread: Case studies in the therapeutic relationship.* Boston: Lahaska Press.

Deahl, M. P., Srinivasan, M., Jones, N., Neblett, C., & Jolly, A. (2001). Evaluating psychological debriefing: Are we measuring the right outcomes? *Journal of Traumatic Stress, 14*(3), 527–529.

DeCarlo, A. (2000–2001, Winter). Rap therapy? An innovative approach to group work with urban adolescents. *Journal of Intergroup Relations, 27*(4), 40–48.

DeJongh, A., van den Oord, H. J. M., & ten Broeke, E. (2002). Efficacy of eye movement desensitization and reprogramming in the treatment of specific phobias: Four single-case studies of dental phobia. *Journal of Clinical Psychology, 48,* 1489–1503.

del Valle, P., McEachem, A. G., & Sabina, M. Q. (1999). Using drawings and writings in a group counseling experience with Cuban rafter children, "los balseritos." *Guidance & Counseling, 14,* 20–29.

Deurzen-Smith, E. van. (1988). *Existential counseling in practice.* London: Sage.

Devilly, G. J., & Cotton, P. (2003). Psychological debriefing and the workplace: Defining a concept, controversies and guidelines for intervention. *Australian Psychologist, 38,* 144–150.

Dyregrov, A. (1997). The process in psychological debriefings. *Journal of Traumatic Stress, 10*(4), 589–605.

EMDR Institute. (2004). *History of EMDR.* Retrieved February 27, 2005, from www.emdr.com/history.htm.

Fletcher, T. B., & Hinkle, J. S. (2002). Adventure based counseling: An innovation in counseling. *Journal of Counseling & Development, 80,* 277–285.

Gass, M. A. (1995). Adventure family therapy: An innovative approach answering the question of lasting change with adjudicated youth? *Monograph on youth in the 1990s, 4,* 103–117 (ERIC Document Reproductive Service No. ED-384468-RC020171).

Gersons, B. P. R., Carlier, I. V. E., Lamberts, R. D., & van der Kolk, B. A. (2000). Randomized clinical trial of brief eclectic psychotherapy for police officers with posttraumatic stress disorder. *Journal of Traumatic Stress, 13*(2), 333–347.

Gladding, S. T. (1995). *Group work: A counseling specialty* (2nd ed.). Englewood Cliffs, NJ: Merrill.

Gladding, S. T. (2001). *The counseling dictionary: Concise definitions of frequently used terms.* Upper Saddle River, NJ: Prentice-Hall.

Gladding, S. T. (2003). *Counseling: A comprehensive profession* (5th ed). Upper Saddle River, NJ: Prentice-Hall.

Gladding, S. T. (2005). *Counseling as an art: The creative arts in counseling* (3rd ed.). Alexandria, VA: American Counseling Association.

Goodman, J. (2003, May). *A baker's dozen.* Workshop presented at the conference of the Michigan College Counselors Association.

Grant, A. M. (2000). Coaching psychology comes of age. *PsychNews, 4*(2), 12–14.

Grant, A. M. (2003). The impact of life coaching on goal attainment, metacognition and mental health. *Social Behavior and Personality, 31*(3), 253–264.

Grant, A. M., & Zackon, R. (2004). Executive, workplace and life coaching: Findings from a large-scale survey of International Coach Federation members. *International Journal of Evidence Based Coaching and Mentoring, 2*(2), 1–15.

Grant, M., & Threlfo, C. (2002). EMDR in the treatment of chronic pain. *Journal of Clinical Psychology, 48*, 1505–1520.

Gutterman, J. T., & Rudes, J. (2005). A narrative approach to strategic eclecticism. *Journal of Mental Health Counseling, 27*, 1–12.

Hertlein, K. M., & Ricci, R. J. (2004). A systematic research synthesis of EMDR studies: Implications of the platinum standard. *Trauma, Violence & Abuse, 5*, 285–301.

Higgins, J. A., & Dermer, S. (2001). The use of film in marriage and family counselor education. *Counselor Education and Supervision, 40*, 182–192.

Hiley-Young, B., & Gerrity, E. T. (1994, Spring). Critical incident stress debriefing (CISD): Value and limitations in disaster response. *NCP Clinical Quarterly, 4*(2). Retrieved January 22, 2005, from www.ncptsd.org//publications/cq/v4/n2/hiley-yo.html.

International Critical Incident Stress Foundation (ICISF). (2004). *Who we are.* Retrieved January 15, 2005, from www.icisf.org/about/affpartners.cfm.

International Coach Federation. (2005a). *About coaching.* Retrieved January 29, 2005, from www.coachfederation.org/aboutcoaching/index.asp.

International Coach Federation. (2005b). *ICF credentialing.* Retrieved January 29, 2005, from www.coachfederation.org/credentialing/en/index.asp.

International Coach Federation. (2005c). *The ICF code of ethics.* Retrieved October 9, 2005, from www.coachfederation.org/eweb/docs/ICF_Code_of_Ethics_01_22_05.pdf.

Isaacson, L. E., & Brown, D. (2000). *Career information, career counseling, and career development* (7th ed.). Boston: Allyn and Bacon.

James, L., & Martin, D. (2002). Sandtray and group therapy: Helping parents cope. *Journal for Specialists in Group Work, 27*, 390–405.

Kant, I. (1952). *The critique of pure reason* (J. M. D. Meiklejohn, Trans.). In R. M. Hutchins (Ed.), *Great books of the western world: Vol. 42. Kant.* Chicago: Encyclopedia Britannica. (Original work published 1781.)

Kennedy, A. (2005, January). Circles in the sand. *Counseling Today*, 16–17.

Knapp, S., & Tjeltueit, A. C. (2005). A review and critical analysis of philosophical counseling. *Professional Psychology: Research and Practice, 36*(5), 558–565.

Koch, G., & Dollarhide, C. T. (2000). Using popular film in counselor education: *Good Will Hunting* as a teaching tool. *Counselor Education and Supervision, 39*, 203–311.

Koehler, J. D. (2002). Vaginismus: Diagnosis, etiology and intervention. *Contemporary Sexuality, 36*, i–vii.

Kraus, R., Zack, J. S., & Stricker, G. (Eds.). (2003). Online counseling: A handbook for mental health professionals. Oxford, UK: Elsevier Science & Technology Books.

Kuhn, T. S. (1970). *The structure of scientific revolutions* (2nd ed.). Chicago: University of Chicago.

Lamprecht, R., Köhnke, C., Lempa, W., Sack, M., Matske, M., & M[ubar]nte, T. F. (2004). Event-related potentials and EMDR treatment of post-traumatic stress disorder. *Neuroscience Research, 49*, 267–273.

Life Coaching Institute. *What is coaching?* Retrieved January 29, 2005, from www.inst.org/coach.

Lytle, R. A., Hazlett-Stevens, H., & Borkovec, T. D. (2002). Efficacy of eye movement desensitization in the treatment of cognitive intrusions related to a past stressful event. *Journal of Anxiety, 16*, 273–289.

MacDonald, C. M. (2003, December). Evaluation of stress debriefing interventions with military populations. *Military Medicine, 168*, 961–968.

Macy, R. D., Behar, L., Paulson, R., Delman, J., Schmid, L., & Smith, S. F. (2004). Community-based, acute posttraumatic stress management: A description and evaluation of a psychosocial–intervention continuum. *Harvard Review of Psychiatry, 12*(4): 218–228.

Marinoff, L. (1999). *Plato not Prozac! Applying philosophy to everyday problems.* New York: HarperCollins.

Marinoff, L. (2003). *The big questions: How philosophy can change your life.* New York: Bloomsbury.

Maxfield, L, & Hyer, L. (2002). The relationship between efficacy and methodology in studies investigating EMDR treatment of PTSD. *Journal of Clinical Psychology, 58*, 23–41.

McCabe, S. (2004). EMDR: Implications of the use of reprocessing therapy in nursing practice. *Perspectives in Psychiatric Care, 40*(3), 104.

McCown, S. S. (2004). *The evaluation of sandtray friendship groups as a tool for improving social interactions in an elementary classroom*. Doctoral dissertation in progress, Minneapolis, MN: Capella University.

McNally, R. J. (2004, April). Psychological debriefing does not prevent posttraumatic stress disorder. *Psychiatric Times*, 71–74.

Multigl, P. (2004). Ontogenesis in narrative therapy: A linguistic-semiotic examination of client change. *Family Process*, 43, 109–131.

National Career Development Association (NCDA). (2005). *What is a career development facilitator (CDF)?* Retrieved January 29, 2005, from http://ncda.org/.

National Crisis Response Team (NCRT) manual. (2004). Introduction. Retrieved January 15, 2005, from www.ojp.usdoj.gov/ovc/publications/infores/crt/intro.htm.

National Christian Counselors Association (NCCA). (2005). *National Christian Counselors Association*. Retrieved February 15, 2005, from www.ncca-usa.com/home.html.

National Organization for Victim Assistance (NOVA). (2005). *About NOVA*. Retrieved January 15, 2005, from www.trynova.org/about/.

New Credential for Distance Counseling. (2004, December). *Counseling Today, 3*.

Newes, S. L. (2001). Future directions in adventure based therapy research: Methodological considerations and design suggestions. *Journal of Experiential Education, 24*, 92–99.

Osuch, E., & Engel, C. (2004). Research on the treatment of trauma spectrum responses: The role of the optimal healing environment and neurobiology. *The Journal of Alternative and Complementary Medicine, 10*, S-211–S-221.

Paden, R. (1998). Defining philosophical counseling. *International Journal of Applied Philosophy, 12*(1), 1–17.

Page, B. J., Jencius, M. J., Rehfuss, M. C., Foss, L. F., Dean, E. P., Petruzzi, M. L., et al. (2003). PalTalk online groups: Process and reflections on students' experiences. *Journal for Specialists in Group Work, 28*, 35–41.

Petersen, S., Bull, C., Propst, O., Dettinger, S., & Detwiler, L. (2005). Narrative therapy to prevent illness-related stress disorder. *Journal of Counseling & Development, 83*, 41–47.

Popper, K. (1963). *Conjectures and refutations*. New York: Basic Books.

Pulley, S. A. (2004, June 17). Critical incident stress management. *eMedicine*. Retrieved January 22, 2005, from www.emedicine.com/emerg/topic826.htm

Raabe, P. B. (2002). Professional philosophy outside the academy: Philosophical counseling. *Philosophical Pathways, 25*. Retrieved January 22, 2005, from www.philosophos.com/philosophy_article_14.html.

Reid, W. M., Ruzycki, S., Haney, M. L., Brown, L. M., Baggerly, J., Mescia, N., et al. (2005). Disaster mental health training in Florida and the response to the 2004 hurricanes. *Journal of Public Health Management Practice, 11*, S57–S62.

Richards, D. (2001). A field study of critical incident stress debriefing versus critical incident stress management. *Journal of Mental Health, 10*(3), 351–362.

Robinson, R. (2004). Counterbalancing misrepresentations of critical incident stress debriefing and critical incident stress management. *Australian Psychologist, 39*, 29–34.

Rogers, E. M. (2003). Diffusion of innovations (5th ed.). New York: Free Press.

Sandplay Therapists of America (STA). (2004). *Welcome*. Retrieved January 18, 2005, from www.sandplay.org/.

School, J., & Maizell, R. (2002). *Exploring islands of healing: New perspectives on adventure-based counseling*. Beverly, MA: Project Adventure.

Segal, J. (2002). *Young women with anorexia nervosa speak out about hospital experiences*. University of New South Wales. Retrieved January 27, 2005, from www.narrativeapproaches.com/antianorexia%20 folder/segal.htm.

Seligman, L. (2001). *Systems, strategies, and skills of counseling and psychotherapy*. Upper Saddle River, NJ: Merrill.

Selye, H. (1956). *The stress of life*. New York: McGraw-Hill.

Shapiro, F. (2002). EMDR 12 years after its introduction: Past and future research. *Journal of Clinical Psychology, 58*, 1–22.

Shapiro, F., & Maxfield, L. (2002). Eye movement desensitization and reprocessing (EDMR): Information processing in the treatment of trauma. *Journal of Clinical Psychology, 48*, 933–946.

Snow, M. S., Ouzts, R., Martin, E. E., & Helm, H. (2005). Creative metaphors of life experiences seen in play therapy. In G. R. Walz & R. K. Yep (Eds.), *VISTAS: Compelling perspectives on counseling 2005* (pp. 63–65). Alexandria, VA: American Counseling Association.

Snyder, M. (1996). Intimate partners: A context for the intensification and healing of emotional pain. In M. Hill & E. D. Rothblum (Eds.), *Couples therapy: Feminist perspectives* (pp. 79–92). New York: Haworth Press.

Sommers, C. H., & Satel, S. (2005). *One nation under therapy: How the helping culture is eroding self-reliance*. New York: St. Martin's.

Stern, L. R. (2004). Executive coaching: A working definition [electronic version]. *Consulting Psychology Journal, 56*(3), 154–162.

Stranger, T., & Harris, R. S. (2005). Marathon group therapy: Potential for university counseling centers and beyond. *Journal of Specialists in Group Work, 30*(2), 145–157.

Sweeney, D. S., Minnix, G. M., & Homeyer, L. E. (2003). Using sandtray therapy in lifestyle analysis. *Journal of Individual Psychology, 59*, 376–387.

Torrey, E. F. (1992). *Freudian fraud: The malignant effect of Freud's theory on American thought and culture*. New York: HarperCollins.

Tuval-Mashiach, R., Freedman, S., Bargai, N., Boker, R., Hadar, H., & Shalev, A. Y. (2004). Coping with trauma: Narrative and cognitive perspectives. *Psychiatry, 67*, 280–293.

Von Emmorik, A. A., Kamphuis, J. H., Hulsbosch, A. M., & Emmelkamp, P. M. (2002). Single session debriefing after psychological trauma: A meta-analysis. *Lancet, 360*, 766–771.

Walker, S. (2004). The evolution of coaching: Patterns, icons and freedom. *International Journal of Evidence Based Coaching and Mentoring, 2*(2), 16–28.

Williams, P., & Davis, D. (2002). *Therapist as life coach: Transforming your practice*. New York: Norton.

Wilson, J. P., Raphael, B., Meldrum, L., Bedosky, C., & Sigman, M. (2000). Preventing PTSD in trauma survivors. *Bulletin of the Menninger Clinic, 64*(20), 181–196.

Zangwill, W. (2004). EMDR and sex therapy. *Contemporary Sexuality, 38*, i–vii.

Ziff, K. K., & Beamish, P. M. (2004). Teaching a course on the arts and counseling: Experiential learning in counselor education. *Counselor Education and Supervision, 44*, 147–159.

CHAPTER ELEVEN

COUNSELING AND SPIRITUALITY
Integrating Wellness into Practice

ANN HUTCHINSON MEYERS

For hundreds of years, the relationship among the mind, body, and spirit has been debated. Philosophers, physicians, and theologians have questioned whether the mind is a separate entity that can influence the body, and have debated if the soul exists and how it influences the physical well-being of the body and mind. These thoughts and many more have made for an uncomfortable relationship between philosophers and scientists, and theologians and medical professionals, within which lay a wealth of information regarding the symbiotic relationship between spirituality and psychology. Professionals of the "hard sciences" have been troubled by the lack of empiricism in studies of the mind–body connection and the influences of spirituality on health, healing, and well-being. Those interested in a more qualitative understanding of these relationships and experiences discount those who regard such research as unscientific and without generalizability. Because of the unrelenting give and take between the concrete and the abstract, many issues regarding spirituality are considered taboo in the academic community.

These same concerns regarding the relationship among the mind, body, and spirit have given way to questions about the place of spirituality in the practice of counseling. Counseling professionals are looking at the use of spirituality as a therapeutic tool in their practices. Along with this new ideology, however, come questions about how to integrate spirituality into counseling, how to develop tools to measure such a construct, and how to evaluate the ethical implications of this new insertion in clinical practice.

In spite of this academic uncertainty, research indicates that a majority of people consider their faith to be an important element in their lives and would like to consider faith as an integral part of any counseling that might take place during a time of crisis (Bergin & Jensen, 1990; Gallup, 1993; Gallup & Lindsay, 1999). In current research about religion and spirituality, definitions are not standardized to allow for the replication of information. With every new study, authors find new concepts and definitions for the terms *religion, religiousness, spirituality, postmodern spirituality, faith, spiritual health*, and *mind–body medicine* (Perrin & McDermott, 1997). Therein lies the difficulty. Without replicated research, how can practitioners know what counseling practices are most effective when working within the spiritual constructs of a client? How can practitioners ensure that appropriate therapeutic guidelines are being met and appropriate ethical boundaries are not being crossed? This chapter will examine the history of emotional and physical healing as it relates to spirituality, as well as the ethical issues of combining spirituality and counseling.

THE HISTORY OF THE MIND–BODY CONNECTION

Since the time of the French philosopher Rene Descartes (1596–1650), dualism, a separation of mind and body, has been the concept that has ebbed and flowed throughout modern scientific ideology. Descartes stated, "It follows that this ego, this mind, this soul, by which I am and what I am, is entirely distinct from my body" (as cited in Hunt, 1993, p. 66). This belief allowed physicians of the fifteenth and sixteenth centuries to escape the control of the church by allowing the work of the "soul" to be handled by the church and the work of the "body" to be handled by the physician.

While practitioners of traditional Western medicine worked diligently to keep the mind and body separate, Eastern and Native American cultures appeared to have an innate understanding of the mind and body as having a symbiotic and natural relationship to the soul and healing. These beliefs were the foundation for the bio-psycho-social–spiritual model of care. Canada, Shin, and Canada (1993) and Nhat Hahn (1998) noted the similarities between the bio-psycho-social–spiritual model of Native Americans, Buddhists, and followers of Confucius in that they all reach toward a hidden source to find the power to heal. Shaman Ribi (1989, p. 69) suggested, "The archaic techniques of the shaman are of great interest for modern psychotherapy because they are a precursor. In contrast to modern psychotherapy, they rest on a foundation of 1,000 years of experience."

Shamans in the Native American community work in tandem with the "spirits" in the healing process, whereas "medicine men" use natural herbs, stories, and tonics to heal the body and soul. In their work, Native American shamans acknowledge that they are receivers of sacred powers to heal mental and physical illnesses through spirits, also believing that mental and spiritual health are inseparable from spiritual and moral health (Hunter, 2005; Ribi, 1990). The interrelated nature of mind and body has been realized throughout generations of Native American healers as common and without question. As suggested by Ribi (1990, p. 76):

> Mind and body are significantly related systems: Processes in one are reflected in the other. Simply consider the way we commonly intuit someone's state of mind from his physical posture and unconscious body manifestations . . . what is happening in our unconscious is betrayed by our body.

Das (1989) compared the similarities in the teachings of Hinduism and Buddhism to the work of both Rogers and Maslow, with their concepts of self-actualization and self-expression. The teachings of Hinduism center on the goal of "self-realization," quite similar to Maslow's self-actualization, with Buddhism's suggestion that self-realization is the way to reach nirvana.

Perhaps it was due to these preexisting cultural beliefs that George Engel (1980) introduced the concept of a bio-psycho-social model of health into the traditional Western practice of medicine. Engel believed that the dualistic way of treating patients, without attending to the emotional, psychological, and spiritual well-being of a patient, was a reductionistic way of approaching the health and wholeness of a patient. By looking at a patient's biological, psychological, spiritual, and social needs, one could see a much clearer picture of the his or her true health. Such an affirmation brought health professionals to a place of understanding that encouraged the integration of spirituality into the practice of healing.

THE BIO-PSYCHO-SOCIAL–SPIRITUAL MODEL OF CARE

In 1946, the World Health Organization defined *health* as the integration of complete physical and social well-being, not just the absence of disease (Perrin & McDermott, 1997). As early as 1948, Frankl viewed the mind-body-spirit integration as the key to physical and emotional well-being. Current literature would suggest that once again the tide has begun to turn to include spirituality into the overall context of well-being (Wolf & Stevens, 2001). The postmodern fascination with spirituality and the supernatural has once again integrated spirituality into many wellness models, viewing the human experience as holistic and multifaceted. Heler's 1984 model of wellness included five aspects: physical, occupational, social, intellectual, emotional, and spiritual aspects of health (Myers & Willard, 2003). Chandler, Holden, and Kolander (1992) took this model one step further to suggest that rather than being fivefold, the model was sixfold, with spirituality being an integral part of the other five aspects of health. As with Heler, Wilber's health model (1995) included six facets of wellness: body, mind, soul, spirit of self, culture, and nature.

DEFINING RELIGION AND SPIRITUALITY

The terms *religion* and *spirituality* are often used interchangeably; this is actually counterfactual, with the two concepts having different meanings. The Latin term for religion is *religio,* meaning a bond between humanity and gods, whereas *religare* means to be bound together (Ingersoll, 1994). For most, the word *religion* refers to a set construct or institution, or the expression of beliefs and rituals that follow the pattern of an organized worship of a god or gods (Standard, Sandhu, & Painter, 2000). Authors often describe religion as a conceptualization of a feeling or a framework in which spirituality is expressed (Ingersoll, 1994). Does that mean that where religion leads, spirituality follows? Not according to Moberg (1971), who suggested that while spirituality might be connected to a specific religion, those who are religious do not necessarily need to be "spiritual." Legere (1984) suggested that religion is the conceptualization of an experience, whereas spirituality is the actual experience itself. So, when analyzing the relationship between spirituality and counseling, the reference being discussed is of a spiritual nature as opposed to the affiliation with an organized religion (Prest & Keller, 1993).

How, then, does spirituality differ from religion, and how does it interface with the healing and wholeness of an individual? One of the problems when working with the concept of spirituality is its ever-changing definition that seems to change from generation to generation (Ingersoll, 1994). The roots of the word come from the Latin word *spiritusí*, or vigor, life, and breath. The Hebrew definition is threefold, meaning breath, wind, and spirit (Debane & Montgomery, 1981).

These definitions show the obstacle to working with spirituality, a transcendent, unobservable, or, as used in recent times, metaphysical concept (Prest & Keller, 1993), although Slife, Hope, and Nebeker (1999) believed that spirituality can be concrete and observable. Jankowski (2002) and Ingersoll (1994) theorized that spirituality has both observable and unobservable elements that, in and of themselves, do not explain the whole experience of spirituality. Spirituality is also seen as something that transcends the egocentric life and moves one into the realm of the scared (Jung, 1933). The theme of transcendence continues in the definition of spirituality by the Association for Spiritual, Ethical and Religious and Ethical Values Issues in Counseling (ASERVIC) in its definition of spirituality: It "moves the individual toward greater knowledge, love, meaning, peace, hope, transcendence, connectedness" (www.counseling.org/aservic/spirituality.html).

The concept that spirituality brings "meaning to life" is one that runs throughout current literature and seems to be a key to the importance of spirituality to the counselor (Myers, 1990; Tillich, 1959). However, because there are as many other definitions of spirituality as there are authors, it is imperative to define the parameters of the term *spirituality* in order to use the concept in modern clinical practice (Curtis & Glass, 2002; Ingersoll, 1994; Perrin & McDermott, 1997).

For this discussion, a combination of definitions will be used from Witmer (1989) and Burns (as cited in Ingersoll, 1994) that conceptualize spirituality as an awareness of the striving for interconnectedness among self, others, and the transcendent, while doing so in relationship to a force that is greater than one's self.

SPIRITUALITY AND COUNSELING PRACTICE

Many of the influential theorists in psychology saw spirituality as a major influence in the developmental and psychological experience. Maslow (1971) saw spirituality as part of the self-actualization process, Piaget (1963) as part of the cognitive process, and Ellison (1983) as an aspect of life that motivates, inspires, and brings meaning to life. The interplay between psychology and faith has historical roots with the inception of psychology coming from the word *psyche*, meaning soul (Haque, 2001). As noted by Jung (1978, p. 337), most of the human condition is touched in one way or another by the soulful or spiritual side of life, suggesting that "everything to do with religion, everything it is and asserts, touches the human soul so closely that psychology least of all can afford to overlook it."

To that end, spirituality can potentially affect many aspects of human relationships and human behavior, as evidenced by the American Psychological Association's inclusion of spiritual and/or religious problems in the *DSM-IV (Diagnostic and Statistical Manual* of the American Psychiatric Association, 1994). In truth, theological ideology is often the foundation of personal values. This perspective, in turn, clarifies spirituality's importance to decision making and personal ideology, thus making it inherently relevant to the practice of psychotherapy (Helminiak, 2001).

Because of the relationship between spirituality and everyday life, one could ask, Is there, or should there be such a thing as a secular therapist? If so, can that therapist work within the client's spiritual belief system without a belief system of his or her own? On the other hand, Are pastoral counselors or counselors who deal with spiritual issues able to effectively work with clients who many not hold personal beliefs like their own or have no belief system at all?

> On a late Thursday afternoon, a new client, Marta, arrived in Sandy's counseling office. Marta explained over the phone that she was experiencing some problems with loss and grief, and Sandy suggested she come in for an appointment. During her initial intake evaluation, Marta burst into tears and told Sandy that four weeks before the appointment she had an abortion after three months of pregnancy. Marta stated that she was unmarried and she could not raise a baby alone. It was after the abortion that Marta says she went to talk with her family pastor who, on hearing of her action, told her that such an action was something that would never be forgiven by God; that her action was murder in the eyes of God. Marta came into Sandy's office stating there was no need to continue her life and that she had contemplated suicide in the last week; that the loss of her life could be no worse in the eyes of God than the life she had already taken.

No matter how hard counselors try to be a part of value-free advice, the values of a counselor are inescapable in the counseling setting (Bergin, 1980; London, 1986). In the case of Marta, Sandy's personal views on religion, abortion, suicide, and pastoral intervention have the ability to color his reaction to, and work with, Marta. During her initial call, Marta had not asked Sandy about his personal religious ideology or background, nor had she asked if Sandy was a counselor who used religion or spirituality as a part of his counseling practices. Although the therapist's views should not pervade the session, it is hard for the counselor's views to not influence the session in some fashion (Bergin, Payne, & Richards, 1996; Tjeltveit, 1999). One problem in maintaining this delicate balance is linked to the reality that many spiritual or religious clients or potential clients mistrust secular or nonreligious counselors. With trust being an essential element in any therapeutic relationship, the need for therapists to be trained to address spiritual issues is essential to an open, healing environment (Richards & Bergin, 2000; Worthington, 1986).

Counselors have quite successfully integrated spirituality into traditional psychological paradigms such as cognitive therapy, behaviorism, and psychoanalysis (Payne, Bergin, & Loftus, 1992). As with any type of cultural context, spirituality is a tool that can be used to gain trust with and connect to the client no matter what technique of psychological ideology a practitioner follows. For example, Bowen's theory of object relations holds an interesting place in the discussion of spirituality in counseling. When the relationship of two (the counselor and the client) becomes a relationship of three (the counselor, the client, and the "higher power"), the relationship is often solidified as if it becomes a three-legged stool (Butler & Harper, 1994). Again, although this may be the case with some clients, not all clients are comfortable with the introduction of this "third party" into the counseling relationship. Such an introduction should be carefully approached by the therapist.

When working with a client and spiritual issues, the counselor should also be aware that there may be a difference in the experience of spirituality between men and women. Miller (1976) and Ballou (1995) theorized that women understand their world through the relationships they create, and through that, a woman understands her spirituality through the people that shape her world. It is often through a woman's faith that she finds her role or purpose and meaning in life. Young (1994) suggests that on an international level, it is through a woman's faith that she is able to raise her social and economic status. Women also see their spirituality intertwined with all aspects of their life and work inside and outside the home, recognizing their work outside the home as contributing to the better good of society and a way of helping others (Cullen, 2003).

Christ (1995) suggests that a woman's spiritual journey involves four distinct experiences: nothingness, awakening, insight, and new naming. The experience of *nothingness* is seen as the struggle of women in a patriarchal world, *awakening* becomes a process of personal empowerment, *insight* becomes self-awareness, and, finally, *new naming* becomes a woman's new identity as she fashions herself and her spiritual experience from a purely woman's perspective.

With reference to the role of spirituality in the life of men, Harris (1997) indicated that this aspect of the inner life has been understudied and is not clearly understood. However, in spite of the lack of research in this area, Harris (1997, p. 34) suggests that there are 10 major aspects to male spirituality as it relates to their life and world:

1. Finding inner wisdom
2. Searching for truth
3. Speaking from the heart
4. Confronting the dark side
5. Loving
6. Working for a better world
7. Passing a test
8. Belonging to something great
9. Following scripture
10. Believing in destiny

Although spirituality has achieved recognition as a factor that can be successfully integrated into the practice of counseling, one must consider the nature of the spirituality experienced by both the practitioner and the client in order to determine how this construct will affect the outcome of their work together. Also, in considering the nature and relationship of spirituality to counseling, the clinician should look at the positive and negative aspects of these belief systems and how they might affect the health and healing of the client.

SPIRITUALITY WELLNESS VERSUS
SPIRITUAL "UNWELLNESS"

Because new models of health have included not only the bio-psycho-social components of health but also the spiritual, one must be able to identify spiritual wellness and ask, If there is spiritual wellness, is there also spiritual "unwellness"? Westgate (1996) proposed that spiritual wellness finds its origins in the basic bio-psycho-social model of health. According to Russell's (1981) model of health, spirituality is the umbrella under which all other aspects of health reside. Spiritual wellness, as defined by Ingersoll and Bauer (2004), does not necessarily deal with religious doctrine but with an individual's values and meaning in life. Most working definitions of spiritual wellness also include dimensions of purpose, compassion, forgiveness, and transcendent beliefs (Chandler et al, 1992; Ingersoll, 1994). Watson (1997) argued that religion (in this case, synonymous with spirituality) is a resource for health and often serves as a context or foundation from which personal and professional values are formed.

Ingersoll and Bauer (2004) believe there are three perspectives of spiritual wellness that one can use in the therapeutic relationship. The *"intrapsychic" perspective* is familiar to most counselors through use of exploration of a client's thoughts, feelings, and emotions, thereby gaining an understanding about their faith structure and belief system as well as their personal "spiritual wellness." *The social perspective* allows the clinician to understand how social dynamics and institutions have affected a person's life and how that, in turn, has left an impact on their belief system/structure. Finally, there is the *cultural perspective,* which, once again, allows the clinician to work within a "we" model of sharing in order to examine similar cultural beliefs and how they fit into the larger social structure.

With the therapeutic understanding of spiritual wellness, there is certainly the implication that with wellness there must be a component of "spiritual unwellness" (Chandler et al, 1992; Lukoff & Turner, 1998). Take, for example, the case of John.

John had been referred to Dave's office by his mother and father. During their initial call to Dave, John's parents suggested they were very concerned about John and believed he had been "brainwashed" by a group of "religious zealots" at his college campus. John's parents told him that in order to receive money to continue college, he must seek counseling.

On John's first visit with Dave, he suggested he was "fine" and in full control of his mental and emotional state. On further questioning, John told Dave that he had become associated with a religious group off campus six months before, that they had become his closest and only friends, and that they made him feel "complete." He went on to say that the group had certain requirements with which he was very comfortable, but his parents were not. These requirements included giving 20 hours a week of volunteer time to the commune where they all lived, moving from his college dorm to the commune, and, finally, giving his tuition money and spending money to the commune and the commune leaders would then give him the money he needed.

John concluded that he had total trust in his new friends and that his parents' concerns were unwarranted. He also noted that the leaders of the commune had suggested that if John's parents did not agree with this new lifestyle, the "Christ-like" thing to do would be to walk away from his family and begin a new life with his new "family" in the commune.

Zinnbauer (2000) noted the importance of understanding the close link between spiritual wellness, spiritual "unwellness," and the mental health of a client; the three, Zinnbauer suggested, are closely linked. For example, the issues of toxic faith/belief (similar to that experienced by the followers of James Jones in Ghana) and unhealthy religious dogmas (as found with the followers of the Branch Dividians in Waco, Texas) show that there are dark sides to the personal experience of spirituality. Bache (1989) explained these as the "exoteric" and "esoteric" sides of religion/belief, with the exoteric being the side of faith that is most often seen in public and the esoteric side of faith being what is considered mystical and private.

It is through the counseling experience that the clinician can gain understanding of a client's faith in order to determine whether a client's faith serves as a positive or negative influence in his or her life. This insight also aids in determining the depth of a client's faith structure and personal development to ensure that the counselor does not step beyond the bounds of the client's personal understanding.

SPIRITUALITY AND THE DEVELOPMENTAL PROCESS

The role of spirituality as an essential part of personality development is rapidly gaining recognition (Beutler & Clarkin, 1990). As has been previously noted, spirituality is considered by many to be part of the developmental process (Kegan, 1982; Noddings, 2003; Piaget, 1963). In that same respect, Gilligan (1982) and Kohlberg (1984) indicated that physical and emotional development begins with an egocentric centering, moving beyond the self to the care of others, and finally to a universal care. Thus, the care of others, often seen as the benchmark of spiritual concern, is seen as much as a developmental process as a belief, and to that end, an area of interest and study.

Fowler's (1981) ground-breaking work on stages of faith development also integrated spirituality as part of the ongoing developmental process. In his work, Fowler proposed that people work through six stages of faith in the maturation process of their spirituality in life:

1. *Intuitive-projective* (age 3–7 years): In this stage, children's belief systems are strongly influenced by the adults around them.
2. *Mythic-literal* (age 7 to puberty): In this stage, children begin to move from a more mythical belief in spirituality/faith to a literal belief with an understanding of the symbols and ideology of specific faiths.
3. *Synthesis-conventional* (puberty to adulthood): This is a time of spiritual evolution in life where a person begins to form his or her own spiritual/faith beliefs, but is still greatly influenced by the community around him or her.

4. *Individuative-reflective* (young adulthood): Here, young adults continue to evolve in their belief systems, but these beliefs become less dependent on the beliefs of others.
5. *Conjunctive*: In this stage of beliefs, a person begins to integrate opposites into his or her belief system as well as experiences a need to assert part of his or her identity into a belief structure.
6. *Universalizing*: The final stage of spiritual formation focuses on the care and concern of others on a global level that reflects an understanding that goes beyond a single belief system.

In order to ensure that a clinician is working within the theoretical and spiritual constructs of the client, the clinician should be aware of the spiritual stages of development in order to assess where the client falls within his or her personal spiritual framework. To move beyond this developmental stage would be counterproductive to the healing process. As with any counseling relationship the Hippocratic oath of "do no harm" and adherence to the profession's ethical standards must be carefully practiced when addressing spiritual issues. This sensitivity can ensure that the emotional and spiritual needs of the client are being met.

PERSONAL VALUES, SPIRITUALITY, AND COUNSELING

As is the case with many counselors, personal experience is drawn on to understand the experience of another. The same can be said about spirituality, with a counselor often drawing on his or her own spiritual beliefs to better understand those of a client. London (1986) suggests, however, that psychoanalysts are trained to be blank screens, behaviorists to be objective, and humanists to be interpersonal mirrors. The problem with this concept is that most researchers agree that therapists' values are inescapable and that their ability to be "value free" is all but impossible. Because of this, the personal values and beliefs of a counselor are often brought into the counseling session (Bergin, Payne, & Richards, 1996). When a counselor and a client's beliefs are similar, this is rarely a problem in that the two can freely exchange ideology.

The problem occurs when there is a conflict or difference in personal values and beliefs, which can occur with some regularity when a client and therapist are discussing religion and spirituality.

Mohammad entered Mark's office late on Thursday night. During his initial call, Mohammad told Mark that he was having problems at work and he needed someone to talk to, so Mark suggested a visit. During his initial intake, Mohammad said that he is a practicing Muslim and that his faith requires him to stop work several times a day in order to pray, explaining that prayers are one of the pillars of Islam and that daily prayer is a compulsory part of the faith. Mohammad went on to explain that his boss has told him to "pray on this own time" and that to stop work for personal reasons might be grounds for dismissal.

Mohammad is taking care of his elderly mother and aunt, and he confides that he must keep his job in order to support his two family members. As Mark listens to Mohammad's story, his internal dialog is conflicted. As a born-again Christian, Mark vehemently disagrees with the teachings of Islam and has been taught through his church that whenever possible, Christians should attempt to "save" practicing Muslims by telling their personal faith story and attempting to convert Muslims to the "true way." As Mark listens to Mohammad, he is conflicted about his correct course of action.

Slife and Richards (2001) indicated that the best way to handle such conflict is for the therapist to work within the traditional objectivist model of science, attempting to find a common ground and a neutral position (method or technique) from which to address the conflicting issues. If a common ground cannot be found, obviously a counselor is ethically required to refer the client to someone better suited to address the needs at hand. It is important, however, for counselors to openly discuss their differences in a caring and sensitive way (Aponte, 1998).

When spirituality becomes a part of the work in a counseling session, Kelly (1990) proposed four ways in which the subject of spirituality/religion might be applicable to the presenting problem:

1. *Religious/Spiritual Issues*: Could deal with a crisis in faith or the role that faith plays in his or her life.
2. *Nonreligious/Spiritual Faith Issues*: Could revolve around the role of faith and the meaning of life in a client's personal or professional life.
3. *Nonreligious/Spiritual Secular Issues*: Could be connected to an issue in faith. These presenting problems could deal with secular issues, such as birth and death, with these issues having spiritual overtones.
4. *Nonreligious/Spiritual Issues with No Connection to Faith*: These issues would not be connected to any part of the client's religious/spiritual journey.

Tan (1996) indicated that when working within a spiritual/therapeutic model, two types of spiritual integration can be used in the counseling session: implicit and explicit. *Implicit integration* has no overt suggestion of religiosity or introduction of religious or spiritual issues in the counseling session but is brought into the session through the counselor's personal belief system and his or her listening and responding techniques. *Explicit integration* does include prayer and the use of various spiritual texts in the session.

When determining whether to use implicit or explicit integration in the counseling session, the counselor or clinician should be careful to initially assess the client's own integration of his or her belief structure into the session in order to evaluate the means of implicit or explicit use of religious imagery, practice, or text. By slowly and carefully learning about the client's deeply personal spiritual walk, the counselor acquires the capacity to include spirituality within the therapeutic context. In addition, dependent on the counselor's depth of understanding of the client's spirituality and the role of spirituality in a specific client's life or worldview, exploration and focus on faith and spirituality can become a foundational platform on which to build counseling interventions.

PROBLEMS ASSOCIATED WITH POSTMODERN SPIRITUALITY

As noted earlier in this chapter, *spirituality* is a term that seems to change from generation to generation, depending on the psychological, emotional, and spiritual needs of the time. Currently, postmodern spirituality has become a prevalent belief structure that finds its value not from the "knowing" but from "experiencing" belief. The unique aspects of postmodern spirituality center on the egocentric need for this belief, whereas in the past, most spiritual or religious beliefs were extrinsically motivated toward the service of others. For many today, experiencing spirituality in a postmodern sense is solely for the experience itself, nothing more. This, in turn, creates a sense of "vertical" spirituality that is an individual relationship between god and the believer (Sider, 1993). The expressed value in this vertical relationship seems to be a personal experience apart from evaluation. Many times, however, an overemphasis on this vertical belief system results in a "private" spirituality that leaves out the importance of community and relationship as is found with "horizontal" belief systems (i.e., those that are primarily traditional religious and spiritual communities of faith) (Greer & Root, 1992).

The positive relationship in a horizontally centered belief system is the sense of connectedness and responsibility that is felt between the individual and the greater community (Sider, 1993). This sense of being a part of something outside of one's self and helping toward the greater good fits well into Maslow's hierarchy of needs toward becoming self-actualized, where postmodern belief systems deal more on the level of fulfilling personal, as opposed to corporate, needs. Also, because a postmodern belief can separate one from a community and unity of ideology, the sense of oneness or "resilient spirituality" seems to be missing (Greer & Root, 1992).

Greer and Root (1992) found that there are three spiritual qualities that help people cope in times of need: (1) a doctrine or set ideology to believe in, (2) a cognitive ability to believe, and (3) a connectedness to others who have the same belief system. Postmodern spirituality seems to alter or completely do away with all three of these qualities in that it is not doctrinally based, it is very subjective, and it is a personal rather than a corporate experience (Greer & Root, 1992).

CLIENT ASSESSMENT OF SPIRITUALITY

From a counselor's point of view, spiritual assessment of a client can be an important tool in diagnosis and treatment because the clinician is better able to understand a client's worldviews, belief system and structure, and how all of these are integrated into his or her everyday values, beliefs, and actions (Kelly, 1994). This assessment often takes place with the intake assessment of a client and can be formal or informal in nature. By inquiring how a client's belief system affects his or her daily life, a clinician can understand whether this belief system is healthy or unhealthy and whether the client's presenting problem is associated with these spiritual beliefs/issues (Richards & Bergin, 1997). These initial questions about a person's belief system can also give the client a valuable opportunity for self-reflection and an invitation to then include these beliefs in the counseling process

(Standard, Sandhu, & Painter, 2000). Although there are literally hundreds of formal spirituality and belief scales, all that is often needed are simple questions about a client's personal spiritual belief system, what those beliefs are, and how those beliefs affect the client's everyday life and the presenting issue for the session. Such a discussion allows the clinician and client to open the therapeutic door to the subject of spirituality or belief and allows the client to feel comfortable in continuing to bring this belief system into future work with the counselor.

TRAINING COUNSELORS TO WORK WITH SPIRITUALITY

The basis of the counseling practice is the story that is told by the client. More often than not, these stories include a religious or spiritual subject. Zeiger and Lewis (1998) indicated that clients' stories (how they view themselves) are integral to the counseling process and imperative in assessing the presenting problem. With clear evidence that most Americans have a personal belief system and that they want to include those beliefs in work with a clinician (Bergin & Jensen, 1990; Gallup & Lindsay, 1999), there seems to be little question that present counselors and counselors-in-training need to be prepared to address these issues with clients in a clinical setting (Bishop, 1992; Kelly, 1994). The Council for Accreditation of Counseling and Related Educational Program (CACREP) included in its *2001 Standards and Procedures Manual* (2001) the need for all training to include work in addressing spiritual issues and needs. In addition, the Association for Spiritual, Ethical, and Religious Values in Counseling (ASERVIC), a division of the American Counseling Association, has published "Competencies for Integrating Spirituality into Counseling" (ASERVIC, n.d.; Cashwell & Young, 2005). This set of nine guidelines for counselor professionals and counselors in training emphasize awareness and sensitivity to spirituality and religious issues within the context of counseling from the perspectives of counselor and client.

Kelly's 1994 study of 341 accredited and non-accredited counseling programs showed that spirituality and religious issues were included as a course component in only 25% of programs. Kelly's 1997 study of 48 CACREP accredited programs showed that slightly more than half (60%) of the programs included training in dealing with spirituality or religious issues in a counseling setting. One reason for this lack of training may be that many faculty members believe they are unqualified to teach techniques aimed at integrating spiritual beliefs in the counseling arena (Young, Wiggins-Frame, & Cashwell, 2000). Of significance is the Young, Cashwell, Wiggins-Frame, and Belaire's (2002) study of 94 CACREP-accredited programs that found 69 percent of these educational curricula include spiritual and religious content. However, consistent with previous research, a significant percentage of this faculty sample did not feel prepared to teach spiritual and religious content. Because the field of counseling has adopted the wellness paradigm that includes bio-psycho-social and spiritual issues as core to the emotional and psychological wholeness of clients, the need for preparing counselors to respond to the spiritual needs of a client is now essential (Bishop, 1992; Kelly, 1994). The incorporation of faculty preparation and methods to increase comfort levels with teaching this content is clearly needed.

Much of the "spirituality" training of current and future counselors is based on their ability to understand personal religious or spiritual beliefs and values and how those beliefs and values might interfere with their ability to demonstrate compassion and empathy toward a client (Burke & Miranti, 1999; Grimm, 1994). In that same regard, current and future counselors should be able to say how their own belief system contributes to personal wellness, general mental health, and effectiveness as a counselor.

Training New Counselors

Most literature agrees that training new counselors to work with spiritual and religious issues requires a teaching environment that is nonthreatening, well balanced, and comfortable for self-exportation and reflection (Burke et al, 1999; Ingersoll, 1994). Hinterhopf (1998, p. 51) offered a process called the "experiential focusing method," which helps to address such issues by allowing one's own experience to "unfold into new, explicit meanings, understandings or insights." Through self-exploration, new counselors are able to understand their own spiritual journey and then apply that knowledge to their work. It is important to note, however, that not only should new counselors be able to understand and articulate a personal faith system but it is equally important for them to be knowledgeable of other belief and value systems. In addition, it is also important for counselors at any point in their professional careers to retain a self-reflective perspective when spirituality does not play a significant role in their lives. Although counselors do not need to agree with or hold the same spiritual belief systems as their clients, they must be knowledgeable about those beliefs and open to understanding how those beliefs impact the views of their clients (Myers & Willard, 2003). It is through this well-balanced and open approach to training that counselors build self-awareness and in turn help to create a nonthreatening and open atmosphere for their clients' own self-explorations.

ETHICAL IMPLICATIONS ON SPIRITUAL INTEGRATION INTO COUNSELING

Quite early in the metamorphosis of psychology, Jung recognized the inherent ethical risk in the integration of spirituality and counseling during instances when "patients force the psychotherapist into the role of priest and expect and demand that he shall free them from distress. That is why we psychotherapists must occupy ourselves with problems which strictly speaking belong to the theologian" (Jung, 1933, p. 278). For years, the subjects of religion and spirituality have been cast off by psychologists because of the field's attempt to validate itself as a scientific domain (Wolf & Stevens, 2001). This, along with the ethical concern that counselors might be working outside their boundaries of competence, have kept the subject of spirituality and counseling at the forefront of many ethical discussions. Obviously, any clinician must work within his or her personal boundaries of competence, which brings us back to the discussion of appropriate training for all counselors (Wolf & Stevens, 2001). As Chappelle (2000) points out, counselors who work outside of their clinical competencies not only cross the line of ethical appropriateness but also run the risk of harming rather than healing their client.

Because of the broad nature of spirituality, it has been thought that a counselor could inhibit a client's growth and healing if the client's values were different from those of his or her therapist, although one should remember that the literature suggests it is all but impossible for a counselor to be value free in working with clients (Sperry & Gilbin, 1996). Although psychoanalysts have been trained to be objective and value free, this is rarely the case, as is acknowledged in the American Psychological Association's Code of Ethics (APA, 2002), which suggests that all counselors work from their own personal views and belief systems, but they are encouraged to keep from imposing those belief systems on their clients. Some authors have voiced concern regarding the ability to remain value free in counseling (Seligman, 1988), although others have suggested that not only is this possible but it is necessary (Richards & Bergin, 1997).

Without question, personal, professional, and belief boundaries must be established early in the therapeutic process. Slife and Richards (2001) suggest that early in the therapeutic process, clients should be told that they have the right to disagree with the counselor and that the client should see such disagreements as productive to the therapeutic process (Richards & Bergin, 1997).

In addition, Slife and Richards (2001) advocate three steps associated with handling spiritual boundary issues. First, there needs to be an acknowledgment if there are theological assumptions or implications that could be a part of the counseling process. Second, counselors must clarify that they are not theologians (unless of course they are), and that they have no authority to address specific theological issues. Finally, clients are encouraged to seek counseling from their personal religious leaders for any specific questions they might have of a religious or spiritual nature. Helminiak (2001, p. 178, p. 165) suggests that it is as important for the client to be open-minded, "especially fundamentalist branches," when dealing with various issues in the counseling setting and suggests that therapists should "avoid issues of religion and theism. . . . For matters of God fall into the domain of religion and matters of religion fall to clergy or theologians."

Anderson and Goolishian (1992) note that a "not knowing" stance when dealing with spiritual beliefs in a therapeutic setting might be a way to avoid ethical concerns. Mrs. Lopez's experience with her counselor provides an example of this posture.

> During the initial interview between Mrs. Lopez and Dr. Wilson, a licensed marriage and family therapist, the client asks, "Are you a Christian, Dr. Wilson?" She discusses how important her faith is to her as she struggles with a marital relationship that is increasingly characterized by angry interactions, loss of emotional connection, and anxiety about the future. Dr. Wilson replies, "Mrs. Lopez, your faith is clearly of great importance to you and perhaps even more so during a very trying time in your life. Tell me more about your question about my spiritual or religious beliefs."

Dr. Wilson can reply as in the example, or in a number of ways while recognizing that he has acquired a vital piece of information about his client. In some settings, Dr. Wilson might readily disclose his faith beliefs, yet doing so might miss an important opportunity to further explore Mrs. Lopez's question. Another option is to assume a stance of "not knowing" by continuing to work from the therapeutic foundation of curiosity about a client's experience.

By asking questions and not imposing personal ideology into the conversation, counselors can guard themselves from exposing their own views and philosophies into the therapeutic process. Miller (1999) proposed two questions that can be used in the therapeutic process to aid in this "not knowing" process. First, it is helpful to ask what it is like to have the spiritual perspective of your client, and second, ask the client to tell you about his or her own personal faith/spiritual/religious life.

SUMMARY

Many agree that there are ethical issues that relate to the inclusion of spirituality in the practice of counseling, and most literature suggests that this inclusion is not only needed but necessary. Current wellness models include spiritual health as an essential component of overall wellness, and so the bio-psycho-social model of care should now include the realm of spirituality.

To be fair, one must concede that the study of spirituality is constantly changing. With that said, the relationship between spirituality and counseling continues to change and evolve. As we learn more about the symbiosis of this relationship and begin to understand more deeply how and if a person's spirituality affects his or her psychological well-being, we will be better able to reflect this relationship in our counseling practices in the future.

DISCUSSION TOPICS/QUESTIONS

1. How do you think the mind and body are connected in relation to spiritual and psychological wellness?

2. As a counselor, would you work any differently with a client presenting a "spiritual" problem as opposed to a "religious" problem? If so, how?

3. Do you agree with Jung's quote that "everything to do with religion, everything it is and asserts, touches the human soul so closely that psychology, least of all can afford to overlook it?" Discuss your rationale.

4. As a counselor, why is it important to compartmentalize your own spiritual beliefs when working with someone who presents with different beliefs than your own? How do you do this?

5. Understanding that spirituality is experienced differently for men and women, how would you work on a "spiritual" issue in couples therapy with a male client and a female client?

6. Discuss the line between spiritual wellness and "unwellness" and how it might be viewed as a relative issue. How are these perspectives affected by cultural and socioeconomic influences?

7. In your initial assessment of a client, what approaches should a clinician use to assess the importance of spirituality in his or her life? Provide a rationale for this aspect of the counseling process as outlined by Fowler's perspective on stages of spiritual development.

8. From a personal point of view, in what ways are you more comfortable with implicit and explicit spiritual integration in a counseling session? Why?

9. Counselors complete academic coursework and clinical training experiences that are designed to prepare them for the "real world" of practice. In your program, how was the interface between spirituality/religion and counseling addressed? How prepared are you to address these issues as they arise in practice? Use a 10-point Likert-type scale to rate your personal sense of preparedness with 1 being "unprepared" and 10 being "very well prepared." Discuss your rating and how you can influence this self-rating over the next year.

10. Imagine that you are a newly hired counselor at a university-based student counseling center with a population that is characterized by multiculturalism and diversity. You have been asked to provide an update to the center's staff about the role of spirituality and religion in counseling. Identify and describe the key points that will serve as the outline for your presentation.

REFERENCES

American Psychiatric Association. (1994). *Diagnostic and statistical manual of mental disorders* (4th ed.). Washington, DC: Author.

American Psychological Association. (2002). *Ethical principles of psychologists and code of conduct.* Retrieved October 12, 2005, from www.apa.org/ethics/.

Anderson, H., & Goolishian, H. (1992). The client is the expert. In S. McNamee & K. J. Gergen (Eds.), *Therapy as social construction* (pp. 25–39). Newbury Park, CA: Sage.

Aponte, H. (1998, February). *Spirituality: The transcendent and practical force.* Paper presented at the meeting of the Chicago Center for Family Health.

Association for Spiritual, Ethical, and Religious Values in Counseling. (ASERVIC). (no date). *Competencies for integrating spirituality into counseling.* Retrieved February 8, 2006, from www.aservic.org/guidelinesfor.htm.

Bache, C. M. (1989). *Lifecycles: Reincarnation and the web of life.* New York: Paragon House.

Ballou, M. (1995). Women and spirit: Two nonfits in psychology. *Women in Therapy, 16,* 9–20.

Bergin, A. E. (1980). Proposed values for guiding and evaluating counseling and psychotherapy. *Counseling and Values, 29,* 99–116.

Bergin, A. E., & Jensen, J. P. (1990). Religiosity of psychotherapists: A national survey. *Psychotherapy: Theory, Research, Practice, Training, 27,* 3–7.

Bergin, A. E., Payne, I. R., & Richards, P. S. (1996). Values in psychotherapy. In E. Shafranske (Ed.), *Religion and the clinical practice of psychology* (pp. 297–325). Washington, DC: American Psychological Association.

Beutler, l. E., & Clarkin, J. (1990). *Systematic treatment selection: Toward targeted therapeutic interventions.* New York: Bantam.

Bishop, D. R. (1992). Religious values as cross-cultural issues in counseling. *Counseling and Values, 36,* 179–191.

Burke, M. T., & Miranti, J. G. (1999). *Counseling: The spiritual dimension.* Alexandria, VA: American Counseling Association.

Burke, M. T., Hackney, H., Hudson, P., Miranit, J., Watts, G. A., & Epps, L. (1999). Spirituality, religion and CACREP curriculum standards. *Journal of Counseling & Development, 77*(3), 251–258.

Butler, M. A., & Harper, J. M. (1994). The divine triangle: God in the marital system of religious couples. *Family Process, 33,* 277–286.

Canada, E. R., Shin, S. I., & Canada, H. J. (1993). Traditional philosophies of human service in Korea and contemporary social work implications. *Social Development Issues, 15*(3), 84–104.

Cashwell, G. S., & Young, J. S. (Eds.). (2005). *Integrating spirituality and religion into counseling: A guide to competent practice.* Alexandria, VA: American Counseling Association.

Chandler, C., Holden, J., & Kolander, C. (1992). Counseling for spiritual wellness: Theory and practice. *Journal of Counseling & Development, 71,* 168–175.

Chappelle, W. (2000). A series of progressive legal and ethical decision-making steps for using Christian spiritual interventions in psychotherapy. *Journal of Psychology and Theology, 28,* 43–53.

Christ, C. P. (1995). *Diving deep and resurfacing: Women writers on a spiritual quest* (3rd ed.). Boston: Beacon Press.

Council for Accreditation of Counseling and Related Educational Programs. (2001). *Accreditation manual.* Alexandria, VA: Author.

Cullen, E. P. (2003). Women's spirituality in the workplace. *America, 189*(8), 1768.

Curtis, C., & Glass, J. S. (2002). Spirituality and counseling class: A teaching model. *Counseling and Values, 47,* 3–10.

Das, A. K. (1989). Beyond self-actualization. *International Journal for the Advancement of Counseling, 12*(1), 13–17.

Debane, R., & Montgomery, H. (1981). *The breath of life: Discovering your breath prayer.* San Francisco: Harper & Row.

Ellison, C. W. (1983). Spiritual well-being: Conceptualization and measurement. *Journal of Psychology and Theology, 11,* 330–340.

Engel, G. L. (1980). The clinical applications of the biopsychosocial model. *American Journal of Psychiatry, 137*(5), 535–544.

Fowler, J. (1981). *The stages of faith.* London: Harper Collins.

Gallup, G. H., Jr. (1993). *Religion in America.* Princeton, NJ: Princeton Religious Research Center.

Gallup, G. H., Jr., & Lindsay, D. M. (1999). *Surveying the religious landscape.* Harrisburg, PA: Morehouse Publishing.

Gilligan, C. (1982). *In a different voice: Psychological theory and women's development.* Cambridge, MA: Harvard University Press.

Greer, N. A., & Root, W. C. (1992). "Desperately seeking Sheila": Locating religious privatism in American society. *Journal for the Scientific Study of Religion, 31,* 346–352.

Grimm, D. W. (1994). Therapist spiritual and religious values in psychotherapy. *Counseling and Values, 38,* 154–165.

Haque, A. (2001). Interface of psychology and religion: Trends and developments. *Counseling Psychology Quarterly, 14*(3), 241–257.

Harris, I. M. (1997). The ten tenets of male spirituality. *Journal of Men's Studies, 6,* 29–53.

Helminiak, D. A. (2001). Treating spiritual issues in secular psychotherapy. *Counseling and Values, 45,* 163–189.

Hinterhopf, E. (1998). *Integrating spirituality in counseling: A manual for using the experiential focusing method.* Alexandria, VA: American Counseling Association.

Hunt, M. (1993). *The story of psychology.* New York: Doubleday.

Hunter, D. (2005). Drawing from Native American tradition in counseling all children. In G. R. Walz & R. K. Yep (Eds.), *VISTAS: Compelling perspectives on counseling 2005* (pp. 133–136). Alexandria, VA: American Counseling Association.

Ingersoll, R. E. (1994). Spirituality, religion, and counseling: Dimensions and relationship. *Counseling and Values, 38*(2), 98–113.

Ingersoll, R. E., & Bauer, A. L. (2004). An integral approach to spiritual wellness in school counseling settings. *Professional School Counseling, 7*(5), 301–309.

Jankowski, P. J. (2002). Postmodern spirituality: Implications for promoting change. *Counseling and Values, 47*(1), 69–80.

Jung, C. G. (1978). *Psychological reflections.* Princeton, NJ: Bollingen.

Jung, C. J. (1933). *Modern man in search of a soul.* New York: Harcourt Brace.

Kegan, R. (1982). *The evolving self: Problems and process in human development.* Cambridge, MA: Harvard University Press.

Kelly, E. W., Jr. (1990). Counselor responsiveness to client religiousness. *Counseling and Values, 35,* 69–72.

Kelly, E. W., Jr. (1994). The role of religion in counselor education: A national survey. *Counselor Education Supervision, 33,* 227–237.

Kelly, E. W., Jr. (1997). Religion and spirituality in variously accredited counselor training programs: A comment on Pate and High. *Counseling and Values, 42,* 7–11.

Kohlberg, L. (1984). *The psychology of moral development.* New York: Harper & Row.

Legere, T. E. (1984). *A spirituality for today. Studies in formative psychology* (5th ed.). Pittsburg, PA: Duquesne University Press.

London, P. (1986). *The modes and morals of psychotherapy* (2nd ed.). New York: McGraw-Hill.

Lukoff, D., & Turner, R. (1998). From spiritual emergency to spiritual problem. *Journal of Humanistic Psychology, 38,* 21–51.

Maslow, A. H. (1971). *Farther reaches of human nature.* New York: Viking.

Miller, G. (1999). *Learning the language of addiction counseling.* Boston: Allyn and Bacon.

Miller, J. B. (1976). *Toward a new psychology of women.* Boston: Beacon Press.

Moberg, D. O. (1971). *Spiritual well being: Background.* Paper presented at the meeting of the White House Conference on Aging. Washington, DC.

Myers, J. E. (1990). Wellness through the lifespan. *Guidepost,* 11.

Myers, J. E., & Willard, K. (2003). Integrating spirituality into counselor preparation: A developmental, wellness approach. *Counseling and Values, 47*(2), 142–156.

Nhat Hahn, T. (1998). *Interbeing: Fourteen guidelines for engaged Buddhism* (3rd ed., rev.). Berkeley, CA: Parallax Press.

Noddings, N. (2003). *Caring: A feminine approach to ethics and moral education.* Berkeley, CA: University of California Press.

Payne, I. R., Bergin, A. E., & Loftus, P. E. (1992). A review of attempts to integrate spirituality and standard psychotherapy techniques. *Journal of Therapy Integration, 2,* 171–192.

Perrin, K. M., & McDermott, R. J. (1997). The spiritual dimension of health: A review. *American Journal of Health Studies, 13*(2), 90–100.

Piaget, J. (1963). *The origins of intelligence in children* (2nd ed., rev.). New York: Norton.

Prest, L., & Keller, J. (1993). Spirituality and family therapy: Spiritual beliefs, myths, and metaphors. *Journal of Marital and Family Therapy, 19,* 137–148.

Ribi, A. (1990). *Demons of the inner world: Understanding our hidden complexes.* Boston: Shambhala.

Richards, P. S., & Bergin, A. E. (1997). *A spiritual strategy for counseling and psychotherapy.* Washington, DC: American Psychological Association.

Richards, P. S., & Bergin, A. E. (2000). *Handbook of psychotherapy and religious diversity.* Washington, DC: American Psychological Association.

Russell, R. D. (1981). *Health education.* Paper presented at the meeting of the National Educational Association. Washington, DC.

Seligman, L. (1988). Invited commentary: Three contributions of a spiritual perspective to counseling, psychotherapy, and behavior change. *Counseling and Values, 33,* 55–56.

Sider, R. J. (1993). *Good news and good works.* Grand Rapids, MI: Baker Books.

Slife, B. D., Hope, C., & Nebeker, R. S. (1999). Examining the relationship between religious spirituality and psychological science. *Journal of Humanistic Psychology, 39,* 51–86.

Slife, B. D., & Richards, P. S. (2001). How separable are spirituality and theology in psychology? *Counseling and Values, 45*(3), 190–207.

Sperry, L., & Giblin, P. (1996). Marital and family therapy with religious persons. In E. P. Shafranske (Ed.), *Religion and the clinical practice of psychology* (pp. 511–532). Washington, DC: American Psychological Association.

Standard, R. P., Sandhu, D. S., & Painter, L. C. (2000). Assessment of spirituality in counseling. *Journal of Counseling & Development, 78*(2), 204–211.

Tan, S. (1996). Religion in clinical practice: Implicit and explicit integration. In E. P. Shafranske (Ed.), *Religion and the clinical practice of psychology* (pp. 365–386). Washington, DC: American Psychological Association.

Tillich, P. (1959). *Theology of culture.* New York: Oxford University Press.

Tjeltveit, A. C. (1999). *Ethics and values in psychotherapy.* New York: Routledge.

Watson, L. M. (1997). Soul and system: The integrative possibilities of family therapy. *Journal of Psychology and Theology, 25,* 123–135.

Westgate, C. E. (1996). Spiritual unwellness and depression. *Journal of Counseling & Development, 75,* 26–35.

Wilber, K. (1995). *Sex, ecology, spirituality: The spirit of evolution.* Boston: Shambhala.

Witmer, J. M. (1989). Reaching toward wholeness: An integrated approach to well being over a life span. In T. J. Sweeney (Ed.), *Adlerian counseling: A practical approach for a new decade* (p. 118). Muncie, IN: Accelerated Development.

Wolf, C. T., & Stevens, P. (2001). Integrating religion and spirituality in marriage and family counseling. *Counseling and Values, 46*(1), 66–77.

Worthington, E. L., Jr. (1986). Religious counseling: A review of published empirical research. *Journal of Counseling & Development, 64*, 421–431.

Young, J. S., Cashwell, C., Wiggins-Frame, M., & Belaire, C. (2002). Spiritual and religious competencies: A national survey of CACREP-accredited programs. *Counseling and Values, 47*, 22–33.

Young, J. S., Wiggins-Frame, M., & Cashwell, C. S. (2000, March). *Spiritual and religious issues in counselor preparation: A national survey*. Paper presented at the meeting of the American Counseling Association. Washington, DC.

Young, K. K. (1994). Introduction. In A. Sharma (Ed.), *Religion and America* (pp. 1–38). New York: State University of New York Press.

Zeiger, M., & Lewis, J. E. (1998). The spiritually responsible therapist: Religious material in the psychotherapeutic setting. *Psychotherapy, 35*, 415–424.

Zinnbauer, B. J. (2000). Working with the sacred: Four approaches to religious and spiritual issues in counseling. *Journal of Counseling & Development, 78*, 108–115.

INDEX